ECHOES OF BATTLE

The Atlanta Campaign

ECHOES OF BATTLE

The Atlanta Campaign

An illustrated collection
of Union and Confederate narratives

Edited by
Larry M. Strayer & Richard A. Baumgartner

BLUE ACORN PRESS

Blue Acorn Press
P.O. Box 2684
Huntington, WV 25726

ISBN 1-885033-30-3

Strayer, Larry M., 1955—
Baumgartner, Richard A., 1953—

Echoes of Battle: The Atlanta Campaign.
An illustrated collection of Union and Confederate narratives detailing 1864's Atlanta campaign in Georgia.

Includes bibliographical references and index.

History — American Civil War

Manufactured in the United States of America

First edition: April 1991
Second printing: August 1991
New edition: May 2004

Cover design by Robin Adkins, River Cities Printing, Huntington, W.Va.

Cover photography

Front: Unknown western Federal infantryman, L.M. Strayer Collection.
Rear: 10th Kentucky (U.S.) Volunteer Infantry color guard (top), Mick Kissick Collection; Corporal Seth Terry, 63rd Ohio Veteran Volunteer Infantry (lower left), L.M. Strayer Collection; Private William A. Halliburton, 6th/7th Arkansas Volunteer Infantry (lower right), Michael Polston Collection; Confederate works in front of Atlanta (background), George N. Barnard, *Photographic Views of Sherman's Campaign.*

Contents

■ The battle of Ezra Church, July 28, 1864, just west of Atlanta. Federal troops belonging to Brig. Gen. Charles R. Woods' division, XV Corps, fire from behind logs and makeshift barricades at a massed line of advancing Confederate infantry. This engraving, published in *Harper's Weekly* on August 27, 1864, was based on a sketch made by combat artist Theodore R. Davis, who traveled with Union forces during the campaign.

The Atlanta campaign

A brief summary of principal events

This chronology was adapted from the Official Records of the War of the Rebellion and preserves the same military terminology as used during the Civil War.

May 5-7, 1864: Skirmishes at and near Tunnel Hill.

May 8-11: Demonstration against Rocky Face Ridge, with combats at Buzzard's Roost and Dug Gap.

May 8-13: Demonstration against Resaca, with combats at Snake Creek Gap and Sugar Valley.

May 13-15: Battle of Resaca.

May 16: Skirmishes near Calhoun and Rome Cross-roads.

May 17: Engagement at Adairsville; action at Rome.

May 18-19: Combats near Kingston and Cassville.

May 20: Skirmish at the Etowah River near Cartersville.

May 25: Battle of New Hope Church.

May 26-June 1: Combats at and near Dallas.

May 27: Battle of Pickett's Mill.

June 9-23: Operations west of Marietta, with combats at Pine Mountain, Lost Mountain, Brush Mountain, Gilgal Church, Noonday Creek, Noyes' Creek and Kolb's Farm.

June 27: Battle of Kennesaw Mountain.

July 3: Confederate Gen. Joseph E. Johnston vacates the Kennesaw line and falls back toward the Chattahoochee River.

July 4: Combat at Ruff's Mill along Nickajack Creek.

July 5-17: Operations along the Chattahoochee River line, with skirmishes at Howell's, Turner's and Pace's ferries.

July 18: Gen. John Bell Hood replaces Johnston as commander of the Army of Tennessee.

July 19: Skirmishes along Peach Tree Creek.

July 20: Battle of Peach Tree Creek.

July 21: Engagement at Bald (Leggett's) Hill.

July 22: Battle of Atlanta. Maj. Gen. James B. McPherson, commander of the Army of the Tennessee, is killed.

July 22-24: Garrard's Federal cavalry raid to Covington.

July 23-August 25: Siege of Atlanta.

July 27-31: McCook's Federal cavalry raid on the Atlanta & West Point and Macon & Western railroads.

July 27-August 6: Stoneman's Federal cavalry raid to Macon.

July 28: Battle of Ezra Church.

August 4-7: Engagements and Union assault at Utoy Creek.

August 10-September 9: Wheeler's Confederate cavalry raid to North Georgia and East Tennessee, with combats at Dalton and other locations.

August 18-22: Kilpatrick's Federal cavalry raid to Lovejoy's Station.

August 31-September 1: Battle of Jonesboro.

September 2: Union occupation of Atlanta.

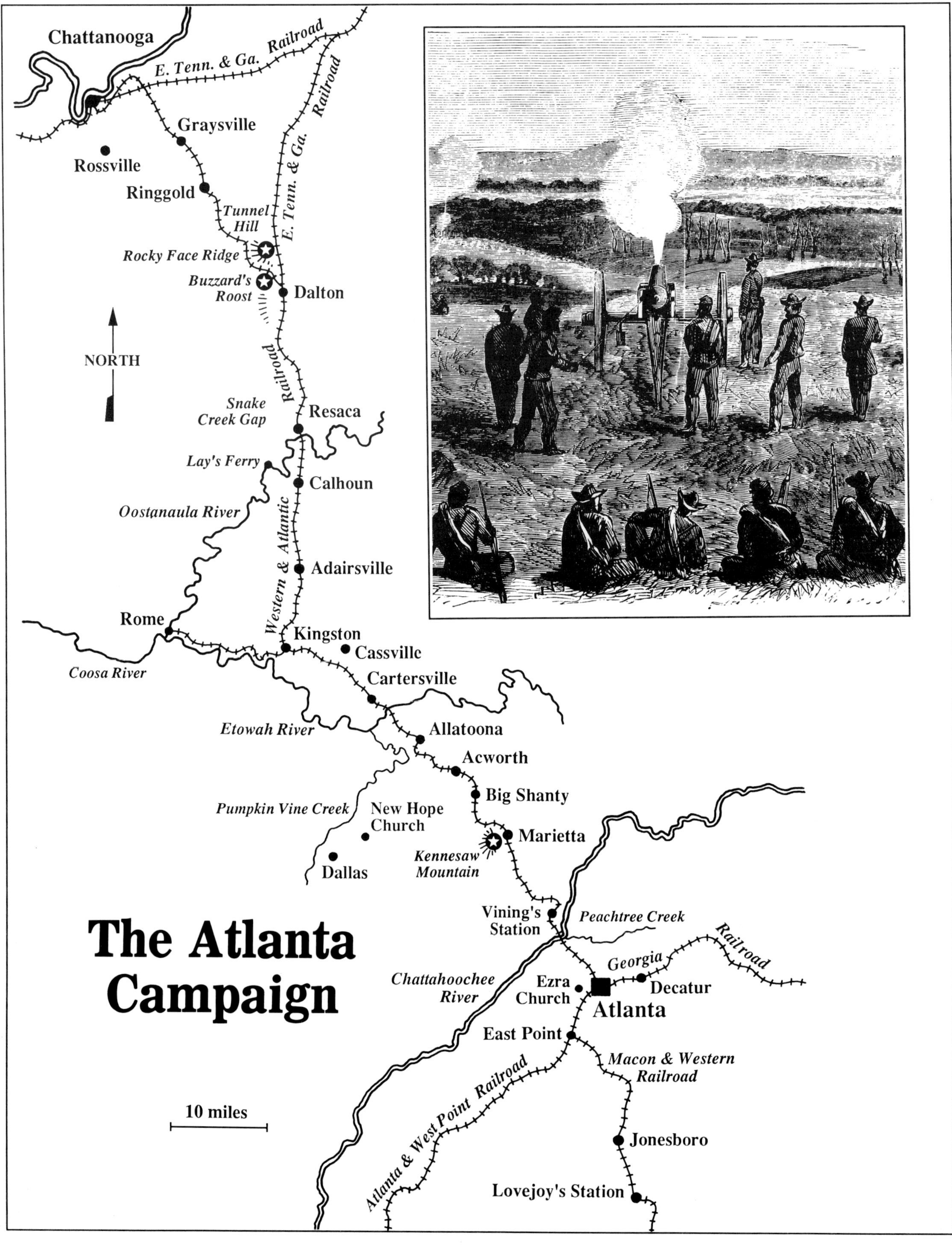
Chattanooga
E. Tenn. & Ga. Railroad
E. Tenn. & Ga. Railroad
Graysville
Rossville
Ringgold
Tunnel Hill
Rocky Face Ridge
Buzzard's Roost
Dalton
NORTH
Western & Atlantic Railroad
Snake Creek Gap
Resaca
Lay's Ferry
Calhoun
Oostanaula River
Adairsville
Rome
Kingston
Cassville
Coosa River
Cartersville
Etowah River
Allatoona
Acworth
Big Shanty
Pumpkin Vine Creek
New Hope Church
Marietta
Dallas
Kennesaw Mountain
Vining's Station
Peachtree Creek
The Atlanta Campaign
Georgia Railroad
Chattahoochee River
Ezra Church
Decatur
Atlanta
East Point
Macon & Western Railroad
Atlanta & West Point Railroad
10 miles
Jonesboro
Lovejoy's Station

'In my judgment, the campaign
for Atlanta has no parallel
in the history
of American military warfare.'

Col. Robert Newton Adams
81st Ohio Veteran Volunteer Infantry

Preface

Fighting for Atlanta: An essence of the reality

When 28-year-old Col. Robert N. Adams rode into Atlanta at the head of his regiment in September 1864, he had seen many sides of war dating back to his enlistment as a private only six days after the fall of Fort Sumter. But few, if any, of his war experiences could match those of the four-month-long military campaign just ended.

"It is difficult to describe a battle to the uninitiated," he later wrote, "so as to give even the faintest idea of the reality. It is still more difficult to describe a campaign ... extending through a period of three months, embracing a march on direct lines of one hundred and forty miles, to say nothing of the here and there marches by the way; a campaign, which was really a continuous battle, of a hundred days' duration."

Thousands of Adams' comrades in blue, as well as their opponents in gray, did try to describe the events of those "hundred days," though to each writer the reality of the skirmish line, a pitched battle or the campaign as a whole was uniquely different. Regardless of rank, no participant saw and experienced exactly the same things as the soldier standing or marching next to him. But gathered together in this collection, the accounts and anecdotes of these men reflect a composite portrait that is characteristic of what most Union and Confederate combatants — especially the common soldiers — experienced during the late spring and summer of 1864 in northwest Georgia.

For this presentation, the editors sifted through hundreds of accounts written by men who fought in the Atlanta campaign. Letters, diaries and journals from private and public collections comprise the majority of primary sources consulted. Some of these have been published over the years, but today are considered obscure. Others are published here for the first time. Memoirs, regimental histories and the Official Records of the War of the Rebellion furnished the other main sources of primary material.

Additional narratives were located in several periodicals published by veterans in the post-war years, most notably *Confederate Veteran, The National Tribune* and *The Ohio Soldier and National Picket Guard.*

Of these three resources, *Confederate Veteran* is the best known. Published monthly from 1893 to 1932, its pages are a treasure trove of minutiae on the Southern armies. However, as with the majority of published Confederate accounts, much more in *Confederate Veteran* deals with the Army of Northern Virginia than the Army of Tennessee. It is indexed and easy to access.

The National Tribune was published by the Grand Army of the Republic from 1877 to 1940, and contains a wealth of information concerning the Federal enlisted man and his officers. It is largely unrecorded by bibliographers as a source of first-hand reminiscences.

The Ohio Soldier and National Picket Guard, a newspaper published in Chillicothe, Ohio, from 1887 to 1902 by John T. Raper, a veteran of the

26th Ohio Infantry, also is an untapped source of material whose articles have remained in obscurity for nearly a century.

Pamphlets published by the Military Order of the Loyal Legion of the United States (MOLLUS), a post-war organization composed of Union officers, further proved to be a valuable resource. Many of the MOLLUS papers are familiar to modern-day historians and readers.

Among available accounts numbering in the hundreds, only those written in a first-person narrative style were selected for the body of each chapter. Shorter passages from these narratives were used as chapter introductions. As a result, more than 260 combatants have been included in this anthology.

In reviewing the material, the editors chose the first-person narrative as the most effective style of conveying an authentic flavor of the campaign. This should not imply that valuable accounts written in third-person style have been neglected or ignored. In fact, many of the photograph captions are drawn from these sources, though slightly rewritten for clarity and limitations of space.

Visually, the editors strove to compile a pictorial record to complement the first-person narrative approach in a manner unlike other treatments of the Civil War. Wartime illustrations by leading artists of the day, original photographs taken during the war or shortly after, and a number of original artifacts were assembled to offer an intimate look at the campaign and its participants.

Some familiar photographs are captioned here correctly and with greater detail than they have appeared previously. These revisions reflect new information obtained through years of research. In an effort to avoid repetition, most of George N. Barnard's often-published photographs of the Atlanta campaign are omitted from this collection.

Instead, more than 280 portraits, many unpublished before, were chosen to illustrate the personal nature of the campaign. Some of the portraits were taken only months — even weeks — before the soldiers fell in battle. These images clearly show how "western" soldiers were clothed, armed and equipped to fight in 1864. It should be noted, however, that by 1864 there were far fewer opportunities for Confederate soldiers to have their portraits made, especially near the front. Hence, their images are much scarcer. Most of those included in this book were taken earlier in the war, when it was fashionable to be photographed armed with muskets, pistols and edged weapons.

While many of the campaign's participants subsequently were promoted, all ranks listed in the text and photograph captions, as best as can be determined, are those which an individual held at the time of his account. In most cases, captions present information relative to a person's involvement in the campaign, with other biographical details added for general interest.

Echoes of Battle does not attempt to detail military operations during the Atlanta campaign, nor does it analyze the strategies and decisions of commanders, or the outcomes of battles. Instead, the following pages offer an essence of the reality which Col. Adams found elusive to describe. Of the ordinary men who shouldered muskets and the officers who led them, the echoes remain ...

■ Col. Robert N. Adams began his wartime service on April 18, 1861, as a 25-year-old private in Company B, 20th Ohio. Discharged three months later, he immediately re-enlisted, was commissioned captain of Company C, 81st Ohio, and by mid-August 1864 had risen to the colonelcy and command of the regiment. On March 13, 1865, he was promoted to brevet brigadier general.

Adams temporarily commanded the 2nd Brigade (to which the 81st belonged), 2nd Division, XVI Corps, three times during the Atlanta campaign. The second occasion occurred July 22 while the battle of Atlanta raged just east of the city. At a critical point in the fighting, Col. August Mersy, the brigade commander, was injured when his horse was shot and pinned him against a fence. Mersy called for Adams, turned the brigade over to him and ordered every man to shout as loud as possible. With Adams' own order, "Forward, double-quick!" the 81st Ohio, flanked by the 12th and 66th Illinois, hurried a mile north to the aid of the embattled XV Corps.

"The boys started with wild yells that would have given credit to a whole tribe of Comanche Indians," wrote Private Thomas J. Shelley of Adams' regiment. That day the 81st captured two stands of Confederate colors and 255 prisoners — at a cost of 11 killed, 52 wounded and 3 missing.

The task would prove so long and bloody

Opposing armies prepare for the struggle

Late in the afternoon of New Year's Eve 1863, Private Robert D. Patrick of Company A, 4th Louisiana, stepped off the train at Dalton, Ga., where the Confederate Army of Tennessee was laying in camp.

"It had ceased raining," he later wrote, "but the ground was one grand loblolly from the tramp of thousands of men and animals, and the running to and fro of supply and baggage wagons. The clouds still looked lowering and the weather was growing colder rapidly. There was nothing to be seen in the vicinity of the depot, except a few houses which looked as though they were deserted, all the fencing and everything about the premises having been torn away by the soldiers I presume. In the distance on all sides, the prospect was anything but cheerful. All looked 'naked, brown and sear,' and the back-ground of this uninviting picture was formed by a chain of dark and gloomy looking hills, which seemed with their frowning rugged sides to preside over this apparently God-forsaken district. After a toilsome walk of over a mile, through mud and water, we at length reached the camping ground of the old 4th, almost worn out ...

"That night the ground froze very hard, and during the remainder of our stay there ... the ground didn't thaw. It was impossible to do any writing on account of the ink's freezing. I would put the inkstand in the warm ashes, but when I dipped my pen in it, it would freeze before I could transfer it to the paper. I never experienced such cold weather, or I never spent such a disagreeable time, as I did during my stay at Dalton."

To the north, soldiers of the Union army shared the Confederates' discomfort. At Strawberry Plains, Tenn., Federal Brig. Gen. Jacob D. Cox was suffering as much as his troops of the 3rd Division, Army of the Ohio. He later wrote:

"On New Year's eve we had a change of weather which rudely broke in upon our dream of a steady and mild winter. It had been raining nearly all day, and we had just turned in about ten o'clock in the evening when a sudden gale sprung up from the northward. The water-soaked ground did not hold the tent pins very well, and the rattling of canvas warned us to look after the fastenings. The staff were all quickly at work, the servants being, as usual, slow in answering a call in the night. The front of our mess tent blew in, and the roof and sides were bellying out and flapping like a ship's sail half chewed up. I caught the door-flaps and held them down to the pole with all my strength, shouting to the black boys to turn out before the whole [tent] should fly away.

Trappings of a soldier

■ Corporal Christopher C. Marsh of Company H, 104th Ohio, sits for a photograph taken January 14, 1864, at Strawberry Plains, Tenn., near Knoxville. Marsh was a 32-year-old farmer from Nimisila, Ohio, when he enlisted on August 2, 1862. He served through the entire campaign without a wound, eventually mustering out with his company on June 17, 1865, at Greensboro, N.C.

Here, he wears a full infantry field kit, including a rolled blanket on his knapsack, and holds an Enfield rifled musket, caliber .577, with bayonet. His patched sack coat is without chevrons, reflecting a practice adopted by some non-commissioned officers to reduce casualties. The wide-brimmed felt hat was a popular substitute for the army cap in the western theater.

Writing home on May 3, 1864, Capt. Henry Richards of the 93rd Ohio recommended the following advice about an enlisted man's field kit to his brother, who was about to enter 100-day army service: "He should take nothing but what he can carry on a march, though I suppose they will not have much of that to do. One blanket, one extra pair of socks, one extra shirt, haversack, canteen and rubber blanket, with half of a shelter tent is all he should take. The pants he wears will last him. A tin plate, knife and fork and spoon, tin-cup and very small tin bucket, with cover, that will hold about a quart, to make coffee in, a little sack for coffee, one for sugar and one for salt, just large enough to hold three days' rations, and a small frying pan completes the outfit. He will find when he carries all these with gun, cartridge-box with forty rounds ammunition, he will have a pretty good load. Nothing is better than Government shoes for the march, and they should be one size larger than he wears at home."

■ Officers of Company H, 118th Ohio. This regiment of the XXIII Corps (Army of the Ohio) was encamped along Mossy Creek, Tenn., in early 1864. In an 1863 photograph, the neat appearance of 2nd Lieut. Sidney F. Moore (left), Capt. Charles Gloyd (center), and 1st Lieut. Amos J. Moore (right) casts a striking contrast to Gen. Jacob Cox's description of the shabby condition of the troops of the XXIII Corps that winter. "They knew as well as I did," Cox wrote, "that [their situation] had grown out of the inevitable fortunes of war, in spite of the utmost efforts of their commanders to get supplies forward as soon as the siege of Knoxville had been raised [in early December 1863]."

Of these three officers, both lieutenants survived the drive to Atlanta and gained promotions; Capt. Gloyd resigned his commission before the campaign began.

"Then we had a lively time for an hour, going from tent to tent to drive the pins tighter and make things secure. We had just got them snug, as we thought, and began to listen to the roaring of the wind ... when a 'stick-and-clay' chimney ... took fire and was near setting the whole encampment in a blaze. This made another short end rush, till the chimney was torn away from the canvas and the fire extinguished. The gale was so fierce that the sparks from the camp-fires rolled along the ground instead of rising, and we should have burned up had not the rain kept the tents soaking wet. It grew cold so fast that by the time we had made the encampment safe, the wet canvas froze stiff. We did not sleep well that night, and we got up in the morning aching with cold. It still blew a gale, though the sky was clear and the thermometer had fallen to zero. It was ... a cold wave from the North, and, as we afterward learned, was exceptional in its suddeness and bitterness along the whole line from Minnesota to northern Georgia.

"On New Year's day morning the ground was frozen solid. The soldiers in the camps had slept but little, for they were obliged to keep awake and near the fires to escape freezing. All huddled about the fires, but the gale was so fierce that on the windward side there seemed to be no radiation of heat ... On the leeward side the smoke suffocated and the sparks burned one, and the men passed from one side to the other doubting which was the more tolerable.

"I spent a good part of the morning going through the regimental camps and giving such encouragement and cheer as I could. The patience and courage of the troops were marvelous, though many of the men were in a pitiable condition as to clothing. They were tatterdemalions in appearance ... Some had nothing but drawers upon their legs, their trousers being utterly worn to rags. Some had no coats and drew their tattered blankets about them, sitting upon their haunches, like Indians, about the camp-fires.

"I estimated that fully one-third of the command had lost and worn out some material portion of their clothing. Whole brigades ... had been without soap for two months. Yet, hungry, cold, ragged and dirty, they responded cheerily to my New Year's greetings, and at this very time the 'veteranizing' was going on without a check until nearly every one of the old regiments re-enlisted for another term."

In Chattanooga, where most of the Federal Army of the Cumberland was encamped, the frigid cold on the first day of 1864 left entire teams of mules dead, standing frozen in their tracks. Two days later, Corporal Bliss Morse of the 105th Ohio wrote to his mother, mentioning the lean and sorrowful looking horses and mules: "Can count more than five hundred dead of both kinds very easily ... and that is a low estimate of the number, too. They lie in squads of thirty or more outside of our camp lines. We think it may be sickly here in the coming spring because of so much carrion around camp."

Twenty-five miles to the southeast, 1st Lieut. Lot D. Young's regiment, the 4th Kentucky, was quartered with the Confederate Army of Tennessee. "Who that spent the winter of '63-'64 at Dalton does not recall some circumstance or incident to remind him of the dreary 'winter of discontent' spent in this mountain fastness of Northern Georgia?" Young wrote. "To many of us it seemed like an age, but withal it was a season of much needed rest and recuperation ... some planning in mind the future campaign and its outcome, others indifferent as to the future and caring but little, willing to entrust all to those at the helm."

A few days before the beginning of the year that trust had been placed

in Gen. Joseph Eggleston Johnston, a battle-scarred native of Virginia who took command of the Army of Tennessee from Gen. Braxton Bragg. The 56-year-old Johnston inherited an army still trying to recover from a severe thrashing suffered at Missionary Ridge, Tenn., on November 25, 1863, after an unsuccessful two-month siege of Chattanooga. Confederate morale and discipline slid to a low ebb during the intervening weeks, which soon became apparent to the general after his arrival at Dalton. "In the inspections, which were made as soon as practicable, the appearance of the army was very far from being 'matter of much congratulation,' " Johnston later recalled.

On January 2, he wrote to President Jefferson Davis in Richmond, assessing what he found in his new command:

"Having been here but six days, during four of which it rained heavily, I have not been able to observe the condition of the army. I judge, however, from the language of the general officers, that it has not entirely recovered its confidence, and that its discipline is not so thorough as it was last spring. The men are, generally, comfortably clothed; a few shoes and blankets are wanting in each brigade, which the chief quartermaster promises to supply very soon.

"According to the return of December 20th, the effective total of the army (infantry and artillery) is not quite thirty-six thousand; the number present about forty-three thousand; that present and absent about seventy-seven thousand. The reports of the adjutant-general show that about four thousand men have returned to the ranks since the battle of Missionary Ridge. My predecessor estimated the enemy's force at Chattanooga, Bridgeport, and Stevenson, at about eighty thousand.

"Major-General Wheeler reports that about two-thirds of his cavalry is with General Longstreet. He has about sixteen hundred in our front; Major-General Wharton has eight hundred and fifty near Rome, and Brigadier-General Roddy, with his brigade, is supposed to be near Tuscumbia — his strength not reported. I am afraid that this cavalry is not very efficient — that want of harmony among the superior officers causes its discipline to be imperfect. I will endeavor to improve it during the winter.

"The artillery is sufficient for the present strength of the army, but is deficient in discipline and instruction, especially in firing. The horses are not in good condition. It has about two hundred rounds of ammunition."

Johnston noted that "the artillery horses were too feeble to draw the guns in fields, or on a march, and the mules were in similar condition; while the supplies of forage were then very irregular, and did not include hay. In consequence of this, it was necessary to send all of these animals not needed for camp service to the valley of the Etowah [River], where long forage could be found, to restore their health and strength."

Rations for his soldiers also were in short supply. When a trainload of provisions arrived near Dalton, a Tennessee private recalled that "soldiers stopped it before it rolled into the station, burst open every car, and carried off all the bacon, meal and flour that was on board. Wild riot was the order of the day; everything was confusion worse confounded. [But] when the news came, like pouring oil upon the troubled waters, that General Joe E. Johnston had taken command of the Army of Tennessee, men returned to their companies, order was restored, and 'Richard was himself again.' "

Improving the quality and quantity of food for his troops was among Johnston's top priorities, and the effort was not lost on the soldiers. "As part of his strategy consisted in feeding his men well, we were living upon

■ Gen. Joseph E. Johnston commanded the Confederate Army of Tennessee from December 27, 1863, until he was relieved by Gen. John Bell Hood on July 17, 1864, three days before the battle of Peach Tree Creek. One of Johnston's enlisted men described him as "rather small of stature, but firmly and compactly built, [with] an open and honest countenance, and a keen but restless black eye, that seemed to read your very inmost thoughts. In his dress he was a perfect dandy. He wore the very finest clothes that could be obtained, never omitting anything, even to the trappings of his horse, bridle and saddle. His hat was decorated with a star and feather, his coat with every star and embellishment, and he wore a bright new sash, big gauntlets, and silver spurs. He was the very picture of a general."

Johnston fought Sherman's overwhelming strength during the first two months of the campaign with a skillful defense, and after the war the two former adversaries became good friends. When Sherman died on February 14, 1891, Johnston served hatless in a freezing rain as an honorary pallbearer. Contracting pneumonia, he died a month later.

■ Private Robert D. Bond of Company G, 1st Arkansas. This regiment of Cleburne's division wintered near Tunnel Hill. One of Bond's messmates, Private William E. Bevens, later recalled: "We had good foraging ground and could get chickens, eggs, butter, so we lived high. [Lieut.] John R. Loftin was captain of the foragers and he was a good one, too. He only got caught once but he lied out of that. We used to go [to Dalton] to see the girls and have parties and sorghum 'candy pulls.' It was a great diversion ..." Bond was wounded on July 22 during the battle of Atlanta. He recovered and rejoined his company, but was captured on December 15, 1864, at Nashville.

the fat of the land, which was poor enough," wrote 1st Sergeant James L. Cooper of Company C, 20th Tennessee. "The contrast to our previous diet was so marked that we imagined we were doing finely. Gen. Johnston gave universal satisfaction, and a marked change was soon perceptible in the army. He infused a portion of his active spirit into his subordinate officers, and the consequence was that we were better clothed, and better provided for in every way than we had been for a year before."

Private Sam R. Watkins of Company H, 1st Tennessee, recalled that Johnston "ordered tobacco and whiskey to be issued twice a week ... sugar and coffee and flour to be issued instead of meal ... old bacon and ham to be issued instead of blue beef. Notwithstanding all this grand transformation in our affairs, old Joe was a strict disciplinarian. Everything moved like clockwork. Men had to keep their arms and clothing in good order. The artillery was rubbed up and put in good condition. The wagons were greased, and the harness and hamstrings oiled. Extra rations were issued to negroes who were acting as servants, a thing unprecedented before in the history of the war."

Another private, Frank A. Roberts of Company C, 2nd Georgia Battalion Sharpshooters, was part of a 10-man mess and remembered its rations coming in good-sized chunks, especially beef. "Sergeant [Henry] Miller was an excellent cook," Roberts wrote, "and he could bake or roast our ration of beef to 'a turn,' and believe me, it was good. At times we had potatoes, which were 'powerful' good with savory gravy he made. Corn bread was our stand-by in that line. This was baked in a big old Dutch oven about fourteen inches in diameter, two bakings of three pones each being required at each of our three meals per day. We used liberally of the little Mexican red peppers for seasoning, which was a most healthy tonic for us. Occasionally bacon, with some kind of green vegetable, varied our bill of fare. We ordered a five-gallon keg of Georgia cane syrup (it cost us only $300), which went splendidly with our corn bread for dessert."

As did many of thc Confederates wintering at Dalton, Roberts and his comrades lived in makeshift cabins and huts. "Our cabins were built of split logs," he wrote, "the cracks being 'chinked' during the severest weather with red clay, thus making a very comfortable house indeed. An ample chimney was constructed of sticks 'chinked' in the same manner as the house; and when the fireplace was piled up with wood [and] set going, we had as comfortable quarters as to warmth as one could wish. Our bedsteads were four posts with end and side pieces nailed to them, and boards were placed so as to give us room to fill in with straw, and over this our quilts and blankets were spread."

Federal troops also were trying to make the best of their surroundings during the long cold snap. On January 9, Sergeant Frank M. McAdams of the 113th Ohio proudly described his new home near McAfee's Chapel, Ga.:

"Our quarters are now completed, and a description of the one in which I am quartered ought to be recorded.

"It is 10 by 14 in its dimensions, 7 ft. high, and covered with our own make of clapboards. The door end stands to the west and the door opens outward. The chimney is also in the west end. The east gable has a six-light window, filled up with glass eight by ten. Our bunks extend from the window toward the fire, leaving a space to the right for a table, which is a homely affair. Four three-legged stools fill the place of chairs, and are real handy things to have around. We have christened our house 'Metropolitan Hall,' the name being in large letters over the door outside. The

dedication took place in due form, several invited guests being present, all of whom, together with the proprietors, took the oath several times. All we lacked in the ceremonies was a brass band and something more to eat. Notwithstanding our comfortable quarters we do not sleep warm of nights. We get up in the night and warm by the fire, and then return to our bunks to sleep."

With the intense cold finally subsiding on January 17, military routine resumed in the 113th's camp. "Dress parade has again been introduced," McAdams recorded in his diary that day. "We now have company drill from 10-11:30 a.m., battalion drill from 2:30 to 4 p.m."

Four days later, McAdams was issued a new Springfield rifled musket. On the 25th, he received "an express box" from home, containing "a greatcoat, an army blanket, a pair of boots, a lot of stationery, dried peaches, dried apples, green apples, canned peaches, two pair socks, apple butter and fifteen postage stamps. Now we will live like brigadiers while these supplies last."

Sergeant Nixon B. Stewart of Company E, 52nd Ohio, remembered that the severity of the winter created a huge demand for extra uniforms and warmer clothing. "It was remarkable how many of the boys overdrew

■ With a photographer's patriotic backdrop behind them, Corporal Thompson E. Osborn, left, and Private Henry S. Howell pose with mess equipment at Rossville, Ga., in April 1864. They belonged to Company F of the 113th Ohio. In June, the regiment was issued new clothing in the field which provoked immediate merriment. One Ohioan recalled that they "looked as if they had just escaped from a band box. They had the new regulation hat; the entire front was covered with emblems and letters designating the company and regiment. John Ryan, a little Irishman of Co. A, 43rd Regiment, who chanced to see them as they passed by, cried aloud, 'Come here quick, Pat, and see the regiment with the multiplication table on their hats. Faith, they look like they could work out anything that comes before them.' "

■ 1st Lieut. Wilbur Fisk Hinman of Company E, 65th Ohio, was typical of many company-grade officers. Enlisting as a private at age 20 in 1861, Hinman soon was appointed first sergeant of his company and within eight months advanced to first lieutenant. At the battle of Chickamauga in 1863, he was wounded during the first day of fighting. When the men of the 65th re-enlisted as veterans in early 1864, Hinman already was one in every sense of the word. Five weeks into the campaign for Atlanta, he attained the rank of captain and took command of Company F. When the regiment finally left the service on November 30, 1865, he commanded the 65th as a lieutenant colonel, but was never mustered at that grade.

After the war, Hinman became a newspaper editor and drew upon his war experiences to produce two classics on the Army of the Cumberland. *Si Klegg and his "Pard"* was published in 1889 as a fictional tribute to the common soldier. This book was so popular that *National Tribune* editor John McElroy produced at least eight subsequent versions. In 1899, Hinman finished *The Story of the Sherman Brigade,* a massive study distinguished for its witty style, large number of wartime portraits and wealth of historical detail. Additionally, Hinman's compilation of Union soldier narratives, entitled *In Camp and Field, Sketches of Army Life,* was released in 1892.

their allowance for clothing," he recalled. "The Government allowed us four dollars a month, and charged us the following prices: Overcoat $7.50, pants $3.50, blouse $3.12, shoes $1.48, boots $2.87, hat $1.68, cap 54 cents, drawers 95 cents, shirt $1.35, dress coat $6.25, woolen blanket $3.25, rubber blanket $2.55, canteen 44 cents, haversack 48 cents, socks 32 cents.

"We must say our clothing was good in quality, as good as we could ask for the price paid, but it was often poorly made."

Feeding and clothing thousands of troops was a logistical nightmare for the commissary and quartermaster departments at Chattanooga. An even greater challenge for the Federal army was finding a way to keep its veteran soldiers in the service after their three-year enlistments were due to expire during the coming summer months. 1st Lieut. Wilbur F. Hinman of the 65th Ohio later explained how this was accomplished and the resulting "veteran craze:"

"Some months previous to this time, the War Department had determined upon a plan by which it hoped to secure the continued service of the large body of soldiers who had already been in the field two years or more, and whose term of enlistment would expire in a few months. It was decided to offer to all such who would re-enlist for 'three years or during the war' a bounty of four hundred dollars each, and a furlough giving thirty days at home, the time going and coming not to be counted. Any company or regiment, three-fourths of whose members should re-enlist, would retain its organization and be accompanied home by its officers.

"The wisdom of this measure was amply shown by its result. Nearly one hundred and forty thousand men re-enlisted under the honorable designation of 'Veteran Volunteers.' These were all *soldiers* — trained and disciplined, inured to hardship, and of tried courage. A regiment of three hundred such men was worth more in an active, arduous campaign than a thousand raw recruits. The armies that fought the great battles of 1864 contained large levies of new troops. The veterans gave to these a steadiness that would otherwise have been wanting.

"It was while in East Tennessee that the 'veteran' excitement broke out in Harker's brigade. It went through the Sixty-fourth and Sixty-fifth [Ohio Infantry regiments] like the small-pox. A day or two after Christmas the commanding officer of each regiment called a 'mass meeting' of its members, at which the orders from Washington were read and the alluring scheme of four hundred dollars bounty and a thirty days' furlough was fully explained. No doubt it was thought that the holiday season was a good time to talk about going home. In this way the boys were vaccinated with the veteran virus. It 'took' right away. They went like sheep over a wall. A 'bell-wether' in each company started it, and the rest almost fell over one another in their haste to get hold of the pen and sign the new roll.

"No doubt the thirty days' furlough was a potent influence in inducing the men to re-enlist. It is impossible for anyone except the soldiers themselves to conceive how great was the temptation. In no other way can it be half so well expressed as in the words of Capt. Brewer Smith, of the Sixty-fifth, in a personal letter to the writer. Said he: 'The boys made up their minds to take three years more of hell for the sake of thirty days of heaven — *home.'* But the great impelling force that moved the veterans was a determination to stand by 'Old Glory' until the rebellion was conquered.

"Before the 1st of January, five-sixths of each regiment had re-enlisted, and then nothing was talked of night or day, but that furlough. No one knew when the regiments would go, and the impatience became almost uncontrollable. Of course, all the veterans could not leave at once, but assurance was given from the highest official sources, that they should be sent home just as fast as they could be spared with safety."

"The veteran feeling is terrific here," wrote Capt. Charles W. Wills of the 103rd Illinois. "Three regiments in our brigade [are] the only ones eligible (that is, that have been in two years) and have re-enlisted almost to a man. 40th Illinois, 46th Ohio and 6th Iowa. In our division there are seven regiments eligible and all have re-enlisted, and are going home in a few days. It is, I think, the grandest thing of the war. I guess no one is more astonished at it than the very men who are enlisting. One of the 40th boys told me that 'about 15 of us were talking about it and cussing it, until every son of a gun concluded to, and did re-enlist.' "

After re-enlistment the troops eagerly awaited transportation home. The journey north involved many days of railroad travel and sometimes was fraught with moments of danger.

"At 5 a.m. [on January 19], our regiment was crowded into the cars and ready to move out of Chattanooga," recalled Private Jacob Adams of Company F, 21st Ohio. "About 8 a.m. we were on the high trestle work at Whiteside Station, the second car from the engine of our train left the rails, bumping along on the ties for a short distance, when the train stopped just as it was hanging on the stringer. Had it gone down, it doubtless would have dragged the whole train with it. We could easily imagine the result if we had fallen from a height of 125 feet to a solid rock below. We were badly frightened, but soon emptied the cars and walked on the ground to the other end of the bridge. After some delay we moved along without further trouble."

Four days later, when the 21st Ohio reached Columbus, the men were sent to Tod Barracks "where the guards were under strict orders to let no one out without a pass," wrote Adams. "We thought we had seen too much service to be cowed or bossed around by tenderfeet who never had seen a Johnny. So a small squad met at the gate and were refused to go out without a pass. Seeing the determined look in our eyes, the guard called the 'Corporal of the Guard' in, and he thought best to call the 'Officer of the Guard.' By that time our whole regiment was at the gate, some with their muskets, awaiting the order, 'forward march,' which someone gave, and the whole regiment passed out. We were then free to go where we wished during the rest of our stay there."

The following day the regiment "turned over arms and accoutrements, drew clothing and dressed ourselves up, got our furlough and were ready to move for Findlay, Ohio," where the 21st originally was recruited and organized.

■ Lt. Col. Charles F. Morse. His regiment, the 2nd Massachusetts, returned from veteran furlough to its camp at Tullahoma, Tenn., in early March 1864. The following month the XII Corps (to which the 2nd belonged) "ceased to exist, and General Slocum issued his farewell order," Morse wrote on April 10. "The officers of our regiment ... brought the band over and paid their respects to the General. Colonel Cogswell made a very good speech; General Slocum tried to reply, but was so affected he could hardly speak, the tears running down his cheeks, but he finally managed to get through, and invited the officers to come in and spend the evening with him. Well, the old institutions are broken up, and we must bear it as philosophically as possible."

Five months later, after the fall of Atlanta, Morse served as the occupied city's provost marshal.

'The sidewalks were filled with a cheering multitude'

Lt. Col. Charles F. Morse
2nd Massachusetts Veteran Volunteer Infantry

The regiment received its orders to go home for its thirty days' furlough January 9, 1864, those who had not re-enlisted remaining in camp at Tullahoma, Tenn. Movements by rail were slow in those days, owing to insufficient transportation, and it was not until the evening of January 18th that the regiment reached Boston. There was a great throng at the Boston and Albany station awaiting it, but no formal reception was given that evening. The men were marched to barracks on Beach Street, and

■ The 73rd Ohio Veteran Volunteer Infantry stands in columns of companies for photographer F.A. Simonds, February 16, 1864, in Chillicothe, Ohio. On this date, the 73rd marched into the city, massed in front of the courthouse and was "presented with a new and beautiful banner, with the names of the principal battles of the regiment inscribed on it," recalled Major Samuel H. Hurst. In spite of inclement weather, a large crowd was on hand for the ceremony.

In the foreground, regimental pioneers shoulder spades and axes. Behind them, four young privates carry battalion guidons used to mark the battalion flanks during drill and battle maneuvers. Two days later, following a month-long furlough, the 73rd left Chillicothe for its former camp in Lookout Valley, Tenn. The regiment began the Atlanta campaign with 318 guns, but suffered casualties of 210 enlisted men and eight officers during four months of fighting.

quartered there for the night; the officers were entertained by Mr. E.R. Mudge at the United States Hotel, and many of them went to their homes for the night.*

The next day, January 20th, was a fine, bright, winter day, not too cold for comfort. At about 9 a.m. the regiment filed out of the Beach Street barracks, and, under the escort of the Boston Cadets, began its march. It was an ovation from the start. The men had spent much of their time the preceding night in polishing their brasses and belts, and brushing up their well worn uniforms. Their rifles and bayonets were burnished to the last degree, and would have passed the inspection of the most rigid West Point martinet. It is difficult to say too much in praise of the appearance of the command on this occasion. The men were veterans in the truest sense, and their whole appearance indicated it. Their march was the easy swing of the old soldier, but in perfect time and alignment, with every face set

* Lt. Col. Charles R. Mudge commanded the 2nd Massachusetts at Gettysburg, where he was killed near Culp's Hill. On July 3, 1863, "at about half-past five [a.m.], Col. Colgrove gave the order to Col. Mudge to advance his regiment and charge the woods opposite us," wrote Morse. "Col. Mudge gave the order 'Forward;' the men jumped over the breastworks and rushed forward with a splendid cheer. We had to cross a little meadow; here was where we suffered so heavily; the enemy was in the woods and we in the open. We reached the opposite woods and commenced firing at the shortest range I have ever seen two lines engaged at. We fought the rebs before us for about ten minutes; then I learned that Col. Mudge had been hit and that I was in command ..."

squarely to the front. Their faces, bronzed by exposure to the sun and the weather, had the expression of hardihood which only comes to men accustomed to meeting dangers and privation. The officers were all young men, hardly one who marched that day being more than twenty-five years old, yet from the military point of view they were entitled to be called veterans. Col. Cogswell, who commanded the regiment, was then in his twenty-fifth year; Capt. Crowninshield, who had been three times wounded, was in his twenty-first year and was the youngest captain, but several other officers of this rank were only a year or two older.

The march was first through the West End of Boston, passing through Arlington Street to Beacon Street — the reception proper really beginning on the latter street. The sidewalks were filled with a cheering multitude, and every window and balcony were crowded with friends, who gave the most enthusiastic greeting to the regiment as it passed. It was a stirring march, to fine martial music, and no one who marched with the regiment that day will ever forget this thrilling episode of his military life.

From Beacon Street the march proceeded through the business streets, where the principal stores had been closed by common consent. On State Street was another ovation from "the solid men of Boston," who filled the street and cheered most enthusiastically as the column marched by. When Faneuil Hall was reached the men filed in, and every inch of available room was immediately filled by the crowds which followed. The galleries were occupied by ladies and many of the immediate friends of the officers and men. The hall was handsomely decorated by flags and streamers, with the State arms and shield on each side of the clock.

The officers and color guard with their shot-riddled battle flag were on the platform, where Governor Andrew and his staff, Mayor Lincoln, General Burnside and other distinguished men were assembled. Governor Andrew [gave] an eloquent address, in which he recounted the services of the regiment and followed its career through its various campaigns. He referred by name to many of those who had fallen in battle, and told the story of the color bearers who fell one after another at Gettysburg, but who never let the flag touch the ground, in a manner which thrilled every one who heard him.

Col. Cogswell made a modest, well-spoken reply to Governor Andrew's speech of welcome, and was followed by General Burnside, who happened to be present in Boston at that time, and who made a few remarks suitable to the occasion.

After the exercises at Faneuil Hall were concluded, the regiment marched to Coolidge Block, Court Street, where the arms and equipments were deposited, and the men received their thirty days' furlough. The officers scattered to their homes to enjoy this brief season of rest, although an active effort was made to secure recruits to take back into the field. This effort entirely failed, mainly owing to the unfortunate policy, then in effect, of creating and filling up new military organizations, rather than placing every recruit in the old regiments or other organized commands.

On Monday, February 22, the regiment assembled at Beach Street barracks, and the next day, at half-past four p.m., left Boston for Tennessee. An entire week was spent on the return trip, and the regiment finally reached its camp at Tullahoma on a dark, rainy morning, where it rejoined the comrades who had been left behind.

■ Private Lorenzo M. Vallen enlisted on December 14, 1863, at Cleveland, Ohio. He was assigned to Company D, 29th Ohio, and joined the regiment when it returned home during veteran furlough. After two years of active service, the 29th mustered fewer than 300 effectives when it re-enlisted almost to a man at Wauhatchie, Tenn. In this photograph, Vallen poses with an overstuffed knapsack, clearly showing his innocence of army campaigning. In the coming weeks, Vallen and thousands of recruits like him would learn the rudiments of army life and prepare for the spring campaign.

Shortly after assuming the Confederate command, Gen. Johnston instituted his own system of granting furloughs to the battle-hardened veterans of the Army of Tennessee. On January 1, Capt. Elbert D. Willett of Company B, 40th Alabama, wrote in his diary: "By General Order 227 a

■ A jeweler-made, silver XIV Corps pin, engraved "W.G.P., Co. F, 16 Ill." The acorn officially was adopted as a corps badge on April 26, 1864, per General Orders No. 62, Department of the Cumberland. It first was worn after the 1863 siege of Chattanooga, when troops of the XIV Corps subsisted for days on acorns gathered near their camps. The above pin belonged to 2nd Lieut. William Porter of Company F, 16th Illinois.

The introduction of such badges bolstered esprit de corps, and strong rivalries sprang up among the Federal armies, as described by another Illinois officer serving in the XV Corps of the Army of the Tennessee: "Our corps don't get along well with these Cumberland and Potomac soldiers. The 4th and 14th Corps Cumberland chaps our men can endure, although much in the spirit [of] a dog chewing a bone, allows another to come within ten feet. The 11th and 12th Corps [reorganized as the XX Corps] Potomac men and ours never meet without some very hard talk. I must do the Yankees the justice to say that our men, I believe, always commence it, and are the meanest set of men that was ever thrown together."

system of furloughs is adopted, to wit: one enlisted man for every thirty men and a leave of absence for one officer where there are three in the Company for duty. Under this order Company B was entitled to two furloughs and a leave of absence for one officer. Lots were cast by the men to decide who should go, and W.L. Lipsey and Bowman Elmore were the lucky ones. They left for home on this day. Their leave will expire on the 20th of January, 1864, then two others will go home."

In another Alabama regiment, the 30th, the members of Company F held a meeting the night of January 28 and unanimously adopted the following resolution: "Whereas the perilous condition of our country necessarily demands the assistance and earnest effort, of every ablebodied man in the field, Therefore — Resolved 1st. That the undersigned members of Company F 30th Ala. Vols., do enlist for the war (it being yet fourteen months until the expiration of our present enlistment) unwilling ever to lay down our arms, or relax our energies, until our country is liberated, and our Confederacy established among the nations of the earth."

However, in spite of such patriotic rhetoric and Johnston's measures to improve morale and discipline, a large number of Confederates still chose to desert their camps around Dalton.

"I see many rebel deserters everyday — saying their cause is hopeless, and there is no further use of fighting," wrote Ohioan Bliss Morse in his diary on January 24. "I am on picket, at the Reserve post. Five have come in from Tunnel Hill, belonging to Texas and Arkansas. One was born in Canada — said they found that one Southern was not equal to five Yankees, and that they *might* match one if he were a very *small one!* They were told that they could with a few negroes and sticks drive the whole horde of Yankees. They seemed to be very downcast and *penitent,* and even *willing* to eat the 'crumbs' of Uncle Sam's table."

Some Southern soldiers failed to return to the army after their furloughs expired, remaining at home or on the lam. One such soldier, Private Bowman Elmore, was among the first enlisted men of the 40th Alabama to receive furloughs. When he did not report back on January 20, further furloughs in his company ceased.

The problem even extended to Maj. Gen. Patrick R. Cleburne's division, which was considered one of the best in the army. Desertions particularly plagued Brig. Gen. Mark Lowrey, who commanded one of Cleburne's brigades of Mississippi and Alabama troops. On March 13, Private Benjamin F. Jackson of Company B, 33rd Alabama, wrote to his wife: "Times are very dull here; the men are so badly disheartened that a good many are leaving here of a night. Some call it deserting. Those that leave call it going to protect their families, which I think is a man's duty. We are expecting every day to be called on to go out in battle again, which I feel but little like doing. I have, ever since this war has been going on, tried to keep in good heart, till now, and I have now given up as for leaving the army. I dont know as I ever shall do that though as for fighting I shall do as little as possible."

Eleven weeks later, Jackson was mortally wounded in the battle of Pickett's Mill.

Penalties meted out to deserters who were caught differed greatly in severity. According to Capt. Willett of the 40th Alabama, "four deserters of Company B, to wit: L., E., E. and E., were captured in Cherokee County, Ala., and brought back. Charges and specifications were preferred, and they were tried by the Corps Court and sentenced, the three E.'s to be marked with letter D on left hip and wear barrel shirt. L. to have his head half shaved, wear barrel shirt ten days and marched

Enlisted men of the Federal IV Corps

■ Six enlisted men belonging to an unidentified regiment of the IV Corps, Army of the Cumberland. Their appearance is typical of the soldiers who fought in the Atlanta campaign. All wear felt hats and five are dressed in fatigue blouses. The sixth man, standing at right, wears a dress jacket with the triangular IV Corps badge pinned on his chest.

Some two months after the campaign began, another member of the IV Corps, Capt. Henry Richards of the 93rd Ohio, wrote to his father on July 11: "The work of the army is very unequally divided, and I think [Gen. George H.] Thomas is very partial to the Fourteenth Corps [which also belonged to the Army of the Cumberland], giving them all post and garrison duty and less of the fighting than any other corps in this Department. There is much grumbling among officers and men on this account, and when this campaign does end there will be more resignations offered than ever before from this corps. When General Baird's Division relieved us yesterday the feeling was manifested by the men calling them Thomas' pets, and saying there's no danger here boys; hold this position till we drive them away again, and build works, and then you can move up again. The boys will have their joke!"

through the Brigade with music and a guard at charge bayonet. So much for deserting the service!"

There were those, however, who were not so fortunate. Sentences passed on deserters in other courts-martial were extreme in their finality, as described by one soldier from Texas:

'Prayers for the man about to die'

Private James Turner
Company G
6th Texas Volunteer Infantry

While in camp, on March 22, we were awakened from sleep during a heavy snow storm and ordered into line. It was very dark and the snow was falling thick and fast. Although we had no idea what we were called out so hurriedly for we took our places in ranks and were marched quietly toward the east until we came to an open field. There just at daylight we were halted and the entire division was formed on three sides of an open

■ The Rev. Charles Todd Quintard served throughout the war as chaplain of the 1st Tennessee. During the winter and early spring of 1864, a religious revival swept through the Army of Tennessee's camps at Dalton and hundreds of soldiers, from privates to generals, were baptized and confirmed. "I was then Chaplain-at-Large under the appointment of the General Commanding," Quintard later wrote. "At Dalton [on April 20] I baptized Brigadier-General [Otho F.] Strahl in his camp in the presence of his assembled brigade, and at night we held services in the Methodist Church at Dalton. I read Evening Prayer ... after which I presented a class for confirmation in which were General Hardee, General Strahl, two other Generals [Shoup and Govan], a number of officers of the line and many privates."

However, not all of the Confederates became converts. 1st Sergeant James L. Cooper of the 20th Tennessee wrote: "For the religiously inclined, there was a considerable revival of religion in the brigade to attract their attention; others, not so pious, could attend the cock fights, and could also take a hand at poker or seven-up. I am afraid those of a pious turn of mind were decidedly in the minority."

square.

Then came a solemn procession made up of a hospital ambulance containing besides the driver, a man sitting on a coffin, and an armed guard marching slowly and silently on each side and in the rear of the wagon. The men in line, their clothing whitened by the thickly falling snow, stood like statues. Not a sound was heard, the deep snow muffled all sound, and in the weird light of the breaking day it seemed as though a phantom procession was passing in review.

The wagon and its guard halted in the center of the open square. The unfortunate occupant descended from the wagon, the coffin was taken out and placed on the snow and the wagon was driven away.

The silent guard stood at attention. The Chaplain's voice could be distinctly heard as he offered up prayers for the man about to die. The prisoner's arms were bound, his eyes were bandaged and he was caused to kneel on the snow beside his coffin. Then the officer commanding the guard, or firing party, gave the commands, "Ready, Aim, Fire!" A puff of smoke, a crashing sound, and the condemned man lay stretched out on the ground. He was not dead and the firing party reloaded their guns and fired another volley at the prostrate form, riddling the man and killing him instantly. It was a horrible sight and seemed to us like a terrible butchery. The man had deserted one of the Alabama regiments, was caught, and was sentenced by Court Martial to death. It was the first and only military execution we ever saw, and was the only one that ever took place in our division.

As soon as the execution was over we marched silently back to camp, and soon had great log fires burning, around which the men clustered and quietly discussed the terrible scene we had just witnessed.

The snow continued to fall and during the day the boys began throwing snowballs at each other. Soon everybody was throwing snowballs and the tragedy of the morning was for a time forgotten. Finally one half of the division was arrayed against the other half, and a regular battle of snowballs began, which kept up until late in the afternoon. Many amusing incidents occurred during the snow fight, and soon after it was over, voices were heard calling, "Come up boys and draw your whiskey." Old Pat [Cleburne] had sent a quantity of whiskey to each regiment, and before very long the men were standing around the fires in steaming groups, yelling at the tops of their voices. This was kept up until midnight.

Snow fighting in the Confederate camps was repeated after each appreciable snowfall that winter and early spring — providing comic relief as well as a few casualties — with field grade officers mixing in and heaving snowballs as energetically as the enlisted men.

'Striped with the tracks of flying snow-balls'

Col. George W. Gordon
11th Tennessee Volunteer Infantry

The Army of Tennessee, commanded by Gen. Jos. E. Johnston, passed the memorable winter of 1863-64 in camp at Dalton, Ga. The winter was one of unprecedented severity — the thermometer registering in January 1864 three degrees below zero. During the cold weather an unusual amount of snow fell for that latitude; and the chief occupations of the soldiers were getting wood, cooking, eating and keeping warm. It was too

cold to drill or indulge in the usual out-door games, "stag dances," etc., tents being too small for these purposes. And as most of the "boys" were *young* men, naturally there was an accumulation of physical energy that constantly sought issue in athletic exercises. When the copious fall of snow came, it brought the opportunity not only for exercise, but for royal sport as well.

Gen. B.F. Cheatham's division of Gen. Hardee's corps was composed of four brigades of Tennesseeans — Maney's, Vaughan's, Carter's and Strahl's, and was camped on one side of a considerable depression in the ground, not sharp enough to be called a ravine, but through which a small branch ran during wet weather. On the opposite summit and slope to this depression, and about three hundred paces from the Tennesseeans, was camped Gen. Walker's division of Georgia troops — also of Hardee's corps.

The day after the snow had ceased to fall, "snow-balling" first began among the men of the same companies and camps, and many interesting, exciting and clamorous contests were had for several hours. But finally a body of Tennesseeans and Georgians became arrayed against each other and very soon the contest became highly exciting. As the news spread through the camps that a fight was on hand between the Georgians and Tennesseeans, division pride and State pride became excited, the small fights ceased, and reinforcements poured in to both sides of the State forces until all interest was absorbed in one grand battle between Georgians and Tennesseeans, in which several thousand men were now en-

■ Diversion from the monotony of camp life: Confederates engage in a March 1864 snowball fight. "They would usually divide off into two grand divisions," recalled Private Sam R. Watkins of the 1st Tennessee, "one line naturally becoming the attacking party, and the other the defensive. The snow balls would begin to fly hither and thither, with an occasional knock down, and sometimes an ugly wound, where some mean fellow had enclosed a rock in his snow ball. It was fun while it lasted, but after it was over the soldiers were wet, cold and uncomfortable. I have seen charges and attacks and routs and stampedes, etc., but before the thing was over, one side did not know one from the other. It was a general knock down and drag out affair."

■ Brig. Gen. William P. Carlin, foreground, with members of his staff at Graysville, Ga., in March 1864. He commanded the 1st Brigade, 1st Division, XIV Corps. In the background, an evergreen stand built by the 104th Illinois holds musicians of the 1st Brigade band, whose members came primarily from that regiment. The light gray stallion was Carlin's personal mount, and was named "Rosey" in honor of Maj. Gen. William Rosecrans.

gaged, making the heavens wild with shouts and the air striped with the tracks of flying snow-balls. Charge after charge was made and repulsed.

For two hours or longer the battle raged, with partially varying successes. The prisoners who were captured in one charge would make their escape under the excitement of the next, and rejoin their comrades in the fight. Sometimes the assaulting columns would have to retreat because their ammunition would give out, and would, in turn, be countercharged and routed by the receiving forces who had held their ground and defended their magazines (large piles of snow-balls as high as a man's head all along the line and prepared beforehand), and were thus supplied with ammunition.

Sometimes these magazines would be charged and captured by massing a force for that purpose. In these charges the supreme efforts made by the defending forces to resist the momentum of the assaulting mass, raised excitement to its wildest height. The place where a magazine was captured was always retaken, but sometimes not until the ammunition had been used up on those making it, or carried away by the enemy into his own lines.

Finally, after alternating successes of a very partial and indecisive character, the battle ceased as if by common consent and the weary combatants "rested upon their arms" — each upon his original ground and upon opposite sides of the depression, and not more than a hundred paces apart. Neither side seemed to be satisfied. Neither was whipped and neither appeared inclined to leave the field. Besides, during this cessation of hostilities, both armies were vigorously engaged in making ammunition, which, with other demonstrations of a hostile character, clearly indicated that the battle was soon to be renewed.

At this moment a messenger, and one of my own command, came running to my quarters and said that he had been sent by the Tennesseeans to ask me to come and command them, and to come mounted; that with a mounted commander to lead them they thought they could win the fight. With my interest already highly excited, it needed no persuasion, and I told my colored boy to saddle my horse immediately. By the time he had done so, the messenger had improvised a flag for me to carry, out of an old bandana handkerchief, about two feet and a half square, and the largest and dirtiest one, I think, I ever saw. I mounted my horse, a beautiful dappled iron grey, and with the bandana flag in my hand, flying to the breeze, I charged to the field — my horse leaping logs, ditches and other obstructions and running faster as I approached the exciting scene.

When I checked up in front of the Tennesseeans (now in battle array) and waving my flag, such a tremendous shout shook the air that the very atmosphere seemed to quiver around and above us. Excitement was now intense, and the men wildly impatient to make the charge.

Immediately after my appearance on horse-back in front of the Tennesseans, a major of Gen. Walker's staff appeared mounted at the head of the Georgians. His coming was greeted with a tremendous shout from *his* men, and was answered by mine with another shout, as if to say "We accept your challenge."

Non-combatants had assembled by the hundreds on the surrounding hills and house-tops to see the fight. General officers and their staffs, at their headquarters, had mounted their horses or ascended higher elevations to witness the impending struggle. All was now ready. After directing the men to fill their pockets, bosoms and hands with balls, and the ordnance officers to follow the line with all the ammunition their details could carry, I ordered the charge.

With a shout that signaled victory, and an impetuosity that seemed irresistible, we dashed upon the brave Georgians, and for a few minutes the struggle was fierce and furious, desperate and doubtful. The air was white with whizzing and bursting balls; men were tripped up, knocked down, covered with snow, or run over. The writer was struck with at least a hundred balls, and his horse by as many more. The momentum of the charging column was too great, however, to be successfully resisted, more especially so when it outflanked both wings of the enemy, which soon gave way. The center then being flanked, and at the same time being sorely pressed in front, also gave way, and his entire army fled in great confusion. The rout on the field was now complete, and the enemy was not only driven therefrom, but through his own camp and into the woods beyond.

The object of the campaign being now accomplished, I ordered the pursuit to cease and the men to return to their camps. As they did so, however, some of them stopped in the deserted camps of the Georgians and plundered their mess chests, which had been well filled by supplies from their friends at home. When I heard of this, and reproved it as not being a legitimate object of the campaign, the reply and defense were in that questionable old maxim, "All is fair in love and war."

So far from this episode of camp life having been a source of unkind feeling between Walker's division of Georgians and Cheatham's division of Tennesseeans, it ever afterward seemed to be rather a bond of sympa-

'This war is a money war'

On February 15, 1864, Sergeant Frank B. Patten of Company A, 92nd Ohio, wrote from Chattanooga to his brother, Preston, expressing his disillusionment with the war and his military service. The letter reads in part:

"Some of the Veterans are beginning to return. They will be coming up most every day for a month or more, just as they left 1 or 2 regts per day. So you see that the army will increase pretty fast as there is a great many recruits comeing up. The 11 OVI & 36 OVI are going for the Veterans. They have just took a fit. One month a go they Swore that they never would go as veterans ...

"You said that you had a notion to Inlist & what I thought a bout it. I have told you before what I thought & will tell you as I told you before that you had better Stay at home. I dont want you to inlist nor I dont want Father to give one cent for bounties or Sanitary Fairs. May be that if they Draft it will bring out Some of the Buternuts. If it dont it wont do any hurt to give them a chance to be drafted & if you are drafted you will be no apter to get killed than you would if you inlist. You wanted to know what I would do if I was not in the army. If I was not in the army nor never had been I should inlist I expect, but that is no Sign that you Should. But if I live to get out of it I Shall not re-inlist. I can make more money in the army than to pack a gun & then I could quit when I got ready & this war is a money war any how. I do not think that this Rebellion will last more than one year but I think that there will be a war after this one but I may be mistaken, but if you will take my advise you will Stay at Home."

In spite of his brother's advice, Preston Patten enlisted in Company A, 141st Ohio — a regiment organized in May 1864 from two battalions (and parts of two others) of the Ohio National Guard. The regiment's service lasted 100 days and consisted of guarding transportation routes between Charleston and Guyandotte, W.Va. The role of the so-called Hundred Days' regiments was important to the overall Federal strategy for 1864, as it freed other regiments from garrison duty and enabled them to join active campaigning.

■ **Officers of the 52nd Ohio pose in April 1864 in their camp at Lee & Gordon's Mills, Ga., located on the site of severe fighting along Chickamauga Creek the previous September. "Many Union soldiers were buried by the enemy on the field," wrote Sergeant Nixon B. Stewart of the 52nd's Company E. "As we strolled over the field we have seen hands, shriveled and blackened in the sun, looking like some mummy ... thrust out of the earth in mute appeal, as a strange memento of the battle." Pictured here are, from left, 2nd Lieut. David F. Miser, Company G (mortally wounded June 19 near Kennesaw Mountain); 2nd Lieut. Julius Armstrong, Company F; 1st Lieut. Frank B. James, Company K (who preserved the original tintype); 2nd Lieut. James H. Donaldson, Company E (killed July 19 at Peachtree Creek); Capt. William Sturgis, Company B (wounded May 14 at Resaca); Capt. Samuel Rothacker, Company G; Lt. Col. Charles W. Clancy (captured July 19 at Peachtree Creek); and Major James T. Holmes (wounded September 1 at Jonesboro).**

thy and union. The writer never afterward passed or met the Georgia division, that its men did not greet him with shouts, often with "Three cheers for the Snow-ball Colonel!"

The Tennesseeans were so enthused with their great victory over the Georgians that they wanted another fight before the "weary sun," then sinking low, "had made his golden set." But as there was not time to seek it with troops in a distant camp and from a different State, they concluded to fight each other. Accordingly, an issue was joined between Maney's brigade, commanded by Col. Hume Feild, mounted, and Vaughan's brigade, commanded by the writer, also mounted.

The dispositions for battle having been duly made, the charge was mutually sounded and when the opposing lines, advancing on each other with great speed and impetuosity, clashed, the shock was tremendous. Men fell right and left, in front and rear. Some were dragged from the field, hatless and coatless, amid the greatest cheering and wildest shouts. The battle raged till all the reserves had been brought into action, when a supreme effort was made by both sides to close the fight with victory.

The writer, venturing too far into the enemy's ranks, had his horse seized by as many of them as could get hold of him, and was thrown to the ground; the rider was grabbed by the head and arms (his bandana flag going down in the wreck), and was being dragged to the enemy's rear when a large squad of his own men seized him by the other end in an effort to recapture him, and he was raised from the ground and actually strung up between the heavens and the earth by the pulling forces at each end of him. At this moment he *felt* that his situation was now serious indeed, and that it was time to stop such "damn foolishness."

So, by vigorous kicking, cussing and yelling to his men to release him, they did so, and he was left a prisoner in the hands of the enemy, but without any serious injury. In the meantime, however, his own men had captured the commander of the enemy, and as neither side now had a leader the men ceased fighting and entered into negotiations for an exchange of prisoners. By the time the exchange was effected, the ardor of the combatants had greatly cooled, and neither side seemed disposed to renew the contest.

In concluding this report of the celebrated snow-ball fight, I suppose the writer can say that he won more "reputation" than in all the other battles in which he participated during the war. With a bowed head to protect his face and eyes from the balls of the enemy, he rode right into and through their ranks, amid a deluging snowstorm of flying missiles, and emerged therefrom with a floating flag, but a hatless head. He congratulates his command and himself that though the battle was intensely boisterous, it was practically bloodless — the only casualties being a few blinded eyes and two or three broken arms, during an action in which not fewer than five thousand men were engaged.

A variety of other amusements also found favor with the Southern soldiers at Dalton; "however, all was not frolic as they were continually reminded that they were in the army and that a war was going on by hearing the Federals having sham battles now and then," wrote Capt. Samuel C. Kelly of the 30th Alabama. Everyone knew that more hard fighting would begin once spring and summer arrived. It was just a matter of time. Meanwhile, the high commands of each side busied themselves with plans and preparations.

In the North, changes in leadership during the month of March spelled trouble for the war-weary Confederacy. Maj. Gen. Ulysses S. Grant was called by President Abraham Lincoln to Washington from Nashville to command all the Federal armies and to personally supervise the Army of the Potomac. Following a meeting with Lincoln, Grant briefly visited Maj. Gen. George G. Meade, who commanded that army at Brandy Station, Va. Grant then returned to his Nashville headquarters.

The man who succeeded to Grant's former western command was Maj. Gen. William Tecumseh Sherman, a 44-year-old West Point graduate from Grant's native state of Ohio. The two men had served together throughout the major campaigns in the west, including the battle of Shiloh and campaigns for Vicksburg and Chattanooga. Both generals possessed an unabiding confidence in the other's judgment, and met one last time in Nashville before Grant made his way back to Washington.

■ Lt. Gen. Ulysses S. Grant, who became commander of all Federal armies in the field in March 1864, outlined his plans for the year to Gen. Sherman in a letter dated April 4. He instructed Sherman: "You I propose to move against Johnston's army, to break it up, and to get into the interior of the enemy's country as far as you can, inflicting all the damage you can against their war resources. I do not propose to lay down for you a plan of campaign, but simply to lay down the work it is desirable to have done, and leave you free to execute it in your own way."

This portrait of Grant was taken in the gallery of F. Gutekunst of Philadelphia, shortly after President Lincoln's assassination.

'A compact army for active operations'

Maj. Gen. William T. Sherman
Commanding
Military Division of the Mississippi

On the 18th of March, 1864, at Nashville, Tenn., I relieved Lieutenant-General Grant in command of the Military Division of the Mississippi, embracing the Departments of the Ohio, Cumberland, Tennessee, and Arkansas, commanded respectively by Major-Generals Schofield, Thomas, McPherson, and Steele. General Grant was in the act of starting East to assume command of all the armies of the United States, but more particularly to give direction in person to the Armies of the Potomac and James, operating against Richmond; and I accompanied him as far as

■ 1st Lieut. Charles T. Schable of Company A, 4th Kentucky Mounted Infantry. At the end of its 30-day furlough, this regiment rendezvoused on March 2, 1864, at Camp Nelson, Ky., where it received orders to recruit and become a mounted unit. Moving to the suburbs of Lexington, Ky., the 4th obtained a full complement of fine horses and began training as mounted infantry — a distinction provided to only a small number of Federal regiments. Armed with breech-loading carbines and able to move quickly on horseback, these regiments usually fought dismounted. The 4th suffered severely during the McCook raid south of Atlanta in late July 1864. Schable, who served for a time as regimental adjutant, appears here as he looked shortly after the raid, when the 4th refitted at Nashville in August.

Cincinnati on his way, to avail myself of the opportunity to discuss privately many little details incident to the contemplated changes, and of preparation for the great events then impending.

After my return to Nashville I addressed myself to the task of organization and preparation, which involved the general security of the vast region of the South which had been already conquered, more especially the several routes of supply and communication with the active armies at the front, and to organize a large army to move into Georgia, coincident with the advance of the Eastern armies against Richmond.

I started at once in a special car attached to the regular train, to inspect my command at the front, going to Pulaski, Tenn., where I found General G.M. Dodge; thence to Huntsville, Ala., where I had left a part of my personal staff and the records of the department ... and there I found General McPherson, who had arrived from Vicksburg, and had assumed command of the Army of the Tennessee. General McPherson accompanied me, and we proceeded by the cars to Stevenson, Bridgeport, etc., to Chattanooga, where we spent a day or two with General George H. Thomas, and then continued to Knoxville, where was General Schofield. He returned with us to Chattanooga, stopping by the way a few hours at Loudon, where were the headquarters of the Fourth Corps.

About the end of March, therefore, the three army commanders and myself were together at Chattanooga. We had nothing like a council of war, but conversed freely and frankly on all matters of interest then in progress or impending. We all knew that, as soon as the spring was fairly open, we should have to move directly against our antagonist, General Jos. E. Johnston, then securely intrenched at Dalton, thirty miles distant.

We discussed every possible contingency likely to arise, and I simply instructed each army commander to make immediate preparations for a hard campaign, regulating the distribution of supplies that were coming up by rail from Nashville as equitably as possible. We also agreed on some subordinate changes in the organization of the three separate armies which were destined to take the field; among which was the consolidation of the Eleventh and Twelfth Corps (Howard and Slocum) into a single corps, to be commanded by General Jos. Hooker. General Howard was to be transferred to the Fourth Corps, and General Slocum was to be ordered down the Mississippi River, to command the District of Vicksburg. These changes required the consent of the President, and were all in due time approved.

The great question of the campaign was one of supplies. Nashville, our chief depot, was itself partially in a hostile country, and even the routes of supply from Louisville to Nashville by rail, and by way of the Cumberland River, had to be guarded. Chattanooga (our starting point) was 136 miles in front of Nashville, and every foot of the way, especially the many bridges, trestles, and culverts, had to be strongly guarded against the acts of a local hostile population and of the enemy's cavalry. Then, of course, as we advanced into Georgia, it was manifest that we should have to repair the railroad, use it, and guard it likewise.

General Thomas' army was much the largest of the three, was best provided, and contained the best corps of engineers, railroad managers, and repair parties, as well as the best body of spies and provost-marshals. He had so long exercised absolute command and control over the railroads in his department, that the other armies were jealous, and these thought the Army of the Cumberland got the lion's share of the supplies and other advantages of the railroads. I found a good deal of feeling in the Army of the Tennessee on this score, and therefore took supreme control of the

'To set the example'

■ Maj. Gen. William Tecumseh Sherman. When the Atlanta campaign opened he took to the field by riding to Ringgold where the Army of the Cumberland began the advance south. Sherman later wrote in his memoirs: "My general headquarters and official records remained back at Nashville, and I had near me only my personal staff and inspectors-general, with about half a dozen wagons, and a single company of Ohio sharpshooters as headquarters or camp guard. I also had a small company of irregular Alabama [Union] cavalry, used mostly as orderlies and couriers. No wall-tents were allowed, only the flies. Our mess establishment was less in bulk than that of any of the brigade commanders; nor was this from an indifference to the ordinary comforts of life, but because I wanted to set the example, and gradually to convert all parts of that army into a mobile machine, willing and able to start at a minute's notice, and to subsist on the scantiest food."

In a letter dated April 10, 1864, Sherman had written from Nashville to Gen. Grant in Washington: "Georgia has a million of inhabitants. If they can live, we should not starve. If the enemy interrupt our communications, I will be absolved from all obligations to subsist on our own resources, and will feel perfectly justified in taking whatever and wherever we can find. I will inspire my command, if successful, with the feeling that beef and salt are all that is absolutely necessary to life, and that parched corn once fed General [Andrew] Jackson's army on that very ground."

This photograph of Sherman, believed to be previously unpublished, was taken in June 1865 in the Chicago portrait gallery of S.M. Fassett. While in the field exactly one year earlier, however, Sherman's appearance was much more non-descript, as Major Charles W. Wills, 103rd Illinois, wrote in his diary on June 11, 1864: "I saw him yesterday — seems to me he is getting fleshy. He don't look as though he had anything more important than a 40-acre farm to attend to."

■ 1st Lieut. Edwin Weller of Company H, 107th New York, was on detached duty with his company near Wartrace, Tenn., during the first four months of 1864. On March 21, he wrote to his future wife: "I have received a dispatch nearly every night for a week past to be on the alert for the Rebs. There is a force of guerrillas prowling up and down the country near the R.R. trying to get below us to the road to destroy the track. They made a dash to the road about twenty miles from us, and attacked a train, ran it off the track and burned it, killing three niggers and taking seven soldiers prisoners. They paroled them after robbing them of their jewelry, money and clothes. Our soldiers killed a few of the gang."

Here, Weller wears a XX Corps badge on his frock coat.

roads myself, placed all the army commanders on an equal footing, and gave to each the same control, so far as orders of transportation for men and stores were concerned.

Thomas' spies brought him frequent and accurate reports of Jos. Johnston's army at Dalton, giving its strength anywhere between forty and fifty thousand men, and these were being reinforced by troops from Mississippi and by the Georgia militia, under General G.W. Smith. General Johnston seemed to be acting purely on the defensive, so that we had time and leisure to take all our measures deliberately and fully. I fixed the date of May 1st, when all things should be in readiness for the grand forward movement, and then returned to Nashville; General Schofield going back to Knoxville, and McPherson to Huntsville, Thomas remaining at Chattanooga.

On the 2d of April, at Nashville, I wrote to General Grant, reporting to him the results of my visit to the several armies, and asked his consent to the several changes proposed, which was promptly given by telegraph. I then addressed myself specially to the troublesome question of transportation and supplies. I found the capacity of the railroads from Nashville forward to Decatur, and to Chattanooga, so small, especially in the number of locomotives and cars, that it was clear that they were barely able to supply the daily wants of the armies then dependent on them, with no power of accumulating a surplus in advance. The cars were daily loaded down with men returning from furlough, with cattle, horses, etc., and, by reason of the previous desolation of the country between Chattanooga and Knoxville, General Thomas had authorized the issue of provisions to the suffering inhabitants.

We could not attempt an advance into Georgia without food, ammunition, etc., and ordinary prudence dictated that we should have an accumulation at the front, in case of interruption to the railway by the act of the enemy, or by common accident. Accordingly, on the 6th of April, I issued a general order, limiting the use of the railroad-cars to transporting only the essential articles of food, ammunition, and supplies for the army proper, forbidding any further issues to citizens, and cutting off all civil traffic; requiring the commanders of posts within thirty miles of Nashville to haul out their own stores in wagons; requiring all troops destined for the front to march, and all beef-cattle to be driven on their own legs.

I accordingly called together in Nashville the master of transportation, Colonel [Adna] Anderson [general superintendent of military railroads], the chief quartermaster, General J.L. Donaldson, and the chief commissary, General Amos Beckwith, for conference. I assumed the strength of the army to move from Chattanooga into Georgia at 100,000 men, and the number of animals to be fed, both for cavalry and draught, at 35,000; then, allowing for occasional wrecks of trains, which were very common, and for the interruption of the road itself by guerillas and regular raids, we estimated it would require 130 cars, of 10 tons each, to reach Chattanooga daily, to be reasonably certain of an adequate supply. Even with this calculation, we could not afford to bring forward hay for the horses and mules, nor more than five pounds of oats or corn per day for each animal. I was willing to risk the question of forage in part, because I expected to find wheat and corn fields, and a good deal of grass, as we advanced into Georgia at that season of the year.

Colonel Anderson promptly explained that he did not possess cars or locomotives enough to do this work. I then instructed and authorized him to hold on to all trains that arrived at Nashville from Louisville, and to allow

Protecting the lines of supply

■ A fortified railroad bridge spans the Cumberland River at Nashville, Tenn. Heavy wooden doors and guard turrets with loopholes enabled Federal defenders to protect the bridge against Confederate cavalry or guerrilla raids. In Gen. Sherman's opinion, "the Atlanta campaign would simply have been impossible without the use of the railroads from Louisville to Nashville, one hundred and eighty-five miles; from Nashville to Chattanooga, one hundred and fifty miles; and from Chattanooga to Atlanta, one hundred and thirty-seven miles. Every mile of this 'single track' was so delicate that one man could in a minute have broken or moved a rail, but our trains usually carried along the tools and means to repair such a break. We had, however, to maintain strong guards and garrisons at each important bridge or trestle, the destruction of which would have necessitated time for rebuilding.

"For the protection of a bridge, one or two log block-houses, two stories high, with a piece of ordnance and a small infantry guard, usually sufficed. The block-house had a small parapet and ditch about it, and the roof was made shot-proof, by earth piled on. These points could usually be reached only by a dash of the enemy's cavalry, and many of these block-houses successfully resisted serious attacks by both cavalry and artillery."

none to go back until he had secured enough to fill the requirements of our problem. At the time he only had about 60 serviceable locomotives, and about 600 cars of all kinds, and he represented that to provide for all contingencies he must have at least 100 locomotives and 1,000 cars.

As soon as Mr. Guthrie, the president of the Louisville & Nashville Railroad, detected that we were holding on to all his locomotives and cars, he wrote me, earnestly remonstrating against it, saying that he would not be able with diminished stock to bring forward the necessary stores from Louisville to Nashville.

I wrote to him, frankly telling him exactly how we were placed, appealed to his patriotism to stand by us, and advised him in like manner to hold on to all trains coming into Jeffersonville, Ind. He and General Robert Allen, then quartermaster-general at Louisville, arranged a ferry-boat so as to transfer the trains over the Ohio River from Jeffersonville, and in a short time we had cars and locomotives from almost every road at the North; months afterward I was amused to see, away down in Georgia, cars marked "Pittsburg & Fort Wayne," "Delaware & Lackawanna," "Baltimore & Ohio," and indeed with the names of almost every railroad north of the Ohio River.

■ Corporal Randolph H. Swan of Company H, 65th Ohio, was photographed during veteran furlough (shortly after his promotion to corporal) and sports a new pair of gauntlets and boots. Later in the spring of 1864, orders were issued prohibiting enlisted men from wearing boots in the upcoming campaign. Reacting to these orders, another Ohioan wrote: "Fortunately for me I sold to Lieut. Kile my $8 boots some days ago, but Green has an expensive pair on hand (feet), which he says will not be thrown away to comply with the order of anybody. Many of the men have boots that have cost high prices, and to be compelled to abandon them and wear shoes will be next to an outrage. I notice that General [Jefferson] Davis wears boots."

Boots or no boots, Swan survived the fighting for Atlanta, but died three months later on December 15, 1864, at the battle of Nashville.

The department and army commanders had to maintain strong garrisons in their respective departments, and also to guard their respective lines of supply. I therefore, in my mind, aimed to prepare out of these three armies, by the 1st of May, 1864, a compact army for active operations in Georgia, and, to make these troops as mobile as possible, I made the strictest possible orders in relation to wagons and all species of incumbrances and impedimenta whatever. Each officer and soldier was required to carry on his horse or person food and clothing enough for five days. To each regiment was allowed but one wagon and one ambulance, and to the officers of each company one pack-horse or mule. Each division and brigade was provided a fair proportion of wagons for a supply-train, and these were limited in their loads to carry food, ammunition and clothing. Tents were forbidden to all save the sick and wounded, and one tent only was allowed to each headquarters for use as an office.

Several times during the campaign I found quartermasters hid away in some comfortable nook to the rear, with tents and mess-fixtures which were the envy of the passing soldiers; and I frequently broke them up, and distributed the tents to the surgeons of brigades. Yet my orders actually reduced the transportation, so that I doubt if any army ever went forth to battle with fewer impedimenta, and where the regular and necessary supplies of food, ammunition, and clothing, were issued, as called for, so regularly and so well.

As Sherman's campaign preparations intensified throughout the month of April, Gen. Johnston readied the Army of Tennessee for the anticipated Federal advance. He later described the limitations of his troop positions around Dalton:

"I supposed, from the information given me by the ranking general officers, that Dalton had not been selected by General Bragg for its value as a defensive position, but that the retreat from Missionary Ridge had ceased at this point, because it was ascertained there that the pursuit had been abandoned by the Federal army. Each division, consequently, was occupying the position it had taken for the encampment of a night, and on it had constructed huts for its winter quarters. These divisions formed two corps: one commanded by Lieutenant-General Hardee, composed of Cheatham's, Breckinridge's, Cleburne's and Walker's divisions; the other, commanded by Major-General Hindman, was composed of his own, Stevenson's and Stewart's divisions.

"Major-General Wheeler, with such of his cavalry as was fittest for active service, amounting to about sixteen hundred, was at the village of Tunnel Hill, on the railroad, seven miles from Dalton, in the direction of Ringgold; his pickets on Taylor's Ridge, in front, and on the left, but extending to the right beyond the Cleveland road. Cleburne's division occupied the crest of Tunnel Hill, on both sides of the wagon-road from Dalton to Ringgold. Stewart's division had one brigade in front of, one in, and two immediately in rear of Mill Creek Gap. Breckinridge was between the Gap and Dalton; Hindman's, two miles southwest of Dalton, except a brigade on the Cleveland road; Stevenson's, near Hindman's; Walker's, three miles east of Dalton; and Cheatham's, near and to the south of Walker's.

"The position of Dalton had little to recommend it as a defensive one. It had neither intrinsic strength nor strategic advantage. It neither fully covered its own communications nor threatened those of the enemy. The railroad from Atlanta to Chattanooga passes through Rocky-Faced Ridge

■ Special office wagon belonging to the Army of the Cumberland headquarters of Gen. George H. Thomas. In this April 1864 photograph, the wagon is parked in Chattanooga, with Brig. Gen. William D. Whipple, Thomas' chief of staff, handing a dispatch to headquarters clerk John Tweedale, a private detailed from the 15th Pennsylvania Cavalry.

On the road to Atlanta, Thomas' large camp came to be called "Thomasville." Gen. Sherman commented: "Most of the general officers except Thomas, followed my example [of baggage reduction] strictly; but he had a regular headquarters-camp. I frequently called his attention to the orders on this subject, rather jestingly than seriously. He would break out against his officers for having such luxuries, but, needing a tent himself, and being good-natured and slow to act, he never enforced my orders perfectly. In addition to his regular wagon-train, he had a big wagon which could be converted into an office, and this we used to call 'Thomas' circus.' "

by Mill Creek Gap, three miles and a half beyond Dalton, but very obliquely, the course of the road being about thirty degrees west of north, and that of the ridge about five degrees east of north. As it terminates but three miles north of the gap, it offers little obstacle to the advance of a superior force from Ringgold to Dalton.

"Between Mill Creek and Snake Creek Gaps, this ridge protects the road to Atlanta on the west, but at the same time covers any direct approach from Chattanooga to Resaca or Calhoun — points on the route from Dalton to Atlanta — or flank movement in that direction, by an army in front of Mill Creek Gap. These considerations would have induced me to draw the troops back to the vicinity of Calhoun, to free our left flank from exposure, but for the earnestness with which the President and Secretary of War, in their letters of instructions, wrote of early assumption of offensive operations and apprehension of the bad effect of a retrograde movement upon the spirit of the Southern people."

As late as March 12, Gen. Bragg, acting as military advisor to President Davis, outlined a plan for Johnston's army to resume offensive operations. The plan, delivered by letter to Johnston on March 18, "prescribed my invasion of Tennessee with an army of 75,000 men," Johnston wrote, "including Longstreet's corps, then near Morristown, Tenn. When necessary supplies and transportation were collected at Dalton, the additional troops, except Longstreet's, would be sent there; and this army and Longstreet's corps would march to meet at Kingston, [Tenn.] on the Tennessee River, and thence into the valley of Duck River."

Johnston did not approve of Bragg's outline. He later explained that "the enemy could defeat the plan, either by attacking one of our two bod-

■ Col. Richard M. Saffell commanded the 26th Tennessee during the campaign. The previous winter he wrote from the regiment's camp near Dalton: "Old Joe Johnston is the man to win the next fight whenever and wherever we meet the foe. This is only my prediction, but time will tell, and if we dont whip them, we will be the most disappointed army that ever fought a battle." Saffell survived the campaign but not the war. He was killed on March 21, 1865, in the battle of Bentonville, N.C.

■ **Opposite:** Private Reuben H. Nations of Company I, 12th Louisiana, was among reinforcements sent to Johnston's Army of Tennessee just as the Atlanta campaign got underway. Belonging to Loring's division of Lt. Gen. Leonidas Polk's Army of Mississippi, the 12th Louisiana arrived by rail at Resaca on May 10. Three days later, the regiment assisted in checking the Federal advance along the Snake Creek Gap road, giving the bulk of Johnston's army time to leave its Dalton-area defenses and take position at Resaca. Nations, a native Georgian, survived the campaign, but suffered the loss of both legs when a shell struck him during a fight near Decatur, Ala., on October 28, 1864.

ies of troops on the march, with their united forces, or by advancing against Dalton before our forces there should be equipped for the field; for it was certain that they would be able to take the field before we could be ready. I proposed, therefore, that the additional troops should be sent to Dalton in time to give us the means to beat the Federal army there, and then pursue it into Tennessee, which would be a more favorable mode of invasion than the other."

On April 30, with the arrival of additional troops, the Confederate Army of Tennessee mustered 37,652 infantry, 2,812 artillery with 112 guns, and 2,392 cavalry.

"The approach of warm weather told us that our work for the summer would soon commence," wrote 1st Sergeant James L. Cooper of the 20th Tennessee, "but I do not think anyone had a thought that the task would prove so long and bloody. Near the latter part of April everything was made ready for action, and every day we listened for the sound of cannon at our outposts."

When Greek meets Greek, then comes the tug of war

Hard service in Georgia with Opdycke's Tigers

At the beginning of the Atlanta campaign in early May 1864, 1st Lieut. Ralsa C. Rice was a seasoned veteran who already had served two and a half years in the Federal army. A native of Kinsman, a small town located in the northeastern Ohio county of Trumbull, Rice went to war in August 1861 as a 23-year-old trooper with Company D, 2nd Ohio Cavalry. A medical certification of disability discharged him from the cavalry in May 1862, but three months later he was back in uniform, this time with the infantry.

A large number of regiments was organizing at Camp Cleveland, Ohio, in the early fall of 1862, and Rice was appointed sergeant and assigned to Company B of the 125th Ohio. Under its Ohio-born commander, Col. Emerson Opdycke, the 125th earned its warlike nickname "Opdycke's Tigers" 12 months later during the battle of Chickamauga, and by the spring of 1864 was considered one of the most dependable regiments in Sherman's army.

"The notoriety and fighting proclivities of a regiment depend upon its commander," Rice later reflected. "If its colonel possesses these characteristics then much may be expected from his followers."

Most of the men under Opdycke's command grew to rely on his military judgment and efficiency, and like Rice, endeared themselves to the man and his methods. "We were being molded into a machine," Rice recalled. "Our colonel could tolerate no delay. He was here, there and everywhere, urging us on. Each one felt that himself was the special object of his attention. Such energetic teachings will long be remembered by the most of us. There was to be no hesitancy, or even mediocrity; promptness was most thoroughly instilled and demanded of all."

During the three months immediately prior to the Atlanta campaign, the 125th Ohio wintered at Loudoun, Tenn., some 30 miles southwest of Knoxville. It belonged to the IV Corps of Maj. Gen. George H. Thomas' Army of the Cumberland, and was closely associated with the 64th and 65th Ohio and 3rd Kentucky Infantry regiments of the 2nd Division's 3rd Brigade.

"Our baggage and all camp equipage left at Chattanooga was brought up," Rice wrote of the stay at Loudoun, "also new clothing and plenty of rations. Material for quarters was found, not in abundance, but enough to enable us to 'patch out.' Our friends at home had worked all the fall to secure for us recruits for the old companies, now reduced far below the minimum number. These new men reached us here and work was at once

begun to 'break them in.' This term is most applicable, from the manner in which the educating was conducted. The unbroken animal if harnessed between two sturdy, well-broken ones, can scarcely go amiss, but go he must; maybe a bit hard on the old ones, but then, we must have exercise."

With winter's relative inactivity nearly at an end, Rice, promoted to first lieutenant on May 3, looked forward "with bright prospects" to the coming campaign. The next four months were to make a lasting impression on him, and comprised more than one-third of his recollections of service with the 125th Ohio written after the war and published in *The National Tribune Scrapbook* shortly after 1900.

In prefacing his account, Rice wrote: "It is not my purpose to enter into any compilation of historical events, or to controvert the writings and sayings of others, but rather a simple narration of facts and scenes as I saw them, and from my own standpoint."

■ Col. Emerson Opdycke was formerly a captain in the 41st Ohio and wounded at Shiloh in 1862. He commanded the 125th Ohio from its organization in the fall of 1862 until he received a flesh wound in the arm on May 14 at Resaca. The regiment so distinguished itself on the second day of fighting at Chickamauga (September 20, 1863) that the division commander, Gen. Thomas J. Wood, gave the 125th its famous sobriquet "Opdycke Tigers." A few days after the battle of Resaca, Opdycke was assigned command of a demi-brigade, until August 6 when he was given permanent command of the 1st Brigade, 2nd Division, IV Corps. He finished the war as a brevet major general of U.S. Volunteers to date from November 30, 1864, when he distinguished himself at the battle of Franklin, Tenn.

1st Lieut. Ralsa C. Rice
Company B
125th Ohio Volunteer Infantry

By the middle of April 1864, spring was all aglow in the Southland. During the previous winter our many discussions developed a consensus of opinion favorable to an early, speedy closing of the war — that one more determined, successful effort must convince the Confederacy of the hopelessness of its cause. We were aware that a campaign was being mapped out and that Gen. Sherman was to lead our Western army. With this we were content, especially as his lieutenants were among the best developed by the war. Each and every one of them had been tried and showed himself fully competent to lead and direct large armies. With such bright prospects all seemed eager for the trial.

There was a general muster called at Chattanooga. Here again the military pageant witnessed was the most imposing, for some 100,000 men were gathered, most of them experienced in the business of war. Neither could we reckon without our host. Bragg had been superceded by Gen. Joe Johnston, known to be one of the ablest generals in the Confederate army. Every effort had been made to create an army able to cope with Sherman. From the most reliable sources, the rebel army which now confronted us numbered 75,000 men, posted behind strong works, or on such naturally defensive positions that fully made up any discrepancy in numbers. "When Greek meets Greek, then comes the tug of war."

On May 8 the movement began. The 125th Ohio began the campaign with 500 men, rank and file; at the end of 100 days but 50 percent remained. Our advance first encountered the enemy at Rocky Face Ridge, a long, sharp mountain spur with an almost perpendicular side toward us. The crest of this ridge runs for a mile or more in an unbroken line, then abruptly terminates in a natural fortress, only needing the replacement of a few stones to make it an impregnable fort. A day or so was occupied in a strong reconnaissance to ascertain, if possible, whether the ridge could be carried by assault.

To Col. Opdycke was assigned the task of making the attempt. We reached the summit in some manner unexplainable amid the plaudits of our comrades below, and drove the enemy along the entire ridge, or until within a short distance of the fort where their artillery swept the crest. Here we remained until night and then went back, leaving the ridge occupied by a

■ 1st Lieut. Ralsa C. Rice of Company B, 125th Ohio, served 10 months with the 2nd Ohio Cavalry before re-enlisting in the 125th. An experienced soldier, Rice was appointed sergeant and later promoted to first lieutenant by May 1864. Both he and his company commander, Capt. Elmer Moses, were wounded during the June 27 assault near Kennesaw Mountain. Rice was struck in the head by a ricocheting bullet, briefly knocking him senseless. After regaining consciousness, he assumed command of the company, leading it until the end of the war.

strong skirmish line. On the day following we were made an attacking party to storm this fort. No scaling ladders were furnished and no shower of artillery shots preceded us. When within striking distance we made our usual rush and reached the fort, where we clung to the sides like bats on a wall. We were kept busy dodging stones which the Johnnies persistently dropped down.

In the meantime, Sherman was hunting for an opening around their flank. In this he was successful. The next morning we found the "Roost" deserted. This high bluff is known by the natives as Buzzard's Roost. Our loss for both days was 50 men, killed and wounded — a pretty serious beginning. We found and took up the trail while yet warm, and followed it down into their deserted camp. Near this camp I saw a number of stout posts set in a row. I was at a loss in finding a purpose. On closer inspection I saw bullet marks in each post and blood stains on the ground. The explanation was now an easy one. Here, tied to each post, deserters had been shot. Thus, the Confederate government under Jeff Davis was making treason odious.

The first town met with was Dalton. Thousands of our soldiers gathered here, converging routes bringing us together. It was a joyous gathering. We had met the enemy and Johnston's great Southern army was in full retreat. Those hills and vales never before or since echoed with such melody. Our bands vied with each other in their selections of patriotic airs: "Hail Columbia," and "Yankee Doodle" put the colored part of the population into ecstacies. To the tune of "The Girl I Left Behind Me" we marched on. We camped for the night within a few miles of Resaca. On the 14th, after marching until about noon, we came to a halt, and from the extensive fire of our skirmishers we judged the enemy was awaiting us.

There was to be no repetition of Chickamauga here. Sherman had his army well in hand, as he always did. The Oostanaula River forms an obstruction here, which the enemy found they could not cross in time to save their trains. At least a day's time must be gained. As if in premeditation a long line of strong breastworks and forts had been constructed, encircling the village of Resaca. These entrenchments now held Johnston's entire army, which Sherman decided to attack and carry by assault if possible. We came on to the field about 2 p.m. and found for once that we were in the rear or reserve line. Surely there was some mistake, some misunderstanding which would soon be discovered and corrected. Our suspense was only momentary, an order coming for us to take the place of a regiment at the front whose ammunition was running low. We marched in by the flank until we were in the rear of the regiment to be relieved. The surface of the ground here was a succession of low ridges with low ground between.

The first line of works, simply a pile of old logs thrown up, was now held by our men. This was constructed by the enemy with an evident purpose of abandonment as they were enfiladed by their artillery in the second line. On our way in we followed the low ground which was covered with brush and an occasional tree. The first thing of note was a cannon shot coming down our line, out of reach, but near enough for discomfort. A trio of officers, Gens. Manson, Cox and Harker, was sitting on a log near where we were then passing. The next shot followed the first one on nearly the same line, lower and more to the right of us. It found these officers and the middle one, Gen. Manson, was struck by it. I was then a lieutenant, following along on the flank of the company, and was just opposite the log mentioned. Gen. Cox was nearest me. He was thrown on the ground by the concussion. On regaining his feet he seemed bewildered. I said, "General, this is a warm place!" "Yes," he replied, "you are right about that." I could not stop to inquire further. I did not see Gen. Cox again until many years after the war. I then reminded him of this incident. Needless to say, I needed no further introduction to him.*

We reached the regiment to be relieved and supposed our advancing would end here. No, this position was too tame for Opdycke. He got old Barney his horse over the logs somehow, and shouting "Forward! Come on, boys!" he rode straight for the enemy, down through one depression and then up another slope, on the crest of which was the enemy's main line. While yet in the lead he was struck by a musket shot, and would have fallen to the ground had not friendly hands prevented. The bullet grazed his side and passed through the flesh of his arm, a painful but not serious wound. Whatever may have been his intentions, we were satisfied to remain where we were. We were ordered to load and fire lying down. Company B was compelled to rise up and advance a few feet to make our shots effective. Company A was on higher ground and suffered severely. We remained here until dark and then were ordered back, not relieved, because we were much in advance of the line then established.

Our loss here was 11 killed and 45 wounded; aggregate 56. We went back to our works a tired, exhausted body of men and soon fell asleep. Shortly past midnight we were brought to our feet, but not to our senses, by a roar of cannon and musketry which shook the earth. A parting salute from the enemy, now again on the retreat, had produced this outbreak. A night attack, generally more imaginary than real, usually has its humorous sides. Our men were asleep a few feet back of the works on ground more dry. I was aroused with the rest, but a new pair of boots were giving me trouble. I had drawn them partly off, and now could not get them either on or off. The delay was just enough for me to recover my wits. I heard Capt. Moses calling for me: "What are you doing back there?" "Oh, I'm just gathering up the arms." I found his sword and belt, and seven muskets abandoned in the haste to obey orders.

In the morning we were marched over that part of the field in our front. The effects of our nighttime cannonade were not apparent until fully a mile and a half had passed. Shooting by moonlight, the aim was a high one but in this instance worked havoc where not intended. The rear of Johnston's army received these shots in profusion — dead men and dead animals lay on the roadway nearly to the river crossing.

The enemy found time to destroy the fine railroad bridge spanning the river at this place. Our ever-available pontoons furnished us a crossing. It looked dubious for our wagons. So much travel had worn out the last trace of a road and with the traveling at its best our trains could barely expect to keep us in provisions. The railroad must be kept running. It was said that Gen. Sherman called the officer in charge of the Construction Corps and asked how long it would take to put the bridge in condition for the crossing of the locomotive. The answer was not satisfactory. "That bridge must be repaired in three days' time." My recollection is that it was ready in the time given.

* Gen. Cox later wrote of this incident: "Newton's men came over part of the ground we had traversed, and as they crossed the open we saw them under the enemy's cannonade, the balls here and there bowling them over like tenpins. Harker's brigade came up to relieve Manson's, which was the most exposed, and Manson and I were standing together arranging the details, our horses being under cover in the edge of the wood. Harker rode up to confer with us and learn the situation, and as we talked, a shell exploded among us, the concussion stunning Manson and a fragment slightly wounding Harker. Manson's experience was a curious illustration of the effect of such an incident. He was unaware of his hurt, and only thought, in the moment of failing consciousness as he fell, that the motion was that of his companions flying upward instead of his own falling; and on coming to himself in the hospital began to speak his sorrow for what he supposed was the death of his friends. He himself never fully recovered from the effects of the concussion."

■ Maj. Gen. Jacob Dolson Cox led the 3rd Division, XXIII Corps, in the campaign. Born in Canada of American parents, he was an Ohio state senator when the war began. As commander of the Kanawha Division, IX Corps, he distinguished himself at South Mountain, Md., in 1862, and upon the death of Gen. Jesse Reno in that battle, assumed command of the corps and led it at Antietam. After the war Cox became governor of Ohio (1866-67) and a Secretary of the Interior (1869-70) in the Grant administration.

■ Private Jesse H. Carey, Company B, 125th Ohio, whose sleep was interrupted by a lizard while in bivouac near Kingston, Ga. Wounded at Chickamauga in 1863, Carey survived the war and mustered out with his company in June 1865.

Our position in the general line was near the center, and in close proximity to the railroad. After crossing the river our advance was necessarily slow; we had to wait until the wings were in position. Skirmishing was an everyday business with us. At no time were we out of earshot of guns. The popping of rifles was incessant and hourly some poor fellow received a shot which ended his career as a soldier.

An erroneous idea prevailed that the enemy had superior rifles, superior ammunition and, with the hands of expert riflemen, were doing this shooting. The fact was their arms, as a general rule, were but the ordinary smoothbore muskets. I took special pains to determine an answer to this question, searching the field after the battle, examining captured arms, and only in one instance saw anything different. On the field after the battle of Peachtree Creek, I found in one cartridge box cartridges of superior make. The paper wrappers were white and strong and the powder of better quality than ours. I at once pronounced them to be of English manufacture. The enemy had a similar idea concerning us, that we had marksmen armed with rifles having telescopic sights. Our Eastern army had a few such weapons, but I only saw one man so armed in our Western army.

In about three days our army was in aggressive shape. The rebels' retreat was more rapid and from this we could understand that they had not reached their next entrenched position.

One evening after a hard day of marching and skirmishing, and just as we were preparing our bivouac for the night, we had an unusual experience. In our front was woodland. Suddenly, like a clap of thunder from a clear sky, a tremendous roar somewhere in the woods greeted our ears. We were quickly in line and double-quicked into the Egyptian darkness. For the first time we saw here the wounded being carried off the field by torchlight. The peculiar effect of this lurid light on our blood-stained comrades is indescribable. We groped about for a while but as the tumult had ceased we had nothing to guide us, and as we thought every man had lost his bearings we camped down then and there. Morning light revealed the fact that we had made our beds on the same ground occupied by the Johnnies the day previous, which they had left without much policing.

Arriving at Kingston we went into camp and were admonished that washing up was in order. We had a fine camp here in an open grove of live oaks. Washing was a simple process for those of us who possessed only the clothes we wore — wade into the water, rub on the soap, swim about for awhile, then crawl out and lie in the sun to dry. In camp we formed the acquaintance of those denizens found in a Georgia forest, a new problem to most of us. Here were scorpions, lizards, centipedes and the most tormenting of all insects — the jiggers of northern Georgia — all dwelling in unity, but, like a swarm of bees, ready to resent any and all intrusion. With the Northern soldier they were always vengeful. Our old doctor, Henry McHenry, with ever-watchful care, had cautioned: "Look out for the scorpion, boys. Their sting is venomous and may prove fatal." Tom Brown of Company B sat down on one of these and with the doctor's admonition ringing in his ears came to me with all the agonies of immediate dissolution depicted in his countenance. I made light of his wound and told him to put off the shuffling of the mortal coil until a more favorable opportunity. I was positively sure that the insect got the worst of the contact. I kept joking him until Thomas complained of feeling better.

Taken collectively, the creatures of the forest and our men were not the best of bedfellows. I sat leaning against a tree, enjoying a quiet smoke with thoughts far away. Near me lay two comrades sleeping as only the just sleep, with the moonbeams gliding through the trees and resting on their upturned faces. With a start and a bound Jesse sprang to his feet, exclaiming, "Holy Moses! What was that?" A swift lizard had run in at the bottom end of his trousers and out at his shirt collar. His streak left behind was that of an icicle, and an electric shock could not have aroused him more effectually.

From here our direction was more easterly, causing another swinging into line. After another three days pressing things we found the enemy opposing our advance with a stubbornness which bespoke of another fortified line.

The Set-To at New Hope Church

The stand here made by the enemy was in a wilderness but little superior to that at Chickamauga. The name given the battlefield was that suggested by the only adornment of all the region: a little frame building built by exiles many years previous and designated "Church of New Hope." Appearances indicated that Johnston had sought seclusion as a means of defense; their works, at least so far as we came in contact with them, were invariably hidden by brush and thickets. A long time was spent in locating their lines so that our approaches might comply as near as possible with their general contour. Our experience in developing the enemy had caused an invention of tactics not laid down in "Hardee."

As I was given an important part — the command of the skirmish line in front of our regiment, then in advance of the brigade — a description of our work will show our style of doing things.

Our captain being away on some detail, I was compelled to act under the command "Company B for skirmishers!" and ordered to report for instructions from Major Bruff. I found him and was given the route and general instructions. We were to advance until the enemy's main line was encountered and then hold our position. The bugle would sound the signals. I ventured to ask if we must comply with the regular skirmish drill. "Take your own way, so long as you get there," said the major. Our line was a short one, only a little more than the regimental front.

At the beginning, brush, brambles and briars must be gotten through, then an open woods with gradual descent of ground for 300 yards, then brush again. On our emerging from the brush we saw the line we were to relieve but a short distance away, engaged in dodging bullets coming from, as near as we could make out, the thicket further down. My instructions to the company were brief:

"Every man for himself. Each must be his own reserve. Take advantage of everything offering protection. We have not a man to spare."

With the sound of the bugle our men deployed at once, and in line behind trees, awaited the signal. I saw an officer, whom I recognized, approaching from the rear on horseback. He had witnessed our preparations and rode up, saying, "Get your men back here in line, then deploy them as you should! Don't you know the tactics better than that?"

I was about to explain to the doughty adjutant my instructions, but a Johnny over there saved me from further humiliation — a bullet came uncomfortably close, quickly followed by another, with an aim most accurate. My inquisitor threw himself off the opposite side of his horse and for a moment I supposed he was hit. But he poked his head out past the animal and said, "Rice, I believe they are shooting at me."

"Yes, I think so."

He gathered himself together, sprang on his horse and, with coattail streaming, I saw no more of him.

With the bugle sounding a charge we ran forward and did not stop to gauge our speed with those on either flank. The breastworks of the enemy

■ Major Joseph Bruff, second in command of the 125th Ohio during the campaign, was slightly wounded at Kennesaw Mountain on June 27. He later commanded the regiment at the battle of Nashville on December 15.

■ Private Nathan B. Hatch, Company B, 125th Ohio, whose close encounter with a "Johnny" at New Hope Church ended with both soldiers exchanging words, not bullets. Hatch was shot through the head and killed June 23 near Kennesaw Mountain.

must be found and the sooner we get there the quicker it will be over with. Their skirmishers were encountered as we entered the brush. They gave us the right of way with their usual hesitancy. A little further we found a ravine, the termination downgrade, with a high bluff bank on the opposite side. We halted in this ravine and found all present and accounted for. I went back a short distance and took position behind a large oak for observation.

I saw that our rush had carried us ahead of the line on both right and left, that the left had stopped at the edge of an open field. On the opposite side I could now make out a line of red clay. I also found to my discomfiture that I was "treed." The Johnnies on the bluff above our boys were making a target of us. On looking out I saw one of these fellows loading his gun. How I longed for my old Springfield, if only for a moment. Sergeant Fitch was the nearest to me. I called for him to come to my relief hastily. I placed my hat on the end of a stick and put it out past the tree. The ruse brought a bullet, making the bark fly. We sprang out, the sergeant took good aim and fired. I heard the bugle again sounding "Forward!"

On gaining the top of the bluff I saw unmistakably the works of the enemy. I noticed at the same time a large fallen tree lying on a line parallel with ours. I assembled the company behind this natural fortification. From it we kept up our part of the demonstration. With no recall or orders to fall back, we remained here until dark. In our last rush Nathan Hatch passed a Johnny behind a tree. Neither had seen the other until this predicament brought them face to face with but a step in between.

"Well, Yank, how is it?" the rebel asked.

"Say it yourself," Hatch answered.

"Well, I don't see why we'uns need to quarrel. You go your way and I'll go mine!" Hatch agreed, and thus a question of much interest to both was settled by arbitration.

Sergeant Fitch went out to the place where he had directed his shot. He came back bringing a haversack with a bullet hole through it, as well as an officer's sword and belt. I exchanged scabbards, the new one a reminder of the sergeant's marksmanship on my behalf. At night our Dutch captain [Capt. Anthony Vallander, formerly of the Prussian Army, in command of Company H] was sent to relieve us. The rebels were shelling the woods back of us. Our position was, of the two, an enjoyable one. The log protected our front and the bullets flying over our heads kept the ground dear in our rear. I was thus free from censure from this direction.

We had sent back no killed or wounded men, and presumably we were set down as not attending to business. The glare of bursting shells in the woods at night is not enjoyable fireworks. Capt. Vallander gave up his search for Company B, went back and reported, "Company B non-est-come-attable." One of his sergeants finally found us and with a portion of Company H, relieved us. Long and continuous shooting had made our nerves impervious to such sounds — even the loud tone of the cannons passed unnoticed. But I very much doubt if we could ever get used to any sudden nocturnal outbreak.

On the night following our skirmish adventure, Capt. Stewart, with companies D and B, was detailed to dig rifle pits along this same front. The line as now established for our outposts did not even reach to the aforementioned ravine. The ground was hard and stony. We well realized that stealth and silence were necessary for the success of our undertaking. In spite of all precautions our picks made much noise. We were nearly through and were congratulating ourselves when a volley of musketry cut the darkness in our immediate front. The shock was too sudden for thought. With a common instinct those pits were hastily abandoned. My flight was arrested at the start by a log, over which I tumbled. I lay there long enough for reaction to set in.

I could hear the sound of flying feet in both directions. The Johnnies had crept up the ravine, hastily fired, then ran back. Here was my opportunity. Capt. Stewart, after coming back on a reconnaissance, found me standing there and questioned, "Didn't you run?"

I answered in as much of an unconcerned tone as I could command: "Run? Why should I run? I have seen nothing to run from."

"Oh yes," he replied, "I see. You were so scared that you couldn't run."

The men came back and we took the precaution of placing the greater part of them in front with muskets cocked. We finished our work without further molestation, aside from the regular picket firing.

The battle of New Hope Church partook more the nature of a siege; for nearly two weeks the firing from both sides was incessant night and day. Several direct assaults were made at the beginning, but the only gain to us was that of pushing our lines closer together. The flanking movement was again resorted to. With such strong works as we possessed men could be spared, a thinner line would suffice and thus a large force was organized into a flanking column, usually of about 20,000 men. Such a force in the hands of such a man as Gen. Hooker was able to take care of itself in any event. On or about June 5 no morning guns greeted us from the enemy. Silence now reigned where tumult had long held carnival. In our pursuit we passed close to the historic church. The roads were poor at best, but now were past usage by man or goat. We gave these thoroughfares the go-by and traveled across lots. Somehow, we managed to keep within gunshot of the Johnnies.

■ Capt. Robert B. Stewart was commander of Company D, 125th Ohio, during the campaign. He was praised by Col. Opdycke as an officer "whose cool management preserved order in the ranks, and whose hazardous examples emulated the boldest and encouraged the faltering." Stewart was later killed in the battle of Franklin on November 30.

Kennesaw Mountain

After five days' hard service, mostly struggling with the elements, we came in sight of Kennesaw Mountain. We did not need to be told that the enemy was again entrenching; we could see them along the sides of this "Gibraltar" of America. Their infantry lines were near the base while each cavern and cleft contained some sort of fieldpiece. The task of enveloping their lines and establishing ours was greatly augmented by frequent hard rain storms. All the lowlands were inundated, the numerous small streams with their ravine-like channels were obliterated, and many the submergings we received in these hidden depths. Fully a week was spent getting into position and nearly all this time in wet clothes. We were fortunate if at night we could find a briar patch in which to make our beds. Officers and men alike were getting desperate to meet the enemy. We went at them with a fury provoked by our surroundings.

One day as we were emerging from one of these lakes we were greeted with a fusilade from the front, indicating something stronger than a skirmish line. About 300 yards across a field was a strong line of earthworks, with here and there an embrasure from which shot and shell were being hurled at us. We were favored by the ground and with a little effort kept out of sight and range. Our regiment had the advance and was halted here until the entire brigade closed up on us. Men were now pretty thick on our side, and such a deluge of lead as we rained down over there prevented the enemy from making even a feeble reply. We kept up our shooting until after dark, expecting at any time an order for us to charge. But no order came. Morning found the rebel works deserted. Our march led us over the ground covered by our fire. I have never witnessed more destructive effects of bullets. On the ground in back of the works an estimate placed the weight of bullets at 100 pounds per square rod. Not a tree or a twig was left standing

■ Survivors of Company H, 125th Ohio, gather for a group portrait at Nashville in the spring of 1865. Standing between the regimental colors is Capt. Anthony Vallander, known as "our Dutch captain," who previously served in the Prussian army. Company H was particularly hard hit during its service — only 22 enlisted men and two officers were mustered out in September 1865.

for some distance back.

The loss to our regiment here was two killed and eight wounded. One incident shows how indifferent men may become to danger under certain circumstances. Back of our firing line on still lower ground the boys had built a fire. Near our end of the fire was a log which made a convenient seat. Our captain noticed that a break in the bank in front exposed this seat to the sight of the enemy, and he cautioned those around to keep off it. In less than a minute one of these men sat himself down on the forbidden seat, and in another moment he was dead, shot through the body. Men's senses seemed numbed by such long exposure.

Following along, now in the advance and then in the rear, this sort of soldiering was getting monotonous. One afternoon there was a change in the program. We were ordered to support the artillery. On our way to the place designated we were compelled to pass through timber so dense as to shut out nearly all light. Just then the rebs thought best to shell this part of their front. Shells dropped in too fast to go unnoticed. Then too, their coming was unlooked for. The captain's Negro servant, Bill, was following closely. With the first explosion Bill fell flat on his face and at once began "crabbing" to the rear. Gaining a little distance he sprang to his feet, leaving behind him only a black streak. With him went all the captain's grub, bed and baggage. Still worse, he did not show up for three days.

Lieut. Collins was killed here, struck by a piece of shell. We quickly got out of range by a flank movement rapidly executed. Arriving on the ground, our alignment was given us and before the ball opened we had built respectable protection, the only available material being logs and stones. My recollection is that there were 18 guns parked here, and all opened up on the sides of the mountain. Guns from hitherto-unnoticed places replied, and as their shots were generally too high they dropped around us alarmingly close. One struck a large stone forming a part of our protection. Bursting, it dismounted a large log on top which was only prevented from falling on us by bayonets thrust into it. I, with several others, was stunned. One large piece of shell sliced the blouse on my shoulder, then cut an ugly gash along the side of the head of one of the company, a wound from which he never fully recovered.

Our loss here was one killed and three wounded. Gen. Harker had a narrow escape. One of the missiles passed so close as to burn the mane of his horse.

"Pretty close call, general."

"Never mind, boys. A miss is as good as a mile. Besides, here is plenty of timber for more generals."

On June 23 we were quietly resting in camp. We had been in the front line all night and now no further duty was expected until our turn came again. We were ordered to fall in and marched a long distance, finally halting in rear of the 100th Illinois on the skirmish line. Here occurred one of those instances of premonition. Robert Rice of our company came and sat down by me and said, "We are going to have a battle today, and I will be killed. I want you to notice that I go as far as anyone in our company."

■ Private Robert F. Rice, Company B, 125th Ohio, whose premonition of death on June 23 proved true later that day when he was killed near Kennesaw Mountain while on the skirmish line.

I saw no indications of a battle and tried to reason with him. While thus engaged we were ordered up to the reserve where, without halting, Companies K, E and B were ordered out on the skirmish line. We quickly deployed and ran out. We found them occupying rifle pits in the edge of woods. We were offered no accomodations with them as their pits were already crowded. We took position behind trees in front of their line and began firing.

I could see no unusual movement of the enemy. So far as I could judge, there was no urgent need of our being there. Our men could not find anything like adequate protection; the trees were all small. Nathan Hatch was the first to be hit. He fell by my side, shot in the head. I then thought of Robert. I saw him several rods in front of everyone else and while I was looking he, too, fell dead. Our best and bravest were falling fast. It was a sorry day for the left wing. Capt. Manchester of Company K was mortally wounded. Our loss here was three killed and 14 wounded.

We were aware that our friends in the North were manifesting impatience — as they expressed it — at the slowness of Sherman. Although men were being shot at the rate of hundreds daily, the work was not progressing fast enough. The argument used in this was that his army was being destroyed piecemeal, by detail. Better to be decided in one great battle, even if the loss should be great. Sherman, above all men, realized the fact that there was no way in all the science of war whereby he could force the enemy to battle on anything like equal terms; that to assault an enemy behind such entrenchments was not only suicidal but defeat almost certain, no matter what the sacrifice.

Still, the clamor went on and had even reached high places. With such pressure our commander felt that he must act in accordance. There was one little chance — one out of a hundred — that some weak spot might be found, that by some freak of fortune a breach might be made. He would try for that chance. A council of war was held, and June 27 was fixed as the day for a general assault. In the details of preliminary orders as promulgated, Gen. Harker was assigned to some minor position, not at all agreeable to him. I should explain here that Harker's brigade of the IV Corps now comprised seven regiments. Col. Opdycke commanded a demi-brigade, the old one of Harker.

By some diplomatic work, Harker succeeded in getting the original order changed. He was given a place in the assaulting line other than where he

■ Capt. Sterling Manchester, commander of Company K, 125th Ohio, was killed along the skirmish line near Kennesaw Mountain on June 23.

In Company D, two out of three officers were lost within eight days of fighting in late June. 2nd Lieut. Freeman Collins was killed by a shell on June 19 during the advance on Noses Creek. And early on June 27, 1st Lieut. Ephraim P. Evans was shot as the 125th advanced to front-line rifle pits. He was among the first of many casualties in the Federal army that day. On July 8, Evans died of his wound in a Chattanooga hospital.

would have been in the natural order of things. At 3 o'clock in the morning we were aroused and ordered to get breakfast and be ready to fall in before sunrise in light marching order. We were taken about three miles where we formed, closed en masse, company front, behind breastworks occupied by a regiment belonging to the XIV Corps.

The sun came up through a dense fog which enveloped us like a mantle, and through which nothing could be seen at any distance. The sun's rays dispelled this so suddenly that before we could deploy the bullets came among us at a fearful rate. Lieut. Evans received a mortal wound and several others were hit, more or less seriously. The officers were called and given instructions. We now learned for the first time the business before us. Col. Moore was in command of the regiment. Col. Opdycke, as division officer of the day, had the task of clearing the way for the assaulting column. In other terms, he had general charge of the skirmish line covering the divisional front.

Our instructions were brief and to the point: "The 125th is chosen to lead in the charge. You will deploy as skirmishers and at the bugle's signal you are to charge and put yourselves inside the works of the enemy, and then create as much confusion as possible; in the meantime the brigade will come to your support. The 125th Ohio has been chosen for a forlorn hope today. Let every man do his best."

My position was on the extreme left of our line, and I had special instructions to keep connection with the line on our left. On the way back to the company I remarked to Capt. Moses, "Pretty severe orders, Captain?"

"Yes," he said. "It means death or captivity to all, if we are lucky enough to reach them."

Our men were made acquainted with the orders and the work expected of them. One man had to be left to guard such baggage as we could dispense with in our run. The captain directed me to detail someone. I saw that he was shirking a dreadful responsibility. I looked the boys over. There was not one wishful look; to do or die was in the face of each and all. I selected the oldest man present. While waiting for the bugle we had time to survey the ground and our prospects in front. My route was to be across an open field for about 200 yards with not so much as a stump to be seen.

Across the way I could but guess the situation. The ground rose abruptly and was covered with timber to my left. About 50 yards distant was, in appearance, a dense copse. While I was making these observations I was accosted by an old Scotch captain belonging to the XIV Corps' regiment at the works. He asked me what we were going to do and I explained.

"Why mon," he said, "ye can nae do that! Ye can nae hole up your han' here!"

I replied, "Captain, I wish you to do me a favor and note the last man over the works when the bugle sounds. When I get back I will hunt you up."

With the first blast of the bugle we were over and away. As soon as the line on our left reached the aforementioned thicket those nearest me broke for this cover. I saw no more of them. This disconcerted me very much as I could not now keep our own alignment and connection with them. I had no time to dwell on any side issues so I kept a straight forward course.

We found the enemy's first line was located on the timber line — an old rail fence had been utilized in the construction of light works. So sudden had been our dash that the Johnnies in this line surrendered almost to a man. The main line was plain to be seen, and from the point where I reached the first line was about 75 yards up a steep incline. A halt was made here — our "wind" was gone. Besides, the prisoners had to be looked after. My first thought was that with these prisoners among us we would not be targets for those above us, but in this we were mistaken. Their bullets kept coming regardless of whom they hit. We compelled the captured men to go back over the ground to the rear. An order was sent down the line to remain where we were for the present, to fire as fast as possible and await further developments. It was very evident that with only a skirmish line our efforts to create confusion among such a body of men would be of no consequence, unless the brigade was in immediate support.

Developments meant, would our brigade be able to come across the field as we had, and at the same time preserve its solid formation? If not, there would be no use or necessity of sacrificing us. By lying flat behind the pile of rails our men could receive fair protection and at the proper time our bullets would make as much commotion as our presence there with clubbed muskets. Again, how were we to pass the rebels' abatis, with no pioneers to clear the way? This obstruction consisted of long logs through which holes were bored at right angles, then long sharpened stakes were driven through. These logs, placed end to end and fastened together with wire, made an obstruction over or through which no man could pass without tools — especially when guarded by a row of muskets not 20 feet distant.

The brigade made three attempts to come across, but was driven back with severe losses each time. At point-blank range for grape and canister, in solid column, company front, no troops could endure such a slaughter. In the meantime our own muskets were worked as never before. From where I lay by looking through between the rails I could see the enemy reinforcing their line. A traverse was in my front, over which they had to climb like a flock of sheep over a fence. Here was a fine chance to test my marksmanship. My right hand had not forgotten its cunning. Three of the boys loaded and passed me their muskets. While thus engaged one of them misfired. I drew it back and proceeded to recap it. I was compelled to shift my position to kneeling. Just then a bullet found a weak spot in the rail and struck me fairly on top of the head. For a brief period there was a blank spot in my memory. I lay there long enough to be reported among the slain in a dispatch sent to a Cleveland newspaper. Learning of this later, and also noting the mistake, I hastened to have it corrected by a subsequent dispatch ("Not killed, but wounded") which reached my family at the same time. I can attribute my escape to my new army hat; it was impregnable to anything but bullets, and these must not be hindered in their flight.

Through some cause the woods caught fire in our front, preventing anything but random shooting. After the third attempt to get his brigade over, Gen. Harker became desperate. Jumping his horse over our works, he, along with his adjutant, Capt. Whitesides of our regiment, came dashing across the field. They struck our line at Company I, Lieuts. Burnham and Dilley being in temporary command. Both these young officers were members of the old organization, warriors tried, and with Harker's cry "Come on, boys!" they rushed to their deaths. Before he reached the abatis, Harker fell mortally wounded. Whitesides also fell with a severe wound, Dilley was killed and my dear old comrade, Thomas M. Burnham, lay there with eight distinct wounds. We got him out as soon as possible but he was wounded to the death. This act of Gen. Harker can well be set down as rash in the extreme. No doubt, in his great disappointment, he had become desperate. Had our regiment been in line of battle and in the position of Company I, Col. Fox, undoubtedly, would have had one more regiment to add to his fallacious standard of fighting regiments — like that entire regiment disappearing in the blowing up of the fort at Petersburg, a wholesale slaughter through rashness.*

■ Capt. Elmer Moses commanded Company B, 125th Ohio, during the first weeks of the campaign. On June 27 at Kennesaw Mountain he was struck twice by bullets, one ball shattering his left thigh bone while another lodged in his leg below the knee. He was never again fit for duty, and was succeeded by 1st Lieut. Ralsa Rice in command of the company.

* Rice's sarcastic mention of Col. Fox refers to Lt. Col. William F. Fox, author of *Regimental Losses in the American Civil War 1861-1865* — a treatise on the extent and

■ Brig. Gen. Charles Garrison Harker, 28-year-old commander of the 3rd Brigade, 2nd Division, IV Corps, was mortally wounded on June 27 while leading a charge of his brigade on Cheatham Hill, about two miles south of Kennesaw Mountain. Gen. Sherman later wrote: "Had Gen. Harker lived I believe we would have carried the parapet, broken the enemy's center, and driven him pell-mell into the Chattahoochee."

We lay there sweltering between fires until 11 a.m., when an order came to fall back. Going back, like going in, was a thing to be dreaded. When all were ready we sprang to our feet and ran the race of our lives. We had made the charge with 260 rifles, and lost 58 men killed and wounded. Company B had three men killed. Our captain was among the number seriously wounded and was compelled to leave us for good. The reunion of the regiment back behind the works was a sorrowful one.

"Boys, if to be hired, what would be your price to repeat that charge?"

"Not for the whole state of Ohio, but if orders came we would cheerfully comply."

Here was the example of that true American soldier. I met my friend, the Scotch captain, and as he clasped my hand he said, "There was nae hindmost, nae last mon. All went o'er at the same time."

Another incident, illustrative of that stand and of Col. Fox: Our surgeon, Dr. McHenry, was belated in getting started from our old camp and on the way down he met one of our men in full retreat. The doctor stopped him and inquired of our whereabouts.

"The 125th Regiment, Doctor? There is no such regiment. I'm the only one left."

It is but just to say that this fugitive was a recent acquisition from some influential source in the North, and he may be running yet for all I know. A grand assault had been made, a general engagement brought on in which hundreds of the bravest, best men that ever followed the flag had been sacrificed, and this, too, against our gallant commander's better judgment; and now, whether satisfactory or not, he would hereafter rule his own household.

Capt. Moses was compelled to leave us here, and on me fell the honor of commanding the old company.

Once again we began stretching the line — our flanking machine was being set in order, the indomitable Hooker made a night's march and in the morning [of July 3rd] was near enough to make his presence felt. We were part of the movement and as soon as it was light eager eyes scanned the mountain. Not a single "bonnie blue flag" disgraced old Kennesaw. "The Johnnies are gone again," was a theme for much rejoicing. Our musical comrade came out with a new song which we sang with great spirit, winding up with "When Hooker goes 'round the flank."

Resuming our march, we made a circuitous one around the base of the mountain; as the line was slow in forming our march was in easy stages. I should mention that the familiar whistle of the locomotive was heard with but little interruption; we were being well fed and cared for.

I have mentioned previously the populace we met. Our morning's march along a deserted road brought us face to face with the only sight of civilization encountered on the leeward side of this historic mountain. This was a domicile by the roadside, and from the appearance it was of remote antiquity. The lady of the house, with arms akimbo, was leaning on the gate, smoking a cob pipe. Our greetings were of that friendly sort, such as "Good morning, madam, how far is it out of the wilderness?" Or, "How far are we from civilization?" and other such questions. She entertained us with a short lecture, thus:

"Yo'uns don't fight we'uns fair. That tarnal Joe Hooker just takes his regiments and fights us endways."

---

nature of the mortuary losses in the Union regiments, with full and exhaustive statistics compiled from the official records on file in the state military bureaus and at Washington, published in 1889. During the war, Fox served in the 107th New York Infantry Regiment.

The speaker was lustily cheered with not one single discourteous remark, and I am pleased to say that same chivalrous spirit was always manifested by our soldiers.

Yes, we had our fun-loving, mischievous boys, full of their pranks, but generally of the harmless sort. One of these met with his own retribution on this morning's tramp. We were passing a deserted camp with a fire yet smoldering by the roadside, and a nearby crackerbox made an inviting seat. Our man must light his pipe. He ran over and contentedly seated himself on the box. There was an explosion — ashes, powder smoke, crackerbox and boy filled the air. Some joker had filled an old canteen with powder, placed it under the box and so arranged it that when pressed down, powder and fire would come in contact. Our hero was badly shaken up, somewhat stunned, but he had learned a new trick which to him was worth several such blow-ups.

Passing around the mountain we came to Marietta, the most beautiful place we had met in the whole Southland. We marched through the suburbs only, but longed for a more extended sight of the town. A few miles further our march slackened, and the same old difficulty was to be overcome. Skirmishing was kept up until dark. In the morning we set out on another tramp for position. A detailed account of this day's trials will show to the reader some of our perplexities.

Rain began falling before we were fairly out of camp. We followed a road so long as its course was in the direction we were traveling. We kept going without gaining distance until about 3 o'clock; then, tired, wet and hungry, we went into a prospective camp. We pitched our dog tents in an old field overgrown with the usual sassafras shrubs. These had to be broken and pounded out of the way before we could stretch our tent cloths. In the meantime, fires were started. But wait, there goes the bugle: "Fall in, boys!" which we did and marched about 100 yards, and again camped. We had the ground about cleared when the same sound greeted our ears. This time we moved farther and were brought up in front of a wood lot, and again stacked arms. We were congratulating our bit of good fortune. Here was an old rail fence. With about 10 minutes of enjoyment we again moved up into the woods. It was dark by this time, and we thought that surely our day's bivouacking was at an end here. But no; our line was facing wrong and another change was imperative. Our next halt was along the low bank of a small stream. The lateness of the hour persuaded a pooling of interests. The officers had a portion of the ground cleared and with a large fire blazing at the foot of the slope, our anticipations brightened, along with the smell of frying meat and boiling coffee.

"The 125th for fatigue duty!" So said the order. Supper did not enter into consideration. We took as much food as we could carry in our hands, eating as we stumbled along. We marched about half a mile and were set to carrying rails with which to build breastworks in an open lot well under water. This employment kept us busy until morning, then we marched away and left our grievances behind. Tomorrow the sun would shine again; thus hope, with its beacon light, was the solace that prevented a total collapse of both soul and body.

At the Chattahoochee

The stand here by the enemy was, like that at Resaca, made to gain time for their trains to cross the river. Their facilities for crossing were better here, and therefore no general engagement followed. Our camp along the Chattahoochee River was enjoyable — dry land, plenty of drinking water and good company. The river was too wide for an exchange of picket greet-

■ Capt. Edward G. Whitesides, 125th Ohio, and adjutant of Gen. Harker's brigade. Just before the assault against the Confederate works of Gen. Alfred Vaughan's Tennessee brigade on June 27, Harker handed money and some trinkets to Whitesides along with instructions to be carried out if the general were killed. According to Capt. Charles T. Clark of the 125th Ohio: "When Harker started to the front he ordered Whitesides to remain at the rifle pits until the 42nd Illinois, last in the column, had passed. He probably intended to keep the captain out of the extreme peril he was himself about to face, but his kind intentions failed. The 42nd passed the works quickly and rushed to the front, and Whitesides hastened on to rejoin the general. On reaching the front he received a ball in his right thigh. He dismounted and found the limb was not broken, but while in the act of remounting his horse was shot and fell dead, throwing the captain to the ground. Two men carried him to the rear, whence he was taken in an ambulance to the hospital and placed on a cot next to one occupied by Harker. The latter said, 'Is that you, my dear boy?' " Harker died an hour later.

■ 1st Lieut. Alson C. Dilley, 125th Ohio, was killed at Kennesaw Mountain. As a sergeant at Chickamauga, Dilley assumed command of Company C when the company commander was shot dead. In his official report of Chickamauga, Col. Opdycke wrote that Dilley distinguished himself "for cool courage and capacity to command under the severest tests."

ings, though an occasional shot from the rebel artillery disturbed us. Back of our camp was one of those hills or peaks only to be met with in a mountainous region. It stood isolated like a large haystack with its summit above the tallest trees. Our company scouts had located this perfect spot for a signal station before we had been in camp an hour. On their report that we could overlook the country for miles around, several of us started on a survey. We had pulled ourselves nearly to the top when our guide stumbled back of us. There, hanging from a tree limb, was the remains of a man completely mummified. Our inquest revealed the fact that he had died from strangulation. From the hill's pinnacle we could see the spires in Atlanta seven miles away — so near and yet so far, with a live rebel army in between.

We were called out one morning in light marching order and sent up the river 16 miles in a forced march to Roswell. This was on July 6, very warm for a Northern man in winter clothing. The vanguard consisted of Col. Opdycke on old Barney, Orderly Sergeant Rufus Woods and myself. The rear guard was miles back. We arrived at Roswell around noon, rested in the shade until evening and then Company B forded the river and went on picket along a lonely wooded road. Gen. Sherman visited our reserve while making a reconnaissance alone and unattended. I remember how well he saluted us when we fell in with presented arms. In the morning we recrossed on a bridge further upstream. Our business here was to aid the cavalry in the destruction of a large factory engaged in the manufacture of clothing for the rebel army. A foreign flag was floating over the establishment, but this did not save it. There were 200 young women working in the factory and what to do with them was the question. The little hamlet could not care for them and neither were they contraband of war. They were finally loaded into wagons and sent to Marietta. Our work here ended, and we marched back to our former camp.

We crossed the river with but little opposition, the IV Corps taking the direct road for Atlanta. We had no doubt that the "Gate City" would not be given up without a great battle and now, with the city within a day's march, we were in constant expectancy. On the afternoon of the first day after crossing the Chattahoochee, we encountered the enemy at Nancy Creek. Our brigade had the advance on this road. The 3rd Kentucky and the 125th Ohio were on the skirmish line, supported by the 64th and 65th Ohio. It was obvious that a determined resistance would be made, the place chosen being one of great natural strength. The road, after crossing the creek, climbed a hill, on the crest of which they had placed a battery of two guns in a substantial earthwork. This was flanked on both sides by heavy timber. The stream alone made the position formidable. The same conditions prevailed here as in all other places to be met with in this part of Georgia. There was so little descent or fall to the streams that they were more like canals with no current, the sluggish water wide and deep while the lowlands along their course were swampy thickets. We were to charge and carry the place with one of our old-time rushes. Here was a "poser" on reaching the creek — it was some 20 feet wide and as many deep in appearance. I found a wooden rail and, making a pontoon of it, with a flying leap I landed near enough to the opposite bank to grab a root and pull myself out. Company B, with men from the 3rd Kentucky, formed an assaulting party and together we rushed through the woods. We reached the Johnnies in time to be of use in aiding their "skedaddle" as they left behind their killed and wounded to our tender mercies. Col. Opdycke witnessed our charge and complimented us.

Sad to relate, old Barney was killed here. He had been with us a long time and shared our dangers as did few other horses in the army. We gave him the burial of a soldier under a tree by the roadside, with a headboard marked "My Horse Barney."

I have heard it said that this horse became mired in the stream and had to be killed, but that is not true. He was fatally shot while on the road. Col. Opdycke was very near us when we made the last charge. We remained at this spot for two or three days and camped near the place where the horse was shot. I assisted in the burial and could not be mistaken. Neither would this noble animal have remained long in a quagmire with so many willing hands to extricate him. Our regimental loss here was one man killed and three wounded. I did not count those of the enemy left on the field, though I remember that a dead colonel lay there and a captain badly wounded. We also captured a number of prisoners.

■ 2nd Lieut. Thomas M. Burnham, 125th Ohio, was mortally wounded at Kennesaw Mountain and died July 13, 1864. He was also wounded at Chickamauga while serving as a sergeant in Company B.

Battle of Peachtree Creek

From the crossing of Peachtree Creek to Atlanta is four miles. From this, we reasoned, the enemy would make but one more stand, fight one more battle. On the morning of July 20 we reached the vicinity of the bridge spanning the creek on the creek road, so called. Much time was occupied in arranging the many divisions of our army for this last advance. To complete the line on the south side of the creek required one division of the IV Corps, and that of Gen. Newton's (ours) was sent over. It should be noted that the line of the creek and that of the road formed a triangle, with the base facing toward Atlanta. Thus, with our line of march following the road there was necessarily an open space formed between our left and the creek. The creek was not fordable at any place along here; troops on the north side could not assist those on the south side. A study of all the surroundings and all the details of this ground must convince the inquirer that Hood, who had succeeded Johnston a few days before, used much strategy in his attack on the 20th. I am persuaded that a charging column of Gen. Bate's rebel division was sheltered in the thick woods near the creek. In the woods, about 300 yards east of the bridge, was a large, strong redoubt entirely out of sight and far enough from the road to escape all observation.

We crossed the bridge shortly after noon. Small earthworks were erected by someone on a slight elevation on the south side, where a few pieces of artillery were in place. Our brigade was in the rear of the division. Slowly we marched until, at a point about 200 yards from the bridge, we filed off to the right side in line of battle, regimental front, where we halted and stacked arms. The 125th was in the advance with our line in the edge of the timber. A bend in the road prevented sight of our brigades in front. About 2 o'clock the sudden roar of both musketry and artillery up ahead brought every man to his feet, and with an instinct born of practice the men grabbed their muskets and fell into line. Our expectant eyes were first greeted with a road full of fugitives fleeing as though their lives depended on their haste. Both Col. Bradley of the 51st Illinois and Col. Opdycke vainly tried to stop and rally these men. Opdycke rode past our flank and observing our line, remarked, "I always know where to find my boys."

He directed Col. Moore to move the regiment on the double-quick diagonally across the road and into the woods. Not finding any enemy there, we made a right-about and went back. Our next formation was in line facing the creek, our regiment on the right of this line which reached nearly to the bridge. The road at this point was along the crest of high ground that descended rapidly to low, flat ground along the creek. This low ground from the woods to the bridge was under pretense of cultivation — stunted corn and weeds, with the latter predominating — surely not good footing for men on the run. We were in position but momentarily when a column of the

■ Lt. Col. David H. Moore took command of the 125th Ohio after Col. Opdycke was wounded at Resaca on May 14. At Rocky Face Ridge on May 9, Moore himself was slightly wounded. The next day he wrote to his wife: "Two more severe days, and this much of the third gone, and I am *nearly* all right. In the charge last night I was hit four times, once by a ball which passed through a corporal's head, struck me in the back of the hip and lodged in the lining of my blouse; that only *stung*. Another stripped my right coat sleeve below the elbow, a fragment of another hit me in the left breast; still another struck my right lower bowels. These last two hurt, but are only *slight;* they do not lay me up." Falling seriously ill just before the fall of Atlanta, he resigned his commission in September 1864.

enemy came out of the woods into the field. They were in solid column, company front. I saw no skirmishers or flankers.

Gen. Newton was overpowered but not overwhelmed. He sent an urgent request to Gen. Thomas for assistance. The messenger met the general at the bridge and Thomas was heard to say, "Go back and tell Gen. Newton that I will reinforce him personally." He crossed over and directed the shooting of the elevated guns we had seen earlier after crossing the bridge. This was the best — the only — thing he could do. The rest of our corps was far in advance following the creek on the opposite side.

We began firing by volley on the first appearance of the Johnnies. "Battalion ready — aim, fire, load!" shouted Col. Moore in regular cadence. The shock of our broadside was terrific. We were evening up matters with June 27 in mind. The range was no more than 100 yards and every shot was telling. The charging rebel column had cleared the woods when the artillery at the bridge opened fire. The enemy's momentum carried them nearly half way from the timber line to the bridge. We fired five volleys in all, our guns sending such a shower of death that the destruction seemed like a massacre. The foremost rebels faltered, and with a charge of grapeshot from the cannons, scattered and ran for the woods.

Probably this maneuver of the enemy was scientific warfare but, in my judgment, had they come out of the woods in line of battle and used their muskets on us the result would have been different. We heard the roar of battle over in the woods to our right and could see the smoke curling up through the treetops. And we could see it farther and farther back. Was Hooker being overpowered? It seemed so. Then came a cheer. That was no rebel yell. Immediately we saw Gen. Hooker riding toward us. With hat in hand he came up and said, "Boys, we have whipped them again!" It was now our turn to shout. We wound up with three cheers for Gen. Hooker.

The 125th lost but two men wounded here. Our rejoicings over, Company B was called for picket. As our line was to be established along the edge of the woods and over the battlefield, we did not hesitate.

After establishing our line of posts, I went to the place where the enemy had come out of the woods. I found their trail and followed it to the end. Dead and dying rebels lay strewn over the ground — a harrowing, pitiful sight. The dead had not that angry look which we ascribe to men fighting for their lives, but rather a sorrowful, frightful one of death by violence. I followed a trail of blood through the weeds to the creek. Here I found a young man in the agonies of death; a grapeshot had torn across his body, disemboweling him. In his pain he had sought the creek and let himself down into the water. Poor fellow, I could do nothing to help him.

One of our pickets reported hearing strange sounds near his post. We made a search and in a ravine found a youth of 17, wounded. We took him to the reserve and found that a bullet had passed through his leg above the knee. We gave him hot coffee and food, and I learned his address, age, etc. As soon as he revived I sent him to the hospital. Though he died soon after, I had the satisfaction of knowing that he had been treated with the utmost kindness on our part. I treasured his address and in later correspondence with his family I gave them all the details, and received from his home, away in Alabama, many thanks for our kindness to their boy.

At daybreak on the 21st, Orderly Sergeant Woods and I made a reconnaissance on our own hook up in the woods in our front. On reaching the aforementioned redoubt, we could not determine in the dim light whether it was occupied or not. So I took the sergeant's musket and fired a shot at the redoubt. Finding it tenantless, we entered the enclosure and there saw evidence that it had but recently been abandoned. On our way back we were met by a messenger from the officer in charge, with an order putting me under arrest for firing out in front. I saw I was "in for it" and, knowing the officer, knew I had nothing to hope for in the way of clemency. Sergeant Woods, however, was a man of resource.

"You go into camp," he said. "I think I can quash this indictment."

He hastened to the tent of Col. Opdycke. We had long since learned who were our friends. The colonel had not yet arisen, but was awakened to receive information from the front.

"Colonel," Woods began, "the rebs have gone from our front."

"How do you know this, sergeant?"

"Lieut. Rice and I went out in front until we reached their works and found them empty." The sergeant explained everything, not omitting the shooting. The colonel expressed his approval and said we had done well.

"By the way, colonel, our lieutenant has been put under arrest for firing my musket."

"Never mind," replied Col. Opdycke. "I will see to this part. There must be more shooting before we are through."

I heard no more from my would-be persecutor.

Reaching the goal

On July 22 we drew up in front of Atlanta and began forming our lines. It was not so difficult here as the ground was more open. We received the usual amount of shelling, but the "feeling for position" was less hazardous.

The first line assigned us did not meet with our approval. We were becoming skilled artisans and competent engineers in this sort of business. We rolled up a few logs and then awaited further developments. We were here entertained by a thing altogether new to us — a 100-pound shot or shell from a siege gun. The sound of these huge missiles flying over our heads was terrifying, especially on first acquaintance. Many fabulous accounts of their great penetration found believers. Unless the aim of the gun was accidental, no one was in danger.

Our conjectures as to the location of the line were correct. A new line was given us with the ground in front having a gradual descent, near enough to the enemy to satisfy the most fastidious. We began work on it as soon as it was dark and worked all night. With heavy logs for the perpendicular, when finished we had a bank of earth 15 feet thick at the base with a slope and large head log surmounting. I stood surveying our work in the dim morning light. I saw Col. Opdycke coming down the line and was sure of commendation.

"You men have worked like beavers," he exclaimed, "but don't you see your works are south? You cannot see the bottom of the ditch in front. There is not slope enough. Send men and have this corrected before daylight."

I saw the error, and getting a spade I was certain I could remedy it without calling for help. I had nearly finished when a bullet warned me that the sun was rising. "Wait a minute, Johnny, I am nearly through." With a last and finishing touch another bullet flew by, missing me, but that well-known "thud" told me plainly that some other body was not so fortunate. Three of the boys were setting up a post for shade. I jumped down and ran to them. Sergeant Fred Knight, one of the best, had received the shot along the spine near the back of his neck. We thought the wound a simple one, as no blood flowed. But its effect proved life-lasting. He died a paralytic some 30 years after.

As we surmised, our conspicuous bank of earth became the special target for this siege gun. Their aim, like the antiquity of the weapon, was of doubtful certainty. This monster bullet in size and shape resembled a camp kettle. "There comes a camp kettle! Lay low, boys!" These shells could be

■ Brig. Gen. John Newton commanded the IV Corps' 2nd Division, which bore much of the brunt of fighting at Peachtree Creek. "Had the enemy obtained this position," he wrote two months later, "the right wing of the army would probably have been rolled back into the angle of Peachtree Creek and the Chattahoochee. Beside the destruction of material, a heavy loss in men would have been the result of such disaster."

■ Orderly Sergeant Rufus Woods, seated at left, and members of Company B, 125th Ohio, were rugged veterans by the time this photograph was taken in the spring of 1865. 1st Lieut. Ralsa Rice, who commanded the company for nine weeks during the campaign, later commented about the veterans' transition to civilian life: "We were not yet aware that our physical condition had underwent that change as to make us barbarians, a class to be feared — dreaded — by the peace-loving citizen at home; that those stains of battle and the wild life in camp would beget lawlessness, and make of us a dangerous element to turn loose in society."

seen by catching the sound overhead, then following with the eye. They were usually 50 feet over our heads, but, dropping fast, they found lodgment in "Cook's Hollow" a half mile in the rear.

These visitants the colored part of our army held in mortal dread. A colony of colored laborers was domiciled in a nearby empty mule wagon. One of the shells passed over quite close by to the wagon, making disturbance enough to break their slumbers. "What's dat? Who dat froin' stones? Who dat nigger foolin' round heah?" When the fact finally dawned on them that one of "dose camp-kittles" was the cause of the intrusion, it was as good as a circus to witness their exodus from that wagon.

Some military genius conceived the project of building a fort on a knoll out in front of our line, and about a half mile to the left of our camp, and that the 125th Ohio should do the work. The site was within short range of the enemy's guns and the idea was considered a dangerous undertaking. We were promised immunity from all other duty while the work lasted. Such an inducement had the desired effect, and one night we marched over carrying our guns and tools and began the work. We were not molested and before morning had our work so well in hand that danger was no longer a factor in the enterprise. We could now work securely by daylight. Each evening we went back to the rear far enough to be out of harm's way and camped in a beautiful grove. We may have nursed that job a little as it required two weeks to complete it. Our rations kept coming in regular quantities and were of good quality.

Our long line of railroad, especially from Nashville to Atlanta, required constant watching and guarding. There were enemies in the rear as well as front. Among the many inaccessible places along the line the "bushwhacker" was found hiding, and he put in his nefarious work to our great annoyance. It required men of nerve to run the locomotives, and to these civilians fabulous wages were paid. We could hardly fail to notice that those men who ran a more dangerous business — that of the guns — received a recompense as nothing in comparison. Guarding the railroad and its trains required several thousand men and thus, our army was depleted as much.

At the siege of Atlanta, Sherman could not muster more than 55,000 muskets. So far the inhabitants of the city had been but little disturbed by our bullets. The distance from our line to the city limits was said to be two miles, certainly not a long shot for our cannons. A short time before the siege was raised, Sherman had brought up and mounted six guns of the most recent construction. Their position was in the works about 200 yards to the right of us. These were of much interest to me and I watched the results eagerly. Each cannon was of steel, long with heavy breech, rifled and threw a projectile about three diameters in length. The sequel showed this shell too long for the rotary motion given by the twist, or pitch, in the rifles. I understood these guns were intended to silence the rebel siege gun. When in readiness they began firing at a rate of one gun per minute. The first shot was fired about 9 p.m. The first shots were with a shell with fuse. This twirl of fire gave the gunner a pretty fair estimate of distance and the proper elevation. It was an interesting spectacle to watch these fiery messengers sailing over the tops of the trees with their long, curved flight, terminating in a crash over in Atlanta. With the proper range found, solid shot was tried.

These, as predicted, failed to keep their equipois, went whirling end over end, producing a peculiar sound not unlike the puffing of a locomotive. This would bring about the shout from some of the boys, "All aboard for Atlanta!" The nocturnal firing would last for an hour or so, to be repeated the following night. This sort of music may have kept the people awake at the other end of the line, but with us the noise became monotonous and we slept on, unawakened and undisturbed.

■ Sergeant James M. Murdock, Company B, 125th Ohio. He survived the campaign, but was killed at the battle of Franklin on November 30.

Flanking Atlanta

We felt that some important movement was in contemplation when all our sick men were sent away, our arms and ammunition received a thorough inspection and, lastly, three days' rations were issued. It came as a "leak-out" that the XX Corps was fortified, resting back at the river; that all our men not in condition for hard service were gathered there. The fact was, as much of this information was allowed to reach us as would establish confidence. On the night of August 25 the movement began, and before morning the whole plan developed in our minds as plainly as if mapped out before us. The corps on the extreme left moved around to the other extreme, passing in the rear of the rest. As soon as the next corps was passed it, too, made a similar movement. We moved out at daybreak, and by sunrise were nearly out of sight of the woods and brush in the rear of the right wing.

So quietly and nicely were these movements executed that the enemy did not mistrust our purpose. Finding us gone, they held a jubilee procession from the city and visited our deserted camps. "The Yanks have gone home," was on every tongue. While this was going on we were marching in good order, camped the first night out in the woods, and in the morning our corps marched to the railroad and began the work of destruction according to infantry tactics. Track the length of a brigade would be turned bottom up into the ditch, then the rails detached, the ties piled up, the rails laid on, and large fires built underneath. When the rails became red hot, men at each end would take a turn around a tree and leave them there to cool. The interests of the stockholders in that railroad were not consulted. Woe would come to the man or men who interfered with our work. Half the men stood at arms, ready for any emergency. The entire IV Corps was engaged on this

■ Capt. Ridgley C. Powers served as acting regimental adjutant of the 125th Ohio during the campaign. After the war he moved to Mississippi to raise cotton, entered politics and became governor of that state in 1871.

railroad contract. The other corps were somewhere in the vicinity, we felt sure.

We kept on with our work from early morning until about 3 p.m., then came a change in the program. A shifting of scenery. There was more of war's alarms: the boom of cannon mingled with the roar of muskets in our front caused us to seize our muskets and hasten to form companies. We were now at a large stream nearly of river dimensions. As we approached a bridge I saw for the first, and only time, Gen. John A. Logan. From the conversation between him and Gen. Stanley we learned quite definitely that there was a fight ahead of us. As soon as the stream was crossed, the IV Corps began forming for battle. Our brigade was sent fully a mile to the left of the railroad. As we swung into line we found ourselves on the extreme flank. When the forward movement began, it became a right half-wheel, causing more speed than any double-quick. It was like "crack-the-whip" from our school-boy days — hang on and run for dear life or get switched off into the bushes. Night was approaching, and with the setting sun the sound of fierce volleys died away. Nothing but the desultory firing of the pickets gave us any idea of our position relative to that of our comrades in other parts of our army.

When we started on our deployment the heavy firing was in front of our right flank. With our swinging around we had kept going so long as we could make headway. When the order to halt and camp where we were came, the darkness was so intense that we could not distinguish one man from another. We were in a ravine, or hollow, filled with brush and small timber. Adjutant Powers came over himself with the guard detail and instructions, and while he was speaking one of my men walked up, saying, "You see that light out there through the brush? That is a rebel hospital. I have just been talking with one of their men. We were getting water at the same place."

With this bit of news Capt. Powers started for the light. I hastily gathered a few men and followed. With the light for a guide, we made our way through the labyrinth as fast as possible. Thus groping, I ran into and stumbled over a pile of arms and legs — hospital gleanings from Hardee's Corps. This was a gruesome tumble, long to be remembered. We entered the first tent reached and were in time to be of assistance to Capt. Powers in settling a dispute between he and the rebel surgeon in charge. Each was determined in the capture of the other. Sergeant Murdock's bayonet settled the controversy in favor of our side. We were in the rear of the rebel army under Hardee. This was their hospital and showed to us what they never would divulge about their losses in battle. I found the inlet and outlet to this retreat, brought up Company B and held the line until morning.

Our night's capture, including the able-bodied personnel belonging to the hospital, was 400. Among these was a "silver band" — not the ordinary brass band; at any rate, their instruments had that appearance and I noticed that some of these horns were considered contraband. During the night we heard heavy explosions in the direction of Atlanta. Our conjectures were verified by word that Atlanta was being evacuated.

With a stroll over the battlefield we spent the forenoon in soldier contentment. The slaughter of the enemy was terrible to behold. They had charged the works of the XV, XVI and XVII Corps, and later the XIV and XXIII Corps added their guns. We had been in a position of our own choosing with ample time to entrench. Nothing but ignorance of our position and numbers had induced this attack. Both Hood and his generals believed our maneuvers to be a simple raid on their railroad. Hardee had passed us during the night, before our railroad work. We heard the rumble of his trains as they passed us. This was the battle of Jonesboro, with no loss to record for our regiment. We followed the remnant of Hood's army on down

to Lovejoy Station, or Cedar Bluffs, then countermarched for Atlanta. One good man was seriously wounded at Cedar Bluffs — Corporal Chester of Company C was struck by a rifle bullet near the heart. Finding lodgment there, no amount of probing could remove it. It became encysted and our comrade is yet carrying nearly an ounce of rebel lead.

Atlanta had fallen and we supposed the campaign to be ended. Gladly we retraced our steps. Nearing Atlanta, we witnessed what became a matter of controversy between Gen. Sherman and Hood. The citizens, as non-combatants, claimed protection, including sustenance in its meaning. It was a difficult matter to provision all our troops let alone a large, populous city. Gen. Hood knew this as well as we. His cavalry at this same time was doing its best to destroy Sherman's supply line. So far as enmity was concerned, he might as well have included his army in the petition. It was a sight incident to war and brought on by the rebels' own indiscretion. Their repentance, if they had any such pangs, came too late.

We were given a view of our conquest and marched through the city's principal streets. Nothing was of greater interest than the bombproof caverns built in the yards on the side of Atlanta next to those long guns of theirs. We made inquiry concerning the damage done and destruction wrought, but found little. One incident was noted where some rebel officers and lady friends were having a dance and a time of social enjoyment. One of our own shells, by its sudden entrance through the walls, broke up the party. The enemy's large siege gun was dismounted and lay in a ditch, but from what force I was unable to learn. All the property owned or controlled by the Confederate government was promptly destroyed, but no individual or private property was molested.

We pitched camp outside the city limits in a fine locality, built a nice camp and prepared to take things easy for a while. But Gen. Sherman was not built that way. Like Grant, he would "press things to the end." After a week's sojourn we were loaded onto railcars and sent back to Chattanooga, where we had started four long months before.

■ Soldiers of Company C, the color company of the 125th Ohio, pose with the regimental color guard in the spring of 1865. 1st Lieut. Ralsa Rice wrote: "Our first flag was carried until Kennesaw Mountain was reached. There a new one was presented to the regiment, sent us by the ladies of Kinsman Township, Trumbull County, Ohio. This we carried to the end. The old one was shot into shreds, and became a present to Opdycke from the regiment." Seated at left center is the company commander, Capt. Edward P. Bates.

Hell has broke loose in Georgia

Opening moves: Rocky Face Ridge and Resaca

Intermingling with the beating of drums and shrill notes of bugle calls, the shouts of officers, cannoneers and teamsters echoed along the hills south of Chattanooga under the warm rays of a midday sun.

It was May 4, 1864, and 60,000 soldiers of Maj. Gen. George H. Thomas' Army of the Cumberland were embarking on a journey Sherman himself described as one "on which the fate of the nation hung." With McPherson's Army of the Tennessee pushing out on the right from Alabama, and Schofield's Army of the Ohio marching from Tennessee on the left, Sherman's "mobile machine" headed confidently in a wide arc toward the Confederate positions around Dalton, Ga. "The day was ideal," wrote Private John Arbuckle of the 4th Iowa Infantry, "when these great columns of Sherman's army, in full swing with banners flying, moved out over Missionary Ridge to meet the enemy and on to Atlanta."

Two nights later outside the small town of Ringgold, Ga., on the Western & Atlantic Railroad, Private Sherman Leland of the 104th Illinois witnessed a demonstration of his comrades' confidence and high morale on the eve of battle. In his journal he wrote: "Soon after dark bonfires were lighted, all tents were illuminated, and cheers rang from one end of the army to the other. Miles away down the valley the cheering commenced, and rolling along like the reverberations of thunder, went from one end of the valley to the other, then turned and, seemingly louder than before, passed back. Mixed with the noise was the firing of wet powder into the air from the muskets, producing miniature fireworks. The celebration was kept up for two hours, when the tumult subsided and naught save a fire here and there indicated that an army of 100,000 men reposed in that valley."

In the same brigade, 1st Lieut. Angus L. Waddle, adjutant of the 33rd Ohio, also remembered the celebratory mood of the night of May 6. "Men were shouting and singing and everything betokened events of importance," he wrote. "Officers from different regiments met in sutlers' tents and as they drank to the success of the cause, exchanged photographs and confidences and, in many instances, entrusted messages of grave import to be given friends in the North in case of their fall; for we were about to engage in what we all knew was a desperate struggle, and one in which many of us were sure to meet a soldier's fate."

The campaign was formally launched on May 7, when the vanguard of Thomas' three corps fired the first shots at a Confederate outpost at Tunnel Hill, seven miles southeast of Ringgold. The small Southern force fell back to Johnston's strongly fortified lines just west of Dalton on Rocky Face Ridge. Its craggy crest bristled with cannon and muskets — a bastion made

■ A Federal cavalryman gazes east across a semi-wooded valley toward Rocky Face Ridge in an official U.S. army photograph taken after the fighting. Major Daniel H. Fox of the 101st Ohio, which assaulted Buzzard's Roost gap at the north end of the ridge on May 11, wrote to his wife: "The Rebs had this gap strongly fortified and commanded by a large number of batteries. The ridge is ... almost precipitous and near the top the rocks rise up about 40 feet, which cannot be scaled only by ladders."

even more ominous with towering cliffs standing sentinel over a flooded gap known locally as Buzzard's Roost. A "terrible door of death," Sherman called it, and he chose to attempt cracking the Confederate defenses by feigning a direct assault on the ridge while simultaneously sending McPherson's army farther south to slip through Snake Creek Gap, strike east for Resaca and sever Johnston's railroad supply line.

On May 8, the movements began. From atop Rocky Face, 1st Lieut. Lot. D. Young of the Confederate 4th Kentucky Infantry watched the Federal military display below. He later wrote: "We could see extending for miles (Sherman's) grand encampment of infantry and artillery, the stars and stripes floating from every regimental, brigade, division and corps headquarters and presenting the greatest panorama I ever beheld. Softly and sweetly the music from their bands as they played the national airs were wafted up and over the summit of the mountain. Somehow, some way, in some inexplicable and unseen manner, 'Hail Columbia,' 'America' and 'The

■ Maj. Gen. David S. Stanley commanded the 1st Division, IV Corps, until July 27 when he replaced Gen. O.O. Howard as commander of the IV Corps. At Tunnel Hill, Buzzard's Roost and Resaca, Stanley credited much of his division's success to the 5th Indiana Battery and the division's chief of artillery, Capt. Peter Simonson. Near sundown on May 14 at Resaca, Cruft's brigade was hit hard by a Confederate infantry assault. Stanley wrote: "Directing their attack more to our rear than flank, the 101st Ohio and 81st Indiana were soon driven back, and the enemy was bursting exultingly upon the open field when Simonson opened on them with canister, which soon broke and dispersed that attack. Had it not been for the timely aid of the battery it would have gone hard with the brigade." A month later, Simonson was killed by a sharpshooter on June 16 while laying out a position near Pine Mountain. "This was an irreparable loss to the division," Stanley wrote. "I have not in my military experience met with an officer who was the equal of this one in energy, efficiency and ingenuity in the handling of artillery."

Star Spangled Banner' sounded sweeter than I had ever before heard them, and filled my soul with feelings that I could not describe or forget. It haunted me for days, but never shook my loyalty to the Stars and Bars or relaxed my efforts in behalf of our cause.

"While thus arrayed in his grand encampment," Young continued, "his banners flying and bands playing, a part of his force (McPherson), like a gladiator, was rapidly and stealthily gliding over the plain west of the mountains to seize Snake Creek and Dug Gaps and strike Johnston in the rear at Resaca. But you know 'the best laid schemes of mice and men gang aft agley.' We arrived there first and gave him a hearty welcome ..."

'The buzzards were on their roosts'

Corporal Joseph Van Nest
Company I
101st Ohio Volunteer Infantry

In the month of April 1864 some changes were made in the company and I was appointed Color Guard, an honorable but not very desirable position. Gilbert Newell of Company C was Color Corporal, Corporal Leonard Cole of Company H was one Color Guard, and myself of Company I the other Color Guard. We had only the two. Our numbers in the regiment were greatly reduced. Company I had the largest company in the regiment; it numbered 54, including men and officers.

We could see by the concentration of commissary stores and the movement of troops that there would soon be a move. At dress parade on the eve of May 3 the order was read that we should be prepared to move the following day. All was bustle and excitement, letters were being written late at night, for most of us realized what was to come, and we made up our marching outfits. I was in the very best of health at this time, and pulled the scales down at 182 pounds — the most I ever weighed, either before or since the war.

We had a number of recruits who came to us during the late winter and spring. This would be new to them, but they followed our course in doing away with all surplus baggage. The next morning the orders were to strike tents and it did not take long to make a dilapidated-looking place of this camp. The sick were left behind and sent to the hospitals.

Our first day's march brought us to Catoosa Springs, quite a prominent summer resort before the war. The grounds were handsomely laid out, there were quite a number of springs and the water in every one tasted different, so it was said. One was called Coffee Spring, and the boys said it tasted like coffee, but I think it was more imagination than anything else. There were other springs called the Red, White and Blue Sulphur Springs, and almost every color of the rainbow. A part of the Rebel army had camped at this place, and I must say that they left it in a much better condition than most places.

The second day our regiment was on the advance, Company H deployed as skirmishers. We soon came to the cavalry outposts and they reported the enemy in our immediate front. We pressed them steadily back. The colors were with the reserve line. I kept a steady lookout in front and watched our boys advance. The firing was not very heavy, and both sides kept under cover as much as they could.

We were advancing down a valley, which was covered in places with thick underbrush, and our skirmishers at times would come onto the

■ On the afternoon of May 8, Kentuckians and Arkansans behind imposing palisades of solid rock poured musketry fire into the ranks of Federals climbing the slopes of Rocky Face Ridge at Dug Gap. Recalled 1st Lieut. Stephen Pierson of the 33rd New Jersey: "Their main line opened furiously upon us, and added to our confusion by sending from the top great boulders rolling down the mountain side."

Johnnies very unexpectedly, and the Johnnies would be surprised at the sudden appearance of the Yanks. Jacob Yeager, who was on the skirmish line, came up to a house very unexpectedly where there were some Rebel officers, and the sudden appearance of the Yanks caused them to leave without some of their accoutrements. Jake got a sword from the house which had been left there by the enemy. It was of very old make, had a white bone handle, the blade was bright and no doubt of the best steel. Jake could not think of leaving that, and when the skirmish line was relieved he brought the sword to me, wanting me to take charge of it for him. I assured him that I would as long as it did not encumber me too much, as I was very much taken with the weapon myself and should have liked to have had it at home.

This was in the fore part of the day. In the afternoon the enemy did not give way so easily, and the firing grew more rapid. We could hear the roar of the cannon to our right, but we kept pressing them back. On looking to the rear we could see no troops in sight and it looked as though we were having this part of the valley to ourselves. There were numerous small knolls we were obliged to pass over, and they would conceal from view any troops that might be in our rear. We well knew there must be a large force not far off to be sent to our support if we needed them.

We soon came in sight of Tunnel Hill. The Rebels had the hilltop well fortified and a number of pieces of artillery there. When we came in sight they sent some shells in our direction and made us hunt our holes, which we did without being told.

We had just passed over a small knoll and were advancing on a low piece of soft ground when all at once a shell struck and the mud flew over some of the boys. "Lay down, lay down!" they shouted. One soldier of Company G by the name of Grant was terribly frightened. I never saw a man jump as far as he did. Some of the mud struck him, and no doubt he

'The opportunity we so much desire'

Marion Light Artillery
In the Field above Dalton
May 10th 1864

dear Pa,

I suppose you have learned before this that the enemy was advancing upon this place and the news is generally known at the rear sooner than we learned it at the Front. Except by the noise of battle we seldom know what is going on more than a mile on each side. Our forces have been in line ever since Friday last and our skirmish lines have been engaged most of the time. I had a fine opportunity of inspecting our position last Sunday being ordered to report to Gen. Cheatham for the purpose of surveying the position for Artillery. We rode out beyond our pickets and saw everything. I think our defences good and cannot be taken except by flanking.

At present I am three miles [from] Dalton on the Tunnel Hill road protecting Mill Creek Gap. Yesterday morning at daylight the Yankees advanced a double line of skirmishers against Bates Division who are in the woods in our front. There was desultory fighting all day from 600 to 2000 yards ahead of us occasionally growing very warm. We repulsed all their advances and just before sun down made a sortie and drove the Yankees from the field.

Our battery has not yet been engaged but we stand with horses hitched ready to go in wherever the enemy advances in force. All day yesterday the shell and bullets fell among us but hurt us but little. We had in the Battery one man badly wounded and one horse killed. This morning the firing commenced at day light and continues — nothing but picket fighting. I do hope the Yankees will assault our lines for I want a victory here to balance those in Virginia and out West. I fear the Yankees will fall back and not give us the opportunity we so much desire. I am of the opinion that such a victory here as Shiloh, Murfreesboro or Chickamauga would end the war speedily ...

Your affectionate son
A.J. Neal

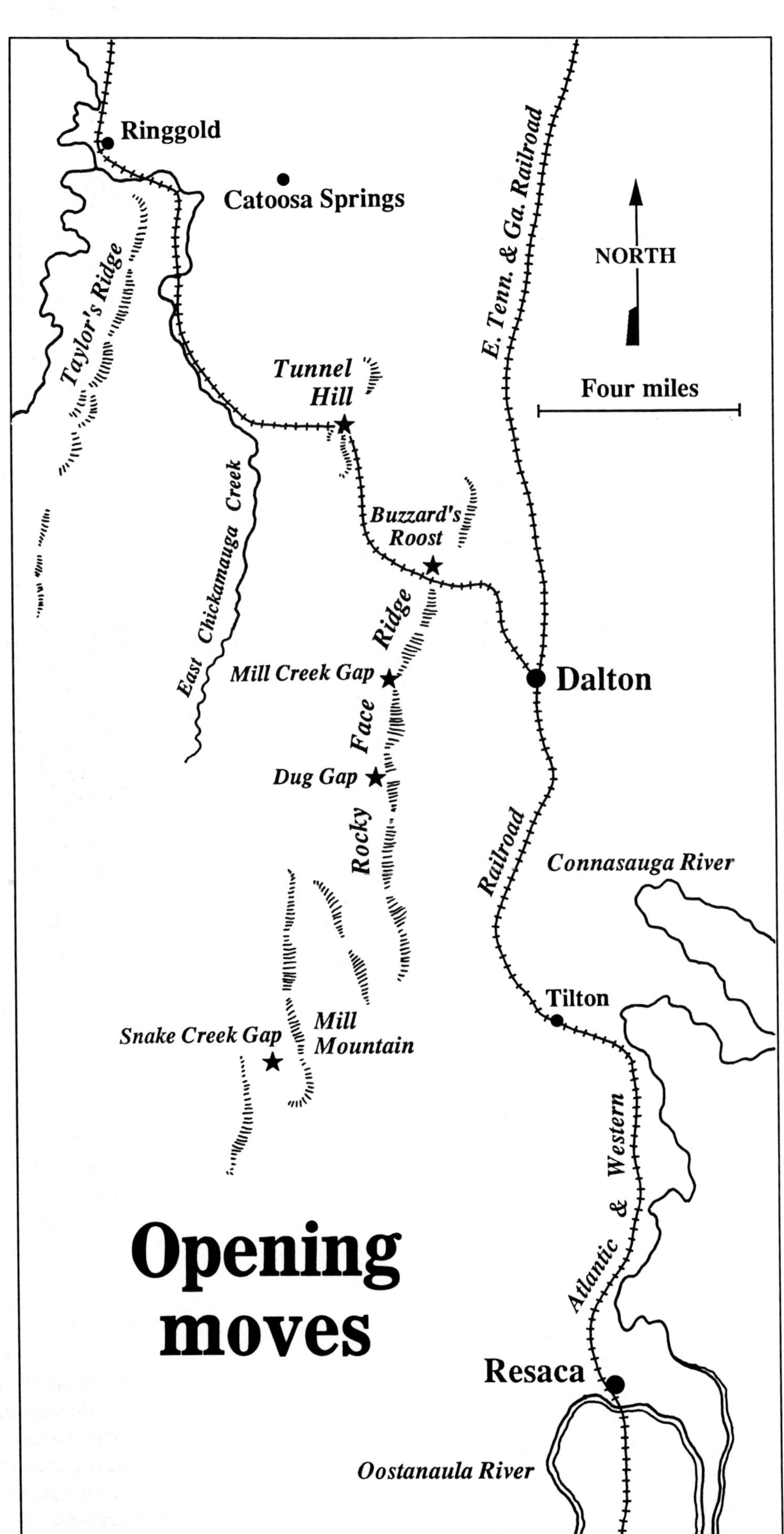

Opening moves

thought he had been hit. He turned very pale and could not speak for some seconds. He was a recruit and this was his first experience. He was large and had red hair and a beard.

This was a close call but luckily no one was hit. We steadily advanced on the enemy on the hill, and I expected we would soon have all we could do, so I left the sword Yeager had given me as I did not wish to have any more load than was necessary. The Rebels would turn their guns on us, and then in opposite directions, as there were troops advancing from different points. In some places they had cut the trees down so they could see us. Our line was still advancing and we were getting closer to their works. Suddenly we saw that there was considerable hustling on the hill, and they limbered up their guns and away they went. We were pushed forward more rapidly up Tunnel Hill, and were the first troops on top. A greater number of tired men I never saw. We laid down any and everywhere when the order came to halt.

Sergeant Newell, Cole and myself struck a soft place in the middle of a road and were soon sleeping soundly. Some time later someone pushed and pulled at me, and said, "Move out of the road. Gen. Thomas is coming!" When we heard that name we soon commenced to move and shout, but old "Pap" Thomas gave orders to not disturb the men. "Let them rest," he said. "I can find my way to the top of the hill."

Gen. Sherman came up later, and we were ordered out of the road to make way for the general and his staff to go to the top of the hill. From the top of Tunnel Hill was a splendid position from which to view the surrounding country in every direction. Far to the rear we could see our troops, and in the front the enemy.

While our officers were still there talking and taking observations of the country, the enemy was doing the same of our lines. A general of some prominence made his appearance on the Rebel side in company with a large number of men on horseback. They came some distance in an open field, stopped and viewed our position with their field glasses. Gen. Stanley ordered the artillerymen to send a shell over with his compliments. The shell was sent, but went over their heads. The Rebels moved some little distance and again stopped. Another shell was sent and it looked to me as though it had exploded right among them. There was a stampede and a hustling to get out of range, and some of the horses were without riders. Whether they were killed, wounded or preferred to take to the brush on foot, I could not tell as I did not ask for the loan of a field glass from our general; neither did he ask my opinion. The Rebels left after this salute.

That night we viewed one of the finest sights I ever saw. We camped on Tunnel Hill and could see the campfires of our troops in the rear, and the enemy's in our front, and it looked as though there were many thousands of them. They seemed to extend for miles and looked beautiful. We seemed to be in the center of a stupendous camp. It was a sight seen but once in a lifetime, and it was beyond description.

Our next move was toward Rocky Face Mountain. This place was a natural fortification — in the valley it was covered with underbrush. We could see no distance, only the mountains in our front where the Rebel sharpshooters were located.

While we lay in this valley in the brush a shell came flying through the air. The Rebels had managed to get some light artillery on top of the mountain, but they could not depress their guns to fire on us direct. So they cut their fuses to explode the shells over us. One exploded over our camp and the pieces came almost too close for comfort for some of the

■ A Federal gun crew fires at Buzzard's Roost in a woodcut published in the May 21, 1864, edition of *Harper's Weekly*. The artist, Theodore R. Davis, traveled with the Army of the Cumberland and drew numerous sketches of the fighting along Rocky Face Ridge and at Resaca. Present during the storming of Dug Gap on May 8, Davis sketched troops of the XX Corps making the assault on the entrenched lines of Gen. Carter Stevenson's division, and wrote to his publisher in a note accompanying his drawing: "Some of our troops, after they had actually climbed the last ridge to the crest of the palisade formation, were hurled from the top by the rebels, who, instead of taking them prisoners, preferred to mangle the brave boys among the rocks beneath."

■ Col. Isaac M. Kirby commanded the 101st Ohio at the beginning of the campaign, and on June 10 succeeded to the command of the 1st Brigade, 1st Division, IV Corps, replacing Brig. Gen. Charles Cruft. "Cool and collected, he had already proven himself reliable under circumstances requiring nerve, decision and pluck," wrote Sergeant Lewis W. Day of Kirby. "While we all rejoiced in his well-merited promotion, the 101st boys felt as though they had met with personal loss. Careful and prompt, Col. Kirby always struck quickly and hard, but he never forgot to look after his men, and his promotion made no change in his bearing toward the boys." Kirby was commissioned a brevet brigadier general on January 30, 1865.

boys, but fortunately no one was killed or wounded.

This Rebel battery made but a short stay on the mountain. Our batteries were camped in the valley, and such a roar of artillery for a few minutes came from our guns that it was a complete surprise to us. They opened on the Rebel guns and that was the last we heard from them. The mountain on the side fronting us was solid rock and almost perpendicular, and some of the shells would strike the face of the mountain and explode.

It was the same evening that some of our bands were playing national airs, when shortly after a Rebel band on top of the mountain struck up "Dixie." The sound of this music I thought was the grandest I had ever heard. The distance appeared to be just right to make it sound well. What few bands the Rebs did have were well versed in their profession. When they had finished, our boys sent up a shout to let them know that their music had been appreciated, much more than their bullets and shells were. Our bands then struck up "Yankee Doodle," and the Johnnies shouted as if they appreciated our music, which I suppose sounded as sweet to them as theirs did to us. There seemed to be a mutual feeling between Yank and Johnny as far as music was concerned.

The following evening some troops were sent to reconnoiter and penetrate the woods at the base of the mountain. They were met with an unexpected reception on the part of the Rebels, and showed that they had a large force in that vicinity. Our troops remained until after dark fighting with them. It was a grand sight to see the flash of the muskets. We could locate their position by the flash of their guns. Whatever the object was in sending our troops there we never knew; we found out, however, that the Rebels were there in strong force.

The next afternoon orders came for Col. Kirby to take the 101st and make an attack on Rocky Face or Buzzard's Roost. We started across an open field in the face of the Rebel sharpshooters. We started on a double-quick and before we got across we felt as if we would like to have doubled our speed two or three times as the bullets fairly whistled round and about us.

I was on the left of Sergeant Newell, who had the colors, and Corporal Cole was on the right side. We kept in line all right until we had passed over about one half of the distance, when suddenly Sergeant Newell took an extra move and left us some distance behind. It came so unexpectedly that I was at a loss to know what occasioned this sudden freak. He was about the first man to reach the opposite side.

When we all got over I asked him what caused him to take such a sudden start. He took his hand and smoothed down his beard, and he had a very heavy one at the time. A bullet had passed through it and cut off quite a handful. He said, "I felt it when it went through my beard, and when they were coming so close as that I was anxious to get across." It was a close shave, but not the kind he wanted.

I do not remember of anyone being hurt while going through the field. When we reached the other side we were protected by the woods and rocks. Our picket lines were stationed in these woods. Our lines were re-formed and we were ordered to march up the mountain.

At the base of the mountain there was a gradual elevation for some little distance. We had not advanced over forty yards when there opened from our right a discharge from artillery of grape and canister. The right of the regiment received the whole charge, and Company A lost a number of its men. We were ordered to lie down when the grape and canister came over us, and as it passed over it sounded just like a flock of quail starting to fly. We could not see the enemy for the thick underbrush, but we could hear them plain enough. It was a terrible position to be in. In front of us was the mountain of almost solid, perpendicular rock, and we could not advance. It was equally bad to retreat while the enemy was discharging their grape and canister. Their firing finally ceased, but the sharpshooters kept picking off all men who exposed themselves.

I have heard of miracles, but never saw one until that day, and that was that Col. Kirby was not killed. He stood up in front of the regiment, fully exposed to the fire and in plain sight of the Rebel sharpshooters, and to me it seemed almost a miracle that he was not shot. I suppose it must have been because he was so thin and split the bullets.

I thought we had been in close quarters before, but this place capped the climax. As we lay there close to the ground the suspense was terrible. We knew not what to expect next. It was now getting dark and we remained there until it was safe for us to retreat down the mountain under cover of the night. That was all that saved us from being cut to pieces. Had it been two hours earlier, the 101st Ohio Volunteer Infantry would have been a thing of the past.

When the order was given to retreat, it was to go as quietly as possible as we did not care to wake them up again if they had gone to sleep. Talk about hornets — I think we had found a whole neighborhood of them. There were many wounded, and also killed, and our right wing suffered greatly. Company A suffered by far the heaviest loss.

It has always appeared to me that there was some neglect on the part of our brigade commander in not trying to relieve us in some way that evening. I may misjudge him, but I thought that we had more than our share of fighting since starting on the campaign. When there was any important move to be made by our brigade, Col. Kirby was ordered to make the move. I think Gen. Cruft had much more confidence in Col. Kirby than in any other officer in the brigade. Gen. Cruft may have been a good general, but I think he failed to show it at the proper time. Some generals get renown by having others do the work while they get the credit, and I think this was the case here.

In going down the mountain that night a peculiar incident occurred, something I had never before heard of. Several men in the regiment became night blind. Lt. Col. McDonald was one of them. It appears they could not see and had to be led down by others. Col. Kirby was considerably excited after we had arrived at the base of the mountain, and could not find the lieutenant-colonel. He was going around inquiring, "Boys, have you seen Mac? Where is Mac?" Receiving no satisfactory answer, he started up the mountain in search of him, thinking he was killed or wounded. He had gone but a short distance when he met some of our boys leading Col. McDonald down. There were others being led, too.

We lost a number of noble men at this place, and I do not know that any important service was accomplished. It was called "Buzzard's Roost," and we found that the buzzards were on their roosts, but not asleep, and also in greater numbers and better prepared than we expected to find them.

The next day we were moved some distance to the right, almost directly in front of Mill Creek Gap. We remained there all day and in the afternoon some heavy Parrott guns were placed in position and fired a number of times in the direction of Dalton. I was standing not far from the guns, watching them load. Just before they fired, one of the batterymen shouted, "Stand on your toes, and open your mouth!" I soon found out the reason for that. The jar of the gun when discharged was fearful, and I did not remain in that vicinity long as I did not fancy the ring of

■ Lt. Col. Bedan B. McDonald assumed command of the 101st Ohio on June 10 after the promotion of Col. Isaac Kirby to brigade command. As a major the previous year at Chickamauga, McDonald temporarily led the regiment until he was captured on September 20. Sent to Libby Prison in Richmond, he escaped in February 1864, rejoined the 101st and was promoted to lieutenant colonel. He led the regiment during the remainder of the campaign and at Franklin, where he was wounded on November 30.

■ Private David F.C. Rhoad, Company G, 36th Alabama, was among the Confederates of Gen. Henry D. Clayton's brigade defending Rocky Face Ridge at Buzzard's Roost from May 7-12. With rock formations and strong rifle-pits for protection, the 36th suffered only eight casualties on the ridge before retiring on May 13. Two days later, however, Rhoad's regiment lost 83 officers and enlisted men in one 25-minute charge at Resaca. Before the month was out, 32 more were added to the casualty rolls, including regimental commander Col. Lewis T. Woodruff, who was seriously wounded on May 25 at New Hope Church. Rhoad survived the campaign and the war, and as a personal protest to Federal victory he never shaved his beard for the rest of his life.

those Parrott guns.

I will not undertake to describe what was in our front at Mill Creek Gap, more than to say that any force sent in there would return as dead and dying. The Rebels had batteries masked to sweep any force that was sent in. It was simply a natural fortification, and there were more buzzards at roost here, too. Our picket line was located at the base of the mountain and they had holes dug in the ground (we called them gopher holes), and usually one or two men in a hole. These pickets were relieved only at night, under cover of darkness, and they would remain there until the next night. We were in front of Mill Creek Gap two days.

On the morning of the third day at daybreak, we were drawn up in line of battle — the whole brigade and more, perhaps. We were ordered to leave all surplus baggage, and that meant blankets, cooking utensils, etc. It looked to us as though we were going to be sent into the gap. A railroad passed through here, and also a small creek called Mill Creek. The railroad company had built a bridge over the creek near the entrance and there were embankments on either side. It was reported that the Rebels had dammed up the creek at this bridge and backed the water over the low ground, and about the only place to cross was on the railroad, and also that the Rebels had it covered with their guns, and if these reports were true, there would not have been a grease spot left of us.

We had been standing in line some little time when we heard a shout from one part of our line. Our attention was directed toward our pickets who were going up the mountain with no resistance being made on the part of the enemy, who, we then learned, had retreated during the night and evacuated their stronghold. You may talk about luck; just about this time we thought ourselves very lucky indeed, for we were certainly highly favored.

As soon as it was found out that they had retreated, our orders were to pack up and fall in line, and off we started after the enemy through Mill Creek Gap which was now perfectly harmless. When we reached the other side where the Rebels had been in camp, we found great stacks of corn meal which the Rebels had left, and which no doubt they could not carry with them. The distance from this place to Dalton was said to be six miles. The roads were in good shape and we made good time after the Johnnies. Just as we sighted Dalton the Rebels were passing through. As our troops were entering on one side, the Rebel rear guard was going out on the other side.

In Dalton there were a number of warehouses and I entered one and got a box of something. On examination it proved to be tobacco. I did not use the weed in this form, it being plug tobacco or chewing tobacco. I had no trouble, however, in getting rid of it for there were many who were greatly in need of it.

We did not stop here very long as we were ordered to advance, and we took the same road that the Rebels were retreating over. It led up the side of the mountain part of the way and the Rebel rear guard would hurl their shells at us when pushing them too hard. Rebel prisoners said the reason they left their stronghold at Mill Creek Gap was because Gen. McPherson had come through Snake Creek Gap some distance to the south of us and would have cut them off, and to avoid capture they were forced to retreat — a flank movement I suppose it would be in military terms. The rank and file of the army were not let into the secrets of our commanding generals. We were expected to do the work laid down by our superiors in rank only. Our army was composed of many intelligent men.

Many of them as privates in the ranks were much more competent to command than some who wore straps.*

'Against such fearful odds'

Private Robert H. Dacus
Company H
1st Arkansas Mounted Rifles

Our brigade opened the campaign, or rather Gen. Joe Hooker opened the campaign by trying to force a passage through Dug Gap and over Rocky Face mountain, west of Dalton, and our brigade was the only troops there, or in reach, to defend the pass.

We had been sent directly from the railroad cars to this point, it being one of the most important picket posts to be guarded. We were sent out on the 7th of May, and on the 8th, just after noon as we were lying around, not dreaming of an attack because the place seemed almost impregnable, the officer in charge of the signal station called out that the enemy was crossing a field two miles west of the gap. Immediately following came the second line. This was signaled down to Dalton, but before this message could be sent the third line had crossed the field; then came the fourth and close after it came the fifth. It began to look like we were going to have something to do.

The signal officer signaled to Gen. Johnston that 10,000 Federals were within two miles of the gap, and it was bound to be taken before help could reach it, and so it really seemed. But our officers were cool-headed, brave and determined men, from Gen. Reynolds, our brigade commander, on down. So instead of making preparations to retreat they had things put in order for doing some of the hardest fighting that we did during the war; nor did we have to wait long until it began.

As soon as they could march the two miles intervening between us and straighten up their lines a little they came marching up the mountain in front of us, they with 10,000 and we with 1,000. But we had the odds in position almost as great as they had in numbers. But their men were brave and daring, as we had plenty of opportunities during the next four months to find out. It looked like a sin to run brave men into such a place for it was almost like driving them into a slaughter pen.

Back of us were Gen. Johnston's men in camp, and not in a shape to bring into battle at once. The enemy knew this, and if they could force a passage over this mountain at that point it would throw them against our army in a way and at a time that they would have been almost helpless. With both sides knowing this they fought with desperate determination.

Gen. Cleburne with his division was sent to our help as soon as possible, but it was getting dusk when he arrived and the fighting was over before his men got in line. Word had met them on the way up that the gap was taken, and when they arrived and found it was a mistake it would have done your heart good to hear the cheers that went up from them for the little band that held its position so long against such fearful odds.

■ Private Ezra A. Fahnestock, Company I, 101st Ohio, had served in the army only 41 days before taking part in his first battle on May 11 at Buzzard's Roost. At age 21, he was a newly-arrived replacement in Corporal Joseph Van Nest's company, and his baptism by fire that day must have been unnerving. Wrote Sergeant Lewis W. Day, a veteran of Company E: "The ground in our rear was so completely swept by continually bursting case shot and canister that it seemed utter destruction to attempt a retrograde movement. We could only hug the rocks and work our muskets with all the vim that was in us. The situation just at the coming of night, in that dark gorge, with the ground seemingly on fire from bursting artillery missiles all about us, was weird and awe-inspiring in the extreme."

* On May 14, Van Nest was badly wounded at Resaca, being hit simultaneously by a shell fragment and bullet in the right leg below the knee. After more than 20 operations, it was not until 1867 that the wound healed. Corporal Leonard G. Cole of the regiment's color guard also was wounded on May 14, as was Van Nest's friend, Corporal Jacob C. Yeager, who suffered a fractured jaw.

■ A XX Corps badge, belonging to a member of the 55th Ohio. General Orders No. 144, issued April 4, 1864, consolidated the XI and XII Corps and designated them the XX Corps, with Maj. Gen. Joseph Hooker commanding. The five-pointed star, the badge of the XII Corps, was retained as the badge of the XX Corps at the suggestion of XI Corps officers. The 55th Ohio served in the 3rd Brigade, 3rd Division. This badge is made of German silver with a blue center — the color of the corps' 3rd Division. A red star designated the 1st Division while white was the color of the 2nd Division. The 55th Ohio's commander, Col. Charles B. Gambee, was killed at Resaca on May 15.

During the engagement a part of our regiment killed the man who placed the first stand of colors on Missionary Ridge during that battle. He had his commission as captain in his pocket when killed, which had been given him for the deed. He also put the first and only stand of Federal colors on Rocky Face mountain that evening, but he forfeited his life in doing it.

With a squad of about 20 men he got on top of the mountain by a flank movement, but about the same number of our men met them as they reached the top and a hand-to-hand fight ensued to see who should hold the ground. This man stuck his flag into the ground and called to his men to rally to it. About this time a one-eyed Irishman by the name of Johnson, a private, but to whom the title of "Capt. Johnson" had been given, shot and killed him. Another of our men jumped at the flag and got hold of the staff and tassel, but one of their men at the same moment sprang at the flag and caught it, tore it off the staff and made his escape with it.

We never knew how many of the enemy were killed and wounded. They carried away all their wounded and all their officers who were killed, both commissioned and non-commissioned. How many privates who were killed and carried away we never knew, but two days later, they not coming back to see anything about their dead, and with the stench from the dead bodies becoming unbearable, a detail was made from our command to bury them. I was on the detail. We found 120 dead, all privates. We also picked up 1,600 stands of arms that had been left by them.

This was our first acquaintance with Gen. Hooker's men, or Fighting Joe Hooker as he was styled by admirers in the North. He had three divisions under him in this campaign. Every man wore a star on his hat. One division wore a red star, the second a white star and the third a blue, and were called the Star Corps of Sherman's army.

This, however, was not our last call from Hooker and his men. Polk's corps, to which we belonged, was on our left center and Hooker on their right center during the campaign just beginning. This arrangement placed us in a position to make us close neighbors for the next four months, sometimes not more than a hundred yards apart. During that time the acquaintance was cultivated with a great deal of assiduity, and I can say this much for Gen. Hooker and his men: Whenever we called upon them, no matter how unseasonable the hour, they were always at home and we might depend upon a cordial reception. And being of true Southern blood and a reciprocal nature, we did our best on all occasions to make their calls, if not pleasant, at least as satisfactory as possible.

Thus, while we were confronting each other in one of the greatest and deadliest conflicts ever recorded in the world's history, there sprang up between us a feeling of intimacy almost amounting to friendship. Sometimes we would agree between ourselves not to fight or shoot at each other for a certain period of time, and during all those four months of almost daily fighting not one of these truces was broken.

'Balls sing about my ears'

Diary of Capt. John William Tuttle Company G 3rd Kentucky Veteran Volunteer Infantry

Sunday May 8th. Our regt. marched about a mile around on the left flank of Rocky Face Ridge and occupied a gap, threw forward skirmishers, and soon brisk firing broke out all along the line. The 125th Ohio went out on a reconnaissance and succeeded in gaining the top of Rocky Face with the loss of four men killed and about twenty wounded. Col. Opdycke sent word back that the rebs were thick in his front and advancing. The 79th Ill. was sent to his support. The 23d A.C. joined on our left. Three or four of their Generals came to see us.

A little after noon our regt. and the remaining regts. of our Brigade marched up on top of Rocky Face. Here we had a fine view of this country for many miles on both sides. Saw three rebel forts and a number of lines of fortifications which appeared to be occupied by rebel cavalry pickets only. Towards night, however, the whole rebel army marched out of their camps about Dalton and bivouacked in Crow Valley down to our left. The camp fires of the two armies presented a spectacle magnificent beyond description. A little before sunset our regt. was sent on picket, though relieved a little after dark, not being its turn for picket. Rebels fired a volley into us during the night and though the balls pattered around us none of us were hurt.

Monday May 9th. When I awoke this morning they were clearing a road to bring two pieces of artilery up the hill to batter down the fort on the ridge in front of us. Our Brigade moved forward about sunrise. Heavy skirmishing was kept up all day by our advance, of which four companies of our regt. under Lt. Col. Bullitt and Maj. Brennan constituted a part. Col. Dunlap and I, under orders from Gen. Harker, remained with the six companies in reserve. Balls sang over us all day long, wounding a few of the reserve.

About noon the 23d A.C. moved in line of battle down Crow Valley and connected with the left of our Division. Our artilery was well handled though one of the pieces was so exposed to the enemy's sharpshooters it could not be used a great deal. About 5 p.m. we received orders to the effect that Gen. Wagner should charge a line of rifle pits on the side of the rebel fort next to Crow Valley and if he succeeded in carrying them our Brigade (Harker's) was to charge directly on the fort. Our advance consisting of detachments from our regiment and the 64th Ohio and probably from another regt. or two of our brigade were to take the lead when they saw us coming.

Through some misunderstanding Col. Mollbane* of the 64th started on the charge before we in the rear were ready for the assault. Our regiment and the 125th Ohio were to charge by the flank on top of the ridge, the 125th in advance of us but as Col. Mollbane and those with him had started we were compelled to support them immediately. Our regt. happened to be nearest ready and started forward at once in double-quick time following the charge of our advance detachments and followed by the 125th Ohio.

I brought up the rear of our regt. and pressed forward with all my might at a lively half hammon. I thought at the time I was nearly to the fort but found afterwards I did not get there by nearly one hundred yards. Met our men rushing to the rear and tried to rally them but failing in that joined them in the retreat. Some of our men got within thirty yards of the fort before they were repulsed.

Wagner made a feeble demonstration on our left and fell back, Wood came up bravely on our right, but was repulsed. Left my haversack nearly as far up as I went toward the fort, being too much exhausted to carry it. Received a painful stab in my right leg from a bayonet of one of our [men] during the scramble on the charge. In the retreat I with some others jumped over the bluff, went back down the hill on the west side. Being

■ Lt. Col. William A. Bullitt, 3rd Kentucky Infantry, was severely wounded at Rocky Face Ridge. Along with the 79th Illinois, the 3rd Kentucky supported the May 9 assault of the 64th Ohio on the ridge. Wrote 1st Lieut. Wilbur F. Hinman of the 65th Ohio: "Lieutenant-colonel Bullitt received a grievous wound, a musket ball passing through his thigh. He was carried to the rear, through the ranks of the Sixty-fifth, which he had recently commanded for four months. Its officers and men had formed for him an exceedingly warm attachment, and the expressions of regret and sympathy for him were many and sincere. He eventually recovered in a measure, but was disabled for life."

* Tuttle's spelling is in error. He refers to Col. Alexander McIlvain, commander of the 64th Ohio, who was mortally wounded a short time later.

■ Brig. Gen. George D. Wagner commanded a brigade in Newton's division, IV Corps. Early on May 7, his troops led Newton's advance toward Tunnel Hill and Rocky Face Ridge, with Harker's brigade following close behind. "Within an hour Wagner's skirmishers found the enemy and brisk firing began at once," wrote 1st Lieut. Wilbur F. Hinman of the 65th Ohio. "The rebels retired stubbornly, taking advantage of fences, trees and rocks, from the shelter of which to give us all the annoyance possible. After proceeding about four miles the advance ran against something so solid that Gen. Newton formed the division in line of battle. We waited an hour for an attack which did not come, and then began 'beating the bush' to see if we could flush the game. We climbed hills and crashed through brier thickets until we were thoroughly exhausted. The rebels had gone to the rear." Wagner's brigade began the campaign with an aggregate strength of 2,007 officers and enlisted men. When he arrived in Atlanta four months later it mustered only 1,015.

crippled in both legs, I could not have got along very well had my retreat not been facilitated by some rebel sharpshooters in trees who made the balls sing about my ears.

Thought the rebels would pursue and did not know how far our men would fall back so considered my chance for a berth in Libby pretty fair, but looking up the hill I saw the stars and stripes waving and made for them. Got nearly to the top of the hill when I sank entirely exhausted. Some of my men came down and helped me up the hill. Rested a few moments, drank some coffee, and returned to the regt. (or the main body of those who remained together). Found they had only fallen back about 200 yards and were behind some works we had thrown up in the morning and were still pegging away at the rebels. Lt. Col. Bullitt was very seriously wounded, Capt. Bristow slightly wounded, though badly bruised. Four enlisted men were killed and 26 wounded out of our regt. The Brigade lost thirty-one killed and one hundred and thirteen wounded. We were relieved a little after dark and retired about where we went into bivouac for the night.

'Go back! Hospital right back there!'

Diary of Capt. Robert S. Chamberlain Company C 64th Ohio Veteran Volunteer Infantry

May 3d. 1864. Ordered to be ready to march at 12 o'clock. Sergeant W.D. Patterson took the colors to carry by order of Col. McIlvain. I turned over to Lieut. Tom Smith, Co. E for Corp. Dillon, one Springfield rifle and accoutrements complete. Had dinner at 10:30, and started at 12 noon. Marched 12 miles, got into camp at eight o'clock p.m. Had supper and went to bed at 9 p.m. Lieut. Shellenberger and I slept together on a rubber blanket and one woolen blanket over us.

May 4/64. 15 miles from Dalton, Ga. Left camp at 6 o'clock. Marched through a very desolate-looking country, resembled that around Corinth [Miss.] and Pittsburg Landing [Tenn.]. Passed several houses, but saw only two able-bodied white men during the day; they were at a mill 12 miles from Dalton. Saw one white-haired old man by the road side. Marched 10 miles and are now on a ridge rather to the right of Dalton. Pioneers are busy felling timber in our front. Clear and warm.

May 5/64. 4 miles from Ringgold, Ga. Clear and cool. Moved about a mile and a half northwest of where we stopped last evening. Are now on a high ridge building breastworks. Have a good situation. Moved a short distance to the left this forenoon. Mail came in this morning but nothing for me. Was detailed for picket this evening. Were posted at the foot of the hill we first took up our position on. Came out on the run almost and by a very roundabout way. Received 18 bayonet scabbards of Holden. Sent my overcoat to the train by Burns.

On picket, Tiger Creek, Ga. May 6/64. Clear and cool. Stayed up nearly all night; all quiet along the line during the night. Slept about an hour and a half. Officer of the day did not trouble us any during the night. Col. Blake, 40th Indiana, came around with him this forenoon. Very warm and sultry all day, but windy. Summer has come I think. Lt. Col. Brown, Brigade officer of the day, left me in command of the post. Feel rather dull after being up all night. Relieved by the 3d Kentucky.

Bivouac 64th Reg't. Ohio Vols. Sat. May 7/64. Called up at half past two a.m. Had our crackers and coffee and were ready to move out at 4 a.m.

Formed and waited orders. Moved out at 7 a.m. and formed the lines on the west side of Tiger Creek and advanced about two miles through the woods; difficult marching through the thick undergrowth of young pines. Heard cannonading on our right about nine o'clock for the first time. Expect to have a hand in ere long. Very warm. Took the road about 12 noon and marched through to Tunnel Hill. The firing that we heard was the troops taking Tunnel Hill and Buzzard Roost Gap. Have not learned how many prisoners were captured, if any. No particulars. Got to camp east of Tunnel Hill about 3 p.m. Went to a stream nearby and took a good wash which made me feel much better. The country we passed through today seemed rather better than what we marched through heretofore, yet it was rough enough. There seems to be a series of ridges in our front that I suppose we will have to clear off. Was to meeting this evening.

Bivouac one mile east of Tunnel Hill, Ga. May 8/64. Clear and warm. Ordered to be ready to move at 6:30 a.m. Going out on a reconnaissance this morning. Hope it may not result in a Chickamauga. Left camp at time ordered and marched out east about two miles, formed line of battle and advanced about one mile and lay in the woods until about 10:30 a.m. when we marched back toward the old camp. Remained there until 2 p.m. and then started for "Buzzards Roost." Had a very warm time getting up the mountain. Found no enemy on the top. Skirmishers drove their pickets off.

Quite a number of the 125th Ohio were wounded. Could see the enemy in their works across the valley on the east side of the mountain. Troops from the XXIII Corps relieved us this forenoon. Saw Brig. Gen'ls. Judah, McLean and Hascall. Skirmishing quite brisk at times. There was no cannonading until after 4 p.m. when a few shots were fired. Regiment rested and got coffee. Men had to go nearly two miles for water. Moved along the top of the ridge about a quarter of a mile and stopped for the night. Men drew rations and lay down with orders to be ready to fall in at a moment's warning.

Rocky Face Ridge, Ga. May 9/64. Were waked up at daybreak and ordered to get our coffee and breakfast immediately and be ready to move at any time. Weather beautiful and clear. Some firing along the picket line and a man wounded occasionally. Two pieces of artillery were brought up before day to wake up the "Johnnies." About nine o'clock we moved to the right along the ridge about a quarter of a mile and built temporary breastworks of stone and lay behind them until nearly noon. Bullets from some of the rebel sharpshooters came over us. One hit William Rodocker between the lips but did not injure him any. A correspondent of the N.Y. Herald was sighting around for items. Gen. Harker talked with him a few minutes after which Harker, Gen'l. Newton, division commander, and Gen'l. O.O. Howard, corps commander (IV A.C.), passed to the front. After they came back we were ordered up to support the 79th Illinois who were on the skirmish line. Here we put up another line of breastworks and we had to keep down behind them too. Every man that showed himself was shot at. We lay here all afternoon waiting for what was to come.

About five o'clock George brought us our coffee. While Lieuts. Shellenberger, Smith and I were eating our frugal meal orders came to us to be ready to move forward. There was some coffee left and I divided it out among the boys as we were ordered to pile up the knapsacks and prepare to fall in. I ordered George to get some more water and make the pot full of coffee to drink after coming out of the action, remarking at the time that it would do those who got out all right a great deal of good.

At 5:45 p.m. orders came to fall in and charge the enemy's works. Capt. Whitesides, A.A.A. Gen'l. on Gen. Harker's staff, gave Col. McIlvain the order to move forward along the top of the ridge by the right flank and started back, remarking, "Well, I must get out of this, I am getting demo-

■ Capt. Robert S. Chamberlain, commander of Company C, 64th Ohio, whose jaw was shattered and chin nearly shot off on May 9 at Rocky Face Ridge. Because of this wound he did not return to active duty, and was discharged on September 23, 1864. The 64th Ohio suffered the second highest number of Federal casualties at Rocky Face Ridge — 21 killed, 65 wounded and 2 missing.

■ 1st Lieut. Thomas R. Smith, Company E, 64th Ohio.

■ 1st Lieut. John K. Shellenberger, Company F, 64th Ohio.

ralized." I thought at the time that was great talk for an officer at such a time, especially one exposed to no more danger than he was.

There were a few balls that flew past us while forming. We moved forward under a murderous fire and got so close to their line of works that I could see the buttons on their coats, probably about 30 yards. They had a decided advantage, being strongly fortified and a superior force. Our line stopped, the men falling thick and fast. I took shelter behind a "black jack oak" when the colonel gave the command to lie down, and was standing there when Wintersteen of Co. C came limping back. I asked him if he was wounded. He said he thought so, but on examination found that he had been struck by a spent ball. He loaded his gun and started forward.

Sergeant Patterson with the colors was standing with his face nearly against my right shoulder, as I stood up on the incline of the root of the tree, his forehead about on a line with my chin, as near as I can tell. The tree was not more than 10 inches in diameter and that distance from the works made us quite a prominent mark for the enemy.

We could hear the bullets hit the tree and see the bark fly as they shot at us. Patterson remarked, "Captain, they might come over and take us in out of the wet." I started to look around the tree to see if anything of that kind was likely to occur. I had not more than looked when a ball — shot from an Enfield musket in the hands of an Alabama soldier* — struck me on the left side of my chin in front of the stomach tooth, passed through the jaw, coming out on the right side three teeth forward of the angle of the jaw, cutting off my chin, except about three quarters of an inch at the corner of my mouth on the left side, and about a half inch on the right side, making an opening in which the small end of an ordinary broomstick could have been laid horizontally against the underside of my tongue.

After being struck I faced to the right to start to the rear and as I did so, Patterson settled back, grasping the flag and staff with both hands in front of him, falling to the ground straight and stiff, apparently as if he had been laid there, and the colors arranged or draped over him as tastefully as if done by the tenderest of female hands.

Here I want to digress a little and pay Patterson a well-deserved tribute, showing the kind of stuff the "American private soldier," the noblest and most genuine type of soldier the world ever saw, was made of. At Chickamauga we suffered for water Sunday afternoon, Sept. 20th. About noon or a little later, I directed orderly Lawrence to detail a man to take the empty canteens and fill them. Sergeant Patterson was given 23 canteens and started for Craw Fish Spring to fill them. The whole army was in the same fix we were, and that being the only spring in that section of the country, there was quite a crowd after water. The drain on the spring had been so heavy that but three or four canteens could be filled at the same time by sinking them in the water. You realize the situation. The upshot of the business was, he did not get back to the regiment till nearly dark, but brought every canteen filled with water — a little muddy — but water all the same. Some of the boys, out of pure mischief, hinted that he did not try to get back so as to escape the fight. I never believed it, but it broke him all up for a time.

When at Cleveland, Tenn., May 2nd/64, Col. McIlvain called on me to furnish a color sergeant as "C" was the only company that had a full quota of sergeants. He spoke of Patterson and told me he had applied for the position, for the reason that his lungs were weak and it hurt him to carry a

* The man who shot Chamberlain and Patterson belonged to Company B, 30th Alabama Volunteer Infantry under Col. Charles M. Shelley, Pettus' brigade of Hood's corps.

knapsack. I sent for him and when he came to my tent I happened to be alone. I told him what was wanted and what would be expected of him. He seemed to realize the gravity of the situation and finally said he would try it, if I was willing. He spoke of what the boys had said about him at Chickamauga, and I told him I thought that was a mistake; they did not mean it, but he insisted some of them did. I told him I never thought there was any truth in it and that he *knew* I never entertained any such idea or thought. I gave him quite a talk and finally said to him, "Well, Patterson! There is one thing you must make up your mind to if you take those colors, *and that is to keep them where they belong or die trying!* You must not disgrace the company by disgracing yourself."

He arose to his feet, assumed the position of a soldier, his throat filled, the tears trickled down his cheeks as he firmly said, "Captain, I'll do it." He delivered his gun and accoutrements and I let Dillon have them, as mentioned before. We had dress parade that evening, the only one Patterson carried the colors for. I see in memory Patterson as he so firmly and determinedly said, "Captain, I'll do it," and as he lay there on Rocky Face with a bullet hole in his forehead, I sometimes have thought the ball that hit me killed him. But to return to my subject.

I faced to the right and started to the rear on the run without stopping to examine the nature of the wound, and ran until I came to where the artillery was stationed. As I passed by I saw Major Coulter. Passing on to the rear I saw a surgeon standing on a big rock, looking at the fight. I asked him to do something for me but he motioned me to go back, saying, "There was a hospital right back there a little to the rear." I sought help from another surgeon standing on a stump viewing the fight, and his reply was the same as the first, "Go back! Go back! A hospital is right back there."

Finally I got back to where the surgeon of the 79th Illinois, Dr. J.W. Young, was dressing a man's thigh, a gun shot wound. He looked up and saw me, and immediately dropped the case he had in hand and fixed some bandages on my chin and over my head, first doubling up my beard so as to partially fill the opening under my chin and check the flow of blood. Here I found my servant George who took my things, sword and belt, haversack, watch and memorandum book, from which I take these notes, thus relieving me of about 25 pounds. Thomas Ward of Co. B and another man carried me from here to where Dr. Anderson, our regimental surgeon, was located with his field hospital. I got off the stretcher, walked to a tree and sat down, and began to feel very faint from the loss of blood, as my wound had bled freely and ran down the front of my clothing into my boots and sounded when I stepped just like I had about a half pint of water in each boot. My coat, vest and pants were saturated with blood. Dr. Anderson came and looked at me, felt in my mouth with his fingers and said, "Captain, you have a very bad wound but it is not serious and can be fixed up nicely, but you'll have to go back where they can perform a 'scientific operation.' " This was the cry of all the surgeons I came to: "Go back! Go back! There is a hospital right back there!" Except Dr. Young of the 79th Illinois. But for him I believe I would have bled to death right there among them.

While sitting by the tree I wanted some water and McClure of Co. E, postmaster of the 64th Reg't., gave me a cup of water and I tried to drink it, but it ran out through my wound as fast as I could pour it in my mouth. McClure got a hickory sprout I pointed to and loosened the bark so it would come off. While doing this a big awkward fellow standing by remarked, "Well, I wonder what he wants with that?" I had it split so as to make a trough of it, put it into my mouth back on the base of the tongue, and McClure poured some water into it, and I thus got what I wanted to drink. I

■ Color Sergeant William D. Patterson, above, of Company C, 64th Ohio, was killed on May 9 while carrying the regiment's national flag at Rocky Face Ridge. With a shattered staff and stained with Patterson's blood, the colors immediately were seized by 1st Sergeant Henry Parr, below, of Company E, who also was shot dead a few moments later.

■ Private Benjamin S. Webb was serving in the ranks of Company G, 30th Alabama, when the 64th Ohio attacked its position on May 9 at Rocky Face Ridge. Bullets fired by this Alabama regiment, belonging to Gen. Edmund W. Pettus' brigade, were responsible for wounding Capt. Robert Chamberlain and killing two color bearers of the 64th Ohio. Webb himself was wounded later in the campaign on July 8 near the Chattahoochee River.

then looked at my awkward friend and he remarked, "Well, he is a Yankee sure enough."

About this time Lieut. Hall of Co. K was brought back with his right wrist broken. Col. McIlvain was also brought back shot through the bowels. As the stretcher on which he lay was set down, he called, "Here, doctor, can you do anything for this?" He then closed his eyes, dropped back on the stretcher and was soon out of his trouble.

After seeing the chances of being carried to the foot of the hill, I came to the conclusion that the only sure way of getting down was to walk, if I could get someone to help me. Well it was that I did so, or I would have to stay on the ridge all night. Corporal William Kelso of my company came along about this time, and I called to him but could not make him hear. McClure, I think it was, told him I was there. He looked at me and said, "Oh, Captain! Is that you?"

"It's what is left of me," I replied, and told him I wanted him to help me to the foot of the ridge. I put my arm around his neck, he gave George his gun and we started. It seemed a long way to the bottom and I thought sometimes I would have to give up and sit down as I was getting weak very fast from the loss of blood. But I kept all my energy together and persevered and finally reached the bottom nearly tired out.

Saw Lieut. Samuel Sterns on the ridge. He looked at me as if he never expected me to live and get well.

I was much surprised at the large number of men we saw on the ridge that were without guns, and apparently doing nothing. I thought to myself, why were they not helping the wounded back?

When almost to the foot of the ridge we met a man coming up with a pair of stretchers. Kelso called to him to come and bring them to us. He did so and getting me on them, they started to the ambulances.

After going a short distance we came to where a very large Negro was standing among some old trash, grain bags, old cloths, etc., that he had gathered up. Kelso being very tired after helping me so far, called to him to come and carry this man a little ways. The darky looked at me and drawing a long breath, stretched himself up to his full height and said he did not feel like it. Poor contemptible hound! I looked at him, and reaching around to the back of my belt as if reaching for my revolver — I had none — I said, "See here! Come and take hold here or you'll be a dead nigger!" He began to move then and helped me to the ambulance.

We had a rough ride to Tunnel Hill over a very rough road, a part of which I marched out over a very different man. George gave me two drinks of water on the way back. We got to the hospital about 10 p.m. and they gave me a pallet of hay on the floor. Saw Babb of Co. C and Brumbaugh of Co. E there. I got permission for George to remain there with me. I sent for Dr. McMahon of our regiment, who was there in charge of the amputating department of our corps. He came immediately and saw me, assuring me that my wound was not dangerous, but told me to get home as quick as I could. After examining my mouth pretty thoroughly, McMahon leaned back on his hunkers, breaking out in a hearty laugh and said, "Damned if they haven't spoiled you for eating green corn this summer." The previous summer after a forced march from Tracy City to Sequatchie Valley we lived on green corn and salt for two or three days. Noticing that I "was used up in the mouth" and a little low spirited, he took that plan to revive me.

After a little while a man came around and took my name, company, regiment, where wounded, etc., etc. Presently a nurse came around and wanted to know if I wanted "any sing." I asked him to get me a drink of water but he was so "Dutch" he could not understand me. After that, George took the bucket that he had and got it full of water and gave me what

I wanted to drink.

No one but those who have experienced the loss of the quantity of blood that I did from this terrible wound can realize how much a bountiful supply of water is appreciated by a wounded man. I would have suffered much more than I did but for the devoted attention of my faithful colored servant George. He wet my head, bathed my face and gave me water to drink whenever I wanted it, and seemed much more solicitous about my welfare and comfort than I did. I could not stir hand or foot or disarrange the blankets over me in the least but he would be up and fix them, asking, "Captain, does you feel any better? Does you want any ting I can git? Oh, I do wish you was at your own home in de norf so you could be took care of and git well."

I slept little during the night, and as a matter of course felt rather sore about the face when morning came. Strange as it may seem, I did not suffer much pain — only when I attempted to move my head or take water.

May 10/64. Got on the train for Chattanooga about 7 a.m. without breakfast, but I could not have eaten any had they ever so much. We were put into freight cars with about six inches of hay spread on the floor of them. There were about 200 wounded men on the train. One of the agents of the Sanitary Commission gave me two oranges, but I could not use them. All the men got oranges as they passed to the train. The train stopped at Ringgold quite a while. Gage, Comstock, Sipe, Marvin and Paulus came to see me. I think by the way they looked at me they thought my time had come. I got Paulus to get my valise and bring it to me, and by doing so saved myself a great deal of trouble.

Arrived at Chattanooga about 2 p.m. and was taken to thc hospital and put in one of the tents. Lieut. Albach of Co. C, 64th Reg't. (who was at Chattanooga awaiting the acceptance of his resignation on account of wounds received at Missionary Ridge), came in shortly, as good luck would have it, and went and got permission to move me into one of the barracks of Div. No. 2, U.S. General Hospital at Chattanooga.

I was very fortunate in getting out of the tent, for there was a hard wind and rainstorm that night that blew all the tents down, adding much to the pain and suffering of the unfortunate occupants.

I found the accomodations much better than I had any idea I would from what I had always heard of the hospitals generally. We were well cared for in the ward I was in. I got along finely and began to improve immediately. I remained in the hospital until the 21st of May when my "leave of absence" came, and I started home in company with Lieut. Albach who very kindly remained to accompany me home as far as Cincinnati, Ohio.

We had a very hard time of it from Chattanooga to Nashville as we had to ride in the second class cars and they were crowded to their utmost capacity. It took 24 hours to make the trip and it almost played me out. Brig. Gen. Judah was aboard the train sick. Saw Henry Thorner of Toledo on the train also. Arrived at Nashville about 3 p.m. May 22nd and put up at Mrs. Kidde's for the night.

May 23/64. Left for Louisville on the 7 a.m. train, where we arrived safely about 5 p.m. and put up at the National Hotel. Remained there until noon of the 24th of May. Got my pay and went aboard the boat which left for Cincinnati. Had a little trouble to get my servant George aboard, for what reason I never have been able to explain, unless it was to make me as much trouble as possible. A pass for him from the post commander settled the difficulty, however — my good friend "Riley" Albach again showing his tact and judgment in obtaining it. Poor George suffered intense mental anguish during Riley's absence while getting the pass, lest he be left behind. His tears of sorrow were turned to joy when Riley returned with the pass

■ Col. Alexander McIlvain, commander of the 64th Ohio. Immediately after the breakdown of his regiment's May 9 assault on Rocky Face Ridge, he heard the cries of a wounded man who was lying just beyond the regiment on the other side of a large rock formation. He directed Capt. Samuel M. Wolff of Company H to send a man to his assistance. Wolff replied: "Colonel, it will be certain death to any man who attempts to pass between those rocks. If you order *me* to go I will obey, but I will not send one of my men. If you wish to put me in arrest, here is my sword."

"I will go myself," McIlvain said. No sooner had he entered a narrow passage between the rocks when he was shot through the bowels, and died a few hours later.

■ Private Daniel P. McClure, Company E, 64th Ohio, assisted Capt. Chamberlain after he was grievously wounded in the mouth and jaw. McClure was postmaster of the 64th, and here wears a IV Corps badge on his jacket. "Each division, brigade and regiment had its postmaster," wrote 1st Lieut. Wilbur F. Hinman, 65th Ohio, who served in the same brigade. "In each (regiment) the cry 'Orderlies for your mail!' always provoked a yell and a scramble for letters. The value of the best possible mail service for the army, to keep the soldiers in good spirits, was fully realized by the government, and no pains were spared to maintain the slender thread of communication between the men in the field and their friends at home. Now and then we would hear that a mail had been captured by the 'Johnnies' and destroyed. Then the boys would vow to take dire vengeance by putting extra bullets into their muskets the first time they had a chance."

and said to him, "George, now you can go up norf wid de Captain." If ever he breathed a sigh of relief he did then. He afterward told me he was afraid they would put him back in slavery if I "lef him dare."

We had a very pleasant trip up the river, arriving at Cincinnati at daylight May 25th. Went to Cincinnati, Hamilton and Dayton Depot and got aboard the train for Toledo. Here, much to my regret, I had to part with my dear friend, companion and brother officer Riley Albach, whose route home was in a different direction from mine.

Many were the thoughts that flitted through my mind as the train sped on toward my Toledo home, bearing me there more dead than alive. I was still weak from the loss of blood and insufficient nourishment, because I was unable to get anything that I could take without the most excruciating pain in getting it into my mouth and pester the wound far enough to swallow. One of the questions that troubled me was whether I would ever be able to eat hardtack again. I knew the chances were against me. If I could not I was just as good as out of the service.

Two miles south of Troy, Ohio, the train ran off the track but fortunately no one was hurt. We were detained about four hours by the accident and did not arrive in Toledo until nearly 9 p.m.

In consequence of the train being late, there were no hacks at the depot and I started out to walk home, about one and a quarter miles distant. I made the trip with the assistance of my faithful servant George, but it seemed sometimes as if I would have to fall by the wayside. I made it, however, and of course surprised the folks very much as they did not know anything about my movements. I did not write and did not try to get anyone to, as my mind was set on getting home, which I did, but in a deplorable physical condition.

'Forward with lusty yells'

Corporal Joseph W. Gaskill
Company B
104th Ohio Volunteer Infantry

With night of May 8 coming on we are ordered to halt and build light defenses, and men not on duty have orders to sleep with muskets in hand and be prepared for quick action if called for. The day has been warm and after a tiresome march over rocky hills and through tangled underbrush we gladly accept this rest between reliefs with muskets as bedfellows.

The boys on the skirmish line are meeting a new method of warfare at the base of Rocky Face Ridge. Rebels occupying the heights are sending down boulders as large as barrels, tearing down the mountainside, crashing through brush and trees, bounding from cliff to cliff in their descent. Our skirmishers are keeping out of range of this bombardment, some taking shelter under projecting cliffs near the mountain base, remaining here for a time as volleys of this new ammunition pass over their heads.

On the following morning we are relieved from picket and return to the regiment. Before noon our pickets are attacked by the enemy who sally forth from their works and a rapid firing is kept up for a short time. In the meantime we advance to support the skirmish line and throw up a light line of defenses when the enemy falls back to fortifications. On May 11 we again move and after marching about 10 miles toward the right of our line we bivouac for the night, continuing the march on May 12, while considerable firing is heard on our left.

During these operations we hear that our old friend Judah, commanding the 2nd Division, from whom we so gladly separated ourselves in Kentucky, is arrested for disobedience of orders, by order of Gen. Schofield. It is reported that at the end of a court-martial Judah is dismissed from service. The boys all express a warm and kindly feeling toward Schofield.*

On May 13 we again move forward and after a march of about 15 miles we form in line of battle fronting the enemy's works at Resaca, Ga.

Here the enemy occupies a strong line of works, also a line of rifle pits at the base of the hill in their front. On May 14 we form in line of battle with fixed bayonets and march forward to a position facing the enemy where he awaits us in plain view of our movements, while we are at the timber's edge facing an open field clear of obstruction except a rail fence where we are forming our lines.

The bugle now sounds the charge when we sweep aside the rail fence and go forward with lusty yells amid the whistling of balls and roar of artillery. Crossing the open field the enemy gives way, abandoning the rifle pits where we take refuge and send in a few rounds of ammunition as the rebs scamper over the hill to their second line of defenses.

We are soon ordered forward to attack the second line located over the crest of the hill, and while advancing to this line of the enemy position we are out of range of his fire until we have almost reached the summit of the hill. On reaching this exposed position orders are given to lie down and engage the enemy as opportunity offers. We remain in this position until dark and are then relieved by other troops and retire to the rear for rations and ammunition.

On the following morning it is found that the enemy has changed position and before evening is in full retreat from defenses fronting Resaca, having been forced to make this move by flank movement of our troops threatening the rear. During our assault on their works the rebels give a wonderful exhibition of bad marksmanship, for nearly all their musketry and artillery is aimed at a safe distance overhead.

The loss in our brigade is about 300 killed, wounded and captured, but only 11 in our regiment. David B. Newhouse is the only sufferer in our company, receiving a slight scalp wound.

Col. Reilly leads the charge mounted on a plug horse and dressed in the uniform of a private soldier. The colonel does not want to lose a good horse or draw any more than his share of the enemy's fire, but he loses his cap and with his hair and galways standing out like porcupine quills he reaches the enemy line with his command. The plug horse, unable to leap the works, lands with his front feet in the ditch and balks, leaving the colonel in a very uncomfortable position. He dismounts and finishes the advance on foot, for he could not coax or swear the animal out of the ditch. The boys think it was the sight of the charging Reilly that frightened the enemy out of their works.

Had we known that this assault on the enemy line was to be but little more dangerous than a foot race we would have felt less timid while preparing to make the charge. Owing to the enemy's bad marksmanship our regiment escapes with this small loss, while other regiments in our brigade meet with stronger resistance, or are perhaps occupying more exposed positions.

Lining up for an assault on the enemy is not a pleasing experience in

■ Private M. Van Buren Treadway, Company I, 47th Ohio, was wounded May 13 at Resaca. One week earlier, following his veteran furlough, Treadway rejoined the regiment and wrote to his parents from a cornfield bivouac 15 miles from Dalton: "The weather is warm hear as it is in Ohio in July. the woods is green and Corn is up three or fore inches high. Mother, iff I was thear to take supper to night I could eat a meal. This is all [awful] fare this time. wee expect a big fight out here at Dalton before maney days." Six days after the battle, Treadway died of his wound. He is buried in the Marietta National Cemetery.

* Gaskill's comments refer to Brig. Gen. Henry Moses Judah, who had been commander for a time of the District of Western Kentucky. When the Atlanta campaign opened he commanded the 2nd Division of the XXIII Corps. But, as Gen. John M. Schofield wrote in his official report of the Army of the Ohio's participation in the campaign, Judah "was relieved of the command of the 2nd Division on the 18th day of May and granted leave of absence on account of physical disability ..."

■ Brig. Gen. Hugh Judson Kilpatrick commanded the 3rd Division, Cavalry Corps. Wounded in the leg at Resaca, he was not fit again for service until mid-August, when he led a largely unsuccessful raid on the Macon & Western Railroad south of Atlanta. "Tell Kilpatrick he cannot tear up too much track nor twist too much iron," Sherman wrote to the cavalryman's commanding officer before the raid. Immediately afterward, Kilpatrick, nicknamed "Kil-Cavalry" because of his rough treatment of horses, boasted that he had disabled the railroad for at least 10 days. However, the next morning Sherman saw Confederate supply trains pulling into Atlanta over the "demolished" tracks. Within days, the cavalry was dismounted and spent the remainder of the campaign in the trenches.

army life. It is difficult to give expression to one's feelings at such a time. Pride and a personal sense of duty and honor sustain as the bugle sounds the charge and all go forward with lusty yells, the screaming of shot and shell seeming to infuse one with a strong desire to reach the harmless end of firearms that are dealing out death in the ranks. Our movements seem that of a connected body with one purpose in view, and one feels that greater safety is found in unity of action. It is said a soldier rarely runs away because of individual cowardice, the cowardice being that of a connected body.

Among the prisoners captured Col. Reilly finds an Irishman, not many years from the old sod, who has been serving in the rebel ranks. But it would never do to print what the colonel said to this prisoner, nor can one describe the manner in which it was said. The colonel fairly foamed at the mouth in his denunciation of his countryman who had taken up arms against his adopted country. Before the frightened prisoner could open his mouth in reply, the toe of Reilly's boot found its mark as the colonel departed.

'Run, Johnny, run!'

Private John Will Dyer
Company G
1st Kentucky Cavalry

We skirmished with the enemy between Snake Creek and Resaca for three days with no serious engagement and no result except our gradual retirement toward the town, but we discovered that there was work not far ahead and made ready for it.

By daylight on the morning of May 14th we were in line confidently expecting an attack and were not disappointed. We were formed across the road leading from town with Companies A, E and G of the 1st Kentucky to the left of the road and the balance of the brigade to the right. There was a field about 150 yards wide in front of our three companies and the balance of the line was in the timber. On the left, some 400 yards to the Oostanaula River, we had no force, but had deployed flankers to watch for a movement from that quarter.

Soon after sunrise we heard firing in front which was quickly followed by the appearance of our pickets, closely followed by Kilpatrick and a Federal brigade in column of fours led by the general. His plan was, when he reached the field, to "right front into line," but owing to the thick growth of bushes on the side of the road this move could not be executed until they reached the field, which was so close to our line that we had easy range and could concentrate our fire on one place, and we emptied saddles and tumbled horses so fast that those who could were glad to withdraw.

As soon as we repulsed the charge we were ordered to withdraw and, after leaving the line and mounting our horses, were ordered to dismount and take our old position. During our absence the enemy removed their dead and wounded, among the latter Gen. Kilpatrick — shot through the thigh. The next charge was made in line and dismounted, which we repulsed handsomely, and were again ordered to retreat.

Lieut. John Lamar and I were the last to leave the field, and just as we turned to leave a ball shattered the lieutenant's heel. I was by his side, prevented him from falling and assisted him to his horse.

We were again ordered back to our place in the line and found the Yankees out in the field and coming on. Capt. Howell sent me over a little hill to

the left to watch for a flank movement and I became engaged in a duel with a Yankee who seemed to be out on the same business as I. There was a little ridge between us on which was a tumble-down fence of four or five rails high. We pulled down on each other about the same time, but he fired first and his ball struck me on the hip, making me flinch and throwing me off my aim. This made me a little mad, and I reloaded in a hurry. Just as he raised his gun to fire I pulled the trigger and *his* ball struck the ground close to my foot.

Did I hit him? Well, I am glad to say I don't know, but I had a good aim at short range and the Springfield rifle that I used had brought squirrels out of the highest trees and I never missed a hog, running or standing, under 200 yards, especially when I was hungry, which my messmates could testify was pretty much all the time.

Before the smoke of my gun could blow away I heard a big racket to my right and rear, and going to the top of the ridge to investigate I saw our line in full retreat with the Yankees following closely. There was no chance for me to regain my company, so I ran down to where Si Bingham, Frank Camp and Coley Bacey were guarding the left, told them the news and we all struck out for the river. They being mounted, arrived first, plunged in and swam across.

By the time I reached the river the Yankees were in shooting distance and I didn't want to be shot down like a dog in the water. To tell the truth, I

■ Shown in line of battle, Confederates of Maj. Gen. Thomas C. Hindman's division fire on assaulting Federals of the XXIII Corps at Resaca on May 14. Gen. Edward C. Walthall, commanding one of Hindman's brigades, wrote a short time later that the Federals unsuccessfully attacked his position with three different lines. When the third line charged, "it was checked before advancing as far as either of the others had done," Walthall reported, "and fled before some parts of my command were able to discharge even a single volley. The enemy's sharpshooters, however, in large numbers secured themselves in the woods opposite my right and center, and so irregular and thickly wooded is the ground that it was found impossible to dislodge them."

■ Sergeant Newton Cannon, Company I, 11th Tennessee Cavalry, daringly rescued a friend during the fighting at Resaca. He later wrote: "The enemy having placed a battery so as to get an enfilade fire on a part of our line, we were ordered to charge it on horseback. Capt. W.R. Garrett, the adjutant of our regiment, leading about 60 of us, reached the guns but had to fall back under heavy fire from other guns. Young Cam Terrill's mare was shot from under him, and I stopped in the open under heavy fire and took him up behind me, amid the cheers of the other boys."

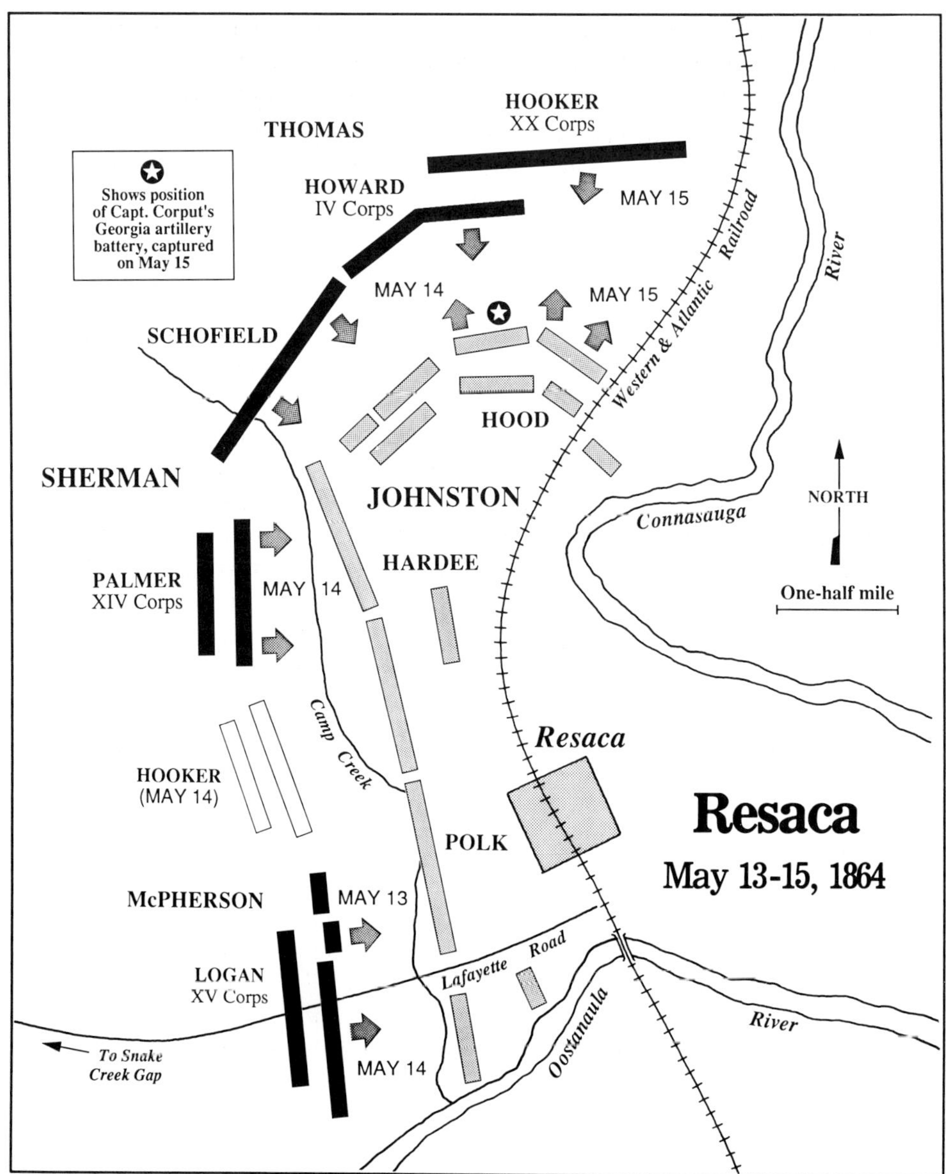

couldn't swim very well anyhow, so I didn't go down into the water for I was afraid I would not come up straight way out of it. I ran up the river bank until I came to the mouth of the Conasauga, which I found too deep to ford, up it to the bridge and crossed at a 2:40 gait.

There is a high, steep hill on the west bank of the Conasauga which extends nearly down to the Oostanaula. This hill had shielded me until I reached the bridge, and although I could see our cavalry passing through Resaca and crossing the bridge, I supposed that our infantry still held the hill. Judge of my surprise when, after going some 200 yards, the bullets began to patter around me like hailstones. On looking around for the cause I saw the top of the hill blue with Yankees, and every one of them trying his marksmanship on me.

Yes, I pulled my freight and pulled it lively. I suppose that I was making Maud S. time, but it appeared to me that I could not have kept pace with a snail. Our breastworks were a thousand yards off and there was nothing to shield me while the bullets were cutting the dust all around. Ye gods, but I felt spotted, and I have no doubt that my eyes would have made good coat hooks. When I had made about half the distance and they had failed to bring me down, the Yanks quit firing and amused themselves, yelling, "Run,

Johnny, run!" Well, I obeyed orders if they were given by Yankees and never stopped running until I tumbled inside of the works.

About this time the Yanks had got a battalion of artillery planted on the hill and from the throats of 32 pieces began to pour shells into us, first in detail and then by volley, and made it so hot that it was dangerous to get out of the ditches. So I just stayed where I was, and by this means participated in the Battle of Resaca. I got caught in this scrape like I did at Chickamauga, unintentionally, but my guardian angel protected me and pulled me through.

All day long the battle raged. After a terrible cannonade which covered us with the clay of our breastworks, the enemy would charge us with his infantry line which we would repulse and charge to the cover of his artillery. The conformation of the ground was such that when their line came within 300 yards of our works, it was within range of their shells which gave us a chance to raise our heads and go at them. While a portion of our force would charge the enemy after repulsing him, others would be repairing the damage done to our works by his artillery. Thus the fight was kept up until nine o'clock at night when hostilities ceased, with honors on our side.

When the trouble quieted down I started out to find my regiment which had been defending a ford on the river below Resaca, where Sherman attempted to cross a force in order to flank us in our position. Our brigade camped in a grove about three miles south of Resaca, where I found them about midnight. Si Bingham had reported me standing on the bank of the river with the Yankees closing in on me, and the general opinion prevailed that I was captured or killed, the latter accepted as most probable.

Acting on this conclusion, my messmates proceeded to administer on my estate, which inventoried one horse, saddle and bridle (my spurs, pistols and gun had shared my fate); one pair of saddle pockets; one gray flannel shirt, well worn and in need of washing and mending; one pair of socks with the feet worn off (also dirty); one testament — the gift of my good, religious sweetheart and not badly worn except on the outside; a few private letters from the girl I left behind me, and others; needlebook with buttons and thread, and my diary.

After locating my messmates I approached them in the dark, halted just outside of the range of their vision and listened. My sudden taking-off did not seem to distress them greatly, but they were greatly troubled over how to distribute my wordly possessions. While standing there listening to the different suggestions and remarks of my comrades, Rip Van Winkle's expression "how soon we are forgotten" came very forcibly to mind, and I could not refrain from feeling a pang of disappointment at the apparent callousness of my most trusted friends.

But the boys finally came to an understanding. They gave my horse to one of the boys whose horse was wounded, the saddlebags to another of the company to carry in my memory. The shirt and sock tops to one of the boys who had neither; my diary to Billy Hughes, to be continued; and my testament and letters to Capt. Howell who was to return them and break the sad news to my mother and sweetheart at the first opportunity.

About the time they had completed their labors I walked in on them and took a hand myself. All begrimed with dust and powder smoke as I was, they failed to recognize me until I spoke, when they piled onto me. But I knew that their demonstrations were prompted by different motives. I would, for a few minutes, as soon have been back in the ditches in front of the Yanks and their guns. But joy never kills, and I pulled through to recover all my belongings except my shirt and socks.

■ Lt. Gen. William J. Hardee commanded a corps in the Army of Tennessee. A native of Georgia, 1838 graduate of West Point and a distinguished veteran of the Mexican War, Hardee was known to his troops as "Old Reliable." He also was famous as the author of *Rifle and Light Infantry Tactics*, commonly referred to as Hardee's *Tactics*, a manual of arms used to drill many soldiers on both sides.

■ 1st Sergeant James L. Cooper, Company C, 20th Tennessee, was 19 years old and the second youngest member of the regiment's color company at the time of the battle of Resaca, where he was wounded in the neck. He previously had been wounded at Missionary Ridge on November 25, 1863, and was hit again at Franklin on November 30, 1864, while serving as an aide to Brig. Gen. Thomas B. Smith. This photograph, taken near the end of the war, shows Cooper after he was promoted to first lieutenant.

'I saw eternity opening before me'

1st Sergeant James L. Cooper
Company C
20th Tennessee Volunteer Infantry

On the night of the 12th our troops evacuated Dalton and marched to Resaca. During the night of the 13th we worked at fortification, and on the 14th, about 12 o'clock the enemy advanced in force, and began a heavy attack. We repulsed several assaults, and about three o'clock we were sitting behind our rail piles waiting for another charge.

At this time I was shot by a sharpshooter who had crawled within a short distance from the works. I was sitting down, closely wedged in by my companions on every side, for the position was very exposed, when all at once I felt a terrible shock and with a sinking consciousness of dying, became insensible. In an instant I recovered my senses, and found myself with my head fallen forward on my breast, and without power to move a muscle. I could hear the blood from my wound pattering on the ground, and thinking I was dying, almost thought I saw eternity opening before me. I felt so weak, so powerless, that I did not know whether I was dead or not.*

The noise of the battle seemed miles away, and my thoughts were all pent up in my own breast. My system was paralyzed, but my mind was terribly active. My head was full of a buzzing din, and the sound of that blood falling on the ground seemed louder than a cataract. I finally recovered the use of my tongue and still thinking I was dying, told the boys that it was no use doing anything for me, that I was a dead man. All this time I could hear remarks around me, which, although very complimentary, were not at all consoling. When first shot one man exclaimed, "By God, they killed a good one that time," another "My God! Cooper's killed!" and several others equal to these.

Finally Capt. Lucas directed the man directly behind me, J. Gee of Co. D, to catch hold of the wound and try to stop the blood. To my surprise he succeeded, and in half an hour, or less time, I had sufficiently recovered my strength to start to the rear. I walked half a mile through perfect showers of balls, and reached the ambulance perfectly exhausted. I was taken to the hospital, and after being exposed to some danger from shells, that night we were taken to the railroad, and then to Atlanta.

I suffered some from my wounds before I reached Atlanta but was well cared for when I was taken to the hospitals. I was about the most forsaken looking object that came to that place, I know, and when I got off the cars felt pretty sheepish. The entire "crystal of my pants" was gone, and I was covered with blood and dirt, so I had reasons for feeling sheepish, being exposed to the sharp eyes of about four hundred ladies. If their eyes were sharp, their hands and hearts were tender as I soon experienced.

After a short time I was carried to Marietta, and here I had a delightful rest for a week; the Yankees moved us however, so we went to Atlanta, I, in

* Cooper was struck in the middle of the throat by a minie ball which passed through his neck and emerged on the right rear side, narrowly missing the spinal cord and jugular vein. Only three months earlier he had returned to his regiment after convalescing from a wound received at Missionary Ridge on November 25, 1863. But after his near-fatal wounding at Resaca, Cooper recovered sufficiently in Atlanta to return to duty by the end of the first week of July, and rejoined the 20th Tennessee along the Chattahoochee River.

■ With skirmishers in front, troops of the XX Corps prepare to attack at Resaca. "As the Federals advanced on the evening of May 14, they presented a grand and imposing spectacle," wrote Private Thomas A. Head of Company I, 16th Tennessee. "Their forces were massed into three columns. As they came up through an open field their ranks closed up into a solid phalanx, and appeared as so many living walls of blue. Their arms glistened in the sunlight, and the columns advanced as steadily as though they were on dress parade."

a car loaded with girls, and took up our abode in the theatre, called the Atheneum.

In the action above, one of my company, John Savage, was killed. Regimental loss about sixty, from a hundred and fifty.

'Death in the pot'

Private Robert Hale Strong
Company B
105th Illinois Volunteer Infantry

Our first little brush with the enemy came at Buzzard's Roost, a mountain pass in upper Georgia. Up to this time (the regiment) had had no big fights and had lost no men by bullets although we had been at "war" for nearly two years.

About this time Company B was on scout. We halted for dinner on a bluff overlooking a creek, with a field beyond the creek and woods beyond that. Just after we halted we heard a peculiar noise in the tree tops. It sounded like a lot of tumble bugs flying through the air. We wondered what caused the noise. Then small twigs began to drop near us. Then we heard guns going off and knew the "tumble-bug" noise was bullets. No one was hit. But it was soon to come.

The army advanced nearly to Resaca, Georgia. Our brigade was ordered to the right flank to support the troops engaged in fighting there. I distinctly

'Give us the ape's proclamation'

Federal Brig. Gen. James D. Morgan, left, commander of the 1st Brigade, 2nd Division, XIV Corps, related an incident that occurred on May 14 while his brigade occupied a gap between Oak Knob and Rocky Face Ridge:

"Yesterday, a corporal of Company I, 60th Illinois, broke from the line and under cover of projecting ledges, got up within 20 feet of a squad of rebels on the summit. Taking shelter from the sharpshooters, he called out:

'I say, rebs, don't you want to hear Old Abe's amnesty proclamation read?'

'Yes! Yes!' was the unanimous cry. 'Give us the ape's proclamation.'

'Attention!' commanded the corporal, and in a clear and resonant voice he read the amnesty proclamation to the rebels whose hands were raised to destroy the fabric of a government established by our fathers. When he arrived at those passages of the proclamation where the negro was referred to, he was interrupted by cries of 'None of your damned abolitionism! Look out for rocks!' and down over his hiding place descended a shower of stones and rocks. Having finished the reading, the corporal asked:

'Well, rebs, how do you like the terms? Will you hear it again?'

'Not today, you bloody Yankee. Now crawl down in a hurry and we won't fire,' was the response, and the daring corporal descended and rejoined his command, which distinctly heard all that passed."

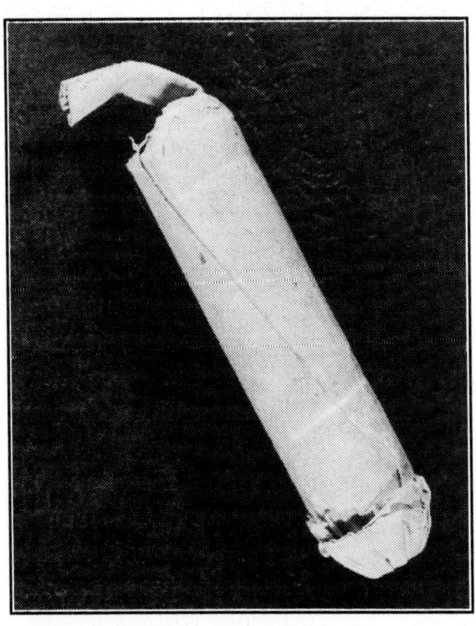

■ U.S. rifled musket cartridge, caliber .58, consisting of a hollow-based, three-grooved bullet powered by 60 grains of black gunpowder, wrapped in paper. The cartridge was opened by tearing the tail between the teeth. In battle, soldiers carried 40 rounds in their cartridge boxes and extra packets of 10 rounds elsewhere on their persons. Black powder created clouds of white smoke that often obscured the enemy.

remember how plain we could hear the whole business: the roar of the artillery, the crack of musketry, the cheers of the Yankees and the yells of the Johnnies. Through it all we were lying in a thick wood and could see nothing. When we would hear the Yankees cheer, our hearts would almost stop beating. Then would come the roar of rebel cannon, and as our boys were beaten back the rebs would nearly split their throats yelling.

We lay there in a fever of impatience until our turn came. We marched around to the left and were ordered to unsling knapsacks and put them in a pile. We left a guard over them and marched almost to the edge of the woods. My company was ordered to advance as skirmishers — that is, in a thin, spread-out line well ahead of the main advance. Skirmishers are likely to see more of the world than anyone else, up to the point when they are suddenly shot.

We were told that just in our front was a rebel fort that had been charged repeatedly, and every charge had been repulsed. Now *we had to take it.* Well, we knew there was "death in the pot" for some of us, wounds of all awful sorts for more of us, and supposed glory untold for the ones who came out alive. We were given 40 extra cartridges to a man and were told not to fire a gun until ordered to do so.

Company B, deployed as skirmishers, led the way out of the woods into an open field and then the work began. We were to advance in a steady line with guns at "shoulder arms" until the order to charge was given. Then the skirmishers were to lie down and let the column charge over us.

We first had to cross a small field and then go through a scattered peach orchard. Then, on a hill beyond, the fort sat waiting. As soon as we skirmishers moved out of the woods onto the field, the rebs began shooting at us. Someone cried out that there was a sharpshooter in a tree sniping at us. So, in spite of our orders not to fire, a dozen of us fired into the tree. The man came tumbling down, legs spread out, and struck the ground with a thud. I remember thinking as he fell that he resembled a big squirrel.

We advanced with no more shooting on our part. The bugle sung out "Skirmishers, lie down," and in the next minute "Charge!" and the rest of the boys went over us with a yell. Most of the skirmishers, I among them, got up and joined the charging column and went up the hill with the rest. We were driven back from the works once, but in a moment we rallied and without waiting for orders — men were dropping all around us, but we had no time to look after them — with a rush and a cheer we drove the rebs from the first line of works back into the second line where their cannon were.

The hill was so steep that the cannon fired over the first line. Then we were reinforced by the 2nd Brigade, and we kept on going and drove the rebs from their guns. Our brigade was ordered back, leaving the 2nd Brigade to hold what we had gained.

A great many amusing and pathetic incidents happened during and after our charge, only a few of which I will repeat. Undoubtedly you remember the massacre of the prisoners captured at Fort Pillow, Kentucky, by the rebel Gen. Nathan Bedford Forrest. Well, when we rushed from the first line that we captured to the second line where the rebel cannon were, we of course captured a good many prisoners. Some of the enemy who refused to run or surrender were killed there. Some crawled under the gun carriages to escape the storm of bullets and bayonets.

One big red-headed man, a cannoneer, crawled out and begged for quarter. He had his shirt off, and on one arm was tattooed in big letters "Fort Pillow." As soon as the boys saw the letters on his arm they yelled, "No quarter for you!" and a dozen bayonets went into him and a dozen bullets were shot into him. I shall never forget his look of fear.*

When we were ordered back to the rear and left the 2nd Brigade to hold the guns that we had captured, the Johnnies had fallen back only as far as another line of works or entrenchments. The cannon were left between the line we captured and the one they still occupied, only a few rods in the rear, and neither they nor our own men could use them.

We fell back not in a body or line of battle as we had advanced, but in squads numbering as many as a hundred, with orders to gather together at a certain place. Leon Palmer and I fell back together. There were a good many dead on the ground, and we had gone only a little way when we heard someone call in a weak voice. We went toward the voice and found a lieutenant of Company G. He had one leg broken and as he fell the leg doubled up under him. It was bent clear back and the bone stuck out through the flesh. He wanted water and to have his leg straightened out. Oh, how he groaned and prayed! He was grit clear through, though, and would not let us carry him off the field. The bullets were flying around us as thick, seemingly, as hail. After doing what we could for him we left him. I don't know what became of him.

When we got back as far as we were supposed to go, we found a line of men posted across the road to stay stragglers from going on farther. Gen. Ward came along with his arm in a sling and said, "Old Pap got it this time, boys." He was pretty drunk and seemed to be proud of his wound.

The ambulance corps kept bringing the wounded back. Shells were still flying over us, some going far to the rear, some bursting right around us. Two men brought a wounded man on a stretcher and set him down near me. I had just lit my pipe, and Mark Naper came to me to get a light for his pipe.

* On April 12, 1864, some 1,500 Confederate cavalrymen under Gen. N.B. Forrest stormed Fort Pillow in Tennessee (not Kentucky, as Strong wrote), about 75 miles above Memphis on the Mississippi River. The yelling Confederates drove the fort's defenders — a majority of them black troops — out of their works and down a bluff toward the river. Many were shot or bayoneted by the attackers who, according to Federal survivors, shouted "No quarter! No quarter!" even after they had surrendered. Strong's mention of the Fort Pillow "massacre" indicates that soldiers of Sherman's army, at least in his regiment, were well informed of this incident which occurred only one month before the Battle of Resaca.

■ Private Robert H. Strong of Company B, 105th Illinois. During the campaign foraging often subsidized government-issue rations, as he later wrote: "If any of the boys while on picket or detached duty saw a fat hen or goose, or a ham hanging handy, or a patch of potatoes, something was mighty apt to stick to his fingers. Many times we cornered a cow and milked her into our canteens. How some of the supposedly high-toned ladies would talk at us for milking their cows! Generally, with the ladies, the worse the circumstances they were in, the more bitter they were about 'Lincoln's hirelings, Yankee scum and bluebellied sons of bitches.' Some said even worse things."

Strong's regiment belonged to the XX Corps. At Resaca, his brigade was commanded by Brig. Gen. William T. Ward and consisted of the 102nd, 105th and 129th Illinois, the 79th Ohio and the 70th Indiana. This last regiment was commanded by Col. Benjamin Harrison, who became president of the United States 25 years later.

■ Brig. Gen. August Willich commanded a brigade in the 3rd Division, IV Corps, at the beginning of the campaign. Born in Germany, he served 19 years in the Prussian army until forced to resign in 1848 for espousing Marxism. He fled to America and in the late 1850s edited a German-language newspaper in Cincinnati. After brief service with the 9th (1st German) Ohio, he was commissioned colonel of the 32nd Indiana — another German regiment — and taught his men the evolutions of Prussian drill. Later, as one of his men recalled: "Gen. Willich had drilled [his] whole brigade to maneuver by bugle signals, the German calls being used which the rebels could not understand. 'The Dutch General and his horn brigade,' they called us." Described as the "antithesis of the stereotyped, spike-helmeted, goose-stepping Prussian officer," Willich believed that volunteer soldiers should be treated "like men, not like dogs." On May 15 at Resaca, he was wounded in the shoulder by a musket ball and did not return to field command.

I turned my pipe upside down to put it on top of his pipe and knock some fire into his, when a shell exploded just over us. A piece of it came down directly between us, breaking both pipes. Another piece killed the wounded man who was on the stretcher. It surely was a close call for Mark and me.

It was during this battle that Lt. Col. Henry F. Vallette, next only to old Col. Dan Dustin in our regiment, got so badly scared that he soiled his breeches. He never got over that scare. Anyway, he left us during our next fight and we never saw him again until we got home.

That night they called for volunteers to bring off the guns that we had been unable to take during the day. A number volunteered and crept up to the breastworks. They dug with spades a gap in the breastworks wide enough to get the guns out and, attaching ropes to them, dragged them away. An officer of some Ohio regiment had charge of the volunteers.

Later that same night the rebs left their works and started for another stronghold. Our brigade was detailed to bury the dead. Of all disagreeable jobs, that was the worst of any I ever took a hand in. It was our first experience, and to carry men to a hole and dump them in was almost too much for me. Some had been dead for three or four days, and the flesh would not hold together to lift them. So we put them in blankets or tied the legs of their pants and their coat sleeves together and gently dragged them to their last resting place.

We came across a rebel hospital with a few rebel surgeons who had been left to care for their wounded. The hospital was simply a shade made of limbs of trees thrown over poles. Near the hospital was a pile of arms, legs, hands and feet that had been cut from the wounded. These had not been buried, just thrown in a pile, and worms had begun to work on them.

On one part of the battlefield the leaves had taken fire, I suppose from shells, and we found a few of the dead who had more or less burned. It is all truly horrible, and if you tell me you don't want anything more on battle scenes, why all right. But so many things come to mind, some worse than these.

'Stay at his guns'

Private Frank Anderson
Company K
4th Tennessee Cavalry
Escort attached to Hood's staff, CSA

As one of Gen. Hood's couriers in the battle of Resaca, I was stationed near a deep cut of the railroad with our corps flag to direct couriers to headquarters. I was immediately in rear of a battery. I was there but a few minutes when it opened fire, which was vigorously replied to by three batteries of the enemy, numbering 18 pieces. One was in front and one on each flank, all playing on our four guns, and I was in a very uncomfortable place.

From a car load of picks on the railroad near me I got one, and soon had a gopher hole in the side of the hill. In a few minutes the infirmary corps passed by me with Col. S.S. Stanton of the consolidated 28th and 84th Tennessee Infantry, who was mortally wounded, and very soon the ambulances commenced passing with our wounded. The dirt road was parallel with the railroad for some distance. As an ambulance with two wounded soldiers was passing a shell exploded, killing both mules. The sudden stop of the ambulance threw the driver on his head, but he was soon up and going through the field as fast as possible. The wounded men were left in the ambulance.

Soon after this, Lieut. F.H. Wigfall of Gen. Hood's staff rode up and ordered me to report to Hood, who was on Gen. Stewart's line to the right of the railroad from where we were. When we found Gen. Hood, Capt. James H. Britton who commanded the escort was the only one with him. All the couriers and staff were off with orders. It was there that Gen. Hood gave the order for the commander of the battery to stay at his guns until he and all the men were killed. They were not to leave the guns under any circumstances. This battery was captured, and it was the only one that was lost on the Atlanta campaign. By some misunderstanding it was placed in front of our infantry and had no support at all.

That night we evacuated the place and crossed the Oostanaula River. When Gen. Hood and staff were crossing the river on the covered bridge the Yankees raised a yell and charged our skirmish line. Gen. Hood about-faced and rode back to Brown's Brigade in Stewart's Division, and told the men how much depended upon them. He told Capt. Britton of the escort company that he could always depend on the Tennessee troops, which made us feel proud as we were all Tennesseeans.

The kind and courteous treatment made the men of the escort company all love Gen. Hood. He was a born gentleman. He never failed to salute a courier, and usually had a kind word for him no matter where he was or what his surroundings. Gen. Stewart was the same way. But these were almost exceptions with the high-ranking officers of our army. Couriers had a hard time, as well as the soldiers in our army, often having to take abuse from superior officers.*

'Taking out the guns'

Lt. Col. Robert Lang Kilpatrick
5th Ohio Veteran Volunteer Infantry

At the time of the battle of Resaca, May 15, 1864, the 5th Ohio Infantry was part of the 1st Brigade, 2nd Division, XX Army Corps. John H. Patrick was colonel of the regiment, I was the lieutenant colonel, and Henry E. Symmes was major. We were all present for duty.

From about noon on the 15th until dusk, the 5th was on the left of the brigade. The brigade most of the time was strung along the top of a ridge, on the left and rear of our 3rd Brigade. Our regiment was not very warmly engaged during the day — our loss was but three killed and 13 wounded.

We had been moving or kept standing in our ranks since early morning; the severe fighting was on our immediate left and on our right front.

■ Lt. Col. Robert Lang Kilpatrick was second in command of the 5th Ohio at Resaca. A native of Scotland, he previously served eight years as a non-commissioned officer in the British army. As a captain in command of Company B, 5th Ohio, he was captured in the Federal retreat from Port Republic, Va., in June 1862, and held captive for more than two months. Following exchange and promotion to a lieutenant colonelcy, he was badly wounded at Chancellorsville which resulted in the amputation of his right arm. Kilpatrick mustered out on August 17, 1864, but was commissioned a captain in the Veteran Reserve Corps in which he served to the end of the war.

* Adjutant George B. Guild of the 4th Tennessee Cavalry later wrote of Anderson: "He was under seventeen years of age when he enlisted in 1861. Company K was at first the escort of General Wharton, and afterwards of different commanding generals of the Army of Tennessee. Anderson was a great favorite, and was frequently called upon by officers to carry their orders to parts of the field where the battle raged hottest and fiercest."

Col. Sidney Smith Stanton originally commanded the 25th Tennessee, then the 84th before the latter was consolidated with the 28th Tennessee in 1863. During the battle of Chickamauga on September 19, 1863, he rallied his regiment by seizing the colors and running to the front, calling his men to follow. Thirty bullets later were found to have pierced the flag while Stanton carried it in the charge. Mortally wounded at Resaca on May 15, he died later the same day.

■ Col. Henry A. Barnum, right, poses with the national colors of the 149th New York, which he rejoined in time to command during the campaign. At Chattanooga seven months earlier, Barnum won the Medal of Honor: "Although suffering severely from wounds, he led his regiment, inciting the men to greater action by word and example until again severely wounded."

The 149th New York was part of Col. George Cobham's brigade of the XX Corps at Resaca, and assisted in the capture of the Confederate works housing Capt. Van der Corput's four Napoleon guns on May 15. Barnum wrote that his men "were so close to the pieces as to be able to touch the muzzles, but could not work them or drag them away, as the lunette was but a few yards distant from the main line of rebel works, which swept the interior of the works in which the artillery was placed."

■ Brig. Gen. John W. Geary commanded the 2nd Division, XX Corps, during the campaign. This portrait was taken by the firm of Schwing & Rudd, Army of the Cumberland photographers.

At dusk, when there was a lull in the fighting, I was preparing to take some rest as I was very tired, when Col. Patrick came to where I was and said, "Our regiment is sold." I asked him what was the matter. He said he had just been informed that Col. Cobham had come over from his part of the line to see Gen. Geary (the division commander), and he understood that the 5th Regiment was to be sent over to Cobham's command for the purpose of securing four pieces of artillery that had annoyed us so much during part of the day. That the rebels had been driven from their guns, but they were so well protected by the rebel infantry fire that it was a difficult matter to get at them, but that during the coming darkness it was thought the guns could be got out. And he had learned through a friend that Geary had decided to send the 5th Ohio to do the work, and that he (Col. Patrick) thought that if such was the case, few, if any, would survive the effort of getting at these guns. He also said, "I am a senior colonel to Col. Cobham and I do not intend to take orders from him."

While we were talking, Gen. Geary came to where we were and said, "Col. Patrick, I want you to take your regiment to the right and front of the 1st Brigade, where you will find Col. Cobham in command on the face of the hill right in front of the ridge, and report to him for duty."

The colonel replied, "General, I am a senior colonel to Col. Cobham, and I don't consider it the proper thing for me to have to report to my junior officer for duty."

Gen. Geary replied (rather angrily, I thought): "Well, you take your regiment over there and form in line in rear of Cobham and support him and render him such assistance as he may need."

We immediately got the regiment together (it was quite dark by this time), and started for Cobham's command — no one in the regiment being in the secret of our destination but the colonel and myself.

We found it a rather difficult task, marching in the dark and over stumps and through brushwood. We must have covered about a mile before we reached our objective point. The regiment was formed in line in rear of Cobham's command, and an order given to rest, but to keep well together. The men lay down and, being tired, many of them fell asleep.

We had not rested many minutes when Col. Cobham came and, addressing Col. Patrick, said: "Colonel, please take your regiment up that hill in your front, and at the top you will find the 111th Pennsylvania Regiment. I want you to relieve that regiment with yours."

Col. Patrick made no reply whatever, and Col. Cobham went away. When he was gone Patrick said to me: "You are tired, and I shall send the regiment up in command of Major Symmes. Pass the word for Major Symmes." The word was passed along the line, but there was no response from the major. A few minutes passed when I said: "It won't do to delay any longer. I will take the regiment up, and I am confident that the first man that I see when I get there will be the major."

The colonel and his adjutant and the assistant surgeon remained where they were, and the regiment marched up the hill. As I had predicted, the first man to address me when we got there was Major Symmes, who made inquiry as to what was up. I satisfied him with regard to our mission in a few words, and felt I had a comrade on whom I could depend; for a better officer than Symmes was not in Geary's division.

There had been considerable firing during our mile march between the opposing forces, but everything was quiet during our progress up the hill. I found the 111th Pennsylvania Regiment deployed along the crest of the hill with their right resting on and covering a redoubt. There were a few men digging in front of the works. I looked into the works and could plainly see the four cannon and what appeared to be many dead and wounded rebels —

■ Col. John H. Patrick, a native of Edinburgh, Scotland, commanded the 5th Ohio at Resaca. Ten days later at the battle of New Hope Church, Patrick was leading a charge on a masked Confederate battery when he was struck in the bowels by a canister shot. He died half an hour later. In this photograph Patrick wears an unusual variation of the XX Corps badge.

■ During the night of May 15, soldiers of the 5th Ohio Infantry, assisted by a detail from the 33rd New Jersey, haul away one of four Confederate artillery pieces captured from Corput's Georgia battery at Resaca. The guns were presented as trophies to Gen. John W. Geary, commander of the 2nd Division, XX Corps, and on May 16 were turned over to Battery E, 1st Pennsylvania Light Artillery.

the result of a severe contest.

The works appeared to have been dug out near the top of the hill, leaving the original ground of the steep slope to serve both as parapet and glacis. The rebel flag still hung to the flag-staff and, with the exception of a few random shots from the rebel riflemen, everything was quiet.

We relieved the 111th Pennsylvania and they retired down the hill, leaving no force whatever between us and the enemy. So far, nothing had been said to me with regard to taking out the guns. I suppose the slight noise occasioned by our relieving the 111th Pennsylvania had awakened the "Johnnies" as they commenced a brisk fire along their line, far away on our right, and for a considerable distance on our left. I ordered our men to lie down and keep a sharp lookout ahead, and not to fire a shot until ordered. I expected the rebels to attempt to re-enter the fort as it was open in the gorge. The firing was kept up on both sides with musketry and artillery for about 20 minutes, but I saw no attempt made to re-enter the fort. I never experienced such a miserable 20 minutes in my life; it seemed to me that our own friends were firing into us about as much as the enemy were, but it finally quieted down.

A short time after the firing ceased an aide-de-camp from Col. Cobham came to me and inquired how we were succeeding in getting the guns out. I said that a party of some other command had been digging in front of the redoubt before the firing commenced, but that during the firing they had disappeared and had not yet returned. The aide-de-camp went away but soon returned, saying: "Col. Cobham's compliments to Lt. Col. Kilpatrick, and orders that he take entire charge of taking the four guns out of the redoubt." Major Symmes was with me at the time and remarked, "If we cannot take the guns out, we can spike them." I reminded the aide-de-camp that it was Major Symmes who made that suggestion, and the aide left us.

I immediately designated Capt. Austin T. Shirer of our regiment as commander of the working party, and gave him Companies G, H, I and K, and afterward reinforced him with his own company (A). The men set to work with the same good will that they were in the habit of using upon all occasions when the reputation of the regiment was at stake. It was now about 12 o'clock midnight. The aide-de-camp returned from Col. Cobham and said that there must be no spiking of the guns. I told him to inform the colonel we were at work doing our best to make a road into the redoubt, and I thought that everything would be all right. The remaining companies of the regiment were placed in such a manner as to defend the working party, and with instructions not to reply to the random shots of rebel sharpshooters.

My greatest difficulty was to go along the line and keep everybody awake and on the alert. I was assisted in my duty in the most efficient manner by my friend Major Symmes; either he or I was in touch with Capt. Shirer and his diggers until the road was completed. When completed, I ordered Capt. Shirer to send the guns down the hill to Gen. Geary's headquarters. He said, "I will need more men for that purpose." Not wishing to reduce my fighting force any more, I dispatched Lieut. Henry Koogle (whom I had appointed to act as adjutant during the absence of the regimental adjutant) to Col. Cobham to ask him to send me 50 men without arms to assist in hauling out the guns; also to report the completion of the road. In a surprisingly short time, 50 men in command of an officer, all of the 33rd New Jersey Regiment, reported to me. I turned them over to Capt. Shirer, who used them to haul out the other two guns as two were on their way down the hill by the time the Jerseymen reported.

It was about this time that Corporal George W. Tyrrell of Company H, 5th Ohio, handed me the rebel flag that he had taken from the flag-staff of the redoubt. It was the usual bunting red flag, with the blue St. Andrew's cross with stars. I handed it in with my official report. Corporal Tyrrell afterward received a medal of honor for the capture of the flag.

When our work was completed, I reported the fact by Acting Adjutant Henry Koogle to Col. Cobham, who in a short time afterward sent his aide-de-camp with orders for me, with the regiment, to report back to our own brigade.

When we reached the foot of the hill I met Col. Cobham. He asked me to halt the regiment for a few minutes, which I did. He then, in a very cordial manner and with a few complimentary words, thanked me and the officers and men under my command for our arduous and successful night's work. By the time we got back to our own brigade, it was past 3 o'clock in the morning.

After very little rest I was again afoot, as I wanted to see Capt. Shirer. I found him near the division headquarters with the four pieces of artillery. He told me that Gen. Geary had ordered him, with a few of his men, to remain in charge of the guns until morning, and until relieved. He afterward reported that, by proper order, he turned the guns over to Knap's battery. The guns appeared to be quite new — twelve pounders.*

■ Col. George A. Cobham Jr., 111th Pennsylvania, commanded the 3rd Brigade, 2nd Division, XX Corps, at Resaca and New Hope Church. At Peachtree Creek on July 20, he was mortally wounded and died the same day. "His loss is deeply felt and deplored throughout the division," wrote Gen. John W. Geary.

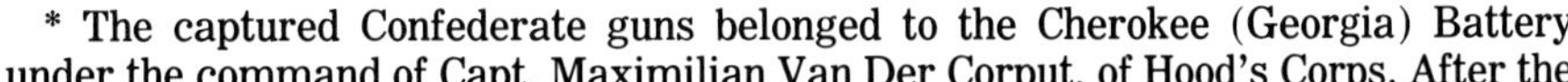

* The captured Confederate guns belonged to the Cherokee (Georgia) Battery under the command of Capt. Maximilian Van Der Corput, of Hood's Corps. After the

■ Although Federals of Brig. Gen. Thomas Sweeny's division crossed the Oostanaula River on May 14, Sweeny ordered his men to return before the day was over, only to send them across again on May 15 to establish an entrenched bridgehead near Lay's Ferry. That afternoon, Confederate Brig. Gen. John K. Jackson, mounted at center, launched the Georgians and Mississippians of his brigade to dislodge Sweeny's division. The attack failed, and after dark Johnston's Confederates left Resaca and retreated south over the Oostanaula toward Cassville.

From the time we relieved the 111th Pennsylvania at the top of the hill until the guns were out and away, I never saw an officer or man of any regiment excepting our own and the 50 men under an officer of the 33rd New Jersey, and the aide-de-camp. I saw no others, excepting those already mentioned, in any way desirous of assisting us in our work, excepting a private of some regiment to me unknown, who appeared to be crazy. He appointed himself to follow me wherever I went. I did my best to get rid of the fellow in a quiet way, but without success. He would say nothing but kept along with me. I did not wish to use forcible means, as that would have caused more noise than was desirable at the time. I could not tell whether he was friendly or not, but he held his musket in a rather disagreeable looking way. I told Major Symmes about my shadow. Symmes got Corporal Kline of his old company to accompany us and said, should the fellow mean mischief, Kline would kill him. After Kline took care of the lunatic I thought no more of him, and do not remember what became of him.

Col. Cobham, under whose temporary command I had been, was a gentleman for whom I entertained great respect for his soldierly qualities. He sealed his devotion for our cause with his life at Peachtree Creek on July

---

battle, and near the scene of this incident, a soldier of the 105th Illinois picked up a letter on the field that was believed to have been written by Corput to his wife almost immediately after the fight of May 15. Part of the letter reads: "The Yankees charged on my battery this P.M. and captured two sections of it. Many of our men and attendants were wounded. It was as daring an exploit as when my brothers were charged at Antietam by a New York Reg. They threw themselves into the front as unconscious of danger as ducks into a pond ... We had to fight Hooker's command here, or else the battery never would have been taken. I hear we are gaining on the Yankees in Va. and we would have whipped them here if it had not been for Hooker's command. They all wore a star ..."

20th. Major Symmes, my well-tried friend, also gave up his brave young life, having died from a wound received in a skirmish with the enemy on the 28th of June.

Col. Patrick also fell, mortally wounded, at the head of his regiment in the attack on the enemy's position at New Hope Church, May 25th.

When Gen. Slocum, who suceeded Gen. Hooker in command of the XX Corps, made his report of the trophies captured in the Atlanta campaign, he gave the 5th Ohio Infantry credit for the capture of four twelve-pounder brass guns and one battle flag at Resaca.

A regiment whose designation I do not now remember had been foraging about the time of the battle of Resaca, and secured several boxes of tobacco. Out of their abundance they sent one box to the 5th Ohio. It was left at the headquarters of the regiment and addressed "To the Regiment that Captured the Rebel Guns at Resaca."

■ Capt. Charles Woeltge, commander of Company I, 111th Pennsylvania, was killed on May 15 at Resaca. This photograph was taken in Buffalo, N.Y., during veteran furlough, less than three months before his death. Note the veteran stripes on Woeltge's sleeves, an unusual adornment for an officer.

This is surely not war, it is butchery

New Hope Church and Pickett's Mill: The horrors of the Hell Hole

Early in the morning of May 16, Johnston had all three corps of his army extricated from the Resaca battlefield, across the Oostanaula River and marching south along the Western & Atlantic Railroad toward Adairsville and Calhoun. Sherman's Federals began an immediate pursuit, occasionally bumping into the Confederate rear which was covered by Wheeler's cavalry.

Johnston was looking for an advantageous location to make a stand, though some of his men were not optimistic of success. On May 17, Private Robert D. Patrick of Company A, 4th Louisiana, wrote in his diary: "The prospects are very gloomy for us at present. Our forces have fallen back across the Oostanaula River and a great many of the men had to jump in and swim the river to prevent being captured. The enemy has taken our batteries on the hills with the guns there-on and have doubtless captured a large number of small arms and a considerable quantity of stores. This looks very bad for our side, but as there are so many rumors, I cannot place much confidence in what I hear, though I have not the slightest doubt that Johnston is retreating ... The wagon train has been passing ever since 12 noon and it is now 5 p.m. and still they come. Johnston is in full retreat and there is no doubt that we have received a good thrashing from the Yankees. I suppose that our train will be ordered away tomorrow morning or maybe before. I am under the impression that we will not stop short of Atlanta, if we are lucky enough to get there."

But late the same day at Adairsville, Johnston made a decision. Twelve miles southeast down the main road lay Cassville — a good place, he reasoned, to lay an ambush. He would send the corps of John Bell Hood and Leonidas Polk there directly, while William Hardee's corps would travel another road 10 miles south to Kingston. Johnston believed that Sherman, once at the fork at Adairsville, would divide his army and follow both roads. In the meantime, Hardee would hurry east to join the bulk of the Army of Tennessee at Cassville, where the reunited Confederates could pounce on the isolated Union left wing.

On May 18, the planned movements were put in motion. "A dry and dusty rode," wrote Private Benjamin M. Seaton of Company G, 10th Texas Infantry, in his diary later that day. "Tired and wore out fer the want of sleep — 3 knights without sleep."

The Federals were equally weary, though the spirits of soldiers in the 33rd Massachusetts were buoyed when a large cache of "secesh" tobacco was found in a house along the regiment's line of march. "Each man of the brigade got his half pound," wrote Col. Adin B. Underwood, "and such a cheering went up."

As they tramped south chewing and smoking the confiscated tobacco, the Bay State soldiers saw ample evidence of the hurried Confederate withdrawal from Resaca. "The roads were strewed for miles with muskets, bayonets and tools," Underwood continued, "and in the temporary hospitals, made of boughs, were dead and dying men, showing the haste of the flight. On the road marched by the Thirty-Third, a poor fellow was left on the operating table, and one of our surgeons kindly took up the operation where the rebel doctor had left it, and finished it."

Upon reaching Adairsville, the Federals found only a small Confederate rear guard to contest their arrival. "Here," wrote Capt. Henry Stone, one of Gen. Thomas' staff officers, "occurred one of the most ludicrous scenes ever witnessed in battle, to which Sherman, in his memoirs, makes a slight allusion. He had not yet given up his boasted method of living under tent-flys; though he was never averse to occupying any convenient house when night or meal-time came. To accomodate his scanty impedimenta, he had a sort of pack-mule train — a motley throng of mules and darkies, loaded down with mess-pans, camp-kettles, and all sorts of noisy implements — which followed closely after his staff and orderlies, like a harlequin escort. Every time this grotesque cavalcade passed a column of troops, it was greeted with derisive laughter, and such chaff as only veteran soldiers know how to indulge in. As Sherman came in sight of his deployed lines, he turned into a large, open field, with all his followers. They had hardly gone their length, when a volley of grape or canister came ripping across the ground, and rattled like hailstones on the side of a large barn just behind them. With one impulse, the whole procession turned tail and stampeded madly to the rear — the tin pans rattling as loudly as the shot on the barn — and was seen no more till next morning."

■ Lt. Col. Gabriel C. Wharton, 10th Kentucky, was the first Federal officer to enter Resaca after Johnston evacuated his positions there and retreated across the Oostanaula River. His brigade commander, Col. George P. Este, wrote: "Before break of day of the morning of [May] 16th, the pickets of our brigade, under charge of Lt. Col. Wharton, were the first to discover the evacuation of their works by the rebels, and the first to occupy them, and, being reinforced, pushed forward and captured some 60 prisoners without loss."

But Sherman wasted no time in pressing the pursuit — and reacted just as Johnston hoped. Sending most of the Army of the Cumberland to Kingston, he ordered the small Army of the Ohio, reinforced by the XX Corps, to Cassville where Johnston waited to spring his trap. For once Johnston would enjoy superiority in numbers — more than 2 to 1. On May 19 he issued a confident proclamation to his waiting troops, who cheered when hearing the words "I lead you to battle." In Gen. Pat Cleburne's division, Private Benjamin Seaton wrote in his diary: "... we antisapate on having a ginerall engagement on tomorrow if everything works out right."

However, everything did not work out right. After Hood's and Polk's corps were deployed, the unexpected appearance of some Federal cavalry on Hood's right caused enough consternation in the Confederate command that Johnston cancelled Hood's attack and pulled back his corps and Polk's to a ridge just southeast of Cassville. They were joined there by Hardee who, by late afternoon, was followed by the Federals rushing east from Kingston. Union artillery immediately opened up with a punishing enfilade fire on the right center of the Confederate line.

In a meeting at Polk's headquarters that night, Hood argued his position was now untenable. Polk concurred and both advised Johnston to withdraw below the Etowah River to fight on a better field. Hardee did not agree, envisioning the possibilities of a victory at Cassville, but in the end Johnston, angry at this stinging turn of events, decided to retreat. It was, he later wrote, "a step which I have regretted ever since." It also

■ Col. Patrick E. Burke, 66th Illinois, commanded a brigade in the 2nd Division, XVI Corps, at Resaca. On May 16, with the Confederates in full retreat after evacuating that town, his brigade fought with Cleburne's rear guard at Rome Crossroads. While preparing to lead a charge on horseback, Burke was shot in the left leg below the knee, shattering the bone. The limb was amputated, but gangrene developed and he died on May 20 before he received further medical treatment.

initiated acrimony between Johnston and Hood that was to last for the next 15 years.

Pulled from their positions and given marching orders, many of the Confederates were puzzled, some were indignant and most were disappointed. In Hood's corps, Capt. E.T. Sykes, assistant adjutant-general of Gen. Edward C. Walthall's brigade, later wrote: "The only recompense to the infantry for this disappointment was the opportunity to witness a fight between the cavalry of the two armies in the plain below — and at which some laughed and said it was like child's play."

On May 20, the Confederates crossed the Etowah with Wheeler's cavalry again covering the retreat. One of the troopers, Private John W. Cotton of the 10th Confederate Cavalry, wrote to his wife: "We have fell back to the South side of hitower[sic] river and give up all north of this river and we are still falling back. I dont no when we will make a stand but general Johnston determed to fite them some where. he has been trying to get them to fite him now for 2 weaks but they wont do it. they keep flanking him and he is oblige to fall back to keep them from cutting him off from his supplies. there has been a rite smart fiting but no regular engagement. I think that we will whip them yet as soon as we can get them to fite us."

From Cassville, also on May 20, Capt. Henry Richards of Company F, 93rd Ohio, wrote to his father: "Our men look haggard and worn out. We have full rations of pork, hard bread, sugar and coffee; nothing else. We have no clothing, tents nor baggage — nothing but what we carry, and as we are obliged to carry three days' rations on our person, it makes a good load for hot weather — though the nights are cold. I still carry my overcoat but will be compelled to throw it away soon if it gets warmer. The rebels are conducting their retreat very well, and are losing but little stores and not many men. It seems to me they must give up one point or the other, and Atlanta is almost the center of their Confederacy, and only fifty-six miles from here. They take all citizens with them as they go, leaving only a few women and children behind. They must be getting pretty thick somewhere ..."

The next day, Private Robert Patrick, 4th Louisiana, wrote in his diary: "They talk about the ravages of the enemy in their marches through the country, but I do not think that the Yankees are any worse than our own army. This morning when the [wagon] train was passing the house of a farmer a lady gave to the men all the milk, butter and butter-milk she had. They were not satisfied with this. They took all the chickens she had, robbed all the nests they could find, went to the stables and took all the fodder and not content with this, pulled down the fences and turned their horses in upon the fields of wheat. I am sorry to say this has been the case all along the road by our army. I saw some beautiful fields all wantonly destroyed. The husband of the lady above mentioned is in the army and as a matter of course, was away from home. War is a terrible thing."

And in two letters to his wife, Quartermaster Sergeant Joel D. Murphree of the 57th Alabama, recorded his thoughts concerning a universal problem in the Confederate ranks: "Ursula, there is no chance to keep clean in the army while on the tramp as we have been for the last two weeks. I am as dirty as a hog and nearly as lousey ... I must say something or you might think I had found a wife up here for the present, and had laid you on the shelf. No such good luck however, in fact I have been in no situation for sweetheart hunting. I have been tormented equal to Job of old until last week. I have been afflicted with Diarrhea, Itch and Piles and part of the time lousey, but thank the Lord for His blessing I am now

clear of all. After a general and thorough greasing for about a week for the itch I yesterday washed off and put on clean clothes from the skin out."

Johnston retired to Allatoona, threw up breastworks and waited. In the meantime, Sherman rested his army around Kingston — a respite to the troops that would last three days. "Clothing had a general wash, the band went serenading generals at night and letters were sent home — the first opportunity since the start from Chattanooga," wrote Col. Underwood of the 33rd Massachusetts.

Another officer, 1st Lieut. Edwin Weller of the 107th New York, wrote to his future wife on May 22: "We officers have been obliged to send all our baggage to the rear — and come down to the same rations that the Pri-

Staples of soldiering: hardtack and coffee

■ Two unidentified Federal "westerners" pose in the field during a coffee break. Having shed most of their equipment, both men hold tin cups or boilers and pieces of hardtack. 1st Lieut. Stephen Pierson, 33rd New Jersey, later wrote of this aspect of campaigning: "We went stripped of every unnecessary thing ... A canteen carried water or coffee, which [a man] boiled for himself in a tin cup or an old tomato can. A tin plate served as frying pan and serving dish. A green stick split at one end and forced over the rim of the plate made a handle to hold it over the fire, *sometimes;* at other times, the plate would lose its balance and into the fire would go the pork or hardtack. The air was sometimes blue on those occasions, not necessarily with smoke. Cooking and eating over, the dishwashing was easy; a hasty run with a few leaves cleaned the frying pan sufficiently; the grease left on was valuable, and back into the haversack it went, rubbing up against the mixture of ground coffee and sugar and hardtack."

Of meals in camp, Corporal Joseph Van Nest, 101st Ohio, remembered: "The way our rations were distributed to the different companies, and then to the messes, was a sight at times and often created much dissatisfaction. Each company would send someone to get the company's rations, and kettles and rubber blankets would come into play to carry them. Then the distribution to the messes — just think of it, taking a spoon for the purpose of dividing food for from two to four men in a mess. Coffee, tea, hardtack, salt, pepper, salt pork, beans, rice, potatoes and molasses at times, also compressed vegetables — a combination of corn husks, tomato skins, carrots and other kinds of vegetables too numerous to mention. When this compressed vegetable compound was first issued to us, we did not know just how to cook it. We got a fair sized piece and it was placed in a small sized camp kettle. It swelled up, and there was enough for two kettles full. It was an article of food that I did not relish, but the German boys of our company praised it highly."

■ Capt. James Compton, Company C, 52nd Illinois. On May 16 near Rome, his division — the 2nd, XVI Corps — struck the flank of Johnston's retreating army. Compton later wrote: "After the engagement at Rome cross-roads, a captured 'Reb' related to me his adventure with a soldier of the 66th Illinois, of the second brigade. This regiment was armed with 16-shooters (Henry rifles) and usually did more than its share of skirmishing. In this engagement, as usual, it was on the skirmish line. The 'Reb' said he saw a 'Yank' and at the same moment the 'Yank' saw him, and each took to a tree. Soon he thought he saw a chance for a shot and fired. 'Then,' he said, 'that Yank just opened up and fired thirteen shots into my tree and the bark and dirt flew powerful; then he called out, 'Surrender or I'll fire a volley into you.' I certainly thought if he were going to fire a volley after those thirteen shots, I had better surrender. So I came out and he took me in. What kind of guns have you all got, anyway?' "

vates live on. Can not get anything else unless we forage for it. I have a man out when on the march foraging for fresh meat — chickens, garden sauce, etc. So I think I shall make out to live. I can live on the same rations that the privates do. I have done it once and can do the same again. A soldier can accustom himself to anything if he is obliged to."

When reveille sounded before dawn on May 23, Sherman had decided to strike directly across country for Atlanta, temporarily leaving behind his railroad supply line, and skirting Johnston's entrenched army at Allatoona. The day was exceedingly hot and choking clouds of dust rose from the roads and tracks as the Federals marched down to the Etowah River.

"Some of the boys prepared to wade, by taking off their shoes and pantaloons," wrote Private Ira S. Owens of Company C, 74th Ohio. "Others went right in, without taking off anything. I did so myself. When about half way across, where the water was nearly breast deep and running very swift, I thought I would go ahead of some who were ahead of me, when I stumbled and fell, losing my gun, and getting a complete wetting, filling my haversack with water and soaking my hardtack. I recovered my gun, which would not have been of much use, should we have an occasion to use it."

With Wheeler's cavalry keeping Johnston apprised of the Federals' movements, the Confederates soon learned that Sherman had cut loose from the railroad and apparently was heading for the Chattahoochee River, the last major water barrier before Atlanta. With this knowledge, Johnston slid his entire army south, hurriedly entrenching again along a heavily wooded line east-northeast of Dallas. Federal infantry reached Dallas at 2 p.m. on May 25, but were stunned when their progress was abruptly and unexpectedly halted by butternut-clad soldiers just east of the small town. Beginning late that afternoon, and continuing for the next week and a half, the echoes of heavy gunfire reverberated through the dense woods around Dallas, New Hope Church and Pickett's Mill — names soon to be added to dozens of regimental colors at a cost of thousands of casualties.

"We have gotten where they cannot flank us now," wrote Surgeon Urban G. Owen, 4th Confederate Infantry, to his wife on May 28. "We were fighting all day yesterday & in places the dead Yankees are lying thick. The wounded are rolling [by] here by ambulance loads every hour, 14 of my Reg't wounded & 5 killed dead on the field."

In a letter to his wife, Capt. Samuel C. Kelly of Company E, 30th Alabama, wrote of the sanguinary fighting: "I thank God for sparing me. We have been under fire three days this week. Our loss, Regimental, is forty or fifty killed and wounded. I am thankful it was no worse. Joe Johnston knows how to manage the Yanks. From accounts their loss is heavy. It is said that in front of Cleburne's division alone our people buried, yesterday, thirty-three hundred. It was tremendous slaughter."

On the Federal side, Major Lewis D. Warner of the 154th New York likened the embattled armies to "two belligerant cats yawling and spitting at each other ... face to face, their advance lines within easy musket range, and each growling and spitting night and day at each other."

And, as Col. Underwood of the 33rd Massachusetts later wrote, "the Wilderness of Georgia [was] the scene of as obstinate fighting as its namesake ... This Georgia thicket was remembered by the soldiers in Sherman's army, for the trials and bloody encounter there, by the expressive sobriquet, the 'Hell Hole.' "

'Darkness so black it could almost be felt'

Sergeant Rice C. Bull
Company D
123rd New York Volunteer Infantry

Our army had been on the campaign 20 days and as it had had no rest, Gen. Sherman decided to halt for two or three days. During that time the railroad in our rear could be repaired and supplies brought forward for the army. In their retreat the enemy had destroyed the railroad in as far as they could by burning bridges, blowing up culverts and tearing up the rails. It was wonderful how rapidly our men could make repairs as we advanced; unless there was unusual work to be done the whistle of the engines could be heard close by us every morning. The bridge over the Etowah was quite long and it would require two or three days to rebuild it. After our morning meal a good many of our men went to the village.

It was a fine little town with four churches, a female seminary, courthouse, many stores and at least 100 residences, some of which were quite pretentious. The people had all left except one family. The stores had been ransacked and wrecked and nearly everything carried away or destroyed. As near as I could see only a few private houses had been disturbed, but during the day some buildings containing Confederate clothing and supplies were burned. As a rule private property was not injured; however, some of the boys searched for tobacco and found a few plugs. The village did present a deserted, deplorable sight.

On May 21st, the day after Johnston's army retreated from Cassville, we were informed there would be no movement for several days. This would not only give us a good rest but time to clean up and do our washing. In service in the field, while we eliminated everything not absolutely necessary, there were some things we had to carry other than what we had on our backs. Our additional clothes consisted of one shirt, one pair of drawers, two pairs of socks and three handkerchiefs. Our underwear contained wool and was thick and very heavy. It took time to wash and dry so we had to know we would halt for at least a day before we could undertake the job. We were near a stream we could use without contamination to our water supply. Nat Rowell and I did our washing. We borrowed a kettle from the regimental commissary for the "boiling" and by ten in the morning were at work. It was a fine warm day so we had no trouble in drying our clothes, after which we took a bath. When we returned to camp that afternoon, wearing our clean clothes, we felt like new men.

Our last day in Cassville was Sunday; had there been any church service in the village many of the boys would have gone. We had, however, service in the open near our camp; our chaplain conducted the service and there was a large attendance. When in camp we were often called in a body to attend church, but in the field it was voluntary. It was surprising so many were at the service that morning. We had no Sunday inspection, so during the afternoon Rowell and I went to see the rebel works. They were the finest we had seen up to that time and it must have taken much labor to build them. Johnston's army could not have reached there more than a few hours before we were in front of them so they must have been constructed prior to the start of the campaign. They were no ordinary breastworks that could be built overnight, but strong elaborate fortifications with redoubts and abatis in front. It looked strange to us that they would abandon such a line without making a defense.

On Monday the campaign was renewed with great vigor. The reveille was sounded at three, before dawn. We were soon up, our blankets rolled and

■ Sergeant Rice C. Bull, Company D, 123rd New York. The night after the battle of New Hope Church he was detailed for picket duty, and later wrote: "It was raining and black as ink and neither side seemed to be desirous to make it more uncomfortable than nature's effort; it was a dismal time and the night was long. From the beginning of the campaign until the battle of New Hope Church we had fine weather. On May 25th the weather changed and I find recorded in my diary that for 21 days it stormed every day. It did not rain continuously but during some part of every day it hit us, usually in thunderstorms of the most violent sort ... After one of these rains the men would be as wet as if they had fallen in a stream."

■ Col. Archibald L. McDougall commanded the 123rd New York until May 25, when he was severely wounded at New Hope Church. Shot through the leg, he was carried from the field with a shattered bone. In spite of treatment at the officer's hospital in Chattanooga, McDougall never recovered and died there on June 23.

strapped to our knapsacks, our tents down and breakfast eaten. At 4:30 the "fall-in" was sounded and we were on the march in the direction of Kingston. After going south 10 miles we halted long enough to get our dinner and have a short rest. We then continued on until we reached the Etowah River, quite a stream flowing toward the west. The engineers had already laid a pontoon bridge which we crossed and continued on for two miles where we camped for the night. It was only three in the afternoon, but with our early start we had made something like 18 miles. Quite heavy cannonading heard at our left told us that some part of the army was up against the enemy. All our corps crossed the river during the afternoon and evening and was lined along the ridge where we camped.

The next morning, which was the 24th, we started early in a southeasterly direction, almost at right angles to the railroad that ran from Kingston to Marietta and Atlanta. Every mile we marched we were getting farther from the railroad upon which we depended for our supplies; and which we had followed all the way from Chattanooga. From Resaca to the vicinity of the Etowah the railroad runs almost due south, but after crossing the river it turns sharply in a southeasterly direction and continues all the way to Marietta, which is beyond the mountain range that centers around Allatoona. Near Marietta there is a pass through which the railroad runs. When Johnston left his position near Etowah, he did not permanently halt his army until he reached the hill country north of Allatoona. Here he formed his line, built strong fortifications, covering the railroad and extending far to the east and west; then waited for Gen. Sherman to advance. However, Sherman did not follow the Confederates into the hills, but leaving a force at Kingston to protect his base of supplies, left the railroad and with the larger part of the army started for the town of Dallas. This place was at least 20 miles from Johnston's left flank and was beyond the hills that surrounded Allatoona. This movement was to force Johnston out of his strong position so as to engage him where the conditions were more equal. This was the flanking shift used time after time in the campaign to compel the enemy to abandon his well-selected positions.

We continued our march the morning of the 25th, starting about 8 o'clock and taking the road leading to Dallas. We swung to the west to avoid the hills around Allatoona, and were gradually working our way back toward the railroad, which had for a short time past been abandoned. Our progress was slow as the road was narrow and our wagon trains were kept so close up to us. They filled the highway making it difficult to make any time. About noon we came to a large creek where our advance had run into a rebel cavalry force; they retreated without a fight but burned the bridge. This was Pumpkin Vine Creek, and like most streams in that region was quite deep with a muddy bottom so could not be forded. Engineers were brought up to build a bridge. It would take some time to do this and our brigade, as it came up, filed into the woods nearby in close order. While waiting we cooked our dinner: coffee, hardtack and pork, an unchanged bill of fare that did not take us more than a half hour to prepare.

After we finished our meal we had to wait for the bridge, which took quite a time as the timbers had to be cut and brought to the site from the surrounding woods. I spread my blanket on the ground intending to get some sleep when Sergeant James Cummings of our company came and sat down by me. Cummings was, I think, the finest soldier in our organization. A physical giant six feet four inches tall, well educated, a man of character and a splendid soldier. He and I had formed a close friendship.

I noticed he seemed melancholy and sad, the very opposite of his usual manner; and I asked him what was the trouble. He answered that for the last few days he had the feeling that he would not survive the next battle; he believed it would be soon and would not be surprised if it came this day. He said he had tried to shake it off but could not, and now believed it was a warning to him. He told me that I was the only one he had spoken to, as he felt almost ashamed to say anything since we might think him cowardly, but he could not throw the feeling off. He said he had consecrated his life to his country's service and if it was necessary for him to die he would rather be killed in action than linger of disease in some hospital. He had strong religious convictions and had no fears in regard to death or the future life. I tried to convince him that it was foolish to give credence to such feelings, saying we all had such "warnings" at times, but they never came true; and it was more than foolish to think of an early battle as it was then so quiet one could hardly imagine the enemy within 50 miles.

While we were talking the "fall-in" sounded and we took our place in line. The bridge was finished and we crossed, our 1st Division taking the road to the right and the 2nd the one to the left. We marched cautiously through the forest and had advanced some two miles, when away to our left we heard the familiar sound of conflict, the first scattering skirmish fire that gradually increased until it was evident that the main lines were engaged with both infantry and artillery.

Our division was halted; soon couriers began to come and orders were given for us to counter-march. We about-faced and started back to the bridge almost at double-quick, then took the way to the left, following after the 2nd Division at full speed. We learned they had met a heavy force of the enemy about three miles from the bridge and had difficulty holding their line, so we were being rushed to their support. As we neared the front there were all the evidences of battle, wounded men being brought back, ammunition wagons and ambulances hurrying to the front, cowardly skulkers who would not stay on the firing line except a bayonet was at their back getting to the rear, men, horses and even mules wild with excitement.

There is nothing that tests men's nerves more than marching up to a line of battle that is already engaged; they know they are soon to take their place on the firing line. While making the advance they can see, hear and think, but can do nothing to take their minds off the dreadful work they know is before them. Until their own battle line is formed and they are facing the front and firing, their nerves are almost at the breaking point; then the strain relaxes and the fear and nervousness passes away. As we neared the firing line the noise was deafening, the air was filled with the fumes of burning powder; the lazy whining of bullets almost spent, the shot and shell from the enemy batteries tearing through the trees caused every head to duck as they passed over us. With all this tumult could be heard the shouts of our men and the yells of the enemy. We had come three miles from the bridge when we halted just in the rear of our battle line, but only long enough to get orders. Then our division was deployed to the right and left; our brigade went to the right at least a half mile through the forest and was then brought to a front.

When all the formation was completed we advanced to relieve the 2nd Division that had been in action for nearly three hours. They had found the enemy in rifle pits and had only been able to hold the position they had first taken very close to their line. As we moved up to the front, our Col. McDougall was just behind our company; he was on foot as it was impossible for him to ride through the underbrush. When we relieved the line in action they dropped back to form the second line in reserve; at that time the enemy's artillery, located in our immediate front, were firing grape. After a discharge from their battery I heard a cry just back of me; turning, I saw the colonel stagger and fall. He was carried to the rear mortally wounded by a grape shot. We took a position a little forward from the line we relieved

■ Lt. Col. James C. Rogers assumed command of the 123rd New York after Col. McDougall was wounded on May 25. The regiment remained that evening on the field at New Hope Church near an entrenched Confederate battery. "At dark, [the 123rd] at once commenced throwing up breastworks of old logs and whatever material was at hand," Rogers wrote. "There were no tools in the regiment, nor would it have been safe to use them, so close were the lines. At 3 a.m., when it was relieved by fresh troops and passed a short distance to the rear, it had completed a line of breastworks, lying behind which during the day our troops were enabled to pick off the rebel gunners and render useless their artillery."

■ Capt. Julian W. Hinkley commanded Company E, 3rd Wisconsin Infantry. At New Hope Church on May 25, this regiment of Gen. Alpheus Williams' division, XX Corps, attacked a Confederate six-gun battery but was halted 60 yards away in a shower of grape and canister. Hinkley recalled: "When we had first come within range of the grape-shot, my scabbard had been struck and cut in two at a point just below where I grasped it with my left hand. Later, when my men had sheltered themselves and had commenced firing, I was again struck ... My attention had just been called to something on the left, when a bullet struck the front of my cap, cutting the figure '3' out of the bugle, and glancing from the bone, cut a gash across my forehead ... I considered it not much of a clip, and thought that in three days at the most I would be back with my company. It was about two months before I rejoined ..."

and fought from a reclining line to keep below the grape shot as far as possible.

In an hour darkness came; our only light was from the flash of the muskets and the greater light of the artillery in action directly in our front. While lying there a thunder shower that had threatened all day broke on us. It was a furious storm, the rain came down in torrents, the lightning was blinding; then the darkness so black it could almost be felt. For a time the thunder drowned out the sound of the artillery which continued to pound away at our line.

During the storm one of the boys, who was quite a wag, lying in a pool of water, turned to Capt. Anderson, who was just behind him, and said, "Now, Captain, if you will just give the order, we will swim over and tackle the Johnnies." This illustrated the degree of familiarity that had become between our men and their officers. It is easy to understand this; our regiment was made up entirely of men from Washington County, and each company of men from the same or adjacent townships; their officers were older men, the friends of their fathers and mothers. About 9:30 the enemy's artillery fire gradually ceased, but there was still quite active skirmishing and bullets whistled around us all night.

Most of the men continued lying on the ground, hugging it closely although the rain was still falling. I was near the right of the company as a file closer in the rear of the men. My friend Cummings arose from a place near me. He had been quiet during all the excitement of the advance and attack, and as far as I could see had not been worried; he had hardly spoken to me. Firing had nearly ended when he arose and, placing the butt of his gun on the ground, stood facing the front. I said, "Jim, you know there are orders not to fire, why do you stand and expose yourself?" He answered, "I don't think there is any more danger in standing here than lying in the mud. I have had enough of that."

He remained standing, leaning on his gun. I do not think it was more than a minute after I spoke to him that I heard a metallic sound, as though one had taken a hammer and hit a tree with it. Cumming's gun dropped from his hands and he and his gun struck the ground at the same time. A bullet had found its mark in his forehead, passing through his brain. We carried him back to the field hospital where he died before morning. In his death our company lost its best soldier.

About ten that night we began to build rifle pits. We had to work quietly as the enemy would send a shower of bullets after any unusual sound. By morning we had works that would protect us from infantry fire. It had become almost a habit with us as soon as we halted close to the enemy to build breastworks; every man would dig in as though his life depended on his work. In many cases it did. It was surprising how quickly we could construct a trench that would protect us from musketry. Each regiment was equipped with spades and shovels which in this campaign were carried by pack mules. In most places the location of our line was in such heavily wooded country that wagons could not follow up closely, while mules could be kept right with us.

In this action our regiment lost 40 men killed or wounded,* including Col. McDougall; he was succeeded by Lt. Col. Rogers. Our Company D had one killed and four wounded. The day after the battle, away to our left, there was heavy skirmishing and artillery action indicating almost a general engagement. In our front it was quiet. It was now known that Gen. Johnston

* Bull was mistaken in his accounting of the 123rd New York's casualties in the fighting of May 25. The correct figures were one killed and 22 wounded. Four of the wounded subsequently died.

was there with his whole army behind well-built works that were far too strong to be captured by direct assault without great loss. In the battle of the 25th both sides had been heavy losers of men; ours was probably the larger as we were the attacking force and we could not claim a victory as we were unable to drive them back. However, we did establish a line close to them and we then kept up a great racket with our skirmishers and sharpshooters.

This engagement is now known as the Battle of New Hope Church; those who fought gave it the name of Hell Hole.

■ The battle of New Hope Church, May 25, 1864. "Every man knew that Hood's Corps was in front and behind the breastworks," recalled a Federal soldier, "and that it would take desperate fighting to dislodge them. Therefore, as the columns of assault moved out they moved with a rush, and though met with the same awful fire as before, scores and hundreds of men surged right up to the breastworks and died there. It was simply slaughter. Sherman had blood to spare, and Hooker poured it out in the dark forest as though human life had no value. The steady sheet of flame pouring over the logs scorched and withered the blue lines until they had to draw away from it."

'Hello, Jim, what's the hurry?'

Private Uriah H. Farr
Company D
70th Indiana Volunteer Infantry

On the afternoon of the twenty-fifth of May it was manifest that a fight was imminent. Troops were hurrying forward, couriers dashing hither and thither, and there was a constant rattle of musketry in front, with an occasional stray ball coming back to where we were slowly marching in column to the front on the sides of the main road, in order that ordnance wagons and ambulances could have free passage. About three p.m. we were hurried forward more rapidly, each of the regiments marching in column side by side at battalion front distance in order to be ready for instant use as support for Coburn's brigade in our front. The rebel line of battle could not be far away from the nearness of the artillery fire of the enemy, the supporting line faring about the same as the front line. Our line was thus pushed up close to the enemy, which resulted in considerable fighting, lasting till dark,

■ Lt. Gen. Alexander P. Stewart succeeded to the command of Gen. Leonidas Polk's corps on June 23 and led the corps for the remainder of the campaign and the war. At New Hope Church, while still a major general commanding a division in Hood's corps, Stewart was responsible for stopping the Federal attack of the XX Corps on May 25. "Like surging waves against the beach, line after line vanished when our angry rifles spat their fire and hungry cannon belched their flame," wrote 1st Lieut. Bromfield L. Ridley, an aide-de-camp on Stewart's staff. "Stewart's old roan was seen all along the line. His quiet way enlisted the love of the division. They begged him to get back, fearing he might be killed, but he rode along as unconcerned as ever. Gen. Johnston sent to know if reinforcements were wanted. The reply was: 'My own troops will hold the position.' And they did."

the battle being known as Dallas Woods or Pumpkin Vine Creek.

I had no gun this day, mine having been ruined by a rebel bullet, but I determined to keep close up and pick one up at the first opportunity. Henry C. Eaton was sick and his gun was turned over to some man of the company who had none, and Eaton was marching with me on the left of our company. As the line of battle was pushed closer and closer to the enemy, and the firing became deadly, Colonel Merrill* who was in command of the regiment, noticed us, and riding to us ordered us to stop in some place of safety (in some ravine we were passing), stating that we were without arms and there was no use of our endangering our lives. But that was not a part of our plan, so we did not stop, but as soon as he left we moved on with the command.

After some half hour he came back down the line again, and seeing us there, peremptorily ordered us to stop, and pointing out a large tree, ordered us to lie down there. We obeyed the order, but discussed the project of keeping close up and if we saw him again to hide; but we had noticed his eye flash forth some fire, a thing not common to him, and we finally decided that he meant that we should obey his order, and that in all probability he would punish us if we did not, so we sat still. After we stopped, our command did not move very far ahead, probably not more than half a mile, where we found it early next morning.

While we were lying there we were treated to some of the scenes of the rear. I saw several men I knew from another regiment, one of whom had been a neighbor and schoolmate. He came rushing back, jumping down the slope quite lively, and I said, "Hello, Jim, what's the hurry?" He checked his flight enough to say that in the advance he had fallen down and hurt his leg, and of course, being crippled, was hurrying to the rear; but he was making good time for a cripple. Perhaps the wind from the enemy's shells and solid shots, which came with fearful velocity, was helping to force him along.

The second night, while everything was still and most of the men were asleep, the enemy's batteries opened on us and poured in a tornado of shells for about an hour, and as our batteries replied the din was terrific. The next day we moved a little to the right and put up a line of works. An old log cabin stood in a field some half-mile to the right and front, and was occupied by sharpshooters, who were doing much damage, but a cannon was brought to the right of our regiment, and the old house was soon knocked to pieces and the sharpshooters fled for their lives amid a shower of bullets from our skirmishers and the huzzahs of our line.

We often listened to the fighting to our right or left, first the cannonading, then a lull, then the hurrahing, sometimes the shrill boyish rebel yell, sometimes the loud, full-voiced, deep-toned, far-sounding chorus of Northern men; then again the roar of cannon, the rattle of musketry, and the awful suspense to the listeners. If, as the noise grew feebler, we caught the wel-

* Lt. Col. Samuel Merrill, an Indianapolis bookstore manager, alternated command of the 70th Indiana with Col. Benjamin Harrison, later president of the United States, who was in temporary command of the 1st Brigade, 3rd Division, XX Corps. Harrison missed nearly all of the campaign in June, being forced into a hospital after suffering the effects of touching a poisonous vine. That month, Merrill wrote to his wife: "One of the horrors of this kind of life is that the men's bodies and clothes are alive and nothing can be done to relieve them as they have no change of clothing and seldom any opportunity to bathe. The officers if they exert themselves and change their clothes frequently can escape the affliction, but the poor private drags his tormented carcass in utter hopelessness to the end of the campaign. Another trouble is produced by wearing thick wool clothes and by eating fat salt pork. Everyone from Colonel to Private is broken out horribly, and cannot enjoy a moment's rest for the intolerable itching."

come cheer, an answering shout ran along to the right or left. But if the far-off rebel yell told of our comrades' repulse, the silence could be felt.

About this time General Hooker was riding through his corps, and as he passed through the Third Brigade, the boys yelled "Hardtack! Hardtack!" and as he came to our brigade he heard the same complaining cry. He went to Colonel Coburn and asked what it meant, and Coburn told him our two brigades were out of rations and had been for some time. There had been some mistake, perhaps; favoritism, perhaps, but be that as it may, Hooker saw that things were righted and we were soon gladdened with the sight of the commissary wagons.

■ 1st Lieut. Alexis Cope, adjutant of the 15th Ohio. Of the heavy Federal losses at Pickett's Mill he later wrote: "The fault was with those high in command, who failed to ascertain the position and strength of the enemy, before sending us to the slaughter. With them must rest the blame. No troops ever went into action with more spirit and vigor, or sustained an unequal combat with more courage and fortitude."

'Why don't they stop those damned bugles?'

1st Lieut. Alexis Cope
Adjutant
15th Ohio Veteran Volunteer Infantry

On the night of May 19 and the morning of May 20 the enemy left our front and retreated across the Etowah River.

The morning of May 20 was foggy, but the fog soon lifted and the weather became clear and warm. We got word that we would not move that day and so made ourselves comfortable. We heard cannonading some distance to the front and supposed the guns were fired by some of our troops who were in pursuit of the enemy. Report came that our railroad train had come into Kingston, and soon after we heard the whistle of an engine and a train ran past us to the front. On the 21st and 22nd we remained in our bivouac of the 20th. There were rumors that we were to go on an expedition, with three-fifths rations for 20 days, cutting loose from our lines of communication.

On the morning of the 23rd we received orders to march at noon, but when the hour came the road was occupied by the XX Corps and we had to wait until it got by. A little after 1 o'clock we moved out taking a road leading in a southerly direction, crossing the railroad nearly at right angles. We were provided with three days' rations which were to last five. Orders directed that no straggling was to be permitted.

After marching about five miles and once getting on the wrong road, we took a direct course over a hill to a road leading to Gillem's bridge over the Etowah River. South of the river we marched through some of the finest country we had yet seen. It bore few marks of the bloody and ruinous struggle which was being waged elsewhere, yet it was now destined to receive its full share of the blighting curse which must fall alike upon all rebellious soil. Just as darkness fell we crossed Euharlee Creek and encamped in the edge of a little village near a mill. As no regular foraging parties had been organized, the men did some individual foraging, with the result that a good supply of fresh pork was added to our rations.

The morning of May 24 we resumed our march, moving steadily in a southwesterly direction until we reached a range of hills. Here the artillery seriously impeded our progress and we halted in a large field. Our men confiscated a large quantity of smoking tobacco, which they found nearby. Col. Gibson heard of it and ordered it equally distributed among the regiments of the brigade. All the men who had pipes soon filled them and those who had none made them out of corn cobs, there being abundant cane for stems all along the road.

Our march now was through beautiful groves of yellow pines which were quite thick on the hills. The road was so crooked we could not tell our exact course, but it seemed more to the east than the day before. We marched

■ Brig. Gen. Alexander W. Reynolds commanded a brigade in Stevenson's division of Hood's corps. The brigade consisted of the 58th and 60th North Carolina and the 54th and 63rd Virginia — the latter two the only regiments from the Old Dominion serving in the Army of Tennessee. At New Hope Church the 54th Virginia lost more than 100 men, many of them taken prisoner. Reynolds, himself a Virginian, was wounded on May 25, but recovered after several months.

steadily on over the hills until 6 o'clock in the evening, when we descended to a small stream and encamped on a hillock nearby. As we were pitching our tents a thunderstorm was approaching. It soon broke above us and continued for two or three hours. But the men were secure in their shelter tents and so escaped the downpour — all except the commissary men who were issuing beef and who were thoroughly drenched. We had marched 11 miles during the day. The advance of our corps was about one mile from Burnt Hickory on the Dallas road.

The morning of May 25 our army was directed to march on Dallas, our corps to follow Gen. Geary's and Gen. Williams' divisions of the XX Corps. About 5:30 p.m. we heard heavy artillery firing at the front, which was so continuous that we knew we had met the enemy in force. It continued for about an hour and the road being then cleared of trains we advanced more rapidly.

A thunderstorm was coming up about that time and the thunder from the clouds mingled with that of our cannon. In the midst of the din there was one mighty peal of thunder — so loud, so deep, so profound that we were awe-stricken. It made our heavy guns sound like the snapping of matches in comparison. It was comforting, as well as awe-inspiring, for it made us remember that God was on His throne and still watching over His world. No one who heard that peal of thunder could ever forget it.

At dusk we crossed Pumpkinvine Creek on a bridge which had been saved by Hooker's men, after the enemy had set it on fire. We soon began to meet large numbers of wounded men from Hooker's corps and were told that they had run into an ambuscade where they met a murderous cross fire of both artillery and musketry. It soon became quite dark and began to rain. For several hours we made but little headway. The roadsides were crowded with wounded men. Large numbers of stragglers had built fires which blinded us and made the darkness almost impenetrable, but we stumbled along a muddy road through a dense forest. About 11 o'clock we were halted, stacked arms along the roadside and laid down on the wet ground, with orders to be ready to move at 3 o'clock next morning.

The morning of May 26, a little before three, the brigade bugler sounded reveille and we heard Col. Gibson caution him not to repeat it. Our bugler was also cautioned not to play. Sergeant Major A.J. Gleason and I went along the line and called on the men to rise and we were soon ready for an emergency.

But little firing was heard during the morning and we were given ample time to get our breakfasts. We waited, expecting to be called on every moment, for over an hour before orders came. Our brigade then marched out in advance, our regiment being in the rear. We marched about two miles on a road leading a little east of south, when we formed in line of battle facing east along the crest of a ridge overlooking quite an opening in the woods. While moving into position the enemy's presence was made known by bullets whizzing over our heads.

Gen. Wood in person superintended the placing of our brigade in position, and when he rode away gave directions to keep close watch on our front and await further orders. The men at once set to work building breastworks of logs and earth, but Gen. Wood told us it was of no use as the line would soon advance. He had barely left us when the advance was sounded and a brisk exchange of shots began on the skirmish line.

The rebel skirmish line seemed to be stronger than was anticipated, as our skirmish line failed to advance. The skirmishers still kept up a desultory fire which gradually slackened and our men resumed the building of a barricade to cover our front.

Gens. Sherman, Thomas, Howard and Wood came along our part of the

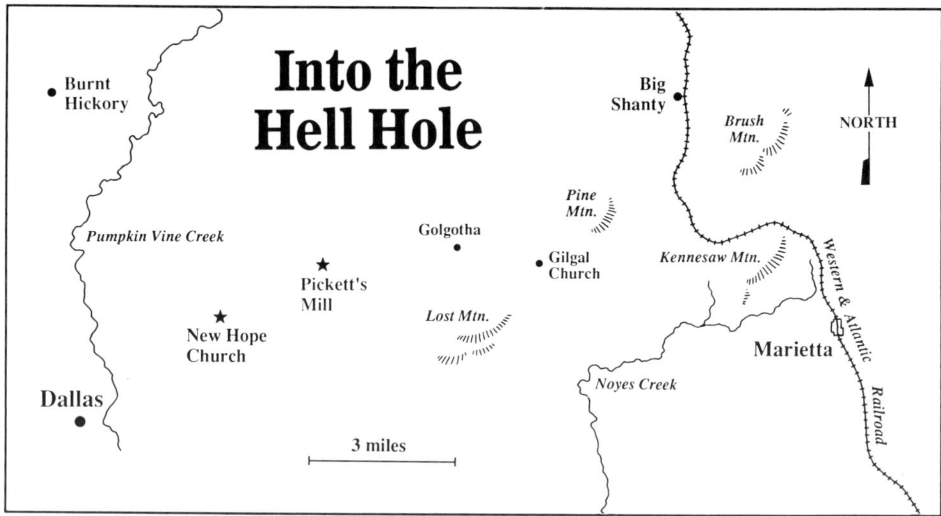

line about noon and examined our position carefully. Dinner was brought up to the line by the company cooks. We had barely time to swallow it when we were ordered by the generals to advance under their observation. We moved forward with little opposition to a point where a good position for a battery was uncovered on our left, and the 6th Ohio was moved forward and placed in such position. The battery opened with effect and we saw the enemy's troops get up and make for the rear. Our skirmishers gradually worked around to the left of the enemy's position in our front, about 200 yards distant, and they were permitted to retire almost unmolested.

The battery to our left now began throwing shells at the enemy's main line, and a battery of the enemy replied quite vigorously. A man in Company B was severely wounded by one of its shells. This same evening Major James P. Hampson of the 124th Ohio, a very popular young officer well known in our division, was mortally wounded and died the next day.

The rebel battery was finally silenced and night came on rather quietly. Our regiment was ordered to relieve the 32nd Indiana on the skirmish line and did so with five companies. The other five companies were placed in reserve behind the works. Our ammunition was replenished, we drew three days' rations and thus made ready for the morrow. The night was still, except for occasional shots between the pickets of the opposing armies. We did not know that the next day we would undergo the severest trial of our entire service.

The morning of May 27 dawned clear and gave promise of a bright warm day. Our skirmishers were relieved by the 29th Illinois and the regiment retired a short distance to the rear of the front line. The timber had been cleared away at a point in our line and a battery of Parrott guns was placed in position and opened on the enemy whose lines were in plain sight, and apparently did some execution. The enemy's battery which we thought was silenced yesterday again opened on us, but was soon silenced again. Our brigade was soon relieved and moved about one mile to the left where we rejoined our division in the rear of the XXIII Corps.

The operations of the 26th had disclosed the position of the enemy in our front and it was decided to make a general attack. His position, however, was so strong that it was decided, if possible, to find and attack his right flank with a view of turning his position. Our division was selected to make this attack. We received our orders about noon and at once began our movement toward the enemy's right. The country over which we moved was quite rough, thickly wooded and covered with a thick growth of underbrush, which made our progress difficult and laborious.

Adrift in the Hell Hole's engulfing darkness

After the troops of Gen. Hooker's three divisions of the XX Corps recoiled from the shock of the bloody and fruitless assaults on the Confederate line at New Hope Church, other Federal units came up to support their comrades in the wildly confused area immediately behind the battlefield. Among these reinforcements was Capt. John W. Tuttle of the 3rd Kentucky Infantry, IV Corps, and he wrote in his diary for May 25:

"Marched at 9 A.M. in the direction of Dallas. Hooker ran into the rebs and fought them all evening. Our Division formed in line of battle a little before dark then moved two or three miles to the left. Was unable to get my horse over the steep cliffs and deep ravines so I got lost from my regt. and indeed from my Division. Met thousands of wounded and stragglers. The rain came down in torrents and it was truly heart rending to hear the groans of the wounded all along for miles as I searched for my regt. It was so dark one could not see his hand before him. Thousands were crowding forward to relieve those who had been fighting — Infantry, Cavalry and Artillery, without the slightest regard to organization for that was impossible. Those relieved came back in swarms, some carrying or leading their wounded comrades. Sometimes a battery would run through the ranks of the Infantry scattering the men in every direction and again some unlucky horseman would ride into a batch of wounded men. All was hurry and confusion and nearly everybody was swearing at the top of his voice. If the rebs had known our condition it would have been an easy matter to have stampeded even the sturdy veterans of the 4th corps."

■ Col. William H. Gibson, 49th Ohio, commanded a brigade in Wood's division of the IV Corps at Pickett's Mill. Before the war he served as Ohio's state treasurer, but was forced from office for alleged complicity in a defalcation of nearly $750,000. Many believed he entered military service in 1861 to wipe clean the stigma of this incident. He distinguished himself at Shiloh and Stone River, and mustered out of the army at the end of the Atlanta campaign. He was brevetted brigadier general to rank from March 1865. As a regimental commander, Gibson "was one of those kind-hearted officers that the boys loved," recalled Corporal William S. Franklin of the 49th's Company H. "Many times during the war, when the soldiers were weary and exhausted with hard marches, hunger and thirst, and we felt like giving up in despair, his eloquent voice would be heard giving cheer, restoring confidence and infusing new life into them."

Our expedition, as we understood, was intended to surprise the enemy and yet, strange to relate, our brigade commander decided to have all orders given by the bugle. This gave the enemy immediate and continuous notice of our movement every step of the way. To the men in the ranks who quickly comprehended the purpose of our movement, this use of the bugle was universally condemned. More than one officer and man exclaimed, "If we are expected to surprise the enemy, why don't they stop those damned bugles?"

But on we went, our bugles blowing. Even when we halted for a short rest the bugles sounded the long, drawn-out note which commanded us to stop. The afternoon was almost consumed by this difficult and tiresome march. We finally came to an open timbered space near a road which wound up a hill toward the enemy's supposed position, and halted on the right of the road. It was reported that we had found the enemy's right flank. Gens. Howard and Wood came up to our position and stopped for a while. There was a sudden and sharp rattle of carbines in our front and a little to our left, and almost immediately came an order for us to advance.

The horses of the lieutenant colonel and I, which had been left behind when we started on our surprise party, had been brought up in the meantime and we mounted them. The regiment was formed in line and advanced up through the open wooded space, our colors floating in a brisk breeze which caught them as we neared the top of the slope.

Suddenly a battery of the enemy, who was strongly posted across the open space a few hundred yards away, opened on our colors. The first shots wounded Lieut. Thomas C. Davis of Company C, as well as a number of the color guard, and the regiment momentarily halted. A terrific fire of musketry opened on our left where Gen. Hazen's brigade was charging, and we received an order to move to the left across the road to the shelter of the woods.

The horses of the field and staff were quickly sent to the rear and, singular to relate, we were thrown into dire confusion by conflicting or misunderstood orders of our regimental commander, Col. Wallace. Before the disorders were corrected, the bugler, Wilson S. Iler, with quick, sharp, clear notes, sounded the advance and we charged forward into the woods and across a steep ravine toward the enemy's position — the left wing of our regiment on the right of our colors and the right wing on their left.

I confess to a momentary fit of complete demoralization over its disorganized condition when it went into action. But there was no diminution in the courage of the men in the ranks, and they rushed forward through the woods, down into the ravine and across it under a murderous fire of artillery and musketry from a line they could not see. They pressed forward up the side of the ravine, found the enemy on its further edge in a position too strong to be successfully attacked, and held on until nightfall when their ammunition was exhausted. They then retired to the rear and closed up their fearfully decimated ranks. While we were holding on to the other side of the ravine and within a few feet at some points of the enemy's works, we suffered from a severe cross and enfilading fire from both the enemy's right and left. This fire did little damage to the men closest to the enemy's line in our immediate front, but was killing the wounded who were lying in the ravine and on its slopes to our rear.

The brigade commander, Col. Gibson, was not with the charging line, but Capt. Cyrus Askew of the 15th Ohio, a member of his staff, was, and I appealed to him to go to the rear, report this deadly cross fire and ask that troops be sent in on our right and left to check it. For some reason Capt. Askew declined to go, but suggested that I go instead. I started to the rear and as I passed into the ravine I saw Capt. Joseph R. Updegrove of Company H, his face and neck crimsoned with blood from a wound behind the ear. I examined his wound, saw it was serious and urged him to go to the rear. He was, for the moment, mentally unbalanced and insisted on remaining with his company, but I sent for Lieut. J.A. Gleason (our sergeant major's brother), who was in command of the pioneers, to take command of the company and went on.

Passing up the slope of the ravine to the rear it seemed almost impossible to escape the bullets and shells of the enemy. The minie balls seemed thick as hornets about a nest which had suddenly been disturbed, and a shell seemed to explode near me almost every step. But I soon reached the thicker woods beyond the ravine where I found Col. Gibson and Gen. Wood, and attempted to explain to them the situation in front. They were both laboring under terrible stress of excitement. Just then Gen. Howard rode up and seeing that I had just come from the front, asked me particularly about conditions on the firing line. I reported and the general said, "Go back and tell the men that I will have troops sent in both on their right and left as soon as I can get them."

I started back and had gone a few paces when one of the enemy's shells exploded apparently right over these officers. Gen. Howard's horse whirled around and the general, putting his armless sleeve before his eyes, exclaimed, "I am afraid to look down! I am afraid to look down!" I at once turned back and told the general that the shell had only torn off the heel of his boot. The general thought it had taken off his leg and seemed much relieved when he knew that only his boot was injured.

When I returned to the firing line I struck it where the 15th Wisconsin of our brigade was still holding on, and by a rapid fire was keeping the enemy down behind their works. If a head showed itself above the enemy's barricade it at once became a target for the riflemen of our line. I passed on to the right, hoping to find the 15th Ohio. It was then growing dark. Failing to find the regiment I went to the rear and found it gathering together its scattered remnants near a house we had noticed when we were resting just before the attack. There had been fearful losses — how great no one could tell — but those who were left closed up their ranks and, together with the remnants of the other regiments of the brigade, moved to a position on a line which had been established along a ridge to our right front.

It was very dark and near midnight before we got into position and protected our line by entrenchments. As we were out of ammunition I took a detail of two men from each company and started out to find the ammunition train. Where it was no one could tell. The woods were thick and dark, but after stumbling about in the darkness for an hour or more the train was found. Each one of the 20 men took a box of cartridges on his shoulder and the detail finally got back to the line.

After the cartridges were distributed and I was about to drop down for a little rest, I heard Col. Wallace, who was lying nearby, groaning. He said he had fallen over a rock as we charged down into the ravine and had wrenched his back. He complained of being cold, although wrapped up in his overcoat and blankets. I took my own blankets, spread them over the colonel and then sank down in the rank, reeking weeds without covering and slept from sheer exhaustion.

On the morning of May 28 I was awakened by one of the enemy's shells exploding in the trees over my head, and went at once to work preparing a list of the casualties in the regiment the day before. Some of the companies had been almost marvelously protected by the inequalities of the ground while others had suffered terribly.

In Company H, out of 49 men carrying guns who had gone into action, only 22 remained — a loss, including Capt. Updegrove, of 56 percent. The losses

■ Col. William Wallace commanded the 15th Ohio at Pickett's Mill where, while charging with his men down into a ravine, he tripped over a rock and badly sprained his back. Sent to hospital at Acworth on June 8, he never returned to the regiment and was discharged from the army on July 19.

■ Maj. Gen. Oliver Otis Howard commanded the IV Corps and, after July 27, the Army of the Tennessee during the campaign. A deeply religious man, the one-armed Howard was well liked by the troops serving under him. On one occasion at Power's Ferry on the Chattahoochee, he was exchanging personal courtesies with soldiers of the 15th Ohio. 1st Lieut. Alexis Cope recalled: "A great many of our men went into the river to bathe and swim and some of them were very noisy and profane. We could see that Gen. Howard was greatly annoyed by their profanity. He finally could stand it no longer, and spurring his horse to the river bank exclaimed: 'My men, I think you should be afraid to use such language if the water is deep.' The rebuke went home, and there was no more swearing while the general was within earshot."

were appalling.* In the space of a little over an hour our division sustained a loss of near 1,500 officers and men. The losses in our brigade of six regiments (two of them small) were 703. In Hazen's brigade of eight regiments, 467. In Knefler's brigade of seven regiments, 301.

Picket firing continued all day and all night, but as we had not been out of hearing of such firing for four weeks we had become accustomed to it, and many of the men not on duty laid down behind our works and slept.

I found time during the day to visit the wounded at the field hospitals, where the surgeons with rolled-up sleeves had worked all night before and were still at work, cutting off legs and arms and otherwise trying to relieve the wounded men. Among those I recall was the regimental bugler, Wilson Iler, whose sunny disposition and cheerful manners endeared him to everyone who knew him.

When he had blown that loud, sharp, clear bugle note which commanded us to charge forward, he had seized the musket of a comrade who had fallen and had gone forward with the line. He, too, was soon laid low by bullet wounds in his arm and leg. His arm had been amputated and, although suffering from pain, he was as cheerful as ever, saying he would soon be back and added, "Adjutant, a bugler only needs one arm." Poor fellow, he died of terrible gangrene at Chattanooga a few days later.

A terrible depression pervaded the ranks this day. It was partially relieved by the arrival of mail which brought letters from home. If it had not been for this and the activities made necessary by the enemy's immediate presence, the depression would have been almost unbearable. Many of the very flower of our young comrades had been killed or fatally wounded, and there were some whose fate was unknown as the enemy still held the ground where the battle was fought.

It was Saturday, and my friend Sergeant Major Gleason in closing his diary for the day, said: "Night came on with the usual amount of desultory firing and we retired to rest at the close of another eventful week. May God forbid that I should be compelled to witness events more painful than those of this week."

'A literal slaughter-pen'

Diary of
Sergeant Major Andrew J. Gleason
15th Ohio Veteran Volunteer Infantry

May 27, 1864 ... The country being quite rough made a great deal of maneuvering necessary to keep in line, which was quite laborious. A large part of the afternoon was consumed in this way before we finally halted in a clear space with rough timber land in our front and rested about an hour. There, Gens. Howard and Wood rode along and gave the order to advance, when skirmishing began at once in the woods in front.

Some time previous to this a sharp rattle of carbines had been heard to our left, indicating that our movement had been discovered by rebel cavalry. Before we advanced the rebels shelled the woods vigorously, one shell bursting in Company C's ranks, injuring several men while we were yet on the reserve. We were ordered to double-quick and soon became exposed to a

* The losses sustained by the 15th Ohio at Pickett's Mill on May 27, 1864, were: killed or died of wounds, 38; wounded, 51; and 15 missing or captured. A number of those captured later died in Andersonville prison. Six members of the 15th Ohio's color guard were successively killed or wounded with the colors, which were finally brought off the field that night by Sergeant David D. Hart of Company I.

galling cross fire of musketry and artillery.

I followed the left of the regiment until a halt was made, dropping behind a convenient log until it moved on, when I reluctantly left my natural breastwork. Moving forward to the crest of a ridge, a severe cross fire was encountered and the line advanced into a ravine close to the rebel works, where it met with a decided check, and having little protection was in a literal *slaughter-pen.*

Here fell gallant Sergeant Ambers Norton, our color bearer, with his life blood staining the flag a deeper crimson. One by one all the color guard, with one exception, were either killed or wounded. Company H, the left color company, seemed almost annihilated. Orderly Mumaugh, Sergeant Miller, Corporal Updegrove and several others were killed, while Capt. Updegrove and many of his men were wounded.

The only protection available was to lie close to the ground or seek cover behind trees and rocks — by no means plenty — until the fire had slackened. No supports had come up and our bugle had sounded the recall as soon as it was apparent the works could not be carried. A galling cross fire scorched the ravine and ridge alike, rendering it almost useless to seek shelter of tree or rock.

I noticed two men taking shelter behind a medium-sized tree on the brink of the ravine, and when one of them was hit in the hand by a minie ball and retired to the rear, I crept to his place behind the other. He was leaning against the tree and would not lie down, although he was not firing. In a few minutes a ball came from the left and struck him squarely in the temple with that peculiar "spat" which once heard is at once recognized as the passage of a bullet through flesh and bone. It killed him so suddenly that he never changed his position, and had I not heard the shot strike and been spattered by his blood and brains I might have believed him still untouched. He was a stranger to me, evidently from another regiment, and being past all human aid I soon left him, going to another tree where I could get a better view of the front.

To my surprise not a soul was visible. The woods were full of smoke and I thought the line could not be far away. The rebel fire still swept the ground like a hailstorm and I deemed it better to quietly await further developments than to try to get away, although our bugle kept blowing the recall.

It was now past sunset and the woods were growing dark, when a wounded man belonging to Company I of our regiment came from the left front, painfully limping toward the rear and, seeing me, asked me to help him as he was nearly exhausted. I arose and taking his roll of blankets in one hand and his arm in the other, led him to the rear as rapidly as his condition would permit. He was severely wounded in the thigh.

Passing on to the right I soon gained the shelter of the ridge and near its foot passed Major McClenahan with a bugler, watching for stragglers from the front and having the recall blown at intervals. Alas! Too many of our brave comrades lay up that bloody ravine, forever beyond the sound of the bugle; many more were so badly wounded as to be helpless, and others were so close to the rebel works that they dared not stir until darkness shielded them.

Pausing for an instant I gave Major McClenahan the little information I possessed and passed on with my charge. We moved more slowly now as we were safer from the enemy's shot and shell, which still swept the forest like a besom. I fell in with stragglers from all regiments of the brigade and division. Nearly every regiment seemed to have lost all formation in the mad and futile charge into the angle of the enemy's works, but I met no one that I knew.

It seemed to be the prevailing opinion that someone (whether Gen. How-

■ Brig. Gen. Thomas J. Wood's 3rd Division of the IV Corps bore the brunt of the fighting — and casualties — at Pickett's Mill. Some 1,469 officers and men of his division "were placed hors du combat in the action," Wood wrote in his official report of the battle. "It may be truly said of it, that it was the best sustained and altogether the fiercest and most vigorous assault that was made on the enemy's entrenched positions during the entire campaign."

■ Private Daniel W. Shideler, Company E, 93rd Ohio, endured skin-drenching downpours while campaigning along Pumpkin Vine Creek. On the evening of May 24, another regiment in Hazen's brigade, the 1st Ohio, halted and stacked arms during a violent thunderstorm. Lightning suddenly struck the stacks and ran along the bayonets of the guns, severely shocking most of the regiment. Surprisingly, however, not a single life was lost.

ard or Gen. Wood was not quite clear), had made a blunder, and a costly one for our division in attacking where we did. The supposed object was to strike the rebels in flank beyond the protection of their works, which would have then been taken in reverse. There had been ample time for reconnoitering, even after the rebel cavalry had discovered our approach. But the blow was delivered at the very strongest part of their line after giving them ample time to reinforce it.

The battle, while covering only our division front, was decidedly our bloodiest so far, and Company H (my own) lost four killed and 16 wounded, so far as known, besides several missing who, it was feared, had also been killed or left severely wounded in the ravine or on its bloody slopes. The losses of Company H were the heaviest of any company in the regiment, and all had suffered terribly. This is surely not war, it is *butchery*.

'There was no safe side to that tree'

Private Daniel W. Shideler
Company E
93rd Ohio Volunteer Infantry

The morning of May 27 broke cloudy and the forenoon was decidedly sultry. The very atmosphere was ominous. The expression was frequently heard during our advance: "Oh, we'll catch it to-day. We'll get into it." My comrades marched steadily and resolutely, it proved for many of them, to their death.

Our brigade was commanded by Gen. Hazen. We formed a line of battle and with fixed bayonets advanced with orders, as we understood it, to charge the rebels wherever found. The march through fields, over hills and hollows, through brush and timber during that hot day was tough on us. In the afternoon we halted on top of a ridge where we laid down, seemingly awaiting orders. We afterward learned that Gen. Hazen and Gen. Wood, our division commander, did not want to make a charge at this point, feeling it would turn out just as it did, and that Hazen received the order a third time before ordering us to advance.

About 5 p.m. the bugle sounded the advance and our brigade moved down into a ravine and up a hill, the left wing striking an open field, the right wing timber. The left of my regiment was in the field.

Here we encountered the rebel skirmishers and drove them across the field to their breastworks. Part of our brigade advanced some of the way across the field, but fell back to the edge of the timber where our line of battle was held. The right of the brigade rested on a ridge at the right of the field, in the timber. I followed a fence at the right of the field, passing through a thicket beyond which I could see a big log, and made a quick run, dropping down behind it.

A lieutenant of the 124th Ohio and another soldier sought protection at my right. The firing was very brisk from both sides. Looking over the log I could see the rebels about 150 yards in our front, and one Johnny in particular drew my attention.

I rested my Enfield on the log and fired at him, dropping down again to reload. I heard a rebel bullet strike the log on the side opposite me.

Again I took a shot at the fellow and dropped behind the log, just in time to hear neighbor Johnny's bullet thud into the log. I reloaded, took another survey and, so I thought, could plainly see Johnny reb. Leveling my gun a third time, I fired and dropped just in time to hear the third rebel bullet hit the log.

At this stage the 124th Ohio lieutenant at my right arose and pointed with his sword in the direction of the rebels. He was at once badly wounded and fell back behind the log again. One of his company ran from the rear to him, and leaning over him, said: "Lieutenant, are you badly hurt?" Scarcely had the words been spoken when he fell, killed outright.

The rebels had charged around on our left and had an enfilading fire on our line, and my log was no protection to me now. So I made another run to a big tree a little in the rear and straightened up behind it.

A rebel bullet from our left passed between me and the tree, knocking the bark into my face and convincing me that there was no safe side to that tree. I beat a retreat to where I found most of our regiment and company under cover of the ridge.

The lieutenant wounded behind the log was the same man who, after our brigade had charged and taken possession of the ridge at Resaca, when a masked rebel battery on our right opened an enfilading fire of grape and canister on our line, persisted in walking up and down the line directing his men to "keep that battery silenced." I never saw him with his regiment again after he was wounded. What became of him and what his name was, I never knew. He was a brave soldier.

Our brigade was relieved about sundown or dusk, and that night built a line of breastworks to the right of the battlefield. The next morning we found our breastworks were endways to the enemy, and of course had to change them.

This was on the 28th and a fearful thunderstorm came up. It seemed as if the clouds were almost in the tree-tops, and peal after peal of thunder rolled and rumbled. Lightning flashed, adding additional gloom to the situation.

Two soldiers in a brigade near us were standing by a tree. One of them said while it was thundering: "That's the kind of cannonading that don't hurt anyone." Scarcely had the words been said when lightning struck the tree and killed both of them, and the shock was felt by our entire brigade.

'Brigade, hell, I have none'

Private Silas Crowell
Company I
93rd Ohio Volunteer Infantry

On May 27 we were ordered to the front, but our movements were slow. We moved to the left toward Laurel Hill to press the rebel right and marched about two and one-half miles before we found any heavy forces. This was about 3 p.m. We were ordered to charge a hill, our brigade in the lead.

We got about two-thirds of the way up when we were met with a galling fire that checked us. We could not see any distance before us on account of the underbrush. With the 23rd Kentucky to our left, the 93rd was on the right of the brigade and advanced almost to the rebel line, and was caught in V-shaped works. We maintained the fight until our ammunition was exhausted. Finally, we were relieved by Gibson's brigade. Our regiment lost eight killed and 42 wounded.

After we had come out of the fight I saw Gens. Howard and Hazen sitting on their horses in the woods. A fragment of the several regiments had rallied around a set of colors, and a lieutenant took charge of us. We passed to the right on a blind road and came near the officers, when the lieutenant halted us, stepped forward and saluted.

■ Capt. John B. Irwin, Company C, 124th Ohio, was mortally wounded on May 27 at Pickett's Mill during the charge of Hazen's brigade against the extreme right of the Confederate line. A fellow officer in his regiment, Capt. G.W. Lewis, recalled: "I moved over to the right of the line, and there saw Capt. Irwin sitting up, his body reclining against a small sapling, smoking a pipe, his face as white as the driven snow. I said, 'Captain, are you wounded?' He replied, 'Yes, it is all day with me.' He was wounded in the right groin." Irwin died in a Chattanooga hospital on June 24.

■ Private Samuel Robbins, Company K, 93rd Ohio, poses with his Enfield rifle and bayonet in the position of order arms. Records indicate that Robbins served in the 1st Ohio Infantry at the battle of First Bull Run, before re-enlisting in the 1st Ohio's three-year organization. He later joined the 93rd Ohio and served with this regiment during the campaign. His black felt hat and commercial sack coat were typical uniform garments of Sherman's army.

"General, where is our brigade?" he said. "We wish to report to our regiments."

Gen. Hazen looked at him a moment. The tears began to roll down his cheeks and he said, "Brigade, hell, I have none. But what is left is over there in the woods."

He addressed us kindly and told us to get all the rest we could. I was an eyewitness to this, and know he did shed tears about his brigade on that day.

It was the bugles which caught us that day. The 32nd Indiana had been on the skirmish line and they drilled by bugle. From some prisoners taken we learned that the rebels were sent double-quick from their left to the right to intercept us. And they did, too. There was only a thin line, but the bugles gave our movements away and the rebel line was reformed so strong that we did not get there.

One of the boys of our company, Christian J. Sensenbaugh, was killed near their works, and after the rebels had left three of us went up to find him if we could. He had been slightly wounded at Chickamauga, pretty severely wounded at Mission Ridge by a piece of shell striking him on the top of the head, and he would often say that if hit a third time it would kill him.

We went to the trees that we took shelter behind during the fight, locating the tree he stood behind when shot, and near it found a grave. We did not know if it was his body. One of the boys who had a spade dug down until he came to his head, but we still could not tell whether it was he or not. One of my companions asked if we remembered the scar on his head. We did, and his head was raised high enough and we could see the scar of the second wound. In that way we identified him.

We left a piece of cracker-box board as his headboard with his name cut on it. His remains afterward were taken up and placed in the cemetery at Chattanooga.

'Men awaiting death laugh easily'

1st Lieut. Ambrose G. Bierce
9th Indiana Veteran Volunteer Infantry
Topographical engineer
Hazen's Brigade, IV Corps

To how many having knowledge of the battles of our Civil War does the name Pickett's Mill suggest acts of heroism and devotion performed in scenes of awful carnage to accomplish the impossible?

Buried in the official reports of the victors there are indeed imperfect accounts of the engagement: the vanquished have not thought it expedient to relate it. It is ignored by General Sherman in his memoirs, yet Sherman ordered it. General Howard wrote an account of the campaign of which it was an incident, and dismissed it in a single sentence; yet General Howard planned it, and it was fought as an isolated and independent action under his eye. Whether it was so trifling an affair as to justify this inattention let the reader judge.

At nine o'clock on the morning of the 27th Wood's division was withdrawn and replaced by Stanley's. Supported by Johnson's division, it moved at ten o'clock to the left, in the rear of Schofield, a distance of four miles through a forest, and at two o'clock in the afternoon had reached a position where General Howard believed himself free to move in behind the enemy's forces and attack them in the rear, or at least, striking them

■ Confederates of Granbury's brigade fire their first volley into an attacking line of Wood's division, IV Corps, on May 27 at Pickett's Mill. One of the skirmishers in front of Granbury's line, Private Posey Hamilton of Company D, 10th Confederate Cavalry, later recalled: "The enemy seemed to select that thick woods to make the attack, but it proved very detrimental to them, as they could not see our men until they were in about twenty yards of them, when they came into the open, and our men were ready, and there was nothing to do but shoot them down. It was most destructive — the greatest loss of life that I ever witnessed. I doubt that there was ever, at any time during the war, as many men killed by so small a force as we had there that day."

in the flank, crush his way along their line in the direction of its length, throw them into confusion and prepare an easy victory for a supporting attack in front. In selecting General Howard for this bold adventure General Sherman was doubtless not unmindful of Chancellorsville, where Stonewall Jackson had executed a similar maneuver for Howard's instruction. Experience is a normal school: it teaches how to teach.

The attack, it was understood, was to be made in column of brigades, Hazen's brigade of Wood's division leading. That such was at least Hazen's understanding I learned from his own lips during the movement, as I was an officer of his staff. But after a march of less than a mile an hour and a further delay of three hours at the end of it to acquaint the enemy of our intention to surprise him, our single shrunken brigade of fifteen hundred men was sent forward without support to double up the army of General Johnston. "We will put in Hazen and see what success he has." In these words of General Wood to General Howard we were first apprised of the true nature of the distinction about to be conferred upon us.

That, then, was the situation: a weak brigade of fifteen hundred men, with masses of idle troops behind in the character of audience, waiting for the word to march a quarter-mile up hill through almost impassable tangles of underwood, along and across precipitous ravines, and attack breastworks constructed at leisure and manned with two divisions of troops as good as themselves. True, we did not know all this, but if any man on that ground besides Wood and Howard expected a "walkover" his must have been a singularly hopeful disposition.

As topographical engineer it had been my duty to make a hasty examination of the ground in front. In doing so I had pushed far enough forward through the forest to hear distinctly the murmur of the enemy awaiting us, and this had been duly reported; but from our lines nothing could be

■ 1st Lieut. Ambrose Gwinett Bierce of Company C, 9th Indiana, served as topographical officer on Hazen's staff during the campaign, until severely wounded near Kennesaw Mountain on June 23 — the day before his 22nd birthday. Hazen had sent Bierce to direct the advance of his brigade's skirmish line. "While engaged in this duty, Lieut. Bierce was shot in the head by a musket ball," Hazen later wrote, "which caused a very dangerous and complicated wound, the ball remaining within the head from which it was removed sometime afterwards." Bierce recovered sufficiently to return to duty three months later. After the war he became a well known author and journalist, especially while writing for William Randolph Hearst's San Francisco *Examiner,* where he was dubbed "the literary dictator of the Pacific Coast." By 1913, however, Bierce became depressed as his reputation and finances waned. In a letter to friends shortly before mysteriously disappearing in Mexico, he wrote: "Goodbye; if you hear of my being stood up against a Mexican stone wall and shot to rags please know that I think it a pretty good way to depart this life. It beats old age, disease or falling down the cellar stairs. To be a Gringo in Mexico — ah, that is euthanasia!"

heard but the wind among the trees and the songs of birds. Someone said it was a pity to frighten them, but there would necessarily be more or less noise. We laughed at that: men awaiting death on the battlefield laugh easily, though not infectiously.

The brigade was formed in four battalions, two in front and two in rear. This gave us a front of about two hundred yards.

We moved forward. In less than one minute the trim battalions had become simply a swarm of men struggling through the undergrowth of the forest, pushing and crowding. The front was irregularly serrated, the strongest and bravest in advance, the others following in fan-like formations, variable and inconstant, ever defining themselves anew. For the first two hundred yards our course lay along the left bank of a small creek in a deep ravine, our left battalions sweeping along its steep slope. Then we came to the fork of the ravine. A part of us crossed below, the rest above, passing over both branches, the regiments inextricably intermingled, rendering all military formation impossible. The color-bearers kept well to the front with their flags, closely furled, aslant backward over their shoulders. Displayed, they would have been torn to rags by the boughs of the trees. Horses were all sent to the rear; the general and staff and all the field officers toiled along on foot as best they could. "We shall halt and form when we get out of this," said an aide-de-camp.

Suddenly there was a ringing rattle of musketry, the familiar hissing of bullets, and before us the interspaces of the forest were all blue with smoke. Hoarse, fierce yells broke out of a thousand throats. The forward fringe of brave and hardy assailants was arrested in its mutable extensions; the edge of our swarm grew dense and clearly defined as the foremost halted, and the rest pressed forward to align themselves beside them, all firing.

The uproar was deafening; the air was sibilant with streams and sheets of missiles. In the steady, unvarying roar of small-arms the frequent shock of the cannon was rather felt than heard, but the gusts of grape which they blew into that populous wood were audible enough, screaming among the trees and cracking against their stems and branches. We had, of course, no artillery to reply.

Our brave color-bearers were now all in the forefront of battle in the open, for the enemy had cleared a space in front of his breastworks. They held the colors erect, shook out their glories, waved them forward and back to keep them spread, for there was no wind. From where I stood, at the right of the line — we had "halted and formed," indeed — I could see six of our flags at one time. Occasionally one would go down, only to be instantly lifted by other hands.

Early in my military experience I used to ask myself how it was that brave troops could retreat while still their courage was high. As long as a man is not disabled he can go forward; can it be anything but fear that makes him stop and finally retire? Are there signs by which he can infallibly know the struggle to be hopeless?

In this engagement, as in others, my doubts were answered as to the fact; the explanation is still obscure. In many instances which have come under my observation, when hostile lines of infantry engage at close range and assailants afterward retire, there was a "dead-line" beyond which no man advanced but to fall. Not a soul of them ever reached the enemy's front to be bayoneted or captured. It was a matter of the difference of three or four paces — too small a distance to affect the accuracy of aim. In these affairs no aim is taken at individual antagonists; the soldier delivers his fire at the thickest mass in his front. The fire is, of course, as deadly at twenty paces as at fifteen; at fifteen as at ten. Nevertheless, there is the "dead-line," with its well-defined edge of corpses — those of the bravest. Where both lines are fighting without cover — as in a charge met by a counter-charge — each has its "dead-line," and between the two is a clear space — neutral ground, devoid of dead, for the living cannot reach it to fall there.

I observed this phenomenon at Pickett's Mill. Standing at the right of the line I had an unobstructed view of the narrow, open space across which the two lines fought. It was dim with smoke, but not greatly obscured; the smoke rose and spread in sheets among the branches of the trees. Most of our men fought kneeling as they fired, many of them behind trees, stones and whatever cover they could get, but there were considerable groups that stood.

Occasionally one of these groups, which had endured the storm of missiles for moments without perceptible reduction, would push forward, moved by a common despair, and wholly detach itself from the line. In a second every man of the group would be down. There had been no visible movement of the enemy, no audible change in the awful, even roar of the firing — yet all were down. Frequently the dim figure of an individual soldier would be seen to spring away from his comrades, advancing alone toward that fateful interspace, with leveled bayonet. He got no farther than the farthest of his predecessors. Of the "hundreds of corpses within twenty paces of the Confederate line," I venture to say that a third were within fifteen paces, and not one within ten.

It is the perception — perhaps unconscious — of this inexplicable phenomenon that causes the still unharmed, still vigorous and still courageous soldier to retire without having come into actual contact with his foe. He sees, or feels, that he *cannot*. His bayonet is a useless weapon for slaughter; its purpose is a moral one. Its mandate exhausted, he sheathes it and trusts to the bullet. That failing, he retreats. He has done all that he could do with such appliances as he has.

No command to fall back was given, none could have been heard. Man by man, the survivors withdrew at will, sifting through the trees into the cover of the ravines, among the wounded who could drag themselves back; among the skulkers whom nothing could have dragged forward.

The left of our short line had fought at the corner of a cornfield, the fence along the right side of which was parallel to the direction of our retreat. As the disorganized groups fell back along this fence on the wooded side, they were attacked by a flanking force of the enemy moving through the field in a direction nearly parallel with what had been our front.

I had been sent by General Hazen to that point and arrived in time to witness this formidable movement. But already our retreating men, in obedience to their officers, their courage and their instinct of self-preservation, had formed along the fence and opened fire. The apparently slight advantage of the imperfect cover and the open range worked its customary miracle: the assault, a singularly spiritless one, considering the advantages it promised and that it was made by an organized and victorious force against a broken and retreating one, was checked. The assailants actually retired, and if they afterward renewed the movement they encountered none but our dead and wounded.

The battle, as a battle, was at an end, but there was still some slaughtering that it was possible to incur before nightfall; and as the wreck of our brigade drifted back through the forest we met the brigade (Gibson's) which, had the attack been made in column as it should have been, would

■ Brig. Gen. William B. Hazen commanded a brigade in Wood's division, IV Corps, at Pickett's Mill. Twenty years after the war Hazen wrote about the May 27 battle: "It is scarcely noticed in any of the reports of the Union commanders, and is ignored by Sherman in his memoirs; but it was the most fierce, bloody and persistent assault by our troops in the Atlanta campaign ... The whole fight was terrific and the slaughter immense. Everybody was morose, and found fault with his superior — the men with their captains, the captains with their colonels, and so on all the way up."

■ 1st Lieut. Sylvanus S. Dixon of Company I, 1st Ohio Infantry, was killed during the assault of Hazen's brigade on May 27 at Pickett's Mill. Lt. Col. Robert L. Kimberly, who commanded the consolidated 1st and 41st Ohio regiments, described their charge: "The battalion had advanced hardly a half dozen paces when it was struck by a withering volley of musketry from the thicket in front and from the right. The enemy's fire was sustained in greater severity than would be possible for a single line, and in advancing twenty paces nearly one-third of the battalion was stricken down."

1st Lieut. Ambrose Bierce noted the depleted strength of Hazen's regiments going into the battle: "The brigade was formed in four battalions, two in front and two in rear. The whole command ... consisted of no fewer than nine regiments, reduced by long service to an average of less than two hundred men each. This gave us a front of about two hundred yards."

have been but five minutes behind our heels, with another five minutes behind its own. As it was, just forty-five minutes had elapsed, during which the enemy had destroyed us and was now ready to perform the same kindly office for our successors. Neither Gibson nor the brigade which was sent to his "relief" as tardily as he to ours accomplished, or could have hoped to accomplish, anything whatever.

[The] losses were considerable, including several hundred prisoners taken from a sheltered place whence they did not care to rise and run. The entire loss was about fourteen hundred men, of whom nearly one-half fell killed and wounded in Hazen's brigade in less than thirty minutes of actual fighting. I remember that we were all astonished at the uncommonly large proportion of dead to wounded — a consequence of the uncommonly close range at which most of the fighting was done.

The action took its name from a water-power mill near by. This was on a branch of a stream having, I am sorry to say, the prosaic name of Pumpkin Vine Creek. I have my own reasons for suggesting that the name of that water-course be altered to Sunday-School Run.

'Like hogs rooting for acorns'

Diary of Capt. Samuel Thompson Foster Company H 24th Texas Cavalry (Dismounted)

May 26 This morning we are marched off early and go in the direction of where the heavy firing was yesterday. We could hear the skirmish firing from the time we started and as we march it gets louder and louder, nearer and nearer.

Now we can hear an occasional bullet whistling past like it was on the hunt of someone. We are marched up in rear of the line of battle, and then follow the line to the right for about two miles where we are put in position as a reserve force. We don't know whether we are on the right, left or center of the army, but the heavy firing has been on our left and front all day today.

Some of our boys (our brigade is separated from everybody) go to the breastworks in front of us to see what soldiers are there, because they have no confidence in any of them except the Arkansas troops (who are nicknamed "Josh'es" and whenever a Texan meets an Arkansas soldier, he says, "How are you, Josh?" Or, "where are you going, Josh?" &c. It is all the time Josh ——). We find Georgia troops in our front and our boys tell them that if they run that we will shoot them, and no mistake, and as soon as they find out that the Texans are in their rear they believe we will shoot them sure enough.

May 27 Remained in our place all night, and this morning Gen. Granbury called for a scout of five men to go around the Yankee army. Col. Wilkes ordered me to send them from my company. They started out early in the day and returned in the afternoon, and reported that they were massing their troops on the right of our army and would flank us before night if we did not stop them some way.

Our brigade was moved off toward the right of our line following the line of breastworks until we came to the extreme right of the infantry, and found some dismounted cavalry deployed in the woods still further to the right. We find some Arkansas troops on the end of our line, and we form on to their right making our line that much longer, and it also puts us just where the scouts said the Yanks were going to try to flank our army.

Our position is in a heavy timbered section with chinquapin bushes as an undergrowth. From the end of the army where the breastworks stop we followed a small trail or mill path, and as soon as our brigade got its whole length in this place the command is to halt. At the same instant the cavalry skirmishers came running back to our lines, saying that we had better get away from there for they were coming by the thousand. These cavalrymen had been keeping up a very heavy fire until our arrival, when it got too hot for them.

Col. Wilkes ordered me to deploy my men and go forward in the woods. I soon had them all in position and started to move forward, but found the enemy close up to our line on the right, so I advanced the left of the skirmish line by a right wheel until the skirmish line and our line of battle behind us were in the shape of the letter V, with our right skirmisher nearly on the line of battle and the left skirmisher was 75 yards from the line.

As soon as the skirmish line was put in position our men commenced firing at the enemy skirmishers who were not more than 40 to 50 yards from us. One of my men, Joe Harrison, who never could stop on a line of that kind without seeing the Yanks, ran forward through the brush but came back as fast as he went, saying that they fired a broadside on him, but didn't hit him. He took his place on the skirmish line behind an oak tree about 14 inches in diameter.

The enemy kept advancing through the bushes from tree to tree until they were (some of them) in 30 or 40 feet of our line. I had three as good men as ever fired a gun killed on this skirmish line — W.J. Maddox, T.I. Doran and T.F. Nolan. The two first named were shot through the neck and killed instantly, the last one was shot in the bowels and died about 15 hours after.

When the sun was about an hour high in the evening we were ordered back to the line of battle. And it seems that the enemy's line of battle was advancing when the order came for the skirmishers to fall back. The frolic opened in fine style as soon as we got back into our places — instead of two skirmish lines the two lines of battle open to their fullest extent. No artillery in this fight — nothing but small arms.

Our men have no protection, but they are lying flat on the ground and shooting as fast as they can. This continues until dark when it gradually stops, until it is very dark when everything is very still, so still that the chirp of a cricket could be heard 100 feet away — all hands lying perfectly still, and the enemy not more than 40 feet in front of us.

About 9 o'clock in the night the order from Gen. Granbury is to "Charge in the woods at the sound of the bugle."

Col. Wilkes sent his adjutant to me with an order to deploy my company in front of our regiment and go in advance of the charge. While deploying my company by the right flank, commencing at the left of the regiment and stop one man about every eight or 10 feet, we took some prisoners who had crawled up to eight or 10 feet of our line of battle. We were finally deployed about 10 feet in front of the line of battle waiting for the bugle to sound the charge.

While waiting (all this time none had spoken above a whisper) we could hear the Yanks just in front of us moving among the dead leaves on the ground like hogs rooting for acorns, but not speaking a word above a whisper. To make that charge in the dark, and go in front at that, and knowing that the enemy were just in front of us was the most trying time I experienced during the whole war.

In about an hour from the time we received Gen. Granbury's order to charge, the bugle sounded the charge and we raised a regular Texas yell, or

■ Maj. Gen. Patrick R. Cleburne led a division in Hardee's corps, and was considered by many on both sides to be among the best division commanders of the war. An Irishman by birth and former soldier in the British army, he fought his brigades savagely throughout the Atlanta campaign. After Pickett's Mill he wrote that the attacking Federals of Wood's division "displayed a courage worthy of an honorable cause, pressing in steady throngs within a few paces of our men, frequently exclaiming, 'Ah! Damn you, we have caught you without your logs.' Now, Granbury's men, needing no logs, were awaiting them ... and as they appeared upon the slope slaughtered them with deliberate aim."

■ Brig. Gen. Hiram B. Granbury commanded a brigade of mixed Texas infantry and dismounted cavalry in Cleburne's division throughout the campaign. Cleburne lauded the actions of the Lone Star soldiers at Pickett's Mill, calling the piles of Union dead and wounded in their front the morning after the battle "a silent but sufficient eulogy upon Granbury and his noble Texans." At Franklin on November 30, Cleburne and Granbury were killed within yards of one another just outside the Federal works. After the war Granbury, Texas, was named in honor of the 33-year-old general.

an Indian yell, or perhaps both together, and started forward through the brush so dark we could not see *anything at all.* We commenced to fire as soon as we started and the Yanks turned loose. The flash of their guns would light up the woods like a flash of lightning and by it we could see a line of blue coats just there in front of us, but the noise we made with our mouths was too much for them. They broke, but not before we were among them with our skirmishers. We were so close that one Yank caught one of my men and told him to "fall in quick as Company C was gone already." My man went about 20 steps with them and stopped beside a large tree until we came up to him again, all of which did not occupy as much time as to write this history of it.

As soon as they broke to run we commenced to take prisoners. We were going down hill, still yelling like all the devils from the lower regions had been turned loose, and occasionally a tree lying on the ground would have from five to 20 Yanks lying down behind the log. We kept finding them as we advanced. All they could say was *"don't shoot! don't shoot!"* Finally we got down to the bottom of the hill to a little branch and under the banks were just lots of them. But just here at this little branch we lost trail of the enemy, and our men were badly mixed up.

After calling and some loud talking for a little time, every man fell into his place when Col. Wilkes ordered me to deploy my company on the hill in front of us and hold the ground until daylight, and said the brigade would go back to where the fight began and make breastworks.

As soon as my company was put in position I discovered that we were on the top of a ridge and the enemy, if near, could see us where we could not see them. So I put my men back about 15 or 20 feet so we could skylight to the top of the ridge.

In the course of half an hour we could see the Yanks lighting their camp fires about a mile or more from us, but immediately in front of us. Their camp appeared to be on a hillside facing toward us. So we could see every fire in the whole camp, and there seemed to be a thousand of them.

One of our batteries that had been put in position nearly in our rear on the line of the fight in the evening sent word to me that they were going to shell the enemy's camp, over our heads. Presently, "BOOM" went a shell which burst right in their midst. The artillery kept up the shelling about an hour, at which time there was not a fire to be seen — nowhere.

I walk from one end of my skirmish line to the other all night, and every man stands on his feet and holds his gun in his hands until daylight. As soon as it gets light we see we have been standing among dead Yanks all night and did not know it.

I go out in front of the line and I find under a little pine bush a Yank knapsack with an oil cloth and blanket strapped to it, and in it is a plug of tobacco, needles, thread, pins &c; all of which except the knapsack I appropriate to my own use.

I also find scattered here and there tin cups, tin plates, haversacks with knife and fork, bacon and crackers, coffee, *surenough coffee.* Oh I am rich; crackers, bacon & coffee.

May 28 About sunup this morning we were relieved and ordered back to the brigade. We have to pass over the dead Yanks of the battlefield of yesterday, and here I beheld that which I cannot describe and which I hope never see again. Dead men meet the eye in every direction, and in one place I stopped and counted 50 dead men in a circle of 30 feet of me. Men lying in all sorts of shapes just as they had fallen, and it seems like they have nearly all been shot in the head. A great number of them have their skulls bursted open and their brains running out, quite a number that way.

I have seen many dead men, and seen them wounded and crippled in various ways, have seen their limbs cut off, but I never saw anything before that made me sick like looking at the brains of these men did. I do believe that if a soldier could be made to faint that I would have fainted if I had not passed on and got out of that place as soon as I did. We learn through Col. Wilkes that we killed 703 dead on the ground, and captured near 350 prisoners.

'The spectacle was revolting'

Lt. Col. Columbus Sykes
43rd Mississippi Volunteer Infantry

In line of Battle,
May 27th, 1864.

My Dear Darling,

We left the Etowah river at 10½ o'clock Monday morning last and after a good deal of maneuvering have taken position between Dallas and Atlanta, some three of four miles from the former place. Our line was formed Wednesday evening. We have been offering the enemy [battle] here for three days, but thus far they have not accepted it. On Wednesday evening they made one or two charges on Stewart's division but were handsomely repulsed with considerable loss. Since then there has been nothing but sharpshooting with some artillery firing.

As I write at 5½ o'clock p.m. a pretty sharp skirmish is going on, and the balls occasionally fall thick around us. This is the seventh day we have offered them fair to open battle since our army retired from Dalton — three days at Resaca, one at Cassville and three here — but thus far they have postponed a general engagement by flanking us on the left. Whether they will continue this flanking process or join the battle is more than I can tell, but of one thing I am assured: they can't keep it up much longer and they must fight us sooner or later; and whenever they do I believe God will grant us a signal victory.

Sunday morning, May 29th

We are still in line of battle, sharpshooting constantly along the lines with frequent interludes of heavy artillery firing. Stewart's loss in the fight on Wednesday was about 175 killed and wounded — the enemy's from 400 to 600.

On Friday evening the 27th, the enemy charged Granbury's and Lowrey's brigades of Cleburne's division. I walked over the battlefield in Cleburne's front yesterday evening. The Yankee loss was terrific — the spectacle was revolting — the ground was almost literally covered with their dead. They were lying piled so thick that I could, had I chosen, have walked over a large portion of the field on their mutilated bodies. Their loss in *dead* could not have been scarcely less than 1,000 or 1,200, their entire loss probably about 4,000 including killed and wounded. The official report of the loss in Granbury's brigade was 35 killed and 120 wounded. Their loss was unquestionably and I think without exaggeration 15 or 20 to our one. The disparity is wonderful and can only be attributed to the over-ruling Providence of God.

Our men captured a large number of trinkets, such as daguerreotypes, letters, etc. I read two of the letters: One from a Yankee girl to her lover, complaining of his inconstancy and apparent faithlessness, and averring that if the engagement was ever broken it would not be her fault; the other

■ Lt. Col. Columbus Sykes, 43rd Mississippi. On May 21, he wrote to his wife from his regiment's position on the south side of the Etowah River: "All the people of wealth above us have left their homes, keeping in rear of our army. Many hundreds of thousands, perhaps millions of dollars of property have been destroyed. Magnificent wheat and clover fields have been desolated, fences burned, etc. On yesterday the Railroad bridge, the dirt road bridge and two pontoon bridges across the river here were burned. Such immense destruction of property is painful to witness." This half-plate ambrotype was taken early in the war when Sykes held the rank of captain.

■ Private James A. Stephens, Company B, 7th Florida, participated in the unsuccessful assault of Gen. J.J. Finley's brigade on May 28 near Dallas. Finley, originally colonel of the 6th Florida, was wounded at Resaca and command of the brigade had passed to Col. Robert Bullock, 7th Florida, when the charge was made against the Federal line. The summer's fighting decimated the ranks of the Florida brigade, but Stephens survived and eventually surrendered with Johnston's army on April 26, 1865. Stephens so admired Johnston that he named his first-born son after the general.

from a sister to her brother giving an account of the festivities at home. The faithless lover and the loved brother are now quietly sleeping beneath southern soil.

I have to write as I have time and opportunity to get paper. Don't be uneasy should you not hear from me regularly. I intend to do my full duty and trust to the Kind and Merciful Guardianship of God for safety. I saw Joe, Frank and Eddie night before last. Joe was slightly wounded in the head at Resaca, but not so severely as to disqualify him for duty. I have met a number of acquaintances. All the Sykes have escaped thus far uninjured — Gus, Summerfield, Turner, Gran, Tom, Edgar and I are here.*

Your devoted husband.

'Good for a 60 days' furlough'

Private John K. Duke
Company F
53rd Ohio Veteran Volunteer Infantry

On May 28th about 12 o'clock we were attacked by the rebels all along the line. Immediately in front of the 53rd Ohio there were three lines in the rebel column. It was Finley's brigade of Florida troops. The enemy in our front was of Bate's division and composed principally of Kentucky and Florida troops.

The charge of the Florida brigade, which the 53rd and 37th Ohio resisted and repulsed, was an extremely gallant one. As they ascended into our semi-circle position where we had a galling fire upon their front, right and left flanks, they came with heads bowed down and their hats pulled over their eyes as if to hide from view their inevitable death. Our murderous fire, while we had them in this death-trap, was that of precision. Our aim was deadly. It seemed as though nothing short of utter annihilation could stop them.

They left 600 dead in the semi-circle. The charge was not checked until their line was shot to pieces, and that within 50 feet of our line of fortifications. Their colors were planted in advance of their line. Then it was that Major [Ephraim C.] Dawes wanted to shoot that color-bearer. Our field officers were in a position where they could see the line and were doing what they could to encourage us to hold our own.

Unfortunately, we ran out of ammunition and Col. [Wells S.] Jones ordered a fresh supply, and Capt. [Charles K.] Crumit of Company D got out of the trenches behind the men and went along with a pick, opening the boxes of ammunition while everyone else was largely protected. Col.

* In early January 1865, Sykes rejoined his regiment in Itawamba County, Miss., during Hood's retreat south following the Confederate defeat at the battle of Nashville. He had just left his home in Monroe County, Miss., where he had been to carry the body of his brother, William, who was killed two months before in a skirmish near Decatur, Ala. On the night of January 5, only a few hours after resuming command of the 43rd Mississippi, Sykes ordered the regiment to bivouac in a skirt of woods. Along with a captain and lieutenant of his command, Sykes bedded down under a large, dead oak tree. In the middle of the night the tree's roots gave way and the oak fell with a loud crash, crushing all three officers. An eyewitness, J.L. Collins of the 43rd, later wrote that Sykes was conscious after being pulled from under the tree, but lamented as he writhed in pain: "Oh, why should I have to die this way. If I only could have died in battle, like my brother did, I could willingly die. Oh, it is too bad, too bad. Tell my dear wife and children I loved them to the last." A short while later he died of his injuries.

Jones and Major Dawes were close together, and they realized that it was a fight to the death — there was no retreat in it. To allow the rebels to break the line at that time would have cost us our trains in back of us. We knew they had a great many more men than we had, but we were able to repulse this attack of overwhelming numbers and helped to save that wing of the army. We took a large number of prisoners, among them the colonel commanding the brigade.

In the center of our regiment a road leading to Lost Mountain was left open for future use, our fortifications coming up to either side. Back of this road a short distance was a section of DeGress' 20-pounder Parrott guns, and in the rear of all, our trains. It was the evident intention of our enemy to force their way through this road and capture our trains. In the heat of the fray Major Dawes apprehended that our line might give way at this point and rushed to the road just as their line was within about 50 feet of ours. Their color-bearer was shot down and immediately the colors were caught up by one of the color-guards. The line began to waver.

Just prior to this, Major Dawes received a severe facial wound. The bullet struck the left side of the lower jaw, carried away the body of the inferior maxilla to near the angle. It took off his lower lip, tore the chin so that it hung down, took out all the lower teeth but two and cut his tongue. It was the most horrible looking wound I saw during my entire army service.

While in the ambulance going to the rear for treatment, he wrote in the dust upon the opposite side, "Good for a 60 days' furlough."

Just prior to his receiving this awful wound he was struck in the back of the head by a glancing ball. This, however, was so small in comparison to the other that but little attention was paid to it. As to the nerve of the major, and how he survived this terrible ordeal, the reader may judge.

He underwent several very difficult surgical operations. It was not until near the close of September 1864 that the most difficult and trying operation was performed upon his jaw. Dr. Blackburn performed the operation at the Officers' Hospital in Cincinnati. He was one and a half hours under the surgeon's knife and steadily refused the use of anesthetics.

This was some four months subsequent to his receiving the wound and the jagged pieces had been put together and a sort of chin formed. The flesh was all cut loose, then a gash cut through the cheeks on both sides of the angle of the jaw; slits were then cut parallel with them so as to get a loose strip of flesh an inch wide, which was only attached to the face at the angle of the jaw. These strips were pulled and stretched so as to meet over an artificial underjaw and teeth to form an under lip. The tightening and stretching of these strips caused the upper lip to be pushed out of place and to protrude, so that a gore had to be cut out on each side and sewed up; then the flesh which had been loosened from the chin was put back and trimmed to fit in with the new under lip.

He lay upon the table unbound, obeying every direction of the operator, turning his head as directed until the agony and the loss of blood exhausted him and only a shiver ran through his frame. About the time they were ready to release him from the table, Dr. Blackburn said, "Major, I must finish up with two more stitches."

The major, to whom no voice was left, raised up one finger to plead for only one. His brother who was present, cried, "Dr. Blackburn, don't touch him." Then the major raised up both fingers and the two stitches were taken.

During the operation he came very near strangling with blood in his mouth, and in a spasmodic effort to get his breath threw out his false

■ Major Ephraim Cutler Dawes, 53rd Ohio. These photographs were taken in March 1864, above, and July 1864. The one below shows the effects of a facial wound he received on May 28 near Dallas, when his lower jaw was shattered by a minie ball. The wound ended his active military service and he was discharged August 31. After the war the 53rd Ohio's members voted unanimously to present Dawes with the regiment's national colors. He was the younger brother of Lt. Col. Rufus R. Dawes, 6th Wisconsin, which belonged to the famed Iron Brigade, Army of the Potomac.

■ Col. Charles C. Walcutt, 46th Ohio, commanded a brigade in the 4th Division, XV Corps, during the campaign. On May 28, his brigade found itself in direct line of Hood's assault near Dallas. "Quicker than thought," he reported, "the enemy attacked us in force, and with the greatest vigor and determination. On the right bayonets were fixed to receive the column that was advancing with such numbers and impetuosity that it seemed they must break through my weak line. After severe fighting of one hour and twenty minutes, my men [followed] the retreating enemy with terrific volleys of musketry; 244 dead and wounded rebels were found in my front." The attack cost Walcutt severely as well — three of his regimental commanders were wounded, two mortally. He was promoted to brigadier general on July 30.

teeth and chin which were not replaced, and it was perhaps well they were not. But this made necessary, a month later, another operation of comparatively limited extent.

The terrible wound eventually healed. He regained his speech much to the satisfaction of himself and friends. By simply a casual glance at his face with a full-grown beard, one would scarcely have detected his wound.

'That's another of your Yankee nutmeg tricks'

Corporal John W. Clemson
Company I
46th Ohio Veteran Volunteer Infantry

The 46th Ohio fought all along the Dallas line and, on account of its superior arms, held the key at Dallas in single line on May 28 when the Johnnies charged three lines deep.

While here our lines were advanced until the 2nd Brigade of the 1st Division, XV Corps, had advanced and entrenched, by actual count afterwards, to within 120 steps of the rebel works. The only guard duty we did was to make a detail of three men from each company as camp-guard at night, with instructions to watch very carefully lest the rebels should surprise us while it was dark. We could plainly see the Confederate works during the day, and no man dare raise his head above the works lest it became a target for watchful sharpshooters.

On June 4, Col. Walcutt of the 46th Ohio thought to give the rebs a surprise. He arranged with the other regimental commanders of the brigade for their regiments to give the accustomed "Yankee yell" as the bugles sounded the charge. The Johnnies would think we were charging their works and fall in line, exposing themselves above the works. This would give the 46th a fair chance at them.

Our boys were armed with Spencer rifles — seven-shooters. They were ordered to load and every man be ready to fire at the sound of the bugle and the yelling of the remainder of the brigade.

All was ready; the bugle sounded the charge. The 46th rose from behind its works, gave the Johnnies seven volleys and fell down again without the loss of a man. The Johnnies did not see the point until the Ohioans had killed and wounded many of them. The rebels evacuated this part of the line that evening, and I went over inside of their works and saw many old hats with bullet holes through them, along with many other marks of death.

The rebels, when they saw the trick we had played on them, heaped all kinds of slurs on the men of the 46th. I will give a few of the remarks. We could plainly talk across from line to line.

"You green-eyed Yankees, that's another of your Yankee nutmeg tricks!" shouted one Johnny.

One of the boys of the 46th called over: "Say, Johnny, how many of you are there over there?"

A tall, lean, lank reb yelled back: "Well, I guess there's enough for another killin'."

"Say, Yank, what kind of guns have you-all got over there?" asked another.

"Wind 'em up on Saturday night and they run all week."

"Why are you-all down here fightin' we'uns? We-all ain't mad at you-all," was a call that especially brought us a laugh.

'A yell the devil ought to copyright'

Diary of
Capt. Charles W. Wills
Company G
103rd Illinois Volunteer Infantry

Near Dallas, Ga., May 27, 1864, 8 a.m.

There has been some very heavy fighting on our left this morning, and everywhere along the line. We have been moving in line since 6 o'clock, supporting skirmishers and the 3d Brigade. Have driven the Rebels about three-quarters of a mile. The XIV Corps must have had a severe fight about 6:30. The bullets have whistled pretty thick this a.m.

Skirmish line, 11 a.m. — Osterhaus and Smith (I think), have just had a big fight on our left. At 8:30 I was ordered to take Companies E, K, B and G, deploy them and relieve the 3d Brigade skirmishers. Deployed and moved forward over one-half mile through the very densest brush — couldn't see six feet, expecting every minute to find the 3d Brigade skirmishers, but they had been drawn in, and we were right into the Rebels before we saw them. Three of my company were wounded in an instant and three of K's taken prisoner, but our boys made the Rebels skedaddle, and all of them got away. Twenty-one Rebels came up in rear of Captain Smith and two of his men. Private Benson shot one of them, and Smith roared out for the rest to surrender, which they did. They (the Rebels) said they would not have been taken if the Georgia brigade had not fallen back. I think that is doing pretty well for four companies of our regiment, running a whole brigade. Firing is very heavy all around us.

Twelve thirty p.m. — A chunk of Rebel shell lit 15 feet from me. Lively artillery firing right over head.

Four p.m. — At 2:15, after firing a few shells, the Rebels set up a yell along our whole front. I knew a charge was coming. At 2:30 another yell was much nearer. My men then commenced firing on them, but they came on yelling pretty well, but not as heartily as I have heard. They came jumping along through the brush more then, making the bullets rain among us. I think they could not fly much thicker. My men did nobly, but they were too many for us, and we had to fall back. I heard their officers halloo to them, "to yell and stand steady," and they were right amongst us before we left. Our line of battle checked them and made them run. I lost A. Huffard — killed; Seth Williams — died in two hours; Wm. Gustine — severely wounded; E. Suydam — ditto; S. Hudson — ditto; H. Stearns — slight wound; J.H. Craig — ditto; F. Cary — ditto; W. Roberts — ditto; W.G. Dunblazier — captured.

Seven p.m. — I tell you this was exciting. My men all stood like heroes (save one), and some of them did not fall back when I wanted them to. The bush was so thick that we could hardly get through in any kind of line. Gustine and Suydam were about 20 feet on my left when they were shot, but I couldn't see them. The Rebels were not 15 feet from them. I had 31 men on the line, and nine killed and wounded, and one prisoner, is considerable of a loss. They took six more of Company K prisoners, but three of them got off. I don't think anyone can imagine how exciting such a fracas as that is in thick brush. As quick as our line started the Rebels running, I went back on the ground and found a lot of dead and wounded Rebels. Every prisoner of the 20th Georgia had whiskey in his canteen, and all said they had all issued to them that they wanted. I never saw such a dirty, greasy, set of mortals. They have had no rest since they left Dalton. On account of my skirmishers

■ Capt. Marcus C. Horton, Company D, 104th Ohio, was killed on May 28 near Dallas while walking behind his regiment's breastworks only 60 yards from a Confederate skirmish line. Regimental historian N.A. Pinney later wrote: "Early in the day, as Capt. M.C. Horton was passing along in the rear of the line, a shot from a rebel sharpshooter hit him in the forehead, and he dropped dead without a struggle or a groan. Capt. Horton was one of nature's noblemen, kind and generous to a fault. He was loved by all who knew him, while his uncomplaining endurance of fatigue, hardships and want, and his coolness in scenes of danger and strife marked him as one of the bravest of the brave. A half dozen of Company D carried him to his resting place ..."

■ Capt. Horton's clothing stencil was among his effects sent to relatives in Ravenna, Ohio, after his death. For many families, such mementoes were cherished for decades as reminders of their personal loss.

■ Capt. Charles Wright Wills, 24-year-old commander of Company G, 103rd Illinois, was the youngest captain in his regiment when the campaign began. After 11 days of fighting along the Dallas line, he wrote in his diary on June 5: "The Rebels run last night. Everything gone this morning slick and clean. Our regiment was the first in their works. I was over their works to-day and find three lines, two of them very strong ... My health continues excellent, and I hope it will until this campaign is over. I am making up for some of my easy times soldiering. The Rebels were awful dirty and the smell in their camps dreadful. We got some 25 prisoners in front of our division. I think one more big stand will wind the thing up. This is the first day since May 26th that I have been out of the range of Rebel guns, and hardly an hour of that time that the bullets have not been whistling and thumping around. I tell you it is a strain on a man's nerves, but like everything else that hurts, one feels better when he gets over it."

losing so heavily, we have been relieved from the line, and are now in rifle pits, and are supporting those who relieved us.

May 28, 1864, 9 a.m.

Still in rifle pits. We have been treated to a terrific storm of shells, spherical case and solid shot. The batteries are in plain sight of each other, and the gunners call it a thousand yards between them. I don't think either battery does very fine work, but they make it more than interesting for us. A conical shell from a 12-pound gun passed through a log and struck a Company C man on the leg, only bruising him. Two solid shot fell in my company works, but hurt no one.

Seven p.m. — Talk about fighting, etc., we've seen it this p.m. sure, of all the interesting and exciting times on record this must take the palm. At about 3:45 p.m., a heavy column of Rebels rose from the brush with a yell the devil ought to copyright, broke for and took three guns of the 1st Iowa Battery which were in front of the works (they never should have been placed there); the 6th Iowa boys, without orders, charged the Rebels, retook the battery and drove them back. They came down on our whole line, both ours and the XVI Corps, and for two hours attempted to drive us out. We repulsed them at every point without serious loss to us, but I believe they are at least 3,000 men short. In our brigade Colonel Dickerman, Lieutenant Colonel 6th Iowa commanding, and Major Gilsey, commanding 46th Ohio, are wounded. Besides these I don't think our brigade lost over 80. It was a grand thing. I did not lose a man and only three companies of our regiment lost any. When the musketry was playing the hottest, Logan came dashing up along our line, waved his hat and told the boys to "give them hell, boys." You should have heard them cheer him. It is Hardee's Corps fighting us, and he promised his men a "Chickamauga," but it turned out a "Bull Run" on their part. It is the same corps our regiment fought at Mission Ridge. Our line is very thin along here, but guess we can save it now. I heard a 40th boy get off an oddity this evening; he said: "If they come again, I am going to yell if there's any danger of their taking us, 'Worlds by Nation Right into line Wheel!' and if that don't scare them, I propose going."

May 29, 1864, 4 p.m.

Have been in the rifle pits all day. We're now expecting a charge from the Rebels, that is, our division commander is. I think they will lose an immense sight of men if they attempt it.

Monday, May 30, 1864.

At dark last night I was put in charge of our brigade skirmish line of four companies; by 9:30 I had everything arranged to our notion. About that time the musketry commenced fire on our left and continued for a half hour; it was very heavy. Some three or four pieces of artillery also opened on our side. That thing was repeated eight times during the night, the last fight being just before daylight. When I was down on the right of the line I could hear the Rebels talking about the fight and saying it was a mighty hard one, and "I wonder whether our men or the Yanks are getting the best of it." These night fights are very grand. I understand this fighting occurred between Hooker and the "Johnnies." Attacks were made by each side, repulses easy. I guess from what little I hear there was a good deal more shooting than hitting on both sides. I think it was the intention for us to move to the left last night, but so much fighting prevented it. I don't know when I have been so used up as this morning, and the whole command is not far from the same condition, but a few hours' sleep made me all right again this morning. The Rebels are much more tired than we; they have had no rest since leaving Dalton. One of their wounded, a captain, told me that one of their surgeons told him their loss since leaving Dalton in killed and wounded would amount to 25,000. That's pretty strong, the third of it or 10,000 I could believe. I was relieved at dark to-day from skirmishing duty.

May 31, 1864.

Generals Sherman, McPherson, Logan and Barry visited our position yesterday. Sherman looks very well. Logan smiled and bowed in return to my salute as though he recognized me. During the fight of the 28th I was standing, when he was riding along our lines on the inside of the rifle pits (with a hatful of ammunition), just over my men. He stopped by me and said: "It's all right, damn it, isn't it?" I returned: "It's all right, General." The Rebels were quite busy last night running troops and artillery along our front both ways. Some think they planted a number of guns opposite us. I hear some of the officers talking as though a fight was expected to-day. Their sharpshooters are making it quite warm here this morning; several men have been struck, but none hurt seriously.

Seven p.m. — The Rebels have just finished throwing 126 shells at us, only 19 of which bursted. We expected they would follow it with a charge, but they hardly will attempt it this late. I think we have lost none to-day in the regiment. Their shells hurt no one. Logan was slightly wounded in the arm yesterday. Colonel Dickerman died this morning.

Five miles west of Acworth, June 1, 1864.

At daylight this morning we left our position on the right and moved over here, six or seven miles, and relieved Hooker's XX Corps, which moved around to the left. It was ticklish business moving out from under at least 30 of the enemy's guns, and we did it *very quietly.* They did not suspect it. We are now within 90 yards of the Rebel works, and the shooting is very lively. Only one of our regiment wounded to-day. I would much rather be here than where we were, for there they shot at us square from three sides, and here they can but from one front. This is dense woods and the ground between our works nearly level. There are two lines of works here, 30 yards apart; we occupy the rear works to-day, but will relieve the 6th Iowa to-morrow and take the front. This is the ground that Hooker had his big fight on on the 25th of May. He lost some 2,000 men killed and wounded. The woods are all torn up with canister, shell and shot, and bloody shoes, clothing and accoutrements are thick.

June 2, 1864.

The 40th Illinois returned to-day, and I was right glad to see them back. We have lost no men to-day. The XVII Army Corps is beginning to come in.* We advanced our works last night, commencing a new line in front of our regiment. The Rebels didn't fire at us once, though they might as well killed some one as not. Colonel Wright and ten men picked out the ground and then I took a detail and went to work. By daylight we had enough of a rifle pit to cover 50 men and had the men in it. I tell you it waked them up when our boys opened upon them. This is getting on the Vicksburg order. The troops are in splendid spirits and everything is going on as well as could be wished. I think this thing will be brought to a focus in a few days.

* The XVII Corps, commanded by Maj. Gen. Frank P. Blair Jr. and belonging to McPherson's Army of the Tennessee, had been on veteran furlough in the North. The two divisions of the corps which arrived in the vicinity of Acworth by June 8 amounted to 9,000 men. Another 1,500 were left by Blair at Allatoona as a garrison force.

■ Lt. Col. George W. Wright, 103rd Illinois. When the campaign began the regiment was commanded by Major Asias Willison, who was wounded by a shell and his horse killed on May 13 at Resaca. He was succeeded by Col. Willard Dickerman, who was mortally wounded 15 days later during the Confederate attack of May 28 near Dallas. Wright next assumed command after being relieved at his own request as acting assistant inspector-general of the XV Corps' 4th Division. But he, too, was not destined to lead the regiment for long. On June 27 at Kennesaw Mountain, Wright himself was severely wounded and disabled for the remainder of the war.

We are not to be whipped

Dangerous duty along the skirmish line

During the entire four months of the Atlanta campaign, scarcely a day went by without the crack or pop of a musket or carbine being heard somewhere along the opposing lines. More often than not, these bullets were directed not at massed infantry formations standing or marching in line of battle, but at individual soldiers sheltering behind trees, bushes, rocks and breastworks. "Indian fighting," Sherman called it, and the constant sniping exacted a heavy toll on the men and officers of both sides who came to specialize in service along the skirmish line.

According to one 19th century military writer, skirmishing embraced "watching the movements of the enemy, reconnoitering, beginning and finishing combats, covering retreats, etc.," and the successful skirmisher needed to be "quick of hearing, keen-sighted, light-footed and clear-headed. Much greater skill and valor are required for fighting and advancing in this manner than in combats in close ranks, where the touch of the elbow and the unity of the command sustain the individual."

Despite the dangers, many of the soldiers who were detailed or volunteered for skirmish duty "soon took to skirmishing like ducks to water, naturally," wrote 2nd Lieut. William Wirt Calkins of Company E, 104th Illinois. "They soon found out that there was a big difference between line of battle fighting and skirmishing. In the former, the soldier is part of a machine, and is seldom called upon to exercise his judgment; in the latter his individuality plays a prominent part."

In the same regiment, Sergeant William H. Conrad of Company E recalled an incident of such personal initiative that occurred while he was on the skirmish line near Dallas on May 30:

"After leaving our line of works and going some thirty rods we came to an open field that sloped off gently from the edge of the woods where we were in the direction of the enemy, who lay in the woods on the opposite side. We could advance a little ways without much danger, but the rebels soon had a fair sight of us. In front of the company lay at a short distance a log about twenty inches in diameter. The log lay endways to us. I saw at once that if I could gain it I would have an advanced and safe position against minie balls, so I ran and reached it safely. I found it was about ten feet long and could be moved. I then beckoned Joe Wilson, who was nearest, to come, which he did, and we moved the log around broadside to the foe. William M. Wilson, John Nattinger and John W. Hart next closed in on the log. We then advanced slowly rolling the log before us, keeping close behind it and firing by volley whenever we saw any rebels. They were concealed in the edge of the woods, and it was hard to get sight of them. Charley Ruger, who was one

of the bravest of the brave and was in the line on the left, got sight of a rebel, jumped up and blazed away. He drew their fire and I thought would be killed before he could lie down. This enabled us to know just where the rebels were and we steered our fort toward them, continuing to fire by volley at every chance ..."

Ten days before this, Lt. Col. Lester B. Faulkner of the 136th New York was in command of Col. James Wood Jr.'s skirmishers near Cassville as Wood's brigade marched in line of battle. The Confederate skirmishers were so close to Faulkner's men that they amused themselves by mimicking his shouted orders, calling to the advancing Federal pickets, "Move up a little on the right, move up!"

And two days later near Cartersville, Corporal Joseph Gaskill of Company B, 104th Ohio, wrote of an encounter with Confederate skirmishers along the banks of the Etowah River:

"In the evening our company is detailed for picket duty and form our lines south of the city along the north bank of the river. With my squad we take a position near the river bank at the burning railroad bridge. Soon after dark we hear voices on the opposite side of the river and do a little scouting along the water's edge where we find rebels are placing picket posts along the south bank of the stream. Securing a safe position in an abandoned turn-table pit we cap our muskets and await developments. All is quiet along the line save the low tones of command given by an officer placing his pickets. We wait and listen for some time until the Johnnies probably conclude the 'Yanks are not thar' and grow bold enough to start a small fire near the water's edge. We see them walking about their fire, then send in six shots that brings a howl from some luckless reb and their firebrands are quickly kicked into the water. This volley draws the enemy's fire on us for a short time then all becomes quiet the remainder of the night. No

■ Col. William Grose's brigade of Stanley's division, IV Corps, pauses during skirmish drill on April 27, 1864, near its camp at Blue Springs, Tenn. The brigade consisted of the 59th, 75th, 80th and 84th Illinois, the 9th, 30th and 36th Indiana, and the 77th Pennsylvania — "eight small regiments [that] won't average over 250 men each," wrote 1st Lieut. Chesley A. Mosman of the 59th Illinois. Here, skirmishers of the 36th Indiana are deployed in open order formation in the immediate foreground. Each alternate file is either loading or ready to fire. In their immediate rear is the reserve, offering support. The rest of the regiment is behind the reserve with its colors at center. Except for the color bearers and mounted officers, the entire regiment is kneeling or lying prone in order to minimize casualties. The other seven regiments are massed in lines of battle as if ready to advance behind the skirmishers. Artillery support is provided by one of the division's two batteries, positioned on the brigade's right flank.

■ Capt. Will D. Neal, Company K, 20th Ohio, was killed on picket duty at Kennesaw Mountain on June 26. Neal Post No. 62, Department of Ohio, G.A.R., was named in Neal's honor in his hometown of Sidney.

more fires are built, the rebs probably contenting themselves with a cold lunch."

Another encounter of skirmishers along a river, this time the Chattahoochee, occurred on July 9 when Federal troopers of Col. James P. Brownlow's 1st East Tennessee Cavalry met Confederate pickets in what, perhaps, was one of the most unusual episodes of the campaign. Brig. Gen. Edward M. McCook reported later the same day: "Brownlow performed one of his characteristic feats today. I had ordered a detachment to cross at Cochran's Ford. It was deep, and he took them over naked, nothing but guns, cartridge-boxes and hats. They drove the enemy out of their rifle-pits, captured a non-commissioned officer and 3 men, and the 2 boats on the other side. They would have got more, but the rebels had the advantage in running through the bushes with clothes on. It was certainly one of the funniest sights of the war, and a very successful raid for naked men to make."

In June, as Sherman's three armies slowly pushed toward Johnston's entrenched lines at Kennesaw Mountain, the skirmishers of each side were the first to meet — with varying consequences, as the following five accounts of skirmishing near Kennesaw attest.

"We now occupy a very strong position, with the enemy in our immediate front," wrote Lt. Col. Charles F. Morse, 2nd Massachusetts, on June 9. "Their pickets and ours are on perfectly good terms: the men off duty meet each other between the lines, exchange papers, and barter sugar and coffee for tobacco."

"Our boys, notwithstanding their severe losses, are in the best of spirits, and enjoy the excitements of the picket line as well as ever they did squirrel shooting at home," wrote Major Lewis D. Warner of the 154th New York. "They will sit for hours, peering from behind their tree, log, or rail pile, with their musket cocked and the finger upon the trigger, waiting patiently for some Johnny to expose his cranium (with the same object in view), and then sights his mark and blazes away, and whether the ball comes within an inch or a rod of his aim, it is all the same, he has shot at a rebel, and perhaps has hit him, and perhaps (which is much the more likely) he only caused the butternut to duck his head and then return the fire. Occasionally the pickets, which are generally within hailing distance, will suspend their fire, and hold a short discourse with each other, generally of the blackguard order, and winding up with 'Take care, rebels, or Yank,' when bang goes the musket, and the conference is at an end, and each looks out for his own head."

"(Our) line was established right up to the line of abatis in front of the enemy's works and within clear, short range of their rifles," wrote Sergeant Lewis W. Day of Company E, 101st Ohio. "It was accomplished by deploying two light lines of skirmishers. Each man in the front line was provided with a short block cut from a pine log, which he could readily handle, and each man in the rear line had (some) thick brush, with the stick sharpened so as to be easily thrust into the ground. The first man advanced crawling on his stomach and rolling his log before him, his comrade following with his brush as soon as the designated line was reached. The brush was set up in front of the log to obscure the sight of the enemy's riflemen, and the boys lying prostrate fell to scraping out an intrenchment. Thus three regiments were quickly and firmly established under the very noses of the enemy."

On June 19, duty on the skirmish line nearly cost one Confederate his life. 1st Lieut. Robert M. Collins, 15th Texas Cavalry, later wrote: "About midnight we were put on the move and went into position about sunrise on the great Kennesaw line. (My) company was amongst those put on picket. We marched deployed as skirmishers quite a mile, through a field of growing

oats, and the slow rain that had been falling all night made the trip through this field very much like wading a river ... By eleven o'clock the enemy was pressing us, and they seemed to be getting bolder and more aggressive every day, while we from the effects of so many times giving up lines and falling back were getting more or less out of hope and timid. There fell several hard rains during the day and on some parts of our line the men at times were in water up to their arm-pits. Between these showers a constant firing was kept up, we doing all we could to hold the line, and the enemy trying to press us out. By sunset our lines were only a few paces apart ... About ten o'clock Lieut. J.L. McCracking, commanding Company E, came out with his company to relieve us. I went back some twenty paces in rear of our line to show him how to deploy his company to cover the ground we were on. I pointed with my sword where his right should rest near the big road, and to a stump where his left must extend to; about this time a dark fleecy cloud that had been over the face of the moon passed off and a Federal who was very near our line took aim at me. He was a good shot, as the ball singed my mustache; the shock was so great I came very near falling. Merrett Matthews standing close by insisted that I was shot, declaring he heard the ball strike me. Another instance of narrow escape and I passed along ..."

"It was man against man — equally courageous, equally self-reliant, equally fervent in his endeavor," recalled Musician Fenwick Y. Hedley of Company C, 32nd Illinois. "Rarely did either see more than a half-dozen of his enemy, more frequently but one, often none at all, sometimes only able to locate his position by the puff of smoke from his rifle. Often the skirmishers were obliged to leave shelter before they had 'warmed their holes,' as they expressed it, to make a sudden dash upon the enemy, for the purpose of securing more ground, and sometimes it was their opponents who stirred them out in turn, and made them take a hurried trip to the rear. At times, having located their enemy's position during the day, they would make a midnight dash, noiselessly, without firing a gun, taking the Gray 'in out of the wet,' and bearing him back as a prisoner. Occasionally the Blue would keep his prisoner with him in his rifle-pit until he was relieved and could take him into camp. In such cases the two fraternized most heartily, the Yankee sharing his provisions with the 'Johnny,' and the latter dividing tobacco with his captor; both 'swapping lies' the while, comparing notes as to where they had met before, and what they did upon that occasion, interspersing these reminiscences with highly imaginative prophecies of the outcome of the campaign."

■ Capt. William Henry Chamberlin, commander of Company C, 81st Ohio, was a professional journalist and wrote the history of the regiment. Promoted to major on August 9, 1864, he resigned from the army only five weeks later.

'Spoiling for a fight'

Capt. William Henry Chamberlin
Company C
81st Ohio Veteran Volunteer Infantry

In the western army, the skirmish line was undoubtedly seen at its best during the Atlanta campaign. The relation of the two armies to each other during those hundred days was almost constantly that of entrenched field works confronting each other, with the ever-watchful skirmish lines between.

Nowhere during the war were the elements of a true soldier more fully developed than in the exercise of skill, endurance, ingenuity and audacity by those who were the eyes and ears of the army. It was a place in which a

■ 2nd Lieut. George W. Miller, Company B, 81st Ohio, was in command of the fourth boat to cross the Oostanaula River on May 14 near Lay's Ferry. Confederate rifle fire killed three soldiers in Miller's boat as it made the crossing — Sergeant James Carrothers of Company F, Private John M. Wiley of Company C, and one of the oarsmen. Miller was promoted to first lieutenant on August 9, but he declined to accept. He was mustered out of the army on December 19, 1864.

man literally offered himself to death. Almost every skirmisher was a target, and he was under constant apprehension of a sudden attack or a sharpshooter's bullet. It was a common thing to hear of these fearful enemies perched in some invisible tree-top and picking off our men. Dangerous as the duties were, there were not wanting men ready to volunteer for the place, and a detail for picket duty, which was the name generally given to the skirmish line of guards, was accepted as a matter of course, quite as cheerfully as a detail for any kind of camp duty.

Although the class of soldiers who were "spoiling for a fight" in the early days of the war had been greatly diminished by actual experience in battle, there was no lack of material for the skirmish line in the Atlanta campaign. It was a post of honor, and certainly afforded enough excitement and adventure to make it a favorite duty to those who grew restless under the monotony that reigned where hostile bullets were not flying night and day. Yet the heroes of the skirmish line had no hope of glory before them. Their deeds never were told in army correspondence, nor recorded in official reports, except in such general terms as "our skirmish line was advanced," or "our skirmishers were driven in." There was no credit to company or regiment, nor did the commanding officers often receive notice, unless their names adorned the list of killed or wounded.

It may be fairly claimed that the troops in the National army in the Atlanta campaign very soon acquired a general condition of efficiency that was not known in the earlier campaigns of the war in the West. Perhaps the feeling of isolation, as Sherman pushed farther and farther away from the North, and from his base of supplies, and penetrated farther and farther into the heart of the South, may have called out the best powers of self-reliance and of courageous co-operation among the soldiers, as a natural result of the promptings of the instinct of self-preservation. Whether from mere instinct or from higher causes, it must be admitted that Sherman's army grew stronger and stronger as it forced its way down through Georgia. Its failures were scored only when it attempted impossibilities.

My service in the Atlanta campaign was with the 81st Ohio Regiment, in the Army of the Tennessee, under McPherson. This command began the flanking strategy of that campaign by penetrating Snake Creek Gap, and appearing before Resaca, in Johnston's rear, May 9, 1864. It happened that four companies of the 81st Ohio Regiment were deployed as skirmishers on this first day of those hundred days of fighting, and that the first man killed in the Army of the Tennessee in the Atlanta campaign was Thomas D. Crosley, a skirmisher of Company B, 81st Ohio, who fell that evening, in front of the Confederate works at Resaca.

A few days later, on the 14th of May, while the main contest at Resaca was in progress, the division to which I belonged — the 2nd Division, XVI Corps — was sent far to the right to effect a crossing of the Oostanaula River, at Lay's Ferry. That point was so strongly defended that a lower point was chosen, where Snake Creek empties into the Oostanaula. Canvas boats, capable of bearing 20 men each, were launched in Snake Creek, under cover of a heavy fire by a brigade, and then a skirmish line was called upon to cross the river in these boats and clear away the force occupying the opposite bank, which was covered with trees and afforded excellent protection to the enemy. It was assuredly a hazardous proceeding. Less than a hundred men could be taken across at one time, and they must go in open boats in full view of the sheltered enemy while crossing the narrow stream.

The command of that line devolved upon me, and I am sure I never entered upon a duty with so little hope of being able to report the result. To me it was the open way to Andersonville. The pontoon boats, which consisted of wooden frames, very light but firm, and covered with strong white canvas, were unloaded and put in order. Their appearance as defensive vessels of war was anything but satisfactory to the soldiers who anticipated a chance of being detailed to cross the river in them. The boys called them "canvas ironclads," "muslin ships" and other names not indicative of implicit trust in their defensive qualities. The 7th Iowa Regiment was detailed to perform the laborious task of carrying these boats to the river, or as near it as practicable.

When all was ready the order was given for the first three boats to proceed. Silently the oarsmen from the Pioneer Corps of the Army of the Cumberland dipped their long oars into the muddy waters of Snake Creek and moved the boats toward the river. Not a word is spoken, except a few hurried injunctions from the leading oarsmen to the others to keep time and pull together. As still as death the white boats, with their living cargoes of blue, move on down Snake Creek. They have nearly reached the river when a startling voice from the rear cries out — "halt!" The hindmost two of the boats hear the order and stop, but the foremost does not, and is already out in the river, where to stop or attempt to turn back would be certain death; while to go forward alone would be simply to go deliberately as prisoners.

What shall be done? Col. Adams quickly decided to order forward the other two boats. Obeying the order without questioning why, they sped forward into the river. The first boat was now nearly across, the second had reached the middle of the stream, but the third, on entering the river had struck on a snag! At this juncture the rebels appeared to have first discovered the movement, and plash! plash! into the water came the balls around the third boat. Happily it was easily got adrift, and bending to their oars right gallantly, those sturdy oarsmen sped the little boat like a dart through that gauntlet of death.

Almost simultaneously with the first three boats came the fourth and fifth, bringing the remainder of Companies B and C, 81st Ohio, under Lieuts. Miller and Irion. With a bound and a yell and a volley the skirmishers were quickly in line under cover of the bank. It seems to me now that every man acted as if he had been drilled in that very movement 50 times before. Commands were anticipated, as if the soldiers were mind readers. In the quickest possible time the line was deployed, the men leaped up the bank and the enemy melted away or surrendered. Three of our skirmishers captured a squad of 11, including one captain and two lieutenants. Only one of our little band — Private David Y. Lyttle — found his way to Andersonville. And, in the fourth boat that crossed, Sergeant Crothers and Private John M. Wiley, 81st Ohio, and one of the oarsmen, were instantly killed.

True, the shouts and shots of the remainder of our brigade, on the opposite side of the river, deceived the enemy as to the force that had crossed, or we all could have been easily captured. For some reason the purpose of laying a bridge was postponed until the next day, but Gen. Johnston, the Confederate commander, says that this demonstration having been reported to him as a crossing of the river, caused him to countermand his order for an attack that day with his main force upon Sherman's left, north of Resaca.

Thus the work of a little skirmish line had the effect to change the plans of the Confederate general and to prevent an attack which would have brought on a "battle of the giants," indeed, for the impetuous Hood's corps would have been pitted against the steadfast Thomas and his Army of the Cumberland.

About the same time of this crossing of the Oostanaula, there was another skirmish advance in front of Resaca. It was when Logan's forces made a charge on the enemy's lines. The skirmish line on the right of the charging

■ Capt. William H. Hill, Company A, 81st Ohio, commanded the second wave of pontoon boats to cross the Oostanaula River at the mouth of Snake Creek on May 14. These reinforcements consisted of four companies from the 81st Ohio, two companies of the 66th Illinois and one from the 12th Illinois. During the third week of August, while walking in camp, Hill was hit in the left hand by a chance bullet, rendering him unfit for duty until the spring of 1865.

■ Bugler Emil Smith, Company G, 39th Ohio, posed for this photograph in Cincinnati during veteran furlough early in 1864. The 39th had more re-enlisted veterans — 534 — than any other regiment from Ohio. Smith wears a commercial sack coat with veteran stripes on the sleeves and has adorned his felt hat with the rifleman's trumpet, doubling as a musician's insignia. The bugler's role was indispensable to successful skirmishing when distance and noise factors made spoken or visual commands impractical.

column was ordered to co-operate by as rapid firing as possible, but not to advance. The officer of the day, in command of this line, gave the necessary orders, and went to a commanding position to watch the result of the charge on the left, and to overlook his own line. Judge of his astonishment when he saw a captain and about 20 of his men on the right of his line, who were separated from the others by a thicket, advancing toward the enemy in direct disobedience of orders. Logan's charge was in progress on the left, and the captain and his score of men were wildly pushing their way toward the sound of the hostile guns. Rushing after them, the officer of the day shouted to them to halt, and waved his hat to interpret his meaning. They couldn't hear his command, and, if they saw his hat, they only thought it meant "Go ahead!"

They went ahead, that little band of 20, the officer of the day going with them when he found that he could not stop them, and, on reaching the Confederate entrenched skirmish line, they saw it vacated and the enemy fleeing. Over on the left Logan's charging column had carried the works, and the Confederates could be seen forming for a counter-charge. The position held by this little squad was invaluable as a point from which to deliver a flanking fire on the enemy in such an event; and yet that handful of men could not hold it a minute against a heavy line. In this emergency the officer of the day resorted to deception. He sent the captain to the farther end of the little line, as far away from him as he could, and the two officers began to give orders to imaginary regiments in the boldest tones they could command.

Meantime, word was sent to hasten re-inforcements from the brigade in rear; but before they could arrive, Col. E.F. Noyes, commanding the troops on the right, seeing the situation, sent four companies of the 39th Ohio to strengthen the little band of skirmishers. The officer of the day says those four big companies looked like a whole division, so welcome was their appearance. They arrived in time to deliver their effectual flanking fire upon the enemy in his counter-charge upon Logan.

The captain who pushed his line forward contrary to orders was Capt. P.R. Galloway, and the officer of the day, whose skirmishers disobeyed him and won a victory that day, was Major E.C. Dawes.

The investment of Kennesaw Mountain developed more fully, if possible, the inventive genius of our picket lines. So close were the lines that there was no cover of timber, or of other kind, the skirmishers could only be relieved at night. Yet the men threw up defensive works and made themselves comfortable, even to making coffee when so near to the enemy that its entrancing aroma could reach their envious nostrils. They learned to make defensive works for the protection even of the coffee pot and campfire. And it was a fact, creditable alike to the efficiency and to the humanity of the administration of army affairs, that letters from home were put into the hands of men under the very brow of Kennesaw, where the enemy could be plainly seen above, strengthening the defenses along the rocky side of that famous mountain.

After Kennesaw was abandoned and the race for the Chattahoochee was in progress, it fell to the lot of McPherson's command to confront the enemy south of Marietta, near Ruff's Mills, on the Fourth of July. By that time, every bivouac meant entrenchment, and the enemy was always found likewise behind works. Here it became my duty, as officer of the day for the brigade, to have charge of the skirmish line. It was sent to the front to occupy a ridge, at the edge of a field, on the opposite side of which, across a low depression, the Confederate works were plainly to be seen.

I must be permitted, at this point, to tell something of what was not a skirmish fight, but a successful charge in line upon the enemy's works on my immediate left. At that point Gen. McPherson had decided to make a breach of the enemy's lines, and had ordered out a brigade for the work, but had hesitated, awaiting fuller information. Gen. Sherman happened along, however, and said that that surely was the point for an attack and that that brigade was the proper one to make it.

Speech making is not, as a rule, looked on with favor in the army. This, however, was an unusual occasion. It was the Fourth of July, and the gallant colonel commanding the charging line of two regiments could not resist the temptation to pass along his line and deliver a few remarks. He said, in substance, that these two regiments had been selected to make this charge because this was the best place to hit the enemy and these men were regarded as able to deliver the blow. He reminded them that the day was the Fourth of July; that it was a "mighty" bad day to be beaten; that none of them wanted the word to go home that these Ohio regiments had been whipped on the Fourth of July; "and," said he, "we are not to be whipped. We are going over those works. Fix bayonets, and see that your guns are loaded and capped, but do not let a man fire a shot until we are over their works and can fire into a retreating enemy. When I give the command, let every man follow me."

The two regiments forming the advance of this storming column had been lying for some hours at the edge of a strip of timber with a wide cleared field behind them. They had no skirmishers out for the reason that the enemy's main line of works was too near. They suffered for water because the enemy's guns swept the field behind them, and several men were killed and wounded that afternoon while trying to get water from a stream back of the line. A road ran toward the works, and it separated the two regiments selected to make the charge. There was some protection immediately in their front in a dense undergrowth, but this had been converted by the rebels into a dangerous abatis for a hundred yards in front of their works by being partly cut off at a height of two or three feet, and the tops bent over and interlaced until progress through the tangled obstruction seemed almost impossible. With this picture of the position, it is easy to see that to cross this space in line and without firing a gun was a task not easy for any soldiers, and not possible of accomplishment by raw or undisciplined troops.

When all was ready, the colonel gave the command and led his men on foot, for no horse could carry him through that thicket. The men followed promptly with an enthusiasm and determination befitting the day and the serious work before them. True, some of them went down under the merciless fire poured upon them as soon as they were seen by the enemy, but the mass plunged through the tangled abatis and, with rare coolness, waited a moment to form something of a connected line at the slope of the red earth of the enemy's works, and then, with resounding cheers, mounted the works, emptied their guns in the faces of the enemy, or of so many as remained to receive the volley, and the work was accomplished.

But the colonel in command of the line did not see its final triumph. A Confederate ball had shattered his left ankle, and he was compelled to halt. Steadying himself as best he could by a friendly stump, he soon saw a lieutenant of his command from whom he learned that his orders had been executed to the very letter; that no gun was fired until the works were reached; and that the enemy had gone toward the right. He asked the officer to notify the troops on his right, who were partly hidden by a woods. This brought an order to me to push the picket line forward, and my men had the task of emerging from the cover of a woods, crossing an open, descending field in the face of an entrenched picket line posted at the bottom of the slope, and also of the main line, behind strong works, located along the

■ Private David. D. Kelley, Company G, 39th Ohio, was among 82 enlisted men who fell wounded in the Federal charge at Nickajack Creek on July 4. When discharged on May 2, 1865, Kelley had served in the army three months short of four years.

■ Maj. Gen. Grenville M. Dodge commanded the XVI Corps from the beginning of the campaign until August 19, when he was wounded in the trenches during the siege of Atlanta. Wrote Capt. W.H. Chamberlin of the 81st Ohio: "The general was making, as was his invariable custom, a personal examination of that portion of his lines in front of Gen. Corse's division, accompanied by a single staff officer and one or two orderlies. Not content with the view from the front line, he followed a little trench cut for the purpose to the outer entrenched picket line. Here, while looking through one of the loop-holes, a rebel sent a ball at him, and inflicted an ugly wound upon his forehead and the top of his head. Half an inch lower would have killed him."

rising ground in plain view beyond. So far as I could see, but one man hesitated, and I think that he was more confused than cowardly, for it only required a word to face him in the right direction.

Down through the field our men dashed, not hesitating nor stopping until they reached the enemy's entrenched picket posts, where a halt was called, as it was not the intention to assault the main works. The position of the Confederate skirmishers was so exposed that some of them dared not attempt to return to their own lines, and a dozen or more were captured by our men. My picket line for the remainder of that afternoon enjoyed a more lively Fourth of July din in closer quarters than they ever cared to hear again. The enemy, however, was preparing to move toward the Chattahoochee, and that night stole away from us and left us to follow.

The colonel who led those regiments on that splendid charge on my left was E.F. Noyes, and his command comprised the 27th and 39th Ohio regiments. In supporting distance behind was the remainder of Gen. Fuller's division.

It was said that when Col. Noyes was designated to make the charge, he asked Gen. McPherson if he had a photographer at hand. Being asked why he wanted a photographer, he replied that he was a good deal better looking then than he should be when that charge was ended, and he wanted his picture taken before the charge. Gens. McPherson and Dodge saw him later in the ambulance on his way to the hospital, and asked anxiously if he was badly hurt. "General," said he, "I got their works and" (pointing to his shattered limb) "they got part of mine; but it's the Fourth of July, and I don't care a continental."

The investment of Atlanta from July 22nd until late in August was in the main a gigantic battle of skirmishers. The picket firing never ceased, day or night. Sometimes it was lazy, scattered and weak, and again swelling into volleys like the beginning of a battle, and now and then being followed by the roar of artillery. Every day brought its lists of casualties into the hospitals.

On one of these days a corporal of the 81st Ohio, Daniel Harpster, single-handed, crept out to a picket post where four Confederate soldiers were entrenched. Boldly pretending that he was strongly supported, he captured the squad and actually marched them into our lines.

One of the most distinguished victims of the skirmish-line firing about Atlanta was Gen. Dodge, the commander of the XVI Corps. He went to the front one morning and, desiring to get a good view of the enemy's position, went out to the advance line. While he was peering above the works, a sharpshooter aimed for his head and hit it, plowing a furrow through the scalp above his forehead, and leaving the general apparently dead. It was an exceedingly narrow escape from death, and retired the general from service for several months.

It was a matter of common occurrence for entrenched skirmishers to get such deadly range of the enemy's batteries that the guns were practically silenced. I remember one instance of this, where a single sharpshooter in the night entrenched himself in a cornfield on the Chattahoochee River, and silenced a gun on the opposite shore the next morning.

At the battle of Jonesboro, September 1, 1864, a somewhat peculiar incident occurred. In front of the 2nd Brigade, 2nd Division, XIV Army Corps, a line of skirmishers, consisting of Companies A and H of the 52nd Ohio Regiment, was sent in advance when the attack was to be made. The enemy was on a ridge, with four guns, in front of these skirmishers. The ascent was steep and over open ground. When the artillery fired the smoke hung low and obscured the view. Taking advantage of this, the line advanced rapidly until the smoke cleared away, and then the men fell flat until the next discharge, and so kept on without firing a gun themselves, until they sprang upon the astonished gunners, overpowered them, turned the guns upon the enemy and, being promptly supported, made the capture of Gen. Govan and several hundred of his Arkansas brigade, with eight pieces of artillery.

The Confederate Gen. Lowrey, in his official report, says that three powerful columns of attack converged on Govan's brigade and overpowered him. While this may be true, it does not remove the fact that, without firing a shot, an expert skirmish line of two small companies ascended the slope in front of four of those guns, captured the guns and turned them on the astonished enemy, and then signaled for the supporting troops to come up. Among the men who took part in this skirmish charge was J.C. Michie. He was there wearing the chevrons of a sergeant, and running the imminent risk of being killed as a sergeant, while at the same time he carried in his pocket three commissions: one as major of colored troops, one as captain of United States volunteers, and one as first lieutenant in the 52nd Ohio Regiment. A less impetuous man would possibly have sought a mustering officer before exposing himself to such chances.

The next day, September 2nd, closed the Atlanta campaign. Jonesboro was abandoned and the two armies parted company at Lovejoy's Station.

It is a noteworthy coincidence that the 81st Ohio Regiment, whose men were foremost on the skirmish line at the beginning of the campaign, also sent out skirmishers at this last engagement at Lovejoy's Station, and that this regiment, as it had given the first victim from the Army of the Tennessee in that campaign at Resaca from the skirmish line, also gave the last at Lovejoy's Station, in the person of John M. Cowman of Company C, who was wounded on the skirmish line, and died eight days afterward.

■ Col. Edward F. Noyes commanded the 39th Ohio until July 4 when he was wounded near Ruff's Mills on Nickajack Creek. Noyes was known as a strict disciplinarian, and it was said of him that he managed to have a greater number of men present for duty than any other equal regiment in the army. In 1872, he was elected governor of Ohio and served one term. From 1877 to 1881, Noyes held the post of U.S. minister to France.

Shot on the Fourth of July

Col. Edward F. Noyes
39th Ohio Veteran Volunteer Infantry

I will relate here a personal experience in connection with the 4th of July down in front of Atlanta near Nickajack Creek. I remember it perfectly well — have had some occasion to.

Early in the day, in the forenoon, under the command of Gen. McPherson, I got my command in line of battle to make the charge alluded to by my friend Chamberlin. "We have been selected to make this charge because they thought we could do it successfully, if anybody could," I said as I went down the line. "And this is the 4th of July, you know, and a bad day to be licked, and we don't want to be. Just fix your bayonets and load your guns, and don't fire a shot."

After we had lain there for an hour or two, Gen. McPherson came around again with some staff officer. The latter came to me and said that Gen. McPherson had made up his mind that the works could not be successfully carried by assault, and I might withdraw my command.

Now, having had my courage all screwed up and having demanded my photograph, I had to withdraw my command and it was a terrible let-down. I felt as if it was a sort of slur. But a little later Gen. Sherman came around, looked all along the line and said, "Here's the place to strike them, and we are going to do it right away. Just tell the commander of your troops to get them in line again."

Little by little I got my command into position and all fixed up, and at six o'clock and 40 minutes — I remember perfectly well the hour — the bugle

'I never saw such a mixup'

Four days after elements of his division of the XVI Corps punctured the Confederate defenses at Nickajack Creek on July 4, 18-year-old Private Chauncey H. Cooke of Company G, 25th Wisconsin, wrote to his father:

I don't know what to say about the way we passed the 4th of July in Georgia. I put in a part of the time reading your old letters, and dreaming in a way of home ...

On the morning of the 4th of July, after drawing our allotment of rations of hard-tack, sowbelly and coffee our regiment marched out to the front to the support of a battery of four pieces that were tossing shell into the woods just in front of us. Very soon the order came to erect temporary breastworks of rails and logs along the edge of the woods, where we stood to shield us from the bullets that kept us dodging behind trees. Here we were ordered to lie down, if need be, to keep out of the way of the bullets aimed at the boys on the front line some 40 rods in our front. It was terrible to be sitting and lying down out of the way of the bullets with no chance to shoot back, and we knew that the boys in front of us were being mowed down like grass. We could see the wounded being carried back on stretchers and we knew that the dead were left where they fell. While the roar of musketry went on in our front we lay flat on our bellies while we munched our hard-tack and ate our raw pork, and expecting every minute an order to advance. Suddenly the firing almost ceased, then it burst out again with terrific fury. Then followed a lull in the firing and a moment after there came a mighty shout and we knew the rebels were whipped. I don't know if we had any orders to advance, but the boys all jumped to their feet and rushed over to the firing line. It was something to see the dead and wounded. Many of the boys were crying like children, running back and forth without hats or guns and cursing the rebels for killing their comrades. The whole army seemed to be turned into a mob. I never saw such a mixup. If the rebels had known it they could have slaughtered us like sheep. No time to say more. Love to all

Your son,
Chauncey

sounded the charge, and my boys, in accordance with what I had instructed them, followed me. But I did not get very far — not more than a third of the way. My right struck the enemy first and they put a minie ball into my ankle joint. I sat down on the stump of a tree and the boys went on, making a hole through the enemy's line — big enough to put their whole army in full retreat before daylight the next morning.

I sat on the stump and looked around. There was a lieutenant there by the name of Lossee, and I saw him laying the flat of his sword across the back of a fellow as hard as he could. I said, "Lossee, what are you doing?"

He said, "I am teaching this fellow how to make a charge." The fellow had sneaked off and got behind a tree, and Lossee was not in a good humor about it.

I said, "When you get through, come back here." He came back and I asked, "Lossee, have we got the works?"

"Yes."

"What are they doing?" I said.

"They are breaking to the right now."

I said, "Go right away to the command on my right (that was Chamberlin's command) — go right over there and ask them to close up and fill the works that have just been vacated, and when you have done that, come back."

He did so, returned and said to me, "Are you hurt?"

"Yes."

"You ought to get out of here," he said.

"Yes."

"Can you get on my back?"

"Yes."

I put my arms around his neck and tried to raise myself, but I could not stand it and said, "I guess I can't go it, Lossee. You'll have to go up and get two or three of the boys and bring them back here." So he set me down again on the stump and went up to get several of the boys. They shouldered me and took me back. As we were going along we met a lot of officers, Dodge, Fuller and Sherman among them.

They said, "Who is that?"

"That is Col. Noyes."

"Are you badly hurt?" they asked me.

"Well," I said, "I will tell you what I think. I was ordered to take those works and I have taken them. And I shouldn't wonder if they had taken one of mine, but it's the 4th of July and I don't give a copper."

They took me back to a field hospital and I sent for old Dr. Monahan of the 63rd Ohio, who was the best surgeon in our part of the army. I said, "I've got a little job for you. Cut that leg off."

He said, "I don't believe it's as bad as that."

But I said, "Don't bother to take the boot off, but cut it off."

He said, "I can't do it until the reaction takes place."

"What reaction?"

"Let me feel your pulse," he said. He felt my pulse and said, "Why, your pulse is all right."

"I guess so. Now go ahead and do it." The next thing I knew my leg was off and I was all right.

Up to that moment I had never had an unpleasant thought, not a regret in connection with my disaster. But the next morning the army was ordered to go on to the front and, as the officers passed by the tent where I was lying, one after another filed out, shook my hand and bade me goodbye and "God save him." They were going to the front for glory, and I was going to the rear disabled, with no further part in the war and no share in the final victory which awaited us. Then I cried like a child — yes, like a child!

■ 1st Lieut. Silas O. Lossee, Company A, 39th Ohio.

■ Major Arthur B. Monahan, surgeon of the 63rd Ohio.

A forlorn hope

Kennesaw Mountain: Bitter standoff at the 'Gibraltar of Georgia'

On June 17, Private Alexander Quincy Porter of the 22nd Mississippi settled down at the top of Kennesaw Mountain, pulled out his diary and began writing: "I am now seated on the highest peak of this mountain. The lines of both armies can be seen more plainly from the Mountain than from the one I was on yesterday. The scenery from the peak is magnificent beyond describing. It gives one an exalted idea of that supreme being who created all things."

From his viewpoint Porter also could see the drifting smoke from muskets and artillery as Sherman's army slowly moved toward Kennesaw. After the bloody fighting of the "Hell Hole" at New Hope Church and Pickett's Mill, Johnston withdrew from the Dallas area on June 4 and slipped to a new entrenched line in rugged country eight miles below Acworth. This position was defined by a string of hills — Brush and Lost mountains anchoring the Confederate right and left, respectively, with Pine Mountain jutting forward in the center. And two miles behind these loomed the imposing, humpbacked ridge of Kennesaw Mountain towering nearly 700 feet above the landscape at its northern end. Johnston established his headquarters at Marietta.

Heavy rains during the first two and a half weeks of June hampered the Federal pursuit, as did the rough terrain. Sergeant Henry E. Price of Company D, 104th Illinois, wrote on June 13: "I can give you no intelligent account of our movements, for we have marched in every conceivable direction, and toward every point of the compass. We have nothing at all with us in the shape of baggage and officers carry theirs the same as the men."

On the same day, another Illinoisan, Capt. Charles W. Wills of Company G, 103rd Illinois, wrote in his diary: "Everything and everybody thoroughly soaked. Our division moved about one-half mile to the left this p.m. Strategy! We moved out into an open ploughed field. You can imagine the amount of comfort one could enjoy so situated, after two days' constant rain, and the water still coming down in sheets. The field is trodden into a bed of mortar. No one has ventured a guess of the depth of the mud. It is cold enough for fires and overcoats. My finger nails are as blue as if I had the ague. There is one consolation to be drawn from the cold, it stops the 'chigres' from biting us. I would rather have a bushel of fleas and a million mosquitoes on me than a pint of 'chigres' — don't know the orthography — They are a little bit of a red thing — just an atom bigger than nothing; they burrow into the skin and cause an itching that beats the regular 'camp' all hollow. The ants here also have an affinity for human flesh and are continually reconnoitering us. I kill about 200,000 per day. Also knock some 600 worms off of me. Great country this for small vermin. I pick enough entomological specimens off me every day to start a museum."

Later in the week, Confederate Capt. Robert D. Smith wrote in his diary: "We have about 20 hours rain in every twenty-four. The weather is very cold for this season of the year and I find my large log fire in front of my tent very comfortable ... The roads are almost impassable for the mud."

The miserable weather, perhaps, created even more havoc for mounted troops. "The country was so boggy that it was almost impossible to move artillery or cavalry outside of the beaten roads," recalled 2nd Lieut. Samuel B. Barron of Company C, 3rd Texas Cavalry. "During this long rainy spell we rarely slept two nights on the same ground and never had a dry blanket to sleep on. There was a great deal of thunder and lightning, and artillery duels would occur either day or night, and sometimes it was difficult to distinguish between the thunder of heaven and the thunder of cannon and bursting shells."

By June 16 Union pressure forced Johnston to abandon his defenses at Pine and Lost mountains and Gilgal Church. On the 19th, Johnston pulled back to the much more formidable Kennesaw line and the Army of Tennessee dug in. More rain began to fall, swelling creeks and further transforming the roads into soupy, viscid mud, and Sherman's advancing troops slowed to a pace that could only be measured in yards. Finally, the Federals themselves entrenched in front of Kennesaw. The stalemate was to last for the next two weeks.

"We are here, and the rebels are across the run on that monstrous big hill," wrote Sergeant Major George M. Wise, 43rd Ohio, to his brother on June 23. "I have nearly unjointed my neck looking up at them ... Our skirmishers are about 4th way up the mountain but it is so steep and rough that it would be almost impossible to storm it."

The frustration of static warfare tugged at the nerves of Sherman, whose mobile, flanking maneuvers since the campaign began had brought his army to within 20 miles of Atlanta. By June 23, the same day that Sergeant Major Wise doubted Kennesaw could be stormed directly, the now thin-tempered general resurrected the idea of frontally attacking the Confederates, an option he had proposed in a telegram to Washington one week earlier: "I am now inclined to feign on both flanks and assault the center. It may cost us dear, but the results would surpass any attempt to pass around."

In his *Memoirs* Sherman wrote of a meeting with his three army commanders, and that "we all agreed that we could not with prudence stretch out any more, and therefore there was no alternative but to attack 'fortified lines,' a thing carefully avoided up to that time."

Accordingly, with a variety of compelling reasons in his mind for doing so, Sherman ordered the attack for June 27 at 8 a.m.

'To deal a little with humdrum matters'

1st Lieut. John Irwin Kendall
Company B
4th Louisiana Volunteer Infantry
Staff officer, Cantey's Brigade
Walthall's Division, Loring's Corps CSA

The activity of the enemy [on the Kennesaw line] was untiring. Every man in our regiment was now needed continually at his post; surprises or

■ Private John H. Clippinger, Company K, 68th Ohio, was killed June 15 near Big Shanty while on the picket line. One of his comrades, Private Myron B. Loop of Company I, later wrote: "Our line of works lay parallel to a large field, on the opposite side of which the enemy were strongly entrenched. To the left of our regiment was a cluster of young trees and blackberry bushes, at which point the lines of the blue and the gray were only a short distance apart. Here it was our regiment met with its first loss on the Atlanta campaign. In the early part of the day, June 15, our pickets opened fire upon the pickets opposed to us. The enemy responded, when a warm engagement took place, resulting in a number of our regiment being killed or wounded." This photograph of Clippinger was taken during veteran furlough only two months before his death.

■ The imprint of Clippinger's clothing stencil appears on the back of his last known portrait, above.

'Every one of them had the itch'

Private Robert Draughon Patrick of Company A, 4th Louisiana, served as a clerk on the brigade staff of Gen. James Cantey during the campaign. On June 1, Patrick wrote in his journal:

Day before yesterday I mounted a mule and went out in search of something to eat, but I did not meet with much success ...

On my return to camp, I stopped at a house and inquired for almost anything to eat in the way of vegetables, chickens, eggs, etc. The house was full of children of all ages and sizes, but all girls. There were several apparently from 18 to 22, one 14 and another 16 years old. I succeeded in purchasing a dozen eggs for which I paid $5.00.

I saw several young babies and I inquired of the old lady if any of her daughters were married, but she said they were not. "Whose little baby is that?" I asked as one of the younger girls came near me with a child in her arms. "That is my daughter's."

"Why I thought you said just now that your daughters were none of them married."

"They are not married. I have three grandchildren but none of my daughters are married. Can't you see how it is?" she said rather sharply. The light broke in upon me and I became aware that I had unwittingly been treading upon very delicate ground. I told her certainly that I comprehended her, but that she must excuse me for my dullness.

She went on to remark that the country was being ruined, that the war was ruining every one and that her girls were not the only that acted so and that all the girls she knew in this settlement had done just as badly as they. One of the girls aged 14 and the best looking one in the party, I had a notion of paying some little attention to, but before I left I ascertained that every one of them had the itch, and it was not the camp itch which I have seen the soldiers have, but it was the 7-year sort. I concluded that it would be better to forego any pleasure of this kind than it would be to contract this disease.

assaults were always probable. Tribute is due and heartily given to the persistent daring of our foe.

Now it was that the splendid organizing genius of Johnston bore fruit in a way not apt to be noticed or much thought of, namely, in the feeding of his men. The rations of the whole army were cooked for us at the rear, at the wagons some miles behind us, and brought up to us at regular seasons by details. This was done at night. The arrangement had its disadvantages, of course. Mismanagement might occur or unforeseen accidents of war delay results; then we had to go without rations until darkness came again. But no other course would have allowed us to hold our positions as long or fight as freely as we did. We could not cook and fight too; we could not have cooked at all. The exposure unavoidable in such work would have sacrificed every one of us. Darkness was doubly welcome to us, therefore. It not only brought us a pause in the fighting; it brought us food. Corndodgers and bacon, or boiled beef, that was all. Unsifted corn meal, often without salt, the meal was; and the beef was poor and tough, but our appetites were huge, and our spirits rollicking, and we ate, joked and thrived.

We were on Kennesaw Mountain long enough to get mail. I remember that half a dozen letters from home fell to my portion. I will be pardoned, I trust, for digressing for a little while, so as to throw some light on one of the trials of the soldier's life not often thought of; that is, the anxiety of not hearing from home. Our soldiers generally fared fairly well in this respect, but in the latter part of the war, it grew increasingly difficult to get the mail up to the front. Men who hailed from the border states had a much harder time than we did who came from the "Deep South." We had several such unfortunates in our regiment and when they got letters, it was always in the roundabout way; by flag of truce, by blockade runners via Europe, by "grape vine telegraph," i.e., by spies, by the hands of private parties, and through the strangest and most unexpected channels, some of them entirely unknown to the recipients.

Such letters would sometimes pass through three or four hands before getting to the man for whom they were intended. Women were the most active, fearless and ingenious emissaries in getting letters through the enemy's line; especially the southern women in the city of St. Louis, Missouri. Some of them suffered banishment for it.

These letters were looked upon as almost sacred, and the greatest pains and the greatest risks incurred to get them to their destination. Yet, many must have been written that never arrived. Sometimes they were months in reaching the addressee. In the same way, our letters written to points in territory over which the armies were fighting would sometimes be months on the way; sometimes they never got there at all.

In the latter part of the war some amelioration came. A system was agreed upon by which letters were sent through the military authorities, but only one page of a sheet could be written upon. You had to confine yourself to the simplest news, such as that you and your friends were well, etc.; no allusion to a battle or military movement was allowed; every letter was open to inspection.

I find recorded in my memoranda about Kennesaw another item, viz., "Keeping Clean on Kennesaw." Humdrum topic, indeed, this may be now, and humble enough, I confess; just as the other one, of "Letters from Home." But I assure my readers that it was not so then with us, who were at Kennesaw, and I adjure you not to think of us up there as unwashed, unsewed and uncombed.

And this arduous task I attempt as material for history, and for the high heroics of history too. I am not to be intimidated in this, my lofty purpose, by sneers from any quarter as to the topic being "humdrum." I claim that any man who kept clean on Kennesaw was a hero. And, therefore, as the officers of our regiment, as a rule did, in the face of enormous difficulties, make honest and tolerably successful efforts to keep clean, they were heroes, and this victory also ought to be emblazoned on their flag.

Cleanliness was a very lively problem with the Confederate soldier at all times; a problem always, when on the march or in a campaign. So great, indeed, were the difficulties always, that general officers, even corps commanders, were not exempt from them.

But if all this was so, under ordinary circumstances, how much more so in a position like Kennesaw? The majority of us honestly preferred and honestly strove to keep clean. But, cooped up as we were, exposed to the blazing, sweltering sun as we were; and cut off during the daytime, almost completely, from all water, in peril of life every time we went to get it, and all this for three weeks in June and July, the task of keeping clean was, to say the least, a hard one. Our baths were confined, as a rule, to the face. And scant they were at that. For the water was brought in our canteens and poured out drop by drop. Every drop was precious. Sometimes a wash basin was in evidence, more often a bucket. Officers of the artillery could use the heavy leather bucket that always hung under the piece to hold water for swabbing out the gun during an engagement. But we of the infantry had no such fortunate utensil, and many were the expedients which had to be devised to meet our need.

As for towels, I confess to some embarrassment in touching that delicate point. A few handkerchiefs (cotton) still existed, owned by the "dressy" among us; they were passed around. Then there was, and still is, an article of dress generally regarded in civilized countries as indispensable, and white in color (I do not say that ours were), the lower parts of which were found handy for use as a towel. And then sometimes we just "dried off."

One of our greatest inconveniences was as to our teeth. Here water became the problem again. As for toothbrushes, there was no difficulty, for they were plentiful in every clump of woods. The twigs of the hickory or the gum, splintered at one end into a sort of tassel, made good toothbrushes. But it amounted almost to a question of conscience, this matter of wasting precious water indulging in such a refinement as brushing the teeth.

The Fourth Louisiana occupied a line of entrenchments on Big Kennesaw, from which it did not stir during the entire period of its stay at this point. In order to protect the men from exploding artillery fire, we built traverses at frequent intervals, so that the various companies were shut off, more or less, from one another.

In these confined recesses, about sixteen or twenty feet square and open only at the rear, each detachment had its little world filled with comedy and tragedy, fun and pathos, heroism and humdrum monotony. In a word the traverses were full of variety, a variety such as no one could imagine who has no experience of such things. For three weeks these little boxes were our homes. Of course, a sameness ran through every day, a monotony, but it was by no means dull. Variety came, but not in the killing and the wounding and the fighting. As to that, every day was like another. But it came in the details, as to how one was killed or wounded, and as to whom, and as to the shape the fighting would take.

These details had a sort of fascination. There was a fascination in the

■ Brig. Gen. James Cantey commanded a division and a brigade in the Army of Tennessee during the campaign. He was "a charming gentleman who had been, before the war, a planter In Alabama," recalled 1st Lieut. John I. Kendall who served for two months on his staff. Though sick much of the summer of 1864, Cantey possessed a "fine side" to his character, as Kendall related: "It was on the night after the battle of Kennesaw Mountain. We were riding along a corduroy road which the troops had constructed ... to meet some exigency of the service. The logs were fresh, the road was unsteady, and as it was dark and the weather bad, riding was not pleasant. The general was leading. The staff was strung out behind. Suddenly Cantey's horse stumbled and fell. The general shot over his head, and falling full length on the rough road, slid for some distance on his face. The sight was comical, in a sense. But we knew better than to let our merriment be heard. We ran of course to Cantey's assistance. Then we found that it was really no laughing matter. He had suffered considerable injuries to his face, where it had rudely scraped against the bark of the pine logs. He said little, but remounted and rode onwards, attending to his duties as quietly as though nothing had happened, and as though he were suffering no pain, though it was unquestionably great. This sort of thing he could endure with calm, when lack of food or of sleep, or mere fatigue put him out of commission."

■ Federal troops leave Ringgold, Ga., by train for the front. The Western & Atlantic Railroad had to be defended from Confederate cavalry raids and marauding bushwhackers, tying up thousands of Sherman's men in order to protect the vital supply line. After traveling from Nashville to Big Shanty, Capt. Alfred L. Hough wrote to his wife on June 24: "I was on the first train over a bridge just rebuilt, and the next train after has not yet got in, another bridge behind us having been destroyed immediately after we passed ... The guerillas are getting troublesome, but are not strong enough to attack the trains. They only make a dash and destroy the road causing delay; we soon rebuild them and a stronger guard is now being put on which we hope will prevent further trouble."

question who would be next to fall, or how or when the next assault would come. Day followed day, night followed night, pretty much the same, each like the other. The sun might shine, the clouds break in torrents on our heads; it made no difference; the routine of death went on before us. Lulls came, of course, but they were only breathing spells, after which we should fight again. We were isolated from the big world without; we were isolated almost completely. Danger and death were our familiars and to their constant presence we adjusted our habits of body and mind. Indifference to both became the normal temper; the novelty of peril and the fear of it wore away; the habits and customs of men in time of peace and safety resumed, to some extent, their sway.

To kill time when not in action, two comrades would, for instance, play marbles with canister or grape shot on the very spots where others had recently fallen. Undisturbed by the bullets singing overhead every now and then, they would pursue the game with glee. Writing letters home was, of course, a common occupation, and such missives were ordinarily in a cheerful tone. I have seen men place a few pieces of wood over their heads on going out to the rising ground behind us to sleep at night, and fall into slumber serenely, with legs and a good part of the body exposed to the dropping shot. These were ostrich tactics, yet men did this repeatedly.

In our cramped little world a variety of characters developed odd habits and idiosyncracies, sudden glimpses into heart depths or heart secrets, hitherto unsuspected; human nature proved itself the kaleidoscope that it is; men showed sides of their nature never revealed before; noble traits were discovered where least expected; and, then, on the contrary, traits not noble cynically revealed themselves. Crowd men together closely, as we were there, on the same general level of living, for any length of time, and the true man comes out, divested of all the veneer of civilization, and, no matter what his original social state, you see him as he truly is — good, bad, brave, or cowardly.

The enemy's artillery kept us, more or less all the time, in trouble. Shells fell at intervals throughout the day and the night. It was, however, only occasionally that this intermittent fire swelled into a serious bombardment. I recall only four or five times during our tragic weeks on Kennesaw that this was the case. On one of these occasions, however, I had occasion to make my way down from division headquarters to the spot where the regiment was stationed, and a curious incident occurred which I cannot refrain from describing.

I had a time of it. The top of the mountain could not be avoided. I had to go over it. It did not take me very long. As I ran forward, I saw a man coming toward me. Suddenly he jumped behind a big tree, and simultaneously a shell burst on the other side of it, scattering its pieces and contents all round him. What made him do that? A sort of instinct. Who can tell? There are more things in heaven and earth than are dreamt of in Horatio's philosophy. That individual, somehow or other, had a feeling of peculiar and impending peril, and acted on it. Perhaps he heard the voice of that particular shell saying, "Where are you? Where are you? Where are you?" Such, we used to declare in those days, was the voice of the shell, when we sat around the camp fires and talked of our experiences. At last that bombardment ceased. We were able, then, to take a little breath and to count up casualties.

'At the base of Kennesaw Mountain'

Diary of Capt. Oscar L. Jackson Company H 63rd Ohio Veteran Volunteer Infantry

June 12th. Raining most of the time and but little fighting today. My company went on the skirmish line in the evening. We had brisk firing but no casualties. We pass a most disagreeable night, rain, mud and not a wink of sleep.

June 13th. Raining, raining. At 7:00 a.m. my company relieved, and tired, wet and muddy we reach camp. No change in the position of our division.

June 14th. Clear this morning, rain apparently over for the present. Brisk skirmishing at the foot of Kennesaw this forenoon and our Parrotts are feeling for the enemy. **3:00 p.m.** We have a couple of guns out near the skirmish line and they are throwing shot and shell at the rail piles from behind which the rebel skirmishers fire at ours. It is amusing to see a shot or shell upset a rail pile and then the Johnny Greybacks leaving that part of the country in a hurry. It is amusing to us but like the fable of the frogs, death to them, for our skirmishers open fire on them as they are stripped of cover.

Our men claim to be able to read the rebel signals and some of their stations are in plain view. It is said the enemy signaled today that their Gen. Polk was killed and his body was on the cars going through Marietta to Atlanta. **7:00 p.m.** We advanced about one-third of a mile, constructed rifle pits and advanced our skirmish line about in proportion.

June 15th. A beautiful day. We are trying to advance our lines this morning. Heavy cannonading and brisk skirmishing. **3:00 p.m.** Are having spirited fighting along our entire line. In front of our corps, the XVI, we are

■ Capt. Oscar L. Jackson, commander of Company H, 63rd Ohio. Five days after the battle of Kennesaw Mountain he was sent to the rear sick to recuperate in a Marietta hospital. While there he wrote in his journal: "I had some experience with the Sanitary and Christian commissions at Marietta. The abuses of the Sanitary are great but not more than in ordinary business among mortals. I am fully satisfied with the workings of both taken as a whole. One thing I observed is that the prejudice against commanding officers is so great that they scarce fare as well at hospitals as the private soldiers. Everyone takes it for granted that officers have money and friends and if these things are illusionary you fare badly." Twenty months earlier, Jackson awoke in another field hospital after he was severely wounded defending Battery Robinette at Corinth, Miss., on October 4, 1862. He laid on the battlefield for several hours, presumed dead, until his servant "Mose" carried him to the surgeons and demanded treatment.

Death of a general

On June 14 at Pine Mountain, Lt. Gen. Leonidas Polk was killed instantly by a shell fired from a Federal battery. After the war several batteries claimed to have fired the fatal round. The following two accounts, however, clearly show that the 5th Indiana Battery, commanded by 1st Lieut. Alfred Morrison, was responsible for Polk's death.

In his memoirs, Gen. Sherman wrote:

By the 14th the rain slackened ... when I reconnoitered, with a view to make a break in their line between Kennesaw and Pine Mountain. When abreast of Pine Mountain I noticed a rebel battery on its crest, with a continuous line of fresh rifle-trench about half-way down the hill. Our skirmishers were at the time engaged in the woods about the base of this hill between the lines, and I estimated the distance to the battery on the crest at about eight hundred yards.

Near it, in plain view, stood a group of the enemy, evidently observing us with glasses. General Howard, commanding the IV Corps, was near by, and I called his attention to this group, and ordered him to compel it to keep behind its cover. He replied that his orders from General Thomas were to spare artillery ammunition. This was right, according to the general policy, but I explained to him that we must keep up the *morale* of a bold offensive ... and ordered him to cause a battery close by to fire three volleys. I continued to ride down our line, and soon heard, in quick succession, the three volleys. The next division in order was Geary's, and I gave him similar orders. General Polk, in my opinion, was killed by the second volley fired from the first battery referred to.

In a conversation with General Johnston, after the war, he explained that on that day he had ridden in person from Marietta to Pine Mountain, held by Bate's division, and was accompanied by Generals Hardee and Polk. When on Pine Mountain, reconnoitering, quite a group of soldiers, belonging to the battery close by, clustered about him. He noticed the preparations of our battery to fire, and cautioned these men to scatter. They did so, and he likewise hurried behind the parapet, from which he had an equally good view of our position; but General Polk, who was dignified and corpulent, walked back slowly, not wishing to appear too hurried or cautious in the presence of the men, and was struck across the breast by an unexploded shell, which killed him instantly.

Private Ezra E. Ricketts of Company H, 90th Ohio, was a skirmisher at the base of Pine Mountain on June 14. He later recalled:

The 1st Division of the IV Corps was fronting Pine Mountain at that time, and I was on the skirmish line almost directly in front of where Polk was killed. The skirmish line had advanced about half-way across the old field, between the two battle lines at that point, when we were ordered to halt and lie down. This was early in the morning and there was quite a fog, and we could not tell just where the enemy was. About 10 o'clock the fog vanished and we could see the rebel works only a short distance from us. We dared not raise our heads up too far to let the rebs know where we were, and were compelled to hug the ground in the hot sun until dark that night before we could get out of there.

I heard the report from a piece of artillery fired, and shortly afterward another report, which came from the direction of where the 5th Indiana Battery was posted. Polk was not mounted when he was killed; he was behind a pine stump, about 10 inches in diameter and three feet high, with field glasses in his hands, taking observations of our lines. Immediately after the first shot I could see a running to and fro of the rebels about the place where General Polk was, at the pine stump, for a few minutes, and then they all disappeared from that place.

On being relieved that evening we were ordered to report to our companies, and in going back passed the place where the 5th Indiana Battery was in position. Uriah Post, a member of the battery whom I was acquainted with and happened to meet when passing, asked me if I heard that the rebel General Polk was killed that day by a shot fired from one of the Rodman guns of their battery.

Gen. Sherman further wrote:

Late in the evening [I returned] to my headquarters at Big Shanty, where I occupied an abandoned house. In a cotton-field back of that house was our signal-station, on the roof of an old gin-house. The signal officer reported ... that he had translated a signal about noon, from Pine Mountain to Marietta, "Send an ambulance for General Polk's body;" and later in the day another, "Why don't you send an ambulance for General Polk?"

trying to advance our skirmish line across an open field under cover of our artillery. **Later.** Great excitement and cheering. Many of the enemy's skirmishers are deserting and coming in to us. Our troops are in great glee, and as the prisoners our men take are sent to the rear along with the deserters, it makes a fine appearance. We have been very successful in advancing our line with little loss. **4:30 p.m.** Our regiment is moving to the front to support the skirmish line. **Later.** We are lying under a pretty sharp fire of musketry but I find room to eat supper which Mac has brought out to me. **Sunset.** The pioneer corps has made rifle pits for us. **10:20 p.m.** Enemy pressing our lines. Our men spring into their places and everything indicates a general attack. **Later.** Firing slackens. Nothing but a skirmish fight.

June 16th. I am sent on the skirmish line with my own company and Company C of our regiment. **Noon.** We are having spirited fighting. We have rifle pits and logs for protection. The enemy have the same about 70 yards distant and the least exposure of a man brings a shower of balls. The general commanding informs me he thinks it probable our lines will be assaulted soon and cautions me to be on my guard. **Later.** Nary an assault. A company of the 27th Ohio on my left is suffering severely. One commanding officer of that company killed and another wounded. **Sunset.** We are relieved. Have had one man killed in Company C and several slight wounds in the two companies.

I have expended some 6,000 rounds of ammunition and my men did not fire without seeing an enemy. Our boys would raise a hat on a ramrod and it would bring a half dozen balls. With a glass I detected the rebels at the same game. But we have seen them bearing off killed or wounded to such an extent that I feel confident we have punished them severely for what we have suffered. At one time we hung a blanket tightly rolled on the corner of a log building nearby us and a rebel shot a bullet into it. On examining it I found the ball in the blanket, though it had passed through 16 thicknesses of a wool blanket.

Gen. Fuller, commanding 2nd Brigade of our division, came to my lines and spoke a little short about my not conforming to the direction of his skirmish line and also about us shooting too much when no enemy was near enough to make it effective. I was well acquainted with him, and I told him I thought his men on his skirmish line were in a poor position and all the entrenching they had done was at least useless, and our boys had great sport at seeing him, half an hour after leaving us, move his skirmish line to conform in direction with ours.

About the time he was ready to leave me he looked to the front through a crack in the log building behind which we were sheltered, and asked me what rifle pits those were which he saw just a few yards in my front. I told him they were the enemy's and just then some sharpshooters rose out of them and fired, which was the signal for the enemy to open briskly on my entire line, dropping balls thickly all around us. The general found the enemy plenty close for shooting and asked me which way I thought the safest for him to get out of that. I showed him and he started on the run. The incident rather gratified me for the short remark he had made about my men firing and "no enemy" as he had expressed himself at first. On our return to camp when we were relieved in the evening we found that our regiment had constructed deep rifle pits and regular gopher holes for shelter of the officers.

June 17th. The usual skirmishing commenced at daylight. We were aroused once last night by an attack on the skirmish line. We lay in position in and near our rifle pits. The enemy's skirmishers' bullets flew over us. We having had men killed and wounded right among us during the day. No man is safe outside the rifle pits.

■ The death of Lt. Gen. Leonidas Polk has been attributed to fire from at least four different Federal batteries, including Hubert Dilger's famous "Buckskin Battery." However, entries from the diary of 1st Lieut. David H. Chandler of the 5th Indiana Battery provide details that clearly indicate who fired the fatal shell.

Chandler wrote: "June 14th. On line in front of Pine Mountain and were not engaged, both armies watching each other. Lieut. Gen. Polk of the rebel army was killed this day by a shell fired from one of the steel guns in the middle section. Genls. Polk, Hardee & Johnston were standing together when a shell exploded near them, a fragment entering the breast of Polk killing him instantly. Of this there is no doubt as several of our officers were looking through their glasses right at them & prisoners captured next day also told how he was killed. Charles McMillen pulled the lanyard & Frank McCollum sighted the piece."

■ Union infantry of Gen. John W. Geary's 2nd Division, XX Corps, assault Confederate rifle pits on June 15 at Lost Mountain. Fighting here lasted six hours and claimed Federal casualties amounting to 82 officers and men killed, 432 officers and men wounded. Chief Surgeon H. Earnest Goodman of the 2nd Division wrote: "Condition of command: Worn out and exhausted by continual marching, building breastworks, and under one continuous fire from May 25. One continual rain after this battle. More suffering among wounded because of the continual rain and being worn out by reason of previous hardship. Ambulance horses and mules so worn out as to be scarcely able to remove wounded to Acworth."

June 18th, 1864. Raining, raining and the men have no shelter. Skirmish firing goes on as usual. The Army of the Cumberland on our right has had considerable of a fight this forenoon and appears to have advanced its lines considerably. **4:30 p.m.** Benjamin McCarter of my company severely wounded by a musket ball in the groin, said by the surgeon to be mortal. I have my tent fly up a short distance in rear of the rifle pits and a few minutes ago a rifle ball went through one of the pins holding it, not more than a foot and a half from the ground and passed on, fortunately hurting no one.

Later. The surgeon now thinks McCarter's wound not so serious and that he may recover. **Dusk.** My company goes out on the skirmish line. **8:00 p.m.** The rebs are very talkative and our boys and they have great sport joking one another as our rifle pits are in good talking distance. The rebs propose that we do not fire during the night, to which our boys agree and a truce is thus made without the officers saying a word. **Later.** The boys keep up conversation till near midnight and nary a shot fired by either party along our line, although firing continues to the right and left of us.

June 19th, 1864. Break of day. Can get no word of the enemy. There is no firing and they will not talk. We are now doubtful whether they are in their rifle pits or not. We fire on their works and get no reply. I guess they are gone.

Daylight. We find that the enemy has evacuated his first line of works. My company is relieved as skirmishers. I examine the ground we have been fighting over on the skirmish line for the last few days and the effects of the shot exceed anything I have ever seen. I do not see how the rebels stayed in their gopher holes at all. The advance of the Army of the Cumberland on our right yesterday, although with severe fighting, has been the cause of the enemy's falling back, as their works in our front, although very formidable, are now untenable.

1:00 p.m. We have advanced our line and find that the enemy has only left his advance, or first series of works, and still holds Kennesaw Mountain and a contiguous line of heavy fortifications. We pass over ground strongly fortified by breastworks and rifle pits and protected by abatis of felled trees on a ground densely crowded with underbrush, chinckapin, etc. I feel well satisfied that the long lines of heavy works we are passing are not occupied by the enemy and that as we are picking our way through tangled brush no shriek of shot or shell is around us.

3:00 p.m. Our skirmishers and artillery are feeling the enemy and there is heavy fighting near by our right.

Sunset. Our skirmish line has reached the base of Kennesaw Mountain and is having brisk work. The mountain is very high and rugged, surpassing Lookout Mountain in these respects. Its top is frequently among the clouds.

Later. We are making a temporary breastwork of logs and stone. There has been considerable fighting both right and left of us. The railroad runs between our present position and the base of the mountain and just now our men run a locomotive down the track to get water in plain view of the enemy, in fact nearer them than our main line. Our men cheered like they were wild, which, with the impudence of the trick, caused the rebels to try to bring their artillery to bear on the locomotive. The distance was short, but the mountain was so high they could not depress their guns enough and the shot and shell flew away over, but some dropped close enough to alarm us for our safety as we thought they could not possibly shell us from the mountain.

June 20th, 1864. All day long there has been heavy cannonading between the opposing armies. It will average 30 shots per minute. The enemy's batteries are on the mountain far above ours but artillerists understand that this is no advantage, but rather the reverse, as it will shatter a gun carriage to depress a piece much in firing.

Sunset. Heavy musketry firing on our right where the Army of the Cumberland is fighting.

Later. Heavy musketry on our right till near midnight, though, I am thankful to say, on our part of the line all is comparatively quiet. Often as I listened to the battle surging along the lines I expected the storm to strike us, and tired out as we were by many days heavy marching, hard fighting and much exposure with little food, the hours were ones of expectation such as civilians never know.

June 21st. Cloudy and raining. Heavy cannonading and the ever accompanying rattle of musketry. The enemy are busy at their works on the mountain in plain view. It is a little amusing to be able to look at an enemy's cannon at short range and know they can scarce hurt you the least, but it is so severe a test on the guns that they seldom try the experiment of depressing their pieces at us; but it would be sufficient to keep a nervous man uneasy wondering if they might take a notion to train their guns on us, seeing them as we did, dropping shells right onto our camp when they fired at the locomotive on the 19th. Our camp is a good one, supplied with water from a mountain stream flowing over rock and does not get muddy at all.

June 22nd. A beautiful summer morning. Heavy cannonading from the enemy's batteries on the mountain. They fire over us, making some commotion among the teamsters who are in the rear but not hurting any men who are in line. **11:00 p.m.** They open briskly on our skirmish line but no change is made in the position of our troops. They are yet cannonading us heavily but our batteries have replied but little all day.

June 23rd. My company and four others of our regiment were sent out

■ 2nd Lieut. Charles M. Harrison was second in command of Company H, 63rd Ohio, during the fighting at Kennesaw Mountain. He assumed command of the company on July 2 after Capt. Oscar Jackson became ill and was hospitalized. Near Decatur on July 22, while Company H was separated from the regiment, Harrison was credited with making a bayonet charge that helped save a Federal artillery battery and a wagon train from being captured.

■ Col. Frederick A. Bartleson, commander of the 100th Illinois, was killed on June 23 while in charge of a divisional skirmish line near Kennesaw Mountain. Surgeon H.T. Woodruff wrote two days later: "The artillery opened all along the line for several moments, and the lines were advanced, the skirmish line advancing and one brigade moving on to their support. The Colonel was killed soon after the commencement of the advance. The left of the line did not advance as fast as the rest, and the Colonel rode out to spur them up. There was a point there which was plainly in view of the Rebel line, and they fired at everyone passing by the opening. A Rebel ball struck the Colonel on the right side, passing through the body and coming out on the left side. His death was probably instantaneous. I have seen many officers and men killed on the field, but never saw one whose death seemed to strike such a blow to everyone as his did. Generals Newton, Wagner and Harker were nearby and came up. The regiment passed in review by the body to take the last look at one they loved and honored." Bartleson had been the first man from Will County, Ill., to enlist in 1861, and as a major lost his left arm at Shiloh. He was captured at Chickamauga in 1863, and spent the next six months in Libby Prison. Exchanged in March 1864, he rejoined the 100th less than two months before his death.

on the skirmish line of our brigade this morning at 6:30.

9:00 a.m. We are at the base of Kennesaw Mountain and shot and shell of both friend and foe pass over our heads, but so far harmless. There is but little firing on the skirmish line. The thermometer is 88 degrees Fahrenheit in a dense, woody shade. **4:30 p.m.** We have been having for the last half hour a grand artillery duel, or in other words a most terrific cannonading. As the fire of both parties goes directly over us the scene is grand, though not without its dangers as a shell or two have burst so near over us that pieces dropped among us, fortunately without serious results. As I write there is one continued hum and buzz of shot and shell.

Sunset. We have just had quite a muss. The 14th Michigan of the XIV Corps, which joins on the right of our corps (XVI), it seems had instructions to make a feint of assaulting Kennesaw Mountain in order to assist operations on some other part of our line. We had no notice of this and in the dense thicket which here covers the ground they moved too far to the left and got in rear of the videttes of my company and opened a heavy fire of musketry on the mountain and on my men. I was eating supper at the time and supposed the enemy were attacking us. The advance line of my men thought so too, as the balls were flying all around them and hitting them, and the sergeant in charge ordered them to fall back on the reserve where I was, but about the same time, discovering that it came from our own men, hastened to have it stopped.

In doing this, Private Michael Butler, an Irishman I had lately enlisted just from the old sod, acted with great gallantry. He ran right in front of the regiment while it was firing, telling them to stop as they were shooting our men, but they did not stop. He clubbed his musket as if for fight and cursed them loudly for their blundering. About this time Major Parks of the 43rd Ohio, chief of the skirmish line, reached the rear of the Michigan regiment and with difficulty got them to understand what they were doing, and in time to see Private Butler's exploit in front of the regiment with his musket clubbed.

The enemy's skirmishers at the commencement of the firing fell back and joined their main line, but seeing our men fall back they hastened to occupy our rifle pits. Sergeant Selby had by this time reassembled his men. I gave him an officer and some more men and he moved out to his position and drove the enemy back, receiving a wound as he did so on the hand, but not sufficient to disable him until he got his men in position.

Dark. We have all things straightened out now except our temper which is badly riled at the needless blunder which cost us several wounded men and could all have been avoided by simply notifying us of what they were ordered to do.

June 24th, 1864. Base of Kennesaw Mountain, Cobb County, Georgia. A beautiful morning. Had a very quiet time on the skirmish line last night, but little firing. **7:00 a.m.** Relieved by the 35th New Jersey.

Saturday, June 25th, 1864. The usual firing along our lines. I have been toward the right of our grand line of battle, through the Army of the Cumberland, this afternoon. They do not have as high mountains in their front as we do on the left center, but some hills. Their lines are well up to the enemy and well entrenched. There was a fine artillery duel at Baird's division, XIV Army Corps while I was there. The firing was at short range, making the dirt fly. Our men evidently blew up a caisson, making quite an explosion. The IV Army Corps is so close to the enemy's works that they do not have a skirmish line at all. The men in the main line have to keep under cover all the time. I took supper with Lieut. Aplin of the 31st Ohio Infantry and returned to my regiment at sunset.

Dark. Our army is concentrating on the right, and in order to occupy a

Lessons learned from war's experience

In its July 6, 1864, edition, the Xenia (Ohio) *Torch-Light* published for its readers excerpts from the journal of Major Robert P. Findley of the 74th Ohio. Among the entries Findley wrote:

Thursday, June 2, 1864

Soldiers are very restless creatures. When in camp they want to be on the march. When marching they want (to be) in camp. When they build a breastwork for the preservation of their lives they are not satisfied to remain safely behind it, but will insist on exposing themselves above it as a mark for the enemy.

At the outstart of the war, a man who would get behind a log or stone was jeered at by his fellows, and the officer who would have stood behind a tree on the skirmish line, cut off his straps to avoid being a target for sharpshooters, and not have exposed his person by standing upright and in exposed positions, would have been stigmatized as a coward. But now, of the officer or soldier who won't take these precautions, if killed or wounded, the expressions of soldiers are "I don't pity him, he had no business exposing himself unneccesarily."

Some yet have the idea that it will gain them a reputation for bravery, and expose themselves accordingly. It is the duty of an officer to take every precaution to preserve his own life and that of his men, consistent with the performance of his duty, and if an officer will expose himself unneccesarily, he cannot consistently require care on the part of his men.

Tuesday, June 21, 1864

We sat in works all day, in a cramped position, our feet half buried in the mud, the sun now boiling hot, and now a drowning rain falling. Our clothing was literally besmeared with the red clay with which this country abounds. We dare not get out of (our) works, lest a sharpshooter would try his hand on us, and the shells occasionally screamed over us.

■ Major Robert P. Findley

I went back a short distance farther, and began plucking leaves and branches off a fallen tree top with which to make a bed for myself. While thus engaged a shell came along, but passed so far above me that I paid no attention to it. But almost immediately another came, passing very near me, and tearing up the ground in its course. I concluded I didn't want leaves bad enough for that and returned to the tent; threw in my leaves, saw I had not enough to make a bed, and on this account went and sat in the ditch near the breastwork.

Shortly after, a shell bursted either *in* or *above* the tent, knocking it down, blacking it with powder and tearing 44 holes in it, some as large as my hand! Had the former shell not driven me away from gathering branches when it did, I would have gotten enough and had I gotten enough, I would have had my bed made, and would have been occupying it when the latter shell came along, and if so, I would have been in a coffinless grave today, instead of as I am. That shell would have torn me to pieces.

■ Maj. Gen. John M. Schofield commanded the XXIII Corps, known as the Army of the Ohio, the smallest of Sherman's three armies. He was an 1853 West Point graduate in the same class as Gens. James McPherson and John Bell Hood. On June 19, Schofield was ordered to move the XXIII Corps and Hooker's XX Corps to attempt sliding by the Confederate left flank along the Kennesaw line. Three days later the Federals ran into Hood's corps at Kolb's Farm, where Hood impulsively launched an attack against his former classmate. Behind hastily constructed works, Schofield's and Hooker's men poured point-blank artillery and musket fire into the ill-fated division of Gen. Carter Stevenson, which suffered 870 casualties.

longer line our division is stretching out. Our regiment is ordered to relieve a regiment of the XIV Corps. **9:00 p.m.** Have got into position behind heavy breastworks.

June 26th. We remain in position. Not much firing today but our regiment had one man killed by the random shots the enemy are firing.

June 27th. Have orders to stand to arms at 8:00 a.m. with 60 rounds of ammunition and canteens filled. **9:00 a.m.** There has been heavy cannonading all along the line and it is said we are going to assault the enemy's works. **Later.** Heavy musketry to our right and we are trying to advance our skirmish or first line up the rugged sides of the mountain.

Sunset. All is quiet. We succeeded in advancing our line with considerable loss, mostly in the 64th Illinois. The result of the fighting on our right, where it was heavy, is unknown.

'Hit that fellow or he will kill the whole of us'

Sergeant Frank Elliot
Battery M
1st New York Light Artillery

About June 20, 1864, the XX Corps was in motion going south around the west end of Kennesaw, which was yet in possession of Johnston.

We were halted to let some regiments pass us. A sergeant with a small bag on his shoulder stopped and said to me: "I have carried this bag today about as far as I care to. It is a bag of musket balls. Will you put it into one of your guns for my benefit?"

I went to the rear chest of my caisson, raised the lid and he dropped the bag in. We moved on a few miles and halted on a long ridge, which we at once began to fortify, facing the works to the east toward Marietta. This ridge ran parallel with the [Western & Atlantic] railroad, and about two miles from it.

By midnight we had everything in good shape for defense. We moved south two miles on June 21. The IV Corps occupied the works as we moved out. After our removal we seemed to be on the same ridge. By midnight we had as good a line of works as those we had vacated. The right or 1st Division [of the XX Corps] was in heavy timber, while a beautiful valley was east of us reaching north of Kennesaw.

This part of the valley was Kolb's farm. I saw no house, only well-fenced fields and an old cotton gin with a large press to the right of it. This stood well to the other side of the open ground.

On the morning of June 22, Gen. Knipe [commanding a brigade in the 1st Division, XX Corps] sent a line of skirmishers (the 123rd New York) into the timber half a mile away on the other side of the farm. The battery section I belonged to followed after. We came to a ridge. When about half way Gen. Knipe said we had better take position there, which we did, and he went over into the timber with his men to ascertain if any of the enemy were lurking in that vicinity.

He certainly found some, for the firing soon became brisk. He came back and sent 200 men to reinforce his skirmishers. He told us to use one of our guns to put a shot through a designated tree-top, and to continue firing, at intervals of about five minutes, about three feet lower each time until he gave us a signal when we were to use both guns. He disappeared for a short time in the woods, and after our third shot he reappeared and waved a white handkerchief.

We delivered about 10 rounds from each gun. Our men did some lively shooting and some lusty cheering and advanced into the woods. A rebel battery in our front opened up and gave us a few shots. Knipe soon came running back to us and said: "We have driven them back. They are trying to build breastworks. They left one poor devil over there with his leg shot off. I am going to fortify this ridge for an outpost."

His brigade came, and after lining up behind the caissons, stacked arms and went to the front to get all the rails in the vicinity. The four remaining guns of our battery came down and stopped beyond the stacked rifles. Rails at a "right-shoulder shift" were coming by the thousands from the front, left and right, and were being laid in line. The skirmishing became animated for a time. Then followed a lull.

Since the campaign opened Hood's corps had been at the right of the rebel lines, but it was reported that Hood was ambitious to try a tilt with "Hooker's soft-bread Potomac boys." Afterward it was said he had requested and secured from Johnston permission to cross his corps over and try a round with Hooker.

About the time we began to fortify that little ridge Hood's three divisions were massing back of the timber. The ridge we occupied sloped down gently for about 12 rods, then dropped rather abruptly for another 10 yards, then a space of level ground, and beyond an upslope to the woods. The cotton gin stood at the foot of the upgrade.

We had begun using our picks and shovels when I noticed that for about two miles toward Kennesaw our main line of works was covered with Yankees, who seemed to be looking at us. They could see the enemy getting in readiness to pounce upon us, as we could not. The skirmish lasted only for a short time. Then came the "zip, zip, zip" of missiles from the muskets of the men in gray, and a new act was on. Some of our men dropped their rails, others put them in place and within five minutes the men of the brigade had recovered their arms and lined up with us behind the rails.

Our skirmishers now came swarming out of the woods at thrice-quick time, not even looking back. They had no occasion to, for not more than 15 rods behind them came a long line of battle, four ranks deep, at double-quick. The other four guns took position on our right and left and we poured into the advancing rebel ranks a rapid and destructive fire; but a second, then a third line came at 80-pace intervals and all merged at the foot of the hill and opened fire on us.

For 30 minutes the scrap was animated and everybody kept busy. I did not see a Yankee who was not doing his very best. The rebel line was much longer than ours; they overlapped our left but the batteries in the main line opened on them and they were forced back to our left front, and soon a similar movement was tried on our right — with the same result.

Their whole force then moved forward under cover of the hill and the firing slackened. We distinctly heard the order "Fix bayonets!" and we were expecting them to try a rush upon us. From the beginning of our service we had never been budged from any place we tried to hold, and we had no thoughts of being driven then.

The 46th Pennsylvania occupied the space between the sections. The old cotton gin was about 40 rods to the front and somewhat to the right, a two-story building about 25 to 40 feet in size. The left half of the first story was open and occupied by a large horse-power engine. We had a fair view of the west end of the building; a stovepipe hole was visible a few feet below the peak.

I was at the right of my gun when a ball crashed through the top of the head of a man standing at arm's length from me. He was a young fellow

■ Brig. Gen. Joseph F. Knipe, formerly colonel of the 46th Pennsylvania, commanded a brigade in the 1st Division, XX Corps, throughout most of the campaign. He described the battle of Kolb's Farm on June 22 "as spirited a little fight as we have had during the present campaign." He claimed losses in his entire brigade that day at only nine enlisted men killed, 58 officers and other ranks wounded, and 20 missing. A month later, however, Knipe lost nearly 30 percent of his 1,000-man brigade in what he termed the "fair, stand-up fight" at Peachtree Creek.

■ Lt. Col. Calvin H. Walker, 3rd Tennessee, was killed on June 22 in the assault of Gen. Carter Stevenson's division at Kolb's Farm. "The artillery of the enemy," Stevenson wrote, "which was massed in large force and admirably posted, was served with a rapidity and fatal precision which could not be surpassed. My loss was heavy — 807 killed and wounded. Among the killed were Cols. Ed. C. Cook, 32nd Tennessee, and C.H. Walker, 3rd Tennessee, both models of the Southern soldier and gentleman." This photograph of Walker was taken in 1861 when he commanded Company H as a captain. He wears a uniform similar to that of U.S. army regulations during the Mexican War.

about 17. He fell on his back and every muscle seemed strained to its utmost tension. His captain, standing near, assisted by another comrade, raised him to his feet, when he opened his eyes, seized the captain's coat collar with both hands and exclaimed: "Captain, am I killed?"

The captain laughed and replied: "You certainly don't act much like a dead man."

But he was dead, and did not hear the captain's reply.

I saw a gun stuck out of the stovepipe hole mentioned, and another rifle ball shattered the stock of a soldier's musket near me. I stepped to the side of my gunner and requested him to blow a shell through that stovepipe hole. He sighted the piece and fired, but the shot went too high by several feet. Out came the rifle again, and down went Charles Hatch, my No. 5, who was coming up with a round in his leather bag. The shot penetrated his right temple and passed out at the base of the brain. He fell about 15 feet back of the gun's trail. I stepped up to him and tried to arouse him, calling him by name. His eyes were wide open, but they were sightless. I then noticed the wound. Evidently he never knew what hit him.

I then said to the gunner: "You shot too high. You must shoot lower and hit that fellow or he will kill the whole of us."

Two comrades with a stretcher were about to carry Hatch's body away. I told them he was as safe there as anywhere, but to leave the stretcher as we might have use for it.

John Dryer, my No. 1, then said to me: "We are out of water and this sponge is dry and sticky, and I am about out of wind. I wish someone would load a few times for me."

I reached for the sponge staff when a ball struck him in the right breast, passing out at a point between the shoulder blade and the spine.

"Frank, I am shot," he said as I caught him under the arms.

"I know it," I replied.

The stretcher was quickly brought, and as I laid him back on it — the blood gushing out between his fingers as he held his hand over the wound — he said: "Frank, I don't care a damn for the wound if we only lick them."

I swabbed the gun and sent the charge home. As I stepped back a musket ball passed close enough to my left ear to be suggestive. My gunner had lost his head and missed again, and I said to him: "You get around here and load this gun. I can hit him," and we exchanged places.

In my two years' previous service as gunner I had fired or aimed a 10-pounder Parrott for more than 1,500 rounds, and with the old gun could have hit a man's face every time at that short range. This gun was a brass 12-pounder Napoleon, and I had not studied the ranges; consequently, my first shot was three feet too high and passed through the roof. My second shot was as much too low. It hit the main part of the engine, knocking it down and the big drive wheel with it. My next aim was correct, and as I gave the finishing turn to the [elevating] screw the fellow shot again and knocked the muzzle-sight off the piece. I gave the order to fire. The shot seemed to burst against the building, three feet below the pipe hole. For an instant the atmosphere in that vicinity was filled with smoke, splinters, clapboards and building materials. There was a hole in the end of the old gin that a mule and cart could have gone through. Some 20 long-legged rebels who were inside concluded that was a good place to make tracks from, and they started for the woods with much cheering from our side, emphasized by a few shots from the infantry boys.

Sergeant Hood, of the right gun, came over and placed his hand on my

'Leather Breeches'

■ Capt. Hubert Dilger was on extended leave from the army of the Grand Duchy of Baden when he commanded Battery I, 1st Ohio Light Artillery. Known throughout the army as "Old Buckskin" and "Leather Breeches," Dilger often volley-fired his six-gun battery, an unusual practice for artillery at the time. His cool tenacity was legendary, as witnessed on June 26 by Lt. Col. Samuel F. Gray of the 49th Ohio, and 1st Lieut. Alexis Cope, adjutant of the 15th Ohio.

According to Cope, he and Gray "were standing together just to the left of our line of works behind a large tree which sheltered us from the enemy's bullets, whose zzt, zzt, was unusually annoying, when a Captain of Artillery, riding a fine horse, came galloping up. Behind him was his battery, the horses at full run. He quickly unlimbered his guns preparatory to opening fire on the enemy. He placed his guns in line ... and commenced firing by file, giving the signal for the discharge of each piece by clapping his hands. He was a splendid figure as he sat on his horse directing the fire of his guns. This battery fire ... was evidently disconcerting to the enemy, who at first fired over him, but they soon got his range and dismounted one of his guns. One of his lieutenants and a number of his men were wounded, so that he made a detail of men to aid in serving the guns after the battery ranks had been depleted. He continued serving his guns for about an hour until the enemy's batteries in our front were silenced, when he limbered up and galloped off as suddenly as he came. We learned afterward that the officer in command of the battery was Capt. Hubert Dilger. He had become quite noted as a sort of free lance in the artillery service. He wore buckskin trousers and the boys called him 'Leather Breeches.' It was said that he would carefully examine the location of the enemy's batteries, get permission to choose his own method of attack and then rapidly lead his battery to a new position, sometimes outside of our skirmish line, and open out on and silence the enemy's guns almost before they knew of his presence. Gen. Stanley was reported as saying, in his quiet, humorously sarcastic way, that 'he was going to order bayonets for Dilger's guns.' "

shoulder and said: "Can you see those fellows in my front? They have fixed bayonets and are going to charge on us."

"Yes," I replied, "I can see them, but the gun sits too low to be brought to bear on them." He went back to his gun.

We loaded with two charges of canister, 12 pounds each. I then thought of the bag of musket balls — over 20 pounds — and they were added to the charge in the gun, which we ran by hand a rod or so to the front and right. A slight depression in the hill led down to Hood's front lines. We forced the gun up on a small pile of rails and thence had a fine view of about 200 of the enemy. I depressed the muzzle, aiming by guess as the muzzle-sight was off, and fired. The gun backed off that rail pile, and the way the grass and gravel and jumping bullets went down that hill was a caution.

The shot mowed a swath 20 feet wide through the rebel line and over 400, with guns in hand, believing there were more to follow, walked up into our lines and were received with great rejoicing as our prisoners.

At this time the enemy appeared to abandon the project of capturing the hill, and large numbers of men in squads of from 10 to 100 would break cover and make for the timber from whence they had come. The rebel line, however, remained under cover of the hill until night let down her sable curtain, when they withdrew, taking their dead and wounded with them.

■ Private Adam L. Eichelberger served for four years in the Marion (Florida) Light Artillery. A native of South Carolina, Eichelberger amassed a considerable fortune as an orange grower in Florida before the war. By the time of the Atlanta campaign he had donated much of his personal wealth to the Confederacy, including money spent for vitally needed commissary supplies. Substantial rations for Southern troops at the front were scarce in the summer of 1864, and even the relief committees came in for a share of abuse, as 1st Lieut. A.J. Neal of the same battery complained in July: "I have had due inquiries and searches made for the box ... sent me but can hear nothing of it. I suppose it was sent to the Griffin R[elief] Committee and as usual taken by them to feed a lot of stragglers. I have been unable to hear anything of the G.R.C. except that on Wednesday they were giving away everything to a parcel of straggling soldiers who had deserted their posts at the front and were plundering and pilfering all over Atlanta. I am getting to think these relief committees are the greatest humbug about the Army. Their attentions are universally directed at those least deserving. I had rather see one dirty ragged soldier return to the Army to stand by us in the trenches than all the Committees about here."

'Waving their infernal flags'

1st Lieut. Andrew Jackson Neal
Marion Light Artillery
Hardee's Corps CSA

In the Field 2 Miles above Marietta
Marion Light Artillery Hexton's Bat.
June 20 1864

Dear Pa,

Lest you should see some mention of yesterday's work and fear some evil I have thought it best to write at the earliest moment.

I had my battery yesterday on the line between Walker's and French's Divisions and from daybreak to dark was in a heavy fight, though there was no general engagement of the lines. Gen. Johnston had changed the lines the night before on account of the enemy's gaining possession of some hills from which they obtained a cross and enfilade fire on our original position. As soon as the enemy discovered this they charged our skirmishers and drove them in and fortified about a half mile from us.

Emboldened by this, next morning they again drove in our skirmishers and brought up their line at daylight and took possession of our breastworks 300 yards in front of our new works. They came up waving their infernal flags and cheering as if they had captured all Rebeldom. There was a heavy rain falling but I had my men at their guns and hurled defiance at them and burst my shell among them finely. I was never more anxious for anything than for them to charge our works but they would come no closer. Directly they brought up their artillery and attempted to fight me but I had the commanding position and drove them out of sight.

As soon as this was accomplished they planted their batteries in the woods at long range and for the long day we stood their concentrated fire as heavy as they could pour it in. Their line burst out a steady flame of fire all the time but did no harm except keeping us close in the muddy trenches. To give you some idea of how steady and close was the fire, our flag that floated from the parapet had 31 holes through it. The flagstaff not much larger than my thumb was hit seven times. The trees behind us were riddled with balls. On one little sapling I counted about 80 balls on the body. The face of the pieces upper part of axles and wheels have hundreds of marks made by balls shot through the embrasures of our works while our canteens, blankets, etc., just in the rear of the portholes were shot to pieces. It is astonishing that our men escape so lightly but I keep them close. To look one moment over the works was to draw a hundred bullets around your head. I am confident I had my cap shot at a thousand times.

The artillery fire was bad as the Yankee batteries could not see me or the smoke of my guns as the rain poured down all day. I lost only four men out of about 40 as I had sent the others off with my horses and caissons a mile to the rear.

Our loss along the line was light, about 50 captured and 100 killed and wounded. The fire was mostly directed at our position because the field in front was clear and I had my battery flag waving. All the troops had their banners down by orders but I had received none and the flag was up when they planted their striped rag before me and there it should have floated if it had caused everything to have been torn to pieces.

About night I received orders to get away as quickly and quietly as possible and I am certain I never obeyed anything with more cheerfulness and alacrity. That night they would have fortified their artillery in the position from which I drove them so strongly that I could have done nothing with them and they would have ruined me.

Yesterday's works have necessitated a change of line and I fear a fall back, but I think we will stand here for a while at least. They gained no advantage yesterday except position. If Grant had been at the head of this army we would have whipped them, but Sherman will not give us a chance. When he marches his men up to the assault God have mercy on the poor wretches. They out-general us in maneuvering by mere weight of numbers, but we can fight them back at any point they wish to try.

Capt. Perry returned yesterday but is not well. I am in fine health and was never more sanguine and confident of eventual success.*

Your Affectionate Son
A.J. Neal

■ Capt. Alvah S. Skilton, commander of Company I, 57th Ohio. Three and a half weeks after the assault at Kennesaw Mountain, Skilton and some 90 others of his regiment were captured during the battle of Atlanta, including nearly all of Company I. Skilton was sent to Confederate prisons in Macon, Ga., and Charleston and Columbia, S.C. He escaped from Columbia the night of November 9, 1864, and nearly reached Federal lines when he was recaptured on January 18, 1865, near Ducktown, N.C. He then was sent to the Asheville Jail, Salisbury Prison and finally to Libby Prison in Richmond, where he was released on April 2, 1865.

'This will be serious business'

Capt. Alvah Stone Skilton
Company I
57th Ohio Veteran Volunteer Infantry

After the Battle of Resaca we marched down to Acworth where we tarried two or three days, which afforded us an opportunity to burnish our accoutrements and arms, write to our friends, pass resolutions of respect for our fallen comrades and obtain the rest we so much needed before we turned our faces toward grim Kennesaw.

* On August 10, Neal was killed by a Federal sharpshooter in the trenches west of Atlanta. Born in 1837 in Zebulon, Ga., he graduated from the University of Georgia in 1856, then studied law in Lebanon, Tenn., before moving to Florida to practice. When the war began he enlisted as a private in the Marion (Fla.) Light Artillery and served with that unit until his death. The same year he graduated from college, his parents, John and Mary Jane Neal, moved from Zebulon to Atlanta, occupying a newly built home on the southwest corner of Washington and Mitchell streets. They resided there until forced to leave by the approach of the Union army.

■ Col. Americus Vespucius Rice commanded the 57th Ohio at Kennesaw Mountain. While leading the regiment during the June 27 assault, he charged to within 20 yards of the Confederate breastworks when he was severely wounded in the right leg, left foot and forehead. Because of these injuries Rice was unable to rejoin the army until June 23, 1865, by which time he had been promoted to brigadier general — at the age of 29, one of the youngest general officers recruited from civilian life.

When we moved, which was on the 14th day of June, it happened that the 57th Regiment of Ohio Veteran Volunteer Infantry had the advance of the infantry column of the XV Army Corps, and I was detailed to take command of the skirmishers, or flankers. We proceeded without interruption until we arrived at Big Shanty — that place made historic two years earlier by the daring deeds of the Andrews-Mitchell Raiders. At this point I was instructed to place all the men under my command, some five or six companies of the 57th, on the right hand, or west, side of the road. This was done and we felt our way carefully through the brush and trees as far as I deemed it prudent to go without support. I reported the results of our observations to Capt. James Wilson, then permanent officer of the day for our brigade, who sent another regiment to relieve us and ordered me to report to Gen. McPherson in person. This I did.

I found the general and his staff at the little log house at Big Shanty that stood between the wagon road and the railroad. I noticed as I approached the place that a large tree had been turned out by its roots almost in front of the cabin, and that a signal officer had placed a glass in the roots in such a manner as to command a good view of the rebel signal station on the top of Big Kennesaw. Near him sat another officer recording the numbers as taken from the rebel signal flags.

I had finished my report to Gen. McPherson and was about to leave when the officer who had been recording the numbers as called to him by the other watching the rebel flag sprang to his feet and in an excited manner exclaimed: "My God, Gen. Polk has just been killed by a solid shot striking him in the stomach!" Gen. McPherson went to him immediately, saying, "What is that you say?"

With a salute the officer reported what he had said before and added that he had obtained his information by reading the rebel signals. Gen. McPherson asked him for his notes and required him to give him the code key, which the officer did by whispering in his ear. After observing the notes attentively for a time, he returned them to the officer with the remark, "It must be so, if you have the right key, for that is what it reads, but we shall know before night."

I returned to the regiment and before night a portion of the 54th Virginia Regiment was brought in as prisoners and corraborated the signal officer's statement.

The fact that an officer had obtained the key to the rebel code was of great importance, but the secret was very foolishly given away by a newspaper correspondent and was one of the reasons why Gen. Sherman would not permit newspapermen to accompany his army. I was told it required all the influence this particular correspondent could command to prevent his being hanged, which he undoubtedly deserved.

Signal officers are usually very discreet and, of course, would have guarded a secret like that sacredly, and it has always been a query in my mind whether or not the correspondent referred to was not standing in that little group near Gen. McPherson when the signal officer was shocked and surprised into making the exclamation he did.

By the evening of the 26th of June the 57th Regiment found itself in a line of works constructed by the men close up to the foot of Big Kennesaw, on the line occupied by Gen. Giles A. Smith's brigade of the 2nd Division of the XV Army Corps.

It had been an exceedingly hot day and the cooling shade of evening was welcome to the tired soldiers who, after a frugal meal, had gathered in groups behind the strong line of works to smoke their pipes, chat about the day's adventures and talk of the progress and probable outcome of the campaign. Many made conjecture as to what would, or what should, be the next move. Quite a few of the men thought themselves competent to advise the general, all agreeing, however, that it would be a flank movement. The only difference of opinion being whether it would be by the left or the right, each having his own pet theory, little thinking of what was in store for them on the morrow.

The short Southern twilight had suddenly ended and darkness settled down upon the camp, hiding alike under its mantle the rocks, trees and stern implements of war. For a time silence reigned, broken only by the low murmur of the voices of the men as they talked of loved ones at home, dead or absent comrades, or told tales and laugh-provoking jokes to pass the time. And I well remember a group that gathered that night about a camp chest under the shadows of the pines to eat a scanty supper by the light of a single tallow candle.

This little group consisted of Col. A.V. Rice, commanding the 57th Regiment; Lt. Col. S.R. Mott, Adjutant M.M. Newell, Quartermaster T.L. Parker and myself. The meal was nearly finished when an orderly was heard inquiring for Col. Rice. On being directed to him he delivered an envelope, gave a salute and rode away into the darkness.

Col. Rice broke the seal deliberately, read the order and without comment passed it to Col. Mott, who read it and gave it to me. So it was read in silence and passed around the table.

It was an order for the brigade to move silently out of the works and proceed to a designated spot near the gap, or depression, between Big and Little Kennesaw mountains, and at daylight on the 27th form part of a forlorn hope, or storm column, in an endeavor to make a lodgment inside the enemy's works.

In an hour the regiment was underway and marched a greater part of the night before we arrived at the place assigned us, which was in a dense field of underbrush and close up to the enemy's works. Here we laid down for a little rest. It seemed as though I had scarcely fallen asleep when I was awakened by someone shaking me and whispering in my ear that Col. Rice wanted me. I reported at once and found that Gen. Giles Smith had sent an order requiring the three ranking officers of each regiment of the brigade to report at his headquarters. Cols. Rice and Mott, and myself as senior captain, proceeded to report at once and were, I believe, the first to arrive.

Gen. Smith had established his headquarters under a hickory tree with a small, circular grass plot about 40 feet in diameter to the south of it. The plot was surrounded by a dense growth of underbrush. In a short time there were assembled here the three ranking officers from each regiment in the brigade and the members of Gen. Smith's staff. When all had reported Gen. Smith addressed us as follows:

"Gentlemen, I have sent for you to advise you of what is expected of us today and to make such provision as is possible to prevent confusion or misunderstanding.

"This column has been selected as a 'forlorn hope' and we are expected to carry the enemy's works in our front. Should we succeed in doing it, we are to hold them at all hazards for at least 10 minutes when ample reinforcements will be sent to enable us to hold the works.

"Gentlemen, this will be serious business and some of us must go down. I do not say this to frighten you, for I know that is impossible, but to impress on your minds that if I fall you must look to Col. Martin of the 111th Illinois for orders. If he falls you must look to Col. Rice of the 57th Ohio."

Turning to Col. Rice, who stood nearest to him, he said, "Of course, Col. Rice commands his regiment. Should he go down, Col. Mott succeeds and in the event of his falling, Capt. Skilton will assume command."

Gen. Smith addressed the officers of each regiment in like manner, call-

■ Brig. Gen. Giles A. Smith commanded the 1st Brigade, 2nd Division (led by his brother, Brig. Gen. Morgan L. Smith), XV Corps, at Kennesaw Mountain. "The ground over which my line of battle advanced proved even worse than was anticipated," he wrote one day after the assault. "A part of the way was low swampy ground, and so densely covered with underbrush as to compel the men to crawl almost on their hands and knees through the tangled vines ... (they) moved gallantly up the ascent, making their way independently as best they could over all obstructions, some nearly gaining the works, but only to be shot down as they arrived." On July 21, Smith was given command of the 4th Division, XVII Corps, and brevetted major general on September 1. On November 24, 1865, he was advanced to the full rank of major general of volunteers, the last such appointment on the basis of seniority made in the Civil War.

■ Lt. Col. John E. Maddux, 116th Illinois, was provost marshal on the division staff of Brig. Gen. Morgan L. Smith, XV Corps, on June 27. While Smith and members of his staff were advancing up a slope near Kennesaw Mountain, "a terrible thud was heard, and all turned to see who had been hit," recalled a member of the 47th Ohio. "At the same instant, Col. Maddux, pale as a corpse, cried out, 'Oh, Gen. Smith, I'm killed, I'm killed!' The general answered, 'Then why in hell don't you go to the rear, and quit howling?' A minie ball had struck the colonel's canteen buckle and fallen down, but his left breast had been bruised over a space six inches in diameter. The buckle saved his life."

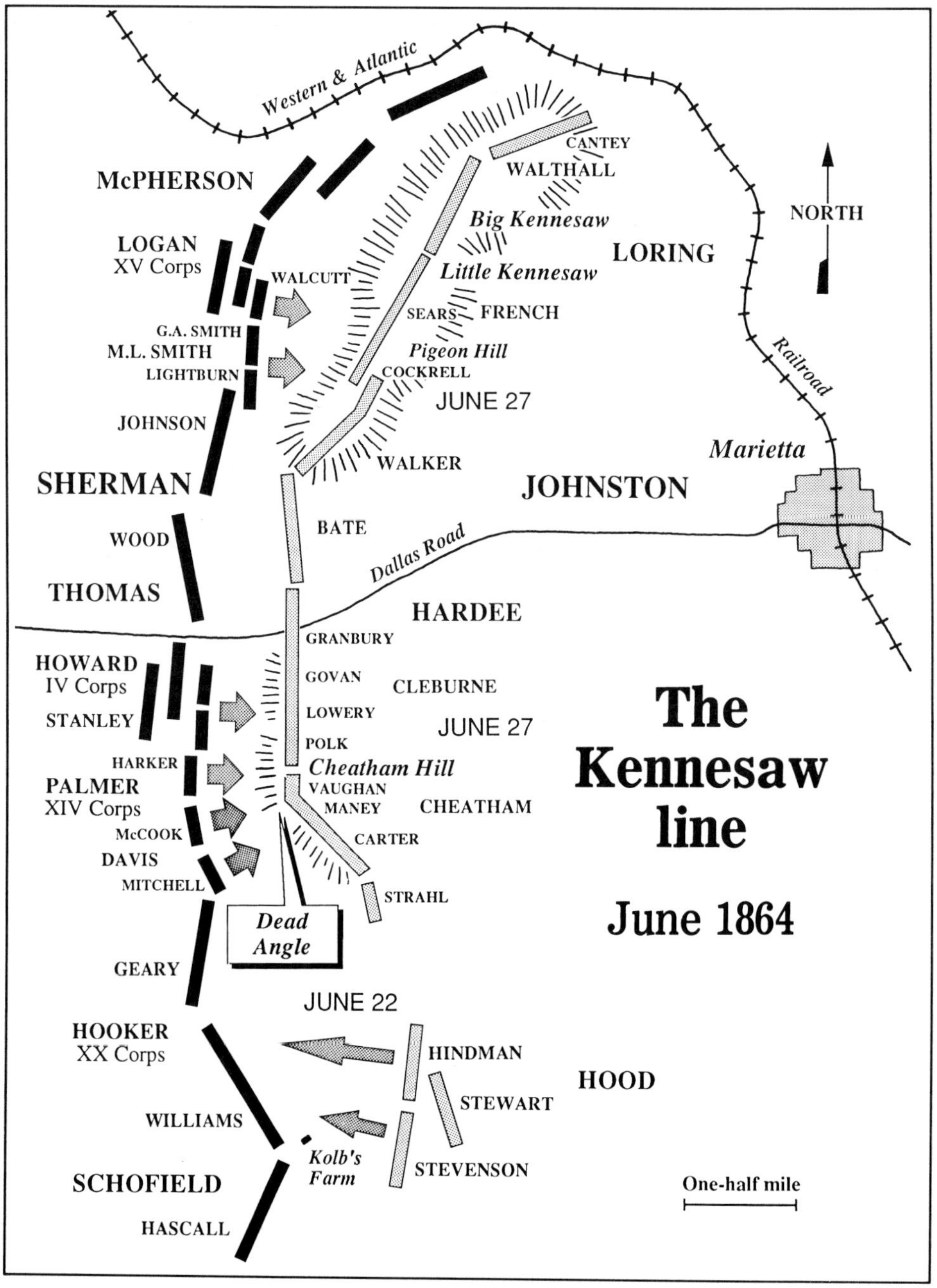

ing each officer by name and rank, thereby showing how perfectly he was acquainted with them and how thorough was his knowledge of his command. When he was finished he said, "Gentlemen, go back to your respective commands, impart this information to your men and when the bugle sounds, charge. And may God bless and protect you all!"

No event of the war has left a more vivid or lasting memory in my mind than this meeting at early dawn under that hickory tree at the foot of Kennesaw. But for how many was it their last meeting on earth, and how few of those who met for that brief consultation are now living and how many of the living are maimed and crippled for life?

We returned to our regiment. The bugle sounded the charge and in an almost incredibly short time we were in the very jaws of death, carrying the enemy's front and outer works. Gallantly the brigade endeavored to perform the task allotted it, but flesh and blood could not endure the withering fire poured into it, and the charge failed.

It cost our beloved colonel one of his legs. Our gallant lieutenant colonel was caught on the mountainside where it was impossible for him to get out until night, where he lay exposed to the burning rays of the sun without food or water, and at evening exposed to one of the most terrific artillery fires I ever witnessed.

When we stopped it happened that I was about 10 feet below the place where both color bearers lay. After remaining quiet in the brush for a time and seeing no chance to do anything more, I whispered to one of the boys to work the national banner down to me, which he did. I hugged the mountainside as close as possible, twisting the flag staff in my hand until the flag was rolled around it. Waiting a while until there was a lull in the firing, I made my way down the mountainside some five or six rods. By this time the boys were beginning to creep out. I gave the flag to Sergeant Samuel Winegardner of Company C, placed him in a protected place and commenced forming the regiment on the colors.

About this time some of the boys came out of the brush carrying Col. Rice who was terribly wounded. I assisted in tying two guns together with a gun strap, put some blankets upon the guns, thus forming a rude stretcher on which we placed the colonel. Raising him onto the shoulders of two of the boys, he was sent to the rear.

In the course of an hour the majority of the regiment had gotten back and formed on the colors. I assumed command and reported to Gen. Smith, who assigned the regiment its position and sent us tools. We built a line of works and remained in them until dark. Soon after dark Col. Mott returned to us uninjured and took command of the regiment.

My recollection is that there was not a regiment of our brigade came out of the charge with the same officer in command that started in with it. The charge at Kennesaw cost us the lives of many, many brave men and inflicted but little injury upon the enemy. It was barren of any good results, and I believe Gen. Sherman has been more severely criticized for this charge than for any other order he ever issued.

■ Sergeant John A. Woodruff, Company K, 57th Ohio. A veteran volunteer who served throughout the campaign, he wears a XV Corps badge on his vest. This photograph was taken at Little Rock, Ark., during the summer of 1865.

'They were nearly all shot down'

Diary of
2nd Lieut. George W. Warren
Company A
5th Missouri Volunteer Infantry
CSA

27th of June, 1864.

Those of us that were sleeping late this morning (having been on picket three consecutive days) were aroused by the most terrific outburst of artillery that the enemy has yet treated us to. Every gun that could reach us was brought to bear on Little Kennesaw. We knew what the shelling foreboded — every man sprang to his arms — Capt. Caniff shouted for each to take his place in the trenches, and in a moment all was ready. I shall always wonder how I got safely across the bald mountain top, through the flying mass of shells and fragments of rock.

The artillery soon slackened its fire and we could hear the volleys delivered by our skirmishers as they met the first line of the enemy. Poor fellows! Few of them could get back up that rugged mountainside in time to save themselves.

In a few minutes the enemy made their appearance, a solid line of blue emerging from the woods a hundred yards below us. We gave them a volley

■ Brig. Gen. Joseph A.J. Lightburn commanded a brigade in the 2nd Division, XV Corps. At Kennesaw on June 27, the Ohio and Indiana troops of his brigade attacked to the immediate right of Giles Smith's brigade, and suffered 171 casualties. "My officers did all that could be done," he wrote the next day, "but the underbrush through which we advanced was so thick that it was impossible to preserve a line. The consequence was the entire line was broken (and) this accounts for the heavy loss of officers." On August 24, Lightburn was struck in the forehead by a spent ball, disabling him for duty for the next six months.

that checked them where they stood. As this line was melting away under our steady fire another pressed forward and reached the foot of the mountain. Behind this came yet another line, but our fire was so steady and accurate that they could not be induced to advance, though their officers could be plainly seen trying to urge them up the hill.

Then came another column, the heaviest that had yet appeared, which made the final as well as the most determined assault, and which stood its ground longer than the others. Some of these men came 20 or 30 yards up the side of the mountain, but they were nearly all shot down which deterred the others from following. Our men shot with unusual accuracy because they had low stone breastworks, which we had constructed with so much labor, on which to rest their guns.

In three-fourths of an hour the attack was over and the Federals were gone, leaving large numbers of their dead lying at the bottom of the hill. I never saw our boys behave with greater coolness and courage. The enemy renewed and kept up their shelling until night, which was most efficiently and gallantly replied to by the batteries of Bledsoe and Guibor.

'Going home to die no more'

Capt. Henry Stedman Nourse
Company H
55th Illinois Veteran Volunteer Infantry

Before us rose the twin summits of Kennesaw, six or seven hundred feet above the plain; and six miles to the west stood Lost Mountain, the southernmost of the noticeable isolated spurs of the Alleghany range. Between and upon these two mountains the Confederates were firmly entrenched. But on the very day of our arrival the smoke of battle could be seen on the far right, gradually sweeping down past Lost Mountain, and on the morrow Johnston's left wing was refused to a new line prudently fortified in anticipation of its necessity, and Kennesaw had become his salient stronghold.

On Sunday, June 19th, we were ordered to the front to join our old brigade. The command now numbered 312 present, **about** 270 being in the ranks for service. After crossing one deserted line of rebel earthworks we came under the fire of the artillery upon Kennesaw, and here Michael Rayding of Company I was instantly killed, being nearly cut in two by a fragment of shell that burst in front of the marching column. He was of German birth, handsome in face and figure, a fine soldier, the first of the veteran volunteers to give up his life.

Reaching the position assigned to us on the lower slope of the mountain, we were formed on the left of the brigade and at once began constructing strong rifle pits. Although persistently annoyed by shells, grape and canister from the artillery on the summit, the work went steadily on until the 21st of June saw our front covered by a finished earthwork with log revetment breast-high, and skidded headlogs atop. The pickets kept up a continuous skirmish on the wooded mountainside, and the roar of artillery duels went on all along the line. The 2nd Division, under Gen. Morgan L. Smith, consisted now of but two brigades, each of six regiments; Gen. Giles A. Smith, his brother, commanding the 1st and Gen. J.A. Lightburn the 2nd:

1st Brigade		*2nd Brigade*	
6th Missouri	127th Illinois	37th Ohio	54th Ohio
55th Illinois	30th Ohio	47th Ohio	83rd Indiana
116th Illinois	57th Ohio	53rd Ohio	111th Illinois

■ Gen. Sherman, seated on horseback at center right, watches his troops move forward on June 27 as artillery shells burst along the sides and summits of Big and Little Kennesaw mountains. Following the attack's failure, Sherman wrote to his wife, Ellen, on June 30: "I begin to regard the death and mangling of a couple thousand men as a small affair, a kind of morning dash — and it may be well that we become so hardened ... The worst of the war is not yet begun."

On the 23rd, a shrapnel shell bursting just in front of us wounded three men: David McKeighan of Company D, and William Walker and Sergeant William Spencer of Company K. Two iron balls passed through the upper part of Spencer's arm, shattering the bone. By a triumph of conservative surgery his arm was saved, two or three inches of the injured humerus being exsected, shortening it by so much. The plucky young sergeant, elated with the prospect of saving his right arm, soon after the operation sent word to his company commander that he was "all right, and even had some advantage in his loss, for he would now be nearer the girls when he shook hands with them than the other boys."

On the right wing, where the obstacles interposed by nature were not unusually difficult, there seemed to be slow but steady onward progress — some gain of road or hill or stream almost daily made; but along our corps' front rose the steep scarp ending abruptly in many places with almost perpendicular ledges of rock, needing no defenders. The rebel pickets shouted down invitations from their safe elevation to our outposts: "Come up and see us." Ours jocularly responded, "We're coming! We're only waiting for our ladders."

No weakening of the Confederate force in our front was obvious, but Gen. Sherman, with the knowledge that Hood's Corps had been withdrawn from before McPherson to reinforce the left of Gen. Johnston's line against the energetic flank movements of Schofield and Hooker, reasoned that the rugged and almost inaccessible heights were probably held by artillery and a noisy skirmish line only, which might be broken through at some weak spot

■ Brig. Gen. Morgan L. Smith, older brother of Gen. Giles A. Smith, commanded the 2nd Division, XV Corps. On June 27 his two brigades, under Gen. J.A.J. Lightburn and his brother, along with a reinforcing brigade from Gen. William Harrow's division, assaulted the Confederate works 400 yards to the right of Little Kennesaw. Morgan Smith wrote the next day: "In addition to the steepness of the ascent, trees had been felled and brush and rocks piled in such a manner as to make it impossible to advance with any regularity. Some of the 55th and 111th Illinois fell on and inside the works. Gen. Lightburn, on the right, pressed on through a swamp where officers and men sank to their knees ... but on account of an enfilading fire, was unable to get nearer than 150 yards [of the] works beyond." A month later, Smith left active field service due to the effects of a wound suffered 19 months earlier at Chickasaw Bluffs, Miss.

by a sudden and determined assault. Upon the rocky watchtower of Kennesaw, however, sleepless eyes noted the slightest change in the features of the map spread out before them, and not a movement was made by day or by night but they marked it, counted its value, guessed its purpose and deliberately made preparations for counteracting it.

The Confederate left wing was now so far refused that Kennesaw was, as it were, the keystone of a semi-circular arch formed by the rebel lines. At briefest notice along the chords of the long curve the reserves could spring to protect sorely threatened points. A successful crushing through of this arc at any important point, however, would almost insure overwhelming ruin to Johnston's army, and Sherman felt that the chance ought to be taken — that even a sanguinary charge, if successful, would be economy of patriots' blood. He took the fearful responsibility, probably against the judgment of all the leading general and field officers in the army, save some few whose judgment was distracted by an itching on their shoulders for a star. In his report Gen. Sherman gives as one chief reason for ordering this assault upon carefully planned entrenchments, that the army needed to be taught that outflanking was not the only mode of offensive warfare. The teacher himself seems to have learned one lesson on the same date. He never again ordered a charge in column upon a well-entrenched foe.

On Sunday, the 26th of June, our division got orders to withdraw from its lines quietly after dark, the 2nd Division of the XVI Corps occupying the vacated position. We marched as we then supposed for a flank movement to the right, but were halted at midnight after proceeding four or five miles, went into bivouac in the woods and slept until daybreak. About seven in the morning the officers were summoned before the brigade commander, Gen. Giles A. Smith, and notified that in half an hour the brigade was to lead in an assault upon Little Kennesaw, then not much more than half a mile distant in our front.* The men were at once instructed to strip for a fight, leaving everything but essentials at the bivouac. One man from each company was detailed to remain as guard over its property.

Few but tried soldiers were in that little band waiting in the forest glade for the dread signal. Though thus surprised with the knowledge that in a few minutes they were to make a desperate dash against ramparts bristling with natural difficulties and defended by practical fighters, yet probably a casual observer would have noted in the occupation or outward manifestations of feeling among these men little to distinguish this from an ordinary group of soldiers resting on a march. A quick breakfast was eaten with appetite, and the pipe smoking and discursive talk went on as usual. But comrades could read in each other's faces signs not always to be seen there; in those of the prominent officers sterner and more rigid facial lines, indicating the load of responsibility they felt resting upon them; in all countenances a more quiet and fixed expression, almost amounting to a slight pallor. The laugh sometimes heard had no heart in it, the arguments no vivacity, the sportiveness rare or spasmodic, and often a faraway look in some eyes told of thoughts wandering to a distant Northern home, perhaps never again to be seen. A few handed to one of the guards, or to the chaplain, a valued watch or keepsake, with brief words of contingent instruction. A few wrote brief notes and placed them in their knapsacks.

The tendency of old soldiers to become fatalists has often been commented on. Examples of this tendency were frequently noticed in the 55th. Tales of premonitions justified by quick-following death or wounds were often in the mouths of comrades, while the examples, probably far more numerous,

* See preceding account of Capt. Alvah Stone Skilton for details of Gen. Smith's prebattle conference with his officers.

of gloomy omens that came to naught, were all forgotten. Men who had marched confidently and undismayed into battle after battle were suddenly on the approach of a fight seen to be out of heart, and save for their pride almost willing to own that their courage had all but left them.

Perhaps these cases of dismal foreboding among us were not more numerous on the morning of June 27th than before other bloody days in our experience, but several are remembered. A sergeant whose past record had proved him exceptionally brave was exceedingly depressed and confessed to his company commander an immovable conviction that if he went into the impending battle he should never see the sun rise again. He asked if he could be saved from the death that stared him in the face, without disgrace. The officer reported the case privately to the senior officer commanding the regiment, Capt. Jacob M. Augustine, who, knowing the worth of the sergeant, ordered him detailed to be left in command of the guard over the regimental property.

There was no one to excuse Capt. Augustine himself. Physically and morally an ideal company commander, tried in battle, march, siege and assault, and never known to falter, he had been conversing cheerfully and displayed his usual calm demeanor. But he had quietly said to his friend and fellow captain sitting beside him that he felt the oppressive shadow of death hanging over him. He handed his friend a pocket-knife "to remember him by," took out a little memorandum book and wrote:

Monday, June 27, 1864.

We marched last night until eleven — got up at seven this morning — are to make an assault upon the breastworks at half-past seven. Our division takes the lead. Now may God protect the right. Am doubting our success.

The order for the forward movement came, and Capt. Augustine's voice in command rang out as sharp and clear as though on parade. The two brigades steadily advanced through the heavily wooded and undulating ground bordering on the headwaters of Noyes Creek, were formed in battle lines and began the charge. At first we were preceded by a regiment armed with magazine rifles and deployed as skirmishers. We soon encountered the fire of the surprised rebel pickets, but without pause dashed over them — killing those who opposed, sending some as prisoners to the rear and driving the rest before us.

The division artillery meantime poured a storm of missiles over our heads into the main works of the enemy. The roar of the cannon behind and before, the bursting shells, rattling of musketry, Union hurrahs and answering rebel yells, made a horrible pandemonium of that little mountain valley, appalling even to the most experienced. Rushing onward about 500 yards beyond the little barricades of the picket line, through dense impeding underbrush and down over a stretch of marshy ground, we crossed the little creek and came out upon an open area at the base of a precipitous, rock-strewn hill. Below the crest, within pistol shot, lay Gen. Loring's veterans — a brigade of French's division — behind strong walls of stone. Up the long incline to the higher ridge of Kennesaw on the left ran a line of rifle pits, the troops in which opened an enfilading fire upon us, while two batteries commanded the ground over which we charged.

Our brigade, as it debouched from the thicket into the open at double-quick step and struck the ledges, all over which a natural growth of stunted, scraggy oaks had been felled, was no longer a column or line, but a swarm of desperate men clambering up between boulders and over tree trunks, and struggling through a tangled abatis of gnarled limbs. The place was almost inaccessible to one unencumbered and unopposed. Nothing we had

■ Capt. Jacob M. Augustine commanded the 55th Illinois at Little Kennesaw Mountain and was fatally wounded during the regiment's charge on June 27. He formerly commanded Company A, part of which he raised in the fall of 1861, and less than three months before his death was elected to the regiment's lieutenant colonelcy, though he never obtained commission to that grade. After being shot in the left breast, he was carried down Kennesaw's slope and died an hour later in the arms of his brother, 1st Lieut. Henry Augustine, who had succeeded to the command of Company A.

■ 1st Lieut. Joseph Hartsook commanded Company K, 55th Illinois, and was wounded in the left shoulder during the June 27 assault at Little Kennesaw Mountain. The injury ended his field service; he was mustered out on November 19, 1864.

surmounted at Vicksburg equalled it in natural difficulties. The troops upon our left, dismayed, fell back without any attempt to cross the open ground at the foot of the slope, and those on the right soon gave way, enabling the enemy to concentrate fire upon us. There could be no concert of action and little leadership; each man had to climb or shelter himself and fight as best he could.

Capt. Augustine was conspicuous, always pressing forward and prominent among the foremost. The impulse of the first rush was quickly lost in the mingled fatigue of climbing and the death of hope at sight of the fearful obstacles ahead. All faltered and advance seemed at an end. Seeing this, and at the same minute hearing and probably misunderstanding the bugle signal for retreat sounded in our rear, Capt. Augustine, sword in hand, climbing in advance a pace or two, and shouting "Forward, men!" stood erect, for one moment the grandest figure in the terrible scene. The next instant he lay prostrate, pierced through the left breast by a fatal bullet. His fall visibly disheartened the regiment, though a few men got closer under the rebel parapet, and attempt at further forward movement ceased. Capt. Shaw, second in command, calmly assumed the duty devolving upon him. Many wounded were dropping back to the rear. Longer exposure to the crossfire from covered marksmen meant only useless slaughter. Gen. Smith again gave the order by bugle call to fall back, and most of the men swept down into the shelter of the forest across the brook. Reforming as a skirmish line along a little ridge, they kept the enemy from making a countercharge or using their artillery, and protected the few living who had failed to retreat so that one by one nearly all crept down and escaped by a desperate run across the open space to the ridge.

At this point tools were brought up and rifle pits begun under a fierce artillery fire from the hill batteries. But at night the brigade was withdrawn to the rear, other troops being aligned in the parallel we had captured from the pickets during the morning's advance. Bands struck up patriotic airs as darkness closed down, and in their tree-canopied bivouac the torn and sadly diminished battalions forgot sorrow and fatigue in sleep. Of the 250 sent into action by the 55th, 12 of the bravest lay stark and cold among the rocks of the hill or by the brook; three had received burial at the hands of comrades in the woodland, and 32 had been borne or found their own way to the hospital for the surgeon's attention.

Capt. Augustine was brought down to the base of the hill by John Sheneman and Joseph Putnam. He was entirely conscious and gave orders to some men nearby to seek shelter behind trees and try to keep down the enemy's marksmen until those yet on the hill could escape. Soon Lieut. Henry Augustine, his brother, was summoned to his side. He died within an hour in his brother's arms, bidding his friends not to mourn for him.

In the same hour, a few paces away by the little stream, another pathetic scene was witnessed. Joseph Putnam of Company F, having helped bring the dying captain to the sheltered spot where he lay, ran to find a stretcher to bear him to the rear. Before he had gone many steps a bullet pierced his thigh, breaking the bone and severing an artery. A sweet singer, jolliest of messmates, loved for his invincible good nature, and respected by all for his courage and cheerful attendance to duty, his heroic death was in harmonious keeping with his life. The rosy-cheeked, curly-headed boy knew that his wound was mortal and told a friend, George Curfman, who attempted to aid him, that he had but a brief time to live. Then he began singing, "We're going home to die no more." As his life's blood pulsed away his voice grew fainter and fainter, but murmured the refrain until forever stilled on earth.

The generous-hearted and dauntless captain of Company E, William C. Porter, leader of a forlorn hope at Vicksburg, was shot through the left thigh, borne from the hill by two of his men, and died from loss of blood about 4 o'clock the same afternoon. The day was intensely hot, and the fatigue of the charge and toilsome climb so accelerated the pulsations of the heart and heated the blood, that several whose wounds might not otherwise have proved fatal perished of depletion before the surgeons could tie their torn arteries. Capt. Porter had married while on veteran furlough and spent his last moments in sending consoling messages to his young wife. The men who placed his body in mother earth, their sad duty done, had not gotten out of sight of the grave when a shell from the rebel batteries struck fairly into the little mound, and bursting, almost uncovered the dead soldier again, as though begrudging him his six feet of Southern soil.

One of the men who went to the captain's assistance when he fell, Adam Gleisner, was shot through the head and died beside him on the hill. He had fought in every battle the regiment was ever engaged in, and bore an enviable reputation for his soldierly behavior.

Capt. N.S. Aagesen, while leading his company well up the slope, had his right arm shattered near the shoulder. He was helped to the rear by his men and finally reached the hospital, where his arm was amputated, leaving him in a pitiable plight, for he had practically lost all use of his left arm from the effects of a wound at Shiloh. Recovering after a long convalescence, he was detailed upon a court of inquiry at Springfield, Ill., and never rejoined the regiment until mustered out with it at Louisville in 1865. He was a Dane by birth and had been in America but two years when the war broke out, going north from Mobile after the fall of Sumter to enlist in the Union cause.

Lieut. Hartsook led Company K in the charge and was wounded on the mountain among the foremost.

Lieut. Lomax and Sergeant Kays of the same company were struck by a bullet while one of them was giving the other a drink from his canteen after the regiment had fallen back, the ball passing through the left thigh of the sergeant into the right hip of the lieutenant.

Bartley Holden, a jovial and plucky Irishman of Company A, was shot down just in advance of Capt. Augustine. James Clark, another faithful soldier of that company, was mortally wounded and died in [an] Allatoona hospital a fortnight after the battle.

George W. Crowell of Company C was instantly killed as he stood upon the trunk of a fallen tree while swinging his hat and shouting "Come on!" to his comrades, he being then as near the rebel line as any man in the regiment. His brother had found a grave on the battlefield of Shiloh.

Henry Curtiss of the same company fell dead just as the charging line reached the base of the hill.

Company E had six men killed, including its captain — nearly half the lives lost in the charge by the 55th. Patrick Moran and James Quigley were among the first to fall. Richard Shanning, a brave veteran, when some of his comrades offered to try to get him to the rear after he was wounded, insisted upon their leaving him and caring for themselves as he believed he could live but a short time. He died before they left him. Charles Merrill, who was known for his coolness in danger, was one of the last to come down from the hill and was shot through the heart facing the enemy as he turned to look back from the foot of the slope.

In every regiment there were probably a few men who, however brave at heart, had legs that could with difficulty be induced to stay anywhere near the front in the hour of battle. These men were sometimes worthy soldiers in all other respects: clean, dutiful and useful everywhere but in a fight. If they had not disgraced themselves too openly they were usually permitted to drift into some menial position, or were detailed where their trades or

■ Private Samuel M. McCracken, Company D, 47th Ohio, participated in the June 27 assault of Lightburn's brigade at Little Kennesaw Mountain. Major T.T. Taylor wrote of the 47th's charge: "Sheets of flame baptise them; plunging shot strike comrades on every hand, and they fall unnoticed by your side. The advance is climbing under tree trunks, jumping over hacked saplings, tearing through the sharpened brush, stepping over fallen comrades ... facing the sheeted flame filled with missiles, giving forth ten thousand shrieks and tones, intensified by the cries of agony and the torture of the wounded." Included among the wounded was McCracken, who died of his injuries on August 5.

■ Lt. Col. William H. Martin, commanding the 1st and 15th Arkansas, called for a truce on June 27 when gunfire along the Federal IV Corps front ignited a brushfire, and the flames burned to death a number of helpless wounded Union soldiers lying between the lines. The Arkansans of Martin's command, left, look on from their breastworks as other wounded Yankees are carried away to safety.

special capacities made them of service to the army. No company in the 55th could be more impatient of the existence of a constitutional coward among them than the always staunch and true Company I. Yet, such a man was in its ranks, who, after escaping from two or three battles, obtained an order placing him on detached service, out of danger. But when Sherman's sweeping order at the opening of the Atlanta campaign sent to their regiments thousands of men who had been long retained in comfortable berths at hospitals or supply depots, this soldier came reluctantly back to his old messmates. After the battle he was found at the foot of a tree some distance to the rear of the creek, shot through the head by a chance ball.

The wounded who could bear being moved were taken from the field hospital after a few days and sent to Allatoona by night in a freight train. It was a terribly painful trip for these mangled men riding over the rough roadway upon mattresses spread on the floors of the cars. When taken out at sunrise most of them were completely exhausted with fatigue and lack of nourishment. But they at once found themselves in the hands of the agents of the Sanitary and Christian commissions, who, with smiling faces and cheerful words of encouragement, administered needed stimulants and food, and soon had them comfortably located in hospital tents.

The assaults made at other points in the lines, though nowhere encountering such insuperable natural obstacles as existed at Little Kennesaw, failed as decidedly to pierce the Confederate defenses. The trial had been gallantly made and, as generally happens when human flesh is hurled against earth and stone defended with military skill by brave veterans, nothing had been gained at all commensurate with the frightful loss of valuable lives. Again resort was had to the strategy of flank movements.

For several days we remained in reserve at the rear of the lines we had captured. Attempts were made by comrades to reach our dead upon Kennesaw by night, but the enemy's pickets were stationed near the foot of the hill and forbade approach. It was nearly a week before a burial party could visit the scene where the bodies were found unburied, though robbed of certain articles of apparel.

The roads which had been in an almost impassable condition on account of heavy rains now dried fast under the hot summer sun. Army stores were rapidly brought to the front. On July 2nd at 4 o'clock in the morning, Gen. Morgan Smith's division moved to the right and halted at noon in rear of the XXIII Corps near Nickajack Creek. That night Kennesaw was evacuated.

■ Private Henry A. Hill belonged to the consolidated 1st/15th Arkansas and helped repulse the Federals attacking Cleburne's division on June 27. Another member of the 1st Arkansas, Private W.T. Barnes of Company G, described the assault's aftermath: "A blaze of fire sprang out among the dry leaves, which were soon ablaze and eating their way toward the gully, which was full of a mass of human beings, squirming around and still piling on each other. At this stage our colonel, Will H. Martin, sang out, 'Boys, this is butchery,' and mounting our head logs, with a white handkerchief, he sang out to the Yanks as well as to our own men: 'Cease firing and help get out those men.' It is needless to add that the Feds never once refused to comply with this request. Our men, scaling the head logs as though for a counter charge, were soon mixed with the Yankees, carrying out dead and wounded Feds with those who a few minutes previous were trying to 'down our shanties.' Together, the Rebs and Yanks soon had the fire beat out and the dead and wounded removed to the Federal side ..."

Hill, however, did not survive the campaign. He was killed 26 days later in the battle of Atlanta.

'They never expected to see me alive again'

Capt. John W.A. Gillespie
Company G
78th Ohio Veteran Volunteer Infantry

In the field, near Kennesaw
Mountain, Ga.,
Tuesday morning, June 28, 1864.

I am indebted to a kind Providence for the privilege of writing today, for certainly no earthly power could have taken me safely through the dangers of the past 48 hours. Yet, why I should have been spared when so many noble "boys in blue" were sent to their long homes is not for me to know. God knows, and that is enough for me to know.

A great battle was fought yesterday in which many lost their lives or were sent to hospitals to suffer from terrible wounds received while trying to drive the rebels from their strong line of works on Kennesaw Mountain.

The night before last, just after coming in off picket, the regiment, with the balance of the brigade, was ordered to make a night march to the extreme left of our lines, which it did. This was done, as we have since learned, for the purpose of attracting the attention of as large a force of the rebels as possible from the extreme left of their lines, on which Gen. Joe Hooker was to make a strong and determined effort to get possession of the railroad in the rear of Marietta. We marched and halted, and halted and marched all night long, and when day began to break in the east we found ourselves directly in front of the rebel works. As soon as it was light enough to see how to work the guns, two of our batteries opened their mouths and began talking in thunder tones to the Johnnies in their works.

Our regiment supported the battery that "opened the ball," and I can assure you that we hugged "mother earth" very closely when the rebel guns began to reply. They did not do so until our own gunners had fired 25 or 30 shots. Then they opened on us with six guns, and from that time until 3 o'clock in the afternoon their shot and shell came shrieking and bursting over our heads, and sometimes a dozen pieces of shell would fall right among us. One shell struck in front of Company G and bounced three times through the company without hurting a man and, surprising as it may seem, each time it struck the earth it passed over three or four of my men.

■ Lt. Col. Greenberry F. Wiles, nicknamed "Old Whiskers" by his men, commanded the 78th Ohio at Kennesaw Mountain. This XVII Corps regiment arrived at the front on June 8 and two days later entered the line under Confederate skirmish fire near Big Shanty. For the next seven days "the skirmishing at this point was very severe," wrote Wiles, "and our loss in killed and wounded considerable. We skirmished at this place continually until June 17, when we dislodged them from their position, which was a strong one." Another nine days of skirmish fighting ensued before the June 27 assault at Kennesaw, in which the 78th participated as a diversionary force on the left of the XV Corps. After the battle of Atlanta on July 22, Wiles assumed command of his regiment's brigade and led it for two months. In documenting the brigade's actions from May to September, Wiles wrote on September 13: "I am aware that my report is lengthy; so was the campaign."

During all the shelling we received we had but two men slightly wounded in the entire regiment.

At half past three the batteries ceased firing and, having accomplished all that had been expected of us on that portion of the field, we were ordered back to the old position in front of our camp. We remained there only a few minutes, being ordered into line again. The fighting on our right at this time was simply terrific, the roar of artillery and musketry being almost deafening, while clouds of smoke kept us from seeing any part of the battle. However, we had enough to look after in our own immediate front, as we soon found out.

The brigade formed in line of battle, two regiments deep, and moved forward a quarter of a mile and prepared to receive the rebels should they charge from their rifle pits, as was reported they were going to do. I was put in command of Companies A and G of our regiment and ordered forward as skirmishers, to go as far as possible without being too much exposed. The woods we had to go through was so thick with a growth of red brush that we could scarcely work our way through it or see 10 steps ahead during our advance. We soon met the rebel skirmishers, however, and received their first fire when our boys let loose their dogs of war and drove them from the woods into their works in an open field.

On the left of our line the rebel rifle pits ran down into the woods and were thickly covered over with red brush. The left of my company got within five steps of the pits before they were aware of it. The rebs immediately opened on us from front and flanks, and being protected by their works had a big advantage and were enabled to pour a raking fire on my men without their being able to return it to much advantage, except to make the Johnnies keep their heads behind the works.

My company had advanced farther than the balance of the line of skirmishers, but owing to the dense undergrowth I did not become aware of it until the affair was over. The rebels had an enfilading fire on my boys for an hour and a half and during that time they tore the earth up all around us, cutting the limbs and leaves from the bushes so that they looked as naked as though a furious hailstorm had passed over them. I never heard balls come thicker or faster, and I hope I never get into such a place again without some chance to return the compliment in full.

Finding we could not advance or retreat, I passed the word along the line for the men to seek the best cover they could and then shoot every rebel who showed his head above the works, an order which was obeyed to the letter. As prisoners afterward stated, our boys killed and wounded several of their men in the works. One big Confederate jumped on top of the works and yelled out, "Surrender, you damned Yanks!" He raised his gun to fire, but before he could pull the trigger John W. Robinson, who was lying on the ground close to me and who had just loaded his Enfield rifle, raised up and fired, killing the fellow instantly. His gun went off in the air and I am sure I don't exaggerate when I say he jumped a full three feet up from the top of the works and fell on the brush outside, stone dead.

Col. Wiles, finding that we had gone farther than was intended we should go, ordered us to fall back to the balance of the line, Capt. Munson calling in a loud voice for us to do so. Knowing it would be impossible to move as a body in any kind of safety, I had the order to fall back one at a time passed along the line, telling the men next to me that when they all got back to call me and then I would try it. The order was obeyed, but in every single instance my boys had a volley fired after them as they ran and dodged among the bushes. But they all got back.

When I heard the signal I jumped to my feet and I am certain I never ran so fast in my life before as I did through the woods yesterday. When I got back the boys all seemed as pleased to see me as though I had been away from them a month. Gen. Leggett and Col. Wiles both said they never expected to see me alive again, after finding we had gone so much farther than was expected of us.

How so many of us escaped wounds or death, God only knows. Corporal Robert Peacock of my company was mortally wounded, a minie ball passing through his bowels. He died last night after suffering intense agony. Private Joseph Dixon was shot through the left thigh, the ball cutting the femoral artery. His leg will have to be amputated and I fear he cannot live.* Both were splendid soldiers and fine looking men, and fell nobly doing their duty. I wrote to the poor old mother of Corporal Peacock in Maryland this morning, and my heart aches to think of how she will receive the news of the death of her darling boy. Yet, hundreds of mothers will weep tears of sorrow when the details of yesterday's great battle reaches them.

Company A had four men wounded, one of whom will die. In all we had one killed and 15 wounded, four or five of whom were only slightly wounded and will soon recover.

The loss in the brigade in killed and wounded is 18, and in the division, eight killed and 43 wounded. The loss yesterday on the right is reported as being very heavy, and as the battle raged fearfully for hours I have no doubt that the reports are true. We have not learned what advantages were gained, if any, but hope to hear by tomorrow morning all the particulars. We have just heard that Col. Dan McCook and Gen. Harker were both killed, and if this be true we have lost two of our bravest and best officers.

'A hard looking set of men'

Journal of
Capt. Robert Davis Smith
2nd Tennessee Volunteer Infantry
Staff officer
Cleburne's Division, Hardee's Corps CSA

June 27 (1864)

At about 10 a.m. the enemy charged our works, they had two lines of skirmishers and three lines of battle in front of our brigade, and seven lines of battle in front of Cheatham's Div. We only had four brigades engaged, Maney's & Vaughn's of Cheatham's Div., Polk & Lowrey of Cleburne's div. The enemy came within five feet of our breastworks and the slaughter was terrific as our troops literally mowed them down. We only lost 12 killed & wounded in our brigade. The enemy could not stand the steady fire of our troops and in a few moments fell back to their breastworks except in front of Maney's brigade, where, it is reported they are fortifying [within] 50 yds of our lines.

About half an hour after the charge, our brigade stopped skirmishing and called to the enemy to stop and come and get their dead & wounded that

■ Sergeant Thomas Clinton Starr, Company I, 78th Ohio. Arriving at Rome on June 5, "we began to see some of the marks of war and the nature of the campaign before us," wrote regimental Chaplain Thomas M. Stevenson. "We pushed on the next morning toward the front, which was then at Acworth. The march was over one continuous battlefield. The country is deserted, the crops all destroyed and fine plantations dug over in the erection of fortifications by both armies. We are now in line of battle, ready to move upon the enemy." A week later at Big Shanty the regiment suffered its first casualties of the campaign — three officers slightly wounded (including Capt. John Gillespie) and one man killed. The dead man was Sergeant Starr, who was shot on the skirmish line and later buried in the Marietta National Cemetery.

* Dixon did survive his wound. The leg was not amputated and he eventually recovered, being mustered out July 14, 1865, at Columbus, Ohio. On July 22, 1864, Capt. Gillespie was captured on Leggett's (Bald) Hill during the Battle of Atlanta. Backed up against the wall of a trench, Gillespie was nearly bayoneted when a Confederate officer restrained the man from running him through. According to Gillespie, "The officer said, 'I see you are a Mason,' and then for the first time I realized that a Masonic pin, on the lapel of my blouse, had been the means of saving my life." From Atlanta he was sent to a prison pen in Macon, then on to a military prison in Charleston, S.C.

■ Capt. William G. Ewin commanded Company A, 20th Tennessee, during the first two months of the campaign. During the artillery bombardment of Kennesaw Mountain before the Federal assault of June 27, Ewin was severely wounded by a shell fragment, necessitating the amputation of his leg.

were in the woods, as the heavy firing had set the dry leaves on fire and the wounded were in danger of being burnt up; during the armistice I succeeded in getting 90 rifles from the field, 7 of them were Henry's patent, 16 shooters.

June 28 (1864)

The enemy have made no demonstrations on our line today and the firing of the skirmishers has been rather lazy. We had to withdraw our skirmishers this p.m. as it was almost impossible for them to stand the stench from the Yankee dead. Both armies have agreed to suspend hostilities tonight so that the dead may be buried. I bought a mare today for the moderate sum of $1,000.00. She moves well and I have only one objection to her; that is she is 10 years old. I forgot to mention that yesterday our brigade captured 40 Yankees, among the number was a lieut. col., they were a hard looking sett of men.

June 29 (1864)

Our brigade has not fired a shot today. The truce has lasted all day as the last of the Yankee dead in front of Cheatham's were only buried at sunsett. I walked all along our line & Cheatham's today and witnessed a sight seldom seen. The troops of both armies were sitting on top of their respective breastworks talking with each other; where, if they had dared to show their heads twenty-four hours ago it would have been shot off. In front of our brigade the Yanks are in full view and their works are between three & four hundred yards off. In front of Maney's brigade the enemy's line is within fifty yards of his at one point. I went up to see it this evening and found the flags of both armies only about 50 yds apart and several colonels talking to each other as if they were the best friends in the world.

I should not be surprised to hear that this salient angle of Cheatham's line (where the lines are so near each other) has been undermined and blown up. The enemy can do it with all ease in thirty-six hours. I consider this the most dangerous part of the line. Had my horse appraised, for $1,400.

June 30 (1864)

Nothing of importance has happened on our part of the line today. Last night at 2 o'clock the enemy attempted to charge our line, but our troops were ready for them and it is reported (by the enemy) that there were 458 dead Yanks in front of our brigade alone. The firing was very heavy for a few moments. We only lost, in our brigade, two killed & three wounded. Some of our brigade met a squad of blue bellies on the half way ground and exchanged late papers, coffee, tobacco &c. They have new weights & measures on our line; the Yanks give a shirt tail full of coffee for a plug of tobacco.

July 1 (1864)

The regular skirmish firing has continued all day. The enemy have advanced their works in front of Maney's Brigade. They are only about twenty-five yards apart now, rather too close for comfort.

July 2 (1864)

There has been very little skirmishing on our part of the line today but the enemy shelled us pretty steadily for about an hour this morning. I don't think they damaged anything. I have named my new horse Marietta. She was slightly wounded this morning by a minie ball. I went to town this evening ... but was disappointed, as everything is being prepared to fall back, as the enemy have flanked us on the left. We left camp at sunset and marched 6 miles toward Atlanta to Smyrna Church and establish a new line. I arrived at my position at 12 o'clock at night. The troops did not leave the line until 11 p.m. I had my horse very badly wounded tonight in the leg. I am afraid that she will never be of any service again. The wound is about eight inches long and one of the muscles is cut almost in two. I had it sewed up tonight and doctored as well as I could.

July 3 (1864) Sunday

I dismounted my wagon master this morning and took his mule as I cannot ride my horse — sent her to the baggage wagons across the Chattahoochee River by my blacksmith. The troops have been busy all day making breastworks. Our brigade has a splendid position. I had some works put up to protect my men and mules as we will be in rather a dangerous place if we have heavy fighting in front. I have been riding nearly all day examining the roads and having new ones cut. I have been sick for more than a month, and I am becoming so weak that I can scarcely get about. I wish they would make haste and have *the big fight* so that I can get some rest or go to a hospital. We are expecting a big fight tomorrow — it is the fourth of July.

■ Private John Arbuckle, Company K, 4th Iowa. "The most severe and trying experiences of the campaign were those we endured in the trenches in front of Kennesaw," he later wrote. "For 26 days, 17 of which were days of continuous rain, we never had our clothes off, or a chance to wash, save dipping up muddy water in the trenches or little driblets from our canteens; never had a cooked meal, and rarely even a cup of hot coffee. During these 26 days in the trenches, at no time was it safe to venture out of them, as strongly fortified lines were in front and above us, extending along the whole length of the mountain. Our only chance for sleep was to make the best of the mud-bedraggled trenches, or, perchance, in the deep darkness creep out to lie down on the water-soaked earth. Such was our condition and personal appearance from grime, mud and burnt powder that we were all but a fright to ourselves. However, whatever else happened, the main thing was to keep our guns in good working order and our ammunition dry."

To stand still was death

Desperate fury at the Dead Angle

At the same time the Federal attacks on Little Kennesaw and Pigeon Hill were breaking down in failure on June 27, Brig. Gen. Jefferson C. Davis' division of the XIV Corps assaulted a hill on the Kennesaw line defended by two entrenched Confederate brigades under the command of Maj. Gen. Ben Cheatham of Hardee's Corps. Cheatham's line, about two miles south of Little and Big Kennesaw mountains, jutted toward the facing Yankees and then cut back eastward to form a sharp-angled salient. Occupying this salient — the "Dead Angle" as it was soon to be known — were the veteran Tennessee troops of Brig. Gens. Alfred J. Vaughan and George Maney. Some 700 yards to the west, the attacking regiments of Col. John Mitchell's and Col. Daniel McCook Jr.'s brigades waited with anxiety for the signal to charge the strong Confederate earthworks. In an attempt to inspire his men, the 30-year-old McCook, a student of military history, walked along the line and recited to them verses of Thomas Macauley's poem depicting the legendary Roman warrior Horatius as he faced battle in defense of a bridge over the Tiber River:

Then out spake brave Horatius,
The Captain of the Gate:
To every man upon this earth
Death cometh soon or late,
And how can man die better
Than facing fearful odds,
For the ashes of his fathers
And the temples of his gods.

Within minutes, signal guns and bugles heralded the advance and, as one Union soldier later wrote, "It became a slaughter of men like beasts in the shambles." The next day Alexander M. Ayers, regimental quartermaster of the 125th Illinois, wrote to his wife: "We have lost in killed 42, wounded 68, making just 110 that we know of today at noon. It is a very rare thing that one Regt. looses as many men as ours did. The men that are now left are all very gloomy and despondent. They are entirely worn out ... The suffering of our wounded is utterly indescribable. Men are shot in every conceivable manner. Our fight was a very small thing compared with the whole army but for our Brigade it is most *terrible.*"

The assault on the Dead Angle cost McCook's brigade 35 percent of its men. It also cost McCook his life.

'We are going to charge the rebel works'

Lt. Col. Allen L. Fahnestock
86th Illinois Volunteer Infantry

Monday morning, June 27, 1864, clear and hot, found us up early with orders to leave our knapsacks, camp equipage and sick in camp and take nothing but our canteens filled with water and haversacks filled with rations. At 7 o'clock we marched out in the following order: 125th Illinois, Col. Oscar F. Harmon commanding; 86th Illinois, Lt. Col. Allen L. Fahnestock commanding; 22nd Indiana, Capt. W.H. Snodgrass commanding; 52nd Ohio, Lt. Col. Charles W. Clancey commanding; and the 85th Illinois, Col. Caleb J. Dilworth commanding, as skirmishers.

While marching to our position a reporter for a New York paper said the 1st Brigade of our division was to charge the rebel works and our brigade was to support them. We had moved but a short distance when we halted. The orderly from Col. Dan McCook, our brigade commander, gave me an order to report to him in person. I rode forward and found him sitting by a tree, and when all the regimental commanders of his brigade arrived he said, "We are going to charge the rebel works in our front."

Addressing Col. Harmon, he continued, "You will command the first line." Turning to me he said, "You will lead the second line, and when you carry the works shove down the headlogs on the rebels, then deploy your regiment to the left and occupy the works." To the others were assigned the following duties: Col. Dilworth would manage the skirmish line, Capt. Snodgrass would lead the third line and Col. Clancey would lead the fourth.

I returned to my regiment, assembled the officers and gave them their orders, and ordered the men to "load at will and not fire a gun until we reached the works." We moved and occupied a hill in front of a spur of Kennesaw Mountain that we were to assault. We laid down in the order assigned and waited for the signal gun. Gen. Charles G. Harker of the IV Corps commanded on our immediate left. While waiting for the signal I went to a small bush where Col. Harmon and Capt. Charles Fellows were sitting in front of the 125th Illinois. We three knelt down on our left knees, each facing the other in conversation. I unloosened my "gorilla whistle" and tore up my letters. Col. Harmon asked me whether I thought we would carry the works. I replied that I thought not, as we had too far to run and the rebels were reinforcing their lines. I also told him that "if we fail to carry the works I will surrender before my men should return over the open field." He agreed with me, but said he thought we *would* carry the works.

I told them that I was sick and had been under the doctor's care all night, and had a dream that I was in a terrible battle but got out safe. Col. Harmon said that he, too, had a dream the previous night — that he was fighting "copperheads up North" and then engaged in a big battle, but did not know how it terminated. Capt. Fellows said he also had dreamed — that his left foot was cut off with a cannon ball, and as he said this he brought his hand down across his left foot. Just as he did so the signal gun fired, at half past 8 a.m. The command was given: "Right shoulder shift arms. Forward!"

The rebels, while we were lying down waiting for the signal gun, were shooting and wounding some of our men. I judged the distance to their works at one-fourth of a mile. At the foot of the hill Gen. James D. Morgan's 1st Brigade lay behind their works. We crossed these and then Noyes Creek, breaking up our lines somewhat. The skirmishers of the 85th Illinois captured most of the rebel picket line. We charged up the mountain side through a strip of timber. Near the top we encountered the rebels in their

■ Brig. Gen. Jefferson C. Davis commanded the 2nd Division, XIV Corps. On the morning of June 27, just prior to the Federal assault on Cheatham's Hill, Davis held a final consultation with Col. Dan McCook, whose brigade was drawn up in column of regiments, each lying prone to avoid Confederate fire. Davis was concealed in a hole behind a large tree stump, directly in rear of the brigade center. As McCook made his way to the stump he cautioned Samuel A. Harper, a sergeant in Company H of his old regiment (the 52nd Ohio), to lie down. After the brief parley between Davis and McCook, Harper heard Davis call out: "Don't be rash, Colonel, don't be rash." McCook answered by quoting in a calm manner the stanzas from the poem "Horatius," which he recited as he walked back to the center of his brigade.

Some six weeks later, Davis was promoted to the command of the XIV Corps.

■ Col. Daniel McCook Jr., mortally wounded on June 27, was a member of the large Ohio family that acquired a wide reputation as the "Fighting McCooks." A former law partner of Gen. Sherman before the war, McCook raised and led the 52nd Ohio until he became a brigade commander in September 1862. After his wounding at the Dead Angle, he was taken home to Steubenville, Ohio, where he died July 18, 1864 — the day after he received a commission as brigadier general.

strong works, in front of which were placed racks staked and wired together. Our men were compelled to break through these obstructions, but after running so far, and receiving so galling a fire, in which Col. McCook fell mortally wounded, many of them were spent. Col. Harmon took command and was instantly killed and fell into the arms of his men. Capt. Fellows rushed forward calling the men to follow, yelling, "Come on, boys, we will take ———" and fell dead a few feet from the ditch.

I ordered a second attempt to carry the works and failed. I then sent Sergeant Major D.E. Ward to find Col. Dilworth, who was then the senior officer in command of the brigade. In passing to our right down the line the sergeant major was wounded. I then went myself and found Col. Dilworth, and explained to him the situation on the left. I found the men nearly all killed and wounded on the right as they struck the angle of the rebel works. The 2nd Brigade on our right, Col. John Mitchell commanding, had retired to the rear, leaving our right exposed to the enemy's cross fire. I asked Col. Dilworth what was to be done, and he asked me my opinion. I told him we could not retreat and I did not now feel willing to surrender, so we agreed to separate the men, make four lines and throw up fortifications while our sharpshooters held the enemy in check. I moved to the left and notified the officers of the several regiments to get the men separated and shove up rails and wood. Soon we had a formidable line of works which enabled us to hold our position. The distance between our works and the enemy's was 27 paces.

After dark we rescued many of our dead and wounded. It was truly heart rending to hear our comrades begging for water, many of whose voices we recognized but were unable to help. My adjutant, Lieut. L.J. Dawdy, was badly wounded and fell at the rebel works and could not get back to our lines, so was compelled to give himself up to the enemy. Capt. Joe Major of Company A also was wounded and lay close to Lieut. Dawdy. After dark two rebels came out and robbed him of about all he possessed. When all was quiet he succeeded in sliding and working himself gradually back down to our pits and landed in our lines.

'Uncover to the right'

Sergeant John H. Brubacker
Company A
86th Illinois Volunteer Infantry

When we reached the enemy's works at the "Dead Angle," the rebel battery on our right and the rebel musketry from the breastworks in our front had decimated our ranks to such an extent that my company, A, did not number quite three platoons. The rebel battery fire had the effect of pressing the right of the brigade toward the left of the "Dead Angle," before reaching which we were somewhat mixed. The regimental organization was pretty badly tangled up.

My company was clustered with the other men of the regiments until, in order to disentangle Company A, I gave the command, "Uncover to the right!" and seeing an opening in the abatis near the "Dead Angle," used by the rebels to pass out to and in from their picket line, I called on the men and led in a rush to gain possession of the passageway at the angle. I fell at this point, as did seven shot dead and 14 wounded who lay in a heap around me. Before we "uncovered" there was a surge of our men in an attempt to carry the rebel works. In the halt the men laid down; in fact, all had fallen to the ground, killed or wounded, or laid down for protection to escape the

An honored Henry

■ Lt. Col. Allen L. Fahnestock, left, commanded the 86th Illinois during the campaign. On the morning of June 27, just before the Dead Angle assault, he loaned his personal Henry rifle and 120 rounds of ammunition to the 86th's principal musician, Fife Major Alason P. Webber, above. Webber's use of the repeating rifle that day earned him a Medal of Honor. The award citation reads: "Voluntarily joined in a charge against the enemy, which was repulsed, and by his rapid firing in the face of the enemy enabled many of the wounded to return to the Federal lines; with others, held the advance of the enemy while temporary works were being constructed." That day in front of the Dead Angle the 86th lost 28 enlisted men killed, 59 officers and enlisted men wounded, and nine missing.

With a magazine under the barrel holding 15 rimfire cartridges — all of which could be fired in less than 12 seconds — the Henry was the most advanced repeating rifle to see service during the Civil War. Fahnestock's privately purchased Henry cost about $38, and is proudly displayed here in an 1863 photograph taken when Fahnestock was a captain in command of Company I.

■ 1st Lieut. Lansing J. Dawdy, adjutant of the 86th Illinois, was wounded and captured at the Dead Angle on June 27. He was discharged April 25, 1865.

fate of their comrades. It was one of those times when veterans act quickly, governed by a judgment acquired by that experience which enables them to size up the situation and weigh the chances of success as clearly as anybody.

When I saw Col. Dan McCook he was to my left and in front of the men. He had almost reached the works and was in the act of leading the few left on the works. He stood erect facing the rebels. I thought that they must have refrained from shooting him down to capture him unharmed. Our men were trying to reach the outside of the embankment which afforded some protection over the point-blank exposed position between us. Just then the right battalion of the brigade, for the regiments had become merged into one line, headed by one of the officers, made a surge to his rescue. His quick eye must have caught the movement, for he made a motion for them to come up to his position. He went forward in the lead and made a lodgment on the breastworks. A fusilading volley which they encountered swept most of them down, although some of them reached the outside of the works. Again the men, moved by the instincts of veterans and the commands of the officers, faced for another effort to rally to our commander, now almost alone.

It was at this moment that I gave the command "Uncover to the right." Lieut. Dawdy, our adjutant, led us; he fell to my right at the foot of the loose earth of the works. All who started with us were now down. As I lay there my stomach revolted and I do not remember ever having felt so sick in my life. As we started, someone said that it was hopeless and hesitated, but about 20-odd of the boys of Company A went forward. As we made the first step in the forward movement I shall never forget the act of two of the boys who had been chums. They reached behind one of the men that separated them and clasped hands as though bidding each other goodbye. I thought it meant a pledge of succor in need or distress and that neither felt hope of surviving the attempt. Both fell, sealing their devotion with their lives.

'For God's sake get down!'

Private S.M. Canterbury
Company C
86th Illinois Volunteer Infantry

The officers and men who made the charge on those works were as brave as ever wore the blue. At the creek at the foot of the hill I was in the rear, but got to the works as soon as any of the boys. I caught up to the front line as we reached the works. I found the brigade all mixed up in one line. In the space I was in I could not tell what was being done very far on the right or left of me. The rebel musketry fire was terrific; to stand still was death.

I realized the safest place was at the works. Col. Dan was in the lead. He said, "Forward with the colors!" When I first reached the works I fell or laid down, and hugged the works as close as I could for protection and to rest, as in running the distance we did, combined with the intense heat, I was about played out. Col. Dan climbed up on the works. For a moment my attention was taken with a rebel on the opposite side from me who was trying to fire under the headlog. When I looked up, Col. Dan was standing on the headlog above me. I heard him say, "Bring up those colors!" I don't know whose colors they were. He grabbed the colors in his left hand, holding them aloft and using his saber in his right hand, parrying the rebels on the other side of the breastworks who were trying to bayonet him. I reached up and took hold of the skirt of his uniform coat and said to him, "Colonel Dan, for God's sake get down, they will shoot you!" He turned partly around, stooping a little, and said to me, "G—d d——n you, attend to your own business." Then the gun was fired; they put the gun almost against him. I know the gun was not more than one foot from his hip when they shot him. I could not tell where he was shot. Had I not pulled on his coat I believe he would have fallen inside the rebel works. Some comrades took him back to the rear; that was the last time I saw him.

My eyes were on the works until I got a chance to crawl back to the top of a felled tree close to the works. The boys in our rear were pouring in a hot fire to keep the rebels down under cover, and to enable those of us at the works to hold our ground. When the colonel fell, we realized those in our rear could not come up and our only chance was to crawl back. While we lay there someone planted the colors in the trench and later a rebel, attempting to capture them, was killed. The spot where Col. Dan stood on the works when he was shot was not far from where the south end of the works jogged off, and was north of the angle.

■ Capt. Joseph Major, commander of Company A, 86th Illinois, who was knocked down near the Dead Angle, played dead amidst a pile of bodies until nightfall and escaped to the Federal line without injury.

'Company A was virtually annihilated'

1st Lieut. L.J. Dawdy
86th Illinois Volunteer Infantry

When the brigade made the charge I took my proper position as adjutant behind the right wing of the regiment, and as we climbed the hill on which the rebel works were situated, I was just to the left and in front of the Dead Angle, being behind Company F. But the nearer I got to those works I could see that abatis was woven thickly in front of the works at that point, and to the right of the angle there was nothing but works with headlogs on top. So it seemed to me that our boys could cross the works at that point — so I pushed out to Company A with the intention of rushing them over.

In the meantime the men had lain down, being as far advanced as those on their left who were to the works, or as near as they could get to them. Their officers did not try to carry them over, but when I called on them they rose to their feet and opened fire instead of going over, and yet they advanced toward the works. But in the meantime the line of rebels to our right poured an enfilading fire into our ranks in addition to that from our immediate front. Hence, Company A was virtually annihilated, losing 23 men out of 40. There it was that I, at about 15 or 20 feet to the right of the angle, was wounded, being not more than 10 feet from the enemy's works. I was unable to get away, so after lying there in the hot sun for five hours, and believing that I could not recover — being shot through the body — I indicated my willingness to be taken over the works, and was therefore taken across, then carried on a stretcher by four Confederates to their field hospital, about 400 yards to the rear.

'Out-possuming any opossum that ever lived'

Private Julius B. Work
Company G
52nd Ohio Veteran Volunteer Infantry

Capt. Joe Major, commanding officer of Company A, 86th Illinois, gave to me an account of how he was knocked down by something — he did not know what — while close to the rebel works in the charge at Kennesaw Mountain. When he regained consciousness he found himself flat on his back just outside the rebel breastworks among many dead and wounded. Our troops had

■ Col. Oscar Fitzallen Harmon, commander of the 125th Illinois, was killed near the Dead Angle on June 27. Before the war he was acquainted with Abraham Lincoln in Illinois, and a few days after Harmon was killed his brother, George E. Harmon, spoke with Lincoln in the White House, informing the president of Col. Harmon's death. George Harmon later recalled Lincoln reaction: "What, my friend Harmon killed?" The president leaned over a table in front of him, resting his head in his hands for a few minutes, then said, "I have not heard of a death for a long time that made me feel so sad."

fallen back about 75 feet and there, hugging the ground closely, were partly protected by the brow of the hill. Spades were trumps, and by diligent digging a new line was soon established, protected by good breastworks.

On the return of consciousness Capt. Major knew he must play himself for dead or he would be forced to crawl over the rebel works a prisoner — as several others were forced to do. Retreat was then impossible. About this time a venturous rebel crawled out over the works, probably for boodle, and crawling around among the dead and wounded, came to the captain, whom he relieved of his revolver, sword, haversack, canteen, pocket-book and hat. Noticing that Major was breathing, the rebel turned a little water into his mouth. But, although nearly dying of thirst, the Yank was afraid to swallow for fear his sham would be detected, and permitted the coveted fluid to run out of his mouth and go to waste in mother earth. The Johnny crawled away and left him, supposing there would soon be another dead Yank.

It was now about 10 o'clock in the forenoon, and during all the balance of that hot 27th day of June, Capt. Major lay flat on his back with the merciless rays of the sun pouring down into his bare face, not even daring to scare the flies from his mouth or nose, or shift his body the least bit to gain a more comfortable position. He could hear the bang, bang of Yankee guns, and the crack of Col. Fahnestock's Henry rifle in the hands of Fife Major Webber — who had gained an advantageous position and was doing all he could to prevent the rebels from raising their heads above their breastworks, for which the government gave Webber a Medal of Honor. When the rebels would reply, the smoke from their guns would almost puff into the captain's face. With the bullets passing both ways, only a few inches above his body, there he lay, out-possuming any opossum that ever lived.

Finally, after a long, long wait, darkness came. Then was his time to attempt an escape from his perilous position. Gathering strength for a supreme effort, he got onto his feet and made a dash for the Yankee line. It was considerably down hill, and he came as near flying as he could. There were many dry twigs and dead leaves on the ground, so he made considerable noise which drew a volley of rebel bullets after him, but fortunately he was not hit.

Coming to our line he did not pause for ceremony or give the countersign, but running up the loose dirt placed his foot on top of the breastworks and leaped clear over men, guns and bayonets. It was my fortune to stand within six feet of where he lit; in fact, he jumped nearly over me, and when we saw who it was and what caused the noise and confusion, I can say of my own knowledge the feeling of surprise, joy and gratitude was simply beyond description. Of course, the first thing required of him was to "give an account of himself." This he did without even waiting for a drink of water. In relating how the rebel robbed him, he moved his hand from place to place, and was just saying "watch" when his hand struck his watch pocket and, to his great surprise, the watch was still there. When he drew it from his pocket and looked at it he could hardly believe his eyes.

'To stay was death or capture'

Sergeant Sam M. Pyle
Company G
52nd Ohio Veteran Volunteer Infantry

The assault of Col. Dan McCook's brigade on Kennesaw Mountain on June 27 I consider about the hottest place, for the time engaged, that we were in.

Our losses were so great that the brigade became mingled into one single line. We made a lodgment at and on the rebel works. Colors were planted several times right up to the works; the 52nd Ohio's at one time were planted in the soft earth at the foot of the rebel works.

After we crossed the creek in our charge up the slope we were under direct musketry fire until we reached the rebel breastworks. It was so withering that I thought at the time that only by chance could any living thing escape. Added to this, to our right and on the enemy's left of the "Dead Angle" they had a battery of eight guns that was pouring double-shotted grape and canister fire into us, enfilading our lines. I judged the distance to be about 500 yards to the battery and realized that the angle was a protection if we could get close to their works. We made a lodgment — the rebels on one side, we holding the other — and we had it "hand to hand." At times we would have been compelled upon one or more critical moments to have surrendered or fall back, but the other regiments of the brigade formed a line just in our rear and, with the energy of despair over our position, they fought like heroes, and by rapid and incessant firing kept the rebels' heads down below the headlogs and top of the breastworks. When they attempted to depress their muskets under the headlogs so as to get range upon those of us lying against the works they had to expose themselves partially, and between those in our rear and those of us at the works we managed to hold our own. But we soon realized that our position was untenable. We could not, in our weakened condition, charge over the works. To stay was death or capture, and we finally succeeded in retiring to where those in our rear had lodged and were doggedly holding the line. Here, 27 paces from the enemy's works with bayonets, tin pans, cups and our hands, we worked as any soldiers can under such circumstances until we had a partial protection, which we strengthened during the night.

Two other incidents from the fight at Kennesaw stand out. Joe Swan of Company G and myself always had a negro servant, although we were not entitled to anything of the sort. We called him "Tom." He was about 16 years old and always on hand in the hottest of the battle. On this occasion, in the charge, Tom was right at my heels with a coffee pot full of coffee, waiting for a chance for me to drink it. As we advanced steady from the start the chance never came, and I heard Tom exclaim, "Dar now, Sergeant, coffee all done spilled." A bullet had struck the coffee pot, wrecking it. Throwing down the useless pot he picked up a dead or wounded soldier's gun and kept right along with us through the charge. All day he pumped lead out of that gun for all it was worth. He was a "sticker," and the boys had a proper consideration and respect for Tom. After our muster-out we sent him back to his home in Tennessee.

It was at Kennesaw that Lieut. David Miser of Company G was shot. We were having our coffee and hardtack, sitting on the ground. After he finished his meal he stood up to stretch himself. Being a tall man he was exposed and made a good mark. A sharpshooter shot him in the breast and later he died in the hospital on Lookout Mountain. He was my chum and I felt his loss as personal. Capt. Rothacker of Company G made it his business to avenge his lieutenant's death and, after deliberate preparation and waiting, he planted a minnie squarely in the sharpshooter's left eye. When we had the truce to bury our dead some rebels told us they had cautioned him not to be reckless, but he "wanted to be smart, and some Yankee called him sure and hard."

The night after the battle the rebels threw lighted cotton balls saturated with turpentine between our works and theirs to prevent a night attack. This was about as inhuman an act as I know of in all my army experience. I do not think I will ever forget the groans and moans of the wounded and dying

■ Col. Caleb J. Dilworth commanded the 85th Illinois during the campaign, until June 27 when he assumed command of McCook's brigade following McCook's mortal wounding and the death of Col. Oscar F. Harmon. Dilworth himself was wounded at Jonesboro on September 1, but recovered before the end of 1864.

■ Capt. Samuel Rothacker, Company G, 52nd Ohio. Just after the failure of the charge at the Dead Angle, the survivors of the 52nd and the rest of McCook's brigade fell back less than 30 paces from the Confederate works. Wrote Major J.T. Holmes of the 52nd: "As illustrating how close to the ground the men were obliged to lie when we dropped back to the little crest, Capt. Rothacker was lying with his head on his hands and the brim of his big black military hat was shot through just by the band within a half inch of his head."

as they lay between them and ourselves, unable to crawl back, and we unable to succor them. I only wished I could.

'A death sentence to every man in the regiment'

2nd Lieut. Milo H. Lewis
Adjutant
121st Ohio Volunteer Infantry

Our brigade received an order about sunset [on June 25] to be ready to move at a moment's notice. We packed up and sat down on our knapsacks to await the notice. Long we waited until sleep overcame us. The earth furnished a ready couch, the knapsack an easy pillow.

Midnight found us sound asleep when the notice came. Reluctantly we arose with much rubbing of drooping eyelids and shuffled unsteadily into line, ready for the word to move on, we knew not whither and cared not to inquire. We needed no injunction to keep quiet as we moved off, the sharp outline of the batteries on Kennesaw, clearly defined in the bright moonlight, exerted sufficient influence to keep us from disturbing the apparent slumber of the gunners. A portion of McPherson's Corps [sic] came to take our place.

Long as we traveled old Kennesaw hung still at our elbow like a dark sentinel, observing our movement with unwavering watchfulness and unfolding, we feared, that which we so much desired should be hidden. The gray tints of morning appeared, and when they gave way to the sunrise of a Sabbath day we halted nearly a mile in rear of our front line, only three miles west of our starting point in a direct line, but twice that far by the way we came.

Most of the day was spent in making up for loss of sleep, but our eyes were opened long enough to notice various movements that indicated the formation of an assaulting column, which was not an agreeable discovery, for we had seen too much of the infernal ingenuity by which the sharpened points of saplings and brush, hacked and bent forward, presented an intricate mass of wooden spears, capable of arresting our charge long enough to allow the defenders, safely sheltered behind massive earthworks, to slaughter us with impunity under the muzzles of their guns while we were trying in vain to tear our way through the frightful obstructions.

Our hope was that we might follow but not lead or form a part of the column selected for sacrifice.

Next morning at daybreak (June 27) we were called up under orders to be ready to move at a moment's notice.

After breakfast our brigade [Mitchell's], with McCook's, was formed in column by regiments. We waited there about two hours for further orders, uncertain yet whether our column was to lead or to act in support of some other column.

Meanwhile, the sun, rising hotter and higher, poured down a fierce heat that was untempered by cloud or breath of stirring air. Wherever the few low bushes around us furnished a scanty shade there we clustered, panted and waited.

At length a messenger was seen delivering an order to the Colonel and all eyes were turned in that direction. The Colonel called me to carry the verbal message to each company commander. It was a simple matter to walk briskly through the scattered ranks and say to each proper officer, "Have your men fall in without knapsacks" — a short announcement, but enough to settle the question as to who was going first. It was our lot.

I had the opportunity to note the effect of these words; how the silence was only broken by company commanders repeating the order; how the men arose from their reclining positions with compressed lips and a far-away look of the eyes, each busy with his own thoughts of home and loved ones, and proceeded to lay aside such articles as must be left behind and might never be needed again.

The feeling that pervaded the ranks may be shown in the remark of a comrade who met the bearer of the message 30 years after: "Forget your face? Never. It rises before me whenever I think of Kennesaw, for it seemed to me you were carrying a death sentence to every man in the regiment."

When the line was formed two companies were deployed in single line to cover the brigade front and two other companies five paces behind them, the remainder of the regiment to follow in line of battle, and behind us the other regiments of the brigade, also in line of battle, one after the other. McCook's brigade joined us on the left in similar formation.

After a heavy outburst of artillery along our lines, which was answered by the enemy's batteries, the signal was given about 9 a.m. and our skirmishers leaped over the works of Morgan's brigade and rushed upon the gray skirmish line without stopping until the enemy was out and our men were in the rifle pits.

This was accomplished before the Confederates opened fire from the main works, but when the heavy column that followed us came nearer the ramparts blazed with a deadly fire of cannon and musketry. This column had to double-quick across a valley a mile wide. The day was fiercely hot so that all were exhausted when they reached the foot of the enemy's works and found their further progress barred by a network of sharpened stakes, impassable to assailants with any semblance of formation.

But it was not in the hearts of these men to retreat. "Dig for your lives!" the word passed along, and with bayonets, tin cups, plates and hands they proceeded to dig themselves under cover while the front ranks were able, at such close range, to direct a continuous fire between the head logs of the enemy's works, creating such a spluttering of lead and splinters that the defenders lay low, apparently well satisfied with having checked the onset and strewn the field with thousands of their assailants with little loss to themselves.

In this manner our earthworks grew up within 35 or 40 paces of the enemy's fortifications, and when tools had been brought forward at night we succeeded in bringing our defenses into condition that enabled us to bid defiance to our rivals next morning.

This description applies to Mitchell's and McCook's brigades. The other two brigades, Harker's and Wagner's, which took part with us in the assault a little to our left, were equally unsuccessful.

'Still the Yankees came'

Private Samuel R. Watkins
Company H
1st Tennessee Volunteer Infantry

The First and Twenty-seventh Tennessee regiments will ever remember the battle of "Dead Angle," which was fought June 27th, on the Kennesaw line, near Marietta, Georgia. It was one of the hottest and longest days of

■ Corporal John H. Boyd, Company B, 121st Ohio, was killed on June 27 near the Dead Angle. His regimental commander, Col. Henry B. Banning, later wrote of the destruction wreaked by the Confederates' first volleys: "The enemy still was reserving his fire, and continued to do so until my command got close up to his ditches ... when he opened upon my single line with grape and canister from both flanks and a full line of small-arms from my front. On the left, the captain of Company B was mortally wounded; the captain of Company G was shot dead; the captain of Company E was shot through the ankle, from which wound he has since died, while the major who was in charge of the left received three mortal wounds. Company I had lost 29 out of 56 men she took into action. Their commander was wounded in the knee, while most of the sergeants were either killed or wounded. In Company B, all of them were either killed or wounded."

■ Private Samuel R. Watkins, Company H, 1st Tennessee, turned 25 years old the day before the fight at the Dead Angle. He was wounded three times during four years of service in the 1st Tennessee, including a shot in the ankle and heel in the battle of Atlanta on July 22.

the year, and one of the most desperate and determinedly resisted battles fought during the whole war. Our regiment was stationed on an angle, a little spur of the mountain, or rather promontory of a range of hills, extending far out beyond the main line of battle, and was subject to the enfilading fire of forty pieces of artillery of the Federal batteries.

On the fatal morning of June 27th the sun rose clear and cloudless, the heavens seemed made of brass, and the earth of iron, and as the sun began to mount toward the zenith, everything became quiet, and no sound was heard save a peckerwood on a neighboring tree, tapping on its old trunk, trying to find a worm for its dinner. We all knew it was but the dead calm that precedes the storm. On the distant hills we could plainly see officers dashing about hither and thither, and the Stars and Stripes moving to and fro, and we knew the Federals were making preparations for the mighty contest. We could hear but the rumbling sound of heavy guns, and the distant tread of a marching army, as a faint roar of the coming storm, which was soon to break the ominous silence with the sound of conflict, such as was scarcely ever before heard on this earth. It seemed that the arch-angel of Death stood and looked on with outstretched wings, while all the earth was silent, when all at once a hundred guns from the Federal line opened upon us, and for more than an hour they poured their solid and chain shot, grape and shrapnel right upon this salient point ... when, all of a sudden, our pickets jumped into our works and reported the Yankees advancing, and almost at the same time a solid line of blue coats came up the hill.

I discharged my gun, and happening to look up, there was the beautiful flag of the Stars and Stripes flaunting right in my face, and I heard John Branch, of the Rock City Guards, commanded by Captain W.D. Kelley, who were next Company H, say, "Look at that Yankee flag; shoot that fellow; snatch that flag out of his hand!"

Column after column of Federal soldiers were crowded upon that line ... but no sooner would a regiment mount our works than they were shot down or surrendered, and soon we had every "gopher hole" full of Yankee prisoners. Yet still the Yankees came. It seemed impossible to check the onslaught, but every man was true to his trust, and seemed to think that at that moment the whole responsibility of the Confederate government was rested upon his shoulders. Talk about other battles, victories, shouts, cheers, and triumphs, but in comparison with this day's fight, all others dwarf into insignificance. The sun beaming down on our uncovered heads, the thermometer being one hundred and ten degrees in the shade, and a solid line of blazing fire right from the muzzles of the Yankee guns being poured right into our very faces, singeing our hair and clothes, the hot blood of our dead and wounded spurting on us, the blinding smoke and stifling atmosphere filling our eyes and mouths, and the awful concussion causing the blood to gush out of our noses and ears, and above all, the roar of battle, made it a perfect pandemonium. Afterward I heard a soldier express himself by saying that he thought "Hell had broke loose in Georgia, sure enough."

I ... shot one hundred and twenty times that day. My gun became so hot that frequently the powder would flash before I could ram home the ball, and I had frequently to exchange my gun for that of a dead comrade.

Colonel H.R. Feild was loading and shooting the same as any private in the ranks when he fell off the skid from which he was shooting right over my shoulder, shot through the head. I laid him down in the trench, and he said, "Well, they have got me at last, but I have killed fifteen of them; time about is fair play, I reckon." But Colonel Feild was not killed — only wounded, and one side paralyzed. Captain Joe P. Lee, Captain Mack Campbell, Lieutenant T.H. Maney, and other officers of the regiment, threw rocks and beat them in their faces with sticks. The Yankees did the same. The rocks came in upon us like a perfect hail storm, and the Yankees seemed very obstinate, and in no hurry to get away from our front, and we had to keep up the firing and shooting them down in self-defense. They seemed to walk up and take death as cooly as if they were automatic or wooden men, and our boys did not shoot for the fun of the thing. It was, verily, a life and death grapple, and the least flicker on our part, would have been sure death to all. We could not be reinforced on account of our position, and we had to stand up to the rack, fodder or no fodder. When the Yankees fell back, and the firing ceased, I never saw so many broken down and exhausted men in my life. I was as sick as a horse, and as wet with blood and sweat as I could be, and many of our men were vomiting with excessive fatigue, over-exhaustion, and sunstroke; our tongues were parched and cracked for water, and our faces blackened with powder and smoke, and our dead and wounded were piled indiscriminately in the trenches. There was not a single man in the company who was not wounded, or had holes shot through his hat and clothing.

Captain Beasley was killed, and nearly all his company killed and wounded. The Rock City Guards were almost piled in heaps and so was our company. Captain Joe P. Lee was badly wounded. Poor Walter Hood and Jim Brandon were lying there among us, while their spirits were in heaven; also, William A. Hughes, my old mess-mate and friend ... who loved me more than any other person on earth has ever done. I had just discharged the contents of my gun into the bosoms of two men, one right behind the other, killing them both, and was re-loading, when a Yankee rushed upon me, having me at a disadvantage, and said, "You have killed my two brothers, and now I've got you." Everything I had ever done rushed through my mind. I heard the roar, and felt the flash of fire, and saw my more than friend, William A. Hughes, grab the muzzle of the gun, receiving the whole contents in his hand and arm, and mortally wounding him. In saving my life, he lost his own. When the infirmary corps carried him off, all mutilated and bleeding, he told them to give me "Florence Fleming" (that was the name of his gun, which he had put on it in silver letters), and to give me his blanket and clothing. He gave his life for me, and everything that he had. It was the last time that I ever saw him ...

■ Brig. Gen. George E. Maney commanded a brigade and later, at Jonesboro, Cheatham's division of the Army of Tennessee. Originally colonel of the 1st Tennessee, Maney served early in the war under Gen. Robert E. Lee in the Cheat Mountain campaign, and with Gen. T.J. "Stonewall" Jackson at Bath and Romney, Va. On June 27, his brigade of Tennessee troops, including the 1st/27th and 6th/9th Tennessee, occupied the apex of the Dead Angle and was responsible for much of the stubborn resistance confronting McCook's and Mitchell's brigades.

'This is a pretty hot place'

1st Lieut. William H. Baxter
Company K
113th Ohio Volunteer Infantry

The sun rose on Monday the 27th of June, 1864, bright and clear. The men went about the duties of the morning untroubled by the knowledge that a dreadful enterprise had been planned for them, had been ordered, and that in three or four hours many of them would be still in death or suffering from shocking wounds.

I had no knowledge of what was before us until H.N. Benjamin, captain on Col. Mitchell's staff, rode up to me and told me that a charge had been ordered, and that when the bugle shall sound it will be to fall in, in order to march to the front line, whence the charge will start.

When the bugle notes did ring clear and loud through the regiment and brigade, I knew what ordeal lay before us. Company K fell into line at company quarters and was counted off. When the company first fell into

■ Col. John G. Mitchell, 113th Ohio, commanded the 2nd Brigade, 2nd Division, XIV Corps. His brigade attacked Cheatham Hill to the immediate right of Dan McCook's brigade at the Dead Angle. Mitchell later wrote: "Our failure to succeed in this assault is owing to the following facts: First, the distance to be passed was too great; second, the excessive heat; third, inadequate support on our right flank. Our loss was very heavy ..." On June 27, the 113th Ohio lost 153 men in 20 minutes, including 10 of 19 commissioned officers who went into the charge.

line we had 63 men, including the two commissioned officers in charge of the company — the first and second lieutenants. On the way from where we camped to the front line, where the charge started, the regiment halted several times. The actions of many discovered that serious thoughts were in men's minds. We all knew that some, perhaps very many, would fall. But who? I or my neighbor?

In due time we arrived at our front line of breastworks and, halting, sat or lay down behind them. Before us were the woods; within that woods were the rebel skirmishers and somewhere behind them were their strong works and their troops.

We sat there some time, I should think 20 minutes at least, perhaps longer. Skirmishing was going on in the woods in our front. Several men were brought back wounded. All felt serious. There was but little laughing or joking while waiting there. While all knew the desperate work before them, and while the question in every mind was "who will escape safe and who will not," each hoping the best, yet courage and resolution was on the faces of the men. The situation of waiting and reflecting under those circumstances is much more trying on men than an immediate advance.

Finally, "Forward!" was commanded. Over the breastworks we jumped, and onward into the woods and toward the rebel works we took our course. The morning was hot, our march hurried and some of the men began to feel exhausted after a time. Occasionally a man would stumble over some obstruction, and several times I found it necessary to encourage and urge such on.

Men began to fall. I remember well seeing Stephen Barr. He fell full length and lay with his head to the foe, his face turned partly upward, his rifle by his side. He had been shot dead through the head near the eye. He died a Christian soldier, for while in camp and during the campaign he daily made his testament his study and led a consistent life. It was not the rule for our men to devote much time to religious matters. The majority sought to be respectable men, but did not trouble themselves much about religion, at least outwardly.

A few paces from Barr, Hiram Hancock lay dead, also shot through the head. But we did not stop for these or others, but pressed on.

In all dangerous places it had been my strong desire to live long enough to know that victory was ours. My thoughts in this instance were similar. They ran: "This is a pretty hot place; I don't know whether I will get out or not; if I am killed I will not know anything about the result and it will make no difference, but if I am wounded I will know the result so there is no use thinking about the consequences, but take what comes."

Suddenly occurred a great shock like the terrific jar of a peal of thunder close at hand. I took a step forward and found my foot give way under me and I fell to the ground. At once I knew I had been wounded. Immediately examining the wound, I found both bones of my leg smashed into pieces a few inches above the ankle. Fearing that I might bleed to death, I rolled up my trouser leg above the knee, took a silk handkerchief from my pocket, tied it tightly about my leg just below the knee and, breaking off a stem of a bush, used it as a lever to twist the bandage so tight that all flow of blood was stopped.

Immediately after I was wounded the charge failed and, men scattering, sought safety as best they could. While I was bandaging my leg a member of my company, John Tway, came up and helped me back some distance until he gave out. The day was hot and he was not strong. Then Sergeant Barber assisted me a short distance until, on his saying he was exhausted, I told him to leave me and save himself, that I would chance it to get back some way. Soon after, I received aid from two men of the 121st Ohio and

Perry Howard of my own company.

Before reaching our own works and while but a short distance from them, Howard, who had hold of my right shoulder, was shot through the arm and side and fell flat as if killed. The other men did not stop to inquire whether he was killed or not, but hurried with me to the works. Howard survived.

After we got over our works the rebels continued a dangerous shelling. There was considerable delay in getting the ambulances brought up near enough to receive the wounded. Back of our works a few rods, behind a gentle rise of ground, quite a number of wounded, including myself, were collected. Here the surgeons were binding up bad wounds temporarily so they could be taken back to the rear. Rebel shells were flying in the air and bursting overhead, which tried the courage of the physicians and caused them occasionally to forget their patients and "duck" their bodies, causing pain to the wounded. They were but men, and to remain steel-nerved amid bursting shells was not their business, and they had not particularly tried to cultivate it.

Finally, after some storming by Col. Mitchell, the ambulances were brought up and I was taken some distance back to a field hospital and laid on the ground with scores of others, waiting to have my leg amputated, for from the first I knew it would have to be done. It began to feel painful and I was anxious to have it done. In a reasonable time my right leg was amputated about four and a half inches below the knee, after which I was laid on a blanket on the ground in a tent. Two of my boys gathered some leaves which they tied in a bundle and placed under my knee for support to keep the raw stump off the ground.

I was not alone. There was plenty of company around me. Among others was James Clabaugh of my company who was shot through the breast, the ball going clear through and inflicting a very bad wound, and no one thought it worth while to spend much time on him as he could not get well; and Joseph Newcomb, also of Company K, who was wounded in the wrist. He was walking about, holding his hand and complaining of the pain, but no one thought his wound serious and expected him soon to recover. Clabaugh got well and was mustered out in June 1865, while Newcomb died of his wound at Nashville on July 24.

I lay that day and night on the ground in the clothes I had worn during the battle, and in the morning found my clothes fly-blown where blood had got upon them. As may be supposed, when morning came I felt quite feeble. In the morning Harry Shepherd, my brother-in-law of the 66th Ohio, XX Corps, came over. He and my brother, Charles T. Baxter, sergeant in my own company, bathed me and put on me some clean underclothes, after which I was put in an ambulance and started for Big Shanty, a railroad station about nine miles back.

My work was done. Others would go on, but I must go back. I had suffered a great misfortune without any compensation. We were shot down by the hundreds while the rebels behind their strong works escaped with scarcely any loss. The whole affair was useless and a mistake, and Sherman's reason given is not creditable to him or any good general. Could we have felt that our enemies had also lost a reasonable number, there would have been some compensation, but for them to have lost almost nothing and to be damaged in nothing, made us feel that we had been a useless sacrifice. If any just reason had been given for the charge we would have felt better. Or even if Sherman had said it was a mistake and should not have been made, but the reason given was not such as to justify him in the loss of a single life in that charge.

Company K was a company added to the 113th Regiment in the beginning of 1864. The majority of the company was seeing its first service, while

■ Lt. Col. Darius B. Warner commanded the 113th Ohio in the attack of Mitchell's brigade on June 27 at Cheatham's Hill. Warner later wrote: "One incident at Kennesaw made an impression on my mind more than all the rest. Certain circumstances in the history of the regiment had made my acquaintance with a particular sergeant of one of the companies, and he became with me a great favorite. When the assault had been made, and we had almost reached the works of the enemy, it became evident that we could not capture them, and I sent word along the line for the men to cover themselves and commence firing. After I thought we were doing well and the men were well hidden under rocks and behind logs and trees, I discovered this favorite sergeant standing out in full view of the enemy, loading and firing as though he were at target practice. I was sure he would be killed, for the rebels seemed to be literally skinning the hill. I turned toward him, and began to motion to him with my right hand to lie down, and while in this position I was shot, and this was the last shake of my right hand."

As a result of the wound, Warner's right arm was amputated. The reckless sergeant, Francis M. McAdams, escaped the battle without a scratch.

■ Lt. Col. James M. Shane, commander of the 98th Ohio, was mortally wounded on June 27 during the assault of Mitchell's brigade. According to wartime journalist Whitelaw Reid, "When [Shane] was told that death was inevitable, he exclaimed, 'My poor wife! Were it not for her — but, O Lord, thy will, not mine, be done.' " Shane's last words before dying were, "Turn my face to the foe, boys."

some of them had seen much service elsewhere. While the company had been under fire with the regiment all along the campaign, until June 27 the regiment in that campaign had been in no place where there had been any serious loss. This was, then, the first desperate place for most of the company. They did their duty well. As brave men they obeyed orders. The loss of the company was heavy. Seven were killed; five more died of their wounds, making 12 deaths. One, Booker Durnell, was captured and died in a rebel prison. Ten or 12 more were wounded, some of them very seriously, so that of the men who went in, one-third died or became valueless to the service.

'Amid a perfect shower of lead'

2nd Lieut. William M. Latimer
Company H
9th Tennessee Volunteer Infantry

The Federal troops concentrated their forces at the foot of the hill at the turn, or elbow, in front of the 1st Tennessee Regiment, Colonel Feild commanding; and the 6th and 9th Consolidated Regiment, of which I was a member, was to his left.

Just before the assault was made we were subjected to the most terrible cannonading it was ever my misfortune to witness. When the firing ceased, the enemy was seen approaching and very close at hand. Then was opened the most destructive close-range fire of musketry I witnessed during the war. The enemy rushed right up to our works. A flag bearer mounted the works and planted his colors on them. One of our boys also mounted and had a tussle with him for possession of the flag, but the Federal carried it back with him. They made a gallant assault and had the satisfaction of retiring, what was left of them, but without making any break in our line.

One of the most thrilling incidents of this battle was Colonel Feild's daring exploit. While the assault was at its closest range, which was so close that the line of breastworks was all that separated the contending forces, Colonel Feild mounted the works with drawn sword and cheered his men to stand the storm, seeming to forget that the leaden missiles of death were as thick as hail. He was struck by a minie ball and rolled into the ditch among his men, and word went down the line that the Colonel was killed. Upon examination it was found that the ball had struck his forehead at the edge of the hair and ranged over the skull. He soon regained consciousness and recovered.

At the time the assault was raging in its fury, Colonel Feild's adjutant came running down the line to the left of the point where our regiment was stationed, with orders that we were to move to the right and fall in behind his regiment, which was out of ammunition. We were ordered to move by the flank, which was done amid a perfect shower of lead, and as we went we stooped very low.

During a part of this engagement General Cheatham, by flag of truce, offered a cessation of hostilities so the enemy could care for his dead and wounded. The reply came that they would "have possession of the field in time to bury their dead and care for their wounded," but the next evening they asked for and obtained permission to bury their dead.

Many of their wounded had died before getting any attention. The pickets were marked to halfway ground between the contending lines; and when they met they "about-faced" and stood back to back, each facing toward his own comrades. The Federals then scooped holes by each dead body, rolled them in and covered them up. Those of us in the ditches the day after the battle could never forget the stench arising from those dead bodies.

We were fatigued and worn out with continued watching and resting on arms in the ditches and were moved to the left on a line of works out of range of the incessant cannonading, it being confined principally to the point of the angle. When we got to our new position we at once doffed our clothing, spread our blankets at the rear of our breastworks and lay down to sleep.

During the night there was a sudden severe bombardment from the enemy. We had just gotten to sleep, and the sudden awakening caused such a panic among the boys that we could scarcely get inside our fort. The order "Fall in line!" was obeyed by some with one leg in their pants, by others with pants in hand, while others were altogether minus. We expected another assault on our lines, but it never came. This false alarm furnished the boys amusement for many days.

'We simply did our duty'

Private James L.W. Blair
Company I
1st Tennessee Volunteer Infantry

We waited anxiously for the Federals to open the fight. We could see some activity in a battery on a hill opposite our position, and about ten o'clock a furious cannonading began. It was very hot, and we had our blankets stretched to shelter us in the trenches; but when the shells began to come our way blankets went down, and we kept out of sight until that part of the programme was finished.

The shelling was to cover the advance of the infantry, and as soon as it ceased we looked down the long, wooded slope and saw the enemy advancing, cheering as they came. Our cartridge boxes were quickly adjusted, every gun was in place, and when the order was given to fire a sheet of flame burst from under the head logs and the missiles of death crashed through the enemy's lines.

The brigades on our right and left, as far as they could reach the enemy, poured in their fire, and a battery on our left shattered their lines with an enfilading fire of grape and canister. For about twenty minutes it was "hot times." The Yankees came on gallantly and some reached the top of our works, but only to come over as prisoners while others fell almost at the muzzles of our guns. Many took refuge behind trees but were picked off. Nine were killed behind one tree.

One new recruit, wearing a straw hat, was seen after the battle behind a rock near our works. We invited him to come in, and he very promptly accepted our invitation. After the smoke of battle cleared away we saw that a part of the attacking force had taken shelter under the abrupt slope of the hill on the right of our regiment and were fortifying.

Being one of the guards on the battlefield while the Federals were burying their dead [on the 29th], the opportunity was presented of passing our compliments, and the Yanks seemed glad to get a chance to talk to a Johnnie about the fight. One big, strapping fellow said that they had two

■ Maj. Gen. Benjamin F. Cheatham commanded a division, and, temporarily on several occasions, a corps in the Army of Tennessee during the campaign. The Dead Angle was a section of his line situated on what became known as "Cheatham's Hill." During the burial truce there on June 29, he and members of his staff left the Confederate works to view progress and converse with Federal officers. An eyewitness, Chaplain George W. Pepper of the 80th Ohio, later wrote: "Cheatham looked rugged and healthy, though seemingly sad and despondent. He wore his 'fatigue' dress — a blue flannel shirt, black neck-tie, gray homespun pantaloons and black slouch hat. At first he was not disposed to be either inquisitive or communicative, but after putting himself outside a few heavy drinks of commissary whisky from the bottle of one of our officers, 'he was himself again,' and made many inquiries about Nashvillians and the Rock City."

Another eyewitness, Sergeant Robert M. Rogers of Company B, 125th Illinois, recalled: "Cheatham's uniform consisted of an old slouch hat, a blue hickory shirt, butternut pants and a pair of cavalry boots. The supports of his unmentionables were an old leather strap, and a piece of web, the general appearance being that of a 'johnny' gone to seed."

■ Capt. Salathiel M. Neighbor, Company D, 52nd Ohio, was severely wounded on June 27 when within 12 feet of the Confederate breastworks at the Dead Angle. Stripping off his sword and belt, he staggered to the rear. The sword was brought back by Col. Charles Clancy of the 52nd, who picked it up after tripping on the belt in making his own way back after the failed assault. Neighbor died of his wound on July 7 at Chattanooga.

divisions — thirty regiments — massed on our front. This was against one regiment of Confederates (in single line) of two hundred men, judging from the size of my company.

We were reinforced near the close of the fight by another regiment of our brigade. I helped to fortify that part of the line and we took pains to make it as safe as digging could make it. The rear of the trench was made deep enough for a man to stand straight without being exposed while loading, then step up, placing the gun under the head log, with which the works were surmounted, fire and step back, load and come again; but there was no *chevaux de frise* in front to retard the enemy's advance. I think the Federal dead were about eight hundred, and our loss was thirteen killed and seventeen wounded. Of course, the First Tennessee does not claim all the honor. We simply did our duty and no man shirked.

A little incident occurred a few days after the battle which reminded us of the "battle of the lightning bugs."* The enemy lying so near us, we were required to watch all night and keep up occasional firing so that sleep was out of the question. We were finally relieved by a regiment of our brigade and allowed to retire a few hundred yards to rest. About midnight we were aroused by a terrific firing, and learned that a Yank had ordered in a loud voice, "Forward, double-quick, charge!" just to see what would happen. The boys had jumped to their guns and poured in volley after volley, which amused the Yankees very much, who were a short distance away lying in their trenches.

'Scared out of my pants'

1st Lieut. Thomas H. Maney
Company B
1st Tennessee Volunteer Infantry

The Federals were massed in regiments and came up quietly with their bayonets gleaming in the bright sun. They were fine-looking fellows and brave. There they stood, not firing for several minutes, but we were pour-

* The so-called "battle of the lightning bugs" occurred along the New Hope Church line in late May, and became a great source of amusement to those Confederates involved, as described by Private Blair: "It was [Gen. James] Cantey's brigade of Alabama troops that did the shooting at the bugs, and my brigade [Gen. Alfred J. Vaughan's] joked them wonderfully about it. A Tennesseean would call to another in the hearing of Cantey's men, 'Say, Gen. Cheatham is going to Atlanta to-day.' His comrade would ask, 'What for?' and the first would shout back, 'To get blacking to put on the tails of the lightning bugs to keep Cantey's men from wasting their ammunition.'

But it was not long before Cantey's men came back at us strong. The Yankees had made a lodgment close up to our lines [at the Dead Angle]. Everything was hanging on a hair trigger; a man on either side dare not show an inch of his hat above the breastworks. It was night, everything perfectly quiet along the entire line, when we were startled by hearing a Yankee just in front of us shout: 'Forward, double-quick, charge!' We thought they were on us, and without waiting for orders poured a volley out in the darkness. The report of our arms was the only sound, and after that died away everything was again quiet. The Yankees, knowing our expectancy, had, out of a pure spirit of devilment, shouted the order, and, anticipating the result, were well under cover when we fired. But this quieted the joke on Cantey, for when we attempted to guy them they would say Gen. Cheatham had gone to Atlanta to buy candles for his babies who were afraid to stay in the dark."

ing musketry into them, and a battery we had on our left was pouring grape and canister into them, and a battery still farther to our left was firing shot and shell among them. They looked as if they had come to stay.

Erelong they made a rush on us, but, brave and gallant as they were, they had foemen to meet them who never quailed. Our regiment was placed along in the works only in single file, about two paces apart, but we had the word passed to us to hold the works at all hazards, and it did look as if we would be pushed back by sheer force. But stand we must, and stand we did.

Some of the enemy were killed on our works. The battle lasted nearly an hour. Then the enemy fell back below the crest of the hill and commenced fortifying, for they had been at work while fighting us. And it was then we discovered that our works were too far beyond the crest of the hill for us to successfully defend them. They were busy burrowing in the ground and sharpshooting at us, and we lost some good men.

We were somewhat reassured, about the winding up of the battle, by a line marching up behind us in our works, and still farther back was another one, and behind them was a detachment of artillery with guns trained on this angle, for it would have been disastrous to our army to have lost this point. I suppose "Old Joe" was afraid they would make another attack, and he was preparing to give them a warmer reception. But they seemed to have had enough. We had as much as we wanted.

We lay there that day, night and the next day. That night we were ordered back to the rear line and on the morning of the 29th were ordered again to the front line, when a flag of truce was raised by the enemy for the purpose of burying their dead. This came none too soon. We had been forced to keep awake all the time as the enemy was only a few yards from us, and, though we had rations, we had lost all appetite owing to the condition of the unburied dead near us. They buried a great many, but I don't know the number. That night we were relieved and marched back to a reserve work about three hundred yards to the rear, to rest and sleep.

On the first night of our rest there was a false alarm. In the darkness a fellow would imagine he saw someone crawling, and then — bang! The report would be answered by several, causing the alarm. Generally such sensations did but little harm. I did not get hurt that night, but got scared out of my pants.

Having pulled off my shoes, socks and pants, I folded them up nicely for a pillow, and was sleeping at a two-forty gait when the din began by bang! bang! boom! boom! while the cry went up all around us: "Fall in, fall in; the enemy are on us!" Some thought that we were still on the front line, and were nearly crazed from loss of sleep. Every man awoke with a start, too dazed to know where to go, but our guns were stacked just before us, and there were the works.

I jumped up, put on my socks, shoes and hat, grabbed what I thought was my pants, jammed one foot through a breeches leg, but it would not go on, simply for the reason that it was my jacket; gave that up as a bad job, looked for the pants and could not find them, so I put on my jacket and fell into line in Texas costume style. Everybody was too much excited to notice my white pants, so after the scare I wrapped my blanket around me and lay down to rest again, promising myself that I would be up with the first peep of day and find my pants before any of the boys could find it out.

But the joke was too good, and I had to tell it and help to laugh at myself for being "scared out of my pants."

■ 1st Lieut. Christopher W. Grimes was second in command of Company C, 52nd Ohio, during the campaign. Twenty-nine men of his company were killed or wounded on June 27 at the Dead Angle, including most of the color guard. Grimes survived the war.

■ A metal clothing stencil belonging to 18-year-old Private Boyd Forbes, Company C, 52nd Ohio. Forbes was killed at the Dead Angle on June 27, and is buried in the Marietta National Cemetery, Section H, Grave 364.

■ Lt. Col. Oscar Van Tassell commanded the 34th Illinois during the campaign. As part of Mitchell's assault on June 27 at Cheatham's Hill, four companies of the 34th were deployed as skirmishers in the brigade's front. Van Tassell wrote: "Advancing on the double-quick, my skirmishers drove in the outposts of the enemy, capturing several prisoners during the charge; some of my men pursuing the retreating foe so far as to die within twenty feet of the rebel works. Corporal George Phipps of Company A, carrying the colors, pressed forward with the intention of planting the Stars and Stripes on the enemy's works, but was wounded before he could accomplish his design; wounded as he was, he brought off the colors, when the skirmishers were ordered back, until a second shot compelled him to drop them, when Lieut. Teeter carried them from the field." The 34th's losses that day amounted to six men killed, 28 wounded and one missing.

'A flag of truce'

Sergeant Major Lyman Widney
34th Illinois Veteran Volunteer Infantry

Camp near Marietta, Ga.
June 30th, 1864.

My dear Parents,

We are still hammering away at the Rebs along the same line, without seeming to accomplish much. We are creeping slowly forward and, of course, they will have to skedaddle before long.

You have heard of the unsuccessful charge made upon the Rebel works on the 27th. Two brigades of our corps were engaged, the 2nd and 3rd. A portion of the 34th was deployed as skirmishers and helped drive the Rebel skirmishers from their line of rifle pits into the main works. Our two brigades charged up to the main works and although unable to carry them, held the ground they had gained and constructed a line of works only 20 yards from the Rebels. They are so close now that a head dare not appear above the works on either side. Our Regt. lost 6 killed and 28 wounded.

If you received the last letter I wrote in pencil you will remember we then lay in front of Kennesaw Mountain exposed to the shells from the battery on top. They favored us with a few dozen shells after I wrote but without hurting any in our Regt., although some men were hurt a short distance from us. Our batteries handled them so roughly that they could not fire while our guns fired at them, consequently they would keep out of sight till all was quiet, and we were running loose through camp away from our works, then they would run up their guns, load and sight them, and before we were aware of it, would fire a whole volley into the midst of our camps, sometimes killing or wounding some unfortunate soldier. Our batteries would then open on them vigorously for 15 or 20 minutes, but the Rebs would lay quietly under cover until another opportunity offered for repeating the dose.

On the night of the 26th we moved from that position 3 miles further to the right of our line, near our present location, and the charge took place next day. We are half a mile in rear of our advance work and the Rebel bullets "zip" around day and night.

Yesterday morning the Rebs sent in a flag of truce proposing an armistice of six hours for the purpose of burying their dead and ours lying between the two lines. It was agreed to and hostilities in our front ceased. I went out within a few steps of the Rebel works where the blue and grey coats were promiscuously mingled together, engaged in friendly conversation. The Rebel works were lined with butternuts with their arms in their hands. Our works were the same but no armed men were allowed on the neutral ground.

I had quite an interesting chat with a Reb lieutenant. While talking with him, Gens. Cheatham and Hindman came out with their staffs and met some of our officers. A Rebel colonel made the introduction and after bowing very politely the whole party sat down on the ground about six feet distant from where I sat on a log, and talked pleasantly together for almost an hour.

Cheatham looked very unlike I supposed a Rebel major general commanding a corps would look. He wore nothing but a rough pair of grey pants tucked under the tops of an unpolished pair of boots, a blue flannel shirt and rough felt hat completed his attire. He had neither coat nor vest and was without any or manner to indicate his rank.

Gen. Hindman was just the reverse. He has a handsome, good natured countenance, and wears an abundance of gold lace and cord. Speaking of prisoners he remarked that a great many of our soldiers had fallen into his hands, and none ever had cause to accuse him of unkindness. A prisoner, said he, ceases for the time being to be a soldier, and should be treated as kindly as possible under the circumstance.

Our men and the Rebs were busily engaged till after two o'clock in burying the dead. When the task was completed the flags were taken down and both parties retreated to their works, and soon the sharp irregular firing along the line showed that the work of death had been resumed.

July 1st. The weather is intolerably hot. We almost roast to death in the shade. We are anxious to have a lull in the campaign, but don't want to stop this side of Atlanta. We were foolish enough to believe before we started out this campaign that we knew what it was to be a soldier, but our conclusion now is that we have heretofore been playing soldier.

We once thought it a good thing to be exposed to the enemy's fire for a few hours. It is the 60th day of the campaign and during that time only 13 days passed that we have not heard the whistle of Rebel balls. The remainder of the time has found us night and day in surmounting danger of being shot. Scores of men in our brigade have been killed or wounded in their tents. We have become accustomed, however, to the constant presence of danger and don't mind it much now unless the firing assumes the proportion of a battle. Our men are hopeful and cheerful and speak of the summer campaign as being the last. They are confident of Grant's success and, too, of our own success, regarded as so certain as that the sun will rise tomorrow morning.

I suppose you are very busy and don't find time for writing often, but I hope you will write as often as you have an opportunity. Letters are the cheapest and most desirable gift you can send.

Yours affectionately,
Lyman

■ Maj. Gen. Thomas C. Hindman commanded a division in Hood's corps until the night of July 3, when he was struck in the eye by a tree branch while riding his horse during Johnston's withdrawal from Kennesaw Mountain. Although a pre-war friend of Gen. Pat Cleburne, he was not well liked by the brigade commanders serving under him. "Hindman never led his division," wrote Gen. Arthur M. Manigault, "but left it entirely to his brigadiers." After the eye injury he "was anxious to get away," Manigault continued, "and everybody else [was] equally so to get rid of him. The accident furnished a very good excuse, and we never saw him again during the war." Hindman was killed in his Helena, Ark., home by an unknown assailant on September 28, 1868.

'We expected hell today'

Lt. Col. Allen L. Fahnestock
86th Illinois Volunteer Infantry

This is what I wrote in my diary, June 28, 1864:

"I hope whoever reads this feeble description of this desperate charge will stop and reflect a moment and think of our position and feelings, laying within 30 steps of a desperate enemy, with our dead and wounded comrades between us, hearing their pitiful cries for help. While the rebel guns were pointed in the direction of the wounded, some of the men crawled up and assisted the poor wounded back to our lines and then to the field hospital, to have their limbs amputated and suffer untold misery. After dark we commenced strengthening our improvised defenses; we have come here to stay. We lost so many of our comrades with so slight a loss to the enemy that we will lose more or rout the enemy from this death trap. The assault on Kennesaw mountain was general along the whole line. The severest losses were in McCook's brigade. We fought hand to hand across the rebel breastworks, in front of our brigade, and planted the colors of some of the regiments in the ditch at the foot of the breastworks of the enemy."

On the 28th of June, Tuesday morning, clear and hot, the 86th Regiment relieved the 125th Illinois on the front line before daylight, keeping up a brisk fire all day. One killed and one wounded reported. Col. Dilworth and myself were trying to arrange some plan to dislodge the enemy. After dark

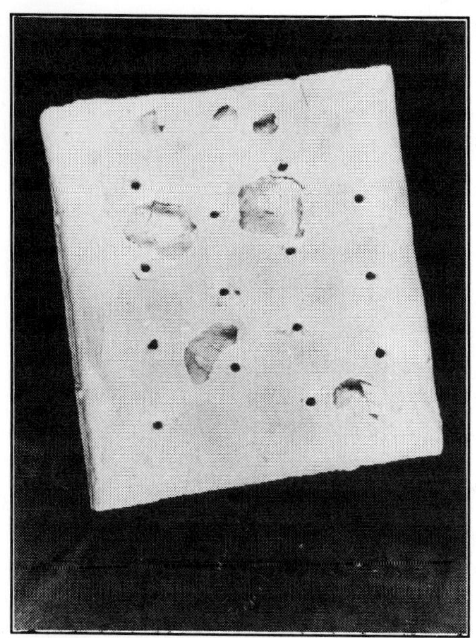

■ Army-issue hardtack. "This was officially called 'hard bread,' " wrote 1st Lieut. Wilbur F. Hinman of the 65th Ohio, "and we bear cheerful testimony to the fact that the adjective part of the name was not misapplied. Others spoke of them as 'crackers' probably because if a man was not careful they would crack his teeth. Some of the commissary people, with a bitter irony that was most exasperating, spoke of them tenderly as 'biscuits.' But they were just as hard by whatever name they were called. It is no exaggeration to say that some of them were so hard that the stoutest teeth in the brigade could make no impression on them. It was like trying to eat a stove-lid. Ingenuity was taxed to its utmost, and every culinary scheme that could be devised was tried on those hardtack. They were fried, roasted, boiled and stewed, but most of the experiments resulted in failure. It was but natural and reasonable to suppose that soaking would soften them, but anybody who acted on this theory made a mistake. Our mess soaked some — soaked them all night, and found in the morning that they had been turned into leather. They would have made a prime article of half soles for army shoes. But, despised and reviled as it was at first, the hardtack became the soldier's best friend [and] there were times when it tasted better than the daintiest morsel that ever passed our lips ..."

I had my men get empty cracker and cartridge boxes, fill them with dirt and shove them in front up the hill. By morning we had good works that would hold about 20 men who could do good execution at so short a range.

June 29, Wednesday morning, clear and hot. The 86th Regiment was relieved by the 52nd Ohio. The dead were still lying between our lines and the smell from the bodies was so offensive, the wind being in our favor, that the rebels requested us to cease firing and have an armistice to bury the dead. We notified our general, J.C. Davis, who came over and sent an officer half way between our lines to meet theirs to make the terms. The Confederates claimed rights to the weapons that lay where our dead and wounded dropped them. Gen. Davis said the arms were ours and if they defeated us they were theirs; if not, they were still ours. We would fight for them. They consented and then commenced the burial of the dead. When our officer was sent to meet the Confederate officer, I counted the steps each made. Ours, 13 steps; the rebel, 14, making 27 steps.

Each side detailed a number of men to dig graves on the top of the ridge. There was one man killed in Company A who had a large roll of money tied around his thigh. His comrade advised me of it.

Lieut. S.T. Rodgers of the 86th had been presented with a sword in his home of El Paso, Ill., and when he was wounded near the rebel works on the 27th he dropped the sword. So in making the detail of men to bury the dead I had a comrade from Company A put on a long coat, and ordered him to secrete the lieutenant's sword under the coat and bring it to me, as it was against orders to remove any of the arms from the field. The sword was found and sent home to Lieut. Rodgers. The other man got the roll of money from his dead comrade.

The Confederate burial party stood with their backs to our works, the Union soldiers with their backs to the rebel works. Moving toward the center both groups dug graves and deposited the dead. I saw several of the rebel generals — Hardee, Cheatham and others. As soon as our poor boys were under the ground the word was given, "Heads down!" and the fight was renewed.

There was a Yankee who came to me and showed me a small looking glass about one inch square attached to a wire that was inserted into a hole bored near the breech of a musket. Lay the musket over the works, cock the gun, look into the glass, and when you see a head, fire. We found we had the right thing in the right place. We now commenced constructing a tunnel to blow up the enemy's works, and by using those glasses on the guns we were able to keep them from doing us any harm.*

June 30, Thursday morning, clear and hot. Heavy firing all night. At one time we expected a charge but we were ready. A few men were wounded in the brigade. The rebel batteries opened on us, doing no damage as their shells passed over. We expected hell today but a heavy thunderstorm came up and dampened their courage, so we got through the day without loss. We could only get rations in after dark.

July 1, Friday morning, clear and hot. The 86th Regiment relieved the 125th Illinois on the front line. There was one killed and several wounded.

* According to Private Samuel Grimshaw of Company B, 52nd Ohio, "the day after the assault we obtained a meager supply of small square mirrors. These we rigged up, attaching them by wire to the butts of our guns, then placing the gun in position on our breastworks. Lying flat on our backs we sighted by the reflection in the glass until we got range of a rebel as he peered over or under their headlogs, and fired. This was very effective." Grimshaw later received the Medal of Honor for heroism on August 6, 1864, when he "saved the lives of some of his comrades, and greatly imperiled his own by picking up and throwing away a lighted shell which had fallen in the midst of the company."

The rebels commenced fighting by throwing stones at us, hurting some men, and sometimes sending over a cold corn dodger. Our men would yell to them, "For God's sake, throw rocks but none of those corn dodgers!" A man in blue would throw over a hardtack and say, "Damn you, take that! Uncle Sam's bread!" The rebels would reply, "Yank, send over some more!"

There was a soldier with a tin bucket in his right hand who stepped over our works and marched over to the rebels. I ordered my men to shoot him, but before they fired he stepped over their works. I supposed he was a spy, but in a short time they yelled over to know why we sent that damn fool over. The man was insane. He belonged to the 2nd Brigade of our division.

We were getting our tunnel well under their works. This night the rebs kept throwing over turpentine balls, keeping up a bright light, thinking we were going to charge them. We intended to mine under their works and blow them up on the 4th of July. We had six killed and wounded today.

July 2, Saturday morning, clear and warm. The 52nd Ohio relieved us on the front line. Continued musketry firing until 12 o'clock that night. Col. Dilworth and myself intended to make a feint about 2 o'clock, have our men ready with guns loaded, fire a few volleys, give a yell and lay low, and if we drew the rebs' fire to immediately charge the works. About 1 o'clock while he and I were talking and making ready, all seemed so quiet that I suggested the rebels had retreated. In a short time a voice from their works asked permission to come over to us, saying the rebels had left. We sent over a guard and found it to be true. So we notified our commander and by daylight the Union army was on the march hunting our enemy. It was a sight to see the rebs' strong works; they even had caves burrowed in the ground. Large trees between the lines were cut down by bullets. Some of the headlogs were so shot to pieces they were sent north as curiosities.

Gen. Joseph Johnston, in an article in Century magazine after the war, says that he repulsed Gen. Sherman's assault on his Kennesaw line, except one brigade of Federals that held a position at one point on his line. That was our brigade. It was the only one that made the charge that day that was not repulsed.

Had we made the charge on the 27th at *daybreak* we would no doubt have carried the works and captured many prisoners.

■ Sergeant Edwin C. Silliman of Company C, 86th Illinois, was credited by some in McCook's brigade with introducing usage of "gun glasses" to the unit a few days before the assault on the Dead Angle. Private Julius B. Work of Company G, 52nd Ohio, later wrote: "Silliman met a IV Corps man trying to sell the glasses. The idea struck him that they could be used to sight the guns of the men in sharpshooting. He bought the whole outfit consisting of 150 mirrors; these he gave to the boys of the brigade. They were about three inches square with a small wire attached by which they were fixed to the stock of the gun. Then by placing the gun on the rifle pit and lying down under cover, the gun could be sighted until you could get the object in line through the sights. The trigger did the rest."

Here they come, boys! By God, a million of them!

Across the Chattahoochee: The clash of arms on Atlanta's doorstep

Shortly after dark on July 2, 1st Lieut. Thomas Maney and 12 men from the 1st Tennessee were detailed to crawl out 30 feet in front of their regiment's breastworks at the Dead Angle to watch for any movement in the opposing Federal entrenchments. It was a serious undertaking, for behind Maney the entire Confederate army was in the process of evacuating its strongly fortified Kennesaw line.

"In crawling out to our posts that night we ran a great risk," Maney later wrote, "for if we shook a bush or made the least noise we would hear the unwelcome 'siz' of a minie ball. We had orders not to fire under any circumstances, so we could not reply. It was our province to watch and listen, and if crowded to jump and run. The men were placed, one by one, in a zigzag line, I having to crawl out in the dark and post each one. We returned one after another until all escaped. It was the officer's duty to go along the line and ascertain if all were doing their duty — lying down and keeping awake. Not much trouble to keep awake that night!

"On one of the tours of inspection I got a little off the line, and, it being crooked, I went clear outside and became so confused that I could not tell whether I was going to my own men or not. Creeping along in this frame of mind, I felt the muzzle of a musket right against my bosom, and then heard the click, click of the cock. Well, the past life of the writer came up before him. All the mean things I ever did were passed in review in a few seconds, for the ordeal was of short duration. I was afraid to catch the gun, for it would make the man at the other end of it pull the trigger. So I asked: 'Who is that?' No answer. Then I said: 'If you are Federals, I'm your meat.' Still no answer. 'If you are Rebs, I am your officer.' No answer yet. The sweat was pouring down my face about that time.

"The soldier took me for a Federal soldier, as my clothes were dark and my hat black, but he lowered his gun. The gun was down and I was down, lying prone on the ground by the soldier. When I realized that it was a man in our regiment who was considered unstable about the head, my scare came on good, for he had no more sense than to shoot. The reaction came to my nervous system and I was as weak as water. If the enemy had come on us then, it would have been impossible for me to rise from the ground. The poor fellow was frightened too, when he saw how near he came to sending me to my long home. At a given signal, about twelve o'clock, we moved back to the works and then on in quick time to catch up with the rear guard."

It was eerily silent as day dawned on July 3 when the first Federals clambered over the Confederate entrenchments. During the night, Johnston's three corps slipped away to another previously prepared line astride the Western & Atlantic Railroad at Smyrna. With the Union Armies of the Ohio and the Tennessee threatening his left flank, the Confederate commander felt it was time to abandon the Kennesaw defenses which so effectively had blocked Sherman for the past two weeks.

"It was the strongest position, and best fortified, I have yet seen," wrote Capt. Henry Richards of Company F, 93rd Ohio, to his father on July 3. "And if we did not outnumber them largely, which enables us to flank them, they could not have been taken."

The Federal pursuit of Johnston's army began immediately. "Our regiment was in the advance [of the XX Corps] that morning," recalled Drum Major William D. Wilson of the 129th Illinois. "Just as we passed around the east side of Kennesaw we discovered some Rebel Cavalry on a slight rise near a Railroad Cut. General Hooker came up and ordered a Battery up and put in position just on the side of the road and near a large cotton gin. As soon as the Battery was in position General Hooker climbed up in this gin to get a good view of the effects of our fire. But the first gun had hardly been fired when the smoke rose out of that Railroad Cut and the Shot and Shells from a masked Rebel battery tore through our Battery, killing horses and men, wounding others, and compelling Gen. Hooker to abandon his place in a hurry."

But the Federals pressed on. On the 4th of July, a section of the Southern line was punctured by troops of McPherson's Army of the Tennessee along Nickajack Creek, and artillery fire hammered elsewhere along the front. "The shells came two each minute from a battery directly in front of our command," wrote 1st Lieut. John Irwin Kendall of the 4th Louisiana. "They cut down a great many limbs from the trees but did practically no harm to our men."

Kendall, along with many other Confederates, expected a general attack by the Yankees to "commemorate" Independence Day. "Hence, when we found their mysterious and mighty 'great thing' held in store for us for the Fourth was nothing more than the old, long-delayed flank movement we had been for some time expecting, we quietly fell back eight miles to another line already staked out for us. This new line was at Vining's Station, on the railroad to Atlanta. At once the men fell to work like beavers, digging trenches. There was every need for haste, for the enemy hovering at our heels would be sure to be on us in the early morning. So we reasoned, as we bent all our energies to throwing up the dirt ... But they did not come. Sherman did not take Johnston's dare at Vining's Station. He was done with frontal attacks [and] fell back on his old reliance, the flanking maneuver. And this it was that got us out of the line. To our loudly expressed disgust, our beautiful works had to be abandoned; we left them on the night of the 4th of July without a fight and took up once more the night march to the rear."

On July 5, the Confederates reached the last major natural barrier in front of Atlanta — the Chattahoochee River — where another line of partially completed defenses was intended to stop or slow "the hovering enemy."

In W.H.T. Walker's division, 1st Lieut. Hamilton M. Branch of Company F, 54th Georgia, wrote to his mother: "We were moved one mile to the left and placed in position behind a portion of the stockade erected by Gen. Shoop [sic], Gen. Johnston's chief of Artillery. This was the strangest sight we have seen since we have been here, it put me in mind of the fortifications I have read of in the account of the first American settlers

■ Sergeant Ambrose Doss, Company C, 19th Alabama, was killed on July 5 along the west bank of the Chattahoochee River. The next day a comrade, J.W. Rouse, wrote to Doss' wife, Sarah: "its with sad heart that I this morining take up my pen to Anounce to you the most painful Intelagence that could posable Be pened to you. your husband is No more on Earth ... Ambrose is gone to the spirit World. he was Killed yesterday About 1 oclock — A Cannon Shot it Struck him in the Right side Nearly Even With the Right Breast and passed Intirely through his Body and through his left Arm Killing him Instantly. When I learned that he Was killed I Got leave from the Col and myself and James G. and John F Rogers and George Eaton Went Back and got the Body of our fallen Brother and Intered it With as much Decency as the Nature of the Case Would admit. it was Knot Done in as Nice a maner As We Would have perfered But fare better then is common with us Soldiers ..."

■1st Lieut. Charles H. Cox, Company E, 70th Indiana. On July 13 he wrote from along the Chattahoochee to his fiancee's brother: "The latest Atlanta papers are at hand — They give gloomy accounts of the condition of the city — Many inhabitants have concluded to remain and be subjected to Yankee rule, with full confidence (so the editor says) the city will soon be wrested again from our infamous hordes. 'I can't see it' in that light and what Mr Sherman takes he generally *freezes* to — Roswell Cotton factory was taken by our forces the other day [July 6] — and with it 700 girls who were working in it — The girls were somewhat alarmed at first, but were soon pacified and seemed pleased at being transferred for the Confed'cy to Uncle Samuel — and said they believed they liked the Yanks the best anyhow, as they wore the best clothes and were the best looking men — A dance was proposed by some of the boys, and agreed upon by the girls who went to work and cleaned out and scrubbed the floor of the largest room — some of our *army* fiddlers were engaged — the dance commenced and all 'was merry as a marriage bell' — when Mr Sherman put a finis to their fun by detaching a squad with a pocket full of matches and soon the buildings were no more. The factories were worth over $1,000,000 — The girls were sent ... to be shipped north I suppose ... mostly are destitute of home ... some lately arrived from England — Some one proposed that they be issued to Officers on 'Special Requisitions,' certifying they are for our own use — "

lives. It was made thus on every little rise and commanding every little valey there were built redouts and block houses and all between these there were rails and logs about 12 feet in length stuck up in the ground close together, the whole forming (as some of the men remarked) a wall between the cornfeds and wheatfeds, and I would have liked it better if the wall had been ½ mile in height and had been built farther north ... I do not know whether we will cross the river or not. Old Joe knows what he is at and will take care of us and do what is best."

Among the first Federal troops of the IV Corps to encounter Confederate skirmishers about two miles from the river was Private Peter Price of Company H, 124th Ohio. He later wrote:

"The firing seemed to grow in volume at times, and our men were getting impatient at the stubborness of the Confederates. From a distance of about 300 yards a squad of the enemy could be seen behind a huge pile of rocks, and above the din of the firing the sharp, penetrating voice of their commanding officer could be heard ordering them to 'shoot low.' The language he used was more forcible than elegant, and punctuated with many startling expletives. He was, in all probability, a graduate of the baggage train; certainly no member of the 'fuhst' families of the South.

"Striking his sword on the stones, he shouted: 'Don't you see them? There they are, damn you, shoot low! Here, come back! Don't run, or I'll cut your damned heart out!' All this could be heard and observed from our position. The fellow's efforts to enthuse his comrades, however, failed, for shortly afterward they broke and ran, and in their retreat the commander proved to be an easy winner in the foot race to the river."

In the meantime, Sherman planned to feint south, flank the Confederates to the north and effect a crossing of the Chattahoochee. Brig. Gen. Kenner Garrard's cavalry division was sent 16 miles upriver to secure the important manufacturing town of Roswell. McPherson briefly demonstrated along the Federal right to deceive Johnston into thinking that an attack there was imminent. But then he pulled out, swung around behind the rest of the army, and marched to Roswell where the Army of the Tennessee formed the extreme left of the Union line. Schofield's Army of the Ohio followed a day later, sliding into the center at Soap Creek between McPherson and Thomas. While the left and center searched for suitable points to cross the river, Thomas' Army of the Cumberland, now on the right, sat poised to keep Confederate attention away from the Federal movements upstream.

On July 8 at the mouth of Soap Creek, troops of Schofield's army were the first over the Chattahoochee. "A special detail of about 60 men out of all the regiments of [Brig. Gen. Robert A.] Cameron's brigade, chosen chiefly for their height, [was] to see if the river was fordable there or not, and to develop the enemy's strength," wrote Capt. George Redway of Company I, 103rd Ohio. "These 60 waded in, single file, carrying arms and ammunition above their heads, walking on a sort of fish-dam, the top of which was over five feet under water part of the way. A few slipped and fell in, but were quickly helped up and on.

"As soon as we reached the south bank of the Chattahoochee we deployed as skirmishers, and so advanced by the right oblique up a 200-foot hill. As it turned out, the Johnnies had not seen us because they were just beyond a bend in the river to our right, and were further concealed by dense woods extending from the river's edge to the top of the hill, and along to the left and front indefinitely. The rest of the brigade followed in the pontoons which rapidly slipped into the creek that emptied into the river at that point."

Sergeant Major Dwight Fraser of the 128th Indiana wrote home of the crossing: "On the night of the 8th we crossed the Chattahoochee River on a Pontoon Bridge. Four Regiments crossed the River in Boats. These Boats were canvas and are used in the Pontoon Bridges. They generally throw over a small force in boats to protect the workers in laying down the Pontoon Bridges. Our regiment was the fifth that crossed the River, but we were too tired to appreciate the greatness of the movement. This was the first bridge that was laid across the river, and our Corps the first of this grand army that effected a crossing. We met with very little opposition from the Rebels and captured the only gun that they had at this point on the river to oppose us."

Troops of McPherson's army soon followed. Wrote Private John F. Brobst of Company G, 25th Wisconsin: "... we jumped into the river and commenced swimming, wading, falling down, rolling and yelling like wild men, and the rebs running for life again, and the result is here we are on the south side of the river building works to keep the rebs back, and I think Atlanta will soon be ours."

The day after Schofield's bridgehead was secured, Garrard's cavalry forced a crossing at Shallowford while other Union cavalry — wading naked — forded the river below Soap Creek. With the construction of additional pontoon bridges, enough Federals crossed by July 9 to seriously threaten Johnston's right flank. Orders to withdraw were issued, and that night the Confederates marched south over the railroad and pontoon bridges — their decking boards covered with cornstalks and straw to muffle the noise. After burning the wooden railroad bridge, Johnston's men fell back to Atlanta's outer ring of fortifications.

"Retreated 6 miles and [are within] 2 miles of Atlanta," wrote Private Benjamin Seaton of Company G, 10th Texas, in his diary on July 9. "And here we have stoped again and perhaps will give them a fight before we leave here. It seams as we have gone as fare as we ought to go unless we intend to give up all of our country and not fight anymore and that is not the idey — it is victory or death."

Quartermaster Sergeant Joel D. Murphree of the 57th Alabama wrote to his wife: "I must confess that I am alarmed about the fate of Atlanta. If Johnston is not reinforced my opinion is Atlanta will soon be lost to the Confederacy and the loss of Atlanta will be the greatest loss we have ever sustained."*

And in his diary, Private Robert D. Patrick of Company A, 4th Louisiana, wrote on July 10: "We have removed our camp inside the breastworks of Atlanta. The bridges over the river were burned this morning by our troops a little before day. I don't believe Johnston can hold Atlanta. I am sorry to admit that as the Frenchman says, I am losing 'the grand confidence.' This is an awful crisis for our young Republic and a short time now will tell the tale, because if Sherman whips Johnston out of Atlanta, we may bid farewell to this part of the country for I have yet to hear of our ever retaking any captured territory."

When the Federals of Thomas' army reached the north bank of the Chattahoochee, many were impressed by the formidable fortifications just evacuated by the Confederates. Capt. Josiah C. Williams of Company C, 27th Indiana, wrote in his diary on July 11:

■ Brig. Gen. Francis A. Shoup was chief of artillery in the Army of Tennessee who designed the novel Confederate fortifications at the Chattahoochee River railroad crossing. Shoup later wrote that "It was not a system of earthworks, but a line of detached log redoubts packed in with earth ... They were called 'Shoupades' ... and such could be held indefinitely by one division against Sherman's entire army." Considered "an educated and disciplined soldier," Shoup was promoted to army chief of staff shortly after the battle of Atlanta when a quick reorganization of the army was effected by Gen. Hood.

* Murphree soon was to suffer two personal losses. Nine of his brothers and brothers-in-law served in Confederate units, and two of the latter were killed in July 1864: Capt. Baily Talbot of the 57th Alabama on July 20 at Peachtree Creek, and Major Shep Ruffin, commanding the 38th Alabama, on July 28 at Ezra Church.

■ Soldiers of the XVI Corps, following the Federal troopers of Brig. Gen. Kenner Garrard's cavalry division, ford the Chattahoochee River on July 10 at Roswell's Ferry. Among the first cavalrymen across were those of Col. Robert Minty's brigade, armed with waterproof, 7-shot Spencer carbines. One trooper recalled: "As the rebel bullets began to splash around pretty thick, the boys sought to keep in this deep water with only the head exposed; they soon discovered that they could throw the cartridge from the magazine (of the Spencer) into the chamber of the piece, by working the lever, as well under water as in the air; hence, all along the line you could see the men bring their guns up, let the water run from the muzzle a moment, then taking a quick aim, fire his piece and pop down again, with only his head exposed. Now, the rebels had never seen anything of this kind before, nor, for that matter had we, and their astonishment knew no bounds. We could hear them calling to each other, 'Look at them Yankee sons of bitches, loading their guns under water!' "

"These are the strongest yet, being provided with bomb proofs ... both flanks resting upon the river; deep trenches with log forts, block-houses — some 40 ft. square for musketeers; these were built about every 75 yds apart in a continuous line along the barricades with lunettes and redoubts for cannon every few rods. Then in front of the barricades was a stockade of straight timbers wedged closely together so that neither man nor beast could get through ... 'Johnny Reb' has a holy horror of anything like a flank movement which has been the main and almost the only beautiful feature of this campaign."

There was little activity along the Chattahoochee front during most of the next week as Sherman rested his troops, brought up supplies to a new base at Vining's Station and awaited reconstruction of the timber railroad bridge over the river. Incredibly, Union engineers built a new 900-foot span in only four days.

But along sections of the river, artillery firing and sniping continued to claim occasional casualties. "Our pickits are now on our Side of the river & the yankee pickits on the other Side & are Keeping up a heavy sharp shooting & cannonading," wrote Private John W. Hagan of Company C, 29th Georgia.

On July 16, Bugler Henry Campbell of the 18th Indiana Light Artillery Battery wrote in his journal: "Just after daylight this morning we fired two shells at a squad of rebels about ¾ of a mile off who were enjoying a quiet breakfast in fancied security. One shell burst right among them, scattering them in all directions and evidently hurting several as we noticed them carrying them away on stretchers."

The next day the tables were turned, as Campbell continued: "The Rebels ... resolved to give us a bombardment. They had the range perfectly and nearly every shot burst above and in the fort and as we could only reply one shot to their 4 they had it all their own way."

Despite such incidents, numerous examples occurred during mid-July of fraternizing along the river banks to pick berries or trade coffee, tobacco, newspapers and trinkets. Men of both sides even bathed together in the Chattahoochee. Many took time to write home, catch up their journals or diaries, and wash and mend dirty, well-worn uniforms.

From the 3rd Wisconsin's camp, Private William Wallace of Company E wrote to his wife: "As soon as you get this, send me some thread for I have been very busy sewing this last week and my thread is nearly all done. I sold my razor, brush and strop yesterday for 2 dollars and a half. It did not pay to pack it around just for shaving myself alone so I will let my beard grow again.

"We are rather short of rations all the time, which makes us growl. Some other corps get more than they want. I guess the fault lies with the cheats of quarter masters we have got. We don't get any of the desecated vegetables and no beans — only 3 times since we left Tullahoma in the spring. There is no need of such work, for Uncle Abe sends us enough if he had only trusty quarter masters, but it is no use talking about it."

On July 15, Lt. Col. Charles F. Morse of the 2nd Massachusetts wrote home: "We are now enjoying a short respite from our exertions, which is very welcome after the campaign's hard work. By a series of movements and operations we have pushed the enemy south of the Chattahoochee, they now picketing their side of the river and we ours.

"The constant retreats of Johnston have, to a certain extent, demoralized the troops belonging in Kentucky, Tennessee, Northern Georgia and Alabama, so that on each occasion of their falling back, hundreds of deserters are brought into our lines; they all say that half the army would do the same if it dared, but they are told fearful stories of our treatment of prisoners and are also closely watched, and, when caught, shot without mercy. The case has occurred, repeatedly, of deserters lying all day in ditches and behind stumps between our picket lines, afraid to stir from fear of being shot by their own men; as soon as night would come, they would come in. Without a single exception, I have seen these men always kindly and hospitably received by our soldiers; it is always, 'How are you, Johnny? We're glad to see you; sit down and have some coffee, and tell us the news.' "

The same day, Sergeant Major Dwight Fraser of the 128th Indiana wrote to his parents: "We are still encamped in the woods and I am getting tired of it. Last night there was quite a severe rain storm here. The wind did much damage by blowing down trees and tree tops; in our regiment two were hurt and one very badly. We have heard of quite a number being crippled in other regiments in the same way. It is too bad for soldiers to have such bad luck after endangering their lives in so many other ways."

And also on July 15, Private Robert Patrick of the 4th Louisiana noted in his diary: "Perhaps, for duration, and the fierce, obstinate nature of the conflict, the present campaign in Georgia is unparalleled in history. Our men have seen a hard time, passing wearied nights of restless anxiety with the cold, damp ground for their beds, sleeping on wet leaves or branches of trees, sometimes on rails to keep them out of the mud, and frequently their rude couches were rendered too hot for them by the pat-

The boys call it 'long Forage'

Receiving good, nutritious food to eat in quantity was a rarity in the Army of Tennessee by the summer of 1864. Many Confederates complained of this in letters home, among them artillery 1st Lieut. Andrew J. Neal, who wrote to his sister Emma on July 13 while his battery was stationed near the Chattahoochee River:

"The box you sent us that was robbed by the Relief Committee was a most provoking circumstance, but no worse than they have to do to set table for the hosts of Quartermasters, Commissaries, stragglers and Dead Heads which congregate at the rear. The troops that build the works, lie in the trenches and do the fighting do not get one-twentieth of the vegetables and contributions that the ladies of the State have so generously stripped their gardens to furnish. I understand that thousands of crate-fulls came up on the cars. Since we left Dalton vegetables have been issued to our Division twice. At Kennesaw while we were doing heavy work and hard fighting I drew rations for 94 men. They issued about a peck of potatoes, six or seven cabbage heads, two squashes and four or five beets. The other issue was as ridiculous, about as bad as when they issued ground peas at Dalton three to the man.

Our men get a vegetable diet by cooking up polk, potato tops, May pop vines, kurlip weed, lambs quarter, thistle and a hundred kinds of weed I always thought poison. I thought it trash at first but the boys call it 'long Forage' and it beats nothing. The commissary gives us bacon and corn bread enough and it is a sorry man that can't fight on that. [What] I hate is the men that do the hard fighting have all the hard living while the crowds at the rear get all that is intended for the front. But I have not nor never will complain of any thing my country gives me."

■ Gen. John Bell Hood led a corps for the first two months of the campaign, until he succeeded Gen. Johnston as commander of the Army of Tennessee on July 17, 1864, by order of Confederate President Jefferson Davis. A crippled left arm from Gettysburg and only a stump remaining of his right leg after Chickamauga did not dampen his ardor for combat, honed earlier in the war as a brigade and division commander. As an administrator and strategist, however, he did not measure up to the task of commanding a corps and an army. After the Atlanta campaign he went on the offensive into Tennessee where his army was crushed at Franklin and Nashville. Hood died of yellow fever in 1879.

tering bullets which came to disturb their slumbers. There is no child's play in soldiering. 'Up to the rack, fodder or no fodder' is the word, to use a vulgar phrase. Our army is like a lion at bay, now and then turning in desperation on their relentless pursuers. They have literally disputed *every inch* of ground from Dalton, down to our present position. Their unexampled, desperate fighting qualities have even won the admiration of the Yankees, and as they say, 'it begets a sad regret that we are not engaged in a holier cause.' "

Sherman resumed the offensive on July 16 when the Army of the Cumberland began a day-long crossing of the Chattahoochee at two ferries. On the 17th, Thomas and Schofield advanced directly on Atlanta toward Peachtree Creek. Simultaneously, McPherson headed in a wide arc for the town of Decatur, where the Army of the Tennessee was assigned to destroy the tracks of the Georgia Railroad before attacking Atlanta from the east.

Johnston did not oppose the Federal crossings. He planned instead to assault Sherman's main force as it crossed Peachtree Creek by driving a wedge between Thomas and Schofield, pushing them back to the Chattahoochee where he would destroy the Federals while their backs were to the river. Just south of Peachtree Creek he deployed Hood's corps to the right, Hardee in the center and Alexander P. Stewart, now in permanent command of Polk's corps, on the left. Wheeler's cavalry was sent to harass and delay McPherson at Decatur.

Everything was set, when about 10 p.m. on July 17 a telegram from the Confederate War Department in Richmond reached Johnston at his headquarters a few miles northwest of Atlanta. The message concluded: "As you have failed to arrest the advance of the enemy to the vicinity of Atlanta, far in the interior of Georgia, and express no confidence that you can defeat or repel him, you are hereby relieved from command of the Army and Department of Tennessee, which you will immediately turn over to General Hood."

When word of Johnston's dismissal circulated through the camps the next morning, widespread indignation permeated the Confederate ranks. "By this act the army was *outraged,*" wrote Capt. Elbert D. Willett of Company B, 40th Alabama, in his diary on July 18. "An older, experienced and successful commander relieved for one untried at this critical period in so important a campaign. It came like a thunder bolt to the army, so unexpected, so undeserved."

Private J.B. Gracey of Company G, 51st Tennessee: "I can bear witness to the spirit of mutiny that filled the minds of the troops, who to a man were ready to throw down their arms and quit. A fatal blunder that removal of Johnston. 'Old Joe' was our idol."

Private David B. Morgan of the 5th Georgia Cavalry: "When Johnston was removed from the army his soldiers almost mutinied; not that they did not trust Hood, but their love for Johnston was so great, and they knew he had such consideration for their welfare, that they felt no one else could take his place. But he appealed to them to continue to be the soldiers under Hood that they had been under him. That was enough. They went forward to their duty and did it nobly."

Less than 24 hours after his dismissal, Johnston was in Macon and 33-year-old John Bell Hood, crippled from two grievous wounds suffered earlier in the war, was in command of the Army of Tennessee.

Though a superb division commander, Hood had yet to prove himself capable of handling larger numbers of troops. The decision to place him in Johnston's stead was made primarily because of his reputation as a

■ Members of Company B, 84th Illinois, in a photograph taken in April 1864 at Blue Springs, Tenn. Between July 12 and 18, the regiment rested along the Chattahoochee not far from Power's Ferry. Regimental Quartermaster Lewis A. Simmons recalled: "Each morning and evening hundreds flocked to the banks of the river, and in swimming and fishing, were as gay and light-hearted as any group of school-boys could be enjoying a holiday or vacation. Besides being of great benefit to the army at this time, by giving the men time to recruit their overtaxed energies, [it enabled] all to be well supplied with new clothing, and have their equipments thoroughly refitted."

bold fighter, who could be relied upon to defend Atlanta by offensive action. The change of command suited Sherman just fine when he learned of it from a smuggled Atlanta newspaper. After two and a half months of playing cat and mouse with the wily Johnston, he professed to welcome the prospects of fighting "in open ground, on anything like equal terms, instead of being forced to run up against prepared entrenchments."

His subordinate, Schofield, agreed. He had roomed with Hood and tutored him in mathematics while both were at West Point in the early 1850s. Schofield advised Sherman that Hood would not wait long to attack: "He'll hit you like hell, now, before you know it."

Proof of the warning was not long in coming. On July 19, Confederate artillery Capt. Thomas J. Key wrote: "Most of Sherman's thieves ... are now skirmishing about two miles from the lines of rifle pits that we are now constructing. Notwithstanding the contrast in numbers, the eventful period of a great battle cannot long be postponed. We have retreated as far as policy or safety will admit."

Within the next 72 hours — at Peachtree Creek on July 20, and a few miles east of Atlanta on July 22 — Hood unleashed two major assaults that resulted in the most ferocious fighting of the summer. And they cost the Confederates dearly.

Of the latter engagement, Col. Robert N. Adams of the 81st Ohio wrote: "The battle of Atlanta was one of a series, but by far the bloodiest and most decisive battle of the campaign. Although the enemy retained pos-

■ Capt. James P. Douglas commanded the 1st Texas Battery — the only one from Texas to serve east of the Mississippi River during the war. It was equipped with two 6-pounder smoothbores and two 12-pounder howitzers. With the battery positioned along the north bank of the Chattahoochee River on July 8, Douglas wrote to his future wife: "The enemy are a few hundred yards in front of us and sharp shooting and cannonading going on about as it has for two months. I still have perfect confidence in our ability to hold Atlanta. The enemy are apparently getting more cautious and rarely ever advance on our works. The lessons Cleburne, Stewart, Cheatham and others have taught them are not forgotten."

Three days later, after the Confederates fell back across the river, he again wrote to his fiancee: "Atlanta is in considerable excitement. Many citizens are moving away and most of the business houses are closed or moving away their effects. I don't yet think Atlanta will be given up. One thing, Johnson [sic] seems determined to preserve his army. It is certainly worth more than cities or states."

session of the city for more than a month after, yet he never recovered from the fearful repulse and terrible slaughter of that memorable day."

'My lost leg'

Brig. Gen. Alfred J. Vaughan Jr.
Cheatham's Division, Hardee's Corps CSA

Soon after Sherman's army was so signally repulsed on the Kennesaw line, he again commenced his flank movement, which forced our army to fall back.

On the 4th of July, 1864, one of the hottest days of the season, our army arrived at Vining Station, just below Marietta, Ga., where it was formed in line of battle, with orders for each brigade to entrench and throw up breastworks.

I was busily engaged all the morning in superintending the work, which was about completed between 12 and 1 o'clock, when, with my staff, I retired to a large spreading oak tree, about 150 or 200 yards in the rear of my line of works, to rest and to eat my scanty rations. No fighting was going on at this time except an artillery duel between a Federal battery some distance off and a Confederate battery on my line.

After I had eaten up all the rations I had, I concluded I would take a smoke. Matches in those days were very scarce and hard to get; so I always carried with me a small sunglass to light my pipe with when the sun was shining. After filling my pipe I noticed that the sun was shining through a small opening in the foliage of the tree under which I was sitting, and I remarked to Colonel Dyer, my Inspector-General, that I could light my pipe through the little opening. He replied that he would bet me a drink of pine-top whisky that I could not. I accepted the bet, and just as I was in the act of drawing a focus on my tobacco, a shell from the enemy's battery came whizzing through the air over my line and exploded just as it struck my foot and the ground, tearing off my foot and making a hole almost large enough to bury me in.

My staff were lying around under the shade of the tree, but none of them were struck by the shell or any of its fragments. Col. Dyer, who was standing over me at the time, had nearly all his clothing torn off, not by the shell or its fragments, but by the gravel that was thrown up against him. He received seventeen flesh wounds, none of which proved very serious. As soon as the shell exploded he involuntarily started to run to get behind a tree. A few days before this Col. Dyer and myself, while walking in the rear of our line on Kennesaw Mountain, noticed that a soldier with all the canteens of his company swung around him, was going after water for his company, when a shrapnel shell came over, exploded and riddled him with balls; yet he walked, or rather ran, some little distance before falling, and then fell dead. Col. Dyer told me that he had this man in his mind's eye while running, and he expected every moment to fall dead.

The shock from the explosion of the shell was very severe, yet the tearing away of my leg was accompanied by neither pain nor the loss of much blood. In addition to the loss of my foot I received another wound on my other leg which was rather remarkable. I had a cut below the knee about four inches long and down to the bone, as smooth as if it had been cut with a sharp knife, yet neither my pants nor underclothing were torn. It was so smooth a cut that when pressed together it healed by first intention. None of us were able to conjecture what made this cut. Before I would allow my removal I made my staff find my sunglass and my pipe.

The rim of my sunglass was broken.

As soon as it was known that I was wounded, the surgeons of my brigade and division came to my assistance, and bound up my wounds as best they could, and gave me some morphine and whisky. I was then put in an ambulance and started to the field hospital. In going to the hospital I passed by Gen. Cheatham's headquarters, who, hearing that I was wounded, came out to sympathize with me, and suggested that as I was looking very pale he thought that some stimulant would do me good, and gave me a stiff drink. I then began to feel pretty good and proceeded on my way to the hospital.

I had not gone very far when I passed Gen. Hardee's headquarters. He had heard of my misfortune and came out to see me. He also said I was looking very pale and that I ought to have some stimulant, and gave me a big drink.

I continued to feel better, and again started toward the hospital, and in a short time passed Gen. Joseph E. Johnston's headquarters. He came out to see me and also said that I was looking very pale, and that some stimulant would do me good. He happened to have some very fine apple brandy, and gave me a big drink, and down it went. From this time on I knew nothing until I awoke on the platform in Atlanta at sunrise the next morning.

The amputation of my leg at the point selected was an unfortunate one for me. My brigade surgeon, Dr. R.W. Mitchell, was absent at the time of my arrival at the field hospital, and the point of selection for the amputation was determined upon by a consultation of surgeons before he returned. If my leg had been cut off higher up it would have relieved me of the many days of suffering I have since experienced.

From Atlanta I was carried on a freight train in a box car, in the hottest of weather, to Macon, Ga. Dr. Mitchell accompanied me, thinking I would die before I reached the place. My sufferings were intense, but I survived, and was taken to Mrs. Josie, the wife of a quartermaster of my division of the army, who cared for and treated me as kindly as if I had been her own child.

Thus I lost my leg, and I have never seen it since.

■ Brig. Gen. Alfred J. Vaughan Jr. commanded a brigade of Tennesseeans in Cheatham's division until he was severely wounded on July 4, losing a foot and lower leg at Vining's Station. The injury caused him considerable pain, and he carried a crutch for the next 35 years until his death in 1899. A native Virginian, Vaughan had gone to war in June 1861 as a captain in command of Company E, 13th Tennessee, but immediately was elected lieutenant colonel of the regiment, and in November 1861, colonel. "I was a disciplinarian while on duty of the strictest school," he later wrote, "which for the first months of the war made me very unpopular with volunteer soldiers, but only one fight was necessary to satisfy them that an undisciplined army was nothing more than an armed mob."

'The most despondent feelings'

Col. Ellison Capers
24th South Carolina Volunteer Infantry

On the 17th of July the commanding general published an address to the army, and announced that he would attack Gen. Sherman's army as soon as it should cross the Chattahoochee River. It was understood that the enemy was crossing at Roswell Factory, beyond the right flank of the army and east of Peachtree Creek, which empties into the Chattahoochee a mile or two east of the railroad bridge.

I had the honor to read the commanding general's address to the brigade, and to congratulate the command upon the prospect of successful battle. The order was received with enthusiasm and the most confident spirit prevailed.

Next day, the 18th, while we were forming to march from our bivouac to the right, a rumor prevailed that Gen. Johnston had been removed from command. After we had marched some distance on the road to Atlanta a courier handed me a circular order from Gen. Hood announcing Gen. Johnston's removal, and his assuming command. Shortly after, the farewell address of Gen. Johnston was received and read to the regiment. It is due to truth to say that the reception of these orders produced the most despondent feelings in my command. The loss of the commanding general was felt to be irreparable.

Continuing the march and passing the general's headquarters, Walker's division passed at the shoulder, the officers saluting and most of the latter and hundreds of the men taking off their hats. It had been proposed to halt and cheer, but Gen. Johnston upon hearing of our intention requested that the troops march by in silence. We marched across the railroad and went into bivouac east of the Peachtree road, some three miles from Atlanta. Thus closed the campaign under Gen. Johnston's command.

■ Col. Ellison Capers commanded the 24th South Carolina during the campaign. Wounded at Vicksburg and Chickamauga, he received a severe third wound at the battle of Franklin on November 30, shortly after his promotion to brigadier general and assuming command of S.R. Gist's brigade. Taken early in the war, this photograph shows Capers in the dress uniform of a colonel of South Carolina Volunteers. He was regarded highly by Gen. Hardee, who called him a "fine disciplinarian, an intrepid warrior and greatly beloved by officers and men." After the war Capers became a bishop in the Episcopal Church.

'Your stocking legs saved us'

1st Lieut. Stephen Pierson
Adjutant
33rd New Jersey Volunteer Infantry

Marietta was ours on the third of July. On the Fourth we were having a little celebration at headquarters in honor of the day and also of our victories, when there came an order for the 33rd to move out and silence a battery that was annoying somebody, somewhere. We did not get into any fight, but, as we passed along a bit of open road, the battery fired a parting shell at us. The shell struck in the soft mud, not far from me. It exploded and literally covered me with mud; face, eyes, nose, ears, clothes, horse, and all were plastered. Blinded for a moment by the mud, and perhaps stunned a bit by the concussion, I reeled and thought I was dead; but I was only very dirty. Where the pieces of that shell went I do not know and am very glad that I did not know by experience then.

The second stage of the campaign was over. The steeples of Atlanta were plainly visible from some of the hills in our new position. From May 25th to July 2nd the fighting, all about Dallas, Pine Knob, Kennesaw, Marietta, had been continuous and severe. Each new position was gained by the one, or lost by the other, only after persistent assaults, or by continuous pressure and struggle, met by obstinate and brave defense.

Johnston's infantry was now massed on the north side of the Chattahoochee in a series of elaborate fortifications, centering upon the railroad bridge. Sherman was pressing him incessantly. By the 7th of July the railroad had been repaired and our supplies were coming abundantly into Marietta. On the 8th, Schofield effected a crossing, with Cox's division, over the Chattahoochee at Shoal Creek, 10 miles above Johnston.

On the 9th, Johnston withdrew to the south bank of the river, burning all the bridges and taking position in the outer line of the defenses he had prepared for Atlanta, four miles outside of the city and two miles from the river at its nearest point.

We were now entering upon the third and final stage of the campaign. Sherman took a few days to study the situation and to lay in a supply of food for men and food for guns. His plan, as finally developed, was to move upon Atlanta by his left flank. Thomas was to cross at Pace's and other ferries, about six miles above the railroad bridge, which would bring him within two miles of Johnston's left and six miles from Atlanta. Schofield was to cross about six miles farther up, some 10 or 12 miles from Atlanta. McPherson was to cross at Roswell, six miles above Schofield's crossing, and 18 or 20 from Atlanta. With Thomas' right as a pivot, Schofield and McPherson were to swing to the right, within supporting distance of each other as far as possible, and so envelop Atlanta from the east.

On the 17th of July the movements began. On the 19th Thomas had made the crossing over Peachtree Creek and was within five miles of Atlanta. We threw up a slight line of works and waited until morning. About noon of the next day, July 20th, the 33rd was ordered out to some high ground in our front to prepare a place for a battery. Gen. Geary went with us. We had just received a mail, the first for some weeks, and I remember, as we passed through the lines in front, I had opened a letter from my father and was reading it. The woods were ominously still; even the birds seemed to have stopped singing. Col. Jackson of the 134th New York rode up alongside of me, put out his hand and said: "Good-bye, Adjutant." I laughed at him, but he said: "There'll be trouble out there." He was right. There was to be trouble and plenty of it.

With no opposition we advanced to the knoll and were about to stack arms preparatory to making a place ready for the battery. The woods were dense; our skirmishers in front had made but small progress. Suddenly and unexpectedly a volley was fired at them and, so close were they to us, that the bullets came on over into our line. Evidently they had not expected our presence at that particular point any more than we had expected theirs, for the firing ceased for a moment. Col. Fourat ordered me to ride out to the open on our left. And there I saw a beautiful sight. Down through the great, open fields they were coming, thousands of them, men in gray, by brigade front, flags flying. Hood was making his first general assault, and it was against Thomas that he was making it. I stopped but a few moments to take it all in, and then rode back to report. Meantime, the force in the woods in our immediate front had sized us up as to numbers and on they came. How the bullets did come in from the front! Our reply was vigorous, too. And for a time we held them. Every moment they could be held was of importance, giving our main line time to be more ready.

But very soon they were wrapping around both our flanks and getting into our rear. The firing was fearfully hot. Our isolated position was no longer tenable and the order to retire was given.

At first it was orderly enough, but, almost surrounded as we were, our line was soon broken and in confusion. I have an indistinct recollection of crossing a little brook and wondering at the splashes made by the rebel bullets as they struck the water. I remember, too, stopping for a rest a moment behind the little line we had left. I suppose I was still somewhat weak from my wound of a month before;* anyway I could not keep up with the others. As I lay there to get breath, the rebel advance came up, and a long, lank Johnny, seeing me said: "Get out of that, you Yankee son of a

■ 1st Lieut. Stephen Pierson, adjutant of the 33rd New Jersey, was only 19 years old during the summer of 1864. After he was wounded in the chest on June 15 at Pine Knob, Pierson recalled: "I was helped up and led back to the field hospital. I suppose I looked pretty white from loss of blood, etc., so Dr. Reilly, our surgeon, poured me out a big drink of whiskey. I had never tasted whiskey before, and, by the time they had found out that my wound was not so very serious and had dressed it, the stuff had gone to my head. I was *fighting mad,* and they tell me my one desire was to get out and kill the fellow who had shot me, and they had to detail a man to keep me from going out to do it."

* Pierson had been wounded on June 15 near Pine Knob, as he here describes: "The hours passed, but the expected orders for change of position never came, and we were caught unprotected. The rebel fire was terribly accurate and demoralizing. Our losses became heavier and heavier as the day wore on; toward afternoon there began to develop a cross-fire from our right flank. The brigade commander ordered out two companies from our regiment to stop it, and the colonel sent me with them. Soon after he came out himself and soon the brigade commander followed. They were anxious about that flank. The firing had then practically ceased and, rather foolishly, I stood up to indicate to them the position of the men. Some fellow on the other side took a shot at the group, and his bullet struck me. The old lieutenant colonel (he was perhaps 40 years old, which seemed very old to us) stooped down, picked me up and placed me with my back against a tree for protection. I am sure it was a real grief to him, for he was fond of me. I was the youngest officer in the regiment (being only 19 years old), and his affectionate name for me was "Bub." There was a hole in the lapel of my coat in front over my breast, where the bullet had gone in, and another hole in the back where it came out. He told me afterward that he feared the bullet had passed through my lung and he expected to see blood pour out of my mouth. Fortunately for me the lung was not wounded."

■ Lt. Col. Enos Fourat commanded the 33rd New Jersey at Peachtree Creek, where the regiment suffered its highest number of casualties during the campaign — 71 officers and enlisted men killed, wounded and missing. Three days after the battle, Fourat wrote of the Confederate onslaught that smashed into his exposed position: "The fire was terrific; the air was literally full of deadly missiles; men dropped upon all sides; none expected to escape. The bearer of our State colors fell; one of the color guard was killed and one or two missing. The enemy were too close upon us to recover the colors; it was simply impossible, and it is with feelings of the deepest sorrow I am compelled to report that our State colors fell into the hands of the enemy ... Gen. Hooker, who before this has complimented the regiment for its gallantry in action, was pleased to say to me, 'Colonel, it is no disgrace to lose your colors under such circumstances; I only wonder that a man of you escaped capture.' "

gun." I got out. Whether he fired at me or not I do not know. Perhaps he had a momentary spasm of pity, the mark was so easy. Perhaps he did fire and missed. Going back further I met the same New York colonel who had bidden me good-bye. He was coming up by the flank. "Where are they, Adjutant?"

"Deploy quickly, Colonel, they are right here," was my answer. Before he could give his order he was wounded, and still further back we were all driven in great confusion and disorder.

I was very blue; it seemed to me that the day was lost. Just then we met Hooker coming forward, magnificent in appearance, mounted on a splendid horse, looking, as he was, the beau ideal of a soldier of the olden type. "Boys," said he, "I guess we will stop here," and stop there we did, and reformed and went back with him, and by nightfall our lost ground was all taken back again. As it was in our own immediate front, so it was along the whole of Thomas' front. Hood was everywhere repulsed. His attack had been a most disastrous and bloody failure. Our own regimental loss in this engagement was very heavy. Six commissioned officers were wounded or captured, and nearly one-half of the men who went into the fight were killed, wounded or captured. One of the color bearers was killed and his colors captured by the enemy.

Just at the left of the gap left in our lines when we were driven back, was our division battery, Bundy's. It was just at the edge, too, of the open field, down which I had seen the enemy coming. Through this gap, and the still longer one to our right, where connection had not yet been made with Williams' division, the rebels swarmed, took Bundy's battery in the flank and attempted to rush it. He wheeled two of his pieces to the right to meet the attack. So hot was the rebel infantry fire that many of the spokes of the wheels of his pieces were almost cut in two by the bullets alone. But Bundy held his ground, drove them off and saved all his guns.

That evening I walked over to the battery and an artillery sergeant, still black and grimy from the fight, told me the story and, as he told it, he leaned against his piece, one arm thrown over it, patting it affectionately with his hand as a mother might pat her child who had been in great danger, but had been saved.

"It was awful, Adjutant," he said, "awful, but your stocking legs saved us."

It was our habit, when the powder in our cartridges became damp and spoiled, to break it off, throw it away, save the bullets and, when we had enough to fill a stocking, to take them over to Bundy for use at close quarters. So that afternoon, when he was so hard pressed, he filled his guns with these and then, at point-blank range, poured it into them. The slaughter was terrible.

"It was awful, Adjutant," said the sergeant, and out yonder in the tangle, piled up they lay, mute evidence of the truth of the sergeant's story.

'A galling fire of minies'

1st Lieut. R.M. Collins
Company B
15th Texas Cavalry (Dismounted)

On the morning of the 4th of July we formed another line near the Chattahoochee River, and by the time we were ready for fight Sherman's advance was in sight. About one o'clock they charged our picket line and drove the men in.

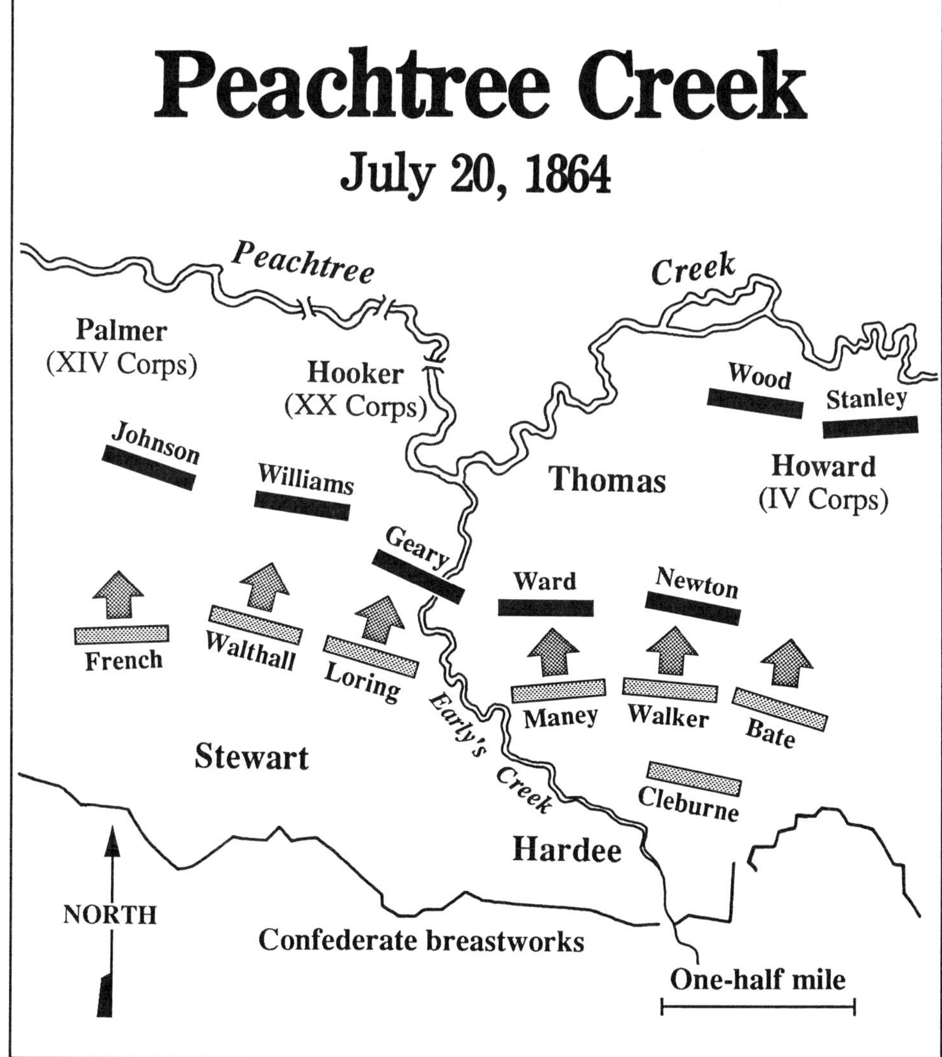

■ Lt. Col. Allan H. Jackson commanded the 134th New York at Peachtree Creek, where he was slightly wounded. The 134th lost 25 officers and enlisted men on July 20, nearly one-fourth of the regiment's total casualties (107) suffered during the campaign.

Capt. Rhoads Fisher, commanding our regiment, ordered Lieut. Harroll, commanding Company A, and myself to take our companies and retake the line of picket works. The Federals were in our advance works and we had to go at them through an open space we had cleared ourselves in front of our main line, a distance of about 200 yards. We all knew that there were but two things we could do — go into the works on them and be killed in the attempt, or refuse to go. We went at them like a herd of wild cattle; they gave us a warm reception but we made them pull their freight.

About sundown they made an effort to retake the works but we repulsed them, a Federal lieutenant was shot down badly wounded near our line. He gave some of the boys his rings, watch and some other things and requested that they be sent to his wife and two children somewhere in Indiana after the war closed. Sometime during the night we were moved back and put on an already fortified line nearer the river. Here Sherman seemed to want to stop and rest a few days and spit on his hands, and God knows that we were more than willing, for we not only needed rest but we wanted time to wash our shirts as well as take a swim in the Chattahoochee.

On the 12th this scientifically fortified line was abandoned, we crossed over the river and lay around loose under the shades of the great oaks and rested until July the 18th; this was a bright Sunday and the boys, instead of all going to hear preaching, had their blankets spread and were playing draw-poker or shaking dice. Along with a majority of my company, I was playing a little game in the deep shade of a great oak, on a big, moss-

■ Brig. Gen. Nathan Kimball commanded a brigade and later a division of the IV Corps, Army of the Cumberland. Of the Confederate assault at Peachtree Creek, he wrote that the rebel infantry charged "with great confidence with a rapidity and an absence of confusion I have never seen equaled ... The troops which attacked our position were Bate's, Walker's and a part of Cheatham's divisions, esteemed among the best in the rebel service ..."

covered flat rock for a table, when Adjutant John Willingham came up and read the order from President Davis removing Gen. Jos. E. Johnston from command and putting Gen. John B. Hood in command of the Army of Tennessee.

The boys all threw down their cards and collected in little groups discussing the new move. They were all dissatisfied, but soon dismissed the whole with the remark "Hell will break loose in Georgia sure enough now." Hood was a bulldog fighter from away back, and President Davis could not have suited Gen. Sherman better had he commissioned him to have made the appointment.

Early on the morning of the 19th, Gen. Hood had the whole army on the move "right in front." We were old soldiers enough by this time to know that this order in our line of march meant that Sherman was making a move to turn our right flank. Our division was moved to and put on a line some two miles east of the Peachtree Creek road. Here we remained overnight.

On the morning of the 20th we were moved still further to the right in the direction of Decatur. We remained here in line of battle until about 3 o'clock in the afternoon, when we were moved in double-quick time back to the Peachtree Creek road, and our division manned a line of works at right angles to this road just in front of a big church house. The right center of Granbury's Texas brigade, being near the road, with Govan's Arkansas brigade, or Joshes, as we boys called them, to our right. I was detailed and put in command of Company C, Lieut. John W. Stewart of Grayson County, Texas, being too indisposed to go into battle with his company. Every movement pointed with the unerring finger of certainty to the fact that somebody was going to get badly hurt, and that in short order.

In front of our brigade was an open field about 400 yards across. About 4:30 o'clock the command was given, "Forward, march!" We quit the works and moved out into the field. The Federals greeted us with terrific fire of shot and shells, but as we were moving down the hill they passed over our heads, doing no damage except that of making a fellow feel like he was very small game to be shot at with such guns.

On we go, now the lines come to the fence of a farm, the line halts and the men take hold of it and just bodily lift it and throw it down. Just at this moment a blinding flash right in our front and a shell explodes. It seemed to be filled with powder and ounce balls. It laid a good many of the boys out, and among the number was Capt. Ben Tyus and myself.

Capt. Tyus was wounded in the ankle while I received an ounce ball in the upper third of my left thigh. As I fell I noticed that about two inches square of my gray Georgia jeans pants had gone in with the shot; this was conclusive that a piece of the shell had passed through my thigh and had necessarily cut the femoral artery, and that therefore I would be a dead Confederate in just three minutes, as my understanding was that the femoral artery cut would let all the blood in a man out in that time.

However, I made a grip on the wound with my right hand, intending to stop the blood as much as possible, and thereby hold on to life long enough to give my past history a hasty going over and to repeat all the prayers I knew. Four big stout fellows picked me up on a litter and started back to the line of breastworks. We had to pass through a galling fire of minies, shot and shell; I was not alarmed at all at this, because my mind was made up to quit the earth and I was now only waiting, as the saying goes, for death to strike me square in the face.

I finally ventured to inquire of one of the men carrying me if I were bleeding much. He was a witty Irishman, and replied, "Not a drap of the rudy current to be seen, Lieutenant."

These words brought back my hope that had already gone over the hills out of sight, and made me remark that an improvement in gait would soon land us out of reach of these Yankee bullets. Then I chuckled in my sleeve when the thought occurred that maybe this wound will win a good furlough, and if it does won't I have fun with those Georgia girls. This may all sound like a strange line of thoughts to run through one's mind in so short a time and under such circumstances, but all this is sound common sense compared to some things we are guilty of doing during our natural lives.

Pretty soon I was dumped over on the safe side of our earthworks, the field surgeon examined my wound and pronounced it an ugly one, but not necessarily fatal. I thanked him from the bottom of my heart for these words.

About 10 of us were piled into an old ambulance and the driver pulled out for Atlanta. We were landed at the City Hall, the commons around this building having been turned into a carving pen, and the doctors had more subjects than they had table room. I was laid on a big broad pine table and four stout men put to hold me, one to each arm and leg, while Doctors D.F. Stuart of Houston and C. Lipscomb of Denton, went into the ugly wound with probes and fingers in search of the missing piece of my Georgia jeans.

Chloroform was too scarce and costly to be used on me, and besides there were so many needing attention that the doctors could not spare time to administer it except in very bad cases; therefore, I had to endure the pain. The ball that struck me was mashed flat on one side to about the size of a quarter, and went in the flat way turning on the femoral artery.

I was then stored away on a nice clean cot in a new tent in a little park just across the street from the Trout House, and remained there overnight and was shipped early next morning along with many others down to a little city on the Macon road called Forsythe.*

■ Maj. Gen. William B. Bate commanded a division in Hardee's corps during the campaign. A native of Tennessee, Bate entered Confederate service in May 1861 as a private in the 2nd Tennessee Infantry, but within 10 months was the regiment's colonel. He was known as a bold, tenacious fighter. During the war he was wounded three times and had six horses killed under him, including two in one morning at Chickamauga.

'You may give it to them, Captain'

Corporal John T. Raper
Acting Ordnance Sergeant
26th Ohio Veteran Volunteer Infantry

At the Battle of Peachtree Creek I was acting ordnance sergeant of the 26th Ohio Infantry. As this is an office unknown to the regulations I will explain that it was my duty to keep the regiment supplied with ammunition and secure the arms and accoutrements of the killed and wounded, and through the colonel of the regiment turn them over to the division ordnance officer, taking his receipt.

On July 19, 1864, we drove the enemy along the Buckhead or Peachtree Creek road, through Buckhead and across Peachtree Creek. The creek here is 30 to 40 feet wide with steep banks of about the same height as the width of the stream, and hills rising sharply on either side. The rebels made a rather stubborn resistance and the skirmishing was brisk and continuous throughout the day. After noon on the 20th our division — Newton's — crossed and took position on top of the first range of hills south of the creek. The crossing was made on the stringers of a partly destroyed bridge, other troops being engaged in tearing down some houses nearby to floor the bridge so the ammunition and the artillery would follow. We gained the position on top of

* After some initial complications with the wound in his leg, and becoming slightly addicted to morphine from 18 straight days of dosages to kill the pain, Collins was moved to Americus, Ga., recovered sufficiently and was pronounced fit again for duty on November 11, 1864.

■ Drummer Hiram D. Throckmorton, Company E, 26th Ohio, poses with his new snare drum, a style one third as deep as a typical, cumbersome army snare. Metal tighteners were also an improvement over the older, rope-tension drums. Throckmorton was a member of the brass band, 2nd Brigade, 2nd Division, IV Corps.

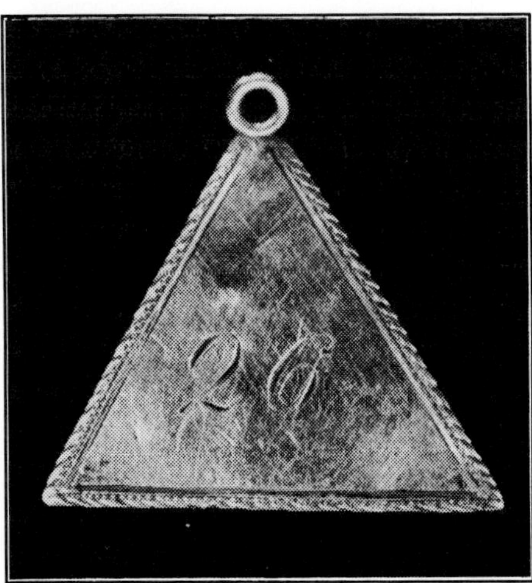

■ A German-silver IV Corps badge worn by a member of the 26th Ohio, the first regiment in the corps to re-enlist as veterans early in 1864. The equilateral triangle was officially adopted by the corps as its badge in April 1864.

the hill almost without resistance and everything in front was quiet — suspiciously so.

Wagner's brigade, to which I belonged, took position on the hill with its right resting on Peachtree Creek road, at right angles thereto, and the left refused; Kimball's brigade on the right of the road and Bradley's in column on the road, the head of the column near the point where Wagner and Kimball joined, and stretching away on the road nearly to the bridge. The division thus formed an immense T, the left of the cross being refused. Wagner's brigade occupied the left portion of the top of the T, Kimball's the right and Bradley's the stem.

The ease with which this position was secured and the remarkable quietness in front had, as intimated, excited suspicion, and the men of Company B, 26th Ohio, commenced a line of works a short distance in front of the line on which they had stacked their arms. A barnyard's numerous cross fences and buildings furnished abundant material. Stakes were driven, rails piled in between them and the whole line took up the work thus begun.

Very little earth had been thrown against this rail barricade when the enemy began his advance; but it was a sufficient protection from the musketry, and the heavy woods in front shielded it from the view of the rebel artillerymen. The enemy came en masse, and our skirmishers lost no time in getting back to the main line. The first one I saw emerge from the woods seemed to be making strides of about 15 feet, and as he came in sight of our line he called out at the top of his voice: "Here they come, boys! By God, a million of them!"

The men in the works immediately set up the cry, "Ammunition, ammunition!" I knew that they had 40 rounds or more; but in the Atlanta campaign they had come to think that 40 rounds were hardly enough to commence a fight with, much less to complete it, and they knew it was nearly three-quarters of a mile back to the bridge which was without a floor, and therefore the ammunition wagons could not cross it. The cry for ammunition and this knowledge made me uneasy, for I took a good deal of pride in the fact that while it had been my duty to supply them, they had never called in vain nor withdrawn from a line of battle, however long the engagement, to replenish their boxes. I didn't know how it was going to be with the closest wagon three-quarters of a mile away, and a "million" rebels in front.

However, I started off with all speed to the bridge. Just before reaching it, and when I was about exhausted, a mounted orderly dashed across the road in front of me. He reined up his horse suddenly at a pile of rails on which an officer was sitting, his elbows resting on his knees which were drawn well toward his body, and field binoculars in his hands directed toward the corner of the woods to left and rear of the position held by Wagner's brigade. As the orderly reined up, the officer took the glasses from his eyes, turned his face and I saw it was Gen. George H. Thomas.

The orderly saluted and said, "Gen. Thomas, Major McGraw presents his compliments and says to inform you that the enemy is moving on him en masse, and it will be impossible to hold his position."

"Orderly, return to Major McGraw, give him my compliments and tell him to hold his position. I will attend to those fellows as soon as they get out from behind the woods," was the reply, with which Gen. Thomas again turned his glasses to the corner of the woods.

From the direction taken by the orderly and Gen. Thomas' fixed attention to the corner of the woods, I inferred that Major McGraw, who commanded the 57th Indiana, was along the creek in front of the advancing column of rebels. So I stopped to see the result. The orderly had scarcely turned his horse when the first rebel line appeared, followed by another and another. The mounted officers were in their positions in rear of the several lines, which were advancing at quick time, each step bringing their left flank closer in line with the point where Gen. Thomas still quietly sat, his eyes riveted to his glasses.

Only once did he take the glasses from his eyes. Bradley's brigade was occupying the road, and for some reason there was momentarily considerable confusion in the ranks which was heightened in Gen. Thomas' vicinity by Col. Opdycke's horse becoming unmanageable and making a scatterment of the men to keep from being trampled on. For just a moment he took his glasses down and looked over his right shoulder. When he looked the disorder was at its height, but he turned back to his glasses as if it did not concern him.

The advancing rebel column was now almost to the creek, its left flank nearly opposite to Gen. Thomas and half a mile in the rear of the left of Wagner's brigade, in which were my friends and comrades. I commenced to think it was high time for Gen. Thomas to "attend to those fellows," and I saw no way in which he was going to do it. Bradley's brigade was not strong enough to rout that column, even though it was fairly on its flank, and no other troops were at hand that I could see.

But Gen. Thomas also seemed to think the time had come. He took the glasses from his eyes, turned his head over his left shoulder, nodded it forward, at the same time saying, slowly, deliberately and distinctly, "Now you may give it to them, captain."

"Fire!" rang out a clear and sharp command, and a dozen or more cannon, which had heretofore been concealed or overlooked by me by reason of intervening undergrowth which here fringed the road, sent their charges of shot, shell and canister tearing straight down the enemy's lines. Load after load as fast as the artillerymen could handle their pieces followed — a continuous shower of murderous iron. No troops on earth could stand that long, for they were taken at a disadvantage, could not reply and were in an open field at point-blank range. A heroic effort was made to maintain lines, but in a minute or less it was apparent that they would go to pieces under the unmerciful pounding of our artillery.*

All this transpired in less time than it takes me to tell it; but I had now regained my wind and must be off. It was an intensely exciting scene from which it was almost impossible to tear one's self. But my duty to keep my regiment supplied with ammunition was imperative.

I continued toward the creek, on the banks of which a pile of ammunition boxes had been carried across the still incomplete bridge. Taking one of the boxes — 1,000 rounds — on my shoulder, and forcing a straggler from my regiment, whom I had found on the way back, to take another, we started for the regiment nearly three-quarters of a mile up the road and along Bradley's line of battle, which was facing eastward.

The pounding of the rebel column by our artillery still continued, and the confusion created in their lines increased. The Johnnies were game, however, and threw out a line of skirmishers in the new direction indicated by our artillery, attempting to change front forward on their left. But they went to pieces in the movement. At the same time Bradley's men leaped over their barricades and charged the tangled mass.

As I passed the edge of the woods with my box of cartridges on my shoulder, the enemy was disappearing in rout where they had first appeared and Bradley's brigade was in pursuit. Before I reached the line of my own

■ Maj. Gen. George H. Thomas commanded the Army of the Cumberland during the campaign. The native Virginian endeared himself to many of the enlisted men in his command, and acquired from them the nickname "Pap." One of these soldiers, Corporal Bliss Morse of Company D, 105th Ohio, wrote in his diary of an encounter with Thomas two days before the battle of Jonesboro: "As we were marching along our Reg. halted near the road side where 'Pappy Thomas' stopped. Our Co. was right beside him. The Gen. looks like some good 'old farmer.' He wore an Army hat — such a hat as many of the boys think a *shocking bad* hat, and besides 'Pap' was really eating *hard bread* for dinner."

* These guns belonged to Battery A, 1st Ohio Light Artillery under the command of Capt. Wilbur F. Goodspeed (acting chief of division artillery), and Battery M, 1st Illinois Light Artillery, commanded by Capt. George W. Spencer.

■ Capt. Wilbur F. Goodspeed, commander of Battery A, 1st Ohio Light Artillery, was chief of artillery for Newton's division, IV Corps, from June 24 to the end of the campaign. Gen. Thomas warmly commended his management of the division artillery at Peachtree Creek, which contributed greatly to checking the Confederate assault and saving the supply trains of the Army of the Cumberland.

brigade the floor of the bridge was completed, Bradley's advance had made the road safe and the ammunition wagons crossed, making an abundant supply a certainty.

Until an intervening obstruction hid Gen. Thomas from view I could still see him sitting in the same position, watching the result of the conflict. I did not notice any of his staff present, but two or three staff officers or orderlies reported to him and dashed off again with orders apparently given in the same quiet way as those I overheard given to the orderly from Major McGraw. The particular business he had in hand just then was to crush and drive back the rebel column, for it had wedged its way through our lines where an interval of nearly two miles existed. His orders were given as deliberately and pleasantly as he might request his orderly to bring him a drink of water; their execution was the breaking of an overwhelming cyclone. Nothing could withstand it; confusion, destruction, death and defeat to the enemy marked its pathway.

'General Walthall ought to promote you'

Private Washington Bryan Crumpton
Company H
37th Mississippi Volunteer Infantry

On the 20th of July the battle of Peachtree Creek was fought. We took the Yanks in our front seemingly by surprise. They threw down their guns and surrendered in droves, and that was our undoing. Too many of our fellows were willing to carry prisoners to the rear. There was no reserve to carry on the victory.

The brigade on our right had to come up through an old field facing a battery and had been unsuccessful. Lieut. Pierce English, gun in hand, and three of us found ourselves on a hill rather behind the battery on our right. We had used up all our ammunition. So we picked up Yankee cartridge boxes, which strewed the ground. Their guns carried a ball about two calibers smaller than ours. So we abandoned the slow method of drawing the rammer to load. We tore the cartridge, placed it in the muzzle, stamped the breech on the ground; the weight of the bullet carried the cartridge home, so we only had to cap and fire. It was almost like a repeating rifle.

There seemed to be no danger in our front. The Yanks had continued their flight, we thought, to the river. We fired on the battery so fast that it almost ceased firing. They turned a gun on us, but fired only once. Probably they were short of ammunition, for the caissons were being rushed forward as fast as the horses could drag them, but we had shot them down. We saw far in the distance a group of horsemen which we took to be a general and his staff. We all loaded, elevated our sights, dropped behind a log and took deliberate aim. In a moment we saw them scampering away.

Old Bill Nicholson, one of our party, had been a Texas Ranger. Returning to Mississippi, his native State, he enlisted, though he had a leg stiff from rheumatism, but that was no bar to service in those days. He brought with him from Texas an old six-shooter, which he buckled around him. It was the joke of the company when "Nick" every few weeks went out into the bushes and tried his pistol at a tree; then for a couple of hours he cleaned and reloaded it. He had never found use for it, but he said the time would come. He was the only man in the company who had a revolver.

On this occasion Bill said to the lieutenant: "Pierce, kill that Yankee." It so happened that not a gun was loaded, and Bill had forgotten his pistol.

Maybe the Yank's gun was empty too, for we saw him twenty steps away dodge into the bushes. A hasty counsel was held, and we decided they were returning and we'd better get out. What had become of the balance of our forces we never did know. We supposed many had gone to the rear with the prisoners and had forgotten to return. With our guns all loaded we started out the way we came in.

On rising a very steep hill in the woods we saw fifty yards away the woods black with Yankees. They had dropped in behind us, but with no idea that there was danger from that direction; they were looking to their front. We all fired into the thickest bunch of them and fairly rolled down the steep hillside. Three of us rushed down a ravine and, after passing a spur, went up another ravine. Poor old Bill Nick went across the spur and we gave him up as lost.

Approaching a road down which General Walthall, our division commander, and staff were riding leisurely, I shouted to him, telling him of his danger. One of his party came galloping, saying: "Go back to the front, you stragglers." With that our lieutenant walked away, demanding that we should go back. I remarked that I'd speak to the General. In a few words I told him that the other brigade hadn't come up, that the Yanks were only a little way down the road. On his expressing great doubt, saying, "We certainly have carried everything," his smart Alec of an aide shouted out as he galloped off: "I'll see." A short distance away he wheeled his horse, and a hundred bullets flew through the woods in his direction.

In the middle of the road there was a brass cannon left by someone. The General said: "You two men remain right here by this gun and when I send you a force pilot them to that hill you were on." My companion was "Chunky" Thompson, called that because he was not chunky. He was as slim as a match and probably six feet and eight inches in height. We looked at the gun and found it loaded, but how to shoot it we did not know. Finally, however, we thought we knew and were determined that we'd fire it if the Yanks came.

After a while the 25th Arkansas came with a very small number of men. Later another bunch, until probably five hundred at last had gathered. Then came a senior colonel drunk as could be. He called for the men General Walthall had left and wanted to know where the hill was. I pointed the direction and suggested modestly that my companion and I, with a few others, should act as skirmishers for there was no telling what changes had occurred. He cursed me, and said he was capable of running that business.

After a time in the wildest confusion we were at the bottom of the hill. I said: "There's the hill, Colonel; I can't tell you what's on top." He ordered the charge. When within twenty or thirty steps of the top a solid blue line of Yanks rose up, and I am sure half of our men fell at the first fire. I fired my gun, then attempted to load it lying down. It had been fired so much that it had gotten clogged, and the bullet hung halfway down the barrel. Standing half bent, trying to ram the bullet home, the gun was shot out of my hand, the stock literally torn into splinters. Fortunately, some of us escaped because the Yanks, firing down the hill, as is most generally the case, overshot us. As I started down the hill I picked up a Yankee gun. Just then the colonel, capless, rode by as fast as his horse could carry him. His drunkeness and foolhardiness had lost the day and fully half his men. Getting back to camp that night, the lieutenant said: "Wash, General Walthall ought to promote you. But for you he would have been killed or captured today."

How we talked of poor old Bill Nick! We mourned him as dead, when about ten o'clock he limped into camp with his empty pistol strapped around him. When asked about it, he said: "They tried to kill me by shoot-

■ Maj. Gen. Edward C. Walthall commanded a division in Stewart's corps during the battle of Peachtree Creek. A native Virginian who was raised in Mississippi, he commanded both the 15th and 29th Mississippi Infantry regiments early in the war. "Walthall was every inch a soldier, and inspired everyone who came near him with the deepest respect and confidence," wrote 1st Lieut. John I. Kendall, who served on Walthall's staff during early August 1864. "He seldom said anything, and especially under fire was cool and collected. When his officers displayed exceptional bravery he said little, but any remissness in the performance of duty was sure to elicit prompt and severe censure."

■ Sergeant Henry E. Price, Company D, 104th Illinois. On July 2 he was injured by a spent ball at Kennesaw Mountain, but returned to duty on the 19th after hospitalization. The next day at Peachtree Creek he wrote in his diary: "At 3 o'clock a.m., moved again and crossed creek. Advancing in line of battle under fire. Halted and built breastworks until ordered to quit." It was his last entry. A few hours later his right thigh and arm were shattered by bullets, and he died soon after. Universally mourned by the regiment, Price's spirit was shown in a letter he had written home the previous November: "If I live to serve out my time, money would not buy my right to say that I had served my country honorably, and if I do not live, the right belongs to our family. I can honestly say, I have never yet been sorry I enlisted."

ing at me, and I don't see how they missed me. Then they undertook to run me down, and I got five of them with my revolver." Think of the weary marches for two years and how, loaded down though he was, he clung to the old Texas weapon, saying: "Some day I'll need it." And that day had come.

'Nothing to do but surrender'

Private Alfred R. Gibbons
Company G
1st Georgia Cavalry

On the 17th day of July the Federals crossed the Chattahoochee River above to our right some distance, and came down on our side so that we had to fall back. This was in the afternoon. We fell back and formed a line of battle and put out a heavy skirmish line. We lost a few men and a number were wounded.

On the 18th we moved and did mostly picketing and scouting. When night came we had just gone into camp when the bugle sounded to saddle up. We were then on the north side of Atlanta and they marched us to the east and southeast of Atlanta. As we passed the infantry and fortifications the bands were playing tattoo, the night roll call. When the band started playing our whole division started yelling, the infantry took it up, so the entire army was yelling and, of course, the Yankees could hear us. This was the last Confederate band I heard play.

The next day, the 19th, we were moved out and ran into a bunch of Yankees near Decatur and Stone Mountain. They were tearing up the railroad near a cut. We opened fire on them and drove them off. We spent that evening and night establishing picket lines to connect with our main earthworks or linc of battle. That night about 50 of us were going through some timber following the branch of a stream. As we came out of the timber into a little flat, open place, on a ridge to the right we saw campfires and heard men's voices not over 200 yards off. We supposed we had come to our regular line, but down this branch we saw men getting water.

Four or five of us rode up and asked them what command they belonged to. We soon found that they were Yankees. We took up three or four behind us, and in the meantime the others upstream had become frightened and ran up the hill where the campfires were. It wasn't long until we heard drums beating and the command to fall in. We pulled out through the brush to the left, what few troops there were with us, and established pickets. The next morning we marched back toward Atlanta.

On the 20th we went into camp about the middle of the afternoon and the regiment was marched out, all except those who had to care for the horses and do the cooking. We took our position to the right of the infantry line and went to work digging trenches. During the night we had orders to move to the right and to give up our works to the infantry that had been brought up. We then went to work throwing up earthworks again.

We had them about half finished at daylight on the 21st. In front of us it was fairly clear — a good deal of timber but no underbrush. To the right was heavy brush and the line extended over a ridge, and was occupied by the Alabama brigade of Martin's division.

It was about daylight when the Federals opened fire on us with artillery all along the line. I saw several of our men falling back. Joseph Hammond, Bud Corbutt, Davy Clark, Moung Ware and myself, five of us together, started back too until we saw our colonel running up the earthworks with a sword in one hand and a revolver in the other, shouting, "1st Georgia, stand to your post!" So we went back, and by that time the Federals were advancing in front. I do not know how many rounds had been fired, but I raised my gun to fire again and as I did so, I saw the 1st sergeant of Company D throw down his gun and shout "I surrender!" I then turned around and saw some of the boys running. A Yankee had the muzzle of his gun within six feet of me and there were others all around me, so there was nothing for me to do but surrender.

The man who captured me was very anxious to get back to the rear, so he led the way and I followed. We had to go some half mile or more, and all the time we were exposed to the firing from the Confederates who had rallied after receiving reinforcements. They drove the Yankees back and recaptured the line of works.

As my captor was taking me back to the reserves, we had to pass over the ridge which had been occupied by the Alabama brigade. When I surrendered my captor did not notice I had a revolver. I was certainly tempted to shoot him, but as the Federal line was between me and the Confederates I did not think I could get away. So I broke my revolver and threw one piece one direction and another in the opposite direction. I also threw my belt away.

We soon came to where the Yankees had charged the Alabama brigade, and there I saw many Yankees dead and wounded. It wasn't long until we came to the Federals' reserve, and as we came up they immediately wanted to know if I had any tobacco. I had two plugs which had been issued to me the day before, but my captor told me not to give it to them. I sold one plug for a dollar greenback.

It wasn't long until I ran across Joe Hammond and Bud Corbutt, whom I had seen only about a half hour before. I was so glad to see them that I had to shake hands with them. Misery loves company.

Toward evening a number of prisoners who had been captured at different intervals were marched to Gen. Frank Blair's headquarters. They had a large flag over his tent. He made us a speech and told us what bad boys we were and that we ought to honor the flag, but I felt more like cutting his throat than listening to his speech.

After he had finished, some others and myself were taken to the commissary wagon and given some pickled pork and hardtack, and then marched back to the timber where they had cut poles and fastened them to the trees. We had to stay inside this barricade. We proceeded to eat our food raw as there was no way to cook it. This was the first food we had had since the day before. Late that evening it poured down rain and, of course, we had nothing to protect us so we had to take it as it came.*

■ Col. Stephen J. McGroarty, commander of the 61st Ohio, had his left arm shattered at the elbow by a minie ball on July 20 at Peachtree Creek. Though the arm was later amputated, he refused to leave the field and remained on his horse, carrying his sword in his right hand and bridle rein in his mouth. However, the wound — the last of 23 he received during the war — incapacitated him for further active service. McGroarty, a native of County Donegal, Ireland, was brevetted brigadier general on May 1, 1865, and died from the effects of his many wounds on January 2, 1870, at the age of 39.

'Our men stood like statues'

Private James Turner
Company G
6th Texas Volunteer Infantry

After the fighting on the New Hope Church line we kept on fighting and slowly retreating toward Atlanta, sleeping when we had a chance to sleep with our guns in hand and without removing our belts or cartridge boxes or

* On July 31, while enroute by train for imprisonment at Camp Chase in Columbus, Ohio, Gibbons jumped from a boxcar near North Vernon, Ind., and escaped. He later recalled, "Well, here I was in the enemy's country, 17 years old, six feet two inches tall, coal black hair almost long enough to tie under my chin, grey jacket and pants,

■ 1st Lieut. Claudius Virginius H. Davis, adjutant of the 22nd Mississippi, was killed on July 20 at Peachtree Creek. Attacking from the center of Gen. W.S. Featherston's brigade, the 22nd had to contend with natural obstacles as well as enemy fire. Regimental commander Major Martin A. Oatis, himself wounded in the battle, later wrote: "We moved on at a double-quick and in tolerable order until midway the field we encountered a boggy marsh overgrown with tall marsh grass and a small creek running through it. At this point we were exposed to a murderous enfilade fire of both musketry and artillery from the left, rendered far more destructive by the grouping of companies and the concentration of the line into masses in order to effect a passage of the marsh and creek by the beaten paths and the open fords. In effecting the passage of this marsh I lost many of my bravest and best officers and men." Three color bearers were shot down in succession until Davis picked up the flag and carried it to the Federal works. While urging the regiment on, he was struck by bullets in the head and chest, killing him instantly.

shoes, sleeping in harness as it were, with bullets and shells constantly flying over and around us. We were constantly under fire. We fought every day and every night as we fell back.

We retreated from Kennesaw during the night of July 2nd and as our company was the last to leave the skirmish line, between midnight and day we saw the stars and stripes displayed at sunrise, on the 3rd of July, on top of the mountain. At Marietta we halted and crossed the Chattahoochee River during the night of July 12th and went into bivouac near the city of Atlanta, where we rested for a few days.

During the forenoon of July 18th there came to us like a clap of thunder from a clear sky the announcement of the removal of General Johnston, whom we all idolized and the appointment of General Hood to the command of the army.

The men were astonished beyond expression and for the first time appeared disheartened. General Hood's order assuming command of the army was read to our command in line, and it was received in absolute silence. Not a cheer was heard and after breaking ranks many unfavorable comments and direful forebodings were indulged in, for our boys felt that a fatal mistake had been made.

Soon after Hood took command the troops began to move and take positions in line. Then followed the battles of Peachtree Creek on July 20, and of Atlanta, on the 21st and 22nd in which we were actively engaged. The battle of Peachtree Creek opened early in the morning and continued all day, and nothing of importance was accomplished. We withdrew from the field of Peachtree Creek soon after dark and marched through the city of Atlanta. We were moved about from place to place during the night and had no chance to lie down or rest.

Just before daylight on the morning of the 21st we were placed on the front line and on the extreme right of the army. We at once began throwing up breastworks, but before we had done much of the work the enemy opened on us a heavy enfilading artillery fire from the left and their well trained guns throwing shrapnel and shells straight down our line played havoc in our ranks. We worked steadily under that murderous fire, digging trenches and throwing up breastworks, but before our works were more than half completed, heavy masses of infantry appeared in our front. Line after line of the enemy came into sight and as the blue columns advanced towards us in perfect formation with flags flying and bayonets flashing in the sunshine, they made a splendid appearance.

Our brigade and regimental officers passed along the line and calling our attention to the advancing columns told us that we must drive them back or die, as the safety of Atlanta and of the Confederate Army depended upon us alone, as we had no support.

The artillery fire ceased and for a brief period a perfect silence reigned. Our men stood like statues watching the advancing hosts. Not one of our men wavered, but on the face of everyone was written a determination to drive them back or die.

When they came within range of our rifles the order to fire was given and a sheet of flame ran along our line. They made charge after charge and after each repulse would form and charge again. After many attempts to

---

wool hat that had lost its shape on account of the weather, a pair of boots that had cost me $200 to have made, and a $1 greenback. What direction to go I did not know." Traveling north, he evaded capture until August 11, when he was arrested for stealing some clothes in Portland, Ind. Confined in jail there until October 14, he was tried, convicted of theft and sentenced to the Indiana Penitentiary for two years, but was released on September 17, 1865.

drive us they fell sullenly back leaving the ground strewn with their dead and wounded.

The only Confederate troops we had on our right were some cavalry men dismounted and fighting on foot, but not being accustomed to meeting infantry charges they fled after the first volley leaving our right flank entirely exposed and enabling the enemy to gain possession of a hill from which point they poured a galling fire down our line. Many of the Federals got over the breastworks and many hand to hand conflicts ensued. Bayonets and clubbed muskets were freely used, but we held our line. It was almost a repetition of New Hope Church, but without its glory, for we could not follow the enemy without exposing our line to an attack from the right and rear, and a forward movement on our part would have opened the gates of Atlanta and caused its capture.

After their infantry retired the enemy again opened a heavy artillery fire on us from the left and from in front while the Federal infantry on our right kept up an enfilading rifle fire down our line. We could do nothing but stay there and take that terrible fire, and to fire back whenever anything came within range.

It was a terrible day and the loss in our brigade was great, but we remained there until darkness set in, and after all our wounded had been removed and our dead buried, we crawled silently away in the dark on our hands and knees leaving the empty trenches to the enemy's force that was trying to envelop us from the right.

We marched back to Atlanta and refilled our cartridge boxes. Then away from the city we went without having the least idea where or in what direction we were going.*

■ Capt. John A. Norris, Company C, 98th Ohio, was severely wounded by a sharpshooter's bullet while reconnoitering at Peachtree Creek on July 20, losing a leg. Wrote Chaplain G.W. Pepper of the 80th Ohio: "Among the numerous wounded officers and soldiers whom I visited in the hospital at Vining Station, none seemed to bear their terrible sufferings with so much composure and cheerfulness as Capt. Norris." Before the war he was a high school teacher in Cadiz, Ohio.

'I say, you are my prisoner, ain't you?'

Col. James C. Nisbet
66th Georgia Volunteer Infantry/26th Georgia Battalion

On the 20th of July we fought the battle of Peachtree Creek. Stevens' Brigade moved out of the works on the Peachtree Road. We were told that the enemy had just crossed Peachtree Creek that morning and were unfortified. My regiment formed into line of battle on the left of the brigade with my left resting on the Peachtree Road.

We advanced, and drove in the enemy's skirmishers. There was a considerable gap on my left. I protested against advancing until this gap was filled; but the order was given — and the line went in with a rush — right up to well-constructed earthworks!

My regiment and that on my right, the 1st Georgia Confederate Infantry, captured the works in our front. But we were not supported. The enemy on my left, not being assaulted, continued to enfilade my line. Seeing fresh troops being rushed up against us, I was certain we could not hold the

* On November 30, 1864, at the battle of Franklin, Tenn., Turner was wounded three times, dragged over the Federal breastworks and taken prisoner. He was sent to Camp Douglas at Chicago and remained there until the close of the war. "Our treatment there was horrible," he later wrote, "and we almost starved to death." From Chicago he was taken to New Orleans "and for some unaccountable reason was confined there for two weeks closely guarded by negro soldiers. We were then taken up the Mississippi River on a steamboat to the mouth of Red River, and were there transferred to another boat which carried us to Shreveport, Louisiana, where we were turned loose."

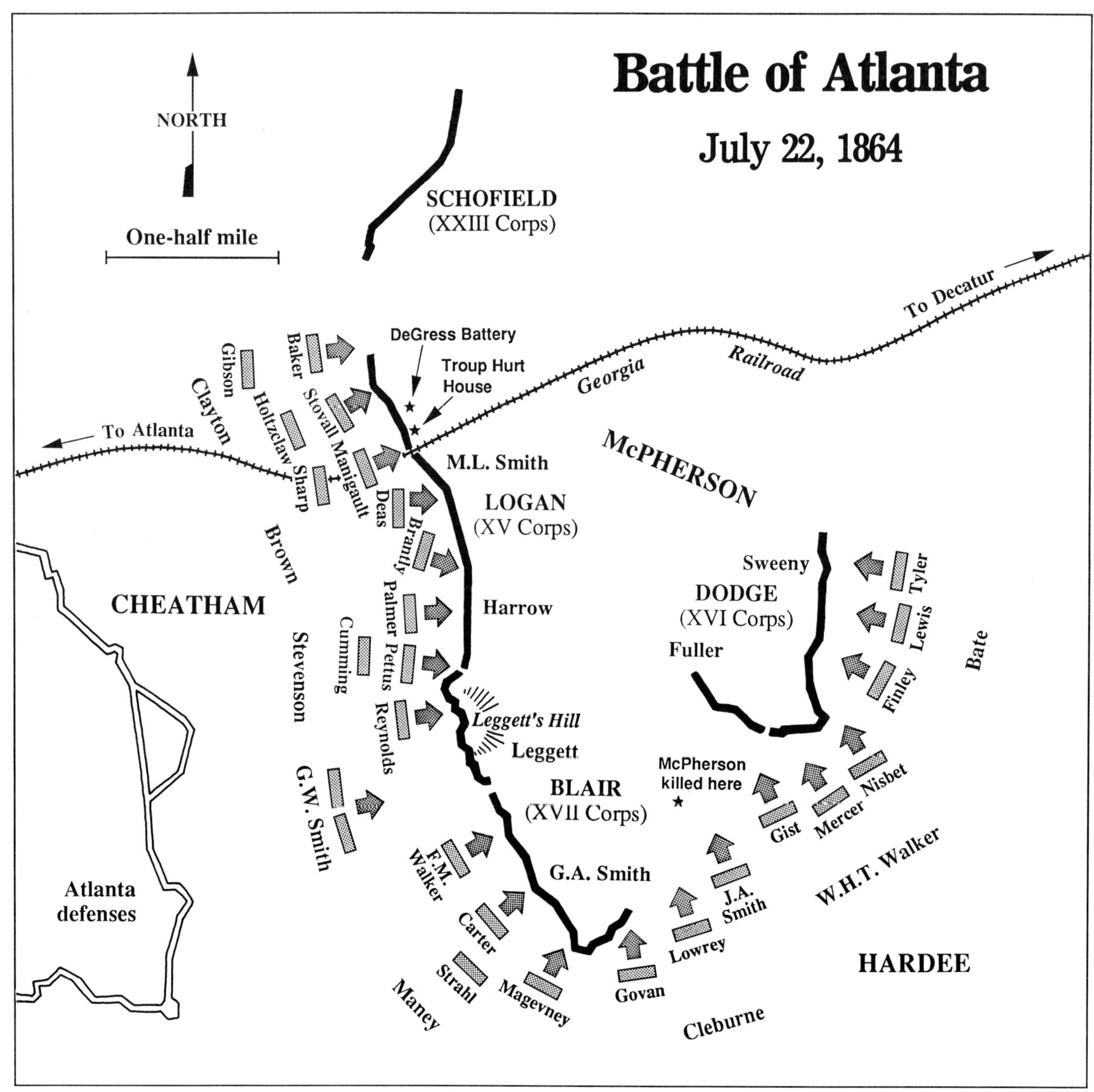

■ **The Confederate battle plan for July 22 called for simultaneous assaults on McPherson's Federal Army of the Tennessee from two different directions. Hardee's corps struck the Federal XVI Corps and part of the XVII Corps early in the afternoon, but the eastward attack of Cheatham's corps against the XVII and XV Corps did not get underway until three hours later. Although the Federal lines came close to breaking, the delay doomed the Confederates' efforts to failure.**

position. This was near the bridge crossing Peachtree Creek. Our brigade commander, Gen. Stevens, rode in, ordered me to fall back and was killed as he gave the order. I ordered the regiment to fall back. Capt. Briggs Moultrie Napier and Capt. Charles J. Williamson both received wounds in carrying Gen. Stevens' body from the field. Lieut. Charles W. Gray was wounded. Capt. Thomas Parks of the Newton County Company was killed. He was a noble, efficient, brave soldier. Never was I under a heavier fire than there — for a brief time.

I thought I would certainly see my "Valhalla" that day. I lost one-fourth of all my officers and men engaged. The firing from both the front and flank was terrific. We abandoned the works and fell back a short distance, as ordered.

We met M.P. Lowrey's Mississippi Brigade of Cleburne's Division, going in. If they had come up sooner, we could have held our captured works. Gen. Lowrey said: "Colonel, you must be mistaken about the enemy being fortified. Gen. Hood informed me that they had just crossed the creek."

I told Lowrey that was a mistake, and offered to deploy my regiment and uncover the enemy's position, which was accepted. I deployed, and drove back their skirmishers who had advanced as we fell back. I halted my line in full view of their breastworks, and waited for Lowrey to come up. After viewing the situation he agreed with me that it would be a useless waste of lives to assault their works again with what force we had. We returned to our original line.

It will be seen that the enemy had crossed Peachtree Creek the evening before and fortified, and that Hood was acting on *misinformation.* The fight was a miserable affair on his part, from start to finish. For the want of concert of action, the army lost many valuable lives and accomplished nothing of benefit.

The next day I was appointed division officer of the day, with instructions to withdraw my pickets that night, very carefully, and join Walker's Division on the McDonough road. This I did successfully. We were very close to the enemy's pickets. I had to go along my outposts and give the order to each regimental officer commanding them. I was afraid to divulge the order generally for fear some craven fellow might desert and give away the whole movement to the enemy.

The night was very dark. I dismounted, tied my horse and crept up cautiously to our line of videttes. I then commenced going down the line, notifying the officers to withdraw. But in going around some obstruction in the swamp I lost my way. I knew that I was close to the enemy's line and tried to be careful. A rotten stick broke under my foot and I quickly dropped down by a tree. A Yank standing not more than 20 feet away heard the noise and fired in my direction. His bullet struck the tree just above my head. I saw him standing a few yards off, and was greatly tempted to put a bullet from my Colt's .44 through him; but it was no time to make a racket.

I was between the lines but got back safely and proceeded with my work until the whole line was withdrawn without detection. I could not find my mare. As I was looking for the place where I hitched her, a squad of our pickets came along leading a horse. It was my mare. They said they had caught her running over to the Yanks. The next morning early we passed down Peachtree Street on our way to join Walker's Division on the McDonough road.

Sherman was shelling the city. The fine residences had been hastily abandoned, the owners leaving their *lares et penates* behind in their hasty flight. We were resting, the men lying about on the streets and sidewalks. One of the men, a tall, lanky "rube," was stalking up and down the sidewalk, oblivious to bursting shells, eating hardtack. A voice from one of the trees said: "Give poor Polly a cracker!" The country youth stopped, and looked around. Again, "Give poor Polly a cracker," came from the tree. Finally he spied the parrot and said: "Gee whillikens, boys, damned if the world hain't coming to an end! Even the birds are talking and begging for bread." Looking up he addressed the parrot: "Sure you are a mighty smart bird, and I'm sorry for you, but you go to hell! This is the first cracker I've seen for two days!"

We marched on through the city, and rejoined Walker's Division on the McDonough road. On the morning of the 22nd of July ... Hardee's Corps was on the move to attack the enemy who had crossed the railroad between Decatur and Atlanta. Walker's and Bate's divisions, finding they were proceeding in the wrong direction, had to change front in an old field. Much

■ Col. James C. Nisbet commanded the 66th Georgia in the campaign until his capture on July 22 during the battle of Atlanta. He spent the remainder of the conflict as a prisoner at Johnson's Island, Ohio. This photo shows Nisbet earlier in the war as a captain commanding Company H, 21st Georgia, Army of Northern Virginia.

■ Maj. Gen. James B. McPherson commanded the Army of the Tennessee, and was killed on July 22 while riding through a strip of woods between the XVI and XVII corps. The only Federal commander of an army to die in battle during the war, McPherson was a personal favorite of Sherman, who later wrote of him: "(He was) a very handsome man in every way, was universally liked, and had many noble qualities." An hour after he died, McPherson was carried by ambulance to Sherman's headquarters and laid on a door wrenched from its hinges. Sherman continued: "While we were examining the body inside the house, the battle was progressing outside, and many shots struck the building, which I feared would take fire ... I ordered his personal staff to go on and escort the body to his home, in Clyde, Ohio, where it was received with great honor, and it is now buried in a small cemetery ... composed in part of the family orchard, in which he used to play when a boy."

valuable time was lost. Gist's Brigade became completely separated from the rest of our division. Maj. Gen. Walker went to find it. Cleburne's Division, however, proceeded, and killed Maj. Gen. McPherson, who, reconnoitering in advance of his corps, rode into Cleburne's line and, on being ordered to halt, tried to escape. When McPherson found he was face to face with the enemy he should have surrendered when ordered to do so.

As we advanced through the field, after correcting our alignment, the enemy could be seen, on or near the Georgia Railroad, placing a battery in position. Gist's South Carolina Brigade of Walker's Division had not yet come up, and the line halted to wait for them. As I have said, Gen. W.H.T. Walker had gone to find Gist and bring him up so as to fill the gap between my left and Cleburne's Division. In the meantime I received orders to move with Stevens' Brigade, which would advance with Bate's Division on our right. I rode over to see Gen. Bate and asked that he would not advance until Gist's Brigade caught up. I told him that there was a gap on my left, made by the absence of Gist's Brigade. Gen. Bate said that so much time had been lost, it was imperative that the line move forward without further delay. So, when Bate moved forward, we advanced. Feeling an insecurity about my left, I put Col. Hamilton in command of the center, Major Newton Hull in command of the right, and I went to the left.

We had orders to push through a swampy branch to reform under the hill and charge a battery which was then playing upon us. There was a fence on my left separating the old field from the woods, a point not far from where Gen. McPherson had been killed. I heard a slight noise over the fence, as of men cocking guns, and looking I saw several Federal soldiers not more than 10 paces from me in the act of throwing up their rifles to shoot. I fell down, and their shots went over me.

Several saw me fall, and it was the impression of the regiment that I had been killed. We had to pass through a marshy thicket of underbrush and briars. I worked my way through, expecting to halt the regiment and reform the line under the hill. I was on foot, as all officers under the rank of brigadier general were required to go into battle dismounted.

I thought the enemy's advanced line was up on the hill, but as I emerged from the thicket I was greeted by a volley from the 39th Ohio Regiment which was lying down — their left not more than 40 yards away. Some 10 men of my left company came out into the field with me. The shots passed over our heads but we were surrounded in an instant by a great number, all exclaiming: "You are my prisoner!"

I was in full uniform. They thought from the stars on my collar that I was a general. Seeing that the jig was up with us, at least for a while, I stood still and said nothing. The battle was roaring all around. There was a contention among my captors as to who had captured me and as to my rank.

As I stood watching the battle surge around us, a young lieutenant took hold of my arm to attract my attention and said: "I say, you are my prisoner, ain't you?"

I said: "It looks that way."

He said: "Well you don't seem *skeered* about it!"

I said: "I have captured thousands of your men, since the war commenced, and always treated them right."

"I'll treat you that way," said he.

No one had asked me for my sword and pistol, but my men had dropped their rifles. In the meantime, having detailed the young lieutenant and a guard to take charge of us, the Federal brigade moved forward. Just then a rear skirmish line came along driving up stragglers. They were Germans. One fellow spied me standing there. Leveling his gun at a charge-bayonet, he said: "Oh! by-tam, youse jest the feller I'se been looking for."

His eyes were fiercely gleaming. I drew my pistol and said: "You stop right there. I will blow your damn head off if you attempt to bayonet me!"

This attracted the attention of my little lieutenant captor, who was watching his brigade advance. He turned and said: "What's the matter?"

I said: "He wants to bayonet me."

Seeing the German, he ran up to him and said: "You stick my prisoner and I will chop your damn Dutch head off."

Then came up the German's fat captain puffing and blowing, who, recognizing his man, said: "Vat for you stop here?"

The lieutenant said: "He wants to stick my prisoner."

The German soldier said: "He ish no prisoner, he vants to shoot me mit hiss pistol."

His captain said: "Say, you vants to keep out of de fight; go on!" and struck the man on the back with the flat of his sword.

The lieutenant said: "We must get to the rear." I told him that his brigade would strike one of our brigades (Gist's) that was coming to fill that gap and that a shower of bullets was going to rake this part of the field directly.

Just then the South Carolina brigade came up and commenced firing, and the minnie balls were whistling by us. I told the lieutenant that we had better lie down in a gulley that was close by. This we did, all piling in together, with a stream of minnie balls passing just over our backs.

The lieutenant said to me: "Now I see where you were mighty right; we couldn't get off this field without getting hit."

I was hoping that the Carolina brigade would drive the Ohio brigade back.

■ At approximately 2 p.m. on July 22, Gen. McPherson and a lone signal officer blundered into a line of skirmishers of Cleburne's division while riding through a wooded gap between Dodge's XVI Corps and Blair's XVII Corps. Ordered to halt, he answered by wheeling his horse around and began to gallop off. Shots rang out and McPherson fell, a bullet hitting him in the back. According to evidence gathered during and after the war by Lt. Col. William E. Strong, XVII Corps inspector-general, the fatal bullet was fired by a corporal in the 5th Confederate Regiment.

■ Private George J. Reynolds, Company D, 15th Iowa, was the last man to see Gen. McPherson alive. According to Lt. Col. William E. Strong, who had spoken with McPherson only minutes before he was shot, Reynolds himself "had received a severe wound in the left arm, a musket ball shattering the bone at the elbow. In going to the rear to find the field hospital, he came across Gen. McPherson, lying on the ground mortally wounded. He raised the dying general's head, placing it upon a blanket, tried to give him a drink of water from his canteen, and asked him if he had any message to communicate. But the general could make no reply and died soon after." Reynolds later received the XVII Corps gold "Medal of Honor."

A large number of wounded men were coming back, some of whom got into the ditch. "How is the fight going?" asked the lieutenant.

"They are cutting our boys to pieces," answered a wounded man.

Then there was a great "rebel yell." My captor jumped up, saying: "Your boys are driving our men back. We must get out of this, or I will be a prisoner."

"If that happens, I will treat you well," said I.

I had strong hopes that our men would come up. However, I could not detain the lieutenant any longer, and a lull coming in the shooting, we were marched off to the rear and turned over to the provost guards. Here we found a good many other Confederate prisoners who had been captured during the day.

My regiment continued on in the fight and acted well their part, but did not lose heavily as they did two days before at Peachtree Creek. Maj. Gen. W.H.T. Walker commanding our division was killed leading the South Carolina brigade. It was in the woods not far from where McPherson lost his life. I think he was killed by the brigade that had captured me.

The fight continued for some time after I was put under the provost guard. There was an enterprising sutler dispensing lemonade, beer, ice cream and other luxuries. This seemed strange to me. I was forcibly reminded of the difference in the resources of our government and the United States. We were glad to get a sufficiency of cornbread, fat meat, sorghum and rye coffee.

The next day I found that Gen. Hood had failed to dislodge Sherman from the Georgia Railroad and that he had only two lines of railroad leading into Atlanta; viz, the railroad to Macon, and that to West Point.

The fine army of Gen. Joe Johnston was thus decimated in five days without any beneficial results. The next day the prisoners captured in this battle — about 600 — were marched to Marietta under the guard of the 6th Missouri Regiment, who treated us quite cleverly. We remained in Marietta one night. The ladies there were very kind. I wrote a letter to my mother, which never reached her, telling of my capture. I suppose the lady I gave it to could not get it through the lines.

The next day we were carried to Chattanooga in box cars. The officers were put in the old jail on Market Street, which had been taken for a military prison. Here was every specimen of disgraceful humanity; a mob of reprobates, deserters, murderers, bounty jumpers and all the other offscourings of the world were huddled together until there was hardly standing room.

A good-looking, well dressed young fellow who said he was a professional bounty jumper scraped up an acquaintance with me. I did not repel his familiarity and kindness for right then I felt the need of a friend. He said he had plenty of money, the proceeds of bounties duly received and "jumped," and insisted on buying from the jail sutler anything I wished to eat. He said: "I am here under charges and am to be court-martialed."

I thanked him for his kindness, and said: "Aren't you afraid you will be shot for your meanness?"

"No," said he, "I will get out and jump another bounty or go in as a substitute and desert. I'm out for all the skads in sight; ain't a-going to fight. *Think your side is right, anyhow!*"

The next day we reached Nashville and were marched out to the penitentiary, which was also used as a military prison. Among the officers of our party was a young lieutenant from South Carolina who had been very argumentative with the guard all along the route. They discussed the constitutional right of secession and he was vehement in the defense of his state's action, which at that particular place and time, I considered inappropriate.

Penned up as we were in a box car, I was obliged to hear it. I had thought that argument was exhausted when we appealed to arms three years before. The little lieutenant seemed to have come from the "fire-eating" class; he impressed me as one who had an undue rice-eating mentality, and needed a cornbread diet. However, when the great doors of the penitentiary opened to receive us, he said: "Boys, I don't know but that South Carolina *was* a little hasty!"

'Hazardous but necessary maneuver'

Brig. Gen. John Wallace Fuller
4th Division, XVI Corps

On the morning of July 22 it was discovered that the enemy had fallen back from the line he had occupied, and the skirmish line in our front was advanced nearly half a mile. Everything seemed unusually quiet, and the new position of the enemy appeared to offer an opportunity to considerably advance our lines. Gen. Dodge came up early in the day and informed me that our corps would take position on the left of the XVII, and as soon as that corps had established its new line we would form on its left. In the meantime my command would retain its present position.

At about 12 midday Lieut. Laird reported with the 14th Ohio Battery. I directed him to park his guns on a little elevation not far from our headquarter tents. He asked if there "would be time to unhitch and water his horses in the brook nearby."

"Oh, yes," was the reply. "We may stay here half the afternoon."

Dinner was announced and Gen. Dodge sat down with us. While we were eating, skirmishing was heard in an easterly direction, almost opposite to that of Atlanta. We dropped knives and forks to listen. The noise grew louder and Gen. Dodge remarked, "There must be some rebel cavalry raiding in our rear," and then said, "You had better post one of your regiments so as to cover our trains."

Capt. Weber of my staff rode into the woods for a regiment, and Gen. Dodge, mounting his horse, rode over to the 2nd Division which had halted nearby. As the firing rapidly increased, almost directly after Gen. Dodge left us another staff officer was sent to order out all the regiments on the double-quick, and to say that I would show them where to form when they arrived.

Riding immediately a few rods to the east, I crossed a little rivulet and was soon on quite high ground. It was an open field from whence could be seen the 2nd Division forming line, facing to the east. As the field seemed such a commanding position, I at once decided to form a line on its westerly side, especially since it was substantially a prolongation of the line of the 2nd Division.

[The field] was nearly square, though rather longer from east to west than from north to south. There was not a tree or shrub, not even a stump, in the field to obscure the view or to afford any shelter. Its westerly side was flanked by the little stream I had just crossed, the banks of which were fringed with bushes not much higher than a man's head. The rivulet, after washing the westerly edge of the field, made a sharp bend to the east, following a deep ravine which skirts the field on the north. On the west and south sides stood the forest. To the south we knew the forest was held by Giles Smith's division of the XVII Corps, half a mile away. But what was there to the east?

As the regiments came out of the woods the line was formed near, and

■ Brig. Gen. John W. Fuller, a native of Harston, Cambridgeshire, England, commanded a brigade and after July 17, the 4th Division of the XVI Corps. On July 22 the four regiments of his 1st Brigade, which he personally handled at a critical moment in the battle of Atlanta, repulsed the Confederates attacking in their front and suffered 364 casualties in the process — half the losses sustained by the brigade during the entire campaign. "More than one-fourth of those who stood in the line of some of our regiments at noon were not present when the sun went down," Fuller wrote. "Many a grave was shutting from sight forever those who had stood manfully in the ranks for years." From February 1862 to April 1864, Fuller commanded the Ohio Brigade, consisting of the 27th, 39th, 43rd and 63rd regiments. In early October 1862, the brigade distinguished itself defending Battery Robinette at Corinth, Miss.

■ Private Bernard McLaughlin, Company G, 39th Ohio, was mortally wounded on July 22 in the battle of Atlanta and died later the same day in a field hospital. In this photograph, taken in Cincinnati during his veteran furlough, McLaughlin wears a government-issue blouse or sack coat and holds the regulation hat of stiff, black felt. These hats usually were worn devoid of decoration in the western armies.

parallel to, the little rivulet on the western edge of the field — near enough the crest to overlook the field and yet have the men partially covered. Kneeling, they would be fully hidden. The 39th Ohio came first, and at the northeast corner formed the left of our line. The 27th Ohio arrived next and was formed on the right of the 39th. The 64th Illinois was formed on the opposite side of the rivulet, slightly in rear, but substantially a continuation of the line to the right. This regiment stretched to the edge of the forest. The 18th Missouri was in reserve behind the 39th Ohio.

Capt. Pollack of my staff rode over to order the 14th Ohio Battery to get ready for action just where they stood; but we could see Laird putting his guns in battery before Pollack reached him. Just behind the battery was posted the 81st Ohio.

We were now in position, with our backs toward Atlanta, facing to the east. As the situation was commanding and the outlook fine, let me note it for just a moment. To our left stretched the 2nd Division of our corps, which could be seen in its entirety. Between their right and us was our battery, not far off, but separated from us by the ravine. As our ground was higher we could see every man and every horse. If we faced about and looked to our rear, we could see the large trains of the Army of the Tennessee pulling out at a trot to the northwest to escape the stray bullets which passed over our heads; while still further off, perhaps a mile away, we could see "Bald Hill," the right of Leggett's division, and to the right of that the XV Corps — all, of course, with their backs toward us, for they were facing Atlanta.

We could not look long, for the skirmishers sent forward to cover our front were coming rapidly back upon us. Orders were now given to keep down until the enemy's line of battle should be near us, and at the signal to rise, fire a volley and charge.

Soon the enemy appeared, and before he was in good musket range our battery opened fire. This seemed a surprise, for he halted and then retired into the woods to reform his line. Very soon, however, he marched out from the forest and moved in good order toward us.

He had come not more than a quarter of the way across the field when the 81st Ohio, across the ravine to our left and in plain sight, charged against a rebel regiment which was threatening our battery. The cheer of this regiment and its gallant charge was so contagious that the men of the 39th Ohio rose to their feet, fired a volley and went for the Johnnies on the double-quick. The 27th, next on the right, seeing the 39th charging the enemy, arose also and joined in the race. It was too soon; our boys had too far to run and the rebels were still so near the woods they could quickly reach shelter. The 39th, however, was in time to capture the colonel, adjutant, a captain and all who did not run of the 66th Georgia, a regiment in Walker's division.

But that part of the rebel line which was not struck by the two Ohio regiments continued marching toward the west, and the extraordinary spectacle presented itself of our men rushing across the field in one direction, while the rebels on their right were marching steadily the opposite way. It is true the enemy kept pretty close to the line of woods to the south, but as they approached the western side they began to widen out into the field.

Directly, the 64th Illinois, partly hidden by a piece of fence and by the bushes which lined the rivulet, opened fire at close range. This regiment was armed with the Henry repeating rifle and could fire 15 volleys without stopping to reload. They demoralized the rebel line in short order so that it began to waver and break.

Just then a fine-looking officer brought another regiment out of the woods. He rode forward, hat in hand, to rally his men; but by this time Col. Sheldon had moved up the 18th Missouri so as to get a flank fire on the rebels, and this proved more than they could stand. The officer who was so conspicuous was immediately shot down, and the whole mass swayed back into the forest. As the last of them were retiring, voices were heard shouting, "Bring off the general!" Some prisoners told us that "the general" was Gen. Walker, the commander of their division.

This combat, though brief, was very sharp. Col. Sheldon, whose regiment buried the rebel dead the next day, told me he found 13 dead rebels in one fence corner.

But the charge of the two Ohio regiments had taken them some distance away from the others, and I went over to see how things looked, intending to order them back. I had scarcely reached them when we saw some rebel regiments formed in column coming out of the woods at the south side of the field. If they pushed on they would come between us and our other regiments. If they deployed to fire they would take us in flank and enfilade our line while we were not in shape to reply.

There was not a moment to lose. We had to change front to the rear on our left; *i.e.,* face about and swing around to the north side of the field. The movement was double-quick for the 27th, for it formed the outside of the wheel and was also nearest the enemy. A heavy fire opened as soon as the movement began, and the men of the 27th, with their backs to the enemy, seemed to think that there was some mistake. They kept stopping and turning about to fire. This broke their formation and they were coming around in a mass.

I had been colonel of that regiment and knew the men would try to do anything called for if they understood what was wanted. I hurried across to meet them at the point where they should halt and face about. There was no time to explain anything for the rebels were coming on in fine style, not more than a hundred yards away. Grasping the colors, I ran a few paces toward the enemy, then turning around stuck the flag staff in the ground, and with my sword showed where to re-form the line.

With a great shout the men came forward and instantly formed. Bayonets were brought down for a charge. Col. Churchill shouted "Forward!" McDowell gave the same command to the 39th, which had faced about and was ready, and away they went for the Johnnies.

As the two regiments rushed on, their line was as fine as if on parade. Instantly the enemy came to a right-about and ran back for the woods. Seeing the enemy would not stand, our line was halted and the men brought up their muskets and sent a volley into the retreating column. They were so close that the effect seemed terrible, and when the rebels had disappeared in the forest the southeast corner of that field was well carpeted with butternut.

While the combats just described were raging, Gen. McPherson sat watching us from high ground in our rear, and when the enemy had been driven the second time from the field he [reportedly] expressed his satisfaction at the result and said, "Well, the XVI Corps is all right; now I'll ride over and see how Giles Smith is getting on."

Putting spurs to his horse he galloped past our right flank, entering the woods by the new road where our men had bivouacked, and over which they marched hardly an hour before. None of us then knew that the enemy had passed our flank, for the dense foliage had hidden everything from view. But almost as soon as McPherson passed out of sight he rode into the rebel line of skirmishers. He was ordered to halt, but lifting his

■ Maj. Gen. William H.T. Walker was killed on July 22 while leading an assault of his division of Hardee's corps in the battle of Atlanta. A native Georgian and Mexican War veteran, Walker had ridden to Hood's headquarters the night before his death. Hood later recalled: "With characteristic frankness ... he wished me to know, before he entered into battle, that he was with me in heart and purpose, and intended to abide by me through all emergencies."

■ At a crucial point in the fighting along the XVI Corps' front on July 22, Confederate troops of Gen. W.H.T. Walker's division began to envelop the right flank of a brigade in Fuller's division. After ordering two of his regiments to change front to meet the threat, Fuller grabbed the national colors of the 27th Ohio, planted the flag less than 100 yards from the oncoming Confederates, above, and rallied his men by waving his sword. Volleys from the brigade's other two regiments, the 64th Illinois (armed with Henry rifles) and the 18th Missouri, helped to break up the attack. Fuller credited fire from the 18th Missouri for the fatal wounding of Walker.

hat to salute his enemies, he reined his horse to the right and endeavored to escape. A volley was fired. One bullet struck him in the back and passed through very near his heart.

A few minutes after McPherson passed us the rebels returned to the edge of the forest, and from the south side of our field opened a heavy fire on us. Capt. Robinson was sent across the ravine in our rear to the 14th Ohio Battery, which by our change of front was now directly behind us, with directions to throw shells over our heads into the edge of the woods. About the same time Col. Morrill was ordered to move the 64th Illinois to the right (now west) until he reached the new road, then to march into the woods a few rods, and thence move upon the flank of the enemy who was making it so hot for us.

Lieut. Laird soon began to drop shells beautifully into the edge of the forest, but Morrill struck a regiment of Cleburne's division almost as soon as he began to move into the woods on the new road. The repeating rifles of Morrill's men again blazed away so rapidly that the rebel regiment was very soon routed. They captured 40 of Cleburne's men and a stand of colors, and sent the prisoners and colors to the rear under guard. They did more, for this advance drove back the rebels who had possession of McPherson's body, and cleared the way for recovering all that was left of our loved commander.

When the 40 prisoners captured by the 64th Illinois were searched, in the knapsack of one was found McPherson's field glass. Another had his gauntlets. But the most important thing found was a note written by Sherman to McPherson only that morning, explaining what he intended to do.

That note could have been seen by nobody but the soldier who took it from McPherson's pocket, and even he could scarcely have read it. I was glad to give assurance of this to my commander when sending the note to him that evening.

But Cleburne's men were not to be driven far by a single regiment, and back they came very soon with reinforcements. They concentrated a heavy fire on the 64th until seven officers and 79 men had fallen. The colonel of the 64th had been severely wounded and sent to the rear. There was no officer who could make up for the loss of Morrill, and when attacked by these fresh troops the regiment was driven out of the woods pell mell, and did not stop until it reached a clump of pines a quarter of a mile to the rear.

From this time on the rebels frequently returned to the south edge of our field where they made a slight breastwork of rails, from behind which they did some wicked firing. Our boys, lying flat as they could, would rise enough to respond, and our battery dropped shells over our heads among the Johnnies so effectively that they never came far into our field, and before night retired from our front.

Toward night we also withdrew from the field. It was fresh and verdant and beautiful under the noonday sun. The storm of battle had swept over it, and evening found only desolation and ruin. Every third man of the 27th Ohio who stood in the ranks at noon, and every fourth man of the 39th Ohio, was now either killed or wounded. A wide strip of rebel dead bordered the side near the forest. Opposite, numerous patches of blue showed where our boys had fallen.

Some incidents of the battle may, perhaps, be of interest. Soon after the second charge described, and while the firing was heavy, Col. Churchill of the 27th Ohio was wounded. He came backward from the line with coat and vest unbuttoned, and, in a sad voice, said to me, "I am sorry to retire, General, but I am wounded."

"Where is your wound, Colonel?" I asked.

He replied in one word: "Abdomen."

We had often discussed the subject of wounds, and it was understood that a wound in the abdomen was generally fatal. As he passed back into the ravine I thought a good soldier and a fast friend was gone. I went forward to see that the major (Lynch) was in command, and I found him, though slightly wounded, so full of pluck and alive in his duty that I took heart again.

Five minutes later, back from the ravine came Churchill. His face, which had been so sad, was now lit up by a smile of at least 500 candlepower. "It was a flank shot," he said. "The bullet only scraped out a little flesh and did not enter my bread basket. So I am going back to command my regiment."

He was back none too soon, for Lynch got a second and frightful wound, and was carried off the field.

Quite late in the afternoon Col. Phillips of Gen. Dodge's staff came over and said the general wanted us to fall back and form on the right of the 2nd Division. This division, on our left when the battle opened, was, after our change of front, directly in our rear now on a line parallel and 300 yards behind us. We had a good many wounded who had not been removed, and who, together with our dead, might fall into the hands of the enemy if we should then retire. So I asked permission to stay where we were until we could get them off. Permission was given. But I soon learned of McPherson's death. I was also told that Gen. Giles Smith had been driven from his entrenched line and some of his regiments had been

■ Col. Mendal Churchill commanded the 27th Ohio in the battle of Atlanta, which he called "the hardest fought battle of the campaign." On the afternoon of July 22, Churchill was wounded when a bullet passed through his clothing and cut the skin. "The wound became quite painful," he wrote. "A metal button had turned the ball sideways and no doubt by that my life was saved. I became very sick and faint, but being refreshed by a drink of water I soon returned to the regiment. Just at this time, Gen. Fuller took the flag of the 27th Ohio, carried it to the front and led the last charge which drove the enemy to final defeat."

■ Lt. Col. Henry T. McDowell, shown here as a captain, commanded the 39th Ohio in the battle of Atlanta. Late in the afternoon of July 22 he assumed command of the 1st Brigade, 4th Division, XVI Corps, after its commander, Col. John Morrill, fell severely wounded. During the campaign the 39th Ohio lost 24 enlisted men killed, eight officers and 158 enlisted men wounded, and two enlisted men missing.

captured.

These statements impressed me; for though we had beaten all the Johnnies who had tried to get a footing in our field, these stories seemed to indicate disaster. If Giles Smith, whom we supposed was fighting on the other side of the woods half a mile away was gone, then we formed an outpost and were in a dangerous place.

We hastened to remove the wounded, and then deploying one regiment as skirmishers to hold the field if they could, we made preparations to withdraw. All retired in line to the position assigned to us. Our skirmishers left on the field were not attacked. After dark there was a tacit truce between the skirmishers of both armies. The rebels removed most of their dead, and ours were brought back and buried in long trenches near some clumps of pine.

One incident of the afternoon led me to watch with special interest the work of those detailed to bury the dead.

When running over from the left of the line to reach the place where the 27th Ohio would come when changing front — the most critical time of the battle — I saw, rushing back from the ranks of the 27th, a soldier whom I thought "demoralized." He was making for the ravine on the north side (rear) of the field. I was hastening to the right and our paths crossed as we came together. I had shouted to him once or twice, "Go back, sir, go back to your regiment!" but, as he paid no attention I struck at him with the flat of my sword.

We were both running fast and I hit harder than I intended. He spun around and faced me with an astonished look, when I recognized a trusted soldier. In an instant he tore open his coat and showed me a bloody wound in his breast. Neither of us spoke, but his face said as plainly as if he had uttered the words, "You see, you were mistaken. I am no coward."

I suppose my face must have answered back some profound apology, for his countenance lighted up with a kind, beaming smile, and then he dropped at my feet. I could not stop to see whether he had fainted, or whether he was dying. But when the dead were brought in that night I looked on with undefined and mournful interest.

One old soldier of the 39th Ohio had a lantern. Nobody knew where he found it, but I told him I wanted to see whom we had lost. Without telling him why, I asked him to show me those who belonged to the 27th Regiment. The lantern showed us the figures of one after another, until at last the face of a young man, wearing the very same smile he had given me that afternoon, lay before us. The old soldier with the lantern seemed to wonder why I wanted to assist in laying this man in his last resting place. I did not explain, but when we had carefully covered him up, merely said, "He was the corporal of my headquarter guard."

'One lived to tell the tale'

Private William E. Bevens
Company G
1st Arkansas Volunteer Infantry

On July 22 we marched 10 miles to the right of Atlanta. Hardee had attacked the enemy in the rear and there had been a terrible struggle which lasted for hours. Toward evening we heard the Yankee bands playing and the soldiers shooting and cheering and we knew they had won.

While Johnston was in command he had preserved his army, and inflicted upon the enemy a loss almost equal to our strength when we began the campaign. Our loss had been about 9,000, which had been filled by the return of the wounded and furloughed men, so that Gen. Hood received an army fully as strong as it was at Dalton. We were as ready to fight as ever, although certainly disappointed at the loss of Johnston. We felt that no other general could do what he had done.

Yet this great military genius was thrown out on the eve of his final and greatest assault upon Sherman, an assault which would have saved Atlanta to the Confederacy. Hood's and Davis' tactics prevailed after that, and the splendid, unconquered army was swept off the earth into the grave. Hood questioned the morale of his army, but as for that our poor little Company G went into line at Atlanta under Hood as true as it ever had under Johnston. We fought for the cause, not the general.

Jim Hensley, a boy who had been wounded severely at Ringgold, returned to the company on the day of the battle. His physician had not reported him fit for duty, but had given him merely a pass to his command. Hensley came to me, saying: "Here, my dear old friend, is a little silver watch I wish to give you, for I shall be killed today."

I told him he had not been reported for duty; that he was still far from well, and begged him not to go into battle, especially as he had a presentiment that he should be killed. He turned his soulful eyes upon me.

"Will, do you think I am afraid because I know I am going to be killed?" Putting his hand on his breast he continued, "I have no fear of death. I am a Christian, and I know I shall be safe in heaven."

With tears we parted. He joined his brave comrades — Jim Murphy, John Baird and George Thomas — on the left of Company G after the line was in motion. They were moving against strong entrenchments heavily defended by abatis. These four boys saw they could crawl under the abatis without being seen and get close to the breastworks. After they started the command was given to oblique to the left, but in the roar of the musketry the boys failed to hear it and went on alone.

There were about a hundred Yankees on the breastworks watching our line which was advancing upon their rear. The four boys crawled close in, prepared and opened up. At the first fire down came four Yankees. They were taken by surprise, not knowing there were any men at their front. The boys kept at their game until the Yankees ran. Then they went forward to take possession of the works. There they found themselves alone and 200 of the enemy entrenched behind a second line.

It was death anyway, so they ran forward firing on the troops with terrible accuracy. One man had a bead on Thomas when Murphy shot the fellow. One hinged for Murphy when Thomas bayoneted him. So they had it — hand to hand. Poor Hensley was killed, Murphy terribly wounded, Baird wounded, but Thomas would not surrender. He bayoneted them until they took his gun, then he kicked and bit until they finally killed him there. Four men had killed 25 Yankees, but only one of the four lived to tell the tale. To question the morale of such men is farcical.

The battle on our left raged all day and we were defeated. Our colonel lost his foot. One third of our regiment was gone. Great numbers were killed and wounded, but the troops were as loyal and fought as bravely as any army on earth. This was Hood's second defeat. In two battles he had lost 10,000 men — more than we had lost in the whole campaign, in 74 days' battles and skirmishes. It would not take long with such tactics to wipe out the rebel army.

■ Private William E. Bevens, Company G, 1st Arkansas, served with this regiment through the entire war, except for a short period in 1862 when he was recovering from a wound received at Shiloh. In 1864, according to Bevens, the commissioned officers of Company G carried and used captured Henry rifles in place of swords.

Fisticuffs at headquarters: When push came to shove

■ XVI Corps commander, Gen. Grenville Dodge, on horseback at center right, above, gestures to an officer during deployment of Brig. Gen. Thomas W. Sweeny's division in assisting a brigade of Fuller's division against attacking Confederates on July 22. By directing Sweeny's troops into battle himself, Dodge greatly incensed the one-armed Irishman, seen standing with a group of officers at left. Three days later, Sweeny accused the English-born Fuller of bolting in the course of the Confederate assault, whereupon Dodge replied that Fuller was not a coward. Sweeny lost his temper in the ensuing argument, accused Dodge of gross mismanagement and finally, called him a liar and a cowardly son of a bitch. With this, Dodge slapped Sweeny and the latter answered by swinging hard with his good arm, striking Dodge on the nose. Other officers who were present quickly separated the two generals while Sweeny, cursing, challenged Dodge to a duel. Fuller, who also was present, then jumped on Sweeny and began to choke him until astonished bystanders pulled everyone apart. Having exhausted all patience, Dodge placed Sweeny under arrest and the Irishman was led away, still cursing, to face a court-martial in Nashville. Though the charges against him eventually were dropped, Sweeny, pictured at right, never returned to his command. He was replaced on July 26 by Brig. Gen. John M. Corse.

'Hardee had struck us endways'

2nd Lieut. Richard Stanley Tuthill
Battery H
1st Michigan Light Artillery

July 22, 1864, dawned in calmness and beauty, presaging a perfect summer day. Our division (Leggett's) extended from north of "Leggett's" (or Bald) Hill, along a road, in earthworks from which we had driven the enemy on the 21st. Our battery had been removed from the hill some distance to the left; one section, under command of Lieut. William Justin, being almost at the extreme of our line, there being only one battery — F of the 2nd Regulars — beyond it.

During the forenoon I passed along our line to its extremity, and saw nothing of a "refused line" on our left. It was "in air." In the woods, quite a long distance to the rear of us, lay the XVI Corps — not in line of battle, but as if halting on the march. A long interval, three-fourths of a mile or more, separated our exposed left flank from the XVI (Dodge's) Corps. Our wagon, mess-chest, campfire, etc., were in the rear of the battery, perhaps 150 yards, at the base of the hill by a small stream of water. I had finished my noonday bean soup, hardtack and coffee, and as everything appeared quiet, I had opened my valise, gotten out my writing materials, and had started to write a letter, giving an account of events since crossing the Chattahoochee, and particularly of the battle of the previous day.

I had but fairly begun my letter when artillery firing was heard from the direction of the city. Dropping my pen and leaving my writing material lying on the open valise, I ran up to the guns to direct the firing of my section, expecting to be back in a few moments. We threw quite a number of shots into the city. Meanwhile, a desultory musketry firing, heard for some time far to our rear — which we supposed was due to Confederate cavalry attacking our wagon trains in the vicinity of Decatur, and which had occasioned us no uneasiness — grew more frequent and distinct. Soon were seen staff officers, evidently bearing important messages, who passed us hurriedly, moving in all directions.

The musketry firing in our rear had grown into a continuous volley and become startling by its nearness. About this time Gen. McPherson, accompanied by one member of his staff, Inspector-General William E. Strong, and one orderly, passing to our immediate rear and into the woods, came unexpectedly upon the enemy, and was instantly killed. McPherson's death was soon known to the army, but fortunately the announcement was accompanied by the information that the command had devolved upon Gen. Logan, who often had demonstrated his ability to handle large bodies of troops on the battlefield, so that nothing like a panic, or even alarm, ensued.

Hardee's corps of four divisions had gotten on our flank and in our rear, and was marching, as it confidently believed, to our certain destruction — and such it might have proved had it not been for the fortunate fact that Gen. Dodge, with two divisions of the XVI Corps, was concealed in the woods there, and, like an aroused and angry lion, sprang to meet the foe. A line of battle was instantly formed, and a desperate fight in the open field resulted. The further advance of the enemy on that part of the line was checked, and he was driven with great loss back into the woods.

Meanwhile, two other divisions of Hardee's corps were marching unobstructedly through the open space between us and the XVI Corps, striking us in the rear and enveloping our exposed left flank.

We turned our guns about and began firing in that direction. Great num-

■ Brig. Gen. Mortimer D. Leggett commanded the 3rd Division, XVII Corps, and suffered six wounds previous to May 1864. Morally strict and of Quaker background, he never smoked, drank liquor or used profane language. Drinking and card playing were always prohibited at his headquarters. His troops renamed Bald Hill, just east of Atlanta, "Leggett's Hill" after his division's fights there on July 21 and 22. This photograph was taken in his wartime home of Zanesville, Ohio.

■ 2nd Lieut. Richard S. Tuthill, Battery H, 1st Michigan Light Artillery. Tuthill's unit was known as "De Golyer's Black Horse Battery" because its original commander, Capt. Samuel De Golyer (who died in August 1863 of wounds received at Vicksburg), selected jet-black horses to pull the battery's 3-inch ordnance rifles. During the Atlanta campaign it was commanded by Capt. Marcus D. Elliott whose artillerists, according to Tuthill, "were nearly all young, some of them mere boys. But braver men or more daring riders never lashed horses on the dead run into the thickest of the fight, or unlimbered guns under a galling fire. In the Atlanta campaign this battery was always at the front, constantly engaged."

bers of our own men, driven from their positions on our left, advancing hurriedly, many of them panic-stricken, passed by us and among us, so that they seriously obstructed the men who were working on the guns.

Hardee had struck us "endways," and his men could be plainly seen occupying the works from which ours had just been driven. The battery of regulars, near the end of our line, had been captured; and Lieut. Justin of our battery had only been able to save his guns by the exercise of great coolness and quickness of movement. No sooner had the regulars been captured than we heard the booming of their guns, and saw their shot ploughing through our line in direct enfilade.

Someone may then have ordered a change of position. The truth is that there was no time to give orders, and I saw neither general nor staff officer there to give them. All I know is that we limbered up our guns and sullenly — for we were much inclined to stay where we were — moved back. Our boys loved their black steel guns, and could not endure the thought of losing one of them. The 3rd Ohio Battery, in our division, had 20-pounder Parrotts — too heavy for field service — and had to leave at least one of them behind, though it was afterward retaken. At least twice, as we were falling back a distance of not more than two or three hundred yards, we unlimbered our guns and fired at the enemy. Then the infantry would move away from us and we would limber up and fall back a little farther, to keep on a line with them.

Seeing then, for the first time since the fight began, our chief of artillery Capt. Williams, I rode to his side and said to him, "For God's sake, Captain, let us stop falling back and fight!" By that time we had reached a position about on a line drawn at right angles to the line occupied by us when the attack was first made, running toward the east from the top of Leggett's Hill. Capt. Williams replied to my remark, "All right! Stop where you are!" It was just the place to form a line of battle. Some general officer may have given an order to stop there. My own belief always has been that the boys did it of their own accord. They had been in so many fights that they did not need a general to tell them where and when to stop running and begin shooting.

In front of us lay an open field containing not more than 20 acres. Beyond this were woods. Pat Cleburne's Texans — whom Force's brigade had driven from this selfsame hillside the day before — desperate and mad, were to make an attempt to wipe out the disgrace of their former defeat. Their line well formed, they emerged from their concealment in the woods, and yelling as only the steer-drivers of Texas could yell, charged upon our division. On the top of the hill, in the apex of the angle of the line of works facing Atlanta and our new line, was a four-gun battery of 24-pounder howitzers, commanded by its boy captain, Cooper. This was Battery D of the 1st Illinois Artillery, better known as "McAllister's Battery." Our six guns were also near this point and distributed along the line for a short distance to the east of it. On came the Texans, but they were met by a continuous volley of musketry and shrapnel, shell and canister from our six rifled Rodmans and Cooper's howitzers. It seemed as if no man of all the host who were attacking us could escape alive; and yet, still yelling, they persisted in their desperate undertaking. Their line was reformed, and again and again they attempted the impossible — to drive the 3rd Division from the line it had decided to hold.

Many of the enemy reached our line; some got across it; many were bayoneted, many killed with clubbed muskets; hand-to-hand conflicts were frequent. But not one inch did the 3rd Division give way. The boys obeyed Logan's well-remembered command to them at Champion Hill — "Give them the cold steel! Give them hell!"

The smell of powder was everywhere. The smoke from the guns was so dense that though a July sun was shining, there was the appearance of a dense fog. Only as the breath of a passing breeze blew the smoke away could the movements of the enemy be discerned clearly; but his unearthly *yell* could be heard above the sound of muskets and cannon. The day being very warm, men and line officers were for the most part without other clothing than hats and shoes, woolen shirts and trousers. I had left my coat and all my traps, including my letters, at the spot where I had suspended my letter writing, and never again recovered them.

The attack made by Cheatham's corps from Atlanta was repulsed bloodily by Frank Blair's heroic men. But beyond the bushy ravine separating the XV Corps, where its line had been weakened by sending troops to strengthen our line fronting to the south, Cheatham had succeeded in breaking through, and was rushing in and forming in line of battle in the works from which our men had been driven. Someone asked that a part of our battery be at once sent to the ravine to shell this forming line. There was at that time comparative quiet in our immediate front, and my section of the battery hurried to the point indicated. The Confederates were there in plain sight. De Gress' battery of four 20-pounder Parrotts had been captured, all of its horses killed, and its guns turned upon us. Taking a position on the edge of the ravine, the boys of my section poured into the forming line of the enemy an enfilading fire of short-range canister — "canned hell-fire," as they used to call it — that no living thing could withstand.

It has been said that this work was done by the massed artillery back a mile or more from the line which had been taken. That artillery had no more to do with breaking the enemy's line than if it had been fired in an opposite direction. The massed artillery on the hill did not begin firing until the enemy had been driven back by the fire of our guns. Then it threw a great number of shells into the woods after the retreating foe — reminding one of the Irishman who, telling of his prowess and achievements in battle, said that he had cut off the legs of an enemy, and being asked why he did not cut off his head, replied, "Some spalpeen had done that before I got there."

Hardly had the enemy been driven from the works to the right of us, and a lull in the firing ensued, when from the open timber in front of the 12th Wisconsin, which regiment was supporting us at the ravine, was seen, riding a magnificent sorrel horse, a fine-appearing young man in the uniform of a Confederate captain of artillery. As I have said, our men were in their shirt-sleeves, and it was impossible, unless at very close quarters, to tell a "Yank" from a "Johnnie."

And so our captain of artillery rode his charger to within a few yards of our line. A thousand rifles, in the hands of men who could hit a squirrel's eye at twice the distance this enemy was from them, were pointed at his breast; a thousand fingers were touching their triggers — the slightest movement of one would have caused the instant death of the poor fellow. But no finger pressed upon the trigger, no shot was fired. It would have been too much like murder. He halted and called out, "What command is this?" Would he turn to escape and be riddled by bullets? It did not seem right that he should die there; he was so young, so brave and so manly-looking. Jumping upon the earthworks I called out to him, "For God's sake, ride over these works or in an instant you will be a dead man!"

At once the situation flashed upon him. He bowed and said, "All right, gentlemen! It's my mistake, I surrender."

He then rode over the works and gave himself up. He shook hands with several of us and presented me a small dagger with pearl and silver-mounted handle, and also with the spurs he wore. It seemed that after the breach in our line had been made, he had been directed to plant his battery at a

■ Lt. Col. Robert Newton Pearson commanded the 31st Illinois at the battle of Atlanta. Under the leadership of the 24-year-old Pennsylvanian, the 31st was rated the best-drilled regiment in the Army of the Tennessee — an accolade not lost on Gen. John A. Logan, who had recruited the unit and became its first colonel in September 1861. Many of the 31st's soldiers hailed from Logan's home county of Jackson in southern Illinois, an area nicknamed "Little Egypt" because large numbers of its residents originally came from slave-holding states and were staunch Democrats, supporting disunion. Pearson served in the regiment at Forts Henry and Donelson as a private, but by September 24, 1864, rose to the rank of colonel, and was commissioned brevet brigadier general in March 1865. He was the brother-in-law of 2nd Lieut. Richard S. Tuthill.

■ Brig. Gen. Manning F. Force commanded a brigade in the XVII Corps, and received a Medal of Honor for his conduct on July 22 during the battle of Atlanta. He also was severely wounded that day when a bullet smashed into his head, narrowly missing his brain but shattering his palate and leaving him temporarily unable to speak. Despite the wound's severity, he recovered sufficiently to rejoin his brigade in October, in time to lead it during the Savannah campaign. In this photograph, taken during the late spring of 1865, Force appears as a major general. On his hat is the XVII Corps badge — an arrow — which was adopted officially in March 1865.

At least 13 corps medals of honor were awarded in the XVII Corps for gallantry on July 22. 1st Lieut. Edmund E. Nutt [see account at right] received one for leading two charges on the Confederates, forcing them back each time. He then organized the defense of Bald Hill until relief finally arrived around midnight.

point near where he had ridden upon us, and supposing his friends were in possession of the entire line, had discovered his mistake too late to escape from capture.

'The sons of bitches are rifling our knapsacks, boys!'

1st Lieut. Edmund E. Nutt
Company A
20th Ohio Veteran Volunteer Infantry

The Battle of Atlanta, July 22nd, 1864, was a peculiar one. Sherman had been flanking Johnston and causing him to fall back mile by mile from Chattanooga to Atlanta. Now Hood had superceded Johnston, and for the first time the Johnnies had an opportunity to retaliate by the flanking process.

Sherman's army had crossed the Chattahoochee and formed a circular line east of Atlanta facing westward. The city was in sight, the XVII Corps on the left or south flank of the line, the 3rd Division completing the extension of the main line with the 20th Ohio on the extreme left, "in air." The 4th Division of the XVII Corps was about a quarter of a mile southwest of us in line, facing southwest. We were on the west side of heavy timber with cleared fields in front. We had driven the Johnnies by heavy skirmishing the morning of the 21st, halting about 10 a.m. when we began entrenchments with all the tools available, working by detail in the afternoon, all night and into the morning of the 22nd. In that 24 hours we had a line of works to be proud of with headlogs, traverses and all the latest improvements, and felt secure.

During the morning we discovered Johnnies passing southward about a mile in our front. They seemed to be on the run the short distance we could see them between patches of timber, and wondered where they were going. Some said to a picnic, some said they were evacuating Atlanta. As usual, many rumors were afloat.

It was a hot day. The men were playing cards and lounging in the shade, and the camp was quiet as the calm before a storm when "Whang!" went a musket shot, apparently about a quarter of a mile south and east to the left flank and rear. The sound was caught by hundreds of alert ears, and all sprang to their feet and faced in that direction. The shot was instantly followed by others and in less than a minute it was a rapid skirmish fire, and seeming to come nearer and nearer.

"Fall in! Fall in!" was the order. The men rushed to and fro, putting on accoutrements, grasping muskets and forming in the line of works with attention directed toward the advancing music, from whence were now coming the well known ping! whing! thud! from left and rear, striking our line on the end. The smoke and roar and roll of musketry proceeding from the plainly defined line of gray and butternut was preceded by our pickets and some of the 4th Division, which had been struck on the flank and run over. Those not killed or wounded were falling back, loading and firing in retreat. Their position between us and the advancing foe prevented us from firing until they arrived, so we were compelled to stand and wait the coming storm.

Some of our boys became panic-stricken and rushed to the rear and reported down the line that the command had all fallen back "cut to pieces" — the old straggler's story. But most "stood the storm." As the Johnnies came to the southeast broad side to our left flank extending to the rear, we climbed our works and faced the rear.

Their line struck the left of the 20th's works, and was received with shot, bayonet thrust, clubbed musket and crash, which for the moment checked that part of their line. Those out of bayonet reach passed on undisturbed, carelessly and impudently passing us by as though we were beneath their notice. As far as we could see through the woods they passed in review, while we poured into their flank a murderous volley. As they were passing we noticed shots coming from over their rear, and looking around we saw the line which was detached by the break our force had made swinging around. They were attempting to capture us from our proper front. We sprang over our works and gave them a volley, which laid many low and scattered the others to cover.

This done, we saw another line following the first, which received our full fire as it advanced. But on it came, closing gaps as they were made by our close-range fire. They, too, struck our line as the first did, and were received in like manner — both parts of the line, and so with a third line. Having use of both sides of our works for each line, we were back and forth six times, each time our numbers growing less and less.

When the third line had passed and the bulk of the rebel army had swept our rear and were heard roaring far down the lines to the north, we were in for it. There was no rear to go to; our supplies were in their hands and reinforcements could not reach us. Every big tree in sight had a Johnny who was loading and firing at us as rapidly as possible. Those we had cut off from their line remained apparently disorganized but full of fight each for himself. They occupied every available spot, were in our trenches and in about half of the works we had dug and made ready for our own use. They brought their flag down one trench within a few feet of our 20th Ohio banner. Crouched down to load, they would rise and fire in our faces, to receive in turn a bayonet or clubbed musket.

Soon there was complaint that our cartridges were scarce. Our ammunition was over in the woods where regimental headquarters were. The trees were sheltering rebs near them. But we must have the cartridges. Who will volunteer to go and get them? Many answered, *"I will!"* But two are enough, so Wilbur Blackburn of Company A and William Nutt of Company F go. Over the works they sprang and with a rapid run reached the boxes, shouldered them, and we watched with breathless anxiety their return with the supply of ammunition, which is now worth more than money to us.

The muskets became hot with rapid firing, but there were plenty lying around cooling with comrades who could use them no more. The tree protection gave the Johnnies the advantage of the trench side of our works, and we have to take the other side.

"The sons of bitches are rifling our knapsacks, boys! Let's jump over and go for them! Up and at 'em, boys!"

Over we went, jumping down on them and mingling with slash and clash. With yells we rushed along the line, taking them in and ordering them over on our side and to pass down the line; recapturing our own boys whom they were holding as prisoners, and thus passing through and among them, neither daring to fire as we were all mixed together. It was a question of audacity how far we could go and be obeyed. Several of these raids were made during the afternoon, and the intermediate time was occupied in crouching to load and reaching over to fire.

Many heroic acts were done by men whose bones are bleaching there. When Bob Elliott discovered his brother Matt lying on the works dead, he said, "Oh, they have killed my brother," and stood boldly up beside him loading and firing until he, too, was shot and soon lying by his side.

The rebs brought two pieces of artillery to the left of our line, but we picked off the gunners and kept them from firing until late in the afternoon,

■ Capt. James B. Walker, 20th Ohio, served on the staff of Gen. Manning Force during the campaign, and was wounded just moments before his commanding officer on July 22. An eyewitness, Private Christian Stucki of Company K, 16th Wisconsin, later recalled: "Capt. Walker, our brigade adjutant-general, was shot first. Gen. Force dismounted to give him assistance and received a bullet [near the] right eye, coming out behind the ear. Our lieutenant colonel ran to give them assistance when he was shot through the thigh. Our stretcher-bearers were ordered out to bring them in, which they did."

■ Col. Robert K. Scott commanded a brigade in Leggett's division, XVII Corps, on July 22. "At the very commencement of the action," Leggett wrote, "even before a shot had been fired upon my lines, Col. Scott was captured by the enemy while returning to his command from a detached regiment. A member of Scott's old regiment, the 68th Ohio, later recalled: "We all believed that he was either killed or captured, or he would have been with his comand. He was a splendid soldier and a bulldog of a fighter. His absence [that day] was a great loss ..." In the same fusillade that fatally wounded Gen. McPherson, Scott's horse was shot dead and he was taken prisoner by men of the 5th Confederate Regiment. After his capture, he was taken to Atlanta and then sent with other Federal officers to Griffin, Ga. Enroute, he leaped from the train at night, but was caught by hounds and brought to Macon. Within two months Scott was exchanged and returned to his command on September 28. In this photograph, taken at the end of the war, he wears a XVII Corps badge on his hat and mourning crepe for President Lincoln around his left arm.

probably 5 o'clock. When they began to enfilade our line with canister, a murderous fire which we could not resist or endure, Col. Wiles of the 78th Ohio, the regiment to our right, moved out to form an opposing line while we held their attention and checked the canister firing all we could.

When this new line was formed we divided into two squads and fell back by turns from one protecting point to another until we arrived in the fort on Leggett's Hill, about the length of two regiments to the right. The Johnnies followed us up closely and reduced our numbers by killed, wounded and prisoners so that not more than half of the squads arrived inside the fort. This was a rebel fort, and was charged and captured on the 21st by Gen. Force's 1st Brigade. As a rebel fort it faced east and south. Gen. Force's command completed the earthworks' circle to the west toward Atlanta, enclosing a large space in the form of a horseshoe with an opening to the north.

With the new line formed by the 78th Ohio and other regiments extending from the fort toward the east, the lines made a right angle. The fort — the point of the angle — was occupied on the inside by Yanks from many disorganized commands, and on the outside by the Johnnies on the southwest sides. They tried to crowd in through the embrasures, and would load behind the earth embankments and fire in at the embrasures — a deadly fire as the fort was full of men.

It was a necessity to stop this destructive work, so we stationed men to watch with loaded guns pointed and ready to pull trigger on the first appearance of an outside shooter, and others to load the guns and hand to them. This gave regular employment to many without the exposure of each moving up to discharge his gun. In this way the passageways in and to the embrasures were soon filled with the dead, and the outside shooting was suppressed. Men were stationed on the earthworks to reach over and fire and pass the guns back to be loaded.

The fort was held. Firing continued 'til after midnight. Men went to sleep loading guns or waiting for them to be loaded, and snoring was a soothing refrain to musketry. Daylight found all who remained, either killed or wounded. The hill could have been walked over on dead men, and piles of dead surrounded the fort, in some places five men deep.

Of this battle I have not told the hundredth part of what occurred in our view and vicinity. It was fought "all around the ring" by both armies, each man on the line had his individual experiences, and like the blind men who went to see the elephant, each touched a different part and received a different impression. Hood's army completely surprised Sherman's army — fought from flank and rear all at the same time, but was routed from the field with terrible slaughter.

'I don't care which side, but get into the works'

Private Myron B. Loop
Company I
68th Ohio Veteran Volunteer Infantry

On the morning of July 22, the 68th Ohio, 2nd Brigade, 3rd Division, XVII Corps, held an advanced position fronting Atlanta. Early we discovered that the enemy had withdrawn from our front, and while engaged in preparing our morning meal we were aroused by the shrill voice of Col. Welles shouting as only he could: "Fall in, men, fall in!"

That earnest voice roused us in an instant, and grabbing our war harness we were soon in rapid motion to the rear to repel, as we supposed, a

Saving the wagons

■ At 1 p.m. on July 22, as the battle of Atlanta raged several miles to the southwest, two divisions of Wheeler's cavalry attacked Decatur, where the Army of the Tennessee's supply wagons were guarded by a single brigade of the XVI Corps. For 90 minutes, Ohio, Wisconsin and New Jersey troops commanded by Col. John W. Sprague, above, desperately resisted the dismounted Confederates, falling back through Decatur's public square to a ridge north of town. The 35th New Jersey was so hard pressed that many of its companies broke down and fought by squads. And a battalion of the 25th Wisconsin became entangled in a swamp, losing its colonel who was wounded and captured. However, nearly all the wagons were extricated safely, including 400 guarded by the 43rd Ohio, which was enroute to Decatur from Roswell when the shooting started.

At left, two members of Company K, 43rd Ohio, who were present at Decatur. Sergeant James McLain, right, was promoted to second lieutenant only a month before the photograph was taken in June 1865. Shortly after the 43rd mustered out at Louisville, Ky., on July 13, McLain was accidentally shot and killed as he sat in camp writing a letter announcing his return home.

■ Twenty-nine years after the Confederate attack of July 22, mounds of earth were all that remained of the works of Leggett's division on Bald Hill. This photograph, looking south, was taken by Private David Auld, a drummer in Company B, 43rd Ohio. During the summer of 1864, the 20-year-old Auld and his brother Demas, 18, also a musician in Company B, served in the often dangerous capacity of stretcher bearers once the fighting began. While carrying a wounded man at Resaca, David was nearly shot in the hand when a bullet splintered his stretcher's handle. He revisited and photographed many of the Atlanta campaign battlefields in 1893.

threatened attack by rebel cavalry upon our corps hospital and XVII Corps headquarters. Upon reaching our position some distance out, imagine our surprise to find in our front, instead of cavalry, a long line of rebel infantry, while at the same time another line of rebel troops was forming across the road in our rear. Our regiment was thus sandwiched between two lines of the enemy who appeared to have been unaware of the position of that little Buckeye band.

From our position, being partly concealed in a dense copse, the commands of rebel officers could be distinctly heard, and prisoners were taken who unknowingly ran into our line. Still the enemy moved on. Something had to be done and done quickly in order to get out of a trap which was about to spring upon us. These were anxious moments, which to waste meant a visit to some Southern prison.

Col. Welles hastily surveyed the ground on our left, and a moment later whispered down the line: "Be cool, men, be cool. Forward by the left flank, march!"

We sprang to our feet and moved to the left on the double-quick, and dropping behind a rail fence which lay in our path poured a volley into the enemy, who were forming in line in an open field on our right. The alarm thus given by the muskets of the 68th was immediately responded to by a battery of artillery, and the battle of July 22 opened in earnest.

The 3rd Division (Leggett's) engaged the enemy so promptly that the 68th was enabled, by making a rapid move to the left and a wide detour of about three miles, to pass around the enemy's right and join our division on Leggett's Hill.

Col. R.K. Scott, commanding the 2nd Brigade, and Capt. A.C. Urquhart, picket officer on Scott's staff, accompanied the regiment in the early morning. But upon our return they took a nearer route than that followed by the regiment, where they encountered a body of the enemy and were taken prisoners.

Upon reaching our division we found our comrades heavily engaged with the enemy who were advancing in solid columns to storm Leggett's Hill. My pen utterly fails me in an attempt to describe in detail the events of that fearful struggle. Nearer and nearer came the line of rebel gray, indicating that they felt able to brush us away, but as they ran against the muskets of Leggett's division they were sent rolling back, suffering great loss.

The next attack came from the direction of Atlanta. We now hastily changed front, as the first attack had come from the east, and again repulsed the enemy in handsome style. The enemy fell back and reformed and returned to the attack, but were again repulsed.

During the afternoon the enemy advanced yet again upon us from the direction of Atlanta, at the same time furiously attacking our flank, using their artillery. If ever we were in a position to fight like demons, it was then.

"Get into the works!" shouted Col. Welles.

"Which side, Colonel?" was asked.

"I don't care which side," he yelled, "but get into the works."

Get in we did, but it was a puzzle to us to know which side would be the safest as the attack came from front and flank, which compelled us to fight first on one side of a barricade of rails and dirt, and then on the other. At one time a portion of our division was on one side firing in one direction, while a little farther along the line the rest of our division was on the opposite side.

The left of our division now swung back to the crest of another hill — the right still resting on the old works — where a few rails were hastily thrown together, and behind these we hugged the ground. Meantime, our muskets blazed defiance to the enemy. Still, on they came, rolling and surging against our lines in another wild and determined effort to take Leggett's Hill. But Leggett's men were just as determined that they should not have it.

We saw the enemy coming to take the hill with officers in front, lines well dressed and following each other in quick succession. Such a scene one does not often behold, even in the wild tumult of battle, for here it was the tidal wave of war beat with its wildest fury against us. Volley after volley of musketry accompanied by the bellowing of heavy guns seemed to have no more effect than so much chaff would have done in the ranks of those advancing hosts.

On came the enemy until they became engaged in a hand-to-hand struggle with the men of Leggett's division. Wild yells rent the air and bayonets clashed together. Men with uplifted blades sought each other's lives, but the swift, unerring ball reached them before the blows were delivered and they fell side by side. The crack of cannon and the roar of musketry were deafening, and the enemy, bent on success, was hurled back only to spring forward with greater fury in a vain effort.

As we glanced right or left we could see it was the same — a struggling mass of men now partly hidden by clouds of smoke, and then in open view. Thus the battle raged till night dropped her mantle over the scene. Little by little the enemy was driven back, and when the shadows of night began to deepen, they gave up the fight and quietly retired from the field.

Wearied with confusion and excitement, we threw ourselves down to

■ 1st Sergeant Webster Clay Shepard, Company H, 68th Ohio, was killed July 22 at nearly the same time as his cousin Benjamin Shepard, a private in the same company. According to another member of the 68th who found their bodies the next morning, "One, it seems, was killed while supporting the head of the other, who had just received a death wound, thus dying in each other's arms."

■ Capt. Paul Wittich, commander of Company E, 37th Ohio, was the only member of his company killed on July 22 during the battle of Atlanta. This regiment, also known as the 3rd German, was recruited from German neighborhoods and communities throughout Ohio, and carried on its rolls 22 officers and enlisted men with the last name of Schmidt.

rest but not to sleep. The voices of comrades calling, hurried here and there, now holding our canteens to the lips of a dying brother, now endeavoring to smooth the couch of a wounded comrade, and now hastily answering a pleading voice: "Oh, give me water!"

July 23 was a sad day for the regiments composing Leggett's division. There was no excitement to keep up our strength as with mute lips we gathered together those who had fallen on the previous day, and with many an aching heart wrapped them in blankets and laid them tenderly away.

'A very slim chance to escape'

Private John Henry Puck
Company G
37th Ohio Veteran Volunteer Infantry

July 3rd we were on the move again, for it was found that the rebels had abandoned their position on the mountain [Kennesaw] caused by our army coming on their flank. After one or two days of marching we came to the Chattahoochee River, which we crossed during a heavy rain and thunderstorm, going into camp late in the afternoon on what I should term the south shore of the Chattahoochee. From this place we marched still further to the left in the direction of Stone Mountain, and many of the boys thought that we were to make another assault on a mountain. But our fears were soon quieted, for instead of attacking rebel soldiers on Stone Mountain we were ordered to attack a rebel railroad known, I believe, as the Georgia Railroad. We diligently went to work to destroy the road, tearing up the track, building fires and heating the rails in the center and then twisting them into all kinds of shapes, in many cases twisting the rails around small saplings and leaving them in that position.

From this place we marched in the direction of Decatur, Ga., but soon swung around further to the left, leaving Decatur in our rear. We encountered the rebels in strong positions some three to four miles from Atlanta, but Gen. Sherman was at his old tricks again and pressed them upon their flanks, forcing them to retreat. On the morning of July 22nd it became known that the rebels in our front were gone and we were early on the move to follow them, but as we came to their abandoned line of works it became evident that our further advance would be disputed.

Our regiment's position was in the front of a 2½-story brick house that stood about 200 yards to the right of the Georgia Railroad, and from 12 to 15 feet back of the breastworks. It was said that some enthusiastic rebel was building this house when the war broke out, and that he said to his workmen that they would first go and whip the Yankees and then come back and finish the house (I will say here that the house was never finished). Gen. Morgan L. Smith, our division commander, had his headquarters at this house and much of the conversation between staff officers was overheard by us. Major Hipp, who was in command of the regiment at the time, made suggestions to Gen. Smith about barricading the railroad and burning a collection of houses and outbuildings that stood to the left oblique in our front. But Gen. Smith would have none of it, saying that the buildings would come in handy for hospital use, and to barricade the railroad would be labor lost, as he was confident that we would take dinner in Atlanta. But we were doomed to disappointment, for the dinner that Gen. Smith promised us that day was not realized until the 1st of September.

It must have been near 2 p.m. when we could see that the rebels were making active preparations for an attack. Major Hipp asked for volunteers to go into the brick house as sharpshooters. Some 12 or 15 of our boys responded, mostly from Companies C and G, I being among the number. Upon reaching the upper story of the house we immediately distributed ourselves in the different rooms and began to break holes through the walls to enable us to fire upon the rebels as they advanced. And none too soon, for we had hardly made our portholes of sufficient size to enable us to see and fire through when the rebels advanced in solid columns. But by the steady fire poured into them they were forced to retreat.

I have always been of the opinion that if Gen. Smith had heeded our major's suggestions, our division would have been spared the humiliation of being driven out of its works — something that had never happened to it before. It seems that the rebels only retreated far enough to come under shelter of the houses aforementioned, and from there marched onto the railroad track and a wagon road running parallel with it. There being a deep cut in both we could not see or hurt them, and I am confident that if a battery with proper support had been stationed at these roads the rebels never could have broken our line. But as there was neither a battery nor infantry there the rebels had an easy task of it. They marched forward at right shoulder arms and opened fire on our line at right angles with such telling effect that our line soon gave way and the rebels again occupied their works.

It was in this engagement that I had the most thrilling experience of any battle that I was ever engaged in during my whole service, for we in the house were in blissful ignorance of what was going on below. We had been ordered to keep a sharp lookout in our front, and the house not having any openings in the sides toward the railroad we could not see what was going on on our left. I presume those of the regiment below were too busy just then to pay any attention to us; in fact, they might not have known that we were in the house. But we were there, and as we thought we were doing our duty in watching our front we were ready to fire on the first rebel who would dare to show himself. Of course, we expected that if they would make another attack it would come from the same direction as the first one. But as 15 to 20 minutes went by and no rebels came into sight we supposed the fight was over. All at once we heard firing on our left but it lasted only a few minutes.

We paid very little attention to this noise, never dreaming that we were in danger or that our line could be broken. But after several minutes we became uneasy. We wanted to see what our boys below were doing, so one of the boys in the room I was in leaned out of the window in order to see the works below. To his horror he discovered that our boys were gone and the works full of rebels. Upon learning this fact we hurried downstairs as fast as we could, but upon reaching the second floor we found that rebel soldiers were already in the house and some of them had started to come upstairs.

Here was a dilemma; to stay in the house meant certain capture and perhaps many months in rebel prisons, and to jump from the second-story window there would be but a very slim chance of escaping, for we did not know if the rebels already were watching every window in the house. But there was no time to investigate. If we were going to try to escape we must act at once. So I, with perhaps a half dozen others, made a break from the window and jumped down. The house had five windows on the side we jumped out, and I chose the center window followed by two more boys of my company.

I should mention here that when we had gone to work in the morning to change front to the rebel works our regiment unslung knapsacks and piled them up in the rear of the house. As I jumped out of the window I came down upon this large pile of knapsacks, which, of course, broke my fall but sent

■ Maj. Gen. John Alexander Logan commanded the XV Corps during the campaign, though for five days following the death of Gen. McPherson on July 22 he was in command of the entire Army of the Tennessee. Nicknamed "Black Jack" on account of his dark eyes, black hair and mustache and swarthy complexion, the Illinois-born Logan was considered a first-rate combat leader by Sherman but, being a pre-war politician, he sometimes antagonized his commander. Logan was very popular with his troops, and to one of them he seemed "a human hurricane on horseback." Another soldier, Private Alvero Curtis of Company E, 81st Ohio, later wrote of Logan after McPherson was killed: "Just at that time it was pretty hot along the line. The rebels were making their desperate charge. They were repulsed and driven back into the woods. Just then I heard a shout: 'McPherson and revenge!' I looked around and saw Gen. Logan going down the line with his hat off. His horse was on a dead run, with two aides just behind him. In a few minutes I heard a voice saying: 'Sing out if they come again. Put the bayonet to them!' It was Gen. Logan, this time going to the right of the line."

■ Confederates of Gen. Arthur Manigault's brigade swarm over the 20-pound Parrott guns of Battery H, 1st Illinois Light Artillery, about 4 p.m. on July 22. The battery commander, Capt. Francis DeGress, later wrote: "The enemy ... was repulsed in my front, but broke through our center, and changing front charged my battery, which I was obliged to leave after spiking the guns, and after all my support had left me." DeGress' guns were retaken a short while later, unspiked and fired at the retreating Confederates, though one of them burst on the third round. The battery's losses on July 22 included 39 horses.

me sprawling on the ground. As I rose to my feet there were several rebels standing at the corner of the house to my right who commanded me to halt. But without taking a second thought I started on a dead run. Better time was never made than I made in that run of perhaps 400 to 500 yards!*

After running this distance I overtook a small squad of our boys and, no rebels being in sight, we started to where one of the boys said our regiment was. We had only gone about 100 yards when Gen. Logan came riding along, ordering us to stay where we were, and in less time than it takes me to tell it he had gathered together 1,200 to 1,500 men from at least a half dozen regiments. After Gen. Logan formed this mixed force into line and made a

* This was the Troup Hurt House, made famous in the mammoth cycloramic painting of the battle of Atlanta on display in that city. The Confederates who nearly captured Puck probably belonged to Company A, 10th South Carolina, which was commanded by Col. James F. Pressley. On July 21, according to Private S. Emanuel of Company A, "a brick house known as the Hurt house, some distance in advance of our line, was considered a good point from which to observe the enemy's movements. Company A was placed in its upper story. The enemy discovering it was occupied, opened fire upon it with artillery. They soon get the range, knocking down the chimneys, which carry in parts of the roof not yet tinned ... J.E. Holmes and others were there injured. That more were not hurt was considered miraculous. Company A was then ordered to rejoin the regiment." During the 10th South Carolina's charge on July 22, "the command pressed on, driving the enemy before it," wrote Emanuel. "By the irony of fate, it captured a number of prisoners from the basement of the house out of which Company A had been driven the day before by the Federal artillery."

short speech, we went forward again with a will, charging our lost position, coming out of the woods a little to the left of the brick house, and capturing a number of prisoners.

Our regiment was in this position until July 25th, when we started on the march again, this time going to the right wing of Sherman's army.

'The lives lost had all been for nothing'

Lt. Col. C. Irvine Walker
10th South Carolina Volunteer Infantry

On the morning of the 22nd of July 1864, news came along the line that Hardee's Corps was off on a secret expedition. How quickly these items of army news spread from regiment to regiment down a long line. The private soldier was always thoroughly posted, and often knew of proposed movements hours before the official orders came.

About dinner time, the arrival of reserves in our rear showed that Hood intended giving us a place in the picture, and the activity of the enemy's pickets proved that they were awake, and expecting some movement. The Yankees run out on their picket line a section of artillery in our front, and gave us a lively shelling. The right of our regiment rested on the Georgia Railroad, we being on the right of our [Manigault's] Brigade. Deas' Brigade, of our Division, was on our right.

We had hardly well finished our dinners when the orders came to advance. The Brigade was soon over the breastworks and formed on the outside. Steadily the line moves forward, supported by Sharp's Brigade, and with Deas' on the right. The enemy's artillery keep up a brisk fire, to which our's replies, firing over the heads of the advancing line. The Yankee picket line is reached, driven in, the 10th Regiment captures the picket reserve, and the section of artillery barely escapes, galloping off ahead of us, and we following close behind, up to within 50 yards of the Federal breastworks. Deas has not been so successful, and our right is exposed to a heavy flanking fire. Sixteen pieces of artillery are belching fire and death into our Brigade. Not quite strong enough to carry the works, we halt and pour in a deadly fire.

A two-story house is just outside of the enemy's line, and covers the left of the 10th and right of the 19th S.C. Regiments. Colonel [James F.] Pressley sends men of both regiments into the upper piazza, where they shoot right down into the enemy's ranks. General Sharp offers to send Colonel Pressley assistance, which is declined. We gather up our ranks, make a desperate charge, mount the Federal breastworks and drive away the enemy. Among the many who fall in the struggle is the gallant Pressley, who is borne from the top of the enemy's fortifications severely wounded in the shoulder.

The Battery captured by the 10th Regiment is at once wheeled around to our side of the lines, and a detail made to man it, if necessary. But limbers being captured, and artillerists sent out from our main line, the guns are safely carried in.

The other pieces captured by the Brigade were so situated that it was impossible to secure them.*

■ 1st Lieut. George W. Eichelbarger commanded Company B, 55th Illinois, at the battle of Atlanta. On July 22, the company was on the extreme left of the regiment near the Georgia Railroad cut. Capt. Henry S. Nourse, commanding Company H, later wrote: "From that position the Confederate column sweeping unopposed up towards our rear from the railway could not be seen. The lieutenant, a fine officer and recklessly brave, hearing no order and seeing no adequate reason for the abandonment of the works, seems to have been stung almost to madness by what he supposed a disgraceful rout, and with tears streaming down his cheeks begged his men to stand firm. When finally forced to retreat, as soon as he could (he gathered) a squad about him (and) insisted upon returning. Lieutenant Eichelbarger was found after the battle, near this spot, shot through the head."

* Of the eight captured Federal artillery pieces, four belonged to Battery H, 1st Illinois Light Artillery, commanded by Capt. Francis DeGress. These 20-pound

■ Major Thomas T. Taylor, 47th Ohio, assumed command of the regiment on July 22 after its commander, Lt. Col. John Wallace, was captured. According to Corporal Joseph Saunier of Company F, which Taylor formerly commanded, the major ran through a strip of woods in order to establish alignment for a new line against the Confederate onslaught near the Georgia Railroad cut. Suddenly, "he came squarely against a column on a narrow road, led by a Confederate mounted on a 'flea specked' gray horse, carrying a flag in one hand and a revolver in the other, who commanded him to 'Halt! Halt!' to which he replied, 'Stranger, this is no place for me to halt.' And as he dodged into the bushes, the officer shot at him without effect."

Having gained a footing on the works, we push to our left, and Sharpe comes up and pushes to the right; together we clear the fortifications for more than half a mile. This attack was on the extreme right, and we were to cooperate with Hardee, who was expected to turn Sherman's left flank. We waited in vain for the sounds of his guns. The Yankees finding no more movement on our part, re-occupied their works on a hill about a quarter or half a mile to our left, brought up a battery which shelled us very heavily, enfilading our line. When it was known that Hardee had not succeeded, Hood withdrew us to the main line of works.

It did seem hard; we had built these breastworks, given them up to the enemy [on the 21st], retaken them at a very heavy sacrifice, and now we had to give them up again. The whole struggle of the afternoon, the lives lost, the suffering inflicted, had all been for nothing. And this was but an example of what happened to us of the Western Army very often; marches, skirmishes, battles, all seemingly with no good result.

'We were in a fearful dilemma'

Private William Bakhaus
Company C
47th Ohio Veteran Volunteer Infantry

Daybreak had just dawned on July 22nd when, from my position on the skirmish line on the Decatur [Georgia] railroad, I heard a clatter of hoofs in my rear, and I at once recognized Gen. Logan and staff approaching me at a gallop. Logan, I noticed, was dressed in his best, as if for a parade.

Upon reaching me, Logan, who was in advance of the party, said to me in his usual plain English, "What in hell are you doing here? Don't you know the town is evacuated?" Not having read the morning papers yet I could not readily reply to his interrogatory. I had been in my position the whole night previous and could not discover any unusual noises in my front, and I thought at the time the question was put to me that the old man was off his base.

Logan and his staff in the meantime had passed on, we skirmishers at his heels. When we arrived at the rebel entrenchments, that the day before were swarming with Johnnies, we found them deserted and Atlanta was in full view. We hastily pressed on, Logan and staff still in the lead, when suddenly there came a rattle of musketry from our front that gave us a firm but polite invitation to halt right there, and we did. Logan and his escort wheeled "about face" in "one time and one motion" and made for the rear. This is the only time I ever saw Gen. Logan show his coattail buttons to the enemy, and under the peculiar circumstances I think he done right. I should have done the same, but I had no horse and had to stay and cover the retreat. My only regret is that I did not stop him long enough to ask him the same question that he put to me a few minutes before. How he and his staff

Parrotts were retaken by the Federals later in the day. The other four guns, 12-pound brass Napoleons, belonged to Battery A, 1st Illinois Light Artillery, commanded by 1st. Lieut. George Echte. He later wrote: "Battery A lost heavy in men and horses. The casualties of the company were 32 men killed, wounded and missing; 55 horses were killed and captured, mostly killed. Shortly afterward our line advanced and drove the enemy from the works they had taken, and recaptured two of the six guns of the battery. The enemy succeeded in drawing away four of them." According to Confederate sources, the four 12-pounders were turned over to Capt. James P. Douglas' Texas Battery of Hindman's division, and used by this battery until recaptured during Hood's retreat from Tennessee in December 1864 after the battle of Nashville.

escaped the shower of balls has always been a mystery to me. As it was he had a very narrow escape and came very near meeting the same fate that McPherson did a few hours later.

Hood had prepared a nice little trap for us and foxy Sherman walked into it, but he won't acknowledge it. But he had his hair pretty well singed that day and made his movements afterward with more caution, for Hood and his cowboy style of fighting were not to be sneezed at.

Our division had advanced in the meantime and occupied the deserted trenches, turning them inside out so they could be adapted for their own use. But we poor skirmishers were between two fires and had to hug the ground very close. I made myself comfortable near a little stone culvert that ran beneath the railroad, from where I could see what was going on in my front and be under cover at the same time. While lying here we received a complimentary shot from one of our own batteries which killed two and wounded six men of our squad, which made us naturally nervous the balance of the day as we were not looking for shots from our rear. The gunner claimed that he thought we were rebels, so he gave us a dose of shrapnel.

While there had been some heavy fighting going on all around us, it was comparatively quiet in our front. But it was only "the calm that precedes the storm," for at about 4 p.m. the familiar rebel yell rang through the woods and down the hill they came in three lines deep. Our major ordered us to "git," and such "gitting" you never saw before, unless you were at Bull Run. Unfortunately, I was strapped to a confounded knapsack. It only contained two gum blankets and some writing materials, but it was all-fired heavy that day and my progress in getting away was not as good as I wished.

Our line that day was very weakly defended by a small brigade. Our left rested on a deep cut in the railroad with no other troops on that flank. The rebels charged "right oblique" and came pouring over the works on our left, and also through the cut, sweeping everything before them and nearly shutting off our retreat. We were in a fearful dilemma. Lt. Col. Wallace ordered us to rally around him, but in this instance I must admit that I did not obey orders, but commanded myself to rally to the rear, and did so in double-quick time.

I have a very vivid recollection of a handsome rebel officer on horseback who invited me earnestly to surrender, saying, "We will treat you like gentlemen," but as I was not a gentleman just then, and had no time to argue the question with him, I made a bold dash for liberty through the scrub oak. Every sapling seemed to be a rebel and would persist in holding me back. I was in such a hurry I cleared a five-foot board fence in one jump.

Finally I reached that precious goal, the rear. Here I paused, and finding myself "all present and accounted for," I adjusted my toilet, reflected on my narrow escape, had a hearty laugh and began to "count noses." I found that our lieutenant colonel and some 50 others of my regiment who had obeyed orders and rallied were all captured. Our six Napoleon guns and four 20-pounder Parrotts of De Gress' battery were also in the hands of the enemy.

The next 20 minutes, however, brought a sudden change. Logan, with fire in his eyes, came dashing down the road at the head of a fresh brigade. I and others joined them, and with bayonets fixed we charged upon the enemy. They gave us one well-directed volley and then beat a hasty skedaddle.

Our greatest loss that day was the death of our beloved Gen. McPherson, who unknowingly had ridden through our unprotected line on our left, and there met his fate. If it had not been for John A. Logan the Battle of Atlanta would in all probability be whistled now in a different tune. He saved the day.

■ Capt. Thomas J. Key, a pre-war newspaper publisher, commanded an Arkansas battery during the campaign. After the battle of Atlanta on July 22, and into the early hours of July 23, Key walked over much of the scarred battlefield where Hardee's corps attacked. "Our forays were bringing off the field small arms, ordnance wagons and other implements of war," he wrote in his diary. "There was no firing during the night, and the pale faces of the dead men seen beneath the mellow rays of the moon gave the scene a ghastly and unearthly appearance ... There was no firing after sunrise in Cleburne's front, and about 10 o'clock a flag of truce was agreed upon to bring off the wounded and bury the dead. The ground was strewn with dead men from both armies, and the foes mingled in the one duty of paying the last sad tribute to the fallen of the battlefield." This daguerreotype of Key was made in the late 1850s, shortly after he moved to Arkansas from Kansas.

■ Eight members of Capt. Francis DeGress' Battery H, 1st Illinois Light Artillery, posed for this group portrait in 1864 during veteran furlough. Seated from left: Sergeant Henry O. Olson, Wagoner Charles D. Roberts, Orderly Sergeant Henry Meyers and Sergeant Frank K. Laha. Standing from left: Bugler Frank B. Moroney, Sergeant John McGeorge, Bugler Wentzel Maschka and Artificer Frederic Dohmeyer.

'Saving his battery'

Capt. Charles D. Miller
Company C
76th Ohio Veteran Volunteer Infantry

The Confederates that got in the rear of the XVII Corps made their appearance late in the afternoon, rushing through a railroad cut upon the flank and in the rear of the 2nd Division of our corps [XV], and most of the division was obliged to fall back and abandon DeGress' battery. This unfortunate occurrence took place in plain view of the troops of our division, as we occupied a high hill but could do nothing to prevent the disaster at the time, as the Confederates flocked into the reverse side of the works on our left rear, and it was necessary for us to change front along our whole line to confront them in line of battle.

Orders came from Gen. Sherman to recapture the battery and abandoned works at any cost, and Gen. [Charles R.] Woods lost no time in marching his division to the left and rear to cover the front of the whole ground in possession of the Confederates.

We moved forward at about 5 o'clock over cleared ground, passing through a valley, and charged up the ascent beyond to the works, the reverse side of which was occupied by the enemy. Never did troops keep better alignment in marching in the face of an enemy. To the right and to the left we could see the straight blue lines with their banners gaily waving in the breeze. When within about 100 yards of the works the enemy opened upon us with a galling fire of musketry, causing considerable havoc in our ranks, but the boys kept straight ahead and accelerated their motion toward the sheet of flame blazing in their faces.

It happened that the 76th Regiment went up opposite the battery, and it was "nip and tuck" which company would get there first. The left wing of the regiment had to pass through a swampy piece of ground which somewhat retarded its motion, and I found my company a little in advance. The firing was very hot and many of the boys were dropping. My first lieutenant (Miles Arnold) was shot three times within two minutes. A rebel color-bearer was shaking a blue flag over the works right in our teeth. I told my boys that the quicker we got there the better, even if we had to fight "hand to hand" over the works, and we sailed in quite lively and were soon in the ditch with the rebs just over on the other side. But they broke out and ran, and my boys gave them a good volley.

I think my orderly sergeant [Hugh F. McDaniel], who was a tall, long-legged man and brave as a lion, was the first man in the division who got into the ditch, and the others were not a minute later in following. I struck the works a little to the right of the battery, and as soon as the boys delivered a volley at the Johnnies running back through the woods I ordered them to move double-quick by the left flank, loading on the jump, toward the guns. We were the first there and we found plenty of rebs about to defend the battery. But we let into them so lively, and with the other troops coming up at the moment, they broke back — leaving some prisoners, some killed, some wounded and, best of all, Capt. DeGress' 20-pound Parrott guns in our hands.

Capt. DeGress soon came up and threw his arms around his pet guns and cried for joy. He thanked the 76th Ohio for saving his battery the second time during the war. This charge ended the battle of Atlanta.

■ Capt. Francis DeGress, commander of Battery H, 1st Illinois Light Artillery. After his four guns were overrun on July 22, DeGress — greatly agitated by their loss — accompanied the XV and XVI corps troops who recaptured his 20-pounder Parrotts. Recalled Private Charles W. Hull of Company A, 76th Ohio: "DeGress came to our line just about 10 feet from me and said, 'My battery is gone.' The enemy turned the guns on us, which caused some commotion. DeGress, with hat in hand, shouted, 'Stand your ground, boys! They are only fooling you. Those guns are all spiked. I know it, for I did it myself.' "

As the Federals charged toward the battery, "Capt. DeGress soon appeared," wrote Private Thomas J. Shelley of Company D, 81st Ohio, "and with a detail of the 81st Ohio turned the guns on the retreating enemy. So zealous were the men in this work that one of the guns burst from its heavy charge." Another 81st soldier later wrote that "the explosion [was] caused by one of our boys [Private Joseph Schum of Company I]. When the gun was unspiked he concluded to give the rebels a double charge of 20-pound shell, remarking as he placed the second shell in, 'Feed 'em, damn 'em; give them double rations!' The gun was fired and torn to pieces, portions of the muzzle going way above the tree-tops, Lieut. Hezekiah Hoover, Co. K, 81st Ohio, being killed and many wounded."

No one's life was safe

Tightening the noose: Atlanta under siege

The spires of Atlanta's churches could be seen plainly from the Federal lines two miles east and north of the Gate City on July 23. But for Sherman's chief engineer, Capt. Orlando M. Poe, they might as well have been as far away as the moon.

Poe described Atlanta's formidable ring of fortifications as "too strong to assault and too extensive to invest," and his commanding general agreed. In the days following the battle of Atlanta on July 22, Sherman decided to sidestep west and south of the city in order to threaten and perhaps cut the Confederates' last remaining railroad supply line. If successful, he hoped to force Hood either to leave the Atlanta trenches and offer open battle or to evacuate the city altogether. More fighting would occur first. But as July gave way to August, the facing lines began to congeal and Atlanta, "now simply a big fort," wrote a chagrined Sherman, found itself under siege.

"Both armies are laying still for the present, watching one another to see how and where the other will jump, just like two great savage dogs," wrote Private John F. Brobst of Company G, 25th Wisconsin, to his girlfriend in early August. "We are close to the city in many places now but there are many bitter weeds grow[ing] between us and there."

The troops settled down to the routine of life in the trenches, broken periodically by informal truces between the lines and bouts of singing at night. However, the shells and bullets continued to fly and the casualties continued to mount.

On August 11, Private Ira S. Owens of Company C, 74th Ohio, wrote in his diary: "Went on picket at night, it being dangerous to relieve pickets in the daytime, the picket-line being within a few rods of the rebel line. It was very disagreeable ... raining a good portion of the time, so as to render sleep impossible. When we got into the pit, it was nearly filled with mud and water; and after daylight it was very risky standing up. We could not stand up, lie, or sit down, but had to remain in a crouching position, which was very tiresome. The pits were about a rod apart, and there were about six men in a pit. Sergeant Slasher, Charley Newman, Faber of Company K, and myself were in the same pit. While Sergeant Slasher was going from one pit to another, he was just in the act of jumping down into our pit when a rebel shot at him, grazing his back. He said it smarted like fire, and got me to examine it; and right across the small of his back was a red streak, but no blood. The sergeant was talking, before that, of going to the regiment for some rations; but he concluded to stay in the pit until after night, and do without his dinner. I had my bayonet shot from my gun in the same pit, the rebs and our men keeping up a constant fire day and night."

The following day, 1st Lieut. William H. Berryhill of the 43rd Mississippi wrote in a letter home: "The Yankees are in gun shot of us and at their old trade ditching up to us. But in some places we are advancing on them by ditching. They want to play Vicksburg on us if they could, but they can't quite come it for we have plenty of good cannon and gunners that are not afraid to fire on them whenever it suits them. The Yanks are beginning to find that Jordan is a hard road to travel after all."

In a diary entry, Capt. Isaac J. Rogers of Company B, 27th Alabama, wrote: "The weather was extremely warm and the troops suffered very much being continually in line of Battle exposed to the hot rays of the Sun. Working and picketing all day and night. I had four holes Shot through my clothes and one through my cap while on this line."

And on August 16, Private Thomas J. Newberry of Company D, 29th Mississippi, wrote home to his younger sisters from Camp Cobb, just outside Atlanta: "I must write you both a few lines to let you know you are not forgotten by your Brother. I am glad to hear you both keep well and hearty. I have no news to write worth your attention only we have a very good band in our Regiment. We have dress parade every week end. The band goes out and plays and a heap of little girls come to see us about your size every evening on dress parade. You both must be good little sisters and be smart and grow fast. You both must write often and tell me the news. Tell all howdy. Goodbye little sisters. Your Brother."

It was the last letter Newberry sent home. Four days later, Chaplain W.T. Hall of the 30th Mississippi wrote to Newberry's father: "It is my painful duty to inform you of the death of your son — a member of the 29th Miss. Regt. I presume, however, that it will be a satisfaction to you and your family to know by letter what you will necessarily learn in some way. Your son fell in the discharge of his duty to his country. He was on picket duty when the fatal shot, a rifle ball, struck him. As far as I know he was killed instantly ..."

■ Capt. Orlando M. Poe was Sherman's chief engineer during the campaign. It was his responsibility to select the Federal lines of entrenchment in late July and August when the Union army sidestepped west and southwest of Atlanta in order to sever the Confederates' railroad supply and communication lines. "Nothing like regular siege approaches were attempted," Poe wrote in 1865. Sherman "always told me that he did not wish anything of the kind done, that he intended to gain possession of Atlanta by operating upon the enemy's lines of communication, until he either brought on a general engagement, in which event he expected to gain a decisive victory, or compel the enemy to evacuate the city, which he could easily do, as the place was not, and it was evident that it could not be, completely invested."

'Golly but dat was a tight shave'

Journal of Private Benjamin T. Smith Company C 51st Illinois Veteran Volunteer Infantry

July 25th. Our army has settled down for a regular siege. And after nearly three months of marching over some pretty rough country, the rest is most welcome. It has been a campaign that will long be remembered by those engaged in it, the enemy leaving no stone unturned to retard our progress. Innumerable skirmishes and many battles have been fought. They selected their ground, wherever nature could aid them, and only retreated when in danger of being outflanked, or to prevent a general engagement; when we confronted them in their strongest position, at Kennesaw Mountain, it was said by them that Sherman was afraid to make a direct attack upon them, always preferring to use his superior forces in flank movements. Whether this was true or not that they (the rebels) had made use of this taunt, in order to cause an attack to be made, or whether the attack was ordered for another purpose, is a question. The facts remain that we did make a fruitless effort upon them in the strongest position they held during the whole of the campaign; true they evacuated directly after, but this was the result not so much from our threatening their front as from our threatening their rear. The aggregate loss to both armies must be con-

■ Maj. Gen. Joseph Hooker, former commander of the Army of the Potomac, commanded the XX Corps during the campaign until late July, when he asked to be relieved in a pique over not being selected to command the Army of the Tennessee after McPherson's death. Sherman, who did not like Hooker, approved the resignation application immediately. He later wrote: "General Hooker was offended because he was not chosen to succeed McPherson; but his chances were not even considered ... I am told that he says that Thomas and I were jealous of him; but this is hardly probable, for we on the spot did not rate his fighting qualities as high as he did ... General Hooker, moreover, when he got back to Cincinnati, reported (I was told) that we had run up against a rock at Atlanta, and that the country ought to be prepared to hear of disaster from that quarter."

siderable. It is true that while the enemy could less afford their losses, it is also true perhaps, that many of our own losses might have been avoided, to some extent.

Over in Atlanta they have planted one of their heaviest guns. It being on a slight elevation we can see it without the aid of a glass; with out looks stationed on the top of a high building they signal to their gunner, how to point the gun so as to do the most damage, aiming at the different groups of Head Quarter tents, with a view to sending some of our general officers to kingdom come. They had our headquarters dead to rights. While one of the boys and myself stood talking together, just as our darkey calls dinner, a big camp kettle from this gun came along and passed a few feet above our heads, making the most infernal noise as it cut the air. We felt the wind from its swift rush as it passed; turning our eyes we saw it strike the side of a tree just below us, taking out a chunk half its size; exploding, it smashed the rear end of one of our wagons and killed a mule that was tied to it. It raised a smoke big enough to hide its work of destruction for a moment. We went to our dinner where our darkey cook stood with his eyes as big as saucers. "Golly but dat was a tight shave," he said as soon as he recovered enough to talk. While we all stood around the board, bang went the old gun again, and pretty soon came another shell, directly in the path of the last, and although it seemed incredible, we saw it strike the selfsame tree, in the same groove its predecessor had made, making it only a trifle broader. We could hardly believe our eyes, and so went down and examined the tree. Sure enough, the evidence was indisputable. The two shells had traversed exactly the same route, varying only a few inches; the distance from the gun to the tree is not less than two miles.

They kept up their fire at intervals the rest of the day and all night; by bed time we had become so familiar with the noise that we did not mind it. The infernal music of the shells varied through a whole octave; if it was traveling very fast it sounded in a high key; if it came more leisurely we dubbed it a bass note, and so the tune went on all night from do to ra with sharps and flats now and then. We felt no apprehension when they played on the upper notes, as that indicated the shell would go far beyond our resting place, but the bass notes might mean it was going to fall short of, or in among us.

At the works just in front of our division a battery of siege guns was placed. This afternoon, while our gunners were working them, driving some of the longest-rifled shells over into the rebel works, I walked over and got on top of our works and stood alongside one of these long guns. Just beside the embrasure, about midway the gun when the gun went off, I could catch the flight of the shell the instant it left the muzzle and follow its whole course, see it strike and explode, showing how quick is the human eye.

'They'll only beat their own brains out'

Major James Austin Connolly
123rd Illinois Volunteer Infantry
Inspector-General
Baird's Division, XIV Corps

Before Atlanta, July 31, 1864.

Dear wife:

It is Sabbath evening, and just one week ago this evening you were writing me the letter which I received yesterday.

There is one good thing about this campaign, and that is that our mail has

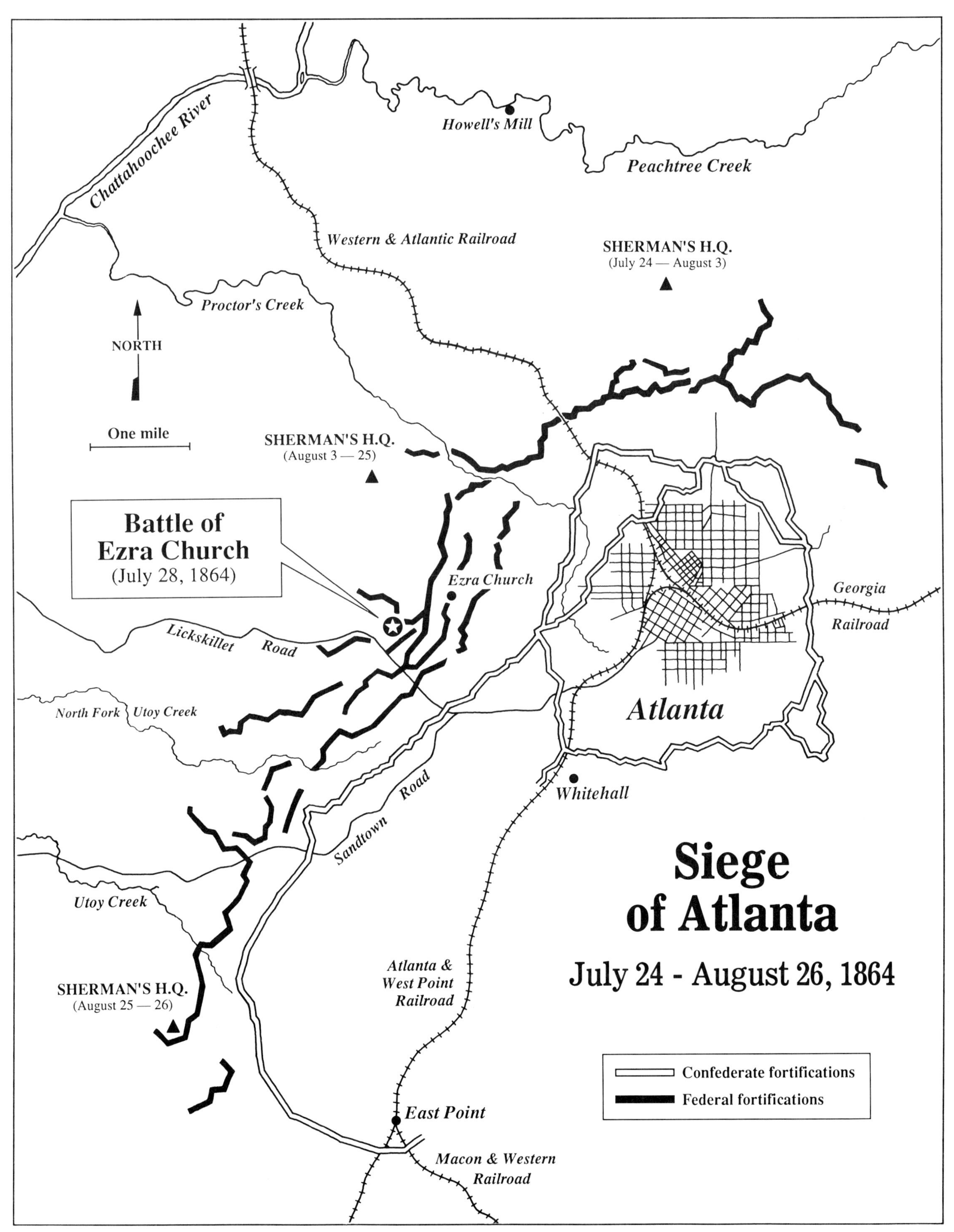
Chattahoochee River
Howell's Mill
Peachtree Creek
Western & Atlantic Railroad
SHERMAN'S H.Q.
(July 24 — August 3)
Proctor's Creek
NORTH
One mile
SHERMAN'S H.Q.
(August 3 — 25)
Battle of
Ezra Church
(July 28, 1864)
Ezra Church
Georgia
Railroad
Lickskillet
Road
North Fork
Utoy Creek
Atlanta
Whitehall
Sandtown
Road
Siege
of Atlanta
July 24 - August 26, 1864
Utoy Creek
Atlanta &
West Point
Railroad
SHERMAN'S H.Q.
(August 25 — 26)
Confederate fortifications
Federal fortifications
East Point
Macon & Western
Railroad

■ Major James A. Connolly, 123rd Illinois, served during the campaign as inspector-general of Baird's division, XIV Corps. Writing to his wife on August 11, Connolly lamented the kind and quality of rations many Federals subsisted on: "I had my first mess of green corn yesterday at dinner, and had some more today, but it is scarce here, and indeed vegetables of all kinds are scarce, almost none to be obtained. The result of this scarcity of vegetables is that a great many cases of scurvy have appeared in this army, even among officers. Oh! if I could only be at home a couple of weeks now, wouldn't I luxuriate on green corn, potatoes, peas, beans, tomatoes, &c., &c.? Talk about bread being the 'staff of life' it's all humbug. I'd give more for an ear of green corn down here than I would for two loaves of bread."

kept up with us in all marches toward the heart of Georgia, and today the little missives come as promptly to the soldier in the trenches before Atlanta as they would if he were at his own northern home. The value of this prompt transmission of mails cannot be too highly appreciated, and the tender and humanizing influence of the dear little home letters, as they are read and re-read by the light of the camp fire, is worth more than all the efforts of army chaplains and Christian Commission men.

On Thursday, the 28th, we had another heavy engagement with the enemy, and as usual they were terribly repulsed in four distinct efforts to break our lines, leaving most of their dead and many of their wounded in our hands.* I was over the ground next morning, and the dead lay just where they had fallen, festering and decomposing in the hot July sun. I rode over a space about 400 yards long by about 75 yards in width, and in that area scanned the faces of 225 dead rebels, and then had not seen more than one-third of those who lay there, but that number satisfied my appetite for blood, and I returned feeling very thankful that I was not a rebel and especially a dead rebel. Colonels, lieutenant colonels, majors, captains, lieutenants and privates lay mingled together on that field of blood, all reduced to the same rank. One colonel, one major and one captain had been buried before I got there. Poor fellows! They fought manfully, like Americans, and I honor them for their valor, even though they fought for a bad cause. The captain who had been buried, had fallen nearer to our line than any other rebel, and he had evidently been decently interred by some Masonic brother in blue, for a head board made out of the lid of a cracker box had been erected at his grave and inscribed with the Masonic "square and compass," and his name "Capt. Sharp, 10th Miss., Buried by the 35th N.J. Vols. I know that he will rise again," all written on it with a pencil, and possibly by the hand of the same soldier that killed him a few hours before. Our men buried 642 rebels on that ground that day, and taking the usual proportions of wounded to killed, their loss on the 28th cannot have been less than 3,500 killed and wounded, and we took 400 prisoners, while our loss cannot have been more than 900 killed and wounded, and no prisoners.

The rebel loss in their several attacks on us since we crossed the river must be fully 20,000, while ours has scarcely reached one third that number. I felt satisfied that the rebels would fight to the bitter end for Atlanta, after we should cross the river, but did not expect them to manifest such senseless desperation. Why it was a perfect murder. We slaughter them by the thousands, but Hood continues to hurl his broken, bleeding battalions against our immovable lines, with all the fury of a maniac. Reason seems dethroned, and Despair alone seems to rule the counsels within the walls of Atlanta. Nothing but defeat and utter destruction stares Hood in the face — he has sense enough to see it, and now, brave traitor as he is, has determined to die fighting, with "harness on his back." Our men would take it as an easy task to repel an assault anywhere on our lines.

In company with Gen. Baird, I chanced to be where Gen. Sherman was during the fighting of the 28th. When the firing commenced, away off, two miles to our right, we didn't know what it meant; Sherman remarked: "Logan is feeling for them and I guess he has found them." The scattering

* The Battle of Ezra Church was fought on July 28 west of Atlanta between troops of the Union Army of the Tennessee under Gen. Oliver O. Howard (appointed to command that army only the day before), and Confederates of Stephen D. Lee's and Alexander Stewart's corps. Sheltered by crude breastworks constructed of logs, fence rails and even wooden pews taken from Ezra Church, the men of Logan's XV Corps were assailed for more than five hours by repeated Confederate attacks. The latter suffered heavy casualties — estimated at 5,000 killed, wounded or captured — while the Federals lost about 600.

musketry, and occasional roar of artillery, swelled louder and louder into the full chorus of battle; presently a staff officer from Gen. Howard dashed up to Gen. Sherman and announced that the enemy were making a heavy and determined assault on Logan's corps, which was on the extreme right of the Army of the Tennessee, now commanded by Gen. Howard; "Good," said Sherman, "that's fine, just what I wanted, just what I wanted. Tell Howard to invite them to attack, it will save us trouble, save us trouble. They'll only beat their own brains out, beat their own brains out." And so, in this confident tone our chieftain talked on gaily, while his boys in blue were reaping the terrible harvest of death. He understood his own strategy, he saw it was working as he had designed, and he was satisfied.

In your letter of a week ago, you congratulated me on our having taken Atlanta. If we have taken it yet I haven't heard of it; and we are in the front line where we will be likely to know it very soon after its capture. I see by the papers that the *correspondents* captured it a week or 10 days ago, but the *army* hasn't got that far yet. True, we can look into the streets of the city from the front lines of this division, but there are several heavy fortifications, filled with huge guns and greybacks, between us and those streets, and they were firing shells, as large as a water bucket, at us yesterday from those very fortifications. One of them struck near our headquarters yesterday and failed to explode; some soldiers dug it up, and on weighing it, found it weighed 65 pounds. I'm just coward enough to dodge all missiles of that size, for I'm sure I couldn't stop their flight if I'd "try my best," and what's the use of a body trying to do what a body knows a body can't do?

A Methodist minister, Rev. George W. Pepper, whom I used to hear preach in Chesterville, Ohio, when I was a small boy, called to see me yesterday and took dinner with me. While he was sitting on a chair in my tent and I was lazily lounging on my cot, one of those big shells came screaming along right over my tent and burst nearby; down on the floor of the tent went my reverend friend, as flat as a frog, and I was so irreverent as to laugh immoderately at the ridiculous figure he cut, sprawling on the floor. He raised up, brushed the dirt off his clothes, and looked as long faced as if he was preaching a funeral sermon, and very soon bade me goodbye. Several shells came our way during dinner, and he made his pastoral call to these headquarters very brief.

A great many such shells passed over our headquarters yesterday, and we had a great deal of sport laughing at each other for our dodging. Falling flat on the ground or jumping behind a big tree are the prevailing modes of dodging these shells. I completely flattened myself on the ground once yesterday, when I thought, from the sound of the shell, it was coming right for me; our medical director, who was sitting near me at the time, also tried to flatten himself, but his pantaloons being very tight he couldn't get down quick enough, though in his vigorous efforts to get down, he succeeded in rending his unmentionables most fearfully, and furnished the rest of the staff a half-hour's laughter. So you see the hours pass lightly with us much of the time, and we levy contributions of merriment from every day as it glides along. ...

'Fight like the devil!'

Col. Wells S. Jones
53rd Ohio Veteran Volunteer Infantry

During the siege of Atlanta our regiment, the 53rd Ohio, was continually engaged in skirmishing with the enemy. We had previously been engaged at Kennesaw Mountain and later we crossed the Chattahoochee, moved on to

■ Brig. Gen. Absalom Baird commanded the 3rd Division, XIV Corps. From July 23 until August 3 (when the XIV Corps was moved to the extreme right of the army), "a constant and venomous skirmish was kept up between the pickets on both sides," Baird wrote, "and our lines were so close that our men in camp were at any moment that they exposed themselves liable to be picked off by the enemy's riflemen. Our batteries and those upon the rebel forts kept up an unceasing exchange of compliments, so that our daily loss in killed and wounded in camp was not inconsiderable. Numerous 20-pounder shells, and shells of sixty-four pounds' weight from the 'old 32-pounder rifle,' came regularly into our camps, a weight of metal entirely out of proportion to our light field pieces."

This photograph of Baird was taken at Morse's Gallery of the Cumberland in Nashville.

■ Col. Wells S. Jones, 53rd Ohio, alternately commanded the 2nd Brigade, 2nd Division, XV Corps, with Gen. J.A.J. Lightburn during the campaign. A physician by profession, Jones was injured in December 1864 at Fort McAllister, Ga., by a spent ball fired by a Confederate sharpshooter. The same bullet killed Capt. John H. Groce of his staff, hitting him in the right temple before striking Jones.

In this photograph, taken in 1865 when he was a brevet brigadier general, Jones wears a XV Corps badge on his coat. Officially adopted in February 1865, this badge consisted of a miniature cartridge box, set transversely on a square, with the motto "40 Rounds" inscribed.

Decatur and, meeting the enemy, drove them into Atlanta.

On July 26 Gen. Sherman began to move the Army of the Tennessee in the rear of the remainder of his army, with a view of forming it on his right. On July 28 the XV Corps began to form in line of battle to gradually wheel around from left to right until it should more closely invest Atlanta on the west side if it did not encounter the enemy. At a point near Ezra Chapel the corps was halted to correct its alignment, the writer at the time commanding the 53rd Ohio, which formed part of the line.

Shortly after we had halted, Gen. Lightburn, commanding the 2nd Brigade, 2nd Division, XV Corps, came to me and said: "I want you to take your regiment and move out into that timber," pointing to a clump of timber some 300 yards in front of the main line, "and form there and charge that hill." He further pointed to a ridge along which the Lickskillet road ran. He said it was occupied by some rebel cavalry that he wanted driven from our front, and suggested to me to be prompt in my actions.

I immediately moved into the timber as directed, and when I fronted my line toward the hill I beheld more rebel infantry, not cavalry, than I had in my regiment. At once I dispatched my orderly to Gen. Lightburn to send another regiment immediately to support me on my left. But before he returned I determined not to wait for the regiment, but charge on the ridge at once. I gave the order to move forward at the double-quick, and it seemed from the alacrity with which the men moved that each vied with the other in seeing who would reach the top first. We took the hill in less time than it takes me to write it, with but little loss as the enemy seemed to fall back promptly toward his main line. This I observed to be some 600 yards in my front, and extending as far as I could see to the right and left.

We had scarcely taken the hill when the regiment I had sent for, the 47th Ohio, formed upon my left. There being no lack of material to shoot at in our front, the two regiments were ordered to open fire all along the line. In fact, that seemed to me to be the only means of staying there at all. Being far out in front of our corps and formed at a half-right angle to the main line, I turned around to look in the direction of my right and rear. Beholding a large body of enemy cavalry there (the cavalry, no doubt, that the generals had seen when I was ordered to charge the hill), and thinking that its presence there was incompatible with the safety of my command, I dispatched my adjutant, Lieut. George W. Cavett, in great haste to Gen. Lightburn, asking him to send me two more regiments to form on my right, fronting the cavalry.

He found Gen. Lightburn with Gen. Smith, the division commander, who rather demurred to sending me more regiments. Instead he sent one of his staff officers with Gen. Smith's compliments to me, who said: "Tell Col. Jones not to be alarmed. There is nothing in his front but some cavalry."

I said to the staff officer: "Give Gen. Smith my compliments, and tell him that I am not alarmed, but that I have Hood's army in my front and cannot whip it with two regiments. I insist that the reinforcements asked for be sent at once."

When they did not make their appearance I took a few men out of my main line and formed a skirmish line on my right, fronting for a short distance in the direction of the cavalry. Believing from the orders that I had received from my generals that they were not aware of the presence of Hood's army in my front, I determined to remain on the hill and make the best fight that I could, as long as I could, so that our main line would fully realize the gravity of the situation and prepare itself at once for the great battle that I saw was coming.

In a few moments Hood advanced his main line in my front, and we remained in position until our retreat which, on account of our proximity to the enemy, partook largely of the nature of a rout. The enemy's line seemed to be about parallel with ours, and I think they were deceived into the idea that our main line was fronting in the same direction that we were. As I retreated in a parallel line with the position I held on the ridge, of necessity I had to pass in front of the XV Corps to get to its right where I desired to reform my command. In hot pursuit the enemy hardly realized what was coming when regiment after regiment in our main line opened up a deadly fire on his front and flank.

Just before I reached the right of our main line I met Major Charles Hipp coming with his regiment, the 37th Ohio, to relieve my right. Not realizing, perhaps, our broken-up condition, he said: "What shall I do?" Having no time to plan a battle in the condition my command was, I said: "Fight like the devil!"

The gallant major brought his men forward into line, but soon received a wound which caused the loss of an arm and entirely disabled him from further participation in the battle. I was unable to stop the retreat of my forces until I reached the right of our line, where I organized them and again moved forward in the direction from which we had retreated. After advancing a short distance we took a house which was occupied by a few rebels who had the temerity to pursue us that far. Taking the accidental line of some rail fences, some of which were made straight by the rails being placed between stakes — affording a pretty good protection for my men — I ordered them to take that position and they hastily carried the rails from the other fences, in that way extending our line to the right and left and presenting quite a formidable front.

From these hastily constructed works we kept up an almost constant musketry fire for more than five hours. The entire XV Corps was engaged at the same time, until the enemy had so exhausted himself by repeated charges that he reluctantly withdrew from the field. The firing was so persistent that often my men would have to stop firing and cool their guns by

■ Buildings in Atlanta (background skyline) can be seen to the east from a portion of the Ezra Church battlefield in a photograph taken in March 1893 by David Auld, 43rd Ohio.

■ Private David Auld, a musician in Company B, 43rd Ohio.

■ Major Charles Hipp lost his left arm while commanding the 37th Ohio on July 28 at Ezra Church, where his regiment anchored the extreme right of the Federal army. "Six companies of the regiment were deployed as skirmishers to cover our right flank," wrote Capt. Carl Moritz, who replaced Hipp as regimental commander. "Soon after two more companies were advanced as advanced pickets on the several by-roads leading to our line. The enemy soon appeared in heavy force in our front and flank, and drove in the skirmish line." Private John H. Puck of Company G recalled: "When everything was confusion our Major was wounded and was seen falling off his horse, and but for the brave act of our color-bearer, Ernst Torgler, would have been captured ..." Torgler, a sergeant from Company G, received the Medal of Honor. The citation reads: "At great hazard of his life he saved his commanding officer, then badly wounded, from capture."

pouring water from their canteens into them so they could load them. Several regiments were sent to me during the battle, with which I extended my line on the right. Owing to the curve in our line, and the slight protection that many of the regiments of the XV Corps had provided themselves with, our loss was trifling compared to that of the enemy.

Thus was begun and fought the battle of Ezra Chapel, which clearly illustrates that great battles were often fought unexpectedly to those who engaged in them.

'Repulsed by the undaunted coffee-coolers'

Private Edwin W. Smith
Company G
54th Ohio Veteran Volunteer Infantry

A few days previous [to the battle of Ezra Church], in one of our gallant charges on hen-roosts and kitchens, my mess had gobbled a coffee-boiler large enough to hold more of that soldiers' precious tonic than Bragg and Warner could both drink in a week, though I would not vouch for it if filled with the genuine old "commissary." We coffee-coolers took turns to carry this huge coffee-boiler, and the day of the battle it happened to be my turn to tote it, which I did, fastened on my gum blanket and swung around on the middle of my back.

Gen. Lightburn had but recently taken command of our squad, and perhaps thinking us somewhat awkward, he thought it best to put us through a little drill. So early in the morning he marched us quite a ways through the woods and underbrush in line of battle. Then commenced a series of the most wonderful evolutions on record. We marched straight to the front, right-about to the rear, filed to the right, then to the left, left-oblique, right-oblique, left flanked, right flanked; in short, having exhausted Hardee's tactics and his own, too, for that matter, as well as our patience, he halted us somewhere in the Southern Confederacy. I have often thought since that the Johnnies and Yanks were playing the game of hide and seek that morning, or perhaps both parties were trying to find Ezra Church and got lost in the brush.

All this time the coffee-boiler clung tenaciously to my back, catching in the brush and briars, which made me think none the more of Lightburn's drill. The 54th Ohio was deployed on the right as skirmishers. We had advanced but a short distance when Major [Israel T.] Moore wanted some of the boys to climb some tall trees and look for Johnnies on the other side of a hill in our front. Another fellow and myself threw off our traps and skinned up the trees. We had just gotten comfortably seated for observation when "zip-zip, ping-ping" told us plainly the rebels could see us, if we could not see them, and that we were a little too high for health.

We hustled down as lively as we could, donned our accoutrements, not forgetting the coffee-pot, and joined our comrades who had found the rebel skirmishers posted behind some stone piles, log house, blacksmith shop, corn-crib and rail fence. Talk about your officers leading and encouraging their men in time of battle. We most generally fought on our own hook, at least we did on this occasion.

Some of us moved to the right and others to the left of the stone piles and buildings, pouring in a close, well-directed fire, cheering and encouraging each other at the same time. Comrades fell badly wounded around us, but still we pressed on.

The rebels, finding themselves flanked, slowly fell back, disputing every foot of the ground. As we took possession of their line we cast our eyes to the front, and there a sight met our gaze that I shall never forget.

At the edge of the woods about 300 yards distant it looked to me as though the whole Southern Confederacy stood in compact line of battle. As far as the eye could reach to the right and left stood a mingled line of yellow and gray in all the pomp, splendor and circumstance of glorious war. Hood was about to make another mighty effort to crush Sherman, and this was the living cyclone that he was in the act of hurling against him.

We halted, gave them a volley, which they noticed no further than to close up their ranks and advance toward us. As we fell back past the buildings and stone piles we gave them another volley. To this they deigned a reply, and such a storm and whiz of bullets I never heard before or since. Ten thousand muskets belched forth, and for a time the air seemed literally filled with lead. How any of us escaped has always been a wonder to me.

We fell back as rapidly as our war harness would permit. I never did such poor running in my life; and that coffee-boiler! How I wished it was a shield or bullet proof. Every moment I expected to get a bullet into it. How it retarded my locomotion! I was tempted a dozen times to throw it, my gun traps and everything else to the Johnnies. They came so close that they called us pet names and ordered us to halt, but we were under Sherman's orders and did not obey Hood worth a cent.

On nearing our lines we were obliged to fall down and crawl on our hands and knees, our men firing over our heads. We were badly scattered; some of the boys and myself fell in with an Illinois regiment. Their volleys checked the exultant foe and gave us a little breathing spell, which was improved by the ordnance boxes being brought to the front at full gallop, knocked to pieces and the cartridges strewed along on the ground.

Charge after charge was made by the massed rebel forces on our single line, but were met and repulsed by the undaunted coffee-coolers with a fearful slaughter. Our guns would get so hot that we could not hold them. Three times when the rebels were driven back we let them cool, and twice poured water in them to clean them out.

At one time when the rebels had met with a bloody repulse, we were letting our guns cool and peering intently into the dense smoke. During this short cessation they had massed their forces in a deep, heavily timbered ravine in our front, and under cover of the smoke had silently moved up close to our line. An ominous stillness like that which precedes the dreadful storm prevailed, and as the battle curtain rolled slowly up it showed their compact lines of yellow and gray standing at right-shoulder shift, coolly taking in the situation and mentally calculating how long it would take to gobble us up.

Our front rank was kneeling, the rear rank standing. The front rank fired just as they were taking aim. The slaughter was terrible. They seemed to melt like wax figures in the flame. Still they rallied, closed up their bleeding, shattered ranks and rushed forward with a dreadful yell, only to meet a withering volley from the rear rank. This swept through their dense lines like a sword blade, causing them to stagger and fall in all directions. Human valor could stand it no longer; they became completely demoralized and amidst the confusion the coffee-coolers pushed out among them, capturing quite a number and several battle flags.

During the many charges and repulses I had noticed a rebel officer mounted on a beautiful white horse making great efforts to rally his men.

■ Capt. James B. Howard, commander of Company G, 49th Tennessee, was killed on July 28 at Ezra Church. An unusually high number of Confederate officers became casualties in this battle — in Walthall's division, Gen. William A. Quarles' brigade alone lost 12 officers killed and 17 wounded. The 49th and 42nd Tennessee under Col. William F. Young were detached from Quarles and ordered by Gen. Walthall personally to support a section of the Jefferson (Mississippi) Artillery near the Lick Skillet Road. Fifteen minutes after the Confederate assault began, Col. Young was badly wounded (losing his right arm) and Capt. Howard was killed. Walthall later wrote: "If it had been possible for the daring of officers and the desperate fighting of the men to have overcome such odds in numbers and strength of position as we encountered that day all along my whole line, the enemy must have been beaten, but double the force could not have accomplished what my division was ordered to undertake."

■ Behind a hastily constructed barricade of fence boards and rails, troops of Logan's XV Corps unload a series of devastating volleys into the ranks of attacking Confederates at Ezra Church on July 28. In Gen. Zachariah Deas' brigade, the 25th Alabama alone lost 125 men out of 173 it took into the battle. Confederate casualties at Ezra Church totaled some 5,000 — including corps commander Lt. Gen. Alexander P. Stewart, who was injured in the forehead by a ricocheting bullet. "It was a slaughter pen, bullets coming from several directions," recalled Private Washington Crumpton of Company H, 37th Mississippi, which belonged to Stewart's corps. "My old haversack had a half dozen bullet holes through it. For ten days my body was not safe from the passage of bullets, some through my clothing and some that barely made my clothes threadbare as they passed, but leaving a sore place on the flesh as if scorched by fire. My case knife in the bottom of my haversack turned two bullets off of me, and my tube wrench and screw driver in my cartridge box was broken by another."

Singling him out I took deliberate aim. I won't say, like Washington's Indian, that I fired 17 times; but I did fire until I got disgusted, and then called on my comrade, Wilson Allison. We took position further to the front behind a large tree and commenced a fusilade on the same officer and white horse. One would fire and the other watch the result. Then we would both try it together. It was no go; like Banquo's ghost he would not go down.

At length, night closed the bloody drama, and tired and begrimed with smoke and powder we sought rest and refreshment. I unslung the coffee-boiler and a few of us dirty-faced, powder-blackened coffee-coolers gratefully partook of the soldier's invigorating beverage.

'Dave, shoot into that gang'

Capt. Emory W. Muenscher
Company I
30th Ohio Veteran Volunteer Infantry

The 30th Ohio, with its comrades of the XV Corps, was in line of battle on a ridge near Atlanta, on which stood a chapel known as Ezra Church. We had been marching most of the previous day, nearly all night and all the forenoon, and hundreds of men had dropped out of the ranks from sheer exhaustion. I had with me but 12 men of my company and the regiment had only about 100.

We had seen no enemy, but there were occasional shots on the skirmish line and my boys began to smell a fight. At their request I went to Lt. Col. [George H.] Hildt, who was in command of the regiment, and asked permission for them to tear down a rail fence a short distance in front of us and throw up a breastwork. He refused, saying that we were going to move on again in a few minutes.

I reported his reply to my boys, but they were not satisfied, and, before long, as we did not move, I went to Hildt with the same request and was again refused. After another wait my boys were becoming so anxious that I went a third time. I suppose that Col. Hildt had either become convinced that the idea was not a bad one, or was getting annoyed at my persistence, for he replied rather impatiently, "Well, do as you please."

The next moment my boys were eagerly pulling down the rails and piling them up. The adjoining companies on each side, seeing what they were doing, immediately followed their example, and it spread like wildfire both ways, and in a few minutes a pile of rails about two feet high extended along our front as far as I could see. It was a lucky thing, for the last rail had hardly been laid on the pile when we heard the well known rebel yell and on they came, two and three lines deep.

The first blow fell entirely on the XV Corps and on the immediate front of our brigade — the 2nd Brigade of the 2nd Division — which was the extreme right of the whole army. The brigade was posted in this order from the right: 54th Ohio, 53rd Ohio, 47th Ohio, 83rd Indiana and 30th Ohio.

Our men kneeled down behind their pile of rails and met the attack with a deadly fire, while I stood on a little hillock about a rod in their rear, where I could look over their heads and direct their fire. The first attack was repulsed, but was renewed time and again with fresh troops, four charges being made on our front and six farther to the right.

During one of the intervals I happened to glance toward our left center, which was covered by a thin forest growth, and saw a rebel officer forming a line for another charge. He had gathered some 30 men about 20 rods away, and I could see scores of men coming from every direction through the woods to join him. I turned to one of my men, David W. Everett, who was standing by my side, and said, "Dave, shoot into that gang."

He raised his gun and fired, and a man near the center of the line went straight down as if a hole had opened in the ground and swallowed him up. The whole group instantly broke and ran.

That one shot had stampeded the whole of them, but the next moment a rebel sharpshooter fired at us as we stood fully exposed. The bullet missed me and struck Everett, and he fell into my arms. I laid him on the ground, opened his clothes and examined the wound. I was scared, for I feared that the ball had cut the intestines. I knew that that was a hopeless case. Fortunately, it had only cut away a chunk of flesh; he was taken to the hospital and recovered.

It was the only instance that I ever heard of where one shot whipped so many men.

The battle of Ezra Church was not a great one, but was a very bloody one for the number of men engaged. Gen. Hardee afterward said: "That so great was the loss in men, organization and morale in that engagement, that no action of the campaign probably did so much to demoralize and dishearten the troops engaged in it."

■ 1st Lieut. Joseph Dickerson, 30th Ohio, was second in command to Capt. Emory Muenscher of Company I during the battle of Ezra Church — having been promoted from Company A only three days before. Another member of the 30th, Private Albert B. Crummel of Company H, recalled: "Dead rebels lay within 20 feet of our regiment's line. Four distinct charges were made on us, and I made four trips among the dead in our front after tobacco, which was scarce with us and always plentiful with our enemy. No sooner were their backs turned than I would be out among the dead and explore their knapsacks for the precious weed. The boys of the 30th Ohio [were grateful for] the long plugs of old Virginia natural leaf I distributed on that day."

'Such a Death Trap'

Capt. John W. Lavender
Company F
4th Arkansas Volunteer Infantry

On the afternoon of July the 28th our Brigade was ordered to advance on the Enemys Brest works on our Extream left near Ezra Church. It was Extreamly warm and we had to advance some Distance through an open Field. The Federal Brest works being in the Edge of the Woods Just out side the Field. When our lines Entered the open Field some three Hundred yards

■ Brig. Gen. William A. Quarles commanded a brigade in Walthall's division. On July 28 at Ezra Church, his troops were on the extreme left of the Confederate line and attacked the extreme right of the XV Corps, hitting Lightburn's brigade. Quarles lost 514 men that afternoon, and wrote nine days later: "The enemy's resistance was stubborn. He was evidently in large force and fighting from behind breast-works. We gained ground upon them but slowly and at heavy cost ... We were at this time near the enemy's works, varying from 25 to 50 paces, and a farther advance with my line of battle, attenuated by casualties to a mere line of skirmishers, would have been fatal to the few left ... My aide-de-camp, Lieut. Ashton Johnson, of St. Louis, Mo., was killed in leading one of the regiments in a charge upon the enemy. Polk G. Johnson, my acting aide-de-camp, had his horse shot under him, and being entirely disabled from duty on the field, requested and was permitted to aid in serving the guns of Yates' [Mississippi] battery. One of my couriers (Hethman) was disabled for duty in a similar manner. Another courier (Private McCollum) was severely wounded." Before the day was over, Quarles lost five of his regimental commanders killed or severely wounded.

From their works they opened a terific Fire of Shells & Small arms on our line.

We held our fire and advanced rapedly as Possable. When aboute half way we opened fire and advanced in Double Quick time. We got near the works but our Fire done Them but Little Damage as they was Protected by Splendid Earth works and was literally mowing our men Down. So our lines was Forced to fall back or all be killed. We fell Back with fearful loss, the worst we had in any one Battle During the war for the number of men ingaged in it. The report was that we went into that Charge with 2600 Guns and lost aboute 1300 Killed and wounded including our Col. H.G. Bunn and nearly all the Field oficers of the Brigade and a great Many company officers. Col. Bunn had his Right arm Broken and wounds in Both Thighs but afterward got well.

This Battle Discouraged our men Badly as they could never understand why they Should have been Sent in to such a Death Trap to be Butchered up with no hope of gaining any thing. If we had succeeded in takeing that one Point we never could have held it but Such is War. We Fell Back to our line in a teriable shattered and Demoralized Condition.

'The wickedness of war'

Chaplain George W. Pepper
80th Ohio Veteran Volunteer Infantry

Here in these woods where Logan's corps was first engaged (on the 28th), there is not a rock or tree, or log, or leaf, but shows the desperate strife. One section of woods is literally cut off, torn down, scattered. Acres of this forest are topped by canister and grape-shot and shell almost as completely as our farmers top their cornfields with a sickle.

At the corner of the cornfield where the corps was engaged, there is a piece of oak rail fence and part of a stone wall. In one length of that fence behind which the rebels were concealed, I count 100 bullet holes. And along that field, and within the distance of 80 rods, we count 1,600 dead rebels, most of them lying on their backs, eyes open, faces black, hands folded on their breasts.

Here lies one upon his side, eyes closed, feet slightly drawn up, his head resting easily upon his knapsack. He looks a weary soldier, sound asleep. I speak to him, he stirs not; put my hand upon him, he will not wake. Dead.

Here is a soldier, a rebel captain, sitting against this tree. His limbs are crossed, and his cap hangs naturally upon his knee. One hand in the breast of his coat, the other hangs by his side. Dead.

Here, leaning against this wall, is a rebel soldier with his leg broken below the knee, and a Union surgeon lying dead across his feet. They are both dead. The surgeon was evidently dressing his wound when he received his death shot, for there is the bandage wound twice around the limb, the other end of which is still in the dead surgeon's hand. The rebel soldier evidently bled to death.

There is a constant stream of our wounded coming in by ambulances. In [a nearby] house is the surgery of the XV Corps. Six surgeons are in attendance; they receive and operate upon each case upon the instant. A wound is dressed in from two to 15 minutes. Amputations are performed in a trice, chloroform being administered. Pools of blood upon the floor are mixed up with the mud that is tracked in. The house's dining table makes a good dissecting bench. Drawers from a bureau are laid upon the floor, bottom up, for a couch to be spread.

In a bed in one small room lay three terribly wounded men, side by side,

'Treated to the fatted calf'

■ Chaplain George W. Pepper, seated at right, and fellow officers of the 80th Ohio. A keen observer and a man of wit, Pepper recorded many incidents of the campaign in a book published only one year after the war ended. He wrote: "It is amusing to witness the demonstration with which our boys receive rebel deserters into the lines on certain occasions. When the armies are lying very close together, as they often are, in battle lines, the disaffected rebels contrive to steal out unnoticed for a time, though they are generally discovered and fired on before reaching our lines. As soon as the soldiers see them coming, they appreciate the situation at once, and cannot resist the temptation to jump up from behind their works, though at the imminent risk of their heads, waving their hats and shouting, 'Good boy! good boy!' 'Come in out of the rain!' 'You're our man!' 'You're making good time!' &c. The first word of salutation is 'Got any tobacco, reb?' The returned prodigal, just escaped from the husks of the rebellion, is then treated to the fatted calf, the hard tack and coffee, which latter is to him a luxury indeed."

the family bedding saturated with their blood. A lieutenant lies in a corner, dead — died before his wound could be dressed. A private sits upon a table, naked to the hips, a musket ball having passed through his body from side to side, three inches below his arm-pits — he talks, is very pale and ghastly, but will live. Another sits on a chair, his leg cut off below the knee with a shell as clean as with a knife. A Kentucky captain, shot through the thigh, is seized with a spasm of pain while being taken from the ambulance into the house. He catches the sleeve of his coat near the shoulder with his teeth and bites, as would a mad dog. Such scenes I witnessed during an hour — and our army was only skirmishing.

The hospital and yard about it presented a spectacle which — how can I describe it? Stretchers, dripping with blood, stand in the pathway. Here come four men bringing on a blanket a pale, bleeding form; in the grass lies a lieutenant with a great wound in his thigh from a grape-shot, from which his life is ebbing; close by him a man with a rifle ball in his back, and nearby, another with a ball through his shoulders. The grass plots are covered with such scenes, and off in the corner of the yard is a blanket spread out, revealing the outline of a human form; we need not lift the covering for we know instinctively that it hides a corpse.

I have heard of the horrors of the battlefield, but they are nothing compared to the horrors of the *hospital.* The glare and excitement are absent, the wickedness of war is revealed.

■ Col. John Thomas Croxton, 4th Kentucky Mounted Infantry, commanded the 1st Brigade, McCook's division, during the raid. Cut off on July 30 along the Atlanta & West Point Railroad near Newnan Station, Croxton and two orderlies found themselves alone, nearly surrounded and unable to reach safety across the Chattahoochee River. He later wrote: "On the following night one of the orderlies was killed by a rebel sentinel. With the other I succeeded, after a good deal of delay and annoyance, in reaching our lines at Sweet Water Town on (August) 12th instant ... I regret beyond expression the loss of so many of those who have been my comrades so long. Perhaps if they had trusted to their heels and less to their carbines the casualty list on our side and the enemy's, too, would have been considerably abridged." At the age of 37, Croxton died less than 10 years later in La Paz, Bolivia, while serving as U.S. minister to that country.

'Eight days and nights in the saddle'

1st Lieut. Granville C. West
Company C
4th Kentucky Veteran Volunteer Mounted Infantry

The 4th Kentucky was now assigned to the 1st Brigade, 1st Cavalry Division, Department of the Cumberland, commanded by Brig. Gen. E.M. McCook, and our colonel — Croxton — took command of the brigade.

It was soon whispered about that there was an important raid or expedition in view. It was not long delayed. "Special Field Orders No. 42, Military Division of the Mississippi, July 25th, 1864," directed "General McCook's and Colonel Harrison's Cavalry to move rapidly on Fayetteville and the railroad beyond and break it if possible." In compliance with this order the expedition moved out at early dawn July 27, 1864.

The command included the 2nd, 4th and 8th Indiana Cavalry and a section of the 18th Indiana Battery, the 5th and 8th Iowa Cavalry, 2nd Kentucky Cavalry, the 4th Kentucky Mounted Infantry, the 1st and 4th Tennessee Cavalry and the 1st Wisconsin Cavalry, with a pontoon train on which to recross the river at some point below.

We moved from the extreme right of our army near the Chattahoochee River, where we had been stationed, crossed the river to the west side and took the road running down the right bank, with the stream between us and the rebel army.

With my company I was assigned to the duty of advance guard with instructions to note carefully all roads and paths leading toward the river, and, if possible, to find some point not guarded by the enemy's pickets where we could make a crossing back to the east side, and, especially, to ascertain the condition of affairs at the little town of Campbellton on the opposite side of the river, for it was thought that would be a good place to cross if it was not guarded.

So, when we reached the road that ran down to the river at that point I concealed my company in the woods so they could not be seen from the town, and, with a file of soldiers, reconnoitered the situation in a lane that gave those in the town full view of us as we emerged from the woods. About two-thirds of the way down the lane it made a sharp turn to the left. At that point a volley of musketry from the pickets in the town warned us that the place was guarded and no crossing could be made there. An orderly came up soon after with instructions from the general to remain where I was until further orders.

It was now late in the afternoon, and as we had not stopped for dinner during the day I instructed my men to hurriedly prepare their food and eat something, as I thought we would have time and I suspected we would be on the move all night.

While I was eating my scanty meal Gen. McCook rode up and dismounted. I invited him to partake of the feast consisting of some fried pork, hardtack and coffee without cream or sugar. I gave him my knife and he took up a cracker and fished a slice of pork out of the pan; my servant handed him some coffee in a tin cup and he ate in silence. He was not at all communicative and seemed to me to be worried and, I thought, a little absent-minded. However, he was then in a position of vast responsibility, in command of an expedition of supreme moment that required all his thoughts, absorbed all his attention, and, knowing that we were engaged in a hazardous and perilous enterprise, I could readily see how it would engage all of his energies.

I gave him all the information I had gathered and told him of the situation so far as I had learned, when he gave me to understand that, in view of the fact that as the river seemed to be picketed by the enemy all along the opposite bank, we would wait there until after dark and then move down through the woods and fields some miles below and try and find a crossing while, perchance, the enemy might sleep.

That night, with as little noise as possible and instructions to keep perfectly quiet, the command moved down the river bottom sometimes in fields and then in woods until a place was found where the road could be made on both banks so the pontoons could be laid, and all night long preparations were being made to cross. The 4th Kentucky dismounted and rigged up a canvas boat and crossed over in that, and immediately took position on the crest of the hill above the river and fortified it the best we could and stood guard while the pontoons were being laid and roads constructed at the approaches. When all was ready the command came over in a grand rush, our horses were brought over and we mounted, and the pontoons were taken up and sent back. It was in the afternoon before everything was in readiness to move, and the command wound itself out of the woods and into the road that led to the town of Palmetto on the West Point Railroad, some 10 or 12 miles away.

The order now was to move rapidly and stop for nothing, to make no halt for any opposition, but to charge in column on every foe found in the road before us. This order was literally carried out, and on every hill in the road was a squad of the enemy to fire on us as soon as we appeared in sight.

Just as it was getting dark we went into Palmetto like a raging storm and here the work of ruin and destruction commenced. The depot was set on fire, telegraph poles and wires torn down, bales of cotton torn to pieces and scattered to the wind and others burned. A number of freight cars loaded with commissary and quartermaster stores, consisting of flour, corn meal and bacon, salt and tobacco for the rebel army, and everything of a public nature were given up to the torch. We left it a scene of fire, of ruin and devastation.

If the conception of this expedition was bold and daring, as it was, I have no doubt the enemy thought it was insolent and offensive in execution. And it *was* insolent. Here we were now almost right under the very guns of the whole Confederate army, and in the midst of the section where their trains and stores were parked in fancied security. In the heart of the enemy's country and the ships and bridges burned behind us.

From Palmetto we took the route east along the rear of Hood's whole army for Fayetteville and the Macon Railroad, and the command tore through that country that night like the concentrated energies of the tornado, cyclone and a holocaust of fire. Everywhere along the route, and especially around Fayetteville, were the parks of tents and wagons loaded with quartermaster, commissary and ordnance stores of the enemy, General Headquarters' and paymasters' wagons, and trains, and hundreds of the finest mules and horses I ever saw. Tents, wagons and stores of all kinds, wherever found, were given up to the torch, and fire completed the work of destruction.

In fact, it was a trail of fire from Palmetto, and the whole heavens were lighted up all night by the flames from burning stores and army equipments. About 300 prisoners, quartermasters, paymasters, commissaries and others were captured and taken along.

When first disturbed in their snug and peaceful beds some of these officers were quite belligerent and swore until the air was blue, demanding in arrogant tones what intruder had abruptly molested their quiet slumbers, and occasionally one would jump up and offer fight, when a carbine stuck under his nose warned him that talk did not "go." There was no time to

■ Brig. Gen. Edward M. McCook, a first cousin to Col. Daniel McCook of the 52nd Ohio, commanded the Cavalry Corps' 1st Division. His raid below Atlanta July 27-30 began successfully, but a delay waiting for Gen. George Stoneman's cavalry division enabled Gen. Joseph Wheeler's Confederate cavalry and an infantry brigade to catch up with the Federal cavalrymen and block their escape routes to the Chattahoochee River. Nearly 1,000 men of his command were captured, though McCook himself made it to safety. Despite the losses, on August 7 he wrote in his official report: "I regard the raid as a brilliant success, and had the forces of General Stoneman been able to unite with mine ... I think we might have successfully carried our arms wherever desired, and accomplished more magnificent results than any raid in the history of this war."

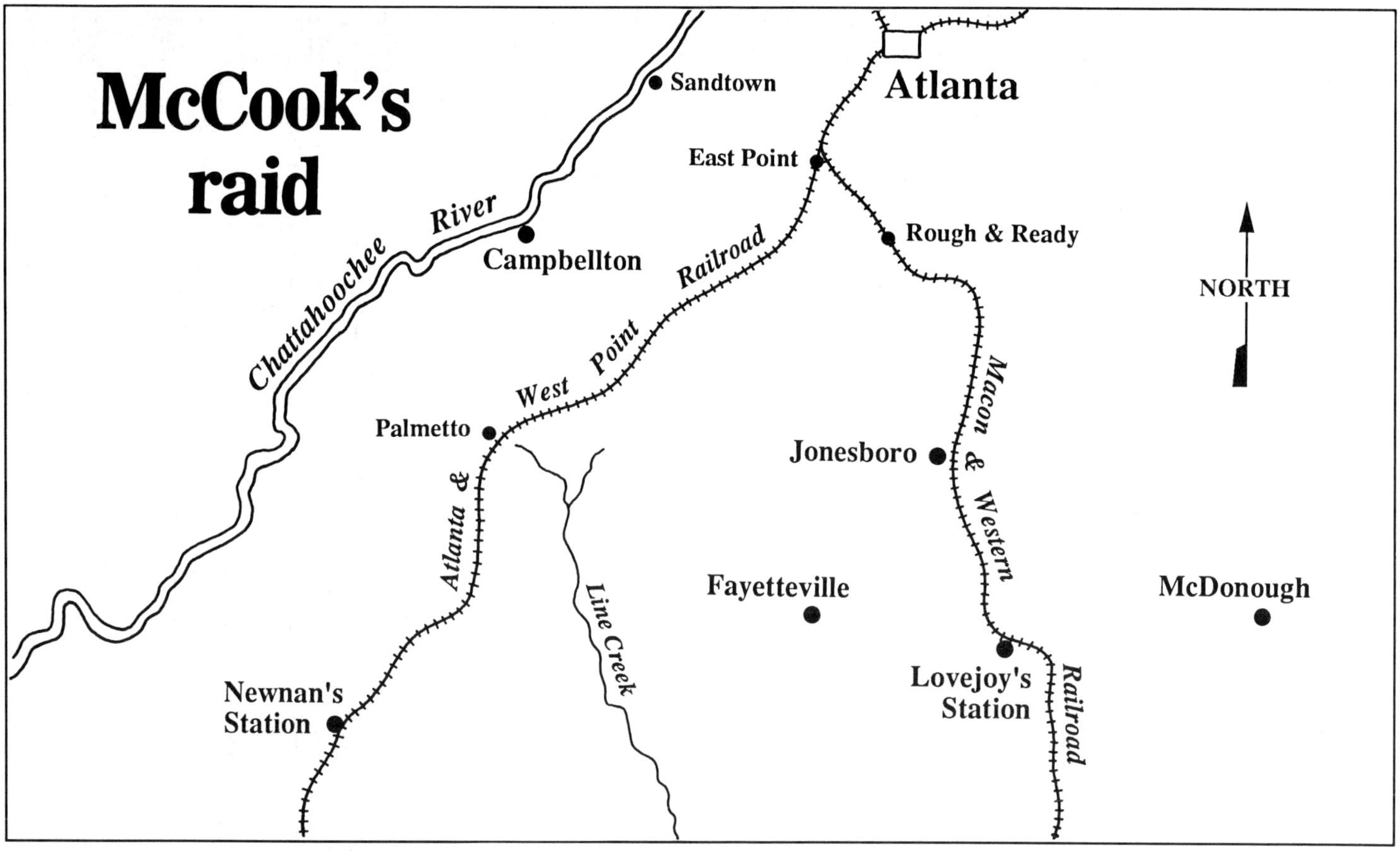

McCook's raid

Sandtown
Atlanta
East Point
Chattahoochee River
Campbellton
Rough & Ready
NORTH
West Point Railroad
Palmetto
Atlanta &
Macon & Western Railroad
Jonesboro
Fayetteville
McDonough
Line Creek
Newnan's Station
Lovejoy's Station

■ 1st Lieut. Charles V. Ray assumed command of Company H, 4th Kentucky Mounted Infantry, after the company commander, Capt. Henry P. Merrill, was captured on July 29. During sharp fighting that day, the regiment also lost 12 men wounded and four killed. Ray was listed among the latter in 1st Lieut. Granville West's official report of the raid, but he eventually made it safely to Federal lines a few days after West filed his report.

listen. But the orders were that no guns should be fired — the saber and fire were the weapons of destruction for the time being.

Paymasters' chests, safes and trunks were broken open, containing hundreds and thousands of dollars of Confederate money. Whenever a soldier saw a chance to make an advantageous trade in horses he generally did so, if he had time to make the change; otherwise he was likely to run his sword or saber into the neck or heart of the horse or mule and leave him dead or disabled, and hundreds of them were thus sabered, maimed or killed. It may be said that this was cruel. Admitted. No one denies that it was cruel. But it was war, and war is cruel.

The Macon Railroad was reached about 7 o'clock in the morning near Lovejoy Station, and two or three miles of the track torn up, ties and bridges and telegraph poles cut and burned, rails twisted and bent, and wires cut and hid away. A lot of cars containing tobacco and other stores valued at thousands of dollars were captured and burned.

At this point we expected to meet Gen. Stoneman who, as we all understood, was to meet us there, as he had started at the same time and was to come around from the left of our army. We remained there nearly all day expecting him and wasted some precious hours in waiting. Had he joined us there and thus united our forces we would have been masters of the situation. We could have whipped all of the rebel cavalry in that section and cut the railroad so the infantry could not follow, and thus have been able to roam at will from Atlanta to Andersonville, and very likely have released the suffering prisoners in that damnable den. Getting no tidings from Stoneman, along in the afternoon the command started to return on the road we came, with our brigade to bring up the rear and the 4th Kentucky as rear guard.

A mile or so from the railroad the head of the column had turned to the left off of the main road, and just as our brigade reached this point the enemy appeared in force in our front and right flank and opened fire from the road and woods to our right. We were in no position just at that moment to run and we had to fight.

The 4th Kentucky dismounted and charged the enemy in our front, and he soon learned that it was best not to be too hasty. He was driven back from our front and concentrated his attack further to the left of my position and near the point where the command in its return movement had left the main road. If he could succeed in his attack at that point it would cut our brigade off from the head of the column that was now probably three or four miles away.

My orders were to drive the enemy before me until I reached a certain position designated in my front. This order was implicitly carried out. One company of the regiment was on my right and moved forward on the same line. After we had driven the enemy to the point where we were to halt, that company was withdrawn from my right and moved in my rear to the left where the enemy had concentrated his main assault, leaving my company alone in that position. This movement separated me entirely from the rest of the command, for the topography of the ground was such that I could not see to my left. I was thus isolated from the regiment and, without further orders, was at a loss to know what to do.

The enemy in my front kept up a rapid fusillade of musketry from the woods in which he was stationed across an open field. But we were in that business also, and held the foe at bay for I had taken a position in a little ravine cut by the erosion of water in the side of the hill, and intended to maintain myself there until I got further orders or there was some change in the situation or movements of the enemy. The battle was raging fiercely to my left and rear on the road the column had moved out on, and it kind of dawned upon me that I was left there to guard the extreme rear, and if the enemy should be successful, of course I was cut off.

In all expeditions of this kind a soldier knows that an occasion may arise, at any moment, when some part of the command has to be sacrificed for the safety of the remainder. The only recompense the soldier has in an emergency of this nature, if recompense it be, is that if he is sacrificed he offers himself as a victim, and thus contributes so much to the safety of his comrades. This is one of the exigencies of a soldier's life.

At this moment the situation looked a little serious and it appeared that we were to be the first victims. I scanned the faces of my men to see the effect of the firing in the rear, and was gratified that no sign of trepidation was visible. They were veterans, and had been in serious situations before in the face of impending danger. If we were to be the first victims it was the determination to die game, and that the enemy who officiated at the sacrifice should be able to boast of a gallant deed in having vanquished a gallant foe.

But the brigade finally got itself into position and gallantly repulsed the attack and drove the enemy out of the road and the field after two or three hours' fighting, and the regiment came back for us and brought our horses which we mounted with feelings of profound relief.

It seemed strange to me that the enemy in my front did not assault my position and try to drive me out, for he was superior in numbers, and I expected every moment to see him move to the attack. But he was probably awaiting the result of the fighting on his immediate right. After they had been whipped and driven out of our front they did not seem to be inclined to renew the attack, as it was now getting toward night, although they had reached the scene of action in large force and were swarming all around us.

We marched during the night, part of the time through woods, fields and by-roads. After some hours we emerged from the woods into a road. Some

■ Maj. Gen. George Stoneman's cavalry command of 6,500 troopers was to rendezvous with McCook near Lovejoy's Station and tear up tracks of the Macon & Western Railroad. But Stoneman never showed up. A day before the raid began he had gained permission from Sherman to ride south to Macon and Andersonville in order to rescue Federal prisoners held there, but only after linking up with McCook. The idea of liberating Andersonville so intrigued Stoneman that he skipped the railroad-wrecking mission and headed for Macon with 2,500 men. He reached Macon on July 30 but was blocked by Georgia state militia and armed citizens. Turning around, Stoneman's men soon were pursued by Wheeler's cavalry, who caught up with them at Clinton on July 31. Although two of his brigades cut their way out, Stoneman and 700 troopers surrendered — and wound up prisoners in the same Macon prison stockade he intended to liberate. He was exchanged in October.

■ Capt. Joshua W. Jacobs, commander of Company A, 4th Kentucky Mounted Infantry, fought off several Confederate attacks at the road barricade early on the morning of July 30. His company was armed with Spencer carbines, while others in the 4th carried Ballard breech-loading rifles. In his report of the raid, 1st Lieut. Granville West wrote: "I do not think it would be out of place here to speak of the utter worthlessness of the Ballard rifle, used by six companies of our regiment. A great many became entirely useless during the action; some bursted from firing; others became useless by the springs which threw out the old cartridge ..." Though the Ballard saw little service during the Civil War, some 3,490 of the rifles and carbines were in use by Union Kentucky cavalry and mounted infantry units as of September 30, 1864.

distance from this point the road crossed a small stream on an old wooden bridge that I learned was known as Line Creek; the 4th Kentucky, of course, still bringing up the rear. As I rode off of this bridge I recognized the lieutenant colonel in the darkness sitting on his horse by the side of the road. He called to me and ordered me to file out of the column and halt, and when the command had all passed to report to Capt. LeRoy, Gen. McCook's adjutant-general. I should say that it was then about 10 or 11 o'clock at night.

As soon as the command had all passed over the bridge and the road was clear, and I ascertained where Capt. LeRoy was, I rode up to him and reported my orders. He says, "Yes; well, the general directs that you remain here at this bridge till daylight and destroy it and then follow on after the command."

To say that I was struck with amazement at such an order at such a time is using a very mild term. The absurdity of the order provoked me, and had not the situation been so serious its naivete would have been amusing. I replied very mildly: "Why, Captain, it might be a difficult matter for the *whole* command to hold this position until daylight."

His laconic reply that "he guessed there would be no annoyance unless it might be by some wandering guerrillas" did not impel me to discredit my own knowledge of the situation. I knew that the whole force we had been fighting in the afternoon was pursuing us, undoubtedly augmented by reinforcements, as the enemy now had time to concentrate his forces in pursuit. He knew where to find us.

I was sure that he would soon be on us and there was no time to lose. I dismounted my company immediately, sent the horses on up the road out of the way, gave the order to tear up the planks on the bridge, throw them into the river as far as we could, and to pile up loads of rails on the bridge preparatory to setting it on fire.

To this proceeding the adjutant-general interposed the suggestion that some of our men might yet be coming up and it would interfere with their crossing to tear up the bridge. There was no time to consider this objection for I was sure that there were none of our men behind who would get to that bridge that night. My information was better than his. I knew the situation and dangers and the necessity for prompt action much better than he did.

Besides, I had been assigned there to an important and responsible duty and I was the commanding officer of the post responsible for its defense, and I proposed to have my own way and follow the dictates of my own judgment in the use of all precautions to prevent disaster to my command. To protect my men was my chief concern, for I had none to lose.

Two sentinels were sent back on the road a hundred yards or so, and a guard stationed under cover to fire on an approaching enemy, and the rest of the company put to the work of ripping up the planks and throwing them into the river, and piling up loads of rails on the bridge ready to be fired, with orders to grab their guns and protect themselves if the sentinels gave alarm.

Within half an hour the sentinel challenged, "Who comes there?" and was answered, "Who are you?" The sentinel again challenged, "Who comes there?" and the response came back, "Who are you?"

The men were ordered to seek cover. I was mad I know, but not enough to make me foolish or reckless, for I had learned to be cool and calm and keep my presence of mind in the midst of danger. But I was sure the safest way was to show a bold front and I yelled to the sentinel, "Tell him it is none of his damned business who you are."

As I expected, this brought a volley of musketry, and the bullets struck in the bank where the men were at work before taking cover. A return volley from my guard drove the enemy back or silenced his fire and all was quiet for a while. As a matter of course it was to be only temporary, and the return of the enemy was expected at any moment. But in the meantime a match had been applied to the pile of rails on the bridge and preparations made to defend it if possible, till it should burn down.

The road, after crossing the bridge, turned sharply to the left under a little ridge or second bank back some two or three rods from the river bank, and, in some distance, turned to the right and cut through this little ridge, leaving high banks. Along the river bank and between that and the road was a high fence and quite a growth of timber which, with a little arrangement of the rails, afforded pretty good protection from the bullets of the enemy and behind which we took position to defend the bridge. To some extent the leaves shaded us from the light of the fire which soon began to creep up through the piles of rails.

In a few minutes a volley of musketry from the other side of the river warned us that the enemy had again appeared. A brisk fire from our rifles again drove him away and silenced his guns. It was not long to wait till they again returned and I knew by the volume of the musketry that the enemy had come in force and the fight was on.

The firing now became general on both sides and continuous. I could readily tell when reinforcements would come up by the fire coming from different points where they would take position. After a while the flames from the burning rails and bridge began to light up our position and make it too conspicuous, and I deemed it prudent to make a change. We ceased firing and led the enemy to believe we had abandoned the defense of the place. I plainly heard the orders from the officer in command to rush on the bridge and throw off the burning rails and put out the fire, and the effort to do so was promptly made.

In the meantime we quietly moved away in the shade of the trees and around the turn of the road, and took position behind the bank where the road had been cut through the little ridge spoken of before. From this point the enemy, trying to extinguish the fire and throwing off the burning rails, could be plainly seen, when a well-directed volley scattered them very rapidly from the bridge and the firing from both sides again became general and furious. This was kept up for some time.

As we were pretty well protected behind the bank I was sure we could keep the enemy away from the fire till it would very seriously damage the bridge. In the course of due time the fire increased to a great bright flame that lighted up the whole creek bottom, and the movements of the enemy could be plainly seen on the opposite shore.

I saw after a little while that he had discovered my location and was moving a force to a point lower down and on a line with my position in the road where he could, without any obstruction, enfilade my whole company with his fire. This movement made the situation very serious and the question "What was to be done?" had to be considered and determined before a volley of musketry from this force swept up the road and over every inch of ground where my company stood.

From what could be seen it is safe to say that the enemy was now fully 1,000 strong on the opposite shore, and I considered that my little band had done all that mortals could do in that situation, and, to avoid the destructive sweep of the impending volley which would surely have annihilated my company, I ceased firing, quietly withdrew, mounted my horses and started on up the road in the darkness I hardly knew where.

The Confederate historian says of this affair: "Wheeler, with a brigade, attacked the Federal rear guard in the small hours of the 30th at Line Creek, where the bridge had been destroyed. After a *stubborn fight* the enemy was dislodged from barricades commanding the passage, and the

■ Maj. Gen. Joseph Wheeler commanded the Army of Tennessee's Cavalry Corps. During the McCook raid, he was in direct command of some 500 Confederate troopers at the Line Creek bridge set ablaze by Lieut. Granville West's rearguard in the early morning hours of July 30. Wheeler called the disastrous McCook-Stoneman foray "the most stupendous cavalry operation of the war." On August 10, he struck out with 4,500 men on a long-range raid of his own to destroy Federal communications and disrupt Sherman's rail supply line. Thirty-five miles of track were ripped up near Marietta, Resaca and Dalton, the bridge burned over the Etowah River, and more than 1,500 horses, mules and cattle were captured. Then Wheeler impulsively veered northeast as far as Knoxville before turning west for Nashville. Federal troops quickly were sent after the raiders, whose depleted ranks eventually were forced into northern Alabama, and it was not until September 9 that Wheeler's survivors rejoined Hood's army.

■ Brig. Gen. Lawrence S. Ross commanded a brigade of Texas cavalry, consisting of the 3rd, 6th and 9th Texas Cavalry regiments and the 1st Texas Legion. On July 30 at Newnan Station, his dismounted brigade attacked McCook's desperate troopers, but had most of its horses captured. "The fighting occurred in thick woods," Ross wrote two days later, "the underbrush concealing the combatants until within a few paces of each other. Friends and foes were mixed up in the struggle, without regard to order or organization, and frequent hand-to-hand encounters were the consequence. Many instances of capture and recaptures occurred during the day, the victor one moment becoming a captive to his prisoner the next." After an hour's fight, Ross' men succeeded in retaking their horses. "Next morning, summing up the fruits of the victory, I found my command had captured 587 prisoners, including 2 brigade commanders, with their staffs, several field and a number of company officers, 2 stand of colors (the 8th Iowa and 2nd Indiana Regiments), 2 pieces of artillery, 11 ambulances and a large number of horses, horse equipments and small-arms."

bridge was constructed over which Wheeler passed and moved on in the intense darkness."

The road ran through a lane between open fields, up gently rising ground to woods on the crest of the hill, probably about three miles from the river, maybe more. Here I came up with the regiment, part dismounted and in line of battle with the road barricaded, and prepared to stay there till daylight as the lieutenant colonel informed me. I reported to him the situation and he directed me to move on up the road a short distance, dismount and await developments.

As I passed through the line and realized that there was a trusty rifle and a good sword between me and the foe, a huge burden seemed lifted from me. The great strain and tension relaxed. I dismounted, threw myself on the ground, put the bridle over my arm, pulled up a pile of leaves and small brush, spread my handkerchief over it for a pillow, and tired, hungry, thirsty, weary and exhausted, I was soon snugly ensconced in the arms of Somnus, blessed sleep, where I was for a few minutes oblivious to the storms of war and the carnage of battle.

This rest was of but short duration, for after a little while the enemy came on up the road, close up to the barricade, and received a murderous volley right in their faces from the company stationed at that point. From this reception they recoiled in confusion, but my rest was broken up and my sleep ended.

The enemy soon rallied his forces and again advanced to the attack and met the same kind of a murderous reception, from which he once more recoiled. Still, he soon renewed his assault in a more extended line to our right and the fighting began to move along our line in that direction. He brought up reinforcements on his left and the fight became general and continuous in a stream of fire all along our front, his line finally extending beyond our position in that direction.

An orderly now came rushing along the road to me with instructions from the lieutenant colonel to move with my command immediately to our extreme right, and he significantly added, "The colonel says drive those fellows back out of the woods."

I hurried through the darkness and woods to the point designated and met the enemy face to face. The rapid fire from our breechloaders was too galling for him and he fell back. We held the ground, but the firing was now continuous and incessant in a blaze of musketry all along the line, and the battle raged from now on in a terrific struggle till the rising dawn of the morning began to appear plainly in the east.

An orderly now came to me with orders to take part of my command and part of Company I and move immediately to our extreme left. I advised my orderly sergeant of the order and told him to do the best he could with that part of the company I left with him, for there was no other officer in my company for duty. While advising the orderly sergeant he spoke of the fact, which I was already painfully aware of, that our ammunition was nearly exhausted. It was a startling fact and too true.

We had now been 72 hours in the saddle and had expended a hundred rounds of ammunition in battle, but it was no time to hesitate or falter. With the little force I gathered from my company and some others we hurried along in the rear of our line across the road and up a little rise of ground to the crest, and here met fresh troops just coming into action. The situation was now so desperate that it justified any act of desperation. A bold, fierce and ferocious assault on this line checked them and drove them back in confusion, and we held the ground.

It was now getting pretty light, and at a glance to my left and rear still further I could see through the open woods, but a few rods away, another line of the enemy advancing at right angles with mine. In fact, the light of the morning disclosed the enemy in every direction and swarming about us, seemingly as numerous as the vandals that pillaged Rome. I hurriedly moved to the left and rear and changed front to meet this new attack, and this brought us on a line parallel with the road not very far behind us.

At this moment a fresh assault was made upon our extreme right, and I realized the terrible fact that the tide of battle in that part of the field was rolling to the rear in a furious and pitiless storm of musketry. Brave endurance could withstand the storm no longer. It was an awful, cruel scene.

In the meantime, the force in my front had come up in speaking distance. The officer in command bawled out at me, "Surrender, you damned Yankee!" At this crisis of supreme peril and desperation I was ready for any desperate deed. I felt as if I could have put a match to a powder magazine, the explosion of which would have blown the earth to atoms. Lashed into vehement and overmastering wrath and the insolence of the demand to surrender, and stung with a realizing sense of approaching ruin that I was powerless to avert, I told him to "go to hell."

At this moment it seemed to me there was one chance left, only one. I knew the force and momentum of a charge of cavalry in column, and I resolved to take the risk to cut my way out or perish, as it was my fixed determination not to submit or surrender while my horse stood up under me and I was able to sit in my saddle.

With me, then and there, were about 70 or 80 men, every one a gallant hero. If they could only feel the impulse to move at the same instant I felt that some of us could go through. This little band of heroes, in the awful confusion, had drifted toward me as if looking and waiting for the final order. The moment was ripe for a final effort. I raised my sword and pointed in the direction of the way to go — for an order could not be heard in the strife — and put the spurs to my horse. It was a reckless move, but the effect was instantaneous. A convulsive tremor, a rush, a crash as of a thunderbolt, and, in defiance of a chorus of demands to surrender, we were out and away and gone.

From near midnight till the rising sun looked upon a pitiful scene of slaughter, the regiment had battled single-handed and alone against the overwhelming odds of a whole division of the enemy's cavalry, repulsed assault after assault, and when the morning came we held the ground, not having yielded or been driven one inch. Until the last moment every soldier faced the foe and succumbed only to sheer brute force when finally borne down and engulfed by an increasing and incoming wave of overwhelming numbers.

Four hundred soldiers were missing, some of them lay stretched unconscious upon the field of battle, some ended a miserable existence in prison, and some of them, poor fellows, have not been accounted for to this hour. Six of my company formed one mess in Andersonville prison, one of whom had saved a five-dollar bill from search of the enemy. He gave this money to the rebel guard to count out all the members of the mess in an exchange of prisoners.

Those of us who cut our way out that morning followed rapidly after the command and overtook them near Newman Station on the West Point Railroad some 10 miles further on. Here it was discovered that infantry had been brought on the cars to intercept our progress and we had now to consider this new force.

Company G of the 4th Kentucky had not been engaged in the battle that morning, having been detailed to guard the horses of the dismounted men, and this company formed a splendid nucleus around which to rally the rest

■ 1st Lieut. Alf Davis, adjutant of the 27th Texas Cavalry, was among the troopers of Ross' brigade fighting McCook's cavalry on July 30 at Newnan Station. The 27th Texas, also known as the 1st Texas Legion, was commanded by Col. Edwin R. Hawkins during the McCook and Kilpatrick raids. In this photograph taken in June 1861, Davis wears an ornately decorated shirt, a Texas star pinned to his felt hat, revolver and a drinking cup and small mess tin attached to his waistbelt. Davis served as a section commander of two guns in the Good-Douglas (Texas) Battery, before transferring to the cavalry in April 1862.

■ Col. Robert Morrow Kelly, commander of the 4th Kentucky Mounted Infantry, was captured along with nearly half the regiment on July 30 near Newnan Station. His troopers, forming the rearguard of McCook's embattled division, repulsed five charges by Brig. Gen. William Y.C. Humes' Confederate cavalry division before they were overpowered and captured. He was exchanged later in 1864 and rejoined the 4th at Pulaski, Tenn. A native of Paris, Ky., Kelly was a boyhood friend and schoolmate of his commanding officer, Col. John Croxton.

of the regiment. Capt. James H. West of that company took command of the regiment, reorganized it in very good order, divided his ammunition among those who had none, and what was left of the regiment stood ready for further duty. It was not long till this additional duty was imposed.

Soon after we came up with the command it turned off to the right of the road through the fields in the direction of the Chattahoochee River, for there was no possible rest for the command now till it could cross that river. We had not gone far in that direction till the enemy again appeared in force in our front and right flank.

The whole brigade was dismounted and moved forward, the 4th Kentucky between the 1st Tennessee and the 8th Iowa Cavalry. We soon engaged the enemy and once more drove him from the field when we again mounted and moved on. But soon after this the whole command came to a halt in the open plain and remained there nearly all afternoon and till it was almost night.

Why Gen. McCook halted there and why he remained there I did not know, could not tell and do not know to this hour. True, the command was surrounded by the enemy, infantry and cavalry in large force, and who could be plainly seen off in the fields and on all the little knolls and elevations around us. He was in force in the woods nearby, to which position he tenaciously held and from which he did not emerge in force. We were skirmishing all afternoon, but the enemy did not seem inclined to attack in force and bring on a general engagement, and he did not. I surmised he was waiting for further reinforcements and every moment made our situation more precarious.

Here our artillery was first brought into use and shells were thrown into the woods at their skirmishers whenever they appeared in reach, till the ammunition was nearly exhausted. At one point their skirmishers ventured too near our brigade and the 4th Kentucky, still game and on the fight, was ordered to charge them, which it did in handsome style, drove them back and captured their horses, but a line of infantry confronted us at that moment and prevented the regiment from bringing away the captured horses. In that charge our last shot was expended, and this left us in that condition which is liable to produce a feeling of helplessness in a soldier.

Why Gen. McCook did not concentrate his forces in an assault on a given point and cut his way out sooner I do not know. I thought then it could be done. Our brigade had done that very thing the evening before after a three-hour fight. We whipped the same enemy virtually and drove him out of the road from before us, mounted our horses and moved away.

It was now once more getting to be nearly night and, of course, the enemy was gathering strength and reinforcements every hour, for the infantry was coming in force on the railroad not far away, and something must be speedily done or all would be lost. The brigade and regimental commanders now appealed to Gen. McCook to allow each one to take care of his own command. He consented and there was instantly a lively scene and movement on that field. Nearly every command came out from there in different directions and without any real, serious difficulty. I thought then, and still think, that in a resolute and determined assault on one point the whole command could have cut its way out at any time during the afternoon.

In the confusion of getting out I got separated with my command from the rest of the regiment and joined Gen. McCook in his movements, and we reached the Chattahoochee some time in the night where we found an old ferry boat and by morning the command was about all over. Then the desire of all was to make straight for camp.

We reached the lines of our army on the 3rd day of August as completely exhausted as men and horses could well be, and still be able to move. Eight days and nights we had been in the saddle without a single hour of rest, free from apprehension and without a single "square meal." We went into camp where the railroad bridge crosses the Chattahoochee north of Atlanta, and I found myself the senior officer present in the regiment and assumed command.

Gen. McCook's adjutant-general came to me and said the general wanted a report from the 4th Kentucky. I told him I did not like to attempt to make a report of the part the regiment had taken in the raid for, being a subordinate, I had heard or received no division or brigade order in person, and I did not consider that I was in possession of sufficient data to do the regiment justice for the gallant part it had borne in the expedition.

He went away, but soon returned and said the general wanted to make his report and that he and the general had spoken of the 4th Kentucky together; that it had done gallant service and that he had himself told the general that I had gallantly defended the bridge that night and acted with the best of judgment, and the general wanted to do justice to the 4th Kentucky in his report.

I hurriedly made the best report I could under the then existing circumstances, but for the want of time and official information I could not and did not do the regiment full justice. But still I think it was a very good report.

After all this, in Gen. McCook's official account of the expedition, he lauds to the skies some of the officers whose regiments did not expend 20 rounds of ammunition on the whole raid, while the 4th Kentucky, which stood between him and the foe for 20 dreadful hours and expended a hundred rounds in actual fighting, is wholly ignored. Another evidence of the fact that for official and complimentary notices a friend at court beats gallantry and bravery upon the field of battle.

■ 1st Lieut. Will F. Hoch, Company G, 4th Kentucky Mounted Infantry. Hoch, Lieuts. Granville West and James McDermott, and about 30 troopers accompanied Gen. McCook when they arrived exhausted in Marietta on August 3 — the largest single body of soldiers left in the 4th Kentucky at the raid's conclusion. Three months later, after promotion to captain and command of Company F, Hoch was severely wounded at Shoal Creek, Ala.

'How we fight at Atlanta'

1st Lieut. Henry O. Dwight
Adjutant
20th Ohio Veteran Volunteer Infantry

Here in the trenches before Atlanta, on this 15th day of August, I propose to give you some idea of the actual manner in which we fight. With us the pomp and show of war has become a matter of poetry rather than of fact. We need no gay dress or nodding plumes to inspire a soldier's pride. Practical utility is what we look at in matters of dress and equipment. Look at most of the pictures. Two-thirds of the pictures in books and papers represent the soldiers with enormous knapsacks neatly packed; officers leading the charge in full dress uniform with their sabers waving in the most approved style. Now this makes a pretty picture, but let me tell you that soldiers don't put on their well-packed knapsacks to double-quick over a half mile of open ground in the hot sun at the *pas du charge*. Limited transportation soon exhausts an officer's stock of white collars. The most elegant dress uniform will become torn and spotted, and the brightly polished boots will become soiled with mud when one is reduced to marching in line of battle through swamps, thickets and briar patches, and then sleeping night after night on the bare ground with only heaven's clouds for an overcoat.

Know ye then, ladies all, yonder pretty-looking officer, with his spotless dress resplendent with gold lace, will present a very different spectacle after a few months of campaigning. Dusty, ragged and unshaven, his appearance is far more in accordance with his surroundings, far more becoming the earnest fighting man that you really suppose he is than if he

■ Lt. Col. John C. Fry commanded the 20th Ohio until he was severely wounded on July 22 during the desperate fighting for Leggett's Hill. In this unusual portrait, Fry's disheveled appearance underscores the rough side of campaigning that even field grade officers endured. The original photograph is part of 1st Lieut. Henry O. Dwight's wartime scrapbook, and is captioned "In front of Atlanta."

were arrayed as you formerly saw him, or as the pictures represent him to be.

Of course, in a war like this upon which we all entered with the art yet to learn, the science has been progressive. Each succeeding year has developed new phases, and under such schooling our soldiers are indeed veterans; men whom practice has perfected in all the mysteries of military life. Each soldier knows that where he used to lie upon his arms all the time, in the face of the enemy, only seeking cover from the shape of the ground, he must now make a strong fortification to enable him to hold his position, and must arrange it to stop pieces of shell from the flank as well as bullets from the front. Had the army been as experienced at Shiloh as it is now, Beauregard would have come up and broken his army to pieces on our fortifications, instead of finding our whole army lying exposed to his attacks on the open field. At Fort Donelson, too, where we had to attack fortifications, we ourselves had no sign of a work upon which we could fall back after each day's repulse; nor did the enemy seem to realize the value of his own works, for instead of quietly waiting the attack he threw away his army by fighting outside his works.

It is now a principle with us to fight with moveable breastworks, to save every man by giving him cover from which he may resist the tremendous attacks in mass of the enemy. Thus, at least, we fight in Georgia in the Atlanta campaign.

Wherever the army moves, either in gaining the enemy's works or in taking up a new line of attack, the first duty after the halt is to create defensive fortifications — rude, indeed, but effective in enabling us to hold our ground against any force. In forming these field-works every man is to some extent his own engineer. The location of the line is selected by the officers, and each regiment fortifies its own front, each company its own ground.

Generally the situation will not allow finishing the works at once, for the enemy will probably attack soon after you take position, which is on a commanding hill or some similar point. So you cause a hasty barricade to be constructed. The front rank takes all the guns and remains on the line while the rear rank goes off in double-quick to collect rails, logs, rocks or anything that can assist in turning a hostile bullet. These they place on the front of the front rank, and in five minutes there is a hasty barricade, bullet-proof and breast-high, along your whole line; not a mere straight work but one varied with its salients and re-entering angles, taking every advantage of the ground and crossfiring on every hollow. You can do this after the enemy forms to charge you while he is feeling you with artillery. Thus, it takes just five minutes to prepare for an assault; and you can hold your line against an attack by three times your number — and that, too, with but slight loss to yourself — if your men be veteran soldiers.

It may be that when your barricade is done you yet have time. Shovels and picks are always carried by your men, and to work they go to complete the frail works. A ditch is speedily made on the inside to stand in. The earth is thrown on the outside of the barricade and the ditch is deepened so that, standing inside, your head will be protected by the parapet. Thus, you speedily have a pretty substantial earthwork with a step inside to stand on when firing, and a ditch to stand in while loading. If you are in the woods, you want to give range to your rifles and have all the thick undergrowth and small trees cut away for 50 paces in front. By felling these all the same way, the bushy tops all turning outward, and trimming off the smaller twigs and leaves, and tangling the tops together, you have a formidable abatis, through which it shall be next to impossible for a line to advance, let alone against the showers of bullets from your men at short range. This done, you

A last letter home

■ 2nd Lieut. William Zay of Company D, 99th Ohio, was wounded during skirmish duty at Utoy Creek, the same day Private Barnhart was killed.

Near Atlanta Georgia
July the 28th / 64

Dear Cousin

It is with pleasure that I take my pen in hand to let you know that I am well at present hoping these poor lines may find you all the same. I received your welcome letter a few days ago and was glad to here from you. it found me behind the breastworks in front of atlanta one mile and a half from the city. the day i received it we had a hard fight on the left of the army. the rebs mast there force on us and made a charge. they came on us with 7 lines and we only had two. but we had works. we fought them as long as we could. they rushed on our works and we had to fall back or be taken prisoners. there force was so much larger than ours that they got in our rear but we soon got reinforcements from the center and drove the hares back. we lost a large number of prisoners in the first charge and also 6 pieces of artilery. but when we charged on them and drove them back we got all of the prisoners back and artilery too. then we took eleven hundred prisoners. our loss killed and wounded was near fifteen hundred. the reb prisoners that we took since then say there loss was over two thousand. there was not many hurt in our regiment. after the fight I went over the battle ground. I could walk over three acres and tramp on nuthing but dead rebs. it was a hard looken site. some with there heads shot off, some with legs and arms off. that was done with our artilery. in front of one of our batteries there was sixteen laying on one pile that was killed with greap and canister. in that charge we lost one of our best generals. he was killed dead on the field. his name was Major General McFerson. after he was shot the rebs got his boddy but when we charged the rebs we got it back again. they took his gold wach and other things.

On the 26th there was hard fighting on the extreme rite by general Howard and the enemy the rebs charged on our men three times and got drove back every time with a heavy loss. the most of our men that was engaged had these sixteen shooters and they just mowed the rebs down. the rebs loss was very heavy and our loss was not so lite. after the fight was over there was a flag of truce sent in to exchange dead. each side was to have one hour. our men got all of our dead off in the first hour but the rebs did not and our men gave them another hour but did not get them all then. but the third hour they got all off. So there loss was supposed to be three to our one. our cavalry went out the other day on the left and got in the rear of the rebs. they captured one thousand head of horses and mules, two trains of cars that was loaded with reb clothing and rations. they burnt both trains captured one hundred and fifty head of beef cattle and tore up 20 miles of railroad and got four hundred prisoners.

We are one mile and a half from atlanta. we can see the town quite plain. we have bin shelling the town for four or five days. our shells has set five big buildings afire in town. the rebs has not got a great many big guns here. there has bin two one hundred pound shells thrown over but did not burst. we have some sixty fore pounders here now. on the 27th there was a regular artilery duel for one hour. it made us hug our works close. Shells bursting all around.

July the 31st —— Nuthing special since the 28th only yesterday there was hard fighting on the rite of us one mile. I don't care whether the rebs come up in front of us any more or not. I have done all the fighting I want to do in this campaign but I am willing to do some more hard fighting to get the city of atlanta. I think we will have it in a weak's time. as it is dinner time I must close so no more. Right soon Libby.

From David A. Barnhart
Co. G 99th OVI
4th Brigade 2nd Division 23 A.C.

Four days later, on August 4, Barnhart was shot and killed near Utoy Creek and buried in Marietta, Ga. He was 23 years old.

A close call

■ Major Horace Park, 43rd Ohio. Early in the Atlanta siege the regiment had no tents and it was common practice for the officers to improvise quarters using their tent flies. Park had just arranged his and laid down to rest using his saddle as a pillow when an artillery duel broke out. Lt. Col. Walter F. Herrick of the 43rd was standing 30 feet away as a Confederate shell exploded near Park's bed, and he was certain the major had been killed. Miraculously, Park emerged unscathed from the brush behind his tattered tent fly as the smoke cleared, and remarked to Herrick, "By God, they make a man move here whether he pays his rent or not." In this studio photograph taken in Louisville, Ky., Park wears an unusual pattern hooded cape with drawstring.

■ 1st Lieut. William H. Kimball, Company D, 47th Ohio. On August 4 he returned to the regiment after one month's sick leave, but was advised to return the following day when his leave officially expired. He answered that his fellow officers were nearly all exhausted, and he felt it was his duty to relieve them at once. Accordingly, Kimball was detached with 40 men of the regiment as advanced skirmishers. Less than two hours later he was shot through the right knee, fracturing the joint. His leg was amputated the following day.

can be making any amount of additions to your work as you have time, all tending to make it impregnable.

Even after you have pronounced the job finished your men will fuss and dig and tinker about the works to make them sure protection. They have no notion of taking a position and then having it taken away from them by a sudden assault. They will cut huge logs 18 inches through and place them on the parapet to protect the head while they shoot through a space left between the log and the parapet. They also have an ingenious plan for preventing these "headlogs" from being an injury to the service. Experience has taught them that a cannonball will sometimes strike one of these huge logs and throw it off the parapet onto the troops inside. As a preventative, skids or stout poles are placed at equal distances along the rifle pits, extending from the parapet across the ditch. The logs being knocked off the top of the breastwork are supposed to roll along these skids over the heads of the soldiers in the ditch until they lodge safely on the bank beyond.

The men will also amuse themselves with devising some new entanglement or snare to annoy the advance of the enemy. They drive palisades — stakes set in the ground with their sharpened points directed outward at an angle of 45 degrees, and so close together that a man cannot pass between them. In front of the palisades they place a strong wire so arranged that it cannot be seen but will trip all comers. They will then imagine how astounded the rebels will be in charging the works when they are suddenly tripped up and fall forward on the sharp palisades.

Your main works being completed, you can rest secure, only putting in an embrasure for a howitzer or two here or there. These howitzers are a fine thing to repel an attack, for they throw nearly a bucketful of small balls at a charge. Your skirmish line, in the meantime, has fortified itself sufficiently for protection and can hold an attacking column long enough for you to form line in the main works before the enemy can get there.

One reads in the papers of the assaults on earthworks, of the repulses, and yet one does not know what is contained in those words — "Assault repulsed." You make up your mind to assault the enemy's works. You have formed line of battle, with a second and third line behind you for support.

You march forth filled with the determination to accomplish the object, yet feeling the magnitude of the undertaking. Two hundred yards brings you to the picket line and here the opposition commences. You dash across the space between the two lines, you lose a few men. The enemy's pickets, after making as much noise as possible, run back to their main works. By this time the enemy is sure you are really coming and opens on you with artillery besides a pretty heavy fire of musketry. This artillery throws the shell screaming through your ranks, producing more moral than physical effect, or throws shrapnel which, bursting in front, scatters myriads of small bullets around. You commence to lose men rapidly. The ball is opened. "Forward, double-quick!" again; and while the whole line of the enemy opens fire from behind their works, your men, mindless of this — mindless of the death intensified, the bullets and the shells — they dash on with wild cheers. The abatis with its tangled intricacy of sharpened branches snares your line. Tripping, falling, rising to fall again, the men struggle through. You get through the abatis, though the minutes are drawn out interminably, and with each step are left brave men to pay for the ground. The firing grows more fierce, the men grow more desperate. Your three lines have been almost reduced to one, and you strike another line of abatis. In this obstruction are the palisades which must be uprooted by force before a man can pass. You stumble, fall, tear your flesh on these stakes, and must stop to pull them up — stop, when every instant is an hour — stop, when you are already gasping for breath; and here open up the masked batteries, pouring canister into that writhing, struggling, bleeding mass — so close that the flame scorches, that the smoke blinds from the guns. Is it any wonder that your three lines are torn to pieces and have to give way before the redoubled fire of an enemy as yet uninjured comparatively? And then the slaughter of a retreat! Oftentimes it is preferable to lie down and take the fire until night rather than lose all by falling back under such circumstances.

This war has demonstrated that earthworks can be rendered nearly impregnable on either side against direct assault. An attack on fortified lines must cost a fearful price and should be well weighed whether the cost exceed the gain. This, then, is what an assault means — a slaughter pen, a charnel house, and an army of weeping mothers and sisters at home. It is inevitable. When an assault is successful it is to be hoped that the public gain may warrant the loss of life requisite. When it is repulsed, tenfold is the mourning.

It was a long time before the men could appreciate the value of these fieldworks. They would grumble and growl, recalling instances without number where the most charming little traps, the most elegant cross-fires, had been prepared with great labor and had never been attacked. I saw some men most beautifully satisfied as to the necessity for defensive works the other day.

On the 22nd of July, before Atlanta, while these men were engaged in grumbling over some newly-finished works which the enemy would not charge, Hardee struck the XVII Corps in flank and rear. His furious onset crushed the flank and the 2nd Brigade of the 3rd Division, to which these grumblers belonged, found themselves suddenly forming the unprotected left of the corps and attacked from the rear in those very works they grumbled so about building. When this attack was made they jumped the works to the front, or outside, and fought that way. This attack repulsed, they jumped back and repulsed an attack from the outside, or real front. Thus they fought, looking for all the world like a long line of these toy monkeys you see which jump over the end of a stick.

Thus they fought for four long hours, cut off from all commanders, corps, division and brigade, cut off from the ammunition trains, and only cheered

■ 1st Lieut. Henry O. Dwight, adjutant of the 20th Ohio, coined a phrase describing the construction of field works during the campaign — "Every man ... his own engineer." Dwight's former regimental commander, Col. Manning F. Force (later promoted to major general), described this concept at a regimental reunion in 1876: "When we were swinging around Atlanta one day, skirmishing the while, the line halted along a rising ground. The men began at once with bayonets, tin cups and sticks to throw up a line of works in their front. Staff officers dashed along to stop them till the engineer [officer] could trace a line. But the engineer, on examination, found no change or improvement to suggest." In a more humorous vein, Private Chauncey Cooke of Company G, 25th Wisconsin, wrote: "The boys make a joke of digging, by saying there is silver in Georgia and they are mining for it."

■ Brig. Gen. Arthur M. Manigault commanded a brigade, consisting of the 10th and 19th South Carolina, and 24th, 28th and 34th Alabama regiments, during the campaign. Of the Confederate defeat at Ezra Church on July 28, Manigault later wrote: "It was one of the many miserable exhibitions of generalship, this whole affair, which was characteristic of the officers of the Army of Tennessee, and one of the numerous instances of which I was a witness and a sufferer."

by the noble example of Gen. Giles A. Smith whose command, broken by the first onset — all except one brigade — had rallied behind the works of the 3rd Division. Firing to front and rear and to either flank, they held their works, only changing front by jumping over the parapet as five assaults were made upon them, successively from front, rear, or flank, until the rebels were checked long enough to make sure the safety of the immense wagon trains already saved by the XVI Corps.

The next works of these men I saw was cause for me to laugh. Experience had taught the utility of fortifications, and they fortified not only the front but facing the rear and every way so that they could hold out if surrounded. They were not going to be caught without ammunition either, for each company had its little powder magazine in a safe place, well stored with ammunition gathered from the battlefield. No grumbling was heard about building the works. All the spare time of the men was devoted to finishing up their pet works, some of them standing off to the side and regarding the effect of each addition with something of the same paternal feeling that an artist exhibits in regarding the power of each master-stroke in finishing his picture.

We hear a great deal about hand-to-hand fighting. Gallant though it would be, and extremely pleasant to the sensation newspapers to have it to record, yet, unfortunately for gatherers of items, it is of very rare occurrence. This year's campaigns have probably seen more of it than any other of the war. When men can kill one another at 600 yards they generally would prefer to do it at that distance than to come down to two paces. Still, as each army grows wiser in military matters, the fighting must naturally become closer and more desperate, and those who have the firmest endurance, the greatest self-control, must win.

This war is not one between mere military machines as soldiers are in Europe, but of rational, thinking beings, fighting with the highest of motives on our side, and with the belief that theirs is the highest of motives on the part of the enemy. When such men are thrown in deadly personal contact with each other the strife is deadly indeed.

On the 22nd of July, in that part of the battle to which I have already alluded, it chanced that I saw hand-to-hand fighting in that same 2nd Brigade aforementioned. A man was actually well-nigh dismembered, the rebels pulling his feet to take him prisoner, and our boys pulling his head to save him. Men were bayoneted, knocked down with the butts of muskets and even fists were used in default of better weapons in that deadly strife. Officers used their dress swords, which they had hitherto considered as mere playthings for the parade, to hack down a troublesome enemy. A rebel colonel, who had laid hold of the colors of the 20th Ohio Regiment, was bayoneted by the color-guard, who at the same instant saved the colors of the 78th Ohio, their bearer, shot through the heart, having dropped the precious flag among the enemy. Men begged for more cartridges as they would for bread and made every one count, as the horrible sight in the ditch testified the next morning.

'A constant state of tension'

Brig. Gen. Arthur Middleton Manigault
Anderson's Division, Lee's Corps CSA

For several days after the battle of [July] 28th, we were shifted about from one position to another, hard at work all the time on entrenchments. On the fourth day, we became settled in a position which we retained during the remainder of the siege of Atlanta. It was about three or four miles from

Atlanta, in a direction S.W., the Lickskillet Road being about a mile on our right, the (Sandtown) road half a mile to our left. Ours was the left brigade of the division, having on our left a Georgia brigade belonging to Clayton's Division, and a very mean one it was. The space for which we were responsible extended a distance of about 450 yards, the line running across a high bald hill, the two flanks reaching to some low ground on each side of it. The parapet and a redoubt for a battery of three guns ran along the outward slope toward the enemy, about 100 yards from the highest part of the hill, the ground rocky and covered with loose stones and broken rock. In front of us for about 200 yards the country was open and generally meadow land. Beyond this it was open, and another hill not quite as high as the one we were on, fronted us. I am somewhat particular in my description, not that it is of much consequence, but because every feature and nook of that location is indelibly fixed in my mind, and I there spent four weeks, the most anxious, exhausting and perilous of any like period during the whole course of my experience as a soldier.

The fighting on the picket line was incessant, and the ammunition daily expended by our detail, consisting of about 175 rifles, for a long time averaged rather more than 6,000 rounds of ammunition daily, or about 35 rounds per man. At times the contest would be desperate, and the enemy frequently repulsed, and I have more than once seen a line of battle in addition to the pickets on duty, driven back and utterly unable to advance. On both sides the shooting was very accurate, the men frequently dropping their (shots) between the lower part of the headlog and the parapet. The slightest carelessness or imprudent exposure of one's person was sure to result in death or a severe wound. This sort of duty coming round as it did nearly every fourth day was particularly trying to the men, as for 24 hours no sleep was to be had. The mind was in a constant state of tension as well as the body, it being necessary to be ready at any moment to repel an attack, and no one knew when to expect it. It must be remembered also that in our main works we were almost as much exposed, the bullets from the sharpshooters and continued fire from the artillery forcing the men to take shelter under the works or in the ditch all day; and even at night the danger was only a little less, excepting for an hour or two immediately after dark, when there was generally a complete cessation.

Our daily loss varied from five men to 55, the two extremes, and would average, I suppose, about 10 or 11. As a general thing more casualties occurred in the main line of works than on the picket line, which can be easily explained from the fact that in the former, owing to the greater distance of the danger, the men would become careless of exposure, and move about as though there was no danger, in spite of the strictest orders to the contrary. An unfortunate cannon ball, or a few well-directed rifle shots, or perhaps accidental ones, would make them keep close for some time, until its effect had worn off, when again they were as indifferent as ever.

With the latter (those on picket) each soldier was on the *qui vive.* He knew full well what would be the consequence of the slightest imprudence on his part, and was constantly being reminded of the danger in which he stood. To judge from the continued firing, the deadliest hate existed between the two opposing lines, yet they would frequently call to each other, asking and answering questions, and from daily contact with each other they knew the names of the different brigades, regiments, and sometimes individuals to whom attention had been called by some cause or other, each organization bearing a different reputation. Thus our men would frequently announce the fact during the night that the following would be a hard day, because such a regiment from Indiana, or some other state, was opposed to them. At another time they would congratulate themselves on the event of some

■ Lt. Gen. Stephen Dill Lee commanded Hood's old corps from July 27 through the end of the campaign. Lee placed much of the blame for the failure of Confederate assaults at Ezra Church and Jonesboro on the men in the ranks. "If all the troops had displayed equal spirit we would have been successful," was his summation of Ezra Church. And of the results of August 31 at Jonesboro, he wrote: "The attack was not made by the troops with that spirit and inflexible determination that would insure success. Several brigades behaved with great gallantry ... but generally the troops halted in the charge when they were much exposed and within easy range of the enemy's musketry, instead of moving directly and promptly forward against the temporary and informidable works in their front. The attack was a feeble one and a failure ..."

■ Maj. Gen. James Patton Anderson commanded Hindman's old division of S.D. Lee's corps from July 30 until August 31, when he was severely wounded at Jonesboro. Of the siege of Atlanta he later wrote: "Instances of persevering skill and courage were manifested daily upon portions of our line along Deas', Brantly's, Sharp's and Manigault's front. In one instance Brantly's men, by rolling logs ahead of them and by digging zigzag trenches, approached so near the enemy's rifle pits as to be able to throw hand-grenades over his breastworks. Our scouts, whenever the darkness of the night favored such operations, penetrated the enemy's picket line and kept us well advised of all his important movements."

other regiment being on duty, as they were known to be averse to carrying on matters in too deadly a spirit.

When the ordinary skirmish firing was going on, and a man on either side happened to be killed or wounded in one of the rifle pits, his comrades would call out, "Cease firing on this pit!" and would stick up his ramrod on the front of the embankment with a piece of white cloth or sheet of paper on the upper end of it. That pit would remain unmolested until the litter bearers made their appearance and carried off the soldier, although during the time, the rest of the lines would go at it just as ever. The wounded man removed and out of range, the ramrod with its indicator would be removed, and hostilities would recommence. How this understanding was arrived at, no one could ever tell me, and how far it extended throughout the armies I do not know; but it was a very common occurrence along our division front, and was very honorable and creditable to both parties. I know that many a man's life was saved by it. It was only during this period, and on this line, that I ever knew this humane arrangement to exist, and it ought to be a matter of great regret that it is not universal.

For the first 10 days of this period I occupied with the staff officers a central position in the breastworks, spending the entire time, night and day, in the ditch of the entrenchment, only leaving it to go along the line, keeping under cover, or to attend to such duties as were necessary; and when exposure could not be avoided, the risk was at all times great, and during the day, even a single individual showing himself for a minute or two would be sure to draw fire on him, either of artillery, or from the sharpshooters.

I estimated that during those 10 days at least 1,500 shot and shell struck or exploded within 20 paces of where we lay. No shot ever fell immediately in our section of the work, although the traverses separating us from the other sections, and not more than 15 paces apart, received several balls, and men were killed on either side of us. The embankment was frequently struck, the balls either grazing the works, or burying themselves in the bank and exploding, in either instance covering us with dust and dirt, producing a sensation not very pleasant. Many fragments of rock, splinters and a few fragments of shells fell in our section, but resulting in no serious injury to anyone.

On one occasion, Lieut. Gen. Lee, making a tour of the lines occupied by his corps, on reaching my brigade, sent for me to accompany him along our front. He was attended by an aide, also by Maj. Gen. Anderson, who had been sent back to the Army of Tennessee, and had been assigned to the command of our division. After inspecting the works and preparations made for defense, it being his first visit, he expressed a desire to get in some position where he could more distinctly see the enemy's works, and proposed going a little back from the works to where the hill was higher, and a good view could be obtained. The spot he pointed out was a very open and exposed one, and where, if a man showed himself for a moment, not only several rifle balls would be sent at him, but he got off well if a shot or two from a rifled cannon did no more than cover him with dust, or explode within a few feet of him.

Being perfectly familiar with the danger myself, and knowing his ignorance of the same, and regarding myself as being somewhat responsible for his safety under the circumstances, I mentioned the danger we would incur, and suggested a point on the edge of the wood in our rear, which offered the same advantages and where we were not so apt to be seen or attract attention.

My suggestion was declined, rather brusquely, and off we started. We soon reached the spot, Gens. Lee and Anderson using their glasses to observe with greater accuracy the enemy's position. I, knowing full well what to expect, did not view the scene with much complacency, expecting every moment that one or more of us would be struck down.

Several rifle balls hummed ominously by us, and we had not been stationary more than 15 seconds, when a severe concussion in our midst, accompanied by a cloud of dust and smoke, and the smart in several parts of the body of each of us from small fragments of rock or loose pebbles, gave notice that a shell had burst amongst us. The report of the gun, the bursting of the shell and the horrid screech which accompanied it, were simultaneous. Fortunately, we had separated from each other a few feet. I turned to see who had fallen, but all were standing. The aide was rubbing his leg where a stone had struck him. Gen. Anderson was picking up his hat, and Gen. Lee brushing from his face and neck the sand and dirt with which he had been deluged.

The shell, a percussion one, had struck and exploded within six or eight feet of us. As no one had been hurt, I was not much put out by the occurrence, and rather pleased than otherwise to notice the disconcerted countenances of my companions who had rejected my counsel. I was determined to say nothing more, however, on the subject. The first shell was speedily followed by several more, fortunately not so well directed. The place was getting disagreeably hot and uncomfortable. The enemy seemed bent upon hurting somebody, and would certainly have done so in a very short time had not Gen. Lee turned to me and remarked that it would have been better had my advice been taken, and proposed that we should seek some temporary shelter. Nothing loath to do so, I pointed out a position occupied by the infirmary corps of one of the regiments about 20 yards off, and into it we slid not very ceremoniously. The enemy had very likely recognized the party as consisting of officers of rank, and before we reached the excavation three batteries were firing away at us, and continued pounding away at our miserable little place of refuge for a full 15 minutes, much to our annoyance and that of the infirmary men, who evidently did not regard us as welcome visitors.

At the end of that time the firing slackened, and we drew out one by one, Gens. Lee and Anderson soon after taking their departure, and so ended the observations of the enemy's position for that day. On the next visit we looked at them from the edge of the wood.

'I sat down and cried like a child'

Capt. Henry Clay Weaver
Company D
16th Kentucky Veteran Volunteer Infantry

South West of Atlanta, Georgia, August 14th 1864

My Darling Nelie:

When I wrote to you last we were on the right of the army at Kennesaw Mountain ... After leaving Kennesaw Mountain we moved to the left and thus advanced on Atlanta. After heavy and desperate fighting day after day we succeeded in gaining a position in full view of the City — after strongly fortifying this we were again moved here to the extreme right of the army.

In front of Atlanta Company D had four of her bravest & best men wounded. This was on the 21st of July. No other calamities befell our noble company until Aug. 6th. Three months ago today we were plunged into the flood of battle at Resaca, and heavily was that day borne on the memory of our company. Having seen nothing since to equal that until the 6th of August, just one week ago on Sunday, when we again confronted a strong & desper-

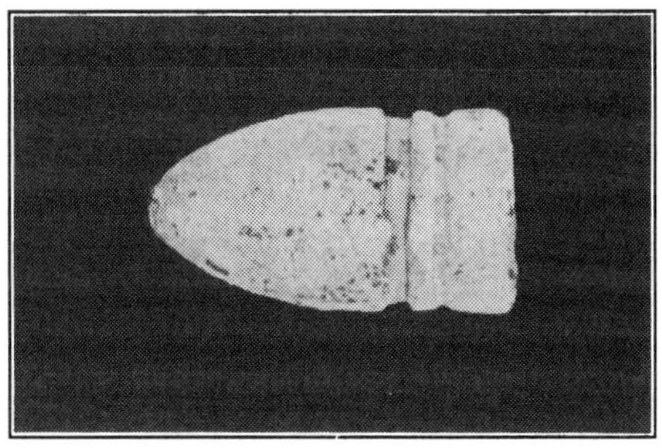

■ Confederate Gardner .577-caliber minie ball.

Whistling a different tune

Soldiers on both sides of the lines during the hot month of August 1864 found diversions to break the monotony of the siege stalemate. One Federal non-commissioned officer, Lyman Widney of the 34th Illinois, wrote in a letter to his family on August 23 about one such method:

"We are six miles from Atlanta but portions of our line are within a mile and a half. At present we are lying on one side of a hill and the Rebels on the other side — half a mile distant. Our breastworks are on the crest of the hill and our pickets a few yards below. The Reb pickets and ours are continually shouting at each other and the hostile 'Minies' fly over our heads to strike the side of a hill in our rear. We are comparatively safe, but a man 15 feet high would stand a poor chance if he stood upright in our camp.

Every few minutes one or more of the spiteful missiles go cracking through the tree tops, each one pitched to a different tune. We have a splendid opportunity for noticing the different notes sounded by them. Some go over with a short 'whisp' as if well greased and sliding through the air. They are the ones that go through a man when he stands in their way. Others come like a young thrashing machine, whirling end over end. They have struck something on their course which has deranged their original motion. They are generally battered into different shapes and emit a sound that is varied according to the form and speed of the ball. The consequence is that there are just as many different sounds as there are different shaped balls. Every hour or so some new note is struck, and is generally greeted by a laugh that runs through the regiment. More balls fly at night than in daytime but that don't prevent us from sleeping soundly."

■ Lt. Col. Henry Granville Stratton, 19th Ohio. Early in the siege he wrote to his sister in a letter dated July 30: "The rebels became so familiar with their little shells that even Hd. Qrs. were obliged to build a bombproof. The boys say you are always very careful to have good works to protect us and to fight in but Hd. Qrs. never appear to think they are in danger. That is generally the case, but close calls from both bullets and pieces of shells have sturred up even the Col. and the result is we now live in a pleasant comfortable habitation, built like a bank barn. We first dug on the sloping side of a rolling spot about ten feet, dug it square and nice, then on the two exposed sides put large oak logs to raise it about the highth of my head then banked well with earth outside covered with a fly and bushes and you have a cool, comfortable safe domocile for four gay lads who enjoy themselves hugely ... For a bed, four short forks driven in the floor so as to leave about eight inches exposed, two short poles at the head and foot, then about a dozen laid lengthwise. On top of this first pine boughs about a foot deep crossed with corn blades and a blanket and you have a spring matress of little cost except a little sweat that is just what we lazy boddies need."

ate enemy (at Utoy Creek, Ga.), and Resaca sank into a mere slight picket skirmish.

Moving out of our works about nine last Sunday, and doubling the picket lines, we moved toward the enemy's breastworks, and then I saw what was coming. Company D was detailed for skirmish duty, it being her time to go on duty. Our regiment was on the right flank of our brigade, connecting it with the 2nd Brigade. I was with the regiment, being still on duty as Adjutant ...

Before we got fairly in position to make a charge, or even to support the skirmish line, the commander of the skirmishers charged the rebels, driving in their skirmishers, and instead of halting in our cover and awaiting for the arrival of the line of battle, rushed forward on the rebel works amid a withering fire of musketry from the enemy behind their works. Many a brave man fell to rise no more during that charge.

Our regiment was nearly a mile on the right of our company, and I began to entertain serious apprehensions for the safety of our Bracken [Ky.] boys, judging from the incessant roll of musketry on our left. The skirmish line pushed up to within 20 feet of the works, and the fire became so hot and so many had fallen & they were falling so rapidly, that they could stand it no longer and were forced to fall flat on the ground and seek every protection behind trees, stumps, logs, &c.

Many an anxious eye was turned back in search of the advancing lines coming to their relief, as they could go no further and it was impossible to get back, but no lines came in sight. For two long hours were these brave boys compelled to lie there within talking distance of the enemy, and every man daring to raise his head was instantly shot.

Finally our lines came in sight, the 100th and 104th O.V.I., 112th Ill. & 8th Tenn. regiments came square up in front of the works & received the deadly fire, whole platoons were swept down at a single volley. Finally they were compelled to fall back, and the rebels were preparing to mount their works and make a counter charge, our skirmish line still being in the perilous position spoken of, and they could actually hear the rebel officers rallying their men to the charge & they must get away from there or be captured. The former at a risk was preferable, and one by one they crawled away among the felled bushes, leaving many of their killed & wounded comrades to the tender mercies of the brutal adversary.

Among the number left on the field were three of our brave boys ... These three noble fellows were killed dead and it was impossible to bring them away. Company D brought off all her wounded among them ... Lieut. Shane was wounded in two places — one toe on right foot shot off and left leg amputated above knee ...

The rebel position could not be taken by a charge, but they were flanked out of it on the following morning, and our killed & a great many of the severely wounded were found still in the field robbed by the rebels of all clothing, watches, pocketbooks, &c. Our brigade suffered more than any other brigade in the corps. I have no idea of the exact number killed, wounded & missing but suppose it will nearly reach 400 in our brigade.

About the time of the charge I was sent to search for the right of the skirmish line & got in the rear of Company D just as they were falling back, and although the bullets were sailing around me like hail, as my men were being carried by me to the rear, groaning and terribly mangled, about a dozen of the survivors collected around me as if I were their only remaining support. I sat down on a log and cried like a child. While here, Gen. Reilly commanding our brigade passed me and I could hear his sobs for 50 yards. We cried the remainder of the evening over the loss of his gallant brigade, the brigade that won for him his glittering stars. On the following morning I was talking with the general in regard to the loss of my company, and he told me that it was the last time for a good while that his brigade should go into such a place as that.

I believe all our wounded boys will get well. Lieut. Shane appeared very lively & I think will recover.

Day before yesterday we were relieved from the front line and we went out beyond the left on a grand reconnaissance. I saw many rebels and long lines of works, but toward dark we fell back to the rear of the army and today, the first for three months, finds the 3rd Division in reserve, away from where the bullets are whizzing and shells bursting and every few minutes a man shot down in camp by your side. We are now almost out of hearing of the small arms except of a night when everything is still.

Since leaving Resaca I have had a thousand hair breadth escapes every day. How I have escaped I cannot tell. I have never even had my clothing pierced by a ball. The only hurt was the bursting of a shell so close to my face that the grains of powder flew into my face.

At Kennesaw Mountain I came very near getting sick and had it not been that we were in the front I would have reported "unfit for duty." But now I am well again and have learned the art of dodging so perfectly that I doubt whether the rebels will ever get me or not ...

■ 1st Lieut. Jacob M. Ruffner, adjutant of the 17th Ohio, was killed August 9 while in command of skirmishers in a section of the Federal line known as the "Belly of Hell." At 6 p.m. that day, when about to be relieved by another officer, he rose up on the breastworks to point out the Confederate line and was shot through the head by a sharpshooter. Earlier in the war he had been a cook for his mess and acquired the nickname "Kate," by which he was universally known in the regiment.

'I am getting tired of this'

Corporal Erastus Winters
Company K
50th Ohio Volunteer Infantry

On the Firing Line, near the Macon R.R.
Southwest of Atlanta, Ga., August 10, 1864.

My Dear Parents, Brothers and Sisters:

I am thankful I have another opportunity afforded me of writing to you all, and to acknowledge the receipt of your kind letter of August 1st.

I was rejoiced to learn you were all well. Glad to tell you also I am enjoying that same blessing, but I must tell you that during the past week we have been in some tough places.

Our corps has kept swinging around on the right flank until we are not far from the Macon railroad. We skirmished with the rebels that it required about all the nerve we had to stay with them, but so far we hold all the ground we have taken.

On August 3rd we took a very commanding position from them, and although they gave us an unmerciful shelling, we had taken a hold, and like bulldogs we held on and fortified the position to suit ourselves.

August 8th the 50th were all on the skirmish line and pushed the rebs back about two miles, Col. Elstner gallantly leading the regiment, but in the last charge we made, where the colonel wanted to drive the enemy from some buildings, we had just started with a yell when the brave colonel fell, shot in the head by a minie ball. He died instantly, but we went on and drove the enemy from those buildings, and away beyond them.

The command of the regiment now fell on Major Gillespie. I don't think there was hardly a man in the regiment but what shed tears when they learned that Col. Elstner was killed, for we all loved him, but that kind voice is hushed in death; we will never hear it pleading with us again to be good boys as we have in the past. Lieut. Reed of Company I went to Cincinnati yesterday with his remains. May they rest in peace.

Joseph Carson of Company K was wounded in the hand this morning by a minie ball while we were eating breakfast in the trenches. I was seated in

■ Hat device worn by a member of Company F, 50th Ohio, consisting of brass insignia affixed to a black wool-covered disc.

■ Lt. Col. George R. Elstner, 22-year-old commander of the 50th Ohio, was instantly killed by a musket ball through the head on August 8 near Utoy Creek. In his journal, 2nd Lieut. Thomas C. Thoburn of Company E described Elstner's death: "Col. Strickland, our brigade commander, told him that he was to take the 50th across the creek and drive the enemy from a wooded ridge beyond that, without saying how he was to do it. While in the timber on our side of the valley, Col. Elstner moved us by the right flank up the stream, perhaps half a mile and then crossed under the cover of intervening trees unmolested by the enemy. While making this movement, Col. Strick galloped up and said, 'Col. Elstner, are you a coward that you are afraid to cross this valley as directed?' 'Col. Strickland, you have called me that for the last time. Get down and take your coat off, and we will settle that right here!' Old Strick wheeled his horse round and plying his spurs galloped away. Elstner was smarting under this taunt, which perhaps made him a little reckless and he exposed himself perhaps unwisely, with the fatal result noted above."

front of him at the time, and my head was near catching the same ball; his wound is slight; he will be all right in a few days. This is the third time he has been wounded since entering the service. At Perryville, Ky., a musket ball entered his breast and came out his back. He is both unlucky and lucky.

Our rifle pits where we are now are not over 200 yards from the rebel rifle pits. We are so close we have to change the pickets after night; our brigade has just finished the 33rd line of breastworks since we came to the front.

I am getting tired of this unceasing pop, pop, popping of the pickets, and boom, boom, boom of the artillery, and the crash of the bursting shells. It's the same thing over every day. "When and how will it end?" is a question we often ask ourselves. Ah well! All good and bad things must end sometime. We are sure we are in the right, and we know the right will conquer in the end, and the end must come sooner or later.

The day that Col. Elstner was killed, the 8th day of August, I was 21 years of age. It was rather a sad birthday for me — but such is life.

The order has just been given for Company K to get ready for the picket line tonight, so I will finish this tomorrow if my life is spared, so I bid you good night.

August 11th, 1864.

I am glad to say this morning that Company K all got back off the skirmish line safe and sound. Everything seems to be quiet along the lines this morning.

It is whispered among the knowing ones that Gen. Sherman is going to try a grand flanking movement, and that troops are already passing our rear toward the right flank. If that be true, look out for startling news from this point before many days.

We draw pretty good rations now and have plenty to eat. It is well that we do, for our work is so hard we could not keep up otherwise.

I have just learned that Lieut. Reed will not go any farther than Marietta, Ga., with the colonel's body, but that Elstner's brother will meet him there and take the body to Cincinnati.

The mail is going out so I will close for this time. Will write again in a few days. My love and best wishes to all.

Near Macon R.R., Southwest of Atlanta, Ga.
August 22nd, 1864.

Dear Parents:

Well, we are still in the same position on the line that we were when I wrote you last.

The Confederate Gen. Hardee's troops are in our front; his pickets and our brigade pickets have compromised and will not fire on each other without warning; they are not much over 100 yards apart. Their butternut clothes are so much the color of dead leaves it is hard to detect them. Since the compromise it has been very quiet in our front. Each party gets out front of their pits and talk to each other a little.

The rebel officers will not allow their men to hold very long chats with our boys. A rebel sergeant came over and gave himself up last night. He reports their lines much weakened in places, as they have had to stretch them out so long to keep us from cutting their railroad. He says if we get possession of the road once, their army would have to leave here in double-quick as that would shut off their supplies.

I understand the enemy's cavalry has cut our road between here and Dalton, but it will not amount to much as they can't hold it long enough to do us any harm. Kilpatrick, on our side, has been trying to cut the Macon road, but so far it has not amounted to anything.

The firing of the pickets was very annoying when we first took positions on this part of the line; the balls would come whistling over our heads pretty vicious; sometimes they would hit the tree-tops and then glance down among us.

The other day Lieut. Pine was sitting in his tent doing some writing when a ball struck a tree over him, glanced down and thumped him on the head. It did him no harm as it was just about spent when it struck him, and only drew a few drops of blood.

The same day a ball came over the works, passed through three or four tents and struck Henry Shepherd on the breast. We all thought the way he yelled that the ball had gone through him. We ran to him and he was holding his hand on his breast, and still kept yelling. We got him to take his hand down and the flattened bullet dropped to the ground. It had not even penetrated his clothes.

When he found out he was still alive he began to curse the rebels, both loud and deep, and I can assure you he called them anything but gentlemen. I never heard a man curse harder. Why, Company K quarters were blue with smoke and smelled of brimstone for an hour afterward. Shepherd is from North Carolina and enlisted in Company K while we were at Knoxville. He has a black and blue lump on his breast the size of a hen's egg where the ball struck him.

We got the first mail this morning that we have received for seven days, but no letters came for me. I trust I will be more lucky next time.

Well, according to the books, I have been in the service two years today. I have one more year to serve, and then if God spares my life I will come home. A year will soon pass away.

There is some movement going on in our rear, and the wise ones say Sherman has a trump card up his sleeve that he intends playing before long. I am satisfied myself that there is trouble brewing for someone, so you can listen for something to drop with a dull thud in this part of Georgia before long.

I close for this time with love and good wishes for you all.*

■ 1st Lieut. Charles R. Pomeroy Jr. commanded Company A, 33rd Ohio, when his regiment stormed a line of works occupied by Confederate skirmishers on August 13 near Utoy Creek. Twenty-eight prisoners were taken at a cost of two killed and five wounded in the 33rd. Regimental commander Lt. Col. James R. Montgomery was severely wounded and Pomeroy, described as a "brave and efficient officer," was killed in the assault. The 33rd's adjutant, Angus L. Waddle, later wrote: "I have always regretted my absence at the time ... as he left a note, written in case of this sad ending, in which he requested me to take charge of his effects. Before I returned they were lost and his friends at home were thus deprived of those souvenirs which would have been so carefully treasured."

'A temporary truce'

Major John H. Widmer
104th Illinois Volunteer Infantry

After the action of August 7th, 1864, the position of the One Hundred and Fourth at Utoy Creek was a peculiarly annoying one.

Our main line was within point-blank rifle range of the rebel skirmish line, which, too, was hidden in a dense growth of pines, the same ground where the sharpshooter who killed Fitzsimmons, Craig and Graves was concealed. Our skirmish line was but a short distance from our main line; while the main line of the rebels was a considerable distance back of their skirmish line, and was out of reach of our skirmishers. The result being, as I judge, a "butcher bill" considerably in their favor. Our men in the main line had to keep very close behind the works, but still several of them were hit and badly wounded by shots from the pines. Corporal Ruble, then color

* Of the individuals mentioned in Winters' letters, Corporal Joseph Carson and 1st Lieut. Edward L. Pine did not survive the war. Carson died February 17, 1865, at Washington, D.C. Pine was severely wounded at the Battle of Nashville on December 15, 1864, and died February 5, 1865.

■ Major John H. Widmer, 104th Illinois, began the war in April 1861 as a private in the 11th Illinois. He was promoted to major and assigned to the 104th in the fall of 1862, and from that time specialized in skirmish fighting. Regimental historian William Calkins wrote: "the qualities that marked Major Widmer as an officer of superior ability, coolness and bravery were more fully developed in the Atlanta campaign ... He was always in splendid physical condition and was called upon oftener than any other officer to take charge of brigade and division skirmish lines and detachments. As such, he came on duty nearly every other day from the opening of the campaign. (He) came to love that kind of fighting, and when the rifle balls were singing merrily and everything going on right, was in his element and perfectly undisturbed." Widmer took command of the 104th after the fall of Atlanta and led the regiment to the close of the war.

bearer, was one of these.*

We had no orders to drive the rebel skirmish line out of their position, and one day the idea occurred to me that a little strategy to make things more even would not be out of the way. I also had some curiosity to know just how their skirmish line was located in the thick pines. So, a little after dark I went to every pit in our skirmish line and told the boys not to fire any more at the Johnnies that night, unless they made a charge. The result was the Johnnies, meeting no reply, stopped firing about midnight.

The left pit in my line was in an old dooryard and on the crest of a little hill. Opposite to it, about forty yards distant, was the nearest rebel pit, just outside of the thick pines. Between these two pits the ground was perfectly clear.

About three o'clock in the morning I went to this left pit of ours and as soon as it was light enough to clearly see the rebel pit I stepped out in front of ours and called out: "Hello, Johnny!" In about two seconds a living fellow in gray clothes rose up in the other pit and replied, "Hello, Yank." I said: "I'm coming over there to make you a visit."

"All right," he replied.

I started at once; he hesitated a little, and then started, meeting me about fifteen steps from his pit. We shook hands, and then I gave him my name and rank, and informed him that I had charge of the skirmish line opposing his, and desired to meet the officer in charge of his line. The man I was talking to was a Lieutenant in, I think, the Forty-second Georgia. He informed me that Captain Howell, of his regiment, had charge of their line. I inquired where the Captain was. He pointed down the line of pits as it ran into the pines, and said the Captain "was in there." I asked him to accompany me, and we started off to find the Captain.

As we went down the line of rifle pits in those pines it may be believed that I kept my eyes wide open to see how the Johnnies were fixed in them. We soon met Captain Howell, to whom I was introduced by the Lieutenant, and I at once proceeded to make known my business. I told the Captain I thought we were conducting a rather barbarous warfare on our part of the line; that we were now and then breaking an arm or a leg, or killing some poor fellow, but we were deciding nothing, only causing suffering; and I proposed a temporary truce, to let the boys on both sides have a chance to shake hands and get acquainted. To all this the Captain, who seemed to be very much of a gentleman, readily assented.

We then agreed to a truce to last until either of us received orders from his commanding officer to resume hostilities, upon receipt of which orders twenty minutes' notice was to be given to the other before any act of hostility was done, and when firing began no attempt should be made to hit an opponent for the first two or three rounds; this to enable every soldier to get safely back to his pit.

Before starting out I had told my boys that if I effected a truce I would signal to them by waving my hat. As soon as the arrangement was completed I went up to the first-mentioned rifle pit and gave the signal. It was laughable to see the way the Blue and the Gray went for each other. They

* Corporal John Ruble of Company G was wounded on August 12. According to Capt. William Strawn of Company F, 104th Illinois, "a stray bullet coming from the right made four holes in the hat of Sergeant John Shay of my company, and then plunged into the neck of the color bearer. The blood spurted out in a stream as large as a man's little finger. I was standing close by and thought an artery had been severed. Our surgeon, fortunately, was near, and being summoned, came quickly and applying his thumb to the wound, bandaged it and sent the man to the hospital. Few of us expected to see him alive again, but in a short time he recovered and resumed his place as color bearer."

'A splendid dash'

1st Sergeant William B. Westerwell
Company K
17th New York Veteran Volunteer Infantry

At the siege of Atlanta ... our second lieutenant was sick, absent; our first lieutenant had just resigned, and our captain was under arrest in his quarters. This accounts for my being temporarily in command of the company.

On August 22 we worked all day building breastworks of logs to protect our tents from the bullets that continually came into our camp from the enemy's rifle pits a few hundred yards in front of our works, and had that day killed one of our men as he was sleeping in his tent and wounded several others as they were walking about the camp.

At dark our work was done and we were congratulating ourselves on the prospect of a good night's sleep. Just as we had finished our evening smoke and were about to "turn in," orders came to form the company. After receiving a fresh supply of cartridges I was ordered to take the company to the skirmish pits and relieve the men who had occupied them for the past 24 hours.

We had strict orders not to fire unless the enemy advanced. We remained very quiet all night, but just as day was breaking were surprised to see the men who occupied the pits on the right of our company leave them and start across an open field for those occupied by the enemy, about 200 yards in front. It was a splendid dash, a captain taking the lead. The pits were captured with most of their occupants, but before our men could turn the pits the enemy made a dash to retake them. This was just the opportunity we were waiting for, as it was an advance and gave us a good excuse for firing, and we gave them the warmest kind of a fire.

This drew their fire, and for a few minutes it was very sharp. Several of our company were wounded, but they dropped down in the pit, out of the way of those still able to shoot. It also helped the troops on our right to drive back the enemy, turn the pits and hold them.

Soon all became quiet, when we sent our wounded to the rear and settled down to wait for something else to happen. During the day the officer who had led the advance came over to our pits, and, inquiring for the officer in command, was directed to me. He seemed surprised at not meeting a commissioned officer — I was only a sergeant — still, he grasped my hand warmly and thanked me for the help given him at the opportune moment in the morning. He was a splendid-looking officer. After an hour's chat he got up from the edge of the pit, where he had sat resting, and as he left he handed me his card, which read: "Henry W. Lawton, Captain, 30th Indiana."

■ Capt. Henry Ware Lawton, Company A, 30th Indiana

Lawton ended his Civil War service in 1865 as a brevet colonel. He remained in the army for the next 34 years, rising to the rank of major general of volunteers on July 8, 1898, and saw active service in both Cuba and the Phillipines during the Spanish-American War. Early on December 19, 1899, he accompanied a mixed command of U.S. infantry and cavalry troops that attacked a 300-man force of Filipino insurgents in the town of San Mateo, Luzon. While walking along the firing line, conspicuous in the white pith helmet he habitually wore, Lawton was struck by a Filipino sharpshooter's bullet and fell dead into the arms of his staff officer.

■ Capt. Joseph P. Fitzsimmons, commander of Company K, 104th Illinois, was instantly killed by a sharpshooter on August 7 while in the act of placing a wood rail on earthworks thrown up by the regiment in front of the Confederates at Utoy Creek. Described by fellow officers as "constitutionally fearless," he was the senior captain in the 104th at the time of his death, though he began the war as a bugler in the 1st Illinois Cavalry. In 1837, when Fitzsimmons was two years old, his father lost his life while attempting to rescue a drowning man.

met and shook hands like old friends. In fact they had met before, but not just in that way. Coffee, corn-bread, hard-tack, jack-knives, tobacco and other inoffensive articles were freely exchanged, instead of deadly bullets. The deep Yankee hurrah and the shrill rebel yell had given way to friendly jokes and conversation.

I made it a point to praise the splendid fighting qualities of their people, and to suggest that if we were again united we could whip the world. This did not seem the least offensive to those with whom I talked. In fact the Lieutenant I first met called me aside and, in a low tone, asked me what would be done with rebel soldiers who voluntarily came into our lines and surrendered. He told me it was the common understanding with them that deserters from their army would be compelled to return. I told him our generals were not fools, and I could assure him such soldiers would receive no worse treatment than that of ordinary prisoners of war; and that I thought it highly probable that they would be sent North and set at liberty upon taking the oath of allegiance to the United States.

About nine o'clock in the forenoon Captain Howell notified me that he had orders to resume hostilities. This put an end to our truce, but it bore fruits well worth the little risk I ran. A night or two after, some twenty-five or thirty of the Johnnies laid down their guns and came into our lines, and I do not remember that we afterwards had a single man hurt by their fire at Utoy Creek. I never made any written report of this truce, but learned, however, that our division commander was not displeased.

'These mournful particulars'

Capt. Everett F. Abbott
Company I
74th Indiana Volunteer Infantry

Headquarters 100th Ind., Marietta, Ga.
August 6th, 1864.

John H. Baker, Esq.,
Dear Sir:

Yesterday I telegraphed from the front to you the intelligence of the melancholy event which has brought deep sorrow upon us, and to yourself, family and relatives, doubtless the most poignant grief. I take the first opportunity of giving you a necessarily hasty account of the circumstances attending the death of your brother.

Our regiment had just advanced and constructed breastworks, upon a hillside, facing the enemy, whose picket line was but a very short distance removed. We were exposed to a fire from rebel pickets, and also from a rebel battery in close proximity to us, but had escaped with the loss of but one man. Our works were well advanced, when Myron passing along the line, stopped at my company and engaged in conversation with me upon the events of the day. We sat down — he by my left side — a couple of rods in the rear of the breastworks, but upon ground considerably higher than that on which they were constructed, as that they, as the sad event proved, furnished little protection. Myron was conversing cheerfully and at the moment was expressing his confidence in the unimpaired bravery and determination of our army, when the fatal musket was fired, the report of which I scarcely noticed, owing to the continued firing which had been kept up. Leaving a sentence uncompleted, Myron raised his arms quickly, fell backward, straightened his body, gave one gasp, and without a groan or struggle, his brave and noble spirit had taken its flight. The ball had struck in the center of his forehead, and passed quite through the head, lacerating it badly. I hesitate at reciting these mournful particulars, and as I write the picture of that face of him whom I cherished as one of my dearest friends, with the life blood gushing through the cruel wound comes before me, but too vividly. But I pass on.

The officers of the regiment sought immediately to make arrangements to have the remains sent to the North, and I was directed to attend to carrying out their wishes. Owing to the great distance which our camp now is from Gen. Thomas' Headquarters, I was unable to get permission to accompany the remains to Chattanooga, in time to start before morning. This morning, however, I started early for this place, where I arrived in the afternoon. I sought immediately to have the body embalmed but the physicians decided that its state was such as to prevent this being done. I have, however, obtained a metallic coffin, placed the body in it, and shall start for Chattanooga by the midnight train, where I shall arrive at one o'clock p.m. tomorrow. I can there have the case properly sealed (which could not be done here) and sent by express to Goshen, to your address. I have sought to do all I could to enable you to obtain the precious remains — all that is left to us of your brother. I regret most deeply that I will not be enabled to do this in such a manner, that I can advise you to open the coffin for a last look of the departed. Causes which must suggest themselves to you have prevented my carrying out my wishes in this respect.

I have received great assistance and everywhere the most earnest sympathy in the performance of the mournful duty which I am seeking to discharge from all the officers and soldiers whom I have met from Elkhart County, of various regiments. Gen. Hascall and Col. Heath have rendered peculiarly valuable assistance.

While feeling that I have lost a friend, proved under diverse circumstances most true and faithful, and than whom scarcely any could have been more dear to me, yet I cannot think to fathom the grief which a brother or a parent experiences, nor to offer to them any adequate condolence; and what I have written, I fear, will rather harrow than console that grief. But I cannot refrain from telling you how much the officers and men of the 74th loved and admired their lamented commander. I suppose there are few colonels who possess to so great an extent as he the affection and confidence of their men, or who would be mourned so truly, if lost. During the short time that I was with the regiment after Myron's death there was to be seen on the countenances and in the conduct of the men all indications that a great calamity had befallen them. It could not well be otherwise, for all knew Colonel Baker to be seeking ever the welfare of the men under his charge, and while avoiding almost studiously all display or ostentation, going forward always in the quiet, and faithful discharge of every duty. When in the presence of danger, in the face of the enemy, he proved himself personally brave, almost to a fault; at other times he showed all that gentle bearing that evinced the true knight. A careful and considerate commander, a brave soldier, a true friend — it is the loss of such a one we mourn, and almost despair of seeing his like again.

The night is growing late and I must close my hasty letter.

Your sympathizing friend,

E.F. Abbott*

■ Lt. Col. Myron Baker, commander of the 74th Indiana, was instantly killed by a sharpshooter on August 5 along a newly established line of works near Utoy Creek. Eulogized by brigade commander Col. George Este as "one of the most gallant and efficient officers in the service," Baker had been arrested by Este earlier in the campaign and his sword taken when Baker complained of his regimental camp ground on May 24. The sword finally was returned, with Baker refusing to accept it several times.

* Twenty-six days after he wrote this letter to Lt. Col. Baker's brother, Abbott himself was killed in the battle of Jonesboro on September 1.

They ran over us like a drove of beeves

Jonesboro: Fierce climax to four months of fighting

The stalemate in front of Atlanta finally exhausted Sherman's limited patience by August 23. After four weeks of shelling the city the Confederates apparently were no closer to caving in. To strangle Hood's remaining life lines the Union commander looked to the south — and decided to attempt with his infantry what the cavalry and artillery had not accomplished.

His plan called again for cutting loose from his own supply line, and severing the last two remaining Confederate rail lines leading to the city — the Atlanta & West Point and Macon & Western railroads. Virtually the entire army would take part. With Garrard's dismounted cavalry temporarily manning the trenches, the XX Corps pulled out of its fortifications on the 25th and marched back to the Chattahoochee to guard the ferries and railroad bridge. The IV Corps followed, then turned south to join the XIV and XXIII corps already west of Atlanta. Finally, the Army of the Tennessee vacated the line the next day and began swinging southwest of Atlanta in what Sherman termed a "grand left wheel."

"That day was a hard one," wrote Capt. Ira B. Read of Company E, 101st Ohio. "We marched till long after dark. Had no chance for dinner and I was so tired and sick that I threw myself on the ground as soon as we halted, and tried to sleep. One of the boys gave me some coffee after a while. I don't think I ever was more tired on a march."

While Read and his comrades marched farther away from Atlanta, the Confederates quickly took possession of the Union trenches. "The enemy evacuated their works in our front last night," wrote Sergeant Edmund T. Eggleston of Cowan's (Mississippi) Battery on August 26. "I visited their abandoned line today. Their works are greatly inferior to ours." The next day he added, "The enemy ... are supposed to be retreating, or massing on our left to flank us out of Atlanta."

His latter conjecture was to be proven correct, but at the time, no one in the Confederate ranks or high command knew exactly where the Federals had gone. Citizens who remained in the city during the siege joined the Atlanta defenders in a joyous celebration. It would take nearly three more days before Hood and his men learned what Sherman was up to. With much of the Confederate cavalry off raiding with Wheeler in Tennessee, not enough horsemen were left to accurately scout the Federals' movements.

Late on August 28, Capt. Read's command struck the tracks of the Atlanta & West Point Railroad, and the purpose of the "grand left wheel" began in earnest the next day for Company E of the 101st Ohio. "Monday was occupied in tearing up the road," wrote Read. "The way it is done is this, the men get along one side of the track as thickly as they can stand and then lift 'all together' and over goes the whole thing ties and all. The ties are then piled up, the iron rails placed on them and the pile is fired. When the rails are hot they bend of their own weight. Sometimes the boys bend and twist them around trees. This makes the destruction complete."

In the same company, Sergeant Lewis W. Day later wrote: "Everything that could be burned was committed to the flames; cedar ties proved to be excellent material for heating the rails, and adjacent trees offered solid supports for bending them; a roaring fire of cedar rails soon destroyed the wooden culverts, and a few pounds of powder blew up the stone ones. The railroad was utterly wrecked — nothing was left, except the roadbed, and even that looked exceedingly disconsolate. We continued this destruction until we met other forces on our right engaged in the same business ..."

Some Federals not on the wrecking crews instead went foraging, and quickly found the surrounding countryside provided welcome diversions to the usual army diet. In his journal, 1st Lieut. Daniel Hayford of Company E, 25th Indiana, wrote on August 29: "The boys found plenty of green corn, which they were not slow in appropriating. I ate four ears myself and many others did much better."

"Our men are living high on the products of the land," wrote Sergeant Francis M. McAdams of Company E, 113th Ohio. "Chickens, hogs, cattle, sheep, geese, turkeys, corn, flour, meal, potatoes and everything eatable is brought in by the quantity. Soldiers have consciences, but they make very little use of them."

To the north, meanwhile, the men of the XX Corps along the Chattahoochee were having "what the boys call a soft thing of it," wrote 1st Lieut. Charles H. Cox of the 70th Indiana. "Strange our corps should be left behind, when we have lost only 8,000 men — and seen more fighting than any other Corps — in the campaign. Being camped on the Chattahoochee, the boys have a big time, bathing and fishing. Occasionally a man is drowned and every person talks about it. If he had been shot on the skirmish line or in battle no one would think of it — such a common occurrence."

Corporal Oliver A. Rea of Company H, 82nd Ohio, was among the troops guarding the Chattahoochee railroad bridge who welcomed "soft" duty after nearly four months of hard campaigning. On August 29 he wrote home: "Perhaps some idea may be formed of our hardships and exposures when I state that yesterday was the first since the 14th of May that artillery or musketry, generally both, could not be heard by us ... As to Gen. Sherman's latest movements we don't know much, but we have all confidence in his ability to perform whatever he undertakes."

On August 30, the rest of the Federal army was ready to strike the Macon & Western Railroad. Not until late afternoon was Hood finally aware of the extreme danger confronting him, though he still believed only half or less of Sherman's forces were below the city. To confront the Federals, he ordered the corps of Lee and Hardee — under Hardee's command — to march hurriedly to Jonesboro. The order was implicitly blunt: attack the enemy and drive them back across the Flint River. In the meantime, Hood would remain in Atlanta with Stewart's corps and the Georgia militia to defend the city.

As the climactic final days of the campaign grew closer, Sherman's troops were flushed with feelings of impending victory. Wrote Sergeant

■ Capt. Alfred W. Bell commanded Company B, 39th North Carolina, during the campaign. Early on the morning of August 27, the 39th and 14th Texas (dismounted) Cavalry were sent out as skirmishers. "After a spirited contest, these two regiments drove the enemy from their rifle-pits on their skirmish line, and advanced until they received the fire from the enemy's main entrenched line," wrote Maj. Gen. Samuel G. French. "Prisoners captured informed me that the XX Corps was there in position ... at Turner's Ferry and at the railroad crossing of the Chattahoochee, [so] I returned to Atlanta and reported the result of my reconnaissance. [On August] 28th, 29th and 30th, nothing of importance occurred on my line. It seemed strange this silence after so long and continuous booming of the artillery. On the 31st my division and the State forces were the only troops in the works immediately around the city."

■ Maj. Gen. Frank P. Blair Jr., brother of U.S. Postmaster-General Montgomery Blair, commanded the XVII Corps during the campaign. As the Army of the Tennessee neared Jonesboro at the Flint River, Blair ordered one of his brigades to reinforce Logan's XV Corps when Logan was attacked by the Confederates on August 31. This brigade, commanded by Col. George E. Bryant, consisted of the 12th and 16th Wisconsin and 31st Illinois. "Works were hastily thrown up," Bryant wrote, "the 12th and 16th Wisconsin being compelled to build traverses and wings to protect themselves from shell and bullets of the enemy. The charge ... extended along the front of the 31st Illinois and seven companies of the 12th Wisconsin, which was successfully resisted at both points." Bryant claimed his three regiments killed, wounded or captured 262 Confederates while losing only seven men of his own wounded, and that "the 31st Illinois, with 200 men, expended in one hour 19,000 rounds of ammunition."

McAdams of the 113th Ohio: "We know nothing of the details of the plan, but are doing our share in the movement with the utmost confidence of its success. What transpires within a day or two from this will make good reading for our descendants."

And of August 30, Sergeant Day of the 101st Ohio later wrote: "Every man seemed to know that a great crisis was approaching, and each nerved himself to do his own particular best ... We were inspired with the notion that it was possible to wind up the campaign in a short time, and this gave zeal and energy and enthusiasm to every move. The lines were kept well closed up — there was little straggling, notwithstanding the intense heat, and every order to advance was obeyed with alacrity. Doubtless [the Confederates], too, felt that the game would soon be ended ..."

'I vill make 'em hell schmell!'

Sergeant Jacob A. Gilberg
Company D
5th Ohio Veteran Volunteer Cavalry

On the great flank movement projected by Gen. Sherman to secure Atlanta, the XV and XVII Corps were sent on the lead under Gen. O.O. Howard, the XV Corps in advance under Gen. J.A. Logan. In the near vicinity of the Flint River it became evident, as the head of the column turned toward Jonesboro, that a heavy force was in front, especially as the cavalry under Gen. Judson Kilpatrick had met with a warm reception during the latter part of the day.

All that day [August 30] the bodyguard, consisting of Companies D and C of the 5th Ohio Cavalry, had been well in the lead of the XV Corps. We were at close carbine range, giving and taking as best we could, now making a dash, now recoiling before greater numbers. It was a hot day's work for us.

At one time, as we emerged deployed through a piece of timber, we sighted a line of rebels but a few rods off; all that intervened was a rail fence. We were debating the feasibility of charging them, but before the fence could be opened they fell back, and we had quite a chase after them, and finally had to desist as their horses were too long-winded for ours.

Night found us in the valley of the Flint River. The many divisions were hurried across, and, moving out, about half went into position. "Shovels" was the order of the night, and by morning there was quite a respectable line of breastworks from right to left. The men had worked all night by reliefs; no fires were built in the front, as the enemy's sharpshooters were in close evidence. Headquarters was made in the river valley and all preparations made for a battle.

In the early morning Gen. Logan and several aides-de-camp rode to the front. The first place we stopped was with Gen. P.J. Osterhaus, he and his mess being at breakfast, seated on the ground around a common mess chest. Osterhaus was on one knee with his left hand full of crackers, a cup of coffee in the right. As Logan rode up he rose to his feet, hooked the handle of the cup on his little finger and gave the common salute.

After a few words between the generals, Logan made the remark: "Well, Gen. Osterhaus, keep your eyes open; they may come any moment."

"All right, General," said Osterhaus. "Youst gif me time my goffee to drink, und I vill make 'em hell schmell!" That was the Dutch of it. It is needless to say that he kept his word.

We moved over to the left, meeting with different generals, with a word of caution and cheer to all from Gen. Logan. He stayed on the left with Gen. Wood, of the XVI Corps, quite a while, going well out to the front. There was no fun in this, as the sharpshooters were getting busy. After giving orders for everything on wheels that was not necessary to the fighting line to go to the rear, the general rode back to headquarters.

I should think it was fully an hour before the first gun was fired by the enemy. It was from a field gun from their right. The shell came over the Union position and plunged into the mud of the Flint River. In an instant all was in an uproar. Volley after volley, the roar of cannons, the shriek of shells, the howl of solid shots, the whizz of minies, filled the air.

At the crack of the first gun I ran for my horse. As I untied him Gen. Logan sprang into the saddle. As it was I was the second man into the saddle. Gen. Logan's horse was on the jump and I hesitated for a second, as my place was in rear of the general staff; but as there was some delay in their mounting, caused by a few having taken off their swords, I gave my horse the spur and was but a few jumps behind the general.

The wagon road to the front was on a slight upgrade, through a bit of woods, large trees, little underbrush, so that one could see a long distance. On we rode, faster and faster — the staff and escort endeavoring to close up. My poor hack was doing his best to keep up with the long strides of Logan's black.

About half way to the front I began to notice the stragglers — cooks of the officers' outfits and various camp attaches — breaking to the rear from both flanks of the corps, all converging to the common center. Soon we saw a four-mule team under full swing coming down the road. Gen. Logan pulled off his hat and waved the driver to pull out of the road. The driver was hatless. He straightened up in the saddle with a scared expression on his face, gave a hasty look behind him as if to assure himself that it was necessary for him to proceed, then swung the blacksnake over the leaders, as though to drive through anything he met.

The general drew his sword and charged straight at the fellow. The driver threw his weight on the lead line, swinging the lead team up a cut bank; the front wheels rose to the edge, but the wagon upset. The staff came up and the general gave orders for the escort to get the team straightened up and out of the way, and we rode on.

Diverging to the right we came in behind the position of Gen. Osterhaus and the 1st Division. Here we halted for a few moments, protected by the works of a six-gun battery. I shall never forget that scene. Osterhaus was walking back and forth in his shirt sleeves, suspenders down like a woodchopper at work, giving directions first here, then there; now to a gunner, now to a rifleman, admonishing the men to lower the muzzles of their rifles and not shoot in the air, for most of the men were loath to get their heads very far above the works as there was a hail of bullets sweeping the line.

The rebels were making their first charge from the protection of the nearby woods, but our fire soon drove them back. How those cannoneers worked their guns! One who never saw an action cannot believe that men could load and fire so fast. Sweating and black with powder, they looked like coal heavers on a river steamboat. But there was no shrinking.

Gen. Logan gave his ordnance officer orders to go back and see that the road was clear for all ordnance transportation. I was selected as his spe-

■ Maj. Gen. Peter J. Osterhaus commanded a division in the XV Corps, composed primarily of Iowa and Missouri troops. He was perhaps the most successful German-born officer of high rank to serve under Sherman during the campaign, although he missed a month of service from July 15 to August 15 because of sickness. At Jonesboro, when the Confederate divisions of Stevenson and John C. Brown attacked his positions about 2:30 p.m. on August 31, Osterhaus' entrenchments had not yet been completed. But as he wrote 10 days after the battle: "The effect of our fire was immediate and terrible; the enemy's line, compact until now, broke and dispersed in all directions. A number came over into our lines; the masses, however, fell back into the timber ... to find protection from our fire. The enemy formed again several times under cover of this timber, and attacked again, though very feebly, showing their first repulse to have been a very severe and decided one."

■ Drummer John McClay, center, poses at the end of the war with fellow 43rd Ohio musician Billy Brown, right, and an unidentified comrade. The cigars do little to disguise their youth. In 1865, McClay was only 15 years old but a veteran of two years' military service.

cial orderly for that day, and back we went. The captain gave the ordnance officer directions to fill all orders that came through me, and then sent me back to the front to go from right to left and see all commanders to get their orders for the various kinds of ammunition wanted, then see that they were brought close to the firing line, and at various times to report to him. Just where to find him was for me to find out. That was one of the hardest day's work I ever did during my four years' service.

From right to left, close to the firing line, was my road to travel; so close at places that but for the thunder of battle one could have talked with the men. I made the course a dozen times that day, and as many trips to the rear to give orders for supplies.

When out of the zone of the hail of bullets I would give a gasp of relief, thankful to have escaped that trip. I would have a few moments of respite in the river bottom, could get a cool drink of water that was so priceless to a thirsty man, linger around for a few moments, watch the wounded being brought in — and there were many by this time — then nerve myself for another ride into that storm of shot. As I would near the battle line I would pull down my hat rim as though to shield my face from the bullets.

Several times the ammunition wagons were stopped before reaching their destination by horses being killed or wounded. This would cause delay. There were some protected places where ammunition for the men could be delivered; where the cartridge boxes could be conveyed along the inner trench and distributed in safety. The head that showed above

John McClay: a dutiful drummer

The drummer boy was one of the essentials in the general make-up of the army and his duties were many and arduous. It was not only the sounding of reveille, taps and the numerous other calls, but also the sounding of the long roll at the midnight hour and awakening the slumbering troops to do battle with the enemy. When in camp the drummer boys were used as orderlies for the commanding officers; when in an engagement they were always found on the battlefield looking after and caring for the wounded and assisting in carrying them from the field of battle, which many times placed them in the most hazardous positions.

So wrote George M. Ziegler in *War Sketches*, a series of articles the former colonel of the 52nd U.S. Colored Infantry penned after the war for a Columbus, Ohio, newspaper. The focus of these sketches was John McClay, a drummer boy belonging to Company H, 43rd Ohio — a regiment that fought in Fuller's and Sprague's brigades of the XVI Corps during the campaign. When Major Horace Park of the 43rd recruited McClay in Columbus in May 1863 he was only 13 years old. The following excerpts are from Ziegler's articles detailing McClay's service in the summer of 1864.

■ There was a German of Co. H who was an inveterate tobacco chewer and with whom the boys always had their sport. In the use of the English language he always managed to get it backwards, and at times created considerable merriment. He was a brave soldier and was always on the firing line.

Near Big Shanty on the second day, Fred, as he was known by the boys, was wounded. Johnny and his companion, with stretcher, looking after the wounded, chanced to run across Fred who had received a terrible wound, the ball entering one side of his face and coming out at the other. He was lying on his back unconscious with the blood gurgling up in his throat.

Johnny, knowing of his tobacco habit, thought he had a chew in his mouth which was strangling him. He dexterously ran his finger into his mouth to remove the tobacco, when Fred's jaws closed down on his finger and held it as firmly as in a vise, until the assistant surgeon came to his relief and pried the man's teeth apart by the aid of a bayonet. And when Johnny was released, the surgeon said, "Now, you little fool, never try that again," and for several days when the boys were out on the field looking for the wounded, they hailed Johnny with "Here is a man that has tobacco in his mouth." But Johnny took the surgeon's advice and never tried it again.

■ The morning following the battle of Jonesboro, Johnny and Sergeant Hugh Dougherty of Co. I were skirmishing around for water, and upon going down in a deep ravine they discovered a nice clear stream. Filling their canteens, they started back for the regiment when Johnny discovered smoke on the opposite side of the ridge.

The sergeant continued on up the hill where they had left the troops, but Johnny's curiosity led him to see what the smoke was. Getting close to it, he discovered a Confederate soldier sitting down beside a tree fast asleep, and upon looking around he saw three others lying on the ground asleep, their guns being stacked.

Slipping around quietly he captured their guns. Laying them down in the tall sage grass which hid them from sight, he slipped back to the sleeping sentinel, and with revolver in his right hand, he jerked the gun away from the sentinel. As he awoke he thrust his revolver into his face, saying, "You are my prisoner." The prisoner replied, "The hell I am."

Keeping his prisoner in front of him, he proceeded to wake up the other soldiers who were not more than 10 paces away. A corporal, upon being awakened, commenced upbraiding the soldier for sleeping on post, when Johnny ordered them to fall in front of him and started for the regiment at the top of the hill.

Carrying the four captured guns on his shoulder, with his revolver in his hand, he came upon the colonel of the 39th Ohio Regt., who said, "Little one, where did you get those fellows?" Johnny replied, "I surrounded them."

He marched them to his own regiment and turned them over to Col. Swayne, who said, "You acted very foolish in running this great risk. What would you have done had the sentinel wakened up and resisted?" Johnny replied, "I would have put him to sleep with my revolver."

Johnny's great feat became noised about the camp that evening and he became the hero of the occasion. The boys declared that he had drowned them with the water from his canteen before capturing them. The prisoners proved to be a picket post holding an outpost which the enemy had failed to notify in their eagerness to get away from Jonesboro.

■ Survivors of Company K, 54th Ohio, pose for a final wartime portrait in August 1865 at Camp Dennison, near Cincinnati. Almost one year earlier, the regiment was in position at Jonesboro on August 31. "About 3 p.m. our pickets were driven in," wrote Major Israel T. Moore, the 54th's commander. "Soon we saw the enemy approaching with three heavy lines of infantry, over open fields, on our left and front. When within good musket-range we opened on them, firing left oblique. They continued to advance under our destructive fire till within 150 to 200 yards of our works, when the first line broke and fell back. Its place was supplied by a line in reserve, but soon all the lines began to waver and fall back in great confusion."

Seated in the second row at far left is Capt. William H. Hunt, purposely difficult to pick out from his men. High casualty rates caused many officers to wear small rank insignia, as seen on Hunt's coat lapels. Others wore no insignia at all.

the log was pretty sure to get a bullet.

During one of these delays the men were running short of cartridges. A sergeant from an Illinois regiment jumped out of the trench in plain view of the enemy, and in a storm of bullets ran back and secured two boxes of cartridges, one under each arm, and returned to his place unharmed.

The enemy made three desperate charges that day, but to me it seemed as though it was one continuous charge. When the battle was over for the day the men could take a little ease, if ease could be had, and count the loss, which was quite heavy. Great numbers were brought into the hospital. I saw piles of arms and legs outside of the field tent, and heard the cries, groans, prayers, even cursings. Hood had shattered his forces against an immovable wall, and to no good; yet it required another defeat for him [on September 1] before he could get the bulk of his army away.

The next day Gen. Sherman, having gotten up more of his forces, placed the XIV Corps on Logan's left and proceeded to finish the work of the day before. I was not on duty that day, as the escort had about two days off to one on for the special duty as orderly work. So, I proceeded to see all that was to be seen. With a number of others I went back to a hill nearby, and, climbing some dwarf trees, had a fine view of the field of operations, though too far off to distinguish individuals.

Soon the XIV Corps, in line of battle, developed from the shelter of the woods, flags flying, guns gleaming in the sunlight — an inspiring sight. As they neared the enemy the crack of guns became audible and soon grew to a continual crash. In a short time they were so enveloped in smoke that all we could see was a flash now and then. The fighting was stubborn for some time, but the enemy had to give back, and the battle rolled on and soon the woods hid the lines from view. At long last, hearty cheers reached our ears. The enemy was in retreat.

The army moved on, and again I was in the saddle.

'They come as a death wave'

Sergeant Major John Williams Green
9th Kentucky Volunteer Infantry
CSA

One day towards the last of August 1864 just before sundown [the enemy] began a terrific cannonading & kept it up until dark but did nothing else. They then quieted down; not even a picket gun was heard in our front that night. The next morning [August 26] our skirmishers reported they had withdrawn from our left. This was reported to Gen. Hood & we were ordered to develop their position. We discovered that their right had been retired & a new position had been taken. It afterwards was learned that part of their force had been withdrawn & sent toward East Point & Jonesboro to flank us & cut off our retreat.

At night on Aug. 28th we were started on a hurried march to Jonesboro. The night was very hot & a most fatigueing march we had of it.

■ Sergeant Major John W. Green, 9th Kentucky. Several weeks after the fight at Jonesboro he returned to the part of the battlefield defended by his regiment. He later recalled: "There was not a twig which had not been cut down by bullets & there were trees as big as my leg which were actually whittled down by minie balls. It seemed a miracle that any living soul could have survived that hailstorm of lead."

Aug. 29th 1864. We reached Jonesboro ahead of the enemy & began fortifying with the few tools we had. The cavalry report to us today that a whole corps of the enemy are pressing on this way. Our regiment is sent out about three miles from town to meet the Yanks. We take up a position in a skirt of woods with an open field in our front. Our cavalry are skirmishing with them. Soon they open their artillery on the cavalry & they fall back through our line & will take up a position in our rear & when we find that we can no longer hold back the enemy's advance we will fall back through the skirmish line formed by our cavalry & thus try to keep back this force of 20,000 Yankees until Gen. Hardee can get here with reinforcements. But I fear any force he can bring will be greatly outnumbered by the enemy as our latest cavalry scouts report that the Yanks are sending 40,000 men here with the determination to break our lines at this point with the hope of capturing Hood's army.

We soon saw the blue coats swarming in the woods on the other side of the field in our front. Our sharpshooters opened with their long-range guns on them & we saw several fall & the others begin to seek cover. They posted a battery in position where it was to a degree masked from sight and began to shell us. We laid still as they were beyond the range of our infantry guns, but our sharpshooters after a while got sight of their battery & made it so hot for them that they deployed a line of skirmishers & advanced against us. When they got within range of our rifles we gave them a volley that killed many of them & drove back the others. Then they formed in double line & advanced against us. We knew we could not drive them back for theirs was a double line & ours only one line in a single rank & they extended way beyond us on each flank.

We fell back behind the cavalry & the enemy advanced very slowly, being evidently afraid that we had a great force for a few of our cavalry would show themselves first in one place beyond our flank & then on the other

■ Lt. Col. John Cripps Wickliffe commanded the 9th Kentucky during the campaign. Possessed of a razor wit that sometimes got him in trouble with superior officers, Wickliffe "relished sport like an English lord ... and it always seemed a relief when he could undo the brass buttons and explode in a general humorous, sportive attack upon all who came in his way — officers, non-commissioned officers, musicians and privates."

flank so as to create the impression that our line extended further than theirs. We kept them back until dark & then left the cavalry to watch them, while we fell back to a point near Jonesboro & began again to entrench.

Aug. 30th. We hear the cavalry skirmishing with them very briskly this morning. We complete our rifle pits & wait, momentarily expecting our cavalry to be driven in & the fight to begin, but the enemy certainly did not realize the fact that we had less than 2,000 men to their 20,000 or more.*

Late in the afternoon of the 30th of August 1864 our cavalry was driven in & we gave the Yanks a few shots from our battery & our infantry skirmishers opened on them & gave them a check.

Our bold stand seems to have the desired effect; they evidently don't believe that so insignificant a force would defy an army of 20,000. They halt for the night knowing that heavy reinforcements are coming to them. But at daylight on Aug. 31st Gen. Hardee has arrived with 10,000 Confederates good & true. But his had been a forced march at night & it was really nearly noon before his entire force had arrived & gotten their rations.

Gen. Hardee determines to attack with his jaded troops. The Yanks have made good use of the past 18 hours. They have chosen a strong position and entrenched within rifle shot of our breastworks. But the order to attack & carry their works is given. As soon as we are called to attention & form outside our works they open artillery & infantry on us. "Forward" is the command. "Hold your fire until you get close to them, then fire & rush on them with fixed bayonets & give them the cold steel."

Soon our men begin to fall, rapidly and steadily we advance — but horror of horrors! Just as we have fired the volley at them & begin to rush on them we come to a deep gully 10 feet wide & fully as deep. No one can jump this gully & at this close range it will be impossible to clamber up the other side of the gully & reform to rush on them with fixed bayonets. The shot & shell & minie balls are decimating our ranks. Forward we rush. The order is given, "Jump into the ditch!" for there we will for a time be out of range of their guns & although the walls of this ditch are so precipitous that we cannot climb out on the other side & renew the assault upon them we are forced to take this shelter & then move out by the flank & withdraw to our former position.

Just as I was about to escape from the terrible fire of shells & minie balls by following our men by a jump into the ditch, I discovered one of our poor boys whose leg had been shattered by a fragment of shell about 20 feet from the ditch struggling to reach that point of safety. Great was his agony & slow his progress & when I ran to his side & helped him into the ditch I thought we both would certainly be riddled by the bullets which were pouring down on us. But finally we both got within its protecting walls before further calamity came upon us.

We got back to our trenches & the infirmary corps had their hands full with the wounded. The field hospital was located far to the rear because no point of safety could be found closer, therefore the litter bearers had more than they could do.

The enemy continued to fill the air with shot & shell. They seemed infuri-

* Late on August 30, Gen. Oliver O. Howard, commander of the Army of the Tennessee, had deployed the XV, XVI and XVII corps, totaling more than 25,000 men, in front of Jonesboro. And the next day Gen. Jefferson C. Davis arrived with the XIV Corps, bringing the Union forces at Jonesboro to 43,000, with the rest of the Federal army within supporting distance. Confederate forces at Jonesboro on August 30 numbered 2,000, but the next day the arrival of Hardee's and Stephen D. Lee's corps raised that figure to 22,000. Lee was ordered back to Atlanta on the night of August 31, leaving Hardee with about 14,000 men to face the entire Union army on September 1.

ated & volley after volley came from their rifle pits. Many of our poor wounded men lay in close range to their works; pitiful cries came for help [and] volunteers were called for to rescue our wounded.

Sept. 1st 1864. Shells and picket guns waken us at daybreak. Some Arkansas troops come to take our position in the trenches & we are marched to the railroad where it is rumored that we will take the cars & hurry to a part of the line near Atlanta, where rumor has it that our line is hard pressed. We wait for hours for the cars to come; the Yanks catch sight of us & open their batteries on us. There is nothing to do but to lie down & take it. Fortunately, however, we had but one man wounded here. The cars at length came & we began to pile into the flat cars which were to transport us, but we were then ordered to get off the cars & hurry on foot to the right of our line at Jonesboro. The enemy were sending an overwhelming force to flank us on our right.

We hurried to the position shown us & could see myriads of the enemy concentrated in our front already advancing against us. A few picks & spades & axes were given us with instructions to work for dear life to erect some defence to enable us to keep the Yanks at bay until night for the remnant of the army had not yet been rescued from Atlanta. We must hold the enemy off until night, by which time our forces in Atlanta could be withdrawn & the army reunited about Lovejoy Station.

We cut & piled some logs & dug for dear life. The Yanks began to shell us but we could not stop. We were two yards apart in our line & we could see them in a large field in our front massing three solid lines of battle to move against us. All the rest of the line on our left was hotly engaged. Just to our left was Govan's brigade & to the left of that was Swett's battery, then our line turned to the left at a rather sharp angle, and in the front of that part of our line the Yanks were keeping up a furious artillery fire and all the shells that passed over Swett's battery landed right in our midst. There was a good-sized tree about six feet in our rear which was cut down by these cannon balls. One shell hit that tree & exploded, killing one man & wounding several. Another shell hit the stump & rolled into the ditch we were digging. The fuze was sizzling, [and] in the next instant it would burst in our midst. Walker Nash had just returned from the rear where he had gone for water, [and] he had a bucket of water in his hand. He saw the danger & dashed the water on the shell, extinguishing the fuze & thus no doubt saved the lives of several of our men.

We have done but little in the way of digging rifle pits before the enemy's first line charges upon us. We drop the entrenching tools & seize our guns, fire a volley into them & go at them with charged bayonets. They fall back hurriedly & we as quickly return to our entrenching because we see four solid lines of battle advancing across a wide field against us.

The battery on our left gives us great annoyance as it enfilades us & thus shoots right down our line. We construct as best we can a transverse defence; but a crack is open just where the transverse joins the front works and an occasional minie ball slips through & brings down one of our men.

A second charge is now made upon us. Two lines coming in solid phalanx determined to overrun our thin gray line, our men being two yards apart. But with steadiness & deadly fire we meet them. They stagger, they waver. Our fire is so sure, so steady we have covered the ground in our front with their dead & dying. They fall back out of this withering fire but a third line advancing to their support presses them on with them. Surely with five times our numbers there is but little chance for us to withstand them. They come as a death wave. Their fire is thinning our slender ranks & surely I never saw men brave death more defiantly than they.

■ Col. John W. Caldwell, commander of the 9th Kentucky, led the 1st Kentucky (Orphan) Brigade at the battle of Jonesboro. When Govan's Arkansas brigade was overrun on September 1, Caldwell was prevented by orders to withdraw his own troops to safety. Many of the Kentuckians were captured and Caldwell succeeded in extricating only 250 of his men. Federal Col. George P. Este, whose troops repulsed an attack by the Orphans the previous day, said the Kentuckians "fought with the greatest determination" and were "confessedly among the best of the rebel army."

■ Capt. Fayette Hewett was adjutant of the 1st Kentucky (Orphan) Brigade during the campaign. Throughout the war he had three horses killed under him in battle, but was never wounded himself, although bullets repeatedly passed through his clothing and hat, and one through his hair.

Just to our left, in front of Govan's brigade, I saw their color bearers, of which each volunteer regiment had two, one to bear the state colors (theirs was New York) & the other the national Stars & Stripes, rush right up to Govan's rifle pits & take their flag staffs & beat our boys in those trenches over the head with the butt of the flag staff. Our boys had exhausted their ammunition. While I rejoiced to see them both fall the next instant (each with a bayonet run through him), I could not help feeling those brave men deserved a tear.

But our own men were surely falling like leaves in wintry weather. Fourqueran of our regiment, who had been on the picket line under command of Lieut. James McAllen & was now fighting on the left of the regiment, cried out, "Oh I am killed! What shall I do?"

I looked at him & he was sitting down in the trenches trying to pull a bullet out of his forehead. I said, "Fourquin (for that is what we called him), I will pull it out & you then run to the rear & go to the hospital."

Just then he got it out & said, "Never mind now, I have it out."

I just then saw Sam Boutcher fall dead from a ball which killed J.E. Adams at the same time. The shot came from a gun poked through the crack between the end of our front trenches & the transverse. Jim McAllen saw it at the same instant & grabbed the muzzle of the gun which a Yank had poked through there, fired it off & killed those two men at one shot. Jim McAllen had someone else to help him bend the gun barrel so that Mr. Yank could not get it out & no other gun could be poked in there to do such murderous work.

Just then Fourqueran, who had again loaded his gun notwithstanding his desperate wound, cried out, "I got him, but oh! I can't fight anymore, my head hurts so." He then took my advice & went back to the hospital.

Their fourth line has now come up to their assistance; they have pressed on regardless of our death-dealing fire until they are lying down flat just on the other side of our works. One great big Yank jumped up on our works & called to Booker Reed, "Surrender, you damn rebels!"

Booker said to him, "The hell you say," & shot him dead on the works.

I had my gun loaded, for notwithstanding I as sergeant major carried ordinarily only a sword, I always carried a gun into a fight with me. I rose from a stooping posture in the trenches to shoot, but just as I looked over our trenches a Yankee with the muzzle of his gun not six inches from my face shot me in the face & neck, but fortunately it was only a flesh wound. It stung my face about as a bee sting feels, but in my knees I felt it so that it knocked me to a sitting posture. But my gun was loaded and thc other fellow had had his shot. I rose & put my gun against his side & shot a hole through him big enough to have run my fist through.

It was now sullen give & take. The enemy, however, were lying down & fired only when one of our men loaded & rose to fire & if our man was not killed he took the best aim; indeed, we were now placing our guns against the man we fired at, but just as we were taking some hope from this slight advantage the enemy captured our battery by just swarming over it.

Govan's line, seeing this, gave way & Lt. Col. Wickliffe seeing we would surely be captured gave orders for us to fall back, but at this instant a message came, "Hold your ground for reinforcements are coming."

We again jumped into our pits & resumed our deadly work. Minutes seemed like hours. Would those reinforcements ever come?

Lieut. Boyd called out, "Never give up, boys!"

Just then a Yank jumped to his feet & shot Lieut. Boyd dead, but Stephen Rowan settled the account for he sent a minie ball crashing through the brain of the man who fired that deadly shot.

Our reinforcements, however, never came. The enemy swarmed over

Govan's works on our left & swung around in our rear. The troops we heard coming in our rear were not our reinforcements so longingly hoped for but blue coats who came up behind us, poured one volley into us from the rear & called again to us to surrender. The right of our regiment was not completely surrounded so they escaped, but for the left there was no escape so we were captured. Many of our other troops were also captured, but the rest of our brigade fell back about one half of a mile & reformed. Capt. Fayette Hewett hurried a battery into position & opened on the advancing enemy so fiercely that they thought it was only our first line they had captured & pursued no further.

This Battle of Jonesboro was the fall of Atlanta. It was a matter of life & death to keep this horde of Yanks from advancing further because Gen. Hood had not yet gotten his army safely out of Atlanta & this was our only road for retreat. Gen. Hardee made a determined stand at this place, notwithstanding the disaster to part of his line. He massed several batteries & concentrated their fire upon that part of the enemy's line that had captured us. If the assistance of these batteries had come to us 15 minutes earlier our line would never have been broken, but they were the first of the troops falling back from Atlanta & after straining every nerve to get to us sooner were only able to get to our hard-pressed troops in time to save us from utter disaster.

Our army had fallen back to Lovejoy Station, thus leaving the enemy in full possession of Atlanta & Jonesboro. They burned the R.R. depot & tore up even the rails leading southward; they piled the rails together & then took the crossties & built great fires over the rails & when red hot they had great big iron hooks for handling the red hot rails which they would take & wind them around a telegraph pole.

We remained here (at a field hospital near the Jonesboro battlefield) for three days. The next day they marched us up to Atlanta & put us in a prison pen which we had used to put Federal prisoners in. It had a large frame building in the center, but not large enough to shelter all of us from the rain or from the sun, both of which we had an abundance of. The rations of hardtack, bacon & coffee were so good that we felt we would soon be growing fat. Every day they sent emissaries in to ask if some did not want to take the oath of allegiance to the United States. They would stick handbills all around offering amnesty & transportation home to any who would take the oath not to fight again in the Confederate army, but I rejoice to say not a Kentuckian would listen to them.

Soon we were sent to Chattanooga & put in a pen with not a bit of shelter. It was a block right in the business part of the city with every house burned down and the charred ruins tumbled in upon themselves. To get a level spot to lie down we had to pile the bricks to one side out of the way.

They seemed to think they had been treating us too good, for the rations now were cold cornbread & cold beef & no coffee & scarcely any water. They put their posters offering amnesty & transportation all around & sent in their emissaries urging the men to go home & stop fighting, saying, "Don't you see the Confederacy is whipped?" But thank God not one of our brigade would listen to them.

They kept us in this discomfort for some time, evidently thinking that the thoughts of home & good rations would cause some to weaken, but if any did, it was very few & I know not one that did. Finally we were put on the cars & sent to Nashville. Here we were put in the penitentiary.

But great was our joy the next day when we learned that Gens. Hood & Sherman had agreed to exchange prisoners captured in and around Atlanta. We were sent by rail to Jonesboro & exchanged 18 days after we were captured.

■ Brig. Gen. Daniel C. Govan commanded the Arkansas brigade of Cleburne's division during the campaign. On September 1 at Jonesboro, Govan and more than 600 of his Arkansas veterans were captured. As the prisoners were escorted to the rear, one of them shouted: "Hurrah for Jeff Davis and the Southern Confederacy!" recalled Capt. Joseph C. Patterson of Company F, 98th Ohio. "The inspector of the XIV Corps came riding along, with pistol in hand, saying, 'Show me the man who did that cheering.' I said, 'Oh, Captain, we can take care of him,' at which Gen. Govan said, 'Men, you are prisoners of war, and if you want to be treated as such, behave yourselves.' "

■ Col. George P. Este, 14th Ohio, commanded a brigade in the 3rd Division, XIV Corps, at Jonesboro. It consisted of the 14th Ohio, 38th Ohio, 10th Kentucky and 74th Indiana. "We never liked him very well in camp," recalled a member of the 14th Ohio, "but I tell you he's a whole team in a fight, and he'd do so well there that all would take to him again and he'd be real popular for a while."

'Nearly all in the works surrendered'

An unknown private
Company C
14th Ohio Veteran Volunteer Infantry

About the middle of August our corps, commanded by Jefferson C. Davis, was lying in works at Utoy Creek, a couple of miles from Atlanta. We could see the tall steeples and the high buildings of the city quite plainly. Things had gone on dull and quiet-like for about 10 days. This was longer by a good deal than we had been at rest since we left Resaca in the spring. We knew that something was brewing, and that it must come to a head soon.

Our little mess — now reduced to three by the loss of two of our best soldiers and cooks, Disbrow and Sulier, killed behind headlogs in front of Atlanta by sharpshooters* — had one fellow that we called "Observer" because he had such a faculty of picking up news in his prowling around headquarters. He brought us in so much of this, and it was generally so reliable, that we frequently made up his absence from duty by taking his place. He was never away from a fight, though. On the night of the 25th of August, "Observer" came in with the news that something was in the wind. Sherman was getting awful restless, and we had found out that this always meant lots of trouble to our friends on the other side.

Sure enough, orders came to get ready to move and the next night we all moved to the right and rear out of sight of the Johnnies. Our well-built works were left in charge of Garrard's cavalry, who concealed their horses in the rear and came up and took our places. The whole army except the XX Corps moved quietly off, and did it so nicely that we were gone some time before the enemy suspected it. Then the XX Corps pulled out toward the north and fell back to the Chattahoochee, making quite a show of retreat. The rebels snapped up the bait greedily. They thought the siege was being raised and they poured over their works to hurry the XX boys off. The XX fellows let them know that there was lots of sting in them yet, and the Johnnies were not long in discovering that it would have been money in their pockets if they had let that "star" crowd alone.

But the rebs thought the rest of us were gone for good and that Atlanta was saved. Naturally they felt might happy over it.

In the meantime we were going through so many different kinds of tactics that it looked as if Sherman was really crazy this time. Finally we made a grand left wheel, and then went forward a long way in line of battle. It puzzled us a good deal, but we knew that Sherman couldn't get us into any scrape that Pap Thomas couldn't get us out of, and so it was all right.

Along on the evening of the 31st our right wing seemed to have run against a hornet's nest and we could hear the musketry and cannon speak out real spiteful, but nothing came down our way. We had struck the railroad leading south from Atlanta to Macon and began tearing it up. The jollity at Atlanta was stopped right in the middle by the appalling news that the Yankees hadn't retreated worth a cent, but had broken out in a new and much worse spot than ever. Then there was no end of trouble all around, and Hood started part of his army back after us.

Part of Hardee's and Pat Cleburne's command went into position in front of us. We left them alone until Gen. Stanley could come up on our left and swing around so as to cut off their retreat, when we would bag every one of

* Private Peter W. Disbrow was killed on August 10, while Private David Sulier lost his life in the Atlanta trenches five days later.

them. But Stanley was as slow as he always was and did not come up until it was too late and the game was gone.

The sun was just going down on the evening of the 1st of September when we began to see we were in it for sure. The XIV Corps wheeled into position near the railroad and the sound of musketry and artillery became very loud and clear on our front and left. We turned a little and marched straight toward the racket, becoming more excited every minute. We saw Carlin's brigade of regulars, who were some distance ahead of us, pile knapsacks, form in line, fix bayonets and dash off with a rousing cheer.

The rebel fire beat upon them like a summer rainstorm, the ground shook with the noise, and just as we reached the edge of the cotton field we saw the remnant of the brigade come flying back out of the awful, blasting shower of bullets. The whole slope was covered with dead and wounded.

When we saw this it set our fellows fairly wild; they became just crying mad. I never saw them so before. The order came to strip for the charge and our knapsacks were piled in half a minute. Lieut. Neubert of our company, who was then on the staff of Gen. Baird, our division commander, rode slowly down the line and gave us our instructions to load our guns, fix bayonets and hold fire until we were on top of the rebel works. Then Col. Este sang out clear and steady as a bugle signal:

"Brigade, forward! Guide center! March!"

Heavens, how they did let into us as we came up into range. The fire they poured on us was simply withering. We walked across the hundreds of dead and dying of the regular brigade, and at every step our own men fell down among them.

Gen. Baird's horse was shot down and the general thrown far over his head, but he jumped up and ran alongside of us. Major Wilson, our regimental commander, fell mortally wounded; Lieut. Walter Kirk was killed and also Capt. Spofford, adjutant-general of the brigade. Lieuts. Cobb and Mitchell dropped with wounds that proved fatal in a few days. Capt. Ogan lost an arm, one-third of the enlisted men fell, but we went straight ahead, the grape and the musketry becoming worse every step until we gained the edge of the hill where we were checked a minute by the brush, which the rebels had fixed up in the shape of abatis.

Just then a terrible fire from a new direction, our left, swept down the whole length of our line. The commander of the 17th New York, Major Grower — as gallant a man as ever lived — saw the new trouble, took his regiment in on the run and relieved us of this, but he was himself mortally wounded.

If our boys were half crazy before, they were frantic now, and as we got out of the entanglement of the brush we raised a fearful yell and ran at the works. We climbed the sides, fired right down into the defenders and then began with the bayonet and sword. For a few minutes it was simply awful. On both sides men acted like infuriated devils. They dashed each other's brains out with clubbed muskets; bayonets were driven into men's bodies up to the muzzle of the gun; officers ran their swords through their opponents; and revolvers, after being emptied into the faces of the rebels, were thrown with desperate force into the ranks.

In our regiment was a stout German butcher named Lieut. Frank Fleck. He became so excited that he threw down his sword and rushed among the rebels with his bare fists, knocking down a swath of them. He yelled to the first rebel he met, "Py Gott, I've no patience mit you!" and knocked him sprawling. He caught hold of a rebel officer and snatched him back over the works by main strength. Wonderful to say, he escaped unhurt but the boys will probably not soon let him hear the last of "Py Gott, I've no patience mit you!"

■ Col. William T.C. Grower, commanding the 17th New York, was mortally wounded on September 1 just before the charge against the breastworks of Govan's brigade at Jonesboro. Gen. Absalom Baird wrote a week later: "The fire of the enemy at this point was most destructive, yet the gallant Colonel carried his regiment into position with a heroic bravery challenging the highest admiration, and was himself almost the first to fall before it. The regiment seeing this, for a moment faltered, but was at once reassured, and the order to charge being given, rushed forward along with the 14th and 38th Ohio, and captured not only the works, but nearly all in them."

George E. Sloat, the 14th Ohio's surgeon, recalled that Grower was "shot through the abdomen, a fatal wound. He begged of me to give him something to end his life, which of course I could not think of doing." Grower died two days later.

■ The color guard of the 10th Kentucky, Este's brigade, XIV Corps, poses shortly after the fall of Atlanta. Corporal Orville B. Young hold's the regiment's national flag which he carried in the Jonesboro assault on September 1. Two days later, Col. William H. Hays of the 10th Kentucky wrote that Young "deserves special mention for the manner in which he discharged his duty when the regiment was checked by a murderous fire within 20 yards of the enemy's works. He ran forward with the flag, calling on his comrades to rally to it. It was the first flag placed on the enemy's works."

The 10th Kentucky, by the queerest luck in the world, was matched against the rebel 9th Kentucky. The commanders of the two regiments were brothers-in-law, and the men relatives, friends, acquaintances and schoolmates. They hated each other accordingly, and the fight between them was more bitter, if possible, than anywhere else on the line. The 38th Ohio and 74th Indiana put in some work that was just magnificent. We hadn't time to look at it then, but the dead and wounded piled up after the fight told the story.

We gradually forced our way over the works, but the rebels were game to the last and we had to make them surrender almost one at a time. The artillerymen tried to fire on us when we were so close we could lay our hands on the guns.

Finally, nearly all in the works surrendered and were disarmed and marched back. Just then an aide came dashing up with the information that we must turn the works and get ready to receive Hardee, who was advancing to retake the position. We snatched up some shovels lying near and began work. We had no time to remove the dead and dying rebels on the works, and the dirt we threw covered them up. It proved a false alarm. Hardee had as much as he could do to save his own hide and the affair ended about dark.

When we came to count up what we had gained, we found that we had actually taken more prisoners from behind breastworks than there were in our brigade when we started the charge. We had made the only really successful bayonet charge of the campaign. Every other time since we left Chattanooga the party standing on the defensive had been successful. Here we had taken a strong line with 10 guns, seven battle flags and over 2,000 prisoners. We had lost terribly — not less than one-third of the brigade and many of our best men.

Our regiment went into the battle with 15 officers; nine of these were killed or wounded, and seven of nine lost either their limbs or lives. The 38th Ohio and the other regiments of the brigade lost equally heavy. We thought Chickamauga awful, but Jonesboro discounted it.

■ Private Joseph Monahan, Company I, 14th Ohio. The youth of many of the enlisted men in the Federal army by the end of August 1864 is clearly evident in Monahan's face. He entered the army in February 1864 at the age of 18, and survived the battle of Jonesboro, in which the 14th Ohio lost 30 men killed — including several whose terms of service had expired, but who volunteered nonetheless to go into action.

'Amid a very hell of carnage'

Sergeant Lee H. Rudisille
Company H
38th Ohio Veteran Volunteer Infantry

All day long we had been stubbornly crowding Hood's army, the XIV Corps keeping the general direction of the railroad. About 4 o'clock in the afternoon the forces in front met with considerable resistance, and the heavy firing away to our right indicated that Hood had been fought to a standstill.

About this time the 3rd Division, XIV Corps, commanded by Gen. Absalom Baird, emerged from a dense woods through which it had been fighting its way most of the afternoon, into an open country of nearly a half mile in extent where the Confederate position could be fairly outlined in front, although partially masked by a belt of timber. This woods, as we afterward learned at fearful cost, was composed principally of post or jack-oak timber, with a heavy undergrowth, that had been slashed and tangled in every conceivable shape, making the ground in front of their works — which were about 10 or 12 rods back from the open — almost impassable.

The division was rapidly advanced across this open country, the left resting on or near the railroad, until it reached a depression in the ground, affording a slight shelter, about 500 yards from the enemy's works. In the meantime, a terrific fusilade had been going on a little to our right and front in which a rebel battery was taking part, but did not seem to be doing much damage, for, as one of the boys said, "They did not elevate their guns low enough." However, a lull soon occurred and word went along the line that the brigade of Regulars had attempted to carry the works in their front but failed.

The 3rd Brigade of Baird's division, which was at that time in reserve, was now marched to the right until it reached about the same ground where the fighting had occurred. We were ordered to unsling knapsacks, fix bayonets and be ready for the order to charge. Instructions also were given to have every gun loaded, but to reserve fire until the works were reached. This brigade was composed of the 14th and 38th Ohio, 10th Kentucky and the 74th Indiana. The 38th and 74th were in the advance with

■ Private Gurden R.B. Dunbar, Company K, 38th Ohio, was killed in the assault of Este's brigade against Cleburne's breastworks at Jonesboro on September 1. The 38th Ohio suffered the highest number of casualties of any Federal regiment at Jonesboro. Of 360 officers and enlisted men present for duty, 72 were killed or died of wounds and another 78 were wounded. Dunbar's older brother William, also of Company K, died of disease the previous November at Chattanooga.

the other regiments in close support.

At the command the brigade went forward at the double-quick up a slight grade, the rebels reserving their fire until the front line of the charging column reached the edge of the timber, and then delivered a volley straight into our faces. But their aim being too high, it did comparatively little execution. The works no doubt would have been reached before they could reload if it had not been for the scraggy, tangled brush the line here encountered. As it was, before the advance had forced its way more than half the distance through, it received a withering fire from the works that thinned the ranks frightfully and staggered it for a moment. But the second line soon came up and joined the remnant of the first, and together they fought their way through to the rebel works amid a very hell of carnage. The battle smoke had become so thick that one could scarcely see anything but the flash of the guns.

The color-bearer of the 38th Ohio was killed while clambering over the brush, well in advance of the line. One of the [color] guards picked up the flag and he, too, went down a moment later. Then another took it, only to leave the impression of his death-grasp upon its staff and moisten its folds with his warm life-blood. Then another and still another of the dauntless and devoted color guard raised the old flag to its place in the hot breath of the battle front, and the fifth man took it onto the works and kept it there until the fight was won. This man was Charlie Donze.

There were two guns of a rebel battery near the right of our regiment, with others still farther to the right. It was near this that the Confederate line was first broken. A portion of our line then swinging to the left took that of the Confederates in the flank and rear, and by this means they were about all gobbled in — the smoke being so thick they could not see that their line had been broken.

Well to their right they were found steadily firing to the front and looked somewhat disgusted when the order to surrender was backed up by a nearness and a rear-ness of Federal bayonets. Even after they had been picked out of their works in this manner and gathered together, one regiment would curse the other for allowing the line to be broken, so much at a loss were they to know how and where it had occurred. They were especially indignant when they saw the weakness of our own line. They comprised Govan's entire brigade, one of the best in the Confederate army, which greatly outnumbered our own after the battle as we had lost over one-third of our number before we reached the works.

Our regiment took only about 300 men into the fight, and of these 152 were either killed or wounded; 20 percent or more of the regiment were buried on the field.

Col. William A. Choate fell mortally wounded within 20 feet of the rifle-pits. A better regimental commander and one more beloved never led men into battle. Altogether it did not leave the 38th with one commissioned officer to a company, my own being commanded on the "march to the sea" by Orderly Sergeant J.D. Gleason.

The 3rd Brigade comprised three of the regiments that in the beginning of the war had formed the nucleus of Gen. Thomas' command in Kentucky, and had marched and fought under his watchful eye and fatherly care ever since. Now, at this brilliant culmination of a summer of battles, he issued a General Order complimenting the troops engaged in this action, in which he stated it was the only instance within his knowledge where a body of troops had charged a superior force behind entrenchments, and not only carried the works but captured those defending them.

'Upon us like an avalanche'

Private Gervis D. Grainger
Company I
6th Kentucky Volunteer Infantry
CSA

On August 31st we were moved around to our left wing, the enemy entrenched beyond a creek about half a mile away. A high bank was on that side of the creek and an open field was between the lines. They had several batteries of from six to eight guns each that commanded the opening. We had only a single line of battle.

We were ordered over the works, lined up in front of them and commanded to charge the enemy. We started at full run. Their batteries opened on us by the dozen with grape and canister, shot and shell. The face of the earth was literally torn to pieces, and how any of us escaped is yet a mystery.

I saw a deep gully to my right, and obliquing toward it I did my best running. I leaped into it only to find six or eight of our boys who had preceded me. How they beat me to it I am unable to say. Others retreated to the works we had left, many were killed on the way, some captured in ditches and gullies, but we were overlooked. The flag was with us and, tearing it from the staff, we buried it in the sand, concealing the staff under the rank grass on the bank. When dark came on we resurrected the flag, the color bearer winding it around his body.

We started, groping our way as noiselessly as possible along the meanderings of the gully, often on hands and knees, passed through the Federal pickets on the way and reached our command about nine o'clock. Major Maxson was with us. Stepping off the breastworks we joined the boys, waving the old flag, which was thought to be lost, in the bright fire light.

Next morning we moved into the village of Jonesboro, awaiting orders to reinforce where most needed. This was often the case with the homeless Orphan Brigade. About one o'clock the long roll was ordered and in 10 minutes we were in a double-quick to our right wing. We were placed in line only one column deep with no support. The enemy could be plainly seen one mile away, forming many columns deep.

We went into the ground like gophers and in a short time had improvised breastworks which, though meager, were better than none. To our left the works were better, having been in construction several days.

We heard the bugle call of the enemy sound, "Forward, march!" and the great cloud of blue coats was moving down upon us. Firing commenced right and left. The blaze of the cannon could be seen all along the line. The Yankees were coming slowly but surely, nor did they break their gait until within 200 yards of our works. Then the whole body, 10 or 12 columns deep, moved down upon us like an avalanche.

Ten pieces of our artillery were playing on them, plowing great roads through their ranks. Amidst this fearful fire from our brave men, on they came to our breastworks. They fought like demons. Bayonets clashed bayonets and swords crossed swords, but over our works they came in spite of the most stubborn resistance I ever saw.

Ten lines to our one was too many for us and great numbers of our boys died in this, their last ditch. I was captured with about 300 others. We were taken up the line and crossed over the breastworks where the fight had been fiercest. Many Federals were wounded and dying in the ditch with our men. The scene on top and at the foot of the works beggars description. In some places they were lying three or four deep, and some guns standing on end

■ Col. William A. Choate, commanding the 38th Ohio, led his regiment on September 1 in the charge of Este's brigade against Confederate positions at Jonesboro. As the troops neared their objective — hastily-prepared trenches dug in woods of scrub oak, the 38th lost three color bearers in rapid succession. In spite of heavy losses, the Buckeyes carried the position, but Choate was shot while raising the regiment's national flag from the ground near the breastworks. He died 11 days later.

■ Private William A. Halliburton, 6th/7th Arkansas, was among the 615 officers and enlisted men of Govan's brigade to be captured on September 1 at Jonesboro. Private Stanard C. Harley, also of the 6th/7th, wrote a short time later: "We were stretched one yard apart, trying to cover the enemy's front. The second assault was made in seven columns with fixed bayonets, guns atrail, and without firing a gun they ran over us like a drove of Texas beeves, by sheer force of numbers. We killed and wounded a great many of them, but our line was too weak." Halliburton was exchanged with Govan's entire brigade on September 19 and survived the war.

with bayonets plunged through the bodies of the victims gave ample evidence of the awful conflict.

In going to the rear, for 300 or 400 yards we had to pick our way through the bodies of the dead, dying and wounded, often stepping over them. At one point we passed where a caisson of a battery, which they had been drawing by hand, had been exploded by one of our shells. Only fragments of the pieces could be seen, but hundreds of the victims covered the ground for 50 yards around.

We spent the night under heavy guard in the valley nearby. A load of corn in the ear was thrown out to us which we parched and ate with a relish, having eaten nothing since morning. They issued rations to us next morning, and also orders that we help bury their dead which we promptly refused to do. About nine o'clock we started on our march for Atlanta and were imprisoned that night in barracks in which we had formerly confined our captives. Thence we were carried by rail to Chattanooga where we were kept in prison a week or thereabouts.*

'There, Stanley, you got one!'

Private Stanard C. Harley
Company C
6th/7th Arkansas Volunteer Infantry

We were in single rank, one yard apart, engaged in an effort to cover Sherman's front of six corps, which made our line very weak. Govan's brigade was the second from the right, occupying a curved back to keep Thomas from striking in the rear of our line. Lewis' Kentucky brigade was on our right, curving still further back.

I suppose it was about 3 o'clock when a brigade composed of the 17th New York Zouaves and the 15th and 16th U.S. Regulars charged our regiment, and we sent them back about as fast or a little faster than they came. Our regiment occupied a level piece of ground that dropped suddenly some six or eight feet in a right oblique direction from our front. The assaulting column fell back behind this low ground. The colonel of our regiment ordered two men from each company forward as videttes to see when the enemy was coming, which we felt sure they would do soon.

A man named Elledge and I were sent forward from our company about 150 yards in front. I was shooting at a line to the left in a field, the rear rank holding the guns while the front rank was doing the mole-digging act — digging as hard as they could. I had my sights raised to 200 yards and had fired, maybe, a half dozen shots, and had my gun loaded and was ready to shoot again when a column of troops came up over the bank to my right. They were about as near our line as I was, and it was a race to see who would get there first. As I had the greater incentive (self-preservation), I beat them back by a neck.

* After this, Grainger and other Confederate prisoners were transported by rail from Chattanooga to Nashville. During the trip Grainger used an old case knife he had found in Chattanooga to cut and saw a hole in the bottom of his boxcar. Southeast of Nashville near La Vergne, Tenn., while the train stopped for wood, he escaped through the hole and traveled on foot, by wagon and mule north to Kentucky in an attempt to reach his home. He remained free for some two weeks until recaptured near Scottsville, Ky., and subsequently was imprisoned in Bowling Green, Louisville and Lexington. In early November 1864 Grainger was paroled.

The 8th and 19th (consolidated) Arkansas were on our left with no enemy in their immediate front, as the assault was made from the right. This regiment was enfilading the left of our regiment, which was making it pretty hot for the assaulting column, especially the right.

There was a hickory tree immediately in my front about 10 feet away, about as large as an ordinary man's body. Behind the hickory tree I squirreled it. I saw a color bearer who was protected from the enfilading fire, but within my range. I brought my gun down, and as I lowered it I noticed that I had my sights raised to 200 yards, so I lowered my gun correspondingly and fired, and he fell — whether killed or not I never knew.

Elledge, who was sent out with me and who always called me "Stanley," even though that was not my name, cried out: "There, Stanley, you got one!" As soon as I fired I squatted behind our little log works, got out another cartridge and looked up to insert it in my gun above me — and there were two Federal soldiers standing above me with fixed bayonets and cocked guns.

I was so frightened that I forgot that I had not loaded my gun, though I had started to do so. I jumped from under their bayonets, placed my gun near one's breast and snapped it, and did the rabbit act at a two-forty rate away from there. Five or six of us ran out, but only one was killed. It is miraculous how we escaped, under the circumstances. The only way I can account for it is that the greater part of the regiment surrendered, which occupied the attention of the men until we got, perhaps, 60 yards away through the thick saplings before they fired at us; and when they did there was a tremendous racket among the saplings around us, which had a wonderful effect on our locomotion.

Our pace was fast. All that kept us from flying was we didn't have our wings with us. We ran a short distance and met Gen. Maney's brigade coming as a reinforcement, and seeing our division commander, Gen. Pat Cleburne, we reported to him what had occurred and he told us to take our places with Gen. Granbury's brigade of Texans, which we did. And thus ended the battle of Jonesboro so far as we were concerned.

■ Col. Charles Hart Olmstead, commander of the 1st Georgia Volunteers, led Mercer's-Smith's brigade of Cleburne's division during the battle of Jonesboro. When his brigade was ordered to the Confederate right to relieve part of Stevenson's division at daylight on September 1, he found that "our new line was not a good one; it was imperfectly laid out and only partially completed, and the enemy had gotten so close onto it that in sending out our pickets to relieve Gen. Stevenson's pickets, some 33 of our men were captured." Earlier in the war, Olmstead served along the Atlantic coast at Fort Pulaski, surrendering its garrison on April 11, 1862, after a two-day bombardment.

'Like a horrible dream'

Col. Charles Hart Olmstead
1st Georgia Volunteer Infantry

After Gen. Walker's fall his division was broken up and its brigades assigned to other divisions.* We were honored by being placed under Gen. Pat Cleburne who commanded *the* fighting division, "par excellence," of the Army of Tennessee. He had seen [our] brigade going into action on the 22nd and had made special request that it might be given to him. Gen. Mercer was returned to his old position on the Georgia coast, and Gen. Argyle Smith was assigned to the command of the brigade. He was on furlough recovering from wounds, so when I returned to duty I, as senior colonel, took his place.

Gen. Cleburne was a distinguished soldier, one of the finest that the war produced upon our side, and I have always felt that it was a privilege to

* Gen. William H.T. Walker, who was killed on July 22 in the Battle of Atlanta.

■ Col. Robert Beckham became the Army of Tennessee's chief of artillery in late July. For the remainder of the campaign he commanded almost as many guns as Sherman had at Atlanta, but faced severe shortages of ammunition and supplies. On September 1 at Jonesboro, Beckham lost two entire batteries during the Federal assault — Key's Arkansas and Swett's Mississippi, comprising eight field pieces. "It was a grand and fearful sight to see that great army coming like a monster wave to ingulf us," wrote Mississippi artilleryman Joseph Erwin of Swett's Battery. "We poured grape and canister into them cutting great gaps in their lines; but they closed them up with fresh men, and came on to the very muzzles of our guns." Three months later, Beckham was mortally wounded on November 29 at Spring Hill, Tenn., when a shell struck a large boulder and hurled a rock fragment into his temple.

serve under him. He was an Irishman by birth, a man of humble beginnings, having in youth been a private in the British army. When the war began he was a practicing lawyer somewhere in Arkansas. Entering the Confederate army, he rose rapidly from one rank to another, filling each place with honor and rising by sheer force of merit. As a division commander he had no superior; whether he would have been equal to higher command cannot be said, though none that knew him doubted it. What specially struck me about him was his perfect grasp of every detail of his division. When on the march we would go into bivouac at night and he would sit on his horse until the last regiment filed off the road — that he might know personally the location of every unit of the command.

In establishing a picket line he always went himself with the engineer officer and saw that the rifle pits were well constructed and mutually supporting. If there was a halt of some days in any one place he invariably utilized the occasion to inspect every musket with his own hands and eyes. As a consequence of this constant and careful supervision Cleburne's division was always in a state of high efficiency, ready for any duty to which it might be called. The brigadiers under him were men of ability and experience: Lowrey of Mississippi, Govan of Arkansas, Granbury of Texas, and our own Argyle Smith, who had the reputation of getting wounded in every fight that he ever went into. Altogether it was a division that one might well be proud of belonging to.

During the month of August little was done by either army; there was always hot firing on the picket lines, but the main bodies were resting and recuperating after the sanguinary engagements of the previous month. We were on the left of the army guarding the railroad between Atlanta and Macon, which was now the road over which our supplies came. The enemy were constantly in evidence in our front, but one morning (I think it was on August 30th) we woke up to find that they had disappeared entirely. Some of us went out to visit the camps they had occupied, and we were much interested to note the ingenuity that had been exercised there to make the men comfortable. On one of the little huts was a placard bearing the words "Good bye Johnny Reb, we'll see you later" — a fact of which none of us had any doubt.

That night Hood held Atlanta with one of his three corps and sent the other two, Hardee's and Lee's, down to Jonesboro, 20 miles south on the railroad, to which point Sherman was pushing his right wing. That was the explanation of its having left our front.

We marched all night long and in the dim gray light of the morning reached the little town and at once went into position to the west of the railroad. It was a misty morning, the air was heavy with moisture, and it muffled the sound of the skirmishing that was already going on, so it seemed as though an army of woodchoppers was at work in the distance. As soon as we were in line, the 54th Georgia Regiment, next to mine, started a fire with the view to getting a little warm breakfast. The blaze felt good to men who had been marching all night, so it was quite provoking when, in adjusting the line of battle, we were compelled to move two or three hundred paces to the left and leave our cheerful fire to others. However, another was soon started, when suddenly a shell from a Yankee battery fell and exploded in the center of the group gathered around the fire we had just left. I don't know how many men were killed, but I could see several of them writhing and struggling and then settling down into the quiet of death. It was a pitiful sight that moved us all greatly.

All that morning we waited, most of the time in line of battle, doing nothing save the shifting of position, sometimes a little to the right and then to the left, while every now and then a man would fall under the fire of the enemy's sharpshooters. It was very trying, much more so than positive action would have been, even though it brought us into greater danger. At last the order to advance was given and on we went; the pace gradually quickening almost to a run. The ground before us was a gentle slope down to where the Flint River wound its way through the lowlands — then upward to the works of the enemy.

As the men went forward cheering, a battery of light artillery commanded by Capt. Beauregard (a son of the general)* followed, the guns leaping and bounding over the uneven surface of the ground, drivers whipping and spurring, horses wild with excitement, cannoneers clinging for dear life to their seats on the caissons and ammunition boxes — as fine an exhibition of warlike power as could be imagined. Again and again at the order *"Action front!"* the teams were brought around in sweeping curves in the full run, the men leaped to their places, the guns were unlimbered and bang!! bang!! bang!! went the shells hurtling over our heads. It fascinated me to watch them.

Nearing the river I happened to strike a boggy place in which my mare sank to the saddle flaps, and every struggle seemed to sink her deeper. Meanwhile, the line was advancing, leaving me, the brigade commander, stuck in the mud. It was an unendurable plight in which to remain for a minute under the circumstances, so I climbed over the mare's head and pushed forward on foot, hoping that Linsky, my orderly, would find Lady Gray and rescue her, which very fortunately he did.

The Flint was a shallow stream through which the division dashed without trouble, then up to the works from which the enemy retreated as we approached. But the fight had gone against us in other parts of the field and we were ordered back to the original position. Returning over the field through which we had charged, I noticed where an entire team of the battery horses had been killed by a shell; the four of them lay in pairs with the harness upon them just as they had been hitched up.

I spoke of the passage of the Flint as having been made without difficulty, and so it was for all excepting Capt. Charlie Russell of the 54th. As that regiment got to the bank and looked at the yellow water of unknown depth, the men hesitated a little before entering the stream. Noticing this, Russell, who was always inclined to be melodramatic, waved his sword and shouted, "Don't be afraid of a little water, men; it's only knee deep. Follow me!" Then he stepped in *up to his neck,* having unfortunately found a place where the current had washed a hole under the bank. Of course, there was a great shout of laughter as the men went by on either side of him through the shallow water.

Gen. Henry R. Jackson's brigade had attacked immediately on our right. On his staff — his adjutant general, I think — was Joe Holcombe, one of my old school mates at Marietta. Poor fellow, he was desperately wounded. I saw him as he was being brought from the field and it grieved me beyond measure to be told that his wound was mortal. He died a few hours after.

That night Lee's corps was hurriedly ordered back to Atlanta and Hardee's corps was left alone to face the largely augmented forces of the enemy at Jonesboro. Cleburne's division was withdrawn from its position on the extreme left of the army and ordered to near the extreme right to fill the gap left by Lee, a division to take the place of a corps. Just before daybreak we filed into the slight works that Lee had hastily constructed the day

■ Orderly Sergeant James Fisher Pray, Company I, 14th Ohio, was killed September 1 at Jonesboro. A comrade recalled that a few days before the battle Pray "had a presentiment that we were going into a fight, and that he would be killed." When the regiment was piling knapsacks prior to the charge, Pray was offered the chance to stay behind and guard them, but he refused. "So he went into the fight and was killed, as he knew he would be."

* 1st Lieut. Rene T. Beauregard, who was in command of Ferguson's (South Carolina) Battery, Martin's Battalion, Hardee's Corps.

■ Officers of the 10th Kentucky shortly after the regiment's bayonet charge on September 1 at Jonesboro. The 10th went into the battle with a depleted strength of 152 rifles, losing five men killed and 26 wounded. Three officers also were shot but survived, including Capt. James M. Davenport (second from right), commander of Company G, who lost his right leg. Seated to his immediate right is Col. William H. Hays, regimental commander; Lt. Col. Gabriel C. Wharton (seventh from left); and Major Henry G. Davidson (ninth from left). Davidson died of disease only weeks later on November 21, 1864, at Louisville, Ky.

Private Henry B. Mattingly of the 10th's Company B received the Medal of Honor at Jonesboro — for capturing the colors of the 6th/7th Arkansas. Company B carried on its roll the names of seven Mattinglys, two of whom died during their service.

before and woefully spread out. We were in them — the men in single line and about a yard apart. As we left the road to go into this position, the field officers all dismounted, giving their horses to the various orderlies who were there to receive them. These were all in a group together, among them a man named Bonny. He was mounted on a miserable old nag that he had picked up somewhere, and was leading a string-halted charger that belonged to our brigadier, the bridles of the two horses being hitched together by a rein. The movement of the troops made a certain amount of noise, though it was done as quietly as possible; it attracted the attention of a Yankee battery located some 700 or 800 yards down the road and they opened upon us with shrapnel. Fortunately, it was too dark for them to see us and they aimed too high, but the whistling of the shells overhead frightened both orderlies and horses, all of whom made a dash for the rear without standing on ceremony.

Bonny was in specially hard luck with his double team when we last saw him. The string-halted horse had gone on one side of a tree, while the other one that he rode took the other side and the most frantic efforts did not get him on an inch. I don't know how he finally got out of the predicament. Bonny was as arrant a coward as ever lived, though very valiant, whenever he managed to get a little whisky. On one such occasion he was heard expressing himself to this effect: "It's a good thing as I ain't in command of this 'ere army — I'm one of the charging kind."

The division was formed in the trenches in the following order by brigades: Govan on the right, then Granbury, Lowrey and Smith (his brigade under my command). The enemy were so close that we could not send out a picket line; in fact, an attempt to do so resulted in the capture of a number of the men. Everything was quiet for a few hours after we got into position; then began a steady firing of both musketry and artillery that lasted throughout the day without serious loss to either side.

In front of Govan's brigade the ground sloped gradually for about 50 yards and then dipped suddenly into a valley which could not be seen from our works. In this depression a heavy storming column of the Yankees was assembled in perfect safety to themselves and unknown to us. About the middle of the afternoon there was a rapid increase of the firing and the division stood in expectancy of the assault that this presaged. It came in an instant upon Govan; the attacking column rising suddenly from the valley, rank after rank, had but a short rush to make and literally ran over his slender line, capturing him and most of his brigade.

Thus the division was pierced, and had supporting troops promptly poured through the gap so made, irretrievable disaster would have befallen Hardee's corps. But the commands on either side were under brave and experienced leaders whose valor had been tested on numberless fields — men ready in resource and not easily flurried by untoward events. Granbury promptly swung back his left wing and Lowrey his right, so that any force attempting to advance through the gap in our line would have had a deadly fire from those two splendid brigades on both flanks. The attempt was not made and night came on without change in the situation.

Hardee's corps was surely most critically placed when night came upon us after two days of unsuccessful fighting. Twenty miles away from the main body of the army and almost surrounded by a largely superior force, the enemy so close we could hear them talking. It was vitally necessary for us to get away from so compromising a position, yet every road was closed to us except the one that leads southward from Jonesboro to Macon. I have read in some accounts of the battle that Howard's army had been ordered to throw itself across the road so as to cut off our retreat absolutely, but that it missed its way in the darkness of the night in marching through the thickly wooded country. However that may be, the road was open and we availed ourselves to it. The order to march came along about 10 o'clock and the men moved out as silently as possible. A certain amount of noise could not be avoided, and that was accounted for to the enemy by sundry calls to the various regiments to come and draw their rations.

We got away from the trenches without molestation, and marching all night reached Lovejoy's Station on the Macon & Western Railroad about daylight. The memory of that night's march is like a horrible dream. I was so tired physically as scarcely to be able to sit on my horse, and the mental depression, deep enough because of our own failure, was the more profound as the red glare in the northern sky and the sullen rumble of distant explosions told that Hood was burning his stores and abandoning Atlanta to Sherman. The long campaign had ended in defeat and disaster.

■ 1st Lieut. Andrew Urban, adjutant of the 70th Ohio, was killed by a sharpshooter on September 3 near Lovejoy's Station as he read to the regiment Sherman's Special Field Order No. 62, announcing the fall of Atlanta. "Oh, boys, I am killed!" he said before falling to the ground, dead. After passing through Urban's chest, the same bullet then struck Private James W. Reed of Company B in the arm.

Atlanta by slow degrees is passing away

The fall of the Gate City

As the pale light of early morning began to illuminate the shattered Confederate breastworks at Jonesboro on September 2, the men of nearly all of Sherman's army soon learned that their adversary once again had vanished.

The previous night, what remained of Hardee's corps evacuated the battlefield and marched dejectedly south to Lovejoy's Station, six miles farther down the Macon & Western Railroad. Hardee was joined there by the two other weary corps of the Army of Tennessee, sent by Hood who earlier on September 1 had decided to abandon Atlanta. The only Confederates remaining in the city were Alabama and Mississippi rearguard cavalry belonging to Brig. Gen. Samuel W. Ferguson's brigade, and a few engineers, assigned to destroy Hood's reserve ordnance train which had neglected to be sent to safety while the railroad was still operating. Just after midnight on the 2nd, the engineers torched the train's five locomotives and more than 80 rail cars containing siege guns, shells, muskets, small-arms ammunition and other equipment. The resulting explosions ripped through the night, severing tracks, flattening a nearby factory, showering the air with fiery debris and creating a blaze that burned until dawn.

A few miles north of the Atlanta defenses vacated only hours before by A.P. Stewart's corps, the newly appointed commander of the Federal XX Corps, Maj. Gen. Henry W. Slocum, listened to the explosions and correctly concluded the Confederates were blowing up their stores. The XX Corps had been left above Atlanta by Sherman to guard the ferries and railroad bridge over the Chattahoochee River, while at the same time keeping an eye on those Confederates manning the city's fortifications as the rest of the Union army slipped around to cut off Hood from the south. At first light on September 2, Slocum sent out reconnoitering parties, the two largest commanded by Col. John Coburn of the 33rd Indiana and Lt. Col. Thomas M. Walker of the 111th Pennsylvania. What occurred in the next few hours touched off a somewhat acrimonious debate between the two officers as to just who had the rightful claim of entering the city of Atlanta first.

Col. John Coburn
33rd Indiana Veteran Volunteer Infantry
2nd Brigade, 3rd Division, XX Corps

On the 2d of September, at 6 a.m., under orders from Brigadier-General Ward, I marched on a reconnaissance from Turner's Ferry to find the position of the enemy toward Atlanta. I had under my command 900 infantry,

composed of 500 men of my brigade, commanded by Captain Crawford, Eighty-fifth Indiana; Captain Baldwin, Nineteenth Michigan; Captain May, Twenty-second Wisconsin, and Lieutenant Freeland, Thirty-third Indiana; and 400 of the Third Brigade, under command of Major Wickham, Fifty-fifth Ohio, together with 40 mounted men under Captain Scott, Seventieth Indiana. Two hundred and forty men were thrown forward as skirmishers and flankers, and so advanced without opposition until we reached the earth-works recently abandoned by us near Atlanta. Here, after a short delay, occasioned by a slight skirmish with a few mounted men and sentinels, we proceeded through the lines of the enemy's works, finding them abandoned.

A brigade of the enemy's cavalry was found to be in the city and we advanced cautiously. I was met in the suburbs by Mr. Calhoun, the mayor, with a committee of citizens bearing a flag of truce. He surrendered the city to me, saying "he only asked protection for persons and property." This was at 11 a.m.

I asked him if the rebel cavalry was yet in the city. He replied that Ferguson's brigade was there, but on the point of leaving. I replied that my force was moving into the city and that unless that force retired there would be a fight in which neither person nor property would be safe, and that if necessary I would burn the houses of citizens to dislodge the enemy; that I did not otherwise intend to injure persons or property of the citizens unless used against us.

I ordered my skirmishers to advance, and they proceeded through the city, the cavalry rapidly evacuating the place. I at once sent dispatches to Brigadier-General Ward, at Turner's Ferry, and to Major-General Slocum, at the railroad bridge, of the occupation of the city by my command. General Slocum came at once to the city. Immediately preceding him came a portion of the First and Second Divisions of the Twentieth Corps. General Ward directed a portion of my brigade to move up from Turner's Ferry, under command of Lieutenant-Colonel Bloodgood, Twenty-second Wisconsin, which reached Atlanta about sunset, and the remainder, under Major

■ Members of Company C, 84th Indiana, pose with the regimental colors (laying in the foreground) in the spring of 1864. On September 2, after the battle of Jonesboro, the 84th was ordered along the Macon Railroad to follow the Confederate retreat toward Lovejoy's Station. "About 4:30 p.m. the general commanding ordered me to move my command on the enemy's lines," wrote Capt. John C. Taylor, commander of the 84th, "which I did, charging and taking his entire skirmish line in the front of my regiment, amounting in all to 27 prisoners — 2 commissioned officers and 25 enlisted men. I was struck on the shoulder by a canister-shot, inflicting a slight wound which caused me to leave the field after turning command over to Capt. [Martin B.] Miller, who held the line taken by me under the most terrific fire of artillery and musketry ..."

■ Col. John Coburn, 33rd Indiana, commanded a brigade in the 3rd Division, XX Corps, during the campaign. The previous year on March 5, 1863, at Thompson's Station, Tenn., he was forced to surrender himself and 1,221 of the Indiana, Michigan and Wisconsin troops of his brigade after a sharp fight against the numerically superior Confederate commands of Nathan Bedford Forrest and Earl Van Dorn. Coburn recalled that when Van Dorn learned which states his troops came from, the Confederate general told his adjutant-general, "These are northwestern men. Treat them well." Coburn was sent to Libby Prison in Richmond, Va., and exchanged within three months.

Miller, the next morning.

Soon after General Slocum's arrival he directed me to move my command, which then occupied the works of the enemy on the southeastern part of the city, to the right of the Augusta railroad. This was done, and General Knipe's brigade was posted on the left of the road in single line, deployed at intervals of three paces ...

The command captured 123 prisoners, including those in hospital. Some 200 small-arms were found in the City Hall, and about 16 pieces of artillery abandoned in the works and burned with the train of cars. The ammunition abandoned had been fired in the night and continued to explode with loud reports after we had entered the city in the forts and among the ruins of the burning shops and buildings where it had been deposited.

The works of the enemy were left almost perfect, and there seemed to have been no attempt at destruction of anything but of the material of war. As we passed through the streets many of the citizens ran gladly out to meet us, welcoming us as deliverers from the despotism of the Confederacy; others regarded us with apprehension and begged to be spared from robbery. I assured them they would be safe from this.

Many of the buildings were found to be much injured by our artillery, but such as will be needed for public use can be taken at once with slight repairs. My command on the reconnaissance behaved with remarkable promptness and energy, and deserved to be first, as they were, of our army to enter the city. The losses in this time are 5 killed and 22 wounded.*

Lt. Col. Thomas M. Walker
111th Pennsylvania Veteran Volunteer Infantry
3rd Brigade, 2nd Division, XX Corps

[My] detachment, consisting of the One Hundred and eleventh Regiment Pennsylvania Veteran Volunteers, Sixtieth New York Veteran Volunteers, and 50 men from each Twenty-ninth Pennsylvania Veteran Volunteers and One Hundred and second New York Veteran Volunteers, together with about 20 men of the Seventh Pennsylvania Cavalry, in all 400 infantry and 20 cavalry, moved on the road from Pace's Ferry to Howell's Mill at 6:45 a.m.

Skirmishers were thrown out to the front immediately after passing the pickets, but we advanced rapidly until after we crossed Nancy's Creek and to where the road turns off to Buck Head. Here the track of a column (cavalry) that had very shortly before moved down the Buck Head road was discovered, and the command halted until the Sixtieth New York could be advanced down the Buck Head road to the junction of the road leading to Howell's Mill. As soon as information was brought me of their having arrived at that point, they were ordered to move in the direction of Howell's Mill and join us there.

We here learned that General Ferguson's brigade of cavalry, which had been encamped near the mill, had moved away a few hours before in the direction of Atlanta. Fording with our horses and passing the command over Peach Tree Creek on a log, we pushed on toward the city.

At the outskirts of the town I met Colonel Coburn, of the Third Division, who had also preceded his column, and discovering that the city was evacuated (there being nothing but the brigade of cavalry before mentioned in the town), we agreed that the two columns should march into town together, when I withdrew my skirmish line and placed them in the column. The two

* Coburn's official report of his command's movements and entry into Atlanta was submitted on September 12, eight days before he was mustered out of the army. He was brevetted brigadier general on March 13, 1865.

columns were placed in position in the rifle-pits, when we went forward to the skirmish line passing through the city.

When in the neighborhood of the City Hall, Colonel Coburn informed me that he had ordered his column to move into the city. I was chagrined at this avowal, that I thought to be in violation of our agreement to come in together, and directed Captain Lambert, Thirty-third New Jersey, of the general's staff, to ride back and order my column in at once. I am happy to state that he did ride, and fast; arrived and delivered the order before it had reached the other column, and, by direction, placing the colors of the One Hundred and eleventh Pennsylvania Veteran Volunteers and Sixtieth New York Volunteers at the head of the column, marched to the City Hall in the following order: One Hundred and eleventh Pennsylvania Veteran Volunteers, Sixtieth New York Veteran Volunteers, detachment Twenty-ninth Pennsylvania Veteran Volunteers, and detachment One Hundred and second New York Veteran Volunteers, when the two colors were at the same time displayed from the roof of the City Hall, amid the cheers and congratulations of the column.

Not being positive, I do not like to set the time of our arrival and entry, but thought it to be near 10 a.m. when we arrived, and in the neighborhood of noon that we marched into the city. I am sure it will be a satisfaction to the general to know officially that a column of his division was the first to march into the city, and that the colors of the One Hundred and eleventh Pennsylvania Veteran Volunteers and Sixtieth New York Veteran Volunteers, Third Brigade of his division, were the first displayed over this stronghold. ...*

■ Lt. Col. Thomas M. Walker assumed command of the 111th Pennsylvania on July 21 following the death of Col. George Cobham at Peachtree Creek. Walker began the campaign with the 111th, but during the first three weeks of July he temporarily led the 29th Pennsylvania — a regiment whose command devolved upon six different officers from May to September 1864.

Despite this debate, by late afternoon and early evening of September 2 the ebullient Federals of Slocum's three divisions walked over the Confederate fortifications and marched with blaring bands into the city. As they did, the exhausted troopers of Ferguson's brigade rode out of Atlanta.

Private G.W. Douglas of the 11th Mississippi Cavalry later recalled: "There was a considerable amount of Confederate stores in the city and these were being appropriated by citizens and soldiers ... A man rolling a barrel of flour on a wheelbarrow, going in the direction of the Yankees, was met by us. On being told that the Yanks were close behind, he turned into an alley. When the head of our column reached the square near the old car shed, it was forced to halt for a few minutes by the great throng of people engaged in pillaging and carrying away government stores. Some of our own men slid from their horses and engaged in the scramble, but obtained nothing very valuable. One fat old chap belonging to Company B secured a box of tobacco, and I had to help him remount with his prize. As soon as we could get through we resumed our march, taking the McDonough road. Halting for a moment on top of the hill, I looked back and could see the blue column entering the square, from which the pillagers had departed in hot haste."

"It can be imagined what was the rejoicing among the troops when it really turned out that Atlanta was taken," wrote Col. Adin B. Underwood of the 33rd Massachusetts. "Loud shouting and cheering ran along the lines, every one had a hurrah for 'Uncle Billy.' The Thirty-third marched ... through the principal streets, the band playing 'Hail Columbia' and 'The Red, White and Blue,' reported to Gen. Slocum and was assigned to comfortable quarters in deserted buildings, and the duty of guarding rebel prisoners. The negroes, black, yellow and white, hailed our men as

* Walker's official report of his column's reconnaissance and occupation of Atlanta was dated September 6, six days before Col. Coburn's report.

■ Maj. Gen. Henry W. Slocum took command of the XX Corps along the Chattahoochee River on August 27. Coming from the post of commander of the District of Vicksburg, he was the permanent replacement for Gen. Hooker, who had resigned in a pique of anger exactly one month before. One of the first things Slocum did after his troops entered Atlanta on September 2 was to send a wire to Washington, informing authorities at the War Department that many of his men had not been paid for eight months, and that paymasters be sent to correct the situation immediately.

their deliverers sent of God. 'Bress de Lord,' they shouted ... 'de Yanks am come, yah! yah! yah!' "

"Most of the citizens that remained in the place," wrote 1st Lieut. Edwin Weller of the 107th New York, "were out at the gates and on the walks to see the Yankees come in, and viewed us with seeming curiosity. They expected no doubt to see a huge set of beings but I rather think they came to the conclusion that we were human, in appearance at least. A majority of those I saw were ladies. Many of them waved their white handkerchiefs at us very politely while some few swung to the breeze the stars and stripes which were cheered enthusiasticly by our boys as we passed."

Many of the Federals were impressed by the city itself. "I doubt if to-day there are many cities in the North, of the same size, which are quieter or cleaner than this one," wrote Lt. Col. Charles F. Morse of the 2nd Massachusetts in a letter home on September 11. "Atlanta is a very pretty place, and less Southern in its appearance than any I have seen ... There are large numbers of elegant residences, showing evidence of a refined population; in a good many cases they are deserted. Our shells destroyed a great deal of property, but I am sorry now that a single one was thrown into the city, for I don't think they hastened the surrender by a day."

Chaplain G.S. Bradley of the 22nd Wisconsin found the bombardment's damage spread unevenly in Atlanta. On September 12, he wrote: "In the northern portion of the city, nearly every house is damaged by shell from *Yankee guns,* and some fine dwellings are nearly demolished, shade trees cut down and fences splintered. In nearly every yard is a bomb-proof, or 'gopher hole,' as the boys call them, in which the families fled for safety when shells came thickest. These 'holes' are about six or eight feet deep, and from eight to twelve feet square, planked over and covered with dirt to the depth of three or four feet, with a little doorway upon the south side. I heard of one instance where a family of six or more, with some friends — young ladies of the neighborhood — were gathered, in the afternoon, during the bombardment. A shell of large size came plowing through the covering and exploded in the midst of them, killing five, and wounding nearly all."

Even generals took time to write home about finally achieving the long-awaited goal of reaching Atlanta. Lt. Col. Morse's division commander penned the following lines on September 3 to his daughters in Michigan:

Brig. Gen. Alpheus S. Williams
Commanding 1st Division, XX Corps

I have dated my letters so long from *Near* Atlanta that it is quite a change to write *"In* Atlanta." Most of our corps came in yesterday evening, the Rebels having evacuated the night previous. We remained in our old camp and works in front of Atlanta until the night of [August] 25th, when the 20th and the 4th corps on our right were withdrawn to cover important operations of the army. Our corps moved to three crossings of the Chattahoochee; Pace's and Furness' ferries and the railroad crossings. We did not march, except to move out of the trenches, until the 4th Corps had withdrawn across our front and taken a new position. It was after 2 o'clock at night before we got away. The Rebs never fired a shot at us and we quietly took up our new positions on the south side of the Chattahoochee. We entrenched ourselves strongly and awaited the progress of events by the rest of the army, which moved southward to strike the Macon Railroad. We heard little from it, but every day we made reconnaissances in force toward Atlanta, getting up to our old line, where the enemy appeared in force.

On the night of the 1st inst. I was awakened from a dream of heavy

■ One of the many bombproof caves dug by residents of Atlanta, in which they sought shelter during the bombardment of the city. Union soldiers frequently referred to the caves as "gopher holes," and many like 1st Lieut. Edwin Weller, 107th New York, were amazed at the amenities they contained. Weller wrote: "Some families had a cave dug in their gardens, floored, carpeted and furnished for living in. It was quite a curiosity to visit those caves soon after we occupied the city and see with what taste and comfort they had arranged them for living in."

thunder in which the earth seemed to tremble. Heavy reports of what I thought artillery firing followed in rapid succession, and for two hours or more the roll of artillery firing seemed to increase, while a red glare lit up the skies in the direction of Atlanta, with fitful shooting up through the clouds that hung over the town. After listening and wondering for an hour or more I concluded that Sherman had driven the enemy near the southeast part of the city and had attacked or was being attacked.

I was strengthened in this belief as toward morning the firing was renewed with more regularity. I inclined at first to the opinion that the reports were explosions, but I had heard distant firing so resembling this, and the line of sound seemed to recede, so my judgment settled down on artillery. We know now it was the explosion of powder shot and shell from eighty-two carloads of Rebel ordnance stores, and the burning of a large car factory. At daylight we started out reconnoitering parties and about noon our advance had entered and occupied the town. I brought up two brigades of my division, reaching this [place] after dark. We entered the town with bands playing. The people say that the Rebel army has gone toward Macon, avoiding the position of Sherman. A good many people are still in town, but my duties on the lines which the Rebs built to protect the town have not yet given me much chance to see this town of greater distances than the original city of Washington. It appears to be scattered over leagues, having a thickly-built business center.

Many [residents] are said to be sincerely Union. As I was marching at the

'Snug huts and quarters'

■ Camp of the 111th Pennsylvania at State Square in Atlanta, looking toward Decatur Street. The Trout House, one of the city's finer hotels, the Masonic Hall (at right), and the Western & Atlantic passenger depot were some of the prominent structures bordering the square. During the occupation, the 111th Pennsylvania, along with the 2nd and 33rd Massachusetts, made up the city's provost guard, under the command of Col. William Cogswell, 2nd Massachusetts. These regiments performed "very pleasant duty ... which was to preserve order, arrest prisoners, keep the ... boots blacked, clothing brushed, guns and brasses shining, and the members themselves generally comfortable," the 33rd's historian later wrote. "To this end, snug huts and quarters were constructed in the city."

Just outside Atlanta, "about 2 miles from the center of the town in a north easterly direction, we ... have a very pleasant camping ground on a high grass knoll," wrote Major Daniel H. Fox of the 101st Ohio. "We have to build shacks and these I much prefer to the timber. We have our quarters fixed up in comfortable shape. We, that is Col. McDonald and myself, have a large new wall tent and have a good pine floor in it and have made us a very comfortable bed and succeeded in getting a couple of good chairs and have a pine table. We are having a shade put up in front of our tent and when that is finished, will be very comfortable indeed as far as the living is concerned."

On September 11, Fox helped the former commander of the 101st, Col. Isaac M. Kirby, prepare his official report of the campaign. "It was rather a tedious job as we, neither one of us, had kept any notes of the different days' operations and had to write from memory. We did not get it completed until near midnight ... It made a very respectable document for length but not much in style as we had no time to review it after it was once written." Fox resigned his commission on September 28, 1864, just 17 days after the report was finished.

head of my column last night through the dark streets, made intensely so by the heavy shade-trees, I heard a window shoved up and a female voice cry out, "Welcome!" I cried back, "Thank you, and the more so as it is a rare sound down here." It did, indeed, seem strange, that voice of welcome where we have met little but battle and carnage, coming so suddenly from the impenetrable darkness. For more than a month we have lain face to face with the heavy works thrown around this city, and day after day have I peered over our trenches to catch some new idea of the position of affairs. Three high, broad parapets seemed to bid defiance, and my curiosity was generally met with sharp efforts to plug my head. Week after week their heavy guns and ours have kept up a roaring, during which we have thrown thousands of projectiles from the twenty-pounder Parrott to the sixty-odd-weight ball into this city.

It seemed, therefore, very strange to march unopposed, as I did last night, through these same hostile works, and especially right alongside of one of those frowning fortresses that lay in my original front and which had killed or maimed hundreds of men of my division. I rode along full of queer sensations and exciting emotions. It was too dark to see much, but there was the principal battlement which had caused so much trouble and injury and not a sound came from it. I could hardly realize that its strong and defiant voice had really been silenced. ...

On arriving here last night I took quarters at a very imposing-looking house, as seen by the dim candle light. A very large room with a broad bed and white counterpane promised a splendid rest, after a fatiguing day. It was the first time in four months I had slept in a house. You will laugh when I tell you that I found the air oppressive and could not sleep. To add to the troubles, the bugs (bedbugs I suppose) worked on me from head to foot. I have never, during the campaign, sleeping under trees, on the ground, or in straw, suffered anything like it from the numberless variety of wood-ticks, jiggers and other festering biters that fill every atom of the dirt of this section. The consequence was, of course, a very disturbed night and the getting up at daylight with a resolution to have my tent pitched and go back to the luxury of my cot and blankets. ...

Writing home and expanding journal and diary entries consumed time for many of Sherman's officers and enlisted men once the remainder of the army moved up from Lovejoy's Station to camps south and east of Atlanta. Just after the XVII Corps marched into the city's outskirts on September 5, an Indiana doctor noted in his diary the date was the day of the military draft in the North, and that his comrades sarcastically hoped that "some of their copperhead neighbors may draw their fortunes today in Uncle Sam's lottery" now that Atlanta had been seized. He also recorded scenes both tragic and comically absurd as his regiment entered the Gate City:

Assistant Surgeon James C. Patten
58th Indiana Veteran Volunteer Infantry

We marched on till we came in sight of the rebel works around Atlanta. Here I saw the most pitiful sight I have ever yet witnessed. A young looking woman was at work by the roadside skinning a cow that had been killed and a little girl some six or seven years old had a piece of the raw bloody meat in both hands devouring it with the eagerness of a starving dog.

We soon came in sight of Atlanta and here all of a sudden Col. Buell concluded that we must begin to put on style and show off. He began to scold because the men had their coats off. He wore a light linen one himself. The men naturally did not like it to be abused so unreasonably, when they were not in fault, and so when showing off time came they became very awkward. One who did not know might have thought them not half drilled.

The Colonel, looking along the line, had his anger stirred by the sight of a man going through the manual with his gun wrong end up. He was almost ready to burst. He fairly boiled over, and putting spurs to his horse went for him. When he got there he could not tell which man it was for all was right when he got there and no one knew anything about him. The Soldiers are all know-nothings. He was mad but how could he help himself. I am glad he did not ask me who it was for I would not have told him nor would I have denied knowing, and at the same time I did not want any fuss with him. We got in order at last and the Colonel who would be a Brigadier, rode away with his staff as proud as a kitten with two tails. He rode straight on through the city and the regt following in such order as pleased themselves and the officers could not see it for they sympathized with the men in the whole matter. My own opinion is that the Colonel had a canteen of something stronger than coffee.

The City is about the size of Evansville and is terribly shattered. I had often heard of the terrors of a bombardment of a crowded city but I never realized it before. Houses were shattered and torn in every shape that can be imagined, some utterly destroyed and some but little injured. Some had shells through the doors, some places the shells had burst inside of a house and torn it all to pieces. After seeing the destruction I no longer wondered at the insane fury with which they (the rebels) charged our works, rushing on as they often did with their hats pulled down over their eyes so that they could not see the certain destruction that awaited them. I am glad that I have taken part in this campaign. I would not for a great deal have missed that ride through Atlanta. It almost paid me for the whole campaign.

On September 3, Sherman had wired Washington, "So Atlanta is ours, and fairly won." Now the majority of his troops were free to rest and recuperate

■ Brig. Gen. Alpheus S. Williams commanded the 1st Division, XX Corps. Like Sherman, Williams did not have a high opinion of most newspaper correspondents who covered the campaign, and was especially distrustful of the reporters working for the Cincinnati *Commercial* and the New York *Tribune*. In letters home in early June, he wrote: "I am not indifferent to the ephemeral praise of reporters, but I cannot sell my self-respect to obtain it. I have seen very few reports of our operations. Those I have seen disgust me with their lies. However, I have got used to these outrageous reports. They are got up by special scribblers, who are kept in many commands. I don't know but one reporter by sight, and he looks like a jailbird. I wish the whole crew were driven out."

■ Major James T. Holmes, 52nd Ohio, commanded a line of skirmishers which led the Army of the Cumberland's advance at Tunnel Hill on May 7. In the months prior to the opening of the campaign, he drilled Col. Dan McCook's brigade at its camp at Lee and Gordon's Mill on Chickamauga Creek. His division commander, Brig. Gen. Jefferson C. Davis, called Holmes "the best drilled officer and ... drillmaster" in the division. On July 19, Holmes assumed command of the regiment following Lt. Col. Charles Clancy's capture shortly after crossing Peachtree Creek. Holmes later led the 52nd's charge at Jonesboro, where he was shot through the knee on September 1. Before the war, as a student at New Athens, Ohio, he was an intimate friend of George A. Custer, who taught school at Cadiz and boarded with Holmes' grandfather. "Custer was quite a lady's man always," recalled Holmes, "and he and I used to go out to see the girls together." The next year Custer obtained his appointment to West Point and Holmes wrote: "That was the first and last school I think that he ever taught."

from the rigors, exhaustion and horrors of the campaign, though the army's postmasters probably found few occasions for relaxation in the days immediately following Atlanta's occupation.

Major James T. Holmes, commanding the 52nd Ohio, was among thousands of Federals sending correspondence to the North during the first three weeks of September. On the 14th, still feeling pain from a leg wound received at Jonesboro, he began a long letter to his parents in Harrison County, Ohio, detailing his service and that of his regiment during the span of the four-month campaign. The letter took Holmes five days to complete.

'Be sure to keep them on the hop'

Major James Taylor Holmes
52nd Ohio Veteran Volunteer Infantry

Headquarters 52nd O.V.I.
Atlanta, Ga., September 14, 1864.

My Dear Parents:

It is ever a gratification and oftimes a pleasure to the way-worn, weary traveler after a haven of rest is reached to review the scenes, the lights and shadows, of his journey, and endeavor to fix in the storehouse of memory all that may be of profit and for future warnings in what has been passed. I sit down tonight by the Gate City of the so-called Southern Confederacy and experience a woof of pleasure with a warp of sorrow as I take up this pen to redeem my promise of a campaign letter.

Thoughts come crowding in swarms for utterance; some steady, calm and quiet; others strange, wild and weird; the mournful and the joyous; the despondent and the exultant. I crowd them all back that a plain narrative of facts may, as I hope it will, interest you and others, who may desire to know of a relative in the army.

On the 3rd day of last May the regiment broke up its camp at Lee and Gordon's Mills, 14 miles south southeast of Chattanooga. This camp, you will remember, was about seven, probably eight, miles from the state line between Tennessee and Georgia and in the latter state. We have been in but the one state since March, or rather December of last year. From the Mills we marched before night to Ringgold and pitched our camp in full view of the gap through Taylor's Ridge of White Oak Mountains, where Hooker fought on the 27th of last November, the second day after the rout from Mission Ridge.

Ringgold and this gap had been left unoccupied by our forces during the month of January, but the enemy showed no disposition to try laying a permanent hold of them. We remained encamped near Ringgold with the army then gathering from Knoxville, Chattanooga and Huntsville.

On the night of the 6th, McCook said to me, "Major, we move in the morning and the 52nd Ohio takes the advance of this army toward Tunnel Hill. I want you to take the lead with three of your best skirmish companies and when you strike them and get them started keep them hopping; give them no time to stop and fight you." He meant the enemy and repeated, "Be sure to keep them on the *hop.*

Bright and early on the morning of the 7th I selected Capt. Sturgis, Capt. Hutchison and Lieut. Lane's companies and deploying them took the road for Tunnel Hill.

The regiment commanded by Lt. Col. Clancey headed the column, the XIV Corps.

A mile through the fields, pine thickets and woods and we found pine bushes chopped across the road, here and there, to prevent our cavalry from charging on their videttes. The skirmishers passed and I, with my bugler and orderly, rode around the obstruction leaving the column to remove their own obstructions. At two miles out, while my line was mostly in thick bushes, bang whiz-z-z, a solitary shot. I listened, "pit it ta pat, pit ta pat" faster and faster went the rebel horsemen until the sound died away in the distance toward Tunnel Hill. Two miles farther on a few rebels let fly as we came in sight of an old house, but it was only fun for the boys, 50 of them probably, to send a very scary volley among them, and as the bugle sounded "Forward!" to laugh as the Johnnies hurried to the rear.

All went quietly then until just as we were coming in sight of Tunnel Hill, about a mile off. I saw their cavalry, 100 or 150 in number, maneuvering for a position to give us a fight. Finally, they opened at the distance of 300 yards. Without the signal, down went every man on the skirmish line flat to the ground and commenced a spirited return of the fire. Gen. Davis himself a short distance back had just told me to be careful as there *might be* a line of battle in the wood in front of me. They hit my horse's right ear and cut through a lock of my hair behind the right ear; in short, they made it quite warm all around. In about a minute, satisfied that I could hoist them without much loss, I ordered the bugler, who stayed by my side, to sound the "Forward." Just as our boys were rising up, a Johnny shouted, "Why don't you send on your cavalry?" You see, they don't like to fight infantry. It is too close work for a cavalryman. Another, as loud as he could shout, said, "Send on your G—d d———d nigger wool." They thought we would send negro soldiers against them. They didn't wait; the skirmish line went for them on the double-quick and away off, as he spurred his horse beyond bullet range, I heard "Bring on your G—d d———d nigger wool."

The cavalry that had been fighting us was routed and the town came in full view. I halted the line and the enemy opened on us with artillery from the edge of the place. Under the personal direction of Gen. Davis I moved my line by the right flank and swept through the place, making the rebel battery get up and dust to avoid capture. We pushed up the hill beyond the town and by order of Gen. Palmer, commanding XIV Corps, I recalled my line of skirmishers, five companies, two having been added as soon as the enemy began to show resistance. I should say seven companies, for I likewise had two from the 125th Illinois.

As I was leading my companies back to the town to camp and rest, for skirmishing is hard work, I met Gen. Davis. Said he, "Major, is there any body of men out this road?" I replied, "General, I just now met about two companies of our cavalry going out to where I drew off my line, and I suppose they are the relief for my line." He rode on with his staff, after telling me to report to the regiment in Tunnel Hill and take rest. As he reached the ground where my skirmishers had stopped and turned back, he and his staff received a volley from probably 30 guns, only one shot taking effect, mortally wounding the horse of his Inspector-General. I could not account for it for a long time. The question with me was how could rebels fire on Gen. Davis from bushes so close at hand when they had not fired at our skirmish line that had just stood on the same ground. In due course of time, a month or six weeks, I satisfied myself that the body of horsemen I had met had been, and were, rebels dressed in our clothes. They had remained in town, took the chance of passing for Yankees, and in the nick of time rode boldly past my skirmish companies as the latter came off the line, and taking shelter behind bushes watched for just such an opportunity as they got, but too eager they missed their mark and Gen. Davis *lives* today.

We remained quartered near the church in Tunnel Hill until the evening of

■ Lt. Col. Charles W. Clancy, left, and Major James T. Holmes, photographed in the 52nd Ohio's camp at Lee and Gordon's Mills in April 1864. Clancy commanded the regiment until July 19 when he was captured at Peachtree Creek by troops of the 15th Mississippi under Col. Michael Farrell. Held prisoner for more than two months, Clancy was exchanged in late September and resumed command of the 52nd from Holmes on November 16, leading it during the Savannah campaign. Despite their close relationship, Holmes repeatedly misspelled Clancy's last name, as seen in Holmes' narrative.

■ 1st Lieut. George A. Masury, adjutant of the 52nd Ohio. Just before the Federal charge at Jonesboro on September 1, he approached James T. Holmes, commanding the regiment. "Major," he said, "I am too sick to go any further." Excused from the assault, Masury was confronted later about the incident and asked to resign his commission. Holmes wrote later in September: "In camp ... Masury was an energetic, driving officer; in the field and in the fight, during four months, he has shown himself neither." Masury resigned under protest, thereby avoiding a court martial.

the 9th, when we moved about two miles out and brought up with the brigade under Rocky Face Ridge, from the top of which rebel sharpshooters plugged their balls down on the heads of devoted Yankees.

Night of the 10th we went on the skirmish line under the very crest of this renowned ridge.

It rained, I cannot tell you how hard. Yea, it poured from dark till morning and we had to sit and take it with the pleasing reflection that daylight would place us almost at the mercy of the enemy on the lofty perch. Morning came and the next night came. Two of our boys had been killed and 10 wounded. The advantage of position and shelter had nearly all been with the enemy, but the regiment, or seven companies on the skirmish line, had fought well, punishing the enemy as badly as they had been punished. I had almost forgotten to say that in the fight at Tunnel Hill I did not lose a man, while the boys emptied three saddles and captured a cavalry horse.

After dark on the 11th we were relieved from the front line and moved some five miles to the right and rear of the army preparatory to passing through Snake Creek Gap and moving on Resaca, which we did during the next day and night. It was dusk when we entered the head of this gap. A little run, as crooked as it can be to get away from where it starts, runs through the six or seven miles of a cut through White Oak Mountains. This stream is called Snake Creek and the gap is named from the stream.

We were most of the dark, drizzly, muddy night of the 12th getting through, but did make it. We reached the exit before day and halted to rest a while.

On the 13th we moved toward Resaca and on the morning of the 14th the work of war began in earnest. As the day advanced the contest thickened. Our brigade was shifted from place to place over the field until shortly after noon when the XXIII Corps, Gen. Schofield, assaulted the enemy's main works. Our division supported him and I never heard such fighting and so long continued on such a small spot of ground. It wasn't more than 40 rods in length. It was here Gen. Sherman was riding along the gun stacks of our regiment when a shell plunked into the ground about 10 feet in front of his horse's head. The animal stopped and turned his head slightly to one side to see what that could mean. The general looked quietly down at it and shook his spurs toward the inquisitive animal's flank, a hint that he meant to move on. It didn't require more than a moment for the whole incident to occur, but in that moment the general showed us he could be as cool as a cucumber under fire.

Sherman ordered the assault to cease and said he wanted the artillery to do that work as it was folly to slaughter men at that point. This day we lost one man standing almost on the spot where the shell struck so close to Sherman. He was cut almost in two by a 12-pound solid shot; he never knew what hurt him.

That night we moved a short distance to the right, occupied a ridge and fortified it. The next day was one of the warm days for us so far as bullets were concerned. We lay on a wooded ridge behind the works we had thrown up. Through the night and from early dawn till dewy eve rebel sharpshooters kept balls whizzing in a complete cross fire amongst the trees, in our ranks, and at a battery that was planted in the middle of the regiment. Our artillery troubled them much and the chief aim of the sharpshooters was to keep cannoneers from working their guns.

There were eight of us lying behind three little logs as a screen from their infernal shots when a sharpshooter put a random shot between the two upper logs that missed Sergeant Major Freeman's arm about three inches, Capt. Barnett's knee two inches, Lieut. James four or five inches, Col. Clancey's head one inch, Adjutant Masury's thigh six inches, grazed my boot

■ Company A of the 52nd Ohio poses at McAfee's Church, Ga., in March 1864 before the opening of the campaign. The 52nd Ohio suffered 253 casualties in the drive to Atlanta, the highest total of any regiment in the XIV Corps. Note the varied number of felt hats worn by the company, which was distinctive of the troops in Sherman's army.

leg, cut Lieut. Duff's pants and drawers on the calf of the leg and plunged through Capt. Sturgis' right leg, entering just below the knee in front, and passing between the two bones came out half way down toward the ankle. It was a remarkable shot. Six inches lower and to the right would have sent it through the whole row of men.

Now and then all through the day someone would be hurt; two were killed. As night settled down the shots commenced falling sparsely and at dark there was only the occasional picket shot.

About half-past eleven and as I had lain down and drawn my blanket over me, a sharp cracking of musketry began a short distance from our left. In a moment every man was up and at his post, weapons in hand. The 12 guns in the center of the regiment were wheeled into position and opened with shot and shell, grape and canister straight to the front and left. We thought they meant to fight us and for about half an hour the scene was strikingly grand and terrible. The 12 guns amid the darkness furnished one of the finest pictures for the artist that mind could imagine. The guns were as close together as they could be worked and the streams of fire that seemed to leap continuously from their deep mouths were only rivalled in grandeur to the senses by their deep-toned thunder upon the stillness of the night.

The rebels were repulsed, and in the morning their works were empty.

From here we marched immediately to the mouth of Snake Creek Gap where we had left knapsacks before the fight. The distance was six miles. Buzzard Roost had been taken by a flank movement on Resaca. The enemy were now on the way to the Etowah and south.

We didn't know where they proposed to stop and fight us next. Gen. Davis' division was selected to sweep through Rome on the extreme right flank of the army, and from our marching ability we were called Davis' Cavalry.

■ Capt. Peter C. Schneider, Company I, 52nd Ohio, was killed July 19 at Peachtree Creek. According to Sergeant Nixon B. Stewart of Company E: "At the time of his death he was 28 and engaged to an excellent young lady of Cleveland. He received a letter from her the evening before the battle, urging him to resign and come home, as she had fears he would be killed in the next battle. When he was found his revolver was in his hand with one barrel empty. A rebel major lay dead within a few feet of him. The hole in the major's head was made by a .32 caliber, the same as the captain's revolver, and the major's bullet had struck the captain in the temple."

We led off for Rome and on the 18th, from that place, I dropped you a line giving you the situation in brief. Had I sat down then to write details of what had occurred I should have written many more things than this account thus far contains, should, in other words, have been more minute, but now it would never do; I shouldn't get through writing in a month at such a rate. In the engagement on the 17th, in sight of Rome, on the north bank of the Oostanaula, we lost no men, although the pluck of the regiment was tried worse than if we had become hotly engaged. Two regiments in the brigade lost, as I think I told you, from 60 to 70 men.

We crossed the Oostanaula on the night of the 18th and on the 20th, leaving our bivouac in the streets of the city, camped in the suburbs until the morning of the 24th.

Rome was deserted, almost, with but few citizens left. I did see one of the prettiest ladies in that place I ever saw, but she was a violent rebel, uncompromising, etc. The country round about is beautiful; there, the two pretty rivers, Oostanaula and Etowah, come together and take the name of Coosa. The city in prosperous days contained about 5,000 inhabitants and was to my eye the most desirable place for permanent residence I had seen in the south. I have had no occasion to change that view since.

On the morning of the 24th we pulled out and after a winding march brought up at Dallas, Paulding County, on the evening of the 26th. The next morning we took position two miles east of Dallas under fire of the enemy and remained there behind works we threw up until the 1st of June, when we moved some miles toward Acworth into works previously constructed by the XXIII Corps. Here we lay within 500 yards of the Johnnies, shooting at them and being shot at until the morning of the 6th, when we found our friends in front gone, flanked out again. This was their position on Pumpkin Vine Creek and the Allatoona Pass.

After resting near Acworth until the 10th we began the movement on the enemy at Kennesaw Mountain and through constant fighting, day by day, always marching, digging or picketing where the guns of the enemy could reach us. Every inch of ground was contested until we came to the base of the mountain. Here again, as at Buzzard Roost, from the crest of the rocky and ragged steep, they could pour the leaden hail down upon our devoted heads. At times they would open two or three six-gun batteries, then — look out; the screech and scream of their shells would very forcibly remind one that he was only flesh and blood, and should one of these nasty creatures come straight to him he couldn't stop it until it would have the better of the argument.

The day they first opened from the top of Kennesaw Mountain with their shells I did a thing that I have often wondered since how I was able to do it.

We were not in works, simply lying out in the open field. They let fly very suddenly and with very respectable aim for the point where I stood; two shells passed just over my head and struck the ground close behind; another burst in the air above and a fourth instantly plowed the ground and burst about 15 feet in front of me. I thought "who can tell how long we'll live," and in the smoke and dust of the bursted shell I folded my arms and stood gazing at the rebel battery, without a feeling of fear, until they slacked up the working of their guns. What possessed me to do it I cannot tell without it may have been an internal assurance that they couldn't or wouldn't hit me. Anyhow, they didn't.

We lay directly under the mountain until the night of the 25th when we were drawn off and marched two miles to the right-hand point of the mountain as you come south. Here we lay until 8:30 o'clock on the morning of the 27th, a day to be remembered while time shall last.

At the hour named, we marched along a ridge through woods until we reached an open field. Here balls from the rebel skirmish line began to disable men in the brigade. We had all learned just before moving into the open field what was to be attempted. The works of the enemy were to be stormed upon a wooded hill opposite the point where our brigade was formed, five regiments deep.

Through the leaves along the crest at less than one-half mile from us, across two open fields, the works of the enemy could be partially seen. There was an ominous stillness in the ranks. All knew that many must fall and each heart communed with itself in the few brief moments of rest. The mother, the wife, the lover, brothers and sisters doubtless occupied the thoughts of many of those brave boys. Some were gazing upon a sun that would only shine in after days to light their graves. Others were feeling themselves perfect men for the last time. Their perfections were soon to be marred.

Here and there was a talkative, restless, profane old soldier. I remember one who had fought at Pea Ridge and many times and places since. Said he, in my hearing, to a comrade: "Aye! God, Jim, that hill's going to be worse'n Pea Ridge. We'll ketch hell over'n them woods." This was uttered in a low tone with mysterious nods toward the opposite ridge.

Our artillery kept pouring its iron messengers upon the devoted spot selected for our assault. The troops on our right and left were ready; on our left a salvo from a six-gun battery told that the instant had come. Away, down the long slope, across the wide bottom, the long lines of men moved with a shout into the face of the foe. When we began to ascend to the works in the edge of the woods the halt and lie-down were ordered, by whom I do not know.

A perfect sheet of lead swept just over us; wounded and bloody men from what were then the front regiments began to pour back past us. "Forward!" came the order at the same instant. The line of every regiment in front of us was broken. Men came rushing down the slope in crowds, breathing hard through fear and physical exhaustion. The tide of retreat swelled until I thought at one moment my part of the regiment, the left wing, would be swept away by the throng.

The first sweep had carried McCook's brigade up to the slight abatis and hundreds of men fell killed and wounded in front of the rebel works. Our charge struck against the sharp point — so far as it had a point — of the angle. The Confederates name it "the dead angle." A glance around showed that we had failed for the time being to carry the line. One-third of officers and men down, success was gone.

Col. McCook had fallen. Col. Harmon, next in command, had been shot down; the brigade had given away, and if truth were told and full justice done, the 52nd saved all that was saved by its nerve and courage for 25 minutes, but in less than that time 85 officers and men bit the dust from our ranks.

Men gave up their lives everywhere, it seemed. You could not say or think who would die or be maimed the next instant. I shall never forget the thud of a minie ball through human flesh; it is a sickening sound, but the saddest sight I saw on that day was each time a poor fellow, near me, would be wounded and start back to the rear only to fall pierced by a death shot after he had ceased fighting. I saw in those few moments several such cases and when you know how eager the wounded man is to get off the field without being killed, you can appreciate in a degree what my feelings were. He is not afraid to die, but after being disabled in the fight he wants to live; that if he must be killed it may be while he himself is able to strike blows as well as receive them.

The other regiments of the brigade were rallied and as the firing slacked

■ 2nd Lieut. James H. Donaldson, Company E, 52nd Ohio, was killed July 19 at Peachtree Creek. "That morning," recalled a member of the same company, he "had drawn a new patent leather haversack, remarking as he put it on, 'I will be a shining mark for the Johnnies.' He was shot through the haversack."

■ 1st Lieut. William H. Lane, Company A, 52nd Ohio, was shot through the left thigh July 20 while on the skirmish line at Peachtree Creek. A week later from the hospital at Vining's Station, he informed Major Holmes that he would return to duty "as soon as able. I am getting along finely and sincerely hope you may escape all danger, for what would the poor boys do now without you? You must be short of officers ..." Lane returned to the regiment in the fall and was promoted to captain in December.

up, the assault having failed, orders were issued to fortify the ground and, until the rebels left July 2nd, it was a constant fight. Night and day the deadly rifle was doing its work. Our boys shot their headlogs and *chevaux de frise* to splinters, killing and wounding from 25 to 50 of them each day, excepting the 29th of June when a truce prevailed to allow the dead lying between the works to be carried off or buried. On that day, Union and Rebel met between the works, shook hands and drank and talked as though they never had tried to kill each other.

If we had carried their works at that point, it would have been goodbye to much of Hood's, or then, Johnston's army. We would have been right in rear of Kennesaw. The point of assault was the *key* to the mountain, but human flesh could not do more than we did and a failure was the result. On the 2nd of July they gave Lieut. Miser, my old orderly sergeant, a mortal wound. He was too brave — carelessness and a reckless spirit despite their attempt to kill him made him, without bravado, expose his person above our works and his life paid the forfeit.

On the 3rd of July we moved from our works where a hovering death had kept our heads for the most part well ducked down and our bodies behind earthworks constantly.

Passing by the suburbs of the neat town of Marietta, some six miles south we discovered our friends again entrenched in front of us. We took matters coolly, stopping and fortifying not far from them and, during the 4th of July, shelling their pickets with 12-pounders.

Next morning they were gone again and we followed until, near the railroad bridge over the Chattahoochee, we found them in a semi-circular work about four miles in length covering the bridge. These were the jaggiest, most unapproachable works I ever saw them in. They were like a row of porcupines on a huge scale; you couldn't go near them even if there was nobody to shoot at you!

These works they abandoned in the night as they had done others all the way from Buzzard Roost and we camped on the northwestern bank of the river and rested until the 18th. From that camp I think I wrote a note home; I know I did.

On the 18th we crossed the river above the mouth of Nancy's Creek and effected the crossing of Nancy's Creek without opposition. On the 20th, however, as we made the crossing of Peachtree the rebels jumped into us and cut our regiment badly. Here Col. Clancey was taken prisoner. The total loss of the regiment was 85 officers and men. Two officers killed and three wounded out of that number.*

I never felt blue in the army until then. Every place I looked I missed familiar faces, some for all time, others for an uncertain period. That fearful word "missing" was written after some names; we did not know what fate it might mean. Here Frank Mc. received his wound, and I bear personal testimony that he was with his company in as hot a place as ever he'll see again.

The rebels were whipped in this fight, too, but it cost some precious blood and sacrifice to do it. When they finally gave way from our front it was to fall back to their works in the outskirts of Atlanta. On the ground between the two lines we found some of our poor fellows dead where our skirmish line had been overpowered at one point; they had been killed and the ground being covered by the guns of both sides it had been impossible to bring the bodies off until the enemy left. Some wounded men lived for 36 hours and

* With the capture of Lt. Col. Clancy at Peachtree Creek, command of the 52nd Ohio was assumed by Major Holmes, who led the regiment for the next four months.

were carried off alive but fly-blown until they were almost yellow. It was a hard sight. I saw two of the 85th Illinois carried off there who were alive; one died soon and the other is living and doing well.

We followed the enemy, thinking they were going out of Atlanta to let us go in, but we missed it. They were not ready to give up Atlanta so easily, and we stopped again in front of strong works. Our brigade was for almost the first time left in reserve and it was here that I lost both my horses, stolen by some of the 10th O.V.C. in the night of the 26th. It's goodbye horses, although no man's $1,500 could have induced me to part with them.

We kept working back and forth until August 7th when our division got into a fight in front of Atlanta and we — the 52nd — never were shelled so before. Down to this time through the campaign they had not, on account of scarcity, thrown one artillery shot to our 10, but here they poured them thick and fast upon us. They couldn't stop our advance and we threw up fortifications within 400 yards of their works, under their fire, and harassed them to our heart's content until the 12th of the month, losing three killed and 14 wounded. This was near Utoy Creek.

On the 12th we drew out of the hot place and enjoyed a kind of rest behind works that the enemy did not shoot at very often.

On the 20th, as I wrote you, our division marched 10 miles and back through rain and mud to cut the Montgomery railroad.

On the 27th the grand movement on the Macon railroad began. After marching, camping, fortifying and maneuvering until 12 midday September 1st, we found ourselves face to face with our enemy once more. Gathering our nerve for what we felt would be the final blow in the Atlanta campaign, after the lines were formed under bursting shells and singing minies, we started across a broad cornfield for the works of the Johnnies. This time we took them and the Johnnies too with their guns, 10 in number. I was knocked out of this fight, but not until we had nearly reached their works. In that whirl and storm of shot and shell I felt exultant at the success and could not have avoided the feeling if I had lost my limb. It was the hour of victory; an hour in which we wiped out old scores with the foe, in which we remembered the graves of Kennesaw and Peachtree.

War gives to men strange turns of nature when battle becomes nature's subject of thought.

In this engagement I lost three killed and 17 wounded, counting myself. The next morning we moved into Jonesboro one-half mile and encamped, while portions of the army went after the routed rebels.

Jonesboro is a very small village strung along the railroad for a mile. It was nearly deserted. I didn't ride through it much as my wound pained me all the time we remained there and I was afraid of it, I'll confess now, although I thought I could take care of it.

On the 4th our brigade brought 1,600 rebel prisoners to Atlanta, and here we are in good quarters resting from our labors.

The 52nd had 470 guns and swords when it left Gordon's Mills. During the campaign it lost in killed, wounded and missing 253. Of these, 16 officers, five of whom are dead. About 100 men are dead. In some cases a man was wounded twice and afterwards killed. Such cases are only classed as killed. Some now with us were wounded as often as three times. No Ohio regiment, if I do say it, has made a bloodier mark during the past four months. We have made our mark in history, but at a fearful cost. Many good and brave men have been snatched from our rolls and our midst forever. There are vacant chairs and lonesome hearthstones in Jefferson, Belmont, Tuscarawas, Van Wert, Cuyahoga, Hamilton and other counties of Ohio that must ever remain vacant and lonesome. The race of the loved one is run. *He gave up his life at his post;* this I say of every departed one of the regiment.

■ Private Thomas H. Kirkland, Company F, 52nd Ohio, was among the regiment's survivors to go into bivouac on the Whitehall road, a mile and a half below Atlanta, on September 5. His commanding officer, Major J.T. Holmes, later wrote: "It was a dull, heavy time for the most part. Our ranks had been fearfully thinned by death and wounds through the previous 118 days of march and battle. The contracted line on dress parade was mournfully eloquent of gaps which had been closed up by moving to the right or left and took the heart and life out of survivors when memory and reflection were allowed to do their perfect work."

■ After entering Atlanta, Union troops dismantled scores of houses, buildings and fences badly damaged in the bombardment. Much of the lumber ended up being used to construct temporary quarters for junior officers and enlisted men during the occupation. "I wish you could see how our shot and shell have torn the houses to pieces," wrote Capt. Ira B. Read of Company E, 101st Ohio, in a letter home on September 18. "On some streets in the more exposed portions of town there is scarcely a house that is not riddled by the shell ... Our camp is in a very pleasant place and I have my tent nicely 'fixed up.' I have a door and two windows in one end with board sides and end, with tent cloth over. My 'furniture' is a stand with three drawers in it, a rocking chair, an armed chair, and a spring seat lounge. The latter article makes a 'gay' bed. I have white dishes to eat off and china cup and saucer. If they will let us stay here this winter, I think I can live quite comfortably."

It was as you know in the action of the 7th of August that John was wounded. The letter sent to his father, I presume, does him justice in the character of a soldier. In bravery his comrades claim he had no superior among them. He had the nerve to dare where others would have quailed.

"Soldier rest, thy warfare o'er,
Sleep the sleep that knows no breaking,
Dream of battlefields no more,
Days of danger, nights of waking."

I have hastily redeemed my promise, indebted to a kind Providence for the life and health to do so. I might elaborate and sentimentalize for pages yet. Let it suffice for me to write, while thousands of hearts mourn the loss of near kinsmen, amid the horrors of war, you are spared thus far both your sons. It is strange, even almost miraculous, that so many escape in battle as do. We cannot tell how it is and yet, God knows, enough perish.*

I began writing on the night of the 14th; this is the 19th. Yesterday in riding down through the city I gathered what I think is a fact. Atlanta by slow degrees is passing away. These soldiers fought for it; their comrades strew the ground with graves from here to Ringgold, 118 miles. The hosts of rebellion held a power here that it is the intention to render naught for all

* Holmes' older brother, Abraham, served as 1st Sergeant in Company G of the 52nd Ohio. Both brothers survived the last seven months of the war.

time to come, no matter what may happen. Gen. Sherman is making a purely military post of the place; citizens are all leaving and all around the city fine houses are leaving, by piece-meal, on the backs of soldiers, in wagons, carts, old buggies and every conceivable vehicle. A house is vacated by a family, some soldier steps inside with a chunk of a rail and bursts off a board; it's goodbye house, for you'll soon see a hundred soldiers carrying away windows, shutters, flooring, weather boarding, studding, etc., etc., *ad infinitum.* All these, to fix up quarters in adjoining camps. So you can see we are comfortable.

The city is scattering; every house has an open lot, or garden, near it, and the result is Atlanta is about two miles in diameter, but it will not be so large by the time we get through with it.

These people bid for these things by their rebellion. They can avert all any day, but they know no such disposition, as a rule.

I have written enough for this time.

We are all well.

Your son,

J.T. Holmes

P.S. Please excuse want of punctuation, if any, as I was too tired to read over so long a paper.

Epilogue

The struggle for Atlanta cost both armies more than 49,000 casualties in killed and wounded — an average of 408 every day of the campaign — while another 17,000 were taken prisoner or deserted. For Sherman, the Federal victory had not come cheap or easy, though it was hailed by many in the North as greatly enhancing President Lincoln's chances for re-election that fall. For Hood, the Confederate defeat and loss of the city were deeply humiliating, and left his army briefly broken in morale.

Union troops settled down in Atlanta for the next 10 weeks. Early in the occupation Sherman ordered all residents removed, "giving to each the option to go south or north, as their interests or feelings dictated," he wrote. "I was resolved to make Atlanta a pure military garrison or depot, with no civil population to influence military measures." The move generated a series of scathing letters to the Union commander from Hood, who called Sherman's order unprecedented "in studied and ingenious cruelty, [transcending] all acts ever before brought to my attention in the dark history of war."

On September 30, Hood struck back with more than words when the Army of Tennessee crossed the Chattahoochee and swung north. Hoping to draw Sherman out of Atlanta, Hood's men cut the Union rail supply line at places from Big Shanty to Tunnel Hill. The Federals did pursue, until the end of October. By then Hood, in Alabama, had decided to push into Tennessee and invade Kentucky if possible. Sherman had other plans. Instead of chasing the Confederates, he envisioned a new campaign across Georgia from Atlanta to Savannah — a great 300-mile "march to the sea." Gen. Thomas and two corps were sent to deal with Hood.

On November 15, one week after Lincoln's re-election, the march began. Before leaving, Federal engineers leveled Atlanta's railroad depot, roundhouse and machine shops, then set fire to them. The resulting blaze soon spread to other buildings — a spectacle surpassing "all the pictures and verbal descriptions of hell," wrote one Union officer.

"Behind us lay Atlanta," Sherman wrote, "smouldering and in ruins, the black smoke rising high in air, and hanging like a pall over the ruined city ... Then we turned our horses' heads to the east; Atlanta was soon lost behind the screen of trees, and became a thing of the past."

Sources

Text

Sources to material quoted in introductory passages and the major accounts of each chapter.

Preface

ROBERT N. ADAMS: "Campaign for Atlanta," *Glimpses of the Nation's Struggle,* Minnesota MOLLUS papers, 1898, 176.

Chapter 1

ROBERT D. PATRICK: *Reluctant Rebel: The Secret Diary of Robert Patrick 1861-1865,* pp. 136-137.
JACOB D. COX: *Military Reminiscences of the Civil War,* Vol. II, pp. 97-100.
BLISS MORSE: *Civil War Diaries & Letters of Bliss Morse,* 105.
LOT D. YOUNG: *Reminiscences of a Soldier of the Orphan Brigade,* 75.
JOSEPH E. JOHNSTON: *Battles and Leaders of the Civil War,* Vol. 4, 260. — *Narrative of Military Operations,* pp. 272-273.
JAMES L. COOPER: "The Civil War Diary of James Litton Cooper, September 30, 1861 to January 1865," *Tennessee Historical Quarterly,* June 1956, 162.
SAM R. WATKINS: *Co. Aytch, Maury Grays, 1st Tennessee Infantry, Or a Side Show of the Big Show,* pp. 112; 113.
FRANK S. ROBERTS: "In Winter Quarters at Dalton, Ga., 1863-64," *Confederate Veteran,* Vol. XXVI, June 1918, 274.
FRANK M. McADAMS: *History of the One Hundred and Thirteenth Ohio Volunteer Infantry,* pp. 60; 62-63.
NIXON B. STEWART: *Dan. McCook's Regiment, 52nd O.V.I.,* 86.
WILBUR F. HINMAN: *The Story of the Sherman Brigade,* pp. 473-476.
CHARLES W. WILLS: *Army Life of an Illinois Soldier: Letters and Diary of the Late Charles W. Wills,* 210.
JACOB ADAMS: *Diary of Jacob Adams, Private in Company F, 21st O.V.V.I.,* pp. 37; 37-38.
CHARLES F. MORSE: *Letters Written During the Civil War, 1861-1865,* pp. 217-219.
ELBERT D. WILLETT: *History of Company B (Originally Pickens Planters) 40th Alabama Regiment Confederate States Army 1862 to 1865,* pp. 53; 54.
COMPANY F, 30th ALABAMA: Kelly, William M., "A History of the Thirtieth Alabama Volunteers (Infantry) Confederate States Army," *The Alabama Historical Quarterly,* Spring 1947, 151.

Abbreviations

MOLLUS — Military Order of the Loyal Legion of the United States.

Official Records — The War of the Rebellion: A Compilation of the Official Records of the Union and Confederate Armies.

The Ohio Soldier — The Ohio Soldier and National Picket Guard.

KMNBP — Kennesaw Mountain National Battlefield Park.

USAMHI — U.S. Army Military History Institute, Carlisle Barracks, Pa.

BLISS MORSE: *Civil War Diaries & Letters of Bliss Morse,* pp. 108-109.
BENJAMIN F. JACKSON: *So Mourns the Dove: Letters of a Confederate Infantryman and his Family,* 80.
JAMES TURNER: "Jim Turner Co. G, 6th Texas Infantry, C.S.A., from 1861-1865," *Texana,* No. 2, 1974, pp. 169-170.
GEORGE W. GORDON: Vaughan, Alfred J., *Personal Record of the Thirteenth Regiment Tennessee Infantry,* pp. 89-95.
SAMUEL C. KELLY: Kelly, William M., "A History of the Thirtieth Alabama Volunteers (Infantry) Confederate States Army," *The Alabama Historical Quarterly,* Spring 1947, 151.
WILLIAM T. SHERMAN: *Memoirs of General William T. Sherman,* Vol. II, pp. 5; 7-10; 11-12; 15; 22.
JOSEPH E. JOHNSTON: *Narrative of Military Operations,* pp. 276-277; 277-278. — *Battles and Leaders of the Civil War,* Vol. 4, 261.
JAMES L. COOPER: "The Civil War Diary of James Litton Cooper, September 30, 1861 to January 1865," *Tennessee Historical Quarterly,* June 1956, 162.

Chapter 2

RALSA C. RICE: "Three Years with the 125th Ohio, Opdycke's Tigers," *The National Tribune Scrapbook,* No. 2, pp. 76; 77; 93; 76; 93-108.
JACOB D. COX: *Military Reminiscences of the Civil War,* Vol. II, pp. 220-221.

Chapter 3

JOHN C. ARBUCKLE: *Civil War Experiences of a Foot-Soldier Who Marched with Sherman,* 52.
SHERMAN LELAND: Calkins, William W., *The History of the One Hundred and Fourth Regiment of Illinois Volunteer Infantry, War of the Great Rebellion 1862-1865,* 200.
ANGUS L. WADDLE: *Three Years with the Armies of the Ohio and the Cumberland,* 66.
LOT D. YOUNG: *Reminiscences of a Soldier of the Orphan Brigade,* pp. 76-77.
JOSEPH VAN NEST: Typed transcript of journal and reminiscences, pp. 54-61, courtesy of Marian B. Till, Sandusky, Ohio.
ANDREW JACKSON NEAL: Typed transcript of letter, May 10, 1864, KMNBP Library.
ROBERT H. DACUS: *Reminiscences of Company H, First Arkansas Mounted Rifles,* pp. 9-11.
JOHN WILLIAM TUTTLE: *The Union, the Civil War and John W. Tuttle: A Kentucky Captain's Account,* pp. 177-180.
ROBERT S. CHAMBERLAIN: Typed transcript of diary and reminiscences, L.M. Strayer Collection.
JOSEPH W. GASKILL: *Footprints Through Dixie: Everyday Life of the Man Under a Musket,* pp. 96-98.
JOHN M. SCHOFIELD: *Official Records,* Series 1: Vol. 38, Part 2, 511.
JOHN WILL DYER: *Reminiscences; Or Four Years in the Confederate Army,* pp. 182-187.
JAMES L. COOPER: "The Civil War Diary of James Litton Cooper, September 30, 1861 to January 1865," *Tennessee Historical Quarterly,* June 1956, pp. 162-163.
ROBERT HALE STRONG: *A Yankee Private's Civil War,* pp. 12-18.
JAMES D. MORGAN: Pepper, George W., *Personal Recollections of Sherman's Campaigns in Georgia and the Carolinas,* 65.
FRANK ANDERSON: "A Courier at the Battle of Resaca," *Confederate Veteran,* Vol. V, June 1897, 297.
ROBERT LANG KILPATRICK: "The Fifth Ohio Infantry at Resaca," *Sketches of War History,* Vol. IV, pp. 246-254.
GEORGE B. GUILD: *A Brief Narrative of the Fourth Tennessee Cavalry Regiment,* 166.

Chapter 4

ROBERT D. PATRICK: *Reluctant Rebel,* pp. 166-167; 168.
BENJAMIN M. SEATON: *The Bugle Softly Blows: The Confederate Diary of Benjamin M. Seaton,* 52; 52.
ADIN B. UNDERWOOD: *The Three Years'*

Service of the Thirty-Third Massachusetts Infantry Regiment, pp. 211; 213; 212.

HENRY STONE: "From the Oostanaula to the Chattahoochee," *Papers of the Military Historical Society of Massachusetts,* Vol. VIII, pp. 400-401.

E.T. SYKES: *Walthall's Brigade, Army of Tennessee C.S.A., 1862-1865,* 569.

JOHN W. COTTON: *Yours Till Death: Civil War Letters of John W. Cotton,* 106.

HENRY RICHARDS: *Letters of Captain Henry Richards of the Ninety-Third Ohio Infantry,* 33.

JOEL D. MURPHREE: "Autobiography and Civil War Letters of Joel Murphree of Troy, Alabama 1864-1865," *Alabama Historical Quarterly,* Spring 1957, pp. 178-179.

EDWIN WELLER: *A Civil War Courtship: The Letters of Edwin Weller from Antietam to Atlanta,* 84.

IRA S. OWENS: *Greene County Soldiers in the Late War, Being a History of the Seventy-Fourth O.V.I.,* 70.

URBAN G. OWEN: "Letters of a Confederate Surgeon in the Army of Tennessee to his Wife," *Tennessee Historical Quarterly,* June 1946, 167.

SAMUEL C. KELLY: Kelly, William M., "A History of the Thirtieth Alabama Volunteers (Infantry) Confederate States Army," *Alabama Historical Quarterly,* Spring 1947, 153.

LEWIS D. WARNER: Dunkleman, Mark H. and Winey, Michael J., *The Hardtack Regiment: An Illustrated History of the 154th Regiment, New York State Infantry Volunteers,* 113.

RICE C. BULL: *Soldiering: The Civil War Diary of Rice C. Bull,* pp. 112-119.

URIAH H. FARR: Merrill, Samuel, *The Seventieth Indiana Volunteer Infantry in the War of the Rebellion,* pp. 117-119.

ALEXIS COPE: *The Fifteenth Ohio Volunteers and its Campaigns, 1861-1865,* pp. 446-448; 449-453; 475-476.

JOHN W. TUTTLE: *The Union, the Civil War and John W. Tuttle: A Kentucky Captain's Account,* pp. 186-187.

ANDREW J. GLEASON: Cope, Alexis, *The Fifteenth Ohio Volunteers,* pp. 454-456.

DANIEL W. SHIDELER: "A New Hope Experience," *The National Tribune,* March 17, 1898.

SILAS CROWELL: "The General Wept," *The National Tribune,* December 31, 1896.

AMBROSE G. BIERCE: "The Crime at Pickett's Mill," *The Collected Works of Ambrose Bierce,* Vol. I, pp. 279-280; 281-283; 285-286; 287-289; 290-296.

SAMUEL T. FOSTER: *One of Cleburne's Command: The Civil War Reminiscences and Diary of Capt. Samuel T. Foster, Granbury's Texas Brigade, CSA,* pp. 81-88.

COLUMBUS SYKES: Typed transcript of letters, May 27 and May 29, 1864, KMNBP Library.

■ 1st Lieut. William C. Stewart, Company E, 23rd Michigan, was killed on May 14 at Resaca — the only officer from that regiment to die in the battle. Commanded by Lt. Col. Oliver L. Spaulding, the 23rd Michigan served in the Army of the Ohio and lost a total of 59 officers and enlisted men, killed or wounded, out of fewer than 300 who went into battle at Resaca.

JOHN K. DUKE: *History of the Fifty-third Regiment Ohio Volunteer Infantry During the War of the Rebellion 1861 to 1865,* pp. 137-140.

JOHN W. CLEMSON: "Surprised the Johnnies," *The National Tribune,* September 30, 1897.

CHARLES W. WILLS: *Army Life of an Illinois Soldier: Letters and Diary of the Late Charles W. Wills,* pp. 248-254.

Chapter 5

WILLIAM WIRT CALKINS: *The History of the One Hundred and Fourth Regiment of Illinois Volunteer Infantry,* 371.

WILLIAM H. CONRAD: *Ibid.,* pp. 334-335.

JOSEPH GASKILL: *Footprints Through Dixie,* 101.

EDWARD M. McCOOK: *Official Records,* Series 1, Vol. 38, Part 2, pp. 760-761.

CHARLES F. MORSE: *Letters Written During the Civil War, 1861-1865,* 169.

LEWIS D. WARNER: *The Hardtack Regiment,* 117.

LEWIS W. DAY: *Story of the One Hundred and First Ohio Infantry,* 219.

ROBERT M. COLLINS: *Chapters from the Unwritten History of the War Between the States,* pp. 219-221.

FENWICK Y. HEDLEY: *Marching Through Georgia,* pp. 107-109.

WILLIAM HENRY CHAMBERLIN: "The Skirmish Line in the Atlanta Campaign," *Sketches of War History 1861-1865,* Vol. III, pp. 182-183; 184-185; 186-195.
— *History of the Eighty-First Regiment Ohio Infantry Volunteers during the War of the Rebellion,* pp. 89-90.

EDWARD F. NOYES: *The Ohio Soldier,* Vol. IV, No. 5, October 11, 1890.

CHAUNCEY H. COOKE: "The Civil War of Private Cooke: A Wisconsin Boy in the Union Army," *Wisconsin Magazine of History,* 1955, pp. 90-92.

Chapter 6

ALEXANDER QUINCY PORTER: Typed transcript of diary, Woodruff Library, Emory University.

HENRY E. PRICE: Letter of June 13, 1864, George Marsh Scrapbook, Illinois State Historical Library.

CHARLES W. WILLS: *Army Life of an Illinois Soldier,* pp. 259-260.

ROBERT D. SMITH: Typed copy transcript of diary, KMNBP Library.

SAMUEL B. BARRON: *The Lone Star Defenders: A Chronicle of the Third Texas Cavalry Regiment in the Civil War,* 195.

GEORGE M. WISE: "Civil War Letters of George M. Wise," *The Ohio Historical Quarterly,* January 1956, 74.

JOHN IRWIN KENDALL: "Recollections of a Confederate Officer," *The Louisiana Historical Quarterly,* October 1946, pp. 1162-1166.

ROBERT D. PATRICK: *Reluctant Rebel,* 175.

OSCAR L. JACKSON: *The Colonel's Diary,* pp. 130-137.

WILLIAM T. SHERMAN: *Memoirs of General William T. Sherman,* Vol. II, pp. 52-53; 54.

EZRA E. RICKETTS: "Killing of Gen. Polk," *The National Tribune,* March 31, 1904.

ROBERT P. FINDLEY: Blackburn, T.W., *Letters from the Front: A Union "Preacher" Regiment (74th Ohio) in the Civil War,* pp. 187; 196-197.

FRANK ELLIOT: "A June Evening Before Atlanta: Cothran's Battery and Knipe's Brigade Repulse Stevenson's Division," *The National Tribune,* October 26, 1905.

ANDREW JACKSON NEAL: Typed transcript of letter, June 20, 1864, KMNBP Library.

ALVAH STONE SKILTON: Typed transcript of reminiscences, L.M. Strayer Collection.

GEORGE W. WARREN: Bevier, R.S., *History of the First and Second Missouri Confederate Brigades, 1861-1865,* pp. 236-237.

HENRY STEDMAN NOURSE: "From Young's Point to Atlanta," *The Story of the Fifty-fifth Regiment Illinois Volunteer Infantry in the Civil War, 1861-1865,* pp. 320-331.

JOHN W.A. GILLESPIE: Letter of June 28, 1864, published in *The Ohio Soldier,* Vol. I, No. 19, December 24, 1887.

ROBERT D. SMITH: Typed copy transcript of diary, KMNBP Library.

Chapter 7

ALEXANDER M. AYERS: Typed transcript of letter, June 28, 1864, Woodruff Library, Emory University.

ALLEN L. FAHNESTOCK: Transcript of diary, KMNBP Library.

JOHN H. BRUBACKER: Work, Julius B., *Reunion of Col. Dan McCook's Third Brigade, Second Division, Fourteenth A.C., Army of the Cumberland,* 1900, pp. 120-121.

SAMUEL M. CANTERBURY: *Ibid.,* pp. 40-41.

LANSING J. DAWDY: *Ibid.,* 35.

JULIUS B. WORK: *Ibid.,* 46.

SAM M. PYLE: *Ibid.,* pp. 61-63.

MILO H. LEWIS: "Closing on Johnston's Army at Kenesaw," *The National Tribune,* August 6, 1925.

SAMUEL R. WATKINS: *Co. Aytch, Maury Grays, First Tennessee Infantry, Or a Side Show of the Big Show,* pp. 156-159.

WILLIAM H. BAXTER: McAdams, F.M., *History of the One Hundred and Thirteenth Ohio Volunteer Infantry,* pp. 342-345.

WILLIAM H. LATIMER: *Confederate Veteran,* Vol. XXV, April 1917, pp. 167-168.

JAMES L.W. BLAIR: "The Fight at Dead Angle," *Confederate Veteran,* Vol. XII, November 1904, pp. 532-533.

THOMAS H. MANEY: "Battle of Dead Angle on Kennesaw Line," *Confederate Veteran,* Vol. XI, April 1903, pp. 159-160.

LYMAN WIDNEY: Typed transcript of letter, June 30, 1864, KMNBP Library.

ALLEN L. FAHNESTOCK: Transcript of diary, KMNBP Library.

SAMUEL GRIMSHAW: Work, Julius B., *Reunion of Col. Dan McCook's Third Brigade, Second Division, Fourteenth A.C., Army of the Cumberland,* 43.

Chapter 8

THOMAS H. MANEY: "Battle of Dead Angle on Kennesaw Line," *Confederate Veteran,* Vol. XI, April 1903, 160.

■ 2nd Lieut. Edgar J. Higby, Company C, 33rd Ohio, was killed at Resaca. At Chickamauga the previous September he had been taken prisoner and was incarcerated in Richmond's Libby Prison. He escaped along with 108 other officers in February 1864, succeeded in reaching the Union lines and upon arrival in Columbus, Ohio, was presented before the Ohio General Assembly, then in session. He returned to his company near Chattanooga just before the start of the campaign. At Resaca on May 14, "while both sides were firing at each other," wrote Adjutant A.L. Waddle of the 33rd, "young Higby, being carried away by the excitement of the occasion, rashly seized a musket from one of his men and standing up to discharge it, received a ball in his forehead. Loving hands bore him from the field and on the next morning I witnessed his rude burial side by side with 13 regimental comrades who had fallen on the same field."

HENRY RICHARDS: *Letters of Captain Henry Richards of the Ninety-Third Ohio Infantry,* 40.

WILLIAM D. WILSON: "Personal Recollections of William D. Wilson, Drum Major, 129th Regiment Illinois Vol. Infty., from Chattanooga to Atlanta, Savannah, Richmond and Washington," Manuscript Section, Indiana Division, Indiana State Library.

JOHN IRWIN KENDALL: "Recollections of a Confederate Officer," *The Louisiana Historical Quarterly,* October 1946, pp. 1170; 1170-1171.

HAMILTON M. BRANCH: "Old Letters," *Georgia Review,* Summer 1961, pp. 123-124.

PETER PRICE: "A Brisk July Day: Sherman's Army Occupies It in Passing the Chattahoochee River," *The National Tribune,* April 28, 1904.

GEORGE REDWAY: "Crossing the Chattahoochee," *The National Tribune,* April 10, 1919.

DWIGHT FRASER: Original letter of July 12, 1864, Indiana State Historical Library.

JOHN F. BROBST: *Well Mary: Civil War Letters of a Wisconsin Volunteer,* 75.

BENJAMIN M. SEATON: *The Bugle Softly Blows: The Confederate Diary of Benjamin M. Seaton,* 56.

JOEL D. MURPHREE: "Autobiography and Civil War Letters of Joel Murphree of Troy, Alabama 1864-1865," *The Alabama Historical Quarterly,* Spring 1957, 182.

ROBERT D. PATRICK: *Reluctant Rebel,* 192.

JOSIAH C. WILLIAMS: Original diary, May-July 1864, Indiana State Historical Library.

JOHN W. HAGAN: *Confederate Letters of John W. Hagan,* 50.

HENRY CAMPBELL: Rowell, John W., *Yankee Artillerymen: Through the Civil War with Eli Lilly's Indiana Battery,* 210.

WILLIAM WALLACE: "William Wallace's Civil War Letters: The Atlanta Campaign," *Wisconsin Magazine of History,* Winter 1973-1974, pp. 101-102.

CHARLES F. MORSE: *Letters Written During the Civil War, 1861-1865,* pp. 175; 176-177.

DWIGHT FRASER: Original letter of July 15, 1864, Indiana State Historical Library.

ROBERT D. PATRICK: *Reluctant Rebel,* pp. 195-196.

ANDREW J. NEAL: Typed transcript of letter, July 13, 1864, KMNBP Library.

ELBERT D. WILLETT: *History of Company B (Originally Pickens Planters) 40th Alabama Regiment, Confederate States Army, 1862-1865,* 74.

J.B. GRACEY: *Confederate Veteran,* Vol. XXVI, September 1918, 385.

DAVID B. MORGAN: *Confederate Veteran,* Vol. XXVI, July 1918, 302.

THOMAS J. KEY: *Two Soldiers: The Campaign Diaries of Thomas J. Key, C.S.A. and Robert J. Campbell, U.S.A.,* 90.

ROBERT N. ADAMS: "The Battle and Capture of Atlanta," *Glimpses of the Nation's Struggle,* Minnesota MOLLUS papers, 1898, 144.

ALFRED J. VAUGHAN JR.: *Personal Record of the Thirteenth Regiment Tennessee Infantry,* pp. 85-88.

ELLISON CAPERS: Capers, Walter B., *The Soldier-Bishop Ellison Capers,* pp. 91-92.

STEPHEN PIERSON: "From Chattanooga

to Atlanta in 1864 ... A Personal Reminiscence," *Proceedings of the New Jersey Historical Society,* 1931, pp. 349; 350-354; 343-344.

R.M. COLLINS: *Chapters from the Unwritten History of the War Between the States,* pp. 224-231.

JOHN T. RAPER: "Gen. Thomas at Peach Tree Creek," *The Ohio Soldier,* Vol. XIV, No. 11, December 31, 1898.

WASHINGTON B. CRUMPTON: *Confederate Veteran,* Vol. XXIX, No. 10, October 1921, pp. 381-382.

ALFRED R. GIBBONS: *The Recollections of an Old Confederate Soldier,* pp. 6-9.

JAMES TURNER: "Jim Turner Co. G, 6th Texas Infantry, C.S.A., from 1861-1865," *Texana,* 1974, pp. 173-175.

JAMES C. NISBET: *Four Years on the Firing Line,* pp. 209-218.

JOHN WALLACE FULLER: "A Terrible Day: The Fighting Before Atlanta July 22, 1864," *The National Tribune,* April 16, 1885.

WILLIAM E. BEVENS: *Reminiscences of a Private,* pp. 56-58.

RICHARD STANLEY TUTHILL: "An Artilleryman's Recollections of the Battle of Atlanta," *Military Essays and Recollections,* Illinois MOLLUS papers, Vol. I, 1891, pp. 296; 298-299; 300; 301; 302-306; 307-308.

EDMUND E. NUTT: "Twentieth Ohio at Atlanta," *The Ohio Soldier,* Vol. VII, No. 21, July 28, 1894.

MYRON B. LOOP: "Sounding the Alarm: The 68th Ohio's Trying Time at the Battle of Atlanta," *The National Tribune,* December 1, 1898.

JOHN HENRY PUCK: Recollections published in *Ninth Reunion of the 37th Regiment O.V.V.I.,* 1890, pp. 48-52.

C. IRVINE WALKER: Rodgers, Robert L., *Who Captured the DeGress Battery? Manigault's Brigade!* pp. 8-11.

WILLIAM BAKHAUS: "The Battle of Atlanta," *The Ohio Soldier,* Vol. II, No. 29, April 27, 1889.

CHARLES D. MILLER: "DeGrasse's Battery," *The National Tribune,* April 23, 1885.

Chapter 9

JOHN F. BROBST: *Well Mary: Civil War Letters of a Wisconsin Volunteer,* 79.

IRA S. OWENS: *Greene County Soldiers in the Late War, Being a History of the Seventy-Fourth O.V.I.,* pp. 81-82.

WILLIAM H. BERRYHILL: *The Gentle Rebel: The Civil War Letters of 1st Lt. William Harvey Berryhill, Co. D, 43rd Regiment, Mississippi Volunteers,* pp. 70-71.

ISAAC J. ROGERS: Barnard, H.V., *Tattered Volunteers: The Twenty-Seventh Alabama Infantry Regiment, C.S.A.,* 65.

THOMAS J. NEWBERRY: "The Civil War Letters of Thomas Jefferson Newberry," *The Journal of Mississippi History,* January 1948, pp. 79-80.

W.T. HALL: *Ibid.,* 80.

BENJAMIN T. SMITH: *Private Smith's Journal,* pp. 172-175.

JAMES AUSTIN CONNOLLY: *Transactions of the Illinois State Historical Society for the Year 1928,* pp. 353-355.

WELLS S. JONES: "How a Great Battle was Begun," *The Ohio Soldier,* Vol. IV, December 6, 1890.

EDWIN W. SMITH: "Battle of Ezra Church: A Coffee-Cooler's Experience," *The National Tribune,* July 5, 1888.

EMORY W. MUENSCHER: "What One Bullet Did," *The National Tribune,* April 27, 1916.

JOHN W. LAVENDER: *They Never Came Back: The War Memoirs of Captain John W. Lavender, C.S.A.,* pp. 97-99.

GEORGE W. PEPPER: *Personal Recollections of Sherman's Campaigns in Georgia and the Carolinas,* pp. 159; 162; 158.

GRANVILLE C. WEST: "McCook's Raid in the Rear of Atlanta and Hood's Army, August 1864," *MOLLUS, District of Columbia War Papers No. 29,* pp. 6-26.

HENRY O. DWIGHT: "How We Fight at Atlanta," *Harper's New Monthly Magazine,* Vol. XXIX, October 1864, pp. 663-666.

DAVID A. BARNHART: Original letter of July 28, 1864, L.M. Strayer Collection.

ARTHUR MIDDLETON MANIGAULT: *A Carolinian Goes to War,* pp. 237-238; 239-240; 241-242.

HENRY CLAY WEAVER: "Georgia Through Kentucky Eyes: Letters Written on Sherman's March to Atlanta," *The Filson Club History Quarterly,* October 1956, pp. 330-332.

LYMAN WIDNEY: Typed transcript of letter, August 23, 1864, KMNBP Library.

ERASTUS WINTERS: *In the 50th Ohio Serving Uncle Sam,* pp. 97-100.

JOHN H. WIDMER: Calkins, William W., *The History of the One Hundred and Fourth Regiment of Illinois Volunteer Infantry, War of the Great Rebellion 1862-1865,* pp. 512-515.

WILLIAM STRAWN: *Ibid.,* 233.

WILLIAM B. WESTERWELL: "How He Met Lawton," *The National Tribune,* July 24, 1913.

EVERETT F. ABBOTT: *History of the Seventy-fourth Regiment Indiana Volunteer Infantry,* pp. 100-101.

Chapter 10

IRA B. READ: "The Campaign from Chattanooga to Atlanta as seen by a Federal Soldier," *The Georgia Historical Quarterly,* September 1941, pp. 274; 274.

EDMUND T. EGGLESTON: "Excerpts from the Civil War Diary of E.T. Eggleston," *Tennessee Historical Quarterly,* December 1958, 349.

LEWIS W. DAY: *Story of the One Hundred and First Ohio Infantry,* pp. 257; 254-255.

DANIEL HAYFORD: "The 25th Ind.'s Share in the Atlanta Campaign," *The National Tribune,* September 22, 1904.

FRANCIS M. McADAMS: *A History of the One Hundred and Thirteenth Ohio Volunteer Infantry,* pp. 99; 98.

CHARLES H. COX: "The Civil War Letters of Charles Harding Cox," *Indiana Magazine of History,* March 1972, 218.

OLIVER A. REA: Letter of August 29, 1864, published in *The National Tribune,* January 27, 1898.

■ 1st Lieut. Henry W. Diebolt, Company A, 27th Ohio, was shot May 27 along the Dallas-New Hope Church line and died the following day. According to wartime journalist Whitelaw Reid, the regiment's pickets "were sharply attacked by the Rebels and driven back ... and two companies of the Twenty-Seventh advanced on the double-quick to re-enforce the guard. The Rebels were driven back, but Captain Sawyer, commanding the skirmish-line, and his First-Lieutenant, Henry W. Diebolt, were mortally wounded; and these two officers, who had served in the same company and eaten at the same table, were laid side by side that evening in a little grave-yard just north of Dallas."

JACOB A. GILBERG: "Battle of Jonesboro: A Day's History by One of Gen. J.A. Logan's Bodyguard," *The National Tribune,* May 6, 1909.
JOHN WILLIAMS GREEN: *Johnny Green of the Orphan Brigade: The Journal of a Confederate Soldier,* pp. 152-162; 165.
14th OHIO PRIVATE: McElroy, John, *Andersonville: A Story of Rebel Military Prisons,* Vol. II, pp. 439-443.
LEE H. RUDISILLE: "The Charge at Jonesboro: The Magnificent Assault by Este's Brigade," *The National Tribune,* August 5, 1909.
— "Atlanta Campaign: What the Brigade did at Jonesboro, Ga.," *The National Tribune,* August 7, 1890.
GERVIS D. GRAINGER: *Four Years with the Boys in Gray,* pp. 19-22.
STANARD C. HARLEY: "A Johnny Reb Writes," *The National Tribune,* June 11, 1914.
CHARLES HART OLMSTEAD: "The Memoirs of Charles H. Olmstead," *The Georgia Historical Quarterly,* March 1961, pp. 46-51.

Chapter 11

JOHN COBURN: *Official Records,* Series 1, Vol. 38, Part 2, pp. 392-393.
THOMAS M. WALKER: *Ibid.,* pp. 319-320.
G.W. DOUGLAS: *Confederate Veteran,* Vol. XXVII, October 1919, 367.
ADIN B. UNDERWOOD: *The Three Years' Service of the Thirty-Third Massachusetts Infantry Regiment, 1862-1865,* 233.
EDWIN WELLER: *A Civil War Courtship: The Letters of Edwin Weller from Antietam to Atlanta,* 104.
CHARLES F. MORSE: *Letters Written During the Civil War, 1861-1865,* 189.
G.S. BRADLEY: *The Star Corps; or Notes of an Army Chaplain During Sherman's Famous March to the Sea,* pp. 149-150.
ALPHEUS S. WILLIAMS: *From the Cannon's Mouth: The Civil War Letters of General Alpheus S. Williams,* pp. 340-342.
JAMES C. PATTEN: "An Indiana Doctor Marches with Sherman: The Diary of James Comfort Patten," *Indiana Magazine of History,* Vol. XLIX, 1953, pp. 409-410.
JAMES TAYLOR HOLMES: *52nd O.V.I., Then and Now,* pp. 244-246; 247-250; 252-253; 182-184; 255-258.

Epilogue

WILLIAM T. SHERMAN: *Memoirs of General William T. Sherman,* Vol. II, pp. 111; 178-179.
JOHN B. HOOD: *Ibid.,* 119.

■ Capt. John S.H. Doty, commander of Company E, 104th Illinois, was killed during the initial Confederate onslaught at Peachtree Creek. A fellow officer, Capt. William Strawn of Company F, later wrote: "Half of Companies A, B, C, D and E were either killed, wounded or captured, to be dragged to the rebel hells called prisons. Company E, next on my right, lost half its men. Captain Doty, my warm personal friend, lay dying with five bullet wounds in his body. He was lying with his head downhill. Realizing his condition he called to me to pray for him. Taking him in my arms and placing him in a better position I administered what consolation I could. His blood saturating my clothing, I held him until he was carried to the rear on a stretcher. He died soon after in the full consciousness that his life had been given to a just cause, and with the hope of the Christian."

Photographs & illustrations

Sources to quotations in captions of photographs and illustrations.

Preface

ROBERT N. ADAMS: Shelley, Thomas J., "Atlanta," *The National Tribune,* September 15, 1887.

Chapter 1

CHRISTOPHER C. MARSH: Richards, Henry, *Letters of Captain Henry Richards of the Ninety-Third Ohio Infantry,* pp. 31-32.
COMPANY H OFFICERS, 118th OHIO: Cox, Jacob D., *Military Reminiscences of the Civil War,* Vol. II, 99.
JOSEPH E. JOHNSTON: Watkins, Sam R., *Co. Aytch, Maury Grays, First Tennessee Infantry, Or a Side Show of the Big Show,* 111.
ROBERT D. BOND: Bevens, William E., *Reminiscences of a Private,* pp. 46; 47.
THOMPSON E. OSBORN & HENRY S. HOWELL: Ziegler, George M., "War Sketches, No. 5," unknown Columbus, Ohio, newspaper circa 1905, L.M. Strayer Collection.
CHARLES F. MORSE: *Letters Written During the Civil War, 1861-1865,* 163.
73rd OHIO: Hurst, Samuel H., *Journal-History of the Seventy-third Ohio Volunteer Infantry,* 110.
XIV CORPS PIN: Wills, Charles W., *Army Life of an Illinois Soldier,* 218.
IV CORPS SOLDIERS: Richards, Henry, *Letters of Captain Henry Richards of the Ninety-Third Ohio Infantry,* 41.
CHARLES TODD QUINTARD: *Doctor Quintard: Chaplain C.S.A. and Second Bishop of Tennessee, Being his Story of the War (1861-1865),* pp. 96-97.
SNOWBALL FIGHT: Watkins, Sam R., *Co. Aytch, Maury Grays, First Tennessee Infantry, Or a Side Show of the Big Show,* 116.
FRANCIS PATTEN: Copy of original letter, February 15, 1864, L.M. Strayer Collection.
52nd OHIO OFFICERS: Stewart, Nixon B., *Dan. McCook's Regiment, 52nd O.V.I.,* pp. 87-88.
ULYSSES S. GRANT: *Memoirs of General William T. Sherman,* Vol. II, pp. 26-27.
WILLIAM T. SHERMAN: *Ibid.,* pp. 31; 28-29.
— Wills, Charles W., *Army Life of an Illinois Soldier,* 258.
EDWIN WELLER: *A Civil War Courtship: The Letters of Edwin Weller from Antietam to Atlanta,* 74.
FORTIFIED RAILROAD BRIDGE: William T. Sherman quoted in Van Horne, Thomas B., *History of the Army of the Cumberland,* Vol. II, 451.
RANDOLPH H. SWAN: McAdams, Francis M., *Every-day Soldier Life, or a History of the One Hundred and Thirteenth Ohio Volunteer Infantry,* 75.
THOMAS' HQ WAGON: Sherman, William T., *Memoirs of General William T. Sherman,* Vol. II, 22.
RICHARD M. SAFFELL: "A Brave Officer: The Letters of Richard Saffell, 26th Tennessee, C.S.A., *Military Images,* Vol. XII, September-October 1990, 18.

Chapter 2

ROBERT B. STEWART: Clark, Charles T., *Opdycke Tigers 125th O.V.I.,* 177.
ALSON C. DILLEY: *Ibid.,* 124.

DAVID H. MOORE: *Ibid.*, pp. 230-231.
JOHN NEWTON: *Official Records,* Series 1, Vol. 38, Part 1, 298.
CHARLES G. HARKER: William T. Sherman quoted in Bailey, Ronald, *Battles for Atlanta,* 71.
EDWARD G. WHITESIDES: Clark, Charles T., *Opdycke Tigers 125th O.V.I.,* pp. 280-281.
COMPANY B, 125th OHIO: Rice, Ralsa C., "Three Years with the 125th Ohio, Opdycke's Tigers," *The National Tribune Scrapbook,* No. 2, 117.
COMPANY C, 125th OHIO: *Ibid.,* 118.

Chapter 3

ROCKY FACE RIDGE: Fox, Daniel H., typed transcript of letter, May 21, 1864, Firelands Historical Society, Norwalk, Ohio.
DAVID S. STANLEY: *Official Records,* Series 1, Vol. 38, Part 1, pp. 221; 223.
DUG GAP: Pierson, Stephen, "From Chattanooga to Atlanta in 1864 — A Personal Reminiscence," *Proceedings of the New Jersey Historical Society,* Vol. XVI, 1931, 334.
BUZZARD'S ROOST: Davis, Theodore R., *Harper's Weekly,* Vol. VIII, No. 388, June 4, 1864, 364.
ISAAC M. KIRBY: Day, Lewis W., *Story of the One Hundred and First Ohio Infantry,* pp. 214-215.
EZRA A. FAHNESTOCK: *Ibid.,* pp. 200-201.
XX CORPS BADGE: Hinkley, Julian W., *A Narrative of Service with the Third Wisconsin Infantry,* 115.
WILLIAM A. BULLITT: Hinman, Walter F., *The Story of the Sherman Brigade,* 520.
GEORGE D. WAGNER: *Ibid.,* 513.
ALEXANDER McILVAIN: *Ibid.,* 519.
DANIEL P. McCLURE: *Ibid.,* 374.
M. VAN BUREN TREADWAY: Copy of original letter, May 7, 1864, L.M. Strayer Collection.
HINDMAN'S DIVISION AT RESACA: Walthall, Edward C., *Official Records,* Series 1, Vol. 38, Part 3, 796.
NEWTON CANNON: *The Reminiscences of Sergeant Newton Cannon,* 52.
XX CORPS AT RESACA: Head, Thomas A., *Campaigns and Battles of the Sixteenth Regiment Tennessee Volunteers,* 126.
JAMES D. MORGAN: Pepper, George W., *Personal Recollections of Sherman's Campaigns in Georgia and the Carolinas,* 65.
ROBERT H. STRONG: *A Yankee Private's Civil War,* 45.
AUGUST WILLICH: Gleason, A.J., "Confusion as to Names," *The National Tribune,* February 11, 1897.
HENRY A. BARNUM: *The Congressional Medal of Honor: The Names, The Deeds,* 713.
— *Official Records,* Series 1, Vol. 38, Part 2, 268.
GEORGE A. COBHAM JR.: Geary, John W., *Ibid.,* 141.

■ Capt. Charles Lane commanded Company K, 81st Ohio, on July 22 during the battle of Atlanta. "While we were forming line," recalled regimental commander Col. Robert N. Adams, "the captain came to me seemingly in a state of great agitation and asked me whether I thought the enemy was there in force. I replied in the affirmative, when the captain drew from his pocket, while tears rolled down his cheeks, a picture of his little boy Charlie, and held it up before me. Looking at the picture with all the interest I could summon under the circumstances, I said, 'Yes, Captain, Charlie is a splendid boy.' But it was not compliments for the boy he was seeking, evidently, as his great agitation at the time indicated. I did not know then his object in showing me the picture, nor do I now know exactly what he wished, but of this I am sure: he acted under what was clearly to him a presentiment, for a moment later our conversation was interrupted by the approach of the enemy and the captain was shot through the head [and instantly killed] while bravely leading his men in the death-grapple that followed."

Chapter 4

GABRIEL C. WHARTON: Este, George P., *Official Records,* Series 1, Vol. 38, Part 1, 806.
STAPLES OF SOLDIERING: Pierson, Stephen, "From Chattanooga to Atlanta in 1864 — A Personal Reminiscence," *Proceedings of the New Jersey Historical Society,* Vol. XVI, 1931, pp. 332-333.
— Van Nest, Joseph, typed transcript of reminiscences, 51.
JAMES COMPTON: "The Second Division of the 16th Army Corps in the Atlanta Campaign," *Glimpses of the Nation's Struggle,* Minnesota MOLLUS papers, 1903, 114.
RICE C. BULL: *Soldiering: The Civil War Diary of Rice C. Bull,* 121.
JAMES C. ROGERS: *Official Records,* Series 1, Vol. 38, Part 2, 48.
JULIAN W. HINKLEY: *A Narrative of Service with the Third Wisconsin Infantry,* pp. 123-125.
NEW HOPE CHURCH: Holmes, James T., *52nd O.V.I. Then and Now,* pp. 199-200.
ALEXANDER P. STEWART: Ridley, Bromfield L., "The Battle of New Hope Church," *Confederate Veteran,* Vol. V, No. 9, September 1897, 460.
ALEXIS COPE: *The Fifteenth Ohio Volunteers and its Campaigns,* pp. 472-473.
WILLIAM H. GIBSON: Franklin, William S., "Under a Terrible Fire," *The National Tribune,* January 27, 1898.
OLIVER OTIS HOWARD: Cope, Alexis, *The Fifteenth Ohio Volunteers and its Campaigns,* 521.
THOMAS J. WOOD: *Official Records,* Series 1, Vol. 38, Part 1, 379.
DANIEL W. SHIDELER: Stewart, Nixon B., *Dan. McCook's Regiment, 52nd O.V.I.,* 107.
JOHN B. IRWIN: Lewis, George W., *The Campaigns of the 124th Regiment Ohio Volunteer Infantry,* 151.
PICKETT'S MILL: Hamilton, Posey, *Confederate Veteran,* Vol. XXX, September 1922, 338.
AMBROSE G. BIERCE: William B. Hazen quoted in O'Connor, Richard, *Ambrose Bierce: A Biography,* 41.
— *Dictionary of American Biography,* Vol. 1, 253.
WILLIAM B. HAZEN: *A Narrative of Military Service,* pp. 256; 258; 259.
SYLVANUS S. DIXON: Kimberly, Robert L., *Official Records,* Series 1, Vol. 38, Part 1, 435.
— Bierce, Ambrose, "The Crime at Pickett's Mill," *The Collected Works of Ambrose Bierce,* Vol. 1, pp. 286-287.
PATRICK R. CLEBURNE: *Official Records,* Series 1, Vol. 38, Part 3, 725.
HIRAM B. GRANBURY: *Ibid.,* 725.
COLUMBUS SYKES: Typed transcript of letter, May 21, 1864, KMNBP Library.

CHARLES C. WALCUTT: *Official Records,* Series 1, Vol. 38, Part 3, pp. 316-317.
MARCUS C. HORTON: Pinney, Nelson A., *History of the 104th Regiment Ohio Volunteer Infantry, 1862 to 1865,* 40.
CHARLES WRIGHT WILLS: *Army Life of an Illinois Soldier,* pp. 254-255.

Chapter 5

GROSE'S BRIGADE: Mosman, Chesley A., *The Rough Side of War,* 186.
GRENVILLE M. DODGE: Chamberlin, William H., *History of the Eighty-First Regiment Ohio Infantry Volunteers,* 139.

Chapter 6

JOHN H. CLIPPINGER: Loop, Myron B., "Rounding Up the Confederacy: Veteran Campaigns of the 68th Ohio," *The National Tribune,* May 16, 1901.
JAMES CANTEY: Kendall, John I., "Recollections of a Confederate Officer," *The Louisiana Historical Quarterly,* October 1946, pp. 1184-1185.
LEAVING RINGGOLD: Hough, Alfred L., *Soldier in the West: The Civil War Letters of Alfred Lacey Hough,* 195.
OSCAR L. JACKSON: *The Colonel's Diary,* 139.
LEONIDAS POLK: Chandler, David H., copy of original diary, L.M. Strayer Collection.
LOST MOUNTAIN: Goodman, H. Earnest, *Official Records,* Series 1, Vol. 38, Part 2, pp. 150; 151.
FREDERICK A. BARTLESON: H.T. Woodruff quoted in Johnson, Kathy, *Colonel Frederick Bartleson,* 7.
JOSEPH F. KNIPE: *Official Records,* Series 1, Vol. 38, Part 2, 42.
CALVIN H. WALKER: Stevenson, Carter L., *Official Records,* Series 1, Vol. 38, Part 3, 815.
HUBERT DILGER: Cope, Alexis, *The Fifteenth Ohio Volunteers and its Campaigns,* pp. 504-505.
ADAM L. EICHELBERGER: Neal, A.J., typed transcript of letter, July 23, 1864, KMNBP Library.
ALVAH S. SKILTON: Typed transcript of journal and letters, Laverne F. Heyman, North Fairfield, Ohio.
GILES A. SMITH: *Official Records,* Series 1, Vol. 38, Part 3, 194.
JOHN E. MADDUX: Thomas T. Taylor quoted in Saunier, Joseph A., *A History of the Forty-Seventh Regiment Ohio Veteran Volunteer Infantry,* 260.
JOSEPH A.J. LIGHTBURN: *Official Records,* Series 1, Vol. 38, Part 3, 222.
SHERMAN AT KENNESAW: *Home Letters of General Sherman,* pp. 299; 300.
MORGAN L. SMITH: *Official Records,* Series 1, Vol. 38, Part 3, 178.
SAMUEL M. McCRACKEN: Thomas T. Taylor quoted in Saunier, Joseph A., *A History of the Forty-Seventh Regiment Ohio Veteran Volunteer Infantry,* 258.
HENRY A. HILL: Barnes, W.T., "An Incident of Kenesaw Mountain," *Confederate Veteran,* Vol. XXX, February 1922, 49.
GREENBERRY F. WILES: *Official Records,* Series 1, Vol. 38, Part 3, 573.
THOMAS CLINTON STARR: Stevenson, Thomas M., *History of the 78th Regiment O.V.V.I.,* 278.
JOHN ARBUCKLE: *Civil War Experiences of a Foot-Soldier Who Marched with Sherman,* 65.

■ 1st Lieut. Norman H. Steffa assumed command of Company K, 76th Ohio, in June 1864. "He is a pretty good officer but a little intemperate," wrote Private Albert M. Sollan of his new commander. On July 22 during the battle of Atlanta, the 76th was ordered to charge and recapture its breastworks near DeGress' artillery battery. In a letter home, Private William Baugh of Company I described what happened next: "After we had taken back the works, we had to go back to where we layed ... and we had to double-quick back up a hill. While we were going up, a ball struck Norman Steffee (sic) in the back and went through his heart. He fell back and died in five minutes. All he said was, 'Oh, help me.' N. Steffee died hard. He looked bad after he was dead, his eyes were wide open. Pop, if his mother asks if he said anything to tell her, tell her he did not. Captain Blackburn has his things. He took them when he died."

Chapter 7

JEFFERSON C. DAVIS: Samuel A. Harper quoted in Work, Julius B., *Reunion of Col. Dan McCook's Third Brigade, Second Division, Fourteenth A.C.,* 84.
ALASON P. WEBBER: *The Congressional Medal of Honor: The Names, The Deeds,* 939.
OSCAR FITZALLEN HARMON: Work, Julius B., *Reunion of Col. Dan McCook's Third Brigade, Second Division, Fourteenth A.C.,* 54.
SAMUEL ROTHACKER: Holmes, James T., *52nd O.V.I. Then and Now,* 185.
JOHN H. BOYD: Banning, Henry B., *Official Records,* Series 1, Vol. 38, Part 1, 703.
JOHN G. MITCHELL: Official Records, Series 1, Vol. 38, Part 1, 680.
DARIUS B. WARNER: McAdams, Francis M., *Every-day Soldier Life, or a History of the One Hundred and Thirteenth Ohio Volunteer Infantry,* pp. 351-352.
JAMES M. SHANE: Reid, Whitelaw, *Ohio in the War,* Vol. I, 1006.
BENJAMIN F. CHEATHAM: Pepper, George W., *Personal Recollections of Sherman's Campaigns in Georgia and the Carolinas,* 105.
— Rogers, Robert M., *The 125th Regiment Illinois Volunteer Infantry,* 99.
OSCAR VAN TASSELL: *Official Records,* Series 1, Vol. 38, Part 1, pp. 685-686.
THOMAS C. HINDMAN: Manigault, Arthur M., *A Carolinian Goes to War,* pp. 193; 195.
HARDTACK: Hinman, Wilbur F., *The Story of the Sherman Brigade,* pp. 67-68; 69.
EDWIN C. SILLIMAN: Work, Julius B., *Reunion of Col. Dan McCook's Third Brigade, Second Division, Fourteenth A.C.,* 121.

Chapter 8

AMBROSE DOSS: Rouse, J.W., typed transcript of letter, July 6, 1864, KMNBP Library.
CHARLES H. COX: "The Civil War Letters of Charles Harding Cox," *Indiana Magazine of History,* March 1972, 210.
FRANCIS A. SHOUP: *Confederate Veteran,* Vol. III, September 1895, 263.

COMPANY B, 84th ILLINOIS: Simmons, Lewis A., *The History of the 84th Reg't. Ill. Vols.,* 185.
JAMES P. DOUGLAS: *Douglas's Texas Battery, CSA,* 109.
ALFRED J. VAUGHAN JR.: *Personal Record of the Thirteenth Regiment Tennessee Infantry,* pp. 14-15.
ELLISON CAPERS: William J. Hardee quoted in Capers, Walter B., *The Soldier-Bishop Ellison Capers,* 75.
STEPHEN PIERSON: "From Chattanooga to Atlanta in 1864 — A Personal Reminiscence," *Proceedings of the New Jersey Historical Society,* Vol. XVI, 1931, pp. 344-345.
ENOS FOURAT: *Official Records,* Series 1, Vol. 38, Part 2, 225.
NATHAN KIMBALL: *Ibid.,* Part 1, 306.
GEORGE H. THOMAS: Morse, Bliss, *Civil War Diaries & Letters of Bliss Morse,* 149.
EDWARD C. WALTHALL: Kendall, John I., "Recollections of a Confederate Officer," *The Louisiana Historical Quarterly,* October 1946, 1187.
HENRY E. PRICE: Calkins, William W., *The History of the One Hundred and Fourth Regiment of Illinois Volunteer Infantry,* pp. 419; 418.
CLAUDIUS V.H. DAVIS: Oatis, Martin A., *Official Records,* Series 1, Vol. 38, Part 3, 887.
JOHN A. NORRIS: Pepper, George W., *Personal Recollections of Sherman's Campaigns in Georgia and the Carolinas,* 192.
JAMES B. McPHERSON: Sherman, William T., *Memoirs of General William T. Sherman,* Vol. II, pp. 76; 78.
GEORGE J. REYNOLDS: Strong, William E., "The Death of General James B. McPherson," *Military Essays and Recollections,* Illinois MOLLUS papers, Vol. I, 1891, 331.
JOHN W. FULLER: "A Terrible Day: The Fighting Before Atlanta July 22, 1864," *The National Tribune,* April 16, 1885.
WILLIAM H.T. WALKER: Hood, John B., *Advance and Retreat,* pp. 181-182.
MENDAL CHURCHILL: Smith, Charles H., *The History of Fuller's Ohio Brigade,* 223.
RICHARD S. TUTHILL: "An Artilleryman's Recollections of the Battle of Atlanta," *Military Essays and Recollections,* Illinois MOLLUS papers, Vol. I, 1891, 294.
JAMES B. WALKER: Stucki, Christian, "At Atlanta," *The National Tribune,* July 28, 1898.
ROBERT K. SCOTT: Leggett, Mortimer D., *Official Records,* Series 1, Vol. 38, Part 3, 565.
— Loop, Myron B., "Sounding the Alarm: The 68th Ohio's Trying Time at the Battle of Atlanta," *The National Tribune,* December 1, 1898.
JAMES McLAIN: Ziegler, George M., "War Sketches, No. 19," unknown Columbus, Ohio, newspaper, circa 1905, L.M. Strayer Collection.

■ 1st Lieut. James A. McQuillen, Company I, 38th Ohio. His non-descript appearance was typical of many Federal line officers during the summer of 1864, especially with the absence of rank insignia on his uniform. McQuillen was wounded in the trenches before Atlanta on July 28, and died in a Chattanooga hospital on October 2. After the war, McQuillen Post 171, G.A.R., in Delta, Ohio, was named in his honor.

WEBSTER CLAY SHEPARD: McElroy, John, *Andersonville: A Story of Rebel Military Prisons ...,* Vol. I, 225.
JOHN ALEXANDER LOGAN: Curtis, Alvero, "Logan at Atlanta," *The National Tribune,* February 22, 1912.
CAPTURE OF DeGRESS' BATTERY: DeGress, Francis, *Offical Records,* Series 1, Vol. 38, Part 3, 265.
GEORGE W. EICHELBARGER: Nourse, Henry S., "From Young's Point to Atlanta," *The Story of the Fifty-fifth Regiment Illinois Volunteer Infantry,* 340.
THOMAS T. TAYLOR: Saunier, Joseph A., *A History of the Forty-Seventh Regiment Ohio Veteran Volunteer Infantry,* 288.
THOMAS J. KEY: *Two Soldiers: The Campaign Diaries of Thomas J. Key, C.S.A. and Robert J. Campbell, U.S.A.,* pp. 98-99.
FRANCIS DeGRESS: Hull, Charles W., *The National Tribune,* September 2, 1909.
— Shelley, Thomas J., *Ibid.,* September 15, 1887.
— 81st Ohio soldier, *Ibid.,* July 5, 1888.

Chapter 9

ORLANDO M. POE: *Official Records,* Series 1, Vol. 38, Part 1, 134.
JOSEPH HOOKER: Sherman, William T., *Memoirs of General William T. Sherman,* Vol. II, pp. 86-87.
JAMES A. CONNOLLY: *Transactions of the Illinois State Historical Society for the Year 1928,* 357.
ABSALOM BAIRD: *Official Records,* Series 1, Vol. 38, Part 1, 743.
WELLS S. JONES: Lewis, Frank M., "Filled with Vicissitudes," *The National Tribune Repository,* Vol. I, No. 1, November 1907, 29.
CHARLES HIPP: Moritz, Carl, *Official Records,* Series 1, Vol. 38, Part 3, 238.
— John H. Puck quoted in *Ninth Reunion of the 37th Regiment O.V.V.I.,* 52.
— *The Congressional Medal of Honor: The Names, The Deeds,* 930.
JAMES B. HOWARD: Walthall, Edward C., *Official Records,* Series 1, Vol. 38, Part 3, 927.
EZRA CHURCH: Crumpton, Washington, *Confederate Veteran,* Vol. XXIX, October 1921, 382.
JOSEPH DICKERSON: Crummel, Albert B., "Ezra Chapel," *The National Tribune,* April 26, 1888.
WILLIAM A. QUARLES: *Official Records,* Series 1, Vol. 38, Part 3, pp. 931; 933.
GEORGE W. PEPPER: *Personal Recollections of Sherman's Campaigns in Georgia and the Carolinas,* 132.
JOHN THOMAS CROXTON: *Official Records,* Series 1, Vol. 38, Part 2, pp. 772-773.
EDWARD M. McCOOK: *Ibid.,* 764.
JOSHUA W. JACOBS: West, Granville C., *Ibid.,* 780.
LAWRENCE S. ROSS: *Ibid.,* Part 3, pp. 964; 965.
HORACE PARK: Ziegler, George M., "War Sketches, No. 6," unknown Columbus, Ohio, newspaper circa 1905, L.M. Strayer Collection.
WILLIAM H. KIMBALL: Saunier, Joseph A., *A History of the Forty-Seventh Regiment Ohio Veteran Volunteer Infantry,* 305.
HENRY O. DWIGHT: Manning F. Force quoted in Wood, David W., *History of the 20th O.V.V.I. Regiment,* 54.
— Cooke, Chauncey, "The Civil War of Private Cooke: A Wisconsin Boy in the Union Army," *Wisconsin Magazine of History,* 1955, pp. 81-82.
ARTHUR M. MANIGAULT: *A Carolinian Goes to War,* 236.
STEPHEN DILL LEE: *Official Records,* Series 1, Vol. 38, Part 3, 763; 764.
JAMES PATTON ANDERSON: *Ibid.,* 770.

HENRY GRANVILLE STRATTON: *Nobly They Served the Union,* pp. 107-108.
JACOB M. RUFFNER: Develling, Charles T., *History of the Seventeenth Regiment,* pp. 83; 91-92.
GEORGE R. ELSTNER: Thoburn, Thomas C., *My Experiences During the Civil War,* pp. 111-112.
CHARLES R. POMEROY: Waddle, Angus L., *Three Years with the Armies of the Ohio and the Cumberland,* 77.
JOHN H. WIDMER: Calkins, William W., *The History of the One Hundred and Fourth Regiment of Illinois Volunteer Infantry,* 370.
MYRON BAKER: Hire, David, original diary, entry of May 24, 1864, L.M. Strayer Collection.

Chapter 10

ALFRED W. BELL: French, Samuel G., *Official Records,* Series 1, Vol. 38, Part 3, 906.
FRANK P. BLAIR JR.: Bryant, George E., *Ibid.,* 570.
PETER J. OSTERHAUS: *Ibid.,* 136.
COMPANY K, 54th OHIO: Moore, Israel T., *Ibid.,* 261.
JOHN W. GREEN: *Johnny Green of the Orphan Brigade: The Journal of a Confederate Soldier,* 166.
JOHN CRIPPS WICKLIFFE: Thompson, Ed Porter, *History of the Orphan Brigade,* 450.
JOHN W. CALDWELL: Este, George P., *Official Records,* Series 1, Vol. 38, Part 1, 811.
DANIEL C. GOVAN: Patterson, Joseph C., "Jonesboro," *The National Tribune,* February 5, 1891.
GEORGE P. ESTE: McElroy, John, *Andersonville: A Story of Rebel Military Prisons ...,* Vol. II, 437.
WILLIAM T.C. GROWER: Baird, Absalom, *Official Records,* Series 1, Vol. 38, Part 1, 752.
— Sloat, George E., "Jonesboro, Ga. An Ohio Surgeon's Account of the Charge," *The National Tribune,* October 2, 1890.
10th KENTUCKY COLOR GUARD: Hays, William H., *Official Records,* Series 1, Vol. 38, Part 1, pp. 817-818.
WILLIAM A. HALLIBURTON: Harley, Stanard C., "A Johnny Reb Writes," *The National Tribune,* June 11, 1914.
CHARLES HART OLMSTEAD: *Official Records,* Series 1, Vol. 38, Part 3, 756.
ROBERT BECKHAM: Erwin, Joseph, *Confederate Veteran,* Vol. XII, March 1904, 112.
JAMES FISHER PRAY: McElroy, John, *Andersonville: A Story of Rebel Military Prisons ...,* Vol. II, 444.
ANDREW URBAN: Connelly, Thomas W., *History of the 70th Ohio Regiment,* 110.

Chapter 11

COMPANY C, 84th INDIANA: *Official Records,* Series 1, Vol. 38, Part 1, 285.
BOMBPROOFS IN ATLANTA: Weller, Edwin, *A Civil War Courtship: The Letters of Edwin Weller from Antietam to Atlanta,* 104.
SNUG HUTS & QUARTERS: Underwood, Adin B., *The Three Years' Service of the Thirty-Third Massachusetts Infantry Regiment 1862-1865,* 234.
— Fox, Daniel H., typed transcript of letter, September 12, 1864, Firelands Historical Society, Norwalk, Ohio.
ALPHEUS S. WILLIAMS: *From the Cannon's Mouth: The Civil War Letters of General Alpheus S. Williams,* pp. 318; 317.
JAMES T. HOLMES: Work, Julius B., *Reunion of Col. Dan McCook's Third Brigade, Second Division, Fourteenth A.C.,* 97.
GEORGE A. MASURY: Holmes, James T., *52nd O.V.I. Then and Now,* pp. 219; 243.
PETER C. SCHNEIDER: Stewart, Nixon B., *Dan. McCook's Regiment, 52nd O.V.I.,* 131.
JAMES H. DONALDSON: *Ibid.,* 130-131.
WILLIAM H. LANE: Holmes, James T., *52nd O.V.I. Then and Now,* 237.
THOMAS H. KIRKLAND: *Ibid.,* 266.
DISMANTLING HOUSES: Read, Ira B., "The Campaign from Chattanooga to Atlanta as Seen by a Federal Soldier," *The Georgia Historical Quarterly,* September 1941, pp. 276; 277.

Sources

EDGAR J. HIGBY: Waddle, Angus L., *Three Years with the Armies of the Ohio and the Cumberland,* 69.
HENRY W. DIEBOLT: Reid, Whitelaw, *Ohio in the War,* Vol. II, 191.
JOHN S.H. DOTY: Calkins, William W., *The History of the One Hundred and Fourth Regiment of Illinois Volunteer Infantry,* pp. 223; 224.
CHARLES LANE: Adams, Robert N., "The Battle and Capture of Atlanta," *Glimpses of the Nation's Struggle,* Minnesota MOLLUS papers, 159.
NORMAN H. STEFFA: Sollan, Albert M., typed transcript of letter, June 28, 1864, Brad L. Pruden Collection.
— Baugh, William G., typed transcript of letter, July 25, 1864, Connecticut Civil War Roundtable Collection, Emory University.

Acknowledgments

The editors wish to thank all the individuals whose valuable assistance, advice and suggestions were instrumental to the completion of this book.

A debt of sincere gratitude is owed to the following people for providing a variety of written and photographic material, as well as giving unselfishly of their time: Brad L. Pruden, Marietta, Ga.; Roger D. Hunt, Rockville, Md.; Steven H. Ward, Dayton, Ohio; Steven J. Adolphson, West Newbury, Mass.; Dr. Richard A. Sauers, Harrisburg, Pa.; Richard F. Carlile, Dayton, Ohio; Dr. Kenneth T. Slack, bibliographer of the Rosanna A. Blake Library of Confederate History, Marshall University, Huntington, W.Va.; Ray Zielin, Chicago, Ill.; Bill Rasp, Jackson, Tenn.; Lee Bernard, Huntington, W.Va.; Lawrence T. Jones III, publisher of the Confederate Calendar Works, Austin, Texas; Herb Peck, Nashville, Tenn.; Mary Michals, audio-visual curator of the Illinois State Historical Library, Springfield, Ill.; Lloyd Ostendorf, Dayton, Ohio; Michael Waskul, Ypsilanti, Mich.; Matthew Burr, Bellevue, Ohio; and Steven Burr, Tallmadge, Ohio.

Appreciation also is extended to: Don Allison, Bryan, Ohio; David Barno, Dayton, Ohio; Gil Barrett, Laurel, Md.; William Brewster, Richmond, Va.; Timothy R. Brookes, East Liverpool, Ohio; Gary B. Carpenter, Ypsilanti, Mich.; the late Wayne Challen, Toledo, Ohio; Robert Coch, Flat Rock, Mich.; Scott Cross, Freeport, Ill.; Henry Deeks, East Arlington, Mass.; Gary Delscamp, Dayton, Ohio; Craig Dunn, Kokomo, Ind.; Craig V. Fisher, Toledo, Ohio; Floyd Flowers, Huntington, W.Va.; James C. Frasca, Croton, Ohio; William A. Frassanito, Gettysburg, Pa.; Pat Davis Fulks, Gulfport, Miss.; Juanita Gray, Cherokee Village, Ark.; John P. Gurnish, Akron, Ohio; Betty Ann Guss, Sandusky, Ohio; Randy Hackenberg, assistant curator of collections, U.S. Army Military History Institute, Carlisle Barracks, Pa.; Michael Hallmark, Dallas, Ga.; Laverne F. Heyman, North Fairfield, Ohio; Christopher Jarvis, Columbus, Ohio; Fred Jolly, Muncie, Ind.; Dennis Keesee, New Albany, Ohio; Paul E. Keller, Berea, Ohio; Dennis Kelly, chief historian, Kennesaw Mountain National Battlefield Park, Marietta, Ga.; Talley Kirkland, Fort Pulaski National Monument,

Savannah, Ga.; Mick Kissick, Albany, Ind.; Michael Klinger, Fort Wayne, Ind.; Charles G. Kratz, Homewood, Ill.; and Michael G. Kraus, Creston, Ohio.

Dr. Kenneth Lawrence, Orwell, Ohio; Roger Long, Port Clinton, Ohio; Chris Magewick, Canton, Mich.; David V. McCullough, Concord, Mich.; Paul McKee, editor of *The Company Wag,* Rockford, Ill.; Harriet Miller, Ft. Lauderdale, Fla.; Mike Miner, Sevierville, Tenn.; David A. Neuhardt, Dayton, Ohio; Andrew Oren, Milwaukee, Wis.; Ronn Palm, Kittanning, Pa.; Scott Patchan, Salem, Va.; Ivan Peterson, Andover, Ill.; Jerry Raisor, Georgetown, Ky.; Paul Reeder, Germantown, Tenn.; Jerry Rinker, South Charleston, Ohio; Harry Roach, editor of *Military Images,* Henryville, Pa.; Don and Jackie Ryberg, Westfield, N.Y.; Ann Sindelar, reference supervisor of The Western Reserve Historical Library, Cleveland, Ohio; Paul M. Smith, McKnightstown, Pa.; Larry Stevens, Newark, Ohio; Betty Strauss, Elkhart, Ind.; Dr. Thomas P. Sweeney, Republic, Mo.; David W. Taylor, Sylvania, Ohio; Richard K. Tibbals, Oak Park, Ill.; Marian E. Till, Sandusky, Ohio; Lyle Thoburn, Chagrin Falls, Ohio; Ken C. Turner, Ellwood City, Pa.; John M. Wedeward, Stoughton, Wis.; Mark Weldon, Ft. Wayne, Ind.; Michael J. Winey, curator of collections, U.S. Army Military History Institute, Carlisle Barracks, Pa.; George F. Witham, Memphis, Tenn.; and George S. Whiteley IV, photographs archivist, Georgia Department of Archives and History, Atlanta, Ga.

And finally, the editors gratefully acknowledge the following publishers for permission to reprint copyrighted material from these works:

Rice C. Bull: *Soldiering: The Civil War Diary of Rice C. Bull,* edited by K. Jack Bauer, copyright 1977, reprinted with permission from Presidio Press, 31 Pamaron Way, Novato, Calif. 94949.

Samuel T. Foster: *One of Cleburne's Command: The Civil War Reminiscences and Diary of Capt. Samuel T. Foster, Granbury's Texas Brigade, CSA,* edited by Norman D. Brown, copyright 1980, reprinted with permission from the University of Texas Press, P.O. Box 7819, Austin, Texas 78713.

John Williams Green: *Johnny Green of the Orphan Brigade: The Journal of a Confederate Soldier,* edited by Albert D. Kerwin, copyright 1956, reprinted with permission from The University Press of Kentucky, 663 S. Limestone St., Lexington, Ky. 40506.

Arthur Middleton Manigault: *A Carolinian Goes to War,* edited by R. Lockwood Tower, copyright 1983, reprinted with permission from the University of South Carolina Press, Columbia, S.C. 29208.

James Cooper Nisbet: *Four Years on the Firing Line,* edited by Bell I. Wiley, copyright 1987, reprinted with permission from Broadfoot Publishing Company, Route 4, Box 508-C, Wilmington, N.C. 28405.

John W. Tuttle: *The Union, the Civil War and John W. Tuttle: A Kentucky Captain's Account,* edited by Hambleton Tapp and James C. Klotter, copyright 1980, reprinted with permission from the Kentucky Historical Society, Old State House, P.O. Box H, Frankfort, Ky. 40602.

Photograph & illustration credits

Private collections

Gil Barrett: 179 (left).
Timothy R. Brookes: 127 (top), 173.
Richard F. Carlile: 80, 90 (right), 99, 166.
Confederate Ordnance: 68 (courtesy of Confederate Calendar Works).
Cumberland Gallery Collection: 14, 17, 18, 19, 20, 23, 28, 29, 30, 31, 33, 34, 35, 39, 41, 43, 50, 51, 62, 66, 69, 72, 73, 74 (top), 77, 78, 79, 88, 89, 90 (left; courtesy of Paul Keller), 91, 97, 112, 114, 115, 116, 119, 120, 125 (top; courtesy of Herb Peck), 126, 132, 133, 135, 136, 137, 138, 139, 141, 143, 153, 154, 159-160 (courtesy of Laverne F. Heyman), 161, 163, 169, 177, 178, 180, 185, 188, 189, 193 (top), 213, 214 (top), 215, 216, 219, 221, 224, 227, 228, 231, 232, 235, 236, 238, 239, 240, 241, 242, 243, 244, 245, 253, 257, 259 (both), 260, 263, 265, 266, 268, 270, 274, 275, 278 (bottom), 279, 285 (top), 287, 294, 296, 304, 307, 308, 309, 313, 320, 322, 325, 326, 327, 331, 336, 337, 340, 341.
Henry Deeks: 286.
Gary Delscamp: 149.
William A. Frassanito: 278 (top).
Pat Fulks: 220.
John P. Gurnish: 13, 193 (bottom).
Michael Hallmark: 199.
William J. Hobday: 158 (courtesy of Confederate Calendar Works).
Joe B. Howard: 261 (courtesy of Confederate Calendar Works).
Roger D. Hunt: 103, 155, 211, 305, 318, 319.
Christopher Jarvis: 164.
Mick Kissick: 306.
Michael G. Kraus: 147.
Peter Lundberg: 124 (courtesy of Confederate Calendar Works).
David McCullough: 107, 277.
Mike Miner: 36.
Richard Nee: 315.
David A. Neuhardt: 190.
Lloyd Ostendorf: 113, 267, 295.
Ronn Palm: 93, 95.
Herb Peck: 156, 207, 254.
Ivan Peterson: 250, 251 (courtesy of Charles G. Kratz).
Michael Polston: 310.
Brad L. Pruden: 127 (bottom), 339.
Bill Rasp: 24, 264.
Paul Reeder: 76 (courtesy of *Military Images*).
Paul M. Smith: 101.
Betty F. Strauss: 118.
L.M. Strayer: 70, 86 (bottom), 196, 214 (bottom), 283, 285 (bottom).
Ken Turner: 21, 22.
Michael Waskul: 134, 314, 335.
George S. Whiteley IV: 123.
John Knox Widmer: 288 (courtesy of Steven J. Adolphson).
Ray Zielin: 98, 100, 129, 162, 167, 168, 234 (bottom), 247.

Public Collections

Rosanna A. Blake Library of Confederate History, Marshall University: 15, 106, 108, 121, 281.
Chicago Historical Society: 145.
Chicago Public Library: 26 (courtesy of Steven J. Adolphson).
Civil War Library & Museum, MOLLUS, Philadelphia: 102 (courtesy of Roger D. Hunt).
Duke University Library: 293.
Fort Pulaski National Monument, Savannah: 311.
Georgia Department of Archives and History: 37.
Illinois State Historical Library: 152, 179 (right), 197, 205, 256.
Indiana Historical Society: 317.
Massachusetts MOLLUS, USAMHI: 11, 46, 56, 59, 131 (courtesy of Scott Cross), 157, 172, 210, 237, 248.
Museum of the Confederacy, Richmond: 171, 187, 204.
New Jersey Historical Society: 209 (courtesy of Roger D. Hunt).
Ohio Historical Society: 276, 298.
Smith County (Texas) Historical Society: 273.
Southern Historical Collection, University of North Carolina: 201.
Western Reserve Historical Society Library: 61.

Published works

Arbuckle, John C., *Civil War Experiences of a Foot-Soldier Who Marched with Sherman*: 175.

Belknap, William W., *History of the Fifteenth Regiment, Iowa Veteran Volunteer Infantry*: 226.

Bevens, William E., *Reminiscences of a Private*: 16, 233.

Bigger, David D., *Ohio's Silver-Tongued Orator: Life and Speeches of General William H. Gibson*: 110.

Brown, Joseph M., *The Mountain Campaigns in Georgia*: 25, 92.

Calkins, William W., *History of the One Hundred and Fourth Regiment of Illinois Volunteer Infantry*: 218, 290, 338.

Cannon, Newton, *The Reminiscences of Sergeant Newton Cannon*: 82.

Capers, Walter B., *The Soldier-Bishop Ellison Capers*: 208.

Clark, Charles T., *Opdycke Tigers, 125th O.V.I.*: 40, 42, 44, 45, 47, 48, 49, 52, 53, 54, 57, 58.

Cope, Alexis, *The Fifteenth Ohio Volunteers and its Campaigns, 1861-1865*: 111.

Cox, Charles H., *Indiana Magazine of History*, March 1972: 200.

Daniel, Larry J., *Cannoneers in Gray*: 312.

Dawes, Rufus, *Service with the Sixth Wisconsin Volunteers*: 125 (bottom).

Day, Lewis M., *Story of the One Hundred and First Ohio Infantry*: 67.

Douglas, James P., *Douglas's Texas Battery, CSA*: 206.

Frank Leslie's Illustrated History of the Civil War: 85, 146, 202, 262, 321, 332.

Green, John W., *Johnny Green of the Orphan Brigade*: 299.

Harmon, Oscar F., *Life and Letters of Oscar Fitzalan Harmon ...*: 182.

Harper's Weekly: 6-7, 8, 65.

Hinkley, Julian W., *A Narrative of Service with the Third Wisconsin Infantry*: 104.

Hinman, Wilbur F., *The Story of the Sherman Brigade*: 71, 74 (bottom), 75.

Indiana at Chickamauga: 289.

Johnson, Rossiter, *Campfires and Battlefields*: 225.

Key, Thomas J., *Two Soldiers: The Campaign Diaries of Thomas J. Key, C.S.A. and Robert J. Campbell, U.S.A.*: 249.

Manigault, Arthur M., *A Carolinian Goes to War*: 280.

McMurray, W.J., *History of the Twentieth Tennessee Regiment Volunteer Infantry C.S.A.*: 84, 174.

Miller's Photographic History of the Civil War: 55, 83, 86 (top), 122, 212, 229, 269, 271, 282, 303, 323.

Payne, Edwin W., *History of the Thirty-fourth Regiment of Illinois Infantry*: 194.

Peddycord, William F., *History of the Seventy-fourth Regiment Indiana Volunteer Infantry*: 291.

Portraits of Companions of the Commandery of the State of Ohio, MOLLUS: 258.

Scofield, Levi T., *The Retreat from Pulaski to Nashville, Tenn., Battle of Franklin, Tennessee, November 30, 1864*: 191, 217.

Smith, Charles H., *The History of Fuller's Ohio Brigade*: 151, 230, 234 (top).

Stewart, Nixon B., *Dan. McCook's Regiment, 52nd O.V.I.*: 328, 329, 330.

Stratton, Henry G., *Nobly They Served the Union*: 284.

Strong, Robert H., *A Yankee Private's Civil War*: 87.

Thomas, Henry W., *History of the Doles-Cook Brigade*: 223.

Thompson, Ed Porter, *History of the Orphan Brigade*: 300, 301, 302.

War Scenes, Views and Pointers on Western & Atlantic RR: 81, 94, 105, 117, 165, 170, 246.

Warner, Ezra J., *Generals in Gray*: 195, 272.

Watkins, Sam R., *Co. Aytch, Maury Grays, First Tennessee Regiment, Or a Side Show of the Big Show* [1952 edition]: 186.

Weller, Edwin, *A Civil War Courtship: The Letters of Edwin Weller from Antietam to Atlanta*: 32.

Wills, Charles W., *Army Life of an Illinois Soldier*: 128.

Work, Julius B., *Reunion of Col. Dan McCook's Brigade ...*: 181, 183, 184, 192, 324.

All maps by Richard A. Baumgartner.

Bibliography

Primary sources

Diaries & correspondence

Berryhill, William H., *The Gentle Rebel: The Civil War Letters of 1st Lt. William Harvey Berryhill, Co. D, 43rd Regiment, Mississippi Volunteers,* edited by M.M. Jones & L.J. Martin, Yazoo City, Miss.: The Sassafras Press, 1982.

Branch, Hamilton M., "Old Letters," *Georgia Review,* Vol. 15, Summer 1961.

Brobst, John F., *Well Mary: Civil War Letters of a Wisconsin Volunteer,* edited by Margaret B. Roth, Madison: University of Wisconsin Press, 1960.

Byrne, Frank L., *The View From Headquarters: Civil War Letters of Harvey Reid,* Madison: The State Historical Society of Wisconsin, 1965.

Connolly, James A., wartime letters published in *Transactions of the Illinois State Historical Society for the Year 1928,* Springfield: Phillips Bros., 1928.

Cooke, Chauncey H., "The Civil War of Private Cooke: A Wisconsin Boy in the Union Army," *Wisconsin Magazine of History,* 1955.

Cooper, James L., "The Civil War Diary of James Litton Cooper, September 30, 1861 to January 1865," edited by William T. Alderson, *Tennessee Historical Quarterly,* Vol. 15, No. 2, June 1956.

Cotton, John W., *Tours Till Death: Civil War Letters of John W. Cotton,* edited by Lucille Griffith, University, Ala.: University of Alabama Press, 1951.

Cox, Charles H., "The Civil War Letters of Charles Harding Cox," edited by Lorna Lutes Sylvester, *Indiana Magazine of History,* March 1972.

Douglas, James P., *Douglas's Texas Battery, CSA,* edited by Lucia R. Douglas, Waco, Texas: Texian Press, 1966.

Eggleston, Edmund T., "Excerpts from the Civil War Diary of E.T. Eggleston," edited by Edward Noyes, *Tennessee Historical Quarterly,* Vol. 17, No. 4, December 1958.

Gillespie, John W.A., letter of June 28, 1864, published in *The Ohio Soldier,* Vol. I, No. 19, December 24, 1887.

Hagan, John W., *Confederate Letters of John W. Hagan,* edited by Bell I. Wiley, Athens, Ga.: University of Georgia Press, 1954.

Harmon, Oscar F., *Life and Letters of Oscar Fitzalan Harmon, Colonel of the 125th Regiment Illinois Volunteer Infantry,* compiled by Lucy Harmon McPherson, Trenton, N.J.: MacCrellish & Quigley Co., 1914.

Hough, Alfred L., *Soldier in the West: The Civil War Letters of Alfred Lacey Hough,* edited by Robert G. Athearn, Philadelphia: University of Pennsylvania Press, 1957.

Jackson, Benjamin F., *So Mourns the Dove,* edited by Alto Loftin Jackson, New York: Exposition Press, 1965.

Jackson, Oscar L., *The Colonel's Diary: Journals Kept Before and During the Civil War by the late Colonel Oscar L. Jackson,* edited by David P. Jackson, Sharon, Pa.: privately printed, 1922.

Key, Thomas J., *Two Soldiers: The Campaign Diaries of Thomas J. Key, C.S.A. and Robert J. Campbell, U.S.A.,* edited by Wirt A. Cate, Chapel Hill: University of North Carolina Press, 1938.

Merrill, Samuel, "Letters from a Civil War Officer," edited by A.T. Votwiler, *Mississippi Valley Historical Review,* Vol. XIV, No. 4, March 1928.

Morse, Bliss, *Civil War Diaries & Letters of Bliss Morse,* edited by Loren J. Morse, Tahlequah, Okla.: Heritage Printing, 1985.

Morse, Charles F., *Letters Written During the Civil War, 1861-1865,* Boston: T.R. Marvin & Son, 1898.

Murphree, Joel D., "Autobiography and Civil War Letters of Joel Murphree of Troy, Alabama 1864-1865," edited by H.E. Sterkx, *The Alabama Historical Quarterly,* Vol. 19, No. 1, Spring 1957.

Newberry, Thomas J., "The Civil War Letters of Thomas Jefferson Newberry," edited by Enoch L. Mitchell, *The Journal of Mississippi History,* Vol. X, No. 1, January 1948.

Owen, Urban G., "Letters of a Confederate Surgeon in the Army of Tennessee to his Wife," edited by Enoch L. Mitchell, *Tennessee Historical Quarterly,* Vol. V, No. 2, June 1946.

Patrick, Robert D., *Reluctant Rebel: The Secret Diary of Robert Patrick 1861-1865,* edited by F. Jay Taylor, Baton Rouge: Louisiana State University Press, 1959.

Patten, James C., "An Indiana Doctor Marches with Sherman: The Diary of James Comfort Patten," edited by Robert G. Athearn, *Indiana Magazine of History,* Vol. XLIX, 1953.

Rea, Oliver A., letter of August 29, 1864, published in *The National Tribune,* January 27, 1898.

Read, Ira B., "The Campaign from Chattanooga to Atlanta as seen by a Federal Soldier," edited by Richard B. Harwell, *The Georgia Historical Quarterly,* Vol. XXV, No. 3, September 1941.

Richards, Henry, *Letters of Captain Henry Richards of the Ninety-Third Ohio Infantry,* Cincinnati: Press of Wrightson & Co., 1883.

Saffell, Richard M., "A Brave Officer: The Letters of Richard Saffell, 26th Tennessee, C.S.A.," *Military Images,* Vol. XII, No. 2, September-October 1990.

Seaton, Benjamin M., *The Bugle Softly Blows: The Confederate Diary of Benjamin M. Seaton,* edited by Col. Harold B. Simpson, Waco, Texas: Texian Press, 1965.

Sherman, William T., *Home Letters of General Sherman,* edited by M.A. DeWolfe Howe, New York: Charles Scribner's Sons, 1909.

Smith, Benjamin T., *Private Smith's Journal,* edited by Clyde C. Walton, Chicago: R.R. Donnelley & Sons Co., 1963.

Stratton, Henry G., *Nobly They Served the Union,* edited by Frederick C. Cross, Walnut Creek, Calif.: 1976.

Thoburn, Thomas C., *My Experiences During the Civil War,* compiled and edited by Lyle Thoburn, Cleveland: 1963.

Tuttle, John W., *The Union, the Civil War and John W. Tuttle: A Kentucky Captain's Account,* edited by Hambleton Tapp & James C. Klotter, Frankfort: The Kentucky Historical Society, 1980.

Wallace, William, "William Wallace's Civil War Letters: The Atlanta Campaign," edited by John O. Holzhueter, *Wisconsin Magazine of History,* Vol. 57, Winter 1973-1974.

Weaver, Henry C., "Georgia Through Kentucky Eyes: Letters Written on Sherman's March to Atlanta," edited by James M. Merrill & James F. Marshall, *The Filson Club History Quarterly,* Vol. 30, October 1956.

Weller, Edwin, *A Civil War Courtship: The Letters of Edwin Weller from Antietam to Atlanta,* edited by William Walton, Garden City, N.Y.: Doubleday & Co., 1980.

Williams, Alpheus S., *From the Cannon's Mouth: The Civil War Letters of General Alpheus S. Williams,* edited by Milo M. Quaife, Detroit: Wayne State University Press, 1959.

Wills, Charles W., *Army Life of an Illinois Soldier: Letters and Diary of the Late Charles W. Wills,* compiled by Mary E. Kellogg, Washington, D.C.: Globe Printing Co., 1906.

Wise, George M., "Civil War Letters of George M. Wise," edited by Wilfred W. Black, *The Ohio Historical Quarterly,* Vol. 65, No. 1, January 1956.

Manuscripts

Barnhart, David A. (99th Ohio), letter of July 28, 1864, L.M. Strayer Collection.

Baugh, William G. (76th Ohio), typed transcript of letter July 25, 1864, Connecticut Civil War Roundtable Collection, Emory University.

Chamberlain, Robert S. (64th Ohio), typed transcript of diary and reminiscences, L.M. Strayer Collection.

Fox, Daniel H. (101st Ohio), letter collection, Firelands Historical Society, Norwalk, Ohio.

Fraser, Dwight, (128th Indiana), letter collection, Indiana State Historical Library.

Hire, David (74th Indiana), original diary, L.M. Strayer Collection.

Neal, Andrew J. (Marion Light Artillery), letter collection, KMNBP Library.

Patten, Francis (92nd Ohio), transcript of letter February 15, 1864, L.M. Strayer Collection.

Porter, Alexander Q. (22nd Mississippi), typed transcript of diary, Robert W. Woodruff Library, Emory University.

Skilton, Alvah S. (57th Ohio), typed transcript of diary and reminiscences, courtesy of Laverne F. Heyman, North Fairfield, Ohio.

Sollan, Albert M. (76th Ohio), typed transcript of letter June 28, 1864, Brad L. Pruden Collection.

Sykes, Columbus (43rd Mississippi), letters of May 21, 27 and 29, 1864, KMNBP Library.

Treadway, M. Van Buren (47th Ohio), letter of May 7, 1864, L.M. Strayer Collection.

Van Nest, Joseph (101st Ohio), typed transcript of journal and reminiscences, courtesy of Marian Till, Sandusky, Ohio.

Williams, Josiah C. (27th Indiana), diaries, Indiana State Historical Library.

Wilson, William D. (129th Illinois), typed transcript of reminiscences, Indiana State Library.

Memoirs, reminiscences & recollections

Adams, Robert N., "Campaign for Atlanta," *Glimpses of the Nation's Struggle. Fourth Series. Papers read before the Minn. Commandery of the MOLLUS,* St. Paul: H.L. Collins Co., 1898.

— "The Battle and Capture of Atlanta," *Ibid.*

Anderson, Frank, "A Courier at the Battle of Resaca," *Confederate Veteran,* Vol. V, No. 6, June 1897.

Arbuckle, John C., *Civil War Experiences of a Foot-Soldier Who Marched with Sherman,* Columbus, Ohio: privately published, 1930.

Bakhaus, William, "The Battle of Atlanta," *The Ohio Soldier,* Vol. II, No. 29, April 27, 1889.

Barnes, W.T., "An Incident of Kennesaw Mountain," *Confederate Veteran,* Vol. XXX, No. 2, February 1922.

Bevens, William E., *Reminiscences of a Private,* privately published, 1913.

Bierce, Ambrose, "The Crime at Pickett's Mill," *The Collected Works of Ambrose Bierce,* Vol. I, New York: Neale Publishing Co., 1909.

Blair, James L.W., "The Fight at Dead Angle," *Confederate Veteran,* Vol. XII, No. 11, November 1904.

Bradley, G.S., *The Star Corps; or Notes of an Army Chaplain During Sherman's Famous March to the Sea,* Milwaukee: Jermain & Brightman Book & Job Printers, 1865.

Buck, Irving A., *Cleburne and his Command,* Jackson, Tenn.: McCowat-Mercer Press, 1959.

Bull, Rice C., *Soldiering: The Civil War Diary of Rice C. Bull,* edited by Jack K. Bauer, San Rafael, Calif.: Presidio Press, 1978.

Cannon, Newton, *The Reminiscences of Sergeant Newton Cannon, from Holograph Material Provided by his Grandson,* edited by Campbell H. Brown, Franklin, Tenn.: Carter House Association, 1963.

Chamberlin, William H., "The Skirmish Line in the Atlanta Campaign," *Sketches of War History 1861-1865, papers prepared for the Ohio Commandery of the MOLLUS, 1888-1890,* Vol. III, Cincinnati: Robert Clarke & Co., 1890.

Clemson, John W., "Surprised the Johnnies," *The National Tribune,* September 30, 1897.

Collins, Robert M., *Chapters from the Unwritten History of the War Between the States,* St. Louis: Nixon-Jones Printing Co., 1893.

Compton, James, "The Second Division of the 16th Army Corps in the Atlanta Campaign," *Glimpses of the Nation's Struggle. Fifth Series. Papers read before the Minn. Commandery of the MOLLUS,* St. Paul: Review Publishing Co., 1903.

Cox, Jacob D., *Military Reminiscences of the Civil War,* Vol. II, New York: Charles Scribner's Sons, 1900.

Crowell, Silas, "The General Wept," *The National Tribune,* December 31, 1896.

Crummel, Albert B., "Ezra Church," *The National Tribune,* April 26, 1888.

Crumpton, Washington B., recollections of Peachtree Creek and Ezra Church, *Confederate Veteran,* Vol. XXIX, No. 10, October 1921.

Curtis, Alvero, "Logan at Atlanta," *The National Tribune,* February 22, 1912.

Dacus, Robert H., *Reminiscences of Company H, First Arkansas Mounted Rifles,* Dardanelle, Ark.: Post-Dispatch Print, 1897.

Dawes, Rufus, *Service with the Sixth Wisconsin Volunteers,* Marietta, Ohio: E.R. Alderman & Sons, 1936.

Douglas, G.W., recollections of Atlanta's evacuation, *Confederate Veteran,* Vol. XXVII, No. 10, October 1919.

Dyer, John W., *Reminiscences; or Four Years in the Confederate Army,* Evansville, Ind.: Keller Printing & Publishing Co., 1898.

Elliot, Frank, "A June Evening Before Atlanta: Cothran's Battery and Knipe's Brigade Repulse Stevenson's Division," *The National Tribune,* October 26, 1905.

Erwin, Joseph, recollections of Jonesboro, *Confederate Veteran,* Vol. XII, No. 3, March 1904.

Foster, Samuel T., *One of Cleburne's Command: The Civil War Reminiscences and Diary of Capt. Samuel T. Foster, Granbury's Texas Brigade, CSA,* edited by Norman D. Brown, Austin: University of Texas Press, 1980.

Franklin, William S., "Under a Terrible Fire," *The National Tribune,* January 27, 1898.

Fuller, John W., "A Terrible Day: The Fighting Before Atlanta July 22, 1864," *The National Tribune,* April 16, 1885.

Gaskill, Joseph W., *Footprints Through Dixie: Everyday Life of the Man Under a Musket,* Alliance, Ohio: Bradshaw Printing Co., 1919.

Gibbons, A.R., *The Recollections of an Old Confederate Soldier,* Shelbyville, Mo.: Herald Print, 1913.

Gilberg, Jacob A., "Battle of Jonesboro: A Day's History by One of Gen. J.A. Logan's Bodyguard," *The National Tribune,* May 6, 1909.

Gleason, A.J., "Confusion as to Names," *The National Tribune,* February 11, 1897.

Gracey, J.B., recollections of Johnston's removal from command, *Confederate Veteran,* Vol. XXVI, No. 9, September 1918.

Grainger, G.D., *Four Years with the Boys in Gray,* Franklin, Ky.: Favorite Office, 1902.
Green, John W., *Johnny Green of the Orphan Brigade: The Journal of a Confederate Soldier,* edited by Albert D. Kerwin, Lexington, Ky.: University of Kentucky Press, 1956.
Hamilton, Posey, *Confederate Veteran,* Vol. XXX, No. 9, September 1922.
Harley, Stanard C., "A Johnny Reb Writes," *The National Tribune,* June 11, 1914.
Hazen, William B., *A Narrative of Military Service,* Boston: Ticknor & Co., 1885.
Hedley, Fenwick Y., *Marching Through Georgia,* Chicago: R.R. Donnelley & Sons, 1887.
Hinkley, Julian W., *A Narrative of Service with the Third Wisconsin Infantry,* Madison: Wisconsin History Commission, 1912.
Holmes, James T., *52nd O.V.I. Then and Now,* Columbus, Ohio: Berlin Printing Co., 1898.
Hood, John Bell, *Advance and Retreat,* Philadelphia: Burk and McFetridge Press, 1880.
Hull, Charles W., recollections of DeGress' Battery, July 22, 1864, *The National Tribune,* September 2, 1909.
Johnston, Joseph E., *Narrative of Military Operations,* New York: D. Appleton and Co., 1874.
Kendall, John Irwin, "Recollections of a Confederate Officer," edited by John Smith Kendall, *The Louisiana Historical Quarterly,* Vol. 29, No. 4, October 1946.
Kilpatrick, Robert L., "The Fifth Ohio Infantry at Resaca," *Sketches of War History 1861-1865, papers prepared for the Ohio Commandery of the MOLLUS, 1890-1896,* Vol. IV, Cincinnati: Robert Clarke & Co., 1896.
Latimer, William H., recollections of the Dead Angle, *Confederate Veteran,* Vol. XXV, No. 4, April 1917.
Lavender, John W., *They Never Came Back: The War Memoirs of Captain John W. Lavender, C.S.A.,* edited by Ted R. Worley, Pine Bluff, Ark.: W.M. Hackett and D.R. Perdue, 1956.
Lewis, Frank M., "Filled with Vicissitudes. Ups and Downs in the History of the 53rd Ohio, from Shiloh to the Grand Review. A Regiment which Spendidly Retrieved its First Mistakes," *The National Tribune Repository,* Vol. I, No. 1, Washington, D.C.: The National Tribune Co., 1907.
Lewis, Milo H., "Closing on Johnston's Army at Kenesaw," *The National Tribune,* August 6, 1925.
Loop, Myron B., "Sounding the Alarm: The 68th Ohio's Trying Time at the Battle of Atlanta," *The National Tribune,* December 1, 1898.
— "Rounding Up the Confederacy: Veteran Campaigns of the 68th Ohio," *The National Tribune,* May 16, 1901.
Maney, Thomas H., "Battle of Dead Angle on Kennesaw Line," *Confederate Veteran,* Vol. XI, No. 4, April 1903.
Manigault, Arthur M., *A Carolinian Goes to War,* edited by R. Lockwood Tower, Columbia: University of South Carolina Press, 1983.
McElroy, John, *Andersonville: A Story of Rebel Military Prisons, Fifteen Months a Guest of the so-called Southern Confederacy. A Private Soldier's Experience in Richmond, Andersonville, Savannah, Millen, Blackshear and Florence,* Vol. II, Washington, D.C.: The National Tribune, 1899.
Miller, Charles D., "DeGrasse's Battery," *The National Tribune,* April 23, 1885.
Morgan, David B., recollections of Johnston's removal from command, *Confederate Veteran,* Vol. XXVI, No. 7, July 1918.
Mosman, Chesley A., *The Rough Side of War: Civil War Journal of Chesley A. Mosman, 1st Lieutenant, Company D, 59th Illinois Volunteer Infantry Regiment,* edited by Arnold Gates, Garden City, N.Y.: The Basin Publishing Co., 1987.
Muenscher, Emory W., "What One Bullet Did," *The National Tribune,* April 27, 1916.
Nisbet, James C., *Four Years on the Firing Line,* edited by Bell I. Wiley, Jackson, Tenn.: McCowat-Mercer Press, 1963.
Noyes, Edward F., recollections of Nickajack Creek, *The Ohio Soldier,* Vol. IV, No. 5, October 11, 1890.
Nutt, Edmund E., "Twentieth Ohio at Atlanta," *The Ohio Soldier,* Vol. VII, No. 21, July 28,1894.
Olmstead, Charles H., "The Memoirs of Charles H. Olmstead," edited by Lilla M. Hawes, *The Georgia Historical Quarterly,* Vol. XLV, March 1961.
Patterson, Joseph C., "Jonesboro," *The National Tribune,* February 5, 1891.
Pepper, George W., *Personal Recollections of Sherman's Campaigns in Georgia and the Carolinas,* Zanesville, Ohio: Hugh Dunne, 1866.
Pierson, Stephen, "From Chattanooga to Atlanta in 1864 ... A Personal Reminiscence," *Proceedings of the New Jersey Historical Society,* Vol. XVI, 1931.
Puck, John H., recollections of the Atlanta campaign, published in *Ninth Reunion of the 37th Regiment O.V.V.I.,* 1890.
Quintard, Charles T., *Doctor Quintard: Chaplain C.S.A. and Second Bishop of Tennessee, Being his Story of the War (1861-1865),* edited by Rev. Arthur Howard Noll, Sewanee, Tenn.: The University Press, 1905.
Raper, John T., "General Thomas at Peach Tree Creek," *The Ohio Soldier,* Vol. XIV, No. 11, December 31, 1898.
Redway, George, "Crossing the Chattahoochee," *The National Tribune,* April 10, 1919.
Rice, Ralsa C., "Three Years Service with the 125th Ohio, Opdycke's Tigers," *The National Tribune Scrapbook, No. 2, Stories of the Camp, March, Battle, Hospital and Prison told by Comrades,* Washington, D.C.: National Tribune, [190-], 3 volumes.
Ricketts, Ezra E., "Killing of Gen. Polk," *The National Tribune,* March 31, 1904.
Ridley, Bromfield L., "The Battle of New Hope Church," *Confederate Veteran,* Vol. V, No. 9, September 1897.
Roberts, Frank S., "In Winter Quarters at Dalton, Ga., 1863-64," *Confederate Veteran,* Vol. XXVI, No. 6, June 1918.
Rodgers, Robert L., *Who Captured the DeGress Battery? Manigault's Brigade!* Atlanta: privately published, 1896.
Rudisille, Lee H., "Atlanta Campaign: What the Brigade did at Joneboro, Ga.," *The National Tribune,* August 7, 1890.
— "The Charge at Jonesboro: The Magnificent Assault by Este's Brigade," *The National Tribune,* August 5, 1909.
Scofield, Levi T., *The Retreat from Pulaski to Nashville, Tenn., Battle of Franklin, Tennessee, November 30, 1864,* Cleveland: Press of the Caxton Co., 1909.
Sherman, William T., *Memoirs of General William T. Sherman,* Vol. II, Bloomington: Indiana University Press, 1957.
Shideler, Daniel W., "A New Hope Experience," *The National Tribune,* March 17, 1898.
Shoup, Francis A., recollections of building Chattahoochee River defenses, *Confederate Veteran,* Vol. III, No. 9, September 1895.
Sloat, George E., "Jonesboro, Ga. An Ohio Surgeon's Account of the Charge," *The National Tribune,* October 2, 1890.
Smith, Edwin W., "Battle of Ezra Church: A Coffee-Cooler's Experience," *The National Tribune,* July 5, 1888.
Stone, Henry, "From the Oostanaula to the Chattahoochee," *Papers of the Military Historical Society of Massachusetts,* Vol. VIII.
Strong, Robert H., *A Yankee Private's Civil War,* edited by Ashley Halsey, Chicago: Henry Regnery Co., 1961.
Strong, William E., "The Death of General James B. McPherson," *Military Essays and Recollections, Papers Read Before the Commandery of the State of Illinois, MOLLUS,* Vol. I, Chicago: A.C. McClurg and Co., 1891.
Sykes, E.T., *Walthall's Brigade, Army of Tennessee C.S.A.,*

1862-1865, Columbus, Miss.: Mississippi Historical Society, 1905.
Thoburn, Thomas C., *My Experiences During the Civil War,* compiled and edited by Lyle Thoburn, Cleveland: 1963.
Turner, James, "Jim Turner Co. G, 6th Texas Infantry, C.S.A., from 1861-1865," *Texana,* No. 2, 1974.
Tuthill, Richard S., "An Artilleryman's Recollections of the Battle of Atlanta," *Military Essays and Recollections, Papers Read Before the Commandery of the State of Illinois, MOLLUS,* Vol. I, Chicago: A.C. McClurg and Co., 1891.
Upson, Theodore F., *With Sherman to the Sea: The Civil War Letters, Diaries & Reminiscences of Theodore F. Upson,* edited by Oscar O. Winther, Bloomington: Indiana University Press, 1958.
Waddle, Angus L., *Three Years with the Armies of the Ohio and the Cumberland,* Chillicothe, Ohio: Scioto Gazette Book and Job Office, 1889.
Watkins, Sam R., *Co. Aytch, Maury Grays, First Tennessee Infantry, Or a Side Show of the Big Show,* Jackson, Tenn.: McCowat-Mercer Press, 1952.
Westerwell, William B., "How He Met Lawton," *The National Tribune,* July 24, 1913.
Winters, Erastus, *In the 50th Serving Uncle Sam: Memoirs of One Who Wore the Blue,* East Walnut Hills, Ohio: privately printed, 1905.
Young, Lot D., *Reminiscences of a Soldier of the Orphan Brigade,* Louisville: Courier-Journal Job Printing Co., no date.

Newspapers & periodicals

Davis, Theodore R., *Harper's Weekly,* Vol. VIII, No. 388, June 4, 1864.
Dwight, Henry O., "How We Fight at Atlanta," *Harper's New Monthly Magazine,* Vol. XXIX, October 1864.

Official records

Davis, George B.; Perry, Leslie J. & Kirkley, Joseph W., Board of Publication. Compiled by Capt. Calvin D. Cowles. *Atlas to Accompany the Official Records of the Union and Confederate Armies,* Washington: Government Printing Office, 1891-1895.
United States War Department, *War of the Rebellion: A Compilation of the Official Records of the Union and Confederate Armies,* Series 1: Vol. 38, Parts 1-5, Washington, D.C.: Government Printing Office, 1891-1902.

Regimental histories

Barnard, H.V., *Tattered Volunteers: The Twenty-Seventh Alabama Infantry Regiment, C.S.A.,* Northport, Ala.: Hermitage Press, 1965.
Barron, Samuel B., *The Lone Star Defenders: A Chronicle of the Third Texas Cavalry Regiment in the Civil War,* New York: Neale Publishing Co., 1908.
Belknap, William W., *History of the Fifteenth Regiment, Iowa Veteran Volunteer Infantry, from October 1861, to August 1865,* Keokuk, Iowa: R.B. Ogden & Son, 1887.
Bevier, R.S., *History of the First and Second Missouri Confederate Brigades, 1861-1865,* St. Louis: Bryan, Brand & Co., 1879.
Blackburn, Theodore W., *Letters from the Front: A Union "Preacher" Regiment (74th Ohio) in the Civil War,* Dayton: Morningside Press, 1981.
Boyle, John R., *Soldiers True: The Story of the One Hundred and Eleventh Regiment Pennsylvania Veteran Volunteers, and of its Campaigns in the War for the Union, 1861-1865,* New York: Eaton & Mains, 1903.
Calkins, William W., *The History of the One Hundred and Fourth Regiment of Illinois Volunteer Infantry, War of the Great Rebellion 1862-1865,* Chicago: Donohue & Henneberry, 1895.
Chamberlin, W.H., *History of the Eighty-First Regiment Ohio Infantry Volunteers During the War of the Rebellion,* Cincinnati: Gazette Steam Printing House, 1865.
Clark, Charles T., *Opdycke Tigers, 125th O.V.I.,* Columbus, Ohio: Spahr & Glenn, 1895.
Connelly, Thomas W., *History of the Seventieth Ohio Regiment, from its Organization to its Mustering Out,* Cincinnati: Peak Bros., 1902.
Cope, Alexis, *The Fifteenth Ohio Volunteers and its Campaigns, 1861-1865,* Columbus, Ohio: Press of the Edward T. Miller Co., 1916.
Davidson, H.M., *History of Battery A, First Regiment of Ohio Vol. Light Artillery,* Milwaukee: Daily Wisconsin Steam Printing House, 1865.
Day, Lewis W., *Story of the One Hundred and First Ohio Infantry,* Cleveland: W.M. Bayne Printing Co., 1894.
Develling, Charles T., *History of the Seventeenth [Ohio] Regiment, First Brigade, Third Division, Fourteenth Corps, Army of the Cumberland, War of the Rebellion,* Zanesville, Ohio: E.R. Sullivan, 1889.
Duke, John K., *History of the Fifty-third Regiment Ohio Volunteer Infantry during the War of the Rebellion 1861 to 1865,* Portsmouth, Ohio: The Blade Printing Co., 1900.
Dunkleman, Mark H. & Winey, Michael J., *The Hardtack Regiment: An Illustrated History of the 154th Regiment, New York State Infantry Volunteers,* Rutherford, N.J.: Fairleigh Dickinson University Press, 1981.
Emanuel, S., *An Historical Sketch of the Georgetown Rifle Guards, Co. A of the Tenth Regiment So. Ca. Volunteers,* privately published, no date.
Guild, George B., *A Brief Narrative of the Fourth Tennessee Cavalry Regiment,* Nashville: 1913.
Head, Thomas A., *Campaigns and Battles of the Sixteenth Regiment Tennessee Volunteers,* Nashville: Cumberland Presbyterian Publishing House, 1885.
Hinman, Wilbur F., *The Story of the Sherman Brigade,* Alliance, Ohio: Press of Daily Review, 1897.
Holm, David D., *History of the Fifth Indiana Battery, compiled and written from the "Field Diary" of Lieutenant Daniel H. Chandler, and from Official Reports of Officers of the Army of the Cumberland,* no publisher, no date.
Hurst, Samuel H., *Journal-History of the Seventy-third Ohio Volunteer Infantry,* Chillicothe, Ohio: [no publisher], 1866.
Kelly, William M., "A History of the Thirtieth Alabama Volunteers (Infantry) Confederate States Army," *The Alabama Historical Quarterly,* Vol. 9, No. 1, Spring 1947.
Kinnear, J.R., *History of the Eighty-Sixth Regiment Illinois Volunteer Infantry,* Chicago: Tribune Co., 1866.
Lewis, George W., *The Campaigns of the 124th Regiment Ohio Volunteer Infantry,* Akron: Werner Co., 1894.
McAdams, F.M., *Every-day Soldier Life, or a History of the One Hundred and Thirteenth Ohio Volunteer Infantry,* Columbus, Ohio: Charles M. Cott & Co., 1884.
McBride, John R., *History of the Thirty-third Indiana Veteran Volunteer Infantry,* Indianapolis: Wm. B. Burford, 1900.
McMurray, W.J., *History of the Twentieth Tennessee Regiment Volunteer Infantry C.S.A.,* Nashville: 1904.
Merrill, Samuel, *The Seventieth Indiana Volunteer Infantry in the War of the Rebellion,* Indianapolis: The Bowen-Merrill Co., 1900.
Ninth Reunion of the 37th Regiment O.V.V.I., Program. Toledo: 1890.
Nourse, Henry S., "From Young's Point to Atlanta," V-IX, published in *The Story of the Fifty-fifth Regiment Illinois Volunteer Infantry in the Civil War, 1861-1865,* Clinton,

Mass: W.J. Coulter, 1887.
Owens, Ira S., *Greene County Soldiers in the Late War. Being a History of the Seventy-Fourth O.V.I.,* Dayton: Christian Publishing House Print, 1884.
Payne, Edwin W., *History of the Thirty-fourth Regiment of Illinois Infantry,* Clinton, Iowa: Allen Printing Co., 1902.
Peddycord, William F., *History of the Seventy-fourth Regiment Indiana Volunteer Infantry,* Warsaw, Ind.: Smith Printery, 1913.
Pinney, Nelson A., *History of the 104th Regiment Ohio Volunteer Infantry from 1862 to 1865,* Akron: Werner & Lohmann, 1886.
Rogers, Robert M., *The 125th Regiment Illinois Volunteer Infantry,* Champaign, Ill.: Gazette Printing, 1882.
Saunier, Joseph A., *A History of the Forty-Seventh Regiment Ohio Veteran Volunteer Infantry,* Hillsboro, Ohio: Lyle Printing Co., 1903.
Secheverell, John H., *Journal History of the Twenty-ninth Ohio Veteran Volunteers, 1861-1865,* Cleveland: 1883.
Simmons, Lewis A., *The History of the 84th Reg't. Ill. Vols.,* Macomb, Ill.: Hampton Brothers, 1866.
Smith, Charles H., *The History of Fuller's Ohio Brigade 1861-1865,* Cleveland: A.J. Watt, 1909.
Stevenson, Thomas M., *History of the 78th Regiment O.V.V.I.,* Zanesville, Ohio: Hugh Dunne, 1865.
Stewart, Nixon B., *Dan. McCook's Regiment, 52nd O.V.I., A History of the Regiment, its Campaigns and Battles, from 1862 to 1865,* Alliance, Ohio: Review Print, 1900.
Thomas, Henry W., *History of the Doles-Cook Brigade,* Atlanta: Franklin Printing, 1903.
Thompson, Ed Porter, *History of the Orphan Brigade,* Louisville: Lewis N. Thompson, 1898.
Underwood, Adin B., *The Three Year's Service of the Thirty-Third Mass. Infantry Regiment,* Boston: A. Williams & Co., 1881.
Vaughan, Alfred J., *Personal Record of the Thirteenth Regiment Tennessee Infantry,* Memphis: Press of S.C. Toof & Co., 1897.
Willett, Elbert D., *History of Company B (Originally Pickens Planters) 40th Alabama Regiment, Confederate States Army, 1862-1865,* Anniston, Ala.: Norwood, 1902.
Wood, David W., *History of the 20th O.V.V.I. Regiment,* Columbus, Ohio: Paul & Thrall Printers, 1876.
Work, J.B., *Reunion of Col. Dan McCook's Third Brigade, Second Division, Fourteenth A.C., Army of the Cumberland,* Chicago: 1900.

Secondary sources

Bibliographies & reference works

Album. *Portraits of Companions of the Commandery of the State of Ohio, Military Order of the Loyal Legion of the United States,* compiled by James J. Briggs, Cincinnati, 1893.
Boatner, Mark M., *The Civil War Dictionary,* New York: David McKay Co., 1959.
Cole, Garold L., *Civil War Eyewitnesses: An Annotated Bibliography of Books and Articles, 1955-1986,* Columbia: University of South Carolina Press, 1988.
Dictionary of American Biography, Vols. I-X, edited by Allen Johnson, New York: Charles Scribner's Sons, 1964.
Dornbusch, C.E., *Military Bibliography of the Civil War,* Vols. I, II and III, New York: The New York Public Library, 1975.
Fox, William F., *Regimental Losses in the American Civil War 1861-1865,* Albany, N.Y.: Albany Publishing Co., 1889.
Fuller, Claud E., *The Rifled Musket,* New York: Bonanza Books, 1958.
Heitman, Francis B., *Historical Register and Dictionary of the United States Army, from its Organization, September 29, 1789, to March 2, 1903,* Vol. I, Washington, D.C.: Government Printing Office, 1903.
Hunt, Roger D., & Brown, Jack R., *Brevet Brigadier Generals in Blue,* Gaithersburg, Md.: Olde Soldier Books, Inc., 1990.
Illinois. Adjutant General. *Report of the ... containing Reports for the Years 1861-66. Revised by Brigadier General J.N. Reece,* 8 vols., Springfield: Phillips Bros. State Printers, 1900-1902.
Jones, Lawrence T. III, *1979 Confederate Calendar,* Austin, Texas: Confederate Calendar Works, 1979.
Kentucky. Adjutant General. *Report of the Adjutant General 1861-1866,* 2 vols., Frankfort: John H. Harney, Public Printer, 1866-67.
McAuley, John D., *Civil War Breech Loading Rifles: A Survey of the Innovative Infantry Arms of the American Civil War,* Lincoln, R.I.: Andrew Mowbray Inc., 1987.
Ohio Authors and Their Books. Biographical Data and Selective Bibliographies for Ohio Authors, Native and Resident, 1796-1950, edited by William Coyle, Cleveland: World Publishing Co., 1962.
Ohio. Roster Commission. *Official Roster of the Soldiers of the State of Ohio in the War of the Rebellion, 1861-1866 ... Compiled under Direction of the Roster Commission ... Published by Authority of the General Assembly,* 12 vols., Akron, Cincinnati, Norwalk: 1886-1895.
Phillips, Stanley S., *Civil War Corps Badges and Other Related Awards, Badges, Medals of the Period,* Lanham, Md.: S.S. Phillips and Assoc., 1982.
Union Soldiers and Sailors Monument Association, Louisville, *The Union Regiments of Kentucky ...,* Louisville: Courier-Journal Job Printing Co., 1897.
United States. Adjutant General's Office. *Official Army Register of the Volunteer Force of the United States Army for the Years 1861, '62, '63, '64, '65, Parts I-VIII,* Washington: 1865.
Warner, Ezra J., *Generals in Blue: Lives of the Union Commanders,* Baton Rouge: Louisiana State University Press, 1964.
———, *Generals in Gray: Lives of the Confederate Commanders,* Baton Rouge: Louisiana State University Press, 1959.

Biographies

Bigger, David D., *Ohio's Silver-Tongued Orator: Life and Speeches of General William H. Gibson,* Dayton: United Brethren Publishing House, 1901.
Capers, Walter B., *The Soldier-Bishop Ellison Capers,* New York: Neale Publishing Co., 1912.
Johnson, Kathy, *Colonel Frederick Bartleson,* Joliet, Ill.: Will County Historical Society, 1983.
Lewis, Lloyd, *Sherman, Fighting Prophet,* New York: Harcourt, Brace & Co., 1932.
O'Connor, Richard, *Ambrose Bierce: A Biography,* Boston: Little, Brown & Co., 1967.

Local histories

Hoehling, A.A., *Last Train from Atlanta,* New York: Thomas Yoseloff, 1958.
Pray, John Lansing, *A Memorial. Record of the Soldier Spirit of Waterville, 1812-1814, 1846-1848, 1861-1865, 1898-1899,* Toledo: The B.F. Wade Printing Co., 1899.

Military histories

Bailey, Ronald H., *Battles for Atlanta,* Alexandria, Va.: Time-Life Books, 1985.

Brown, Joseph M., *The Mountain Campaigns in Georgia,* Buffalo, N.Y.: Matthews, Northrup & Co., 1890.
Connelly, Thomas L., *Autumn of Glory: The Army of Tennessee, 1862-1865,* Baton Rouge: Louisiana State University Press, 1971.
Cox, Jacob D., *Atlanta,* New York: Charles Scribner's Sons, 1882.
Daniel, Larry J., *Cannoneers in Gray: The Field Artillery of the Army of Tennessee, 1861-1865,* University, Ala.: University of Alabama Press, 1984.
Horn, Stanley F., *The Army of Tennessee: A Military History,* New York: The Bobbs-Merrill Co., 1941.
Indiana at Chickamauga, 1863-1900, Report of Indiana Commissioners Chickamauga National Military Park, Indianapolis: Sentinel Printing Co., 1900.
Johnson, Rossiter, *Campfires and Battlefields: A Pictorial Narrative of the Civil War,* New York: The Civil War Press, 1967.
Kerksis, Sydney C. & Wallace, Lee A., *The Atlanta Papers,* Dayton: Morningside Press, 1980.
McDonough, James L. & Jones, James P., *War So Terrible: Sherman and Atlanta,* New York: W.W. Norton & Co., 1987.
Miles, Jim, *Fields of Glory: A History and Tour Guide of the Atlanta Campaign,* Nashville: Rutledge Hill Press, 1989.
Moat, Louis Shepheard, editor, *Frank Leslie's Illustrated History of the Civil War,* New York: Mrs. Frank Leslie, 1895.
Reid, Whitelaw, *Ohio in the War: Her Statesmen, Her Generals and Soldiers,* Cincinnati: Moore, Wilstach & Baldwin, 1868.
Rowell, John W., *Yankee Artillerymen: Through the Civil War with Eli Lilly's Indiana Battery,* Knoxville: University of Tennessee Press, 1975.
Tennesseans in the Civil War: A Military History of Confederate and Union Units with Available Rosters of Personnel, Parts I-II, Nashville: Civil War Centennial Commission, 1964-1965.

Newspapers & periodicals

Cross, Scott, "The Blue Springs Images," *Military Images,* Vol. X, No. 1, July-August 1988.
Ziegler, George M., "War Sketches," No. 1-19, [unknown Columbus, Ohio, newspaper circa 1905].

Pamphlets

War Scenes, Views and Pointers on Western & Atlantic R.R. and Nashville, Chattanooga & St. Louis Ry., Philadelphia: Art Press, Loughead & Co. [no date].

Index

D

E

F

G

H

M

N

O

P

U

V

W

X

Y

Z

About the authors

Echoes of Battle: The Atlanta Campaign is **Larry M. Strayer's** first book-length publication. A Civil War photo historian and longtime student of the war's western theater, he served respectively as a photograph contributor and consultant to the Time-Life series *The Civil War* and *Voices of the Civil War.* The Toledo native holds a history degree from Ohio University and is employed in the legal department of the LexisNexis Group. A former president of the Dayton Civil War Round Table, he is married with four children.

Richard A. Baumgartner is a former award-winning journalist who worked between 1975 and 1991 for Gannett and Knight-Ridder newspapers in West Virginia and California as a feature writer, artist, designer and graphics editor. A Milwaukee native, he is a graduate of the University of Missouri School of Journalism. Among his published works are the books *Buckeye Blood: Ohio at Gettysburg, Kennesaw Mountain June 1864* and *Blue Lightning: Wilder's Mounted Infantry Brigade in the Battle of Chickamauga,* which received the 1999 Alexander C. McClurg Award. A full-time researcher and writer, he resides in Huntington, West Virginia.

Echoes of Battle: The Atlanta Campaign was the 1994 recipient of the Richard B. Harwell Award, presented by the Civil War Round Table of Atlanta.

Other Titles of Related Interest Published by Blue Acorn Press

Echoes of Battle
The Struggle for Chattanooga
Richard A. Baumgartner & Larry M. Strayer

Buckeye Blood: Ohio at Gettysburg
Richard A. Baumgartner

Kennesaw Mountain June 1864
Richard A. Baumgartner

Seventh Michigan Cavalry
of Custer's Wolverine Brigade
Asa B. Isham

Dan McCook's Regiment
52nd Ohio Volunteer Infantry 1862-1865
Nixon B. Stewart

History of the 2nd West Virginia Cavalry
Joseph J. Sutton

Too Young To Die
Boy Soldiers of the Union Army 1861-1865
Dennis M. Keesee

History of the 41st Ohio Veteran Volunteer Infantry
Robert L. Kimberly & Ephraim S. Holloway

History of the 126th Ohio Volunteer Infantry
John H. Gilson

Two Wars
The Autobiography & Diary of Gen. Samuel G. French, CSA
Samuel G. French